UNIVERSITY OF
WOLVERHAMPTON

BÉLA BARTÓK

COMPOSER RESOURCE MANUALS
VOLUME 40
GARLAND REFERENCE LIBRARY OF THE HUMANITIES
VOLUME 1926

COMPOSER RESOURCE MANUALS

GUY A. MARCO, *General Editor*

STEPHEN COLLINS FOSTER
A Guide to Research
by Calvin Elliker

HENRY PURCELL
A Guide to Research
by Franklin B. Zimmerman

CLAUDIO MONTEVERDI
A Guide to Research
by Gary K. Adams
and Dyke Kiel

CARL MARIA VON WEBER
A Guide to Research
by Donald G. Henderson
and Alice H. Henderson

GIOVANNI BATTISTA PERGOLESI
A Guide to Research
by Marvin E. Paymer
and Hermine W. Williams

CLAUDE DEBUSSY
A Guide to Research
by James R. Briscoe

ALESSANDRO AND
DOMENICO SCARLATTI
A Guide to Research
by Carole F. Vidali

GUILLAUME DE MACHAUT
A Guide to Research
by Lawrence Earp

EDWARD ELGAR
A Guide to Research
by Christopher Kent

ALBAN BERG
A Guide to Research
by Bryan R. Simms

BENJAMIN BRITTEN
A Guide to Research
by Peter J. Hodgson

BÉLA BARTÓK
A Guide to Research,
Second Edition
by Elliott Antokoletz

BÉLA BARTÓK
A GUIDE TO RESEARCH,
SECOND EDITION

ELLIOTT ANTOKOLETZ

GARLAND PUBLISHING, INC.
NEW YORK AND LONDON
1997

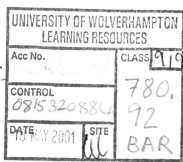

Library of Congress Cataloging-in-Publication Data

Antokoletz, Elliott.
    Béla Bartók : a guide to research / by Elliott Antokoletz. — 2nd ed.
        p.   cm. — (Composer resource manuals ; vol. 40)
    (Garland reference library of the humanities ; vol. 1926)
        Includes index.
        ISBN 0-8153-2088-4 (alk. paper)
        1. Bartók, Béla, 1881–1945—Bibliography.   I. Title.   II. Series.
    III. Series: Garland composer resource manuals ; v. 40.
    ML134.B18A7   1997
    016.78'092—dc21   96-39298
                                                                                    CIP
                                                                                    MN

Cover photograph of Béla Bartók some time after 1940. Photograph by Ernst Nash, courtesy of Bartók Records.

Printed on acid-free, 250-year-life paper
Manufactured in the United States of America

Composer Resource Manuals

In response to the growing need for bibliographic guidance to the vast literature on significant composers, Garland is publishing an extensive series of research guides. This ongoing series encompasses more than 50 composers; they represent Western musical tradition from the Renaissance to the present century.

Each research guide offers a selective, annotated list of writings, in all European languages, about one or more composers. There are also lists of works by the composers, unless these are available elsewhere. Biographical sketches and guides to library resources, organizations, and specialists are presented. As appropriate to the individual composer, there are maps, photographs, or other illustrative matter, glossaries, and indexes.

For Juana

Béla Bartók some time after 1940. Photograph by Ernst Nash, courtesy of Bartók Records.

CONTENTS

PREFACE
To the Second Edition

Since the publication of *Béla Bartók: A Guide to Research* in 1988, materials on the life and music of the Hungarian composer have been flooding the field of Bartók research. The proliferation of scholarly work, including publication of previously unknown or unpublished primary-source documents--letters, autograph manuscripts, essays, and editions of the music--as well as secondary-source studies, has been accelerated by the many international conferences, symposia, and festivals held in 1995 to commemorate the fiftieth anniversary of Bartók's death. These developments have necessitated work on a revised and expanded edition of the original volume.

During the past year alone, four international conferences in the United States and Hungary have inspired several major publications of collected lectures that are expected to pave the way for a more well-rounded and integrated picture of the Hungarian composer's multifaceted contributions to twentieth-century music and scholarship. These commemorative conferences have provided opportunities to bring together outstanding senior scholars and promising younger colleagues devoted to Bartók studies in order to evaluate the most current research with respect to the man, pianist, folklorist, and composer.

One of these publications, *Bartók in Retrospect* (item no. 1138), combines the lectures of the first and last conferences of the commemorative year: the International Bartók Conference at Radford University in Virginia (item no. 1161), held in conjunction with the fifteenth annual Bartók-Kabalevsky International Competition (item no. 1140), and Bartók in Retrospect: A Pre-Conference International Symposium of the Society for Ethnomusicology at the University of California, Los Angeles (item no. 1139). Collectively, these lectures address the most recent research into Bartók's life, his career as ethnomusicologist, and folk music materials with respect to his fieldwork, transcription techniques, classification methodology, and influences on his compositions. They also address theoretic-analytical approaches to his music with respect to compositional technique, style, aesthetics, compositional process (sketches, drafts, revisions, editions), and performance authenticity.

Studia musicologica 36/3-4 (1995) is based on lectures presented at the International Bartók Colloquium 1995 (item no. 1160) in Szombathely, Hungary, which was similar to the latter two conferences in intention and scope. The essays in this issue of *Studia musicologica* could not be annotated separately in this new edition of the *Guide,* since the indexes were completed before the appearance of the journal volume. Another volume, *Bartók and His World* (item no. 1131), based on lectures presented at The Bard Music Festival Rediscoveries: Béla Bartók and His World (item no. 1130) at Bard College in New York, differs from the other conference volumes in its more specialized approach to recent Bartók scholarship. The volume editor's stated intention was to close the gap in Bartók scholarship that has resulted from socio-cultural and linguistic barriers to Western scholars. The volume provides information that has been isolated from the international audience, including many historical sources that have been unavailable outside the Hungarian language. Furthermore, both the Szombathely and Bard occasions each featured many concerts of Bartók's works by major performers. The School of Music at the University of North Carolina, Greensboro, also commemorated the fiftieth anniversary of Bartók's death with a three-day international symposium of concerts and lectures, entitled *Focus on Piano Literature: Béla Bartók,* though without projected publication of the lectures.

Other collected volumes published during the past decade also point to extensive international research that has been contributing to a more comprehensive and integrated perspective of the Bartók field. The main general volume is *The Bartók Companion* (item no. 1158), which, in contrast to the long-available *Companion* volumes on Beethoven, Mozart, and other composers, was published for the first time only in 1993. Fifteen international scholars discuss Bartók's aesthetics, style, musical language, and compositional processes, his activities as pianist, teacher, and ethnomusicologist, and other issues of biographical, historical, philosophical, folkloristic, compositional, theoretical, and analytical significance. In the same year, the *Companion* editor also brought back into print Halsey Stevens's classic monograph on Bartók (item no. 243) in its third edition.

In spite of these developments in Bartók research, there have been few new bibliographic surveys of the Bartók literature since the original publication of this *Guide,* and none of these addresses the broad spectrum or provides an update. Nevertheless, each in its own way provides some important perspective and brings to our attention some little-known items. David Clegg's concisely annotated "Select Bibliography of Articles and Interviews by and About Bartók Published in Britain Between 1904 and 1946" (item no. 1103) is directed toward a special body of literature produced during Bartók's lifetime. The unannotated listing in Gábor Kiss's "A Bartók Bibliography, 1980-1989" (item no. 1110) is useful for some new items not included in the original publication of this *Guide.* The more specialized, unannotated list by Yves Lenoir in his "Bibliographie de Denijs Dille sur Béla Bartók" (item no. 1112) covers the writings of the original director of the Budapest Bartók Archívum exclusively.

By the end of the fifty-year period following Bartók's death, the extant Bartók sources have been determined and are being made available for study and evaluation, thanks to the foresight of the Bartók heirs, the

Hungarian Republic, the trustees of Bartók's New York estate, and charitable donations to public institutions. These developments have led to new writings on primary-source documentation and the compositional process (item nos. 981-1058 *passim*), preparatory work on the thematic catalogue and complete critical edition (item nos. 1018 and 1024-1026, especially), corrected printed editions (item nos. 983 and 991), performance authenticity (item nos. 1059-1091 passim), and other areas of Bartók research. The intention in this enlarged edition of the *Guide* has been to include the most updated authoritative writings in these categories.

Given the ever-widening scope of the Bartók literature and the seemingly unattainable goal of reflecting the entire field of Bartók research thoroughly, one can only look forward to each new edition for some sense of fulfillment in this task. It is my hope that this new edition will at least serve as an important intermediary stage toward a more complete and definitive picture of the composer and his music.

Elliott Antokoletz
Austin, Texas
June 1996

PREFACE
To the First Edition

Since his death in 1945, Béla Bartók has been recognized, along with Igor Stravinsky and members of the Vienna Schoenberg circle, as one of the major figures of twentieth-century music. In addition to his stature as a composer, Bartók had established himself during his lifetime as a piano virtuoso, pedagogue, editor of a significant body of keyboard music (from the Baroque through Romantic eras), linguist, and humanitarian. In the field of ethnomusicological research, he has been universally recognized for his pioneering work in collecting, transcribing, analyzing, and classifying thousands of folk melodies from Eastern Europe, North Africa, and Turkey.

Increasing interest in Bartók's music since 1945 has been reflected by the number of score publications, recordings, concerts, and international festivals devoted to the composer. Conferences and scholarly publications dealing with Bartók's life and works have been flourishing in the last several decades as well. The massive and complex nature of the literature has created the need for an updated and annotated bibliographic reference source to keep pace with these scholarly developments. This *Guide to Research* is intended to fill this need.

There are many relatively brief, topically nonspecific, and generally unannotated bibliographies appearing within larger studies of Bartók's life and works. Although there have been several publications devoted exclusively to providing bibliographic information, or at least to substantial bibliographic listings within larger volumes, they lack updated information and for the most part do not include annotations and topical ordering that would increase their usefulness for Bartók researchers. Nevertheless, several of these substantial bibliographic listings deserve special mention for their pioneering efforts in coping with the growing Bartók literature and research problems. The excellent compilation by Halsey Stevens (see item nos. 1120 or 243) is the most extensive early Bartók bibliography (up to the date of its publication in the early 1950s) to provide a significant list of books and articles by and about Bartók. Stevens also provides a comprehensive list of Bartók's musical compositions, including basic publisher and dedication information. The unannotated, chronologically ordered bibliography by András Szőllősy (item no. 1125), which appeared several years later, is exclusively based on a selective list of primary-source writings. This bibliography provides useful publication information (including reprinted and translated versions, etc.) not found in Stevens. The book by József Ujfalussy (item no. 250), which appeared in 1971, incorporates and expands Szőllősy's primary-source list. It includes the list of Bartók's writings up to the composer's death and the first posthumous publications but not subsequent translations. The main area of Ujfalussy's expansion of the Szőllősy list is seen in the newly added discography as well as in his unannotated bibliography of secondary sources. Ujfalussy also provides some basic topical subdivisions for the otherwise alphabetically ordered entries. A more updated selective bibliography by Todd Crow (item no. 1145), which contains 315 excellently chosen entries, is intended as a listing of the most significant books and articles on Bartók between 1963 and 1973. The more recent compilation by András Wilheim (item no. 1128), published in 1981, is quite useful for its intensive focus on the major books, dissertations, and articles produced between 1970 and 1979. While also limited by its lack of annotations, its year-by-year ordering provides us with a chronological view of research developments in the Bartók world during this decade in which the Bartók literature continued to flourish. William Austin's bibliographic listing in his larger book on twentieth-century music (item no. 1096) was prepared as a supportive bibliography for his Bartók chapter. However, because the source annotations are too brief and general, this list does not readily lend itself to in-depth scholarly research.

Bartók's scholarly contributions have been published and translated into many languages in approximately fifteen volumes devoted to folk music (exclusive of several volumes that have remained unpublished) and in numerous essays. These essays range from the study of folk music to diverse aesthetic, stylistic, and technical questions in connection with both traditional and contemporary art-music as well as broader political and social issues. In the interest of providing the most complete and well-rounded picture of Bartók's multifaceted contributions as well as providing direct insight into his personality, psychology, and philosophical attitudes, the intention in this *Guide* is to compile systematically as many of Bartók's published writings as are available. These primary-source writings are organized into several categories in Chapter II. Bartók's published essays, books, and other primary-source documents, which include approximately 200 items, are presented in chronological ordering within each of these categories to reflect both the evolution of his thinking and its correlation with historical events. Furthermore, each annotation includes a comprehensive listing of the main journals or books in which the cited original publication was subsequently reprinted or translated. These are the criteria for the selection of the primary-source entries.

Selection of the secondary-source entries is based on very different criteria from those of the primary sources. Extensive international work in the field of Bartók research since the 1930s--including detailed discussions of his folk-music investigations, analyses of his musical compositions and of his surviving sketches, as well as studies of his career and personality--has, in part, necessitated a selective rather than comprehensive approach to the vast literature on Bartók. My own research led me to study the archival materials in New York and Budapest, to do an extensive review of the secondary   sources, and to maintain personal contact (at international Bartók conferences, in joint lectures, and through correspondences) with widely recognized scholars in the Bartók field. These experiences led to my awareness of the main issues and problems in Bartók research as well as to the names of those scholars who have appeared in the literature most frequently over a significant period of time and have been most widely quoted. This has permitted me to make judgments regarding scholarly value and/or uniqueness of contribution. On this basis, I have been able to make a calculated reduction of the original 2,500 items I had collected and indexed to a final listing of about 700 items. This final selection is intended as a representation of the core of the literature on Bartók. At the same time, many excellent contributions that deserve to be part of this core were excluded, since they tend toward duplication of discussions that have been developed more substantially in other writings. On the other hand, certain items that were largely repetitions of other items were included when such items also contributed some unique information.

Several other, more specific criteria have also been basic in selecting the secondary-source items. The extreme diversity of Bartók's activities as scholar and composer dictated the need for representation in many areas of scholarly research. In addition to the varied categories that are subsumed under the general chapter topics (see Contents), a more detailed breakdown of subjects dealing with the stylistic and technical features of the musical language also determined the selection of items: due to the numerous theories that have been applied to Bartók's music, a varied and extensive number of special studies are required to provide adequate representation in dealing with his musical language. Since certain theories have been more widely recognized than others, they have received greater representation in the entries. The inevitable result has been some repetition of information in certain items, such repetition being acceptable when these items also provided important additional, sometimes unique information.

Comprehensive international representation also seemed necessary in the selection of the secondary-source writings. The international relevance of Bartók's ethnomusicological activities and the resulting interest in Bartók's methodological approach among scholars of different national backgrounds have made the wide international selection of items in this volume imperative. Another significant determinant has been the diversity and distinctness of the many theoretical approaches to Bartók's music on the international level. Such diversity appears to be influenced to some extent by geographical separation, which has prevented accessibility to or familiarity with those national folk sources as well as archival materials relevant to Bartók research. Language barriers have also contributed to some extent to the lack of integration of information and the fostering of distinct "schools" of theory and analysis. However, no less significant in the development of internationally diverse and often contradictory approaches to Bartók's musical language is the complexity and diversity of that language itself.

The secondary-source selections also include as many scholars as possible who worked with Bartók or knew him personally. In general, priority has been given to those who have been involved extensively with the primary sources. These include writings based on first-witness reports and interviews with Bartók as well as writings dealing with the folk-music collections, sketches, manuscript drafts, letters, and other primary-source documents.

The intention in this volume is to make the greatest amount of information on Bartók accessible with the least amount of effort for the reader. Certain basic information is therefore provided in the annotations in order to facilitate library research. The annotations are aimed at providing concise yet specific and, when necessary, detailed description of content. In those cases where the content of an item is self-evident from the citation itself, in-depth annotation seems unnecessary. Reference is also made to the inclusion of bibliographies, indexes, music examples, facsimiles, illustrations, and other such supportive materials. In addition, most of the items are provided with ISBN, ML, and/or Dewey classification numbers where these numbers are appropriate and available. However, some of the early Hungarian or other European journals in which Bartók's own writings were originally published have been unavailable or difficult to obtain in the United States. Since many of these journals are housed at the National Széchényi Library in Budapest, the special accession numbers employed by that library are given in the citation. These special numbers are preceded by the letter "H" or, occasionally, "HA," "HB," or "HC." In several cases, where I had no access to the original publication, annotations were made from reprints or translations (usually German, French, or English) of the original primary-source article or book. In fewer cases, where the original page numbers had not been supplied in bibliographic sources that otherwise refer to the original publication, I have indicated "n.p." in my citation. However, the annotation of each primary-source item includes the main publications in which reprints or translated versions of the original subsequently appeared. Where annotations of secondary-source items were obtained from *RILM Abstracts,* the *RILM* number and year are given.

Information used to compile the complete list of Bartók's published compositions in Chapter I was derived from several sources: the Dille catalogue (see item no. 1106), the Szöllösy/Ujfalussy catalogues (item nos. 1125/250), the chronological list of works compiled by Halsey Stevens (see item no. 243), the Somfai/Lampert list in the *New Grove* entry on Bartók, and finally the available information contained in the published musical scores themselves. Since it has been impractical to retain the numbering system as established by Dille and Szöllösy in their catalogue listings of Bartók's musical compositions--my listing is by genre rather than by an exclusively chronological ordering--I have used my own numbering system in this *Guide.*

Béla Bartók: A Guide to Research has been compiled with the intention of providing Bartók scholars and students with a tool to facilitate research into historical, biographical, theoretical, analytical, pedagogical, and ethnomusicological issues. Performers and concert-goers should also find this *Guide* a useful source that provides access both to scholarly and general information on the teaching, performance, and appreciation of Bartók's music. If I have closed some of the bibliographic gaps that have been a source of obstruction in Bartók research, then I feel my task will have been fulfilled.

Elliott Antokoletz
Austin, Texas
October 1987

ACKNOWLEDGMENTS

I am pleased to have this opportunity to thank a number of people who have provided me with invaluable advice and assistance in both scholarly and practical matters. First, I should like to express my deep gratitude to my colleague and friend, Dr. Benjamin Suchoff (former Trustee of the Estate of Béla Bartók and Curator of the New York Bartók Archive), for his assistance in providing me with certain essential information regarding a number of primary-source items as well as other materials that were not readily available. His willingness and eagerness to share his special knowledge based on long experience with the Bartók sources have served to make this *Guide* a more valuable and accurate tool for research. Our many years of discussions of Bartók have not only contributed greatly to my acquisition of indispensable tools for Bartók research but have been a source of inspiration in working with the Bartók materials as well. This has led to our joint authorship of a book, *The Sources of Béla Bartók's System of Composition,* in progress.

Regarding practical matters, I should like especially to thank my student, Allison Claire Welch, for the many months she spent formatting and typing the original draft from my numerous and sometimes illegible index cards. Her own research dealing with Bartók's sources and theoretical approaches has not only permitted her to do more accurate work in this task but has also led to a Master's thesis that represents a valuable contribution to this volume. Her assistance was made possible by a generous grant in 1985 from the University Research Institute of The University of Texas at Austin for which I am also grateful.

Special acknowledgment must be made to my dear friend, Judit Frigyesi, with whom I have been in correspondence since our lectures at the 1981 International Bartók Symposium in Budapest, for her thorough proofreading and correcting of the Hungarian and other language diacritical markings. I must also thank her for some suggestions regarding the list of musical compositions as well as having brought to my attention several significant bibliographic items for inclusion. I want to express my appreciation to my student, Christiane Topel, for aiding me with some of the more difficult translations of a number of items from the German as well as from the Russian. I am also grateful to my student, Victoria Fischer, who is presently writing her D.M.A. treatise on special musicological issues and performance problems in Bartók's *Bagatelles* for piano, Op. 6, for bringing to my attention certain discrepancies in several items regarding publication dates of certain musical and scholarly sources.

This *Guide* might not have entirely reflected the importance of certain areas of Bartók research if it were not for my association and correspondences with several of my Hungarian colleagues. I am pleased to be able to take this opportunity to thank László Somfai (Head of the Budapest Bartók Archívum), with whom I have been in correspondence since our first meeting at the Bartók Seminar-Conference at the University of Pittsburgh in 1975. It was shortly after he had become familiar with my work on certain theoretical principles in Bartók's music that he suggested I further extend my research into the area of Bartók's folkloristic sources and ethnomusicological writings. I am grateful to Dénes Bartha, who directed the Seminar-Conference in Pittsburgh, for having invited me to participate in that event. My friendship and interactions with other major Hungarian Bartók scholars over the past several years have also contributed to my broader knowledge of Bartók research. These include Vera Lampert (archivist at the Budapest Bartók Archívum from 1969 to 1978) and János Kárpáti (Library Director at the Ferenc Liszt Academy in Budapest). Their visits to my home during their invited lectures at The University of Texas led to inspiring discussions of Bartók's music. The entries of the main writings of these scholars in this volume attest to the valuable contributions they have made to the field of Bartók research.

To Olga Buth, Music Librarian of the Fine Arts Library at The University of Texas at Austin, I must express thanks for providing me with her special expertise not only in searching for materials but also for her advice on classification numbers, computer terminals, and other such practical library matters.

I am most grateful and indebted to my son, Eric, for his aid and advice in the use of the Macintosh computer. His knowledge of word processing, formatting, and all of the many operations necessary for working with the various drafts and final copy have saved me countless hours of labor.

I am also pleased to have this opportunity to thank Péter Bartók for kindly providing me with the frontispiece photograph of his father, which was taken by Ernst Nash during Bartók's residence in the United States between 1940 and 1945.

Finally, I should like to thank Garland for requesting that I compile this *Guide,* and to express special appreciation to Dr. Guy A. Marco, Marie Ellen Larcada, and Pamela Chergotis for their editorial advice and assistance.

*   *   *

Grateful acknowledgment is made to a number of colleagues and friends for their assistance in the preparation of this revised and enlarged edition. I should like to express my gratitude to Benjamin Suchoff, Ferenc László, Jürgen Hunkemöller, László Somfai, and Malcolm Gillies for supplying me with updated bibliographic listings and other materials in connection with their own writings on Bartók, and to Péter Bartók and Nelson Dellamaggiore for providing me with a personal copy of the new manuscript-facsimile publication of Bartók's *Viola Concerto.* Further acknowledgment is gratefully made to Malcolm Gillies for having provided me with information about first performances of several of Bartók's chamber works of the 1920s, his suggested emendations of which are listed in his book review in *Music and Letters* (August 1989): 428-30, and have been incorporated into this new edition.

I am especially grateful to Judit Frigyesi, Ferenc László, and Alicja Usarek for providing me with translations of certain Hungarian, Romanian, and German language materials, respectively.

Finally, I should like to extend my thanks to Dr. Guy A. Marco and Leo Balk for requesting that I update the original publication and to Phyllis Korper for her intelligent and meticulous copyediting of the manuscript. This new edition has also given me the opportunity to correct errors found in the original publication.

HISTORY OF BARTÓK'S MUSICAL DEVELOPMENT: AN INTRODUCTION

1. Basic Sources of Bartók's Style

Béla Viktor János Bartók (March 25, 1881-September 26, 1945) was born in the town of Nagyszentmiklós in the Torontál district of Hungary. When two-thirds of Hungarian territory was distributed among Romania, Yugoslavia, and Czechoslovakia after the signing of the Treaty of Trianon in June 1920, Bartók's birthplace was absorbed into the western tip of Romania and renamed Sînnicolau Mare. This national tragedy was to have great psychological ramifications for Bartók in the course of his personal and musical development. He recurrently expressed his grief and pessimism and advocated a philosophy based on his desire for brotherhood among nations. The evolution of his musical aesthetics is a direct reflection of his philosophy. As a result of his broad international interests and activities, he was to absorb both divergent folk- and art-music sources into a highly original musical language and style.

In the late nineteenth and early twentieth centuries, several conflicting musical forces became evident in Europe, the most prominent of which were German late Romanticism, French Impressionism, and the folk music of Eastern Europe. Increasing nationalist demands during the decades of international tension prior to the First World War contributed to the independent developments of these forces. Non-Germanic composers began to react against the ultra-chromaticism of the Wagner-Strauss period as they turned away from the long tradition of German musical hegemony toward the new spheres of influence in France and Eastern Europe. These conditions served as the social and musical framework from which Bartók's art was to emerge.

Bartók's pioneering musical role is best understood in the context of international political developments. As part of a dual monarchy, Hungary was absorbed into the German political sphere as a member of the Triple Alliance (which included Germany, the Austro-Hungarian Empire, and temporarily Italy), so that, in 1918, Hungary suffered defeat along with Germany and Austria. Ruled by the Germanized Magyar aristocracy, the Hungarian peasants and the national minorities (especially Romanians, Serbo-Croatians, and Slovaks) opposed the domination of their country by the Austrian Habsburgs. Intense nationalistic sentiment had already burst forth in the Hungarian Revolution of 1848, which was led by the patriot Lajos Kossuth. While the Hungarians achieved independence, this autonomy was short lived. In 1849 Austria, with the aid of both Russia and the rebellious Slavic and Romanian minorities, ruthlessly suppressed Kossuth's nationalist regime.

2. *Early Germanic Musical Influences from 1897 to 1902*

Bartók ardently felt the nationalist spirit, but his musical training and knowledge were deeply rooted in the Germanic tradition. His early compositions, dating from the 1890s in Pozsony (now Bratislava, capital of Slovakia), reveal a distinctly Brahmsian style, which was transformed during his student days at the Royal Academy of Music in Budapest (1899-1903) by his intensive studies of the chromatic scores of Wagner (particularly *Tristan und Isolde*). However, Bartók soon became discouraged with the possibilities of further evolving his style in the Germanic tradition.

This problem was temporarily resolved when he heard a performance of Richard Strauss's symphonic poem, *Also sprach Zarathustra,* by the Philharmonic Orchestra on February 2, 1902, which led Bartók out of a period of stagnation: the Strauss work contained "the seeds for a new life."[1] In the same year Bartók transcribed Strauss's *Ein Heldenleben,* for piano solo: his memorized, virtuoso performance made a profound impression in Budapest and later, on January 26, 1903, at the Tonkünstlerverein in Vienna.

His own compositions began to reveal the harmonic, tonal, and motivic influences of Strauss. This idiom guided him toward the creation of a new type of chromatic melody, later exemplified in such works as movement I of his *First String Quartet* (1908-1909).[2] Although the chromatic line of the quartet evokes the romantic restlessness expressed in the musical thread of Wagner's *Tristan und Isolde,* Bartók's freer tonality (largely achieved by sudden major-minor mixtures) and an almost continuously dissonant texture (based on pervasive use of appoggiaturas and sevenths) may be primarily associated with the more daring harmonic fabric of Strauss's works, for example, his opera *Elektra* (1906-1908).[3] Both the Bartók quartet and Strauss opera are based on the assumptions of triadic harmony, but their constantly shifting tonalities frequently result in polytonal relations.

---

[1] See Bartók's "Selbstbiographie," which originally appeared in several versions, the first in *Musikblätter des Anbruch* (Vienna) 3/5 (March 1921): 87-90; see also Béla Bartók, *Essays* (New York: St. Martin's Press, 1976), p. 410.

[2] Elliott Antokoletz, *The Music of Béla Bartók: A Study of Tonality and Progression in Twentieth-Century Music* (Berkeley and Los Angeles: University of California Press, 1984), p. 14.

[3] This relationship should not be construed to mean that the quartet is influenced by the opera but, rather, that they demonstrate parallel developments. While the general impact of Strauss' idiom on Bartók was decisive, he expressed a specific dislike for *Elektra* in an essay written in 1910; see "Elektra. Strauss Richard operája," *A zene* (Budapest) 2/4 (April 1910): 57-58.

Straussian characteristics can also be observed in other works of the same year. Both the early *Concerto for Violin and Orchestra,* Op. posth., and *Two Portraits* for orchestra are based on the same leitmotif, D-F#-A-C#, which is also recognizable in the *First String Quartet* as well as No. XIV of the *Fourteen Bagatelles,* Op. 6, for piano. This leitmotif has programmatic significance, symbolizing the violinist Stefi Geyer with whom Bartók was in love. In addition to the romantic feature, these works are also structurally related: Bartók had incorporated the first movement of the then unpublished *Concerto*[4] into the *Two Portraits,* with some alteration, and combined it with an orchestral version of No. XIV of the *Bagatelles.* [5]

3. Influence of Liszt, the Magyar Nóta, and First Contact with Authentic Hungarian Folk Music (1902-1905)

In the spring of 1903 resurgent patriotic movements throughout Hungary further roused Bartók's nationalism. He adopted national dress, spoke Hungarian rather than German, and dropped the prefix "von" from his family name, i.e., some of his early compositions were signed "Béla von Bartók." As a patriotic gesture he wrote *Kossuth,* a symphonic poem on the life of the revolutionary hero.[6]

Stemming from Bartók's piano studies with István Thomán, one of Liszt's most gifted pupils, we now find the influence of Liszt as much in evidence as that of Strauss. Bartók had already given his debut in Budapest in October 1901, with a performance of Liszt's *Sonata in B Minor.* The characteristic style of Liszt's *Hungarian Rhapsodies* is apparent in Bartók's "Fantasy II" and "Scherzo" from *Four Piano Pieces* (1903), *Rhapsody for Piano,* Op. 1 (1904), and especially *Kossuth.* At the same time, other works written between 1902 and 1905 had also begun to reveal Bartók's inclination toward the development of a new national style, in particular, the *Four Songs* set to the folk-like texts of Lajos Pósa, *Violin Sonata,* and the *Piano Quintet.*

This new style, derived from Hungarian urban folk song (that is, popular art song or "Magyar nóta"), developed in the nineteenth century from a similar type of German urban folk song known as the "Volkstümlichlied." These songs, usually with piano accompaniment, are generally strophic in form with an architectonic (or rounded) ABA structure. Numerous Hungarian imitations were composed by amateurs from the educated classes and disseminated along with the verbunkos

---

[4]Published posthumously by Boosey & Hawkes (London) in 1958.

[5]Halsey Stevens, *The Life and Music of Béla Bartók* (New York: Oxford University Press, 1954; revised 1964. Third edition, prepared by Malcolm Gillies, Oxford: Clarendon Press, 1993), p. 265.

[6]*Béla Bartók Letters,* ed. János Demény, trans. Peter Balaban and István Farkas, rev. Elizabeth West and Colin Mason (London: Faber & Faber; Budapest: Corvina Press, 1971), p. 29.

(recruiting dance) and csárdás by urban Gypsy bands.[7] (The "Magyar nóta" was not exclusively urban, however, since Gypsy bands were invited to peasant gatherings in small villages as well.)

In 1904, however, and quite by chance, Bartók first came into contact with authentic Hungarian folk music. He heard a peasant girl named Lidi Dósa singing a popular art song with modal inflection and attenuated stanzaic structure. Her rendition was remarkably different from the Gypsy-styled café versions, which he originally thought, as did Liszt and Brahms, to be the authentic folk music of his country.

Thus, Bartók was impelled to investigate the musical repertory of Lidi Dósa's native Transylvanian village and its environs as a new source for his own compositions. Together with Zoltán Kodály (1882-1967), with whom Bartók had formed a lasting relationship at the end of 1905, the two young composers visited Hungarian villages in July of 1906 to collect and record peasant music: Bartók in the eastern part of the country, Kodály in the north.

4. Bartók's First Folk-Music Investigations, His Discovery of Debussy, and Early Compositional Results (1905 Through World War I)

Various composers in the late nineteenth and early twentieth centuries turned to the modalities of their native folk music as the basis for composition, but it was Bartók who most thoroughly and extensively transformed these modes into the materials of a new musical language. In his autobiography Bartók discussed the influence of these sources.[8]

In his desire to move away from traditional Western influences, Bartók had to find the means for deriving new pitch structures to harmonize both authentic folk melodies of Eastern origin and his own original inventions, which might include imitations of folk melodies. The folk tunes themselves showed him new ways of harmonization. Using Edison phonograph cylinders, he and Kodály were able to record multiple thousands of melodies on the spot and later transcribe (notate), analyze, and order them according to a modified classification system developed by Ilmari Krohn.[9] In Bartók's early explorations into the sources of Hungarian peasant music, certain musical styles became apparent. He found that the peasants, in their oral musical tradition, naturally tended to transform the elements of their music, giving rise to

---

[7] See Béla Bartók, *The Hungarian Folk Song,* ed. Benjamin Suchoff (Albany: State University of New York Press, 1981), pp. xv-xvi; also see Benjamin Suchoff, "Ethnomusicological Roots of Béla Bartók's Musical Language," *The World of Music* (1987): 2.

[8] "Selbstbiographie," *Musikblätter des Anbruch* (March 1921): 87-90; see also *Essays,* p. 410.

[9] Finnish ethnologist (1867-1960). Later, Bartók independently developed his own methodological approach to the classification of musical folklore.

numerous variants of one or another melody.[10] Some peasant groups who had been minimally exposed to outside cultural influences (as with a segment of the Romanian population) tended to preserve their old traditions without change. Other peasant groups, having had intercommunication with surrounding tribes and with urban centers, absorbed foreign elements into their existing music, creating a new style that probably began its development only at the turn of the eighteenth century. Thus, Bartók found older and newer styles present alongside one another in some nations (e.g., the Moravians and the Slovaks), while a single homogeneous style several centuries old was preserved in other nations.

Among the Hungarian peasants, the newer style developed in the nineteenth century side by side with the older traditions, gradually replacing them. Peasants found it desirable to imitate certain cultural features of the upper classes from the towns, thereby absorbing and transforming them into a new yet entirely homogeneous Hungarian peasant style. Furthermore, with greater intercommunication, foreign elements from neighboring peoples (e.g., especially from the Romanians and Slovaks, coming mostly by way of the West) infiltrated Hungarian villages. This acculturation resulted in melodies exhibiting heterogeneous ethnic characteristics. Thus, of the diversely collected folk materials, Bartók distinguished three categories: (1) melodies in the old Hungarian peasant-music style; (2) melodies in the new Hungarian peasant-music style; and (3) a group of diverse melodies exhibiting no unity of style.[11] Bartók considered the old and new styles far more significant than the mixed style, and it is these that pervade his own musical compositions. These early investigations culminated in Bartók's many articles and his classic study, *A magyar népdal* (The Hungarian folk song), published in Budapest in 1924.

As Hungarian cultural life was becoming reoriented toward that of France, Bartók found yet another source for his musical language in the works of Debussy.[12] Bartók's appointment in 1907 as a teacher of piano at the Academy of Music in Budapest was important for his development in both areas. Firstly, it permitted him to settle in Hungary and continue his investigations of folk music. Secondly, at the instigation of Kodály, who was also appointed as composition teacher there, he began to study the music of Debussy thoroughly. According to the contents of Bartók's library (now in the Bartók Archívum in Budapest), Bartók purchased Debussy's *String Quartet* and other works during October 1907, and,

---

[10]See Bartók, "Hungarian Peasant Music," *Musical Quarterly* 19/3 (July 1933): 267-289, and *Essays*, p. 81.

[11]See Bartók, *Essays*, p. 84.

[12]See Bartók, "Hongrie," *La revue musicale* 2 (December 1938): 436.

between 1907 and 1911, a number of the piano pieces, including *Pour le piano, L'isle joyeuse, Images I* and *II,* and *Préludes I.*[13]

Bartók's own *Quatre nénies* (Four Dirges), Op. 9a, reveals significant connections with the Debussy works, not only in the use of a French title but also in the prominent use of pentatonic formations in the *Second Dirge.* Bartók was surprised to find in Debussy's work "pentatonic phrases" similar to those in Hungarian peasant music, attributing this to influences of folk music from Eastern Europe, particularly Russia.[14] More extensive similarities between the musical languages of Bartók and Debussy may be seen in the use of modal and whole-tone formations, for example, in Bartók's *First String Quartet* (1908-1909) and his opera, *Duke Bluebeard's Castle* (1911). The opera libretto by Béla Balázs, like that of Debussy's *Pelléas et Mélisande,* finds its inspiration in Maurice Maeterlinck's dramatic symbolism, so the pervasive interactions of modal and whole-tone materials similarly found in the symbolist-impressionist contexts of these two operas hardly appear to be coincidental.

The *Eight Hungarian Folk Songs* for voice and piano (1907-1917) were among Bartók's earliest folk-song arrangements for concert performance. The first five were collected in 1907 during his folk-song expedition to the Csík District of Transylvania. The last three were collected from Hungarian soldiers in 1916-1917, when expeditions to the villages were severely restricted by the war, and are based on soldiers' texts. Both sets were joined in one volume and published in 1922. Six of the eight songs belong to the old style, four of which are exclusively pentatonic, and pentatonic segments are prominent in the vocal lines of two of the songs that are otherwise modally heptatonic.

5. Expanded Folk-Music Investigations and First Mature Compositions

Following his initial investigations of Hungarian folk music in 1906, Bartók also began to explore the folk music of other nations. Unlike Kodály, whose folk-music activities remained limited to the Hungarian villages, Bartók's increasingly international interests led him to collect the melodies of the Slovaks in the autumn of the same year and of the Romanians in the summer of 1909. In 1910, he made his first attempts to collaborate with Slovaks and Romanians in a project for the publication of scientific studies of his respective folk-music collections. In 1913, his collecting tours also took him to the Biskra District in Algeria, where he recorded Arab folk music. These as well as his other expeditions were to result in the collection, transcription, and analysis of thousands of melodies from Eastern Europe (Bulgaria, Hungary,

---

[13] See Anthony Cross, "Debussy and Bartók," *Musical Times* 108 (1967):126.

[14] Musorgsky is a major forerunner of this tendency, and there is evidence that Debussy acquired certain features of folk music primarily from the Russian composer.

Romania, Ruthenia, Slovakia, and Yugoslavia), from North Africa, and in 1936 from Turkey. His scholarly contributions in the field of folk-music research have been published in various languages in many books and a substantial number of shorter essays.[15]

Bartók's expanded folk-music research also resulted in wider influences that were absorbed into his own musical compositions. The Slovak collection provided source material for *Four Slovakian Folksongs* for voice and piano (the first three ca. 1907, the fourth in 1916); the fifth piece of the *Fourteen Bagatelles,* Op. 6, for piano (1908; based on a Slovakian folksong from the province of Gömör); the second volume of piano pieces from *Gyermekeknek* (For Children, 1908-1909); and, between 1917 and 1924, transcriptions for vocal solo, and male and female choruses.

In the *Bagatelles,* which represented for Bartók "a new piano style that appeared in reaction to the exuberance of the romantic piano music of the nineteenth century,"[16] we find, in addition to the general exploitation of progressive compositional techniques (e.g., polytonality in No. I, ostinato rhythmic patterns in Nos. II and V, and modally derived fourth chords in No. XI), experiments with the irregular rhythm (No. V) and tritone (e.g., Nos. VIII, XI, and XIII) of the Slovaks. Bartók's Romanian research also broadened the scope of his compositions, leading to an early arrangement of a Romanian folksong in the fifth of the*Vázlatok* ("Sketches," 1908-1910) and a number of other transcriptions in 1915, including the *Sonatina, Romanian Folk Dances from Hungary, Romanian Christmas Songs (Colinde),* which are all for piano,*Two Romanian Folksongs* for a four-part women's chorus, and *Nine Romanian Songs* for voice and piano (unpublished). Influences from his Arab folk-music research in 1913 are evident in movement III of his *Piano Suite,* Op.14 (1916), and the *Second String Quartet* (1915-1917). Bartók's plans to expand his sphere of research to Russian folk music were prevented by the outbreak of World War I in 1914, and, two years later, Romania's military involvement forced discontinuation of further expeditions to Transylvania.

6. Toward Synthesis of Divergent Art- and Folk-Music Sources

Despite the reaction against the prevailing Germanic influences in Budapest at the turn of the century and the search for new sources of artistic inspiration, many of Bartók's compositions continued to manifest certain characteristics prevalent in the Germanic musical tradition. Fundamental features of this tradition were to be absorbed into his compositions and eventually synthesized with those of the peasant melodies and French musical sources. However, in his early mature works of 1908-1909, these sources were only juxtaposed in a given movement

---

[15]See below, under "Primary Sources."
[16]See Bartók, *Essays,* pp. 432-433.

or work, rather than being synthesized, fused, or transformed into a unified style.

In terms of the Germanic style, the *First String Quartet,* like Strauss's opera *Elektra,* is historically transitional in its interaction of triadic harmonies with chromatic melodic lines that unfold according to nonfunctional voice-leading patterns.[17] Both works epitomize late Romantic music on the threshold of a new chromatic idiom. However, while Strauss never crossed that threshold, Bartók's *First Quartet* was only the beginning of his new chromaticism. At the same time, we also find the "parlando-rubato" style of Eastern European folk music as well as direct references to certain impressionistic passages of Debussy's *String Quartet* in the quiet flow of inverted parallel triads. These three divergent sources are also reflected throughout the work by the juxtapositions of chromatic, pentatonic/modal, and whole-tone passages.

The latter two sources (Hungarian folk music and French impressionism) are especially evident in Bartók's opera *Duke Bluebeard's Castle* (1911), the libretto inspired by Maeterlinck's symbolist drama. Bartók dedicated the work to his first wife, Márta Ziegler, whom he married in the autumn of 1909. The opera was rejected as unperformable in a competition for a national opera because its genuine Hungarian qualities were unrecognizable to an audience accustomed to hearing Italianate or Germanized settings of Hungarian texts. Due to the failure of this work as well as of the New Hungarian Musical Association (UMZE), which Bartók and other young Hungarian composers organized to promote new Hungarian music, Bartók withdrew from public musical life in 1912.

Due to the outbreak of World War I in 1914, Bartók had to give up much of his ethnomusicological fieldwork. As a result, he devoted more of his time to the systematic arrangement of the large quantities of folk material he had accumulated. This new stage in work with the folk material and the greater amount of time that he was able to spend in composing partly account for the developments in his compositional creativity.

The first products of this period, in addition to the Romanian and Slovak settings mentioned earlier, were the one-act ballet, *The Wooden Prince* (1916), on a Balázs libretto, the *Piano Suite* (1916), two sets of songs of five songs each, *Öt dal,* Op. 15 (1915) and *Öt dal,* Op. 16 (1916), the latter composed to poems of Endre Ady, and the *Second String Quartet* (1915-1917). The works of this period, especially the *Second Quartet,* reveal a greater fusion of those diverse sources found in his earlier compositions, with a tendency toward more pervasive manifestations of the folk-music sources, including the influences of

---

[17]With the disappearance, in the early part of the twentieth century, of the traditional triad as the basic harmonic premise, greater importance was placed on the interval as a primary means of harmonic and melodic integration.

Arab folk music. Furthermore, the *Second Quartet* reveals, more than any of Bartók's preceding works, a greater transformation of traditional modal elements into abstract pitch formations and marks a radical break from the harmonic progression in the *First Quartet.*

7. End of World War I to Mid-1920s

The war ended with the defeat of the Alliance, the fall of the Habsburg Empire, and severe political and economic deterioration. The revolution in 1918 brought an independent republic under Count Mihály Károly, whose more liberal rule was soon replaced by the communist dictatorship of Béla Kun in March 1919. Kun's overthrow by Romanian soldiers in July 1919 paved the way for the extreme nationalism of Admiral Miklós Horthy, who was made regent in 1920. Despite these conditions, Bartók was able to produce several significant works between 1918 and 1920, including the *Three Studies,* Op. 18, for piano (1918), the one-act pantomime *The Miraculous Mandarin,* Op. 19 (1919), on a libretto by Menyhért Lengyel, and the *Eight Improvisations on Hungarian Peasant Songs,* Op. 20, for piano (1920). All three works now reveal remarkable developments in style and musical language.

The *Studies* deal with specific pianistic problems not occurring in the etudes of Chopin, Debussy, Stravinsky, or Prokofiev.[18] Although they encompass a smaller range of expression, they are technically and tonally beyond anything occurring in his earlier piano works. Particularly notable is the new concern with the extensions and contractions of the pianist's hand. While the *Studies* were premiered with the Ady songs (*Öt dal,* Op. 16) and the *Piano Suite,* Op. 14, at one of the "composer's concerts" arranged for Bartók in 1919, the *Mandarin* was not to be performed in Budapest during his lifetime, despite the profound and striking quality of the music. Part of the antagonism it aroused was due to the nature of its plot.

After the signing of the Treaty of Trianon in 1920, Hungary had lost much of her pre-war territory to surrounding nations, including Romania, Czechoslovakia, and the Kingdom of Serbs, Croats, and Slovenes (the Former Yugoslavia).[19] This national loss was also a personal tragedy for Bartók: the severed territories were no longer open to the Hungarian folk-music collector. Conditions since the end of the war had already led Bartók to consider an extended leave of absence from his teaching position at the Academy of Music, as expressed in a letter of October 23, 1919.[20]

Although Bartók ultimately remained in Hungary and continued to teach at the Academy, he was forced to shift his activities during this

---

[18] Stevens, *The Life and Music of Béla Bartók,* p. 125.

[19] Failure to recover these territories led to the Hungarian alliance with Nazi Germany in 1941.

[20] *Béla Bartók Letters,* ed. Demény, p. 144.

period more toward composition and an intensive concert career. This change of activity can be observed in part in his approach to those compositions that continued to include authentic folk melodies, the approach now best described as composing with folk song rather than folk-song arranging.

In the *Eight Improvisations on Hungarian Peasant Songs,* Op. 20, for piano (1920), the underlying tunes themselves, which were collected from Felsőiregh (in the District of Tolna), Hottó (Zala), Kórógy (Szerém), Csíkgyimes (Csík), Lengyelfalva (Udvarhely), and Diósad (Szilágy), are secondary to the added materials: the elements of the tunes are systematically developed, modified, and transformed into highly abstract pitch sets and interactions.

The significance of Bartók's change of activities in the 1920s can also be seen in his increased contact with international composers and their works. In his two *Sonatas for Violin and Piano* (1921 and 1922), Bartók came closer than in any of his other works to a kind of atonal chromaticism and harmonic serialization typical of the expressionistic works of the Schoenberg school. At about the same time, Schoenberg was producing his first completely serial twelve-tone works.[21]

In Bartók's works written in the mid-1920s, the transformation of his musical language into further abstractions (or at least fusions) of the modal elements of folk music may have been given some direction toward extreme systematization by his contact with other contemporary composers and their works: in 1921 he met Ravel and Stravinsky in Paris, through the musical writer Henri Prunières, and in 1922 he participated with members of the Schoenberg circle, Stravinsky, Milhaud, Hindemith, Busoni, and others in the first performances of the International Society for Contemporary Music (ISCM). It was at this time that interest in Bartók as a composer was fostered in Britain by two young composer-critics, Philip Heseltine (Peter Warlock) and Cecil Gray.[22] This contributed to his first substantial recognition outside of Hungary.

In the next couple of years, Bartók produced little because of his heavy concert schedule and work at the Academy. His most successful work at this time was the *Dance Suite* for orchestra (1923), which was also arranged for solo piano (1925). The work reveals an increased economy of material based on a synthesis of a wider variety of folk sources than previously; the first and fourth dances show certain Arab influences, the second, third, and ritornel Hungarian, and the fifth

---

[21]Bartók once commented that he "wanted to show Schoenberg that one can use all twelve tones and still remain tonal": Yehudi Menuhin, *Unfinished Journey* (New York: Alfred A. Knopf, 1977), p. 165.

[22]See Malcolm Gillies, *Bartók in Britain: A Guided Tour* (Oxford: Clarendon Press, 1989), especially the chapter, "1922: In the Limelight," pp. 30-49. Gillies also explores, more widely, Bartók's many visits to Britain on concert tours between 1904 and 1938.

Romanian; all of these sources are synthesized in the finale.[23] Other scholars also point to the combination of modal folk sources in this work.[24]

8. *Final Period (1926-1945)*

Following *Village Scenes* (1924) for voice and piano, based on five Slovak folk songs, Bartók moved into a new phase of productivity in terms of piano composition. In the year 1926 alone, he composed the *Sonata, the Out of Doors* cycle of five pieces, *Nine Little Piano Pieces, First Piano Concerto,* and several short compositions that were eventually to become part of the *Mikrokosmos* (completed in 1939), a collection of 153 progressive pieces in part written for didactic purposes.

At the time of the ISCM in London three years earlier (1923), Bartók had met the American composer Henry Cowell. Impressed by the latter's use of tone clusters, Bartók asked him if he could use them in his own compositions. Although these piano works of the mid-1920s bear little relationship to the percussive sonorities as conceived by Cowell, they nevertheless tended toward greater textural and harmonic density. While Bartók composed these works partly out of the practical necessity of providing himself with concert repertoire, they also represented in many ways a new stage in the synthesis of his musical language.[25] The *Piano Concerto,* first performed at the ISCM at Frankfurt on July 1, 1927, is representative of the new percussive style, in which the melody is in a simpler folk-like style while the harmonic dimension is more abstract and dissonant.[26] Another source is also apparent in this as well as the other piano works of this year. Bartók toured Italy during 1925, during which time, in addition to his own performances of Baroque Italian music, he was inspired to investigate contrapuntal techniques in the keyboard works of Benedetto Marcello, Michelangelo Rossi, Azzolino Bernardino della Ciaia, Girolamo Frescobaldi, and Domenico Zipoli, transcribing some of their works for piano.[27]

---

[23]Stevens,*The Life and Music of Béla Bartók,* p. 270.

[24]Benjamin Suchoff, "The Impact of Italian Baroque Music on Bartók's Music," *Bartók and Kodály Revisited,* ed. György Ránki (Budapest: Akadémiai Kiadó, 1987), pp. 187-188.

[25]For a detailed study of the stylistic and structural problems in these works, see László Somfai, "Analytical Notes on Bartók's Piano Year of 1926," *Studia musicologica* 26 (1984): 5-58.

[26]Stevens, *The Life and Music of Béla Bartók,* p. 68.

[27]In addition to a variety of folk sources, the impact of Frescobaldi's toccatas and della Ciaia's Canzone on the *First Concerto* is demonstrated by Suchoff in "The Impact of Italian Baroque Music on Bartók's Music," *Bartók and Kodály Revisited,* ed. György Ránki (Budapest: Akadémiai Kiadó, 1987), p. 189.

At the ISCM concert in Baden-Baden on July 16, 1927, Bartók performed his own *Piano Sonata* on the same program as Berg's *Lyric Suite* for string quartet. Shortly afterward, Bartók completed his *Third* and *Fourth String Quartets* (September 1927 and September 1928, respectively). Although the Bartók works show little stylistic resemblance to the lush romantic textures of the *Lyric Suite,* one may observe a superficial yet striking similarity in their common use of exotic instrumental colors as well as certain common assumptions underlying their symmetrical pitch relations. This comparison is not meant to suggest that Bartók was influenced by Berg's use of pitch symmetry but, rather, that these quartets of the two composers reveal parallel historical developments; Bartók had already exploited principles of inversional symmetry in No. II of his *Bagatelles,* Op. 6, for piano, in 1908, and many works since then.[28]

Bartók's move toward ever-greater abstraction and synthesis of divergent art- and folk-music sources had reached its most intensive stage of development in the *Fourth Quartet.* The large-scale arch form of the five-movement plan serves as a carefully constructed framework within which Bartók organizes diversified melodic, harmonic, and rhythmic formations into a highly systematic network of interrelationships. Despite the more abstract medium, rhythmic and structural properties of folk music are nevertheless still very much in evidence. Elements from Hungarian and other folk sources provide materials that contribute to the distinctive styles of the different movements. The cello line that opens the slow movement is in the parlando-rubato rhythm of the old Hungarian folksong style, or the *horă lungă* (long song) that Bartók discovered in Romanian folk music,[29] and is accompanied by a typical Eastern-European bagpipe-like drone. The complex tempo-giusto dance rhythm of the last movement includes an unequal-beat rhythmic ostinato (3 + 2 + 3/8) typically occurring in Bulgarian folk music.

The year 1928 was one of the most prolific for Bartók. In addition to the *Fourth Quartet,* he wrote two *Rhapsodies* for violin and piano, both arranged for violin and orchestra, the *First Rhapsody* appearing in a version for cello and piano as well. Both works are prominently founded upon certain folk characteristics which foreshadow Bartók's renewed interest in folk-music settings. That same year Bartók participated in the International Folk Music Congress in Prague, and his new folk-song arrangements and transcriptions during the next decade reveal his increasing interest in folk texts.

The *Twenty Hungarian Folksongs* for voice and piano were composed in 1929, followed by *Four Hungarian Folksongs* for mixed chorus, a cappella (1930), *Transylvanian Dances* for orchestra (1931),

---

[28]See Antokoletz, *The Music of Béla Bartók,* p. 21 and Chap. VI.

[29]See Péter Laki, "Der lange Gesang als Grundtyp in der internationalen Volksmusik" [The long song as basic type in international folk music]. *Studia musicologica* 24/3-4 (1982): 393-400.

which are a transcription of the earlier *Sonatina* for piano (1915), *Hungarian Sketches* for orchestra (1931), *Székely Songs* for male chorus, a cappella (1932), *Hungarian Peasant Songs* for orchestra (1933, which are transcriptions of pieces from the *Fifteen Hungarian Peasant Songs* of 1914-1917), *Hungarian Folksongs* for voice and orchestra (1933, which are transcriptions of pieces from the *Twenty Hungarian Folksongs* of 1929), *Twenty-Seven Choruses* for two- and three-part children's or women's chorus (1935), and *From Olden Times,* on old Hungarian folk- and art-song texts, for three-part male chorus, a cappella (1935), as well as many pieces from the *Mikrokosmos* for piano (1926-1939).

As in the earlier *Rhapsody,* Op. 1 (1904), the *Second Sonata* for violin and piano (1922), and later *Contrasts* for violin, clarinet, and piano (1938), and the general characteristics of many other Bartók compositions, the two *Rhapsodies* are based on highly ornamented folk materials and are divided into the conventional lassú (slow "parlando rubato") and friss (quick "tempo giusto") of the *Verbunkos* style.[30] The Gypsy association is also evident in the use of the dulcimer-like cimbalom in the orchestral version of the *First Rhapsody.*

In the increasingly repressive political atmosphere of the 1930s, Bartók withdrew from performing his own works in Budapest. In 1930 he also composed one of several planned cantatas to express his ideal view of the brotherhood of neighboring nations--Romania, Slovakia, and Hungary. The *Cantata Profana,* which is the only completed work of the group, represents the most explicit musical embodiment of his philosophy.[31] Throughout his life, Bartók felt a deep personal commitment to the principles of national independence and artistic freedom.[32] Stylistically, the *Cantata* reveals a neoclassical approach in its use of earlier forms and procedures, including canon, fugue, aria,

---

[30]"Verbunkos" (from the German "Werbung"), or "recruiting," was a Hungarian dance that served as a method of enlistment during the imperial wars of the eighteenth century. The main part of the dance, which consisted of the alternation between slow and quick figures, was performed by a group of hussars led by a sergeant. The musicians, who were mostly gypsies, accompanied them with simple folk tunes and improvised instrumental accompaniments. The idiom was developed by Hungarian violin virtuosi in the early nineteenth century and has survived primarily in the csárdás; see John S. Weissmann, "Verbunkos," *The New Grove Dictionary of Music and Musicians,* ed. Stanley Sadie (6th ed., London: Macmillan, 1980), pp. 629-630.

[31]In a letter of January 10, 1931, Bartók asserted his ideals of international brotherhood. See *Béla Bartók Letters,* ed. Demény, p. 201.

[32]Serge Moreux, in *Béla Bartók, sa vie, ses oeuvres, son langage* (Paris: Richard-Masse, 1949), p. 81, has suggested that the *Cantata Profana* was a protest against the restrictions of the Regent of Hungary, Miklós Horthy.

cadenza, turba, and double choruses as well as an orchestral introduction resembling the opening of Bach's *St. Matthew Passion.* The fusion of all these familiar features into a highly systematic network of relationships produces one of Bartók's most personal expressions.

During the 1930s, Bartók continued his folk-music research primarily with institutional sources. He attended the International Congress of Arab Folk Music in Cairo in 1932, studied Romanian folk music at the Bucharest Phonogramme Archives in 1934, began work on the publication of his Hungarian folk-music collection in the same year, became a member of the Hungarian Academy of the Sciences in 1936, and visited Turkey for his last folk-music collecting tour that same year.

During this period, he composed the *Second Piano Concerto* (1931), *Forty-Four Duos* for two violins (1931), *Fifth String Quartet* (1934), *Music for Strings, Percussion, and Celesta* (1936), commissioned by Paul Sacher, whom Bartók met in Basel in 1929, *Sonata for Two Pianos and Percussion* (1937), *Contrasts* (1938), which was dedicated to Benny Goodman and Joseph Szigeti, *Violin Concerto* (1938), completion of the *Mikrokosmos* (1939), *Divertimento* for string orchestra (1939), and *Sixth String Quartet* (1939).

Bartók's first performance of the *Second Piano Concerto* in 1933 was his last concert in Germany. Finally, in October 1937, he withdrew permission for the broadcasting of his works by the radio stations of Fascist Italy and Nazi Germany and transferred publication of his music from Universal Edition in Vienna, which was becoming nazified, to Boosey and Hawkes in London in 1937. In April 1938, in a letter to Mrs. Müller-Widman in Switzerland, Bartók expressed his concern about the progress of Nazi power in Eastern Europe, following Germany's unprovoked attack on Austria. Fearful that Hungary, too, would fall under German domination and contemplating the possibility of emigration, Bartók requested his Swiss friend to "give shelter" to his manuscripts.[33]

9. Last Years in the United States (1940-1945)

After the death of his mother in 1939, Bartók no longer had reason to remain in Europe, and so, in October 1940, he and his wife emigrated to New York City. These last years were difficult for Bartók both because of exile from his native national sources and general lack of acceptance of his performances of his own music, which led to severe financial straits. However, a grant from Columbia University made it possible for Bartók to work on the Parry collection of Yugoslav folk-music recordings (held at Harvard University) from March 1941 to the end of 1942, at the same time editing his own Romanian and Turkish materials.

Bartók's health began to decline in 1942, and he gave his last performance in January 1943, in which he and his wife played the *Concerto* arrangement of his *Sonata for Two Pianos and Percussion.* In the same year, Bartók composed the *Concerto for Orchestra.* Several

---

[33] See *Béla Bartók Letters,* ed. Demény, p. 267.

important events led to its composition:[34] (1) his discovery of a recording of Dalmatian two-part chromatic folk melodies while transcribing Yugoslav folk music at Columbia University; (2) a request from his London publisher Ralph Hawkes in 1942 for "a series of concertos for solo instrument or instruments and string orchestra . . . or combinations of solo instruments and string orchestra"; (3) a broadcast in 1942 of the Shostakovich "Leningrad" *Symphony No. 7,* in which Bartók, surprised to hear repetitions of a theme that "sounded like a Viennese cabaret song," was to satirize the work by using a variant of this theme in the *interrotto* of movement IV of the *Concerto;* and (4) a commission by Koussevitzky in 1943 for an orchestral work to be performed by the Boston Symphony Orchestra. This *Concerto,* which appears to be Bartók's most popular work, is based on the most extensive "synthesis of Eastern folk-music materials and Western art-music techniques."[35]

In late 1943 Yehudi Menuhin commissioned the *Sonata for Solo Violin,* which Bartók completed for him in 1944, during a period of temporary improvement in his health. His last two works, the *Third Piano Concerto* and *Viola Concerto,* were composed simultaneously in 1945, the latter work left as an incomplete, fragmented piano version just a few weeks before his death on September 26. This work, commissioned by violist William Primrose, was reconstructed by Tibor Serly from Bartók's first draft.[36] Thus, in his contributions to the aesthetics and techniques of modern composition and musicological methodology, Bartók was to serve as one of the most influential models for both composers and musical folklorists since the end of World War II.

---

[34]See Benjamin Suchoff, "Program Notes for the Concerto for Orchestra," *Béla Bartók: A Celebration* (New York: Book-of-the-Month Records, 1981), pp. 6ff.

[35]Ibid.; for a detailed analysis of this work in terms of progression and integration, based on the interaction of diatonic, octatonic, and whole-tone sets, as well as the generation of interval cycles, see Antokoletz, *The Music of Béla Bartók,* Chaps. VII and VIII.

[36]See Tibor Serly, "A Belated Account of the Reconstruction of a 20th Century Masterpiece," *College Music Symposium* 12 (1975): 7-25; see also Sándor Kovács, "Reexamining the Bartók/Serly Viola Concerto," *Studia musicologica* 23 (1981): 295-322.

Béla Bartók

I. PUBLISHED COMPOSITIONS ACCORDING TO GENRE: WITH PUBLISHERS, ARCHIVES, COLLECTIONS, AND CATALOGUES

Publishers

In this list of the main publishers of Bartók's music, only current publishers' addresses are given. These are offered as a source of inquiry regarding practical matters related to Bartók's musical scores.

Archive Edition, Dover, New York
    180 Varick Street
    New York, N. Y. 10014

Bárd Ferenc és Fia, Budapest
    (published Bartók's early pieces)

Boosey and Hawkes, Inc., New York
    24 East 21st Street
    New York, NY 10010-7200

Boosey and Hawkes Music Publishers Limited, London
    295 Regent Street
    London W1R 8JH

Magyar Kórus, Budapest
    (originally a private publisher of Bartók's choruses but
    taken over by the state in 1950; no longer exists)
    For copies of the music, write to:
    Országos "Széchényi" Könyvtár
    1827 Budapest

Rózsavölgyi és Társa, Budapest
    (one of Bartók's publishers from 1904 to 1915)

Rozsnyai Károly, Budapest
    (published some of Bartók's works from 1903 to 1910)

Universal Edition A. G. , Vienna
    Postfach 3
    A-1015 Wien

Universal Edition (London) Limited
   Music Publishers
   2/3 Fareham Street, Dean Street
   London W1V 4DU

Zeneműkiadó Vállalat (= Editio Musica), Budapest
   Vörösmarty Tér 1
   H-1370 Budapest
   Postacím: 322

Archives and Collections

Bartók Archívum, Budapest
   László Somfai, Director
   Magyar Tudományos Akadémia
   Zenetudományi Intézet
   Budapest I., Táncsics Mihály u. 7.
   H-1250 Budapest Pf. 28

Bartók Hagyaték (Bartók estate)
   in the Bartók Archívum
   Budapest I., Táncsics Mihály u. 7.
   H-1250 Budapest Pf. 28

Országos Széchényi Könyvtár
   (Széchényi National Library)
   Polláck Mihály-tér 10
   1827 Budapest

Péter Bartók's Collection
   (Former New York Bartók Archive)
   Péter Bartók, Director
   Bartók Records
   P.O. Box 399
   Homosassa, Florida 34487

Some of Bartók's manuscripts are housed in the following libraries:

British Library (London)
Library of Congress (Washington, D.C.)
Paul Sacher Stiftung (Basel)
Pierpont Morgan Library (New York)
Stadt- und Landesbibliothek and Österreichische
   Nationalbibliothek (Vienna).
University of Pennsylvania (Philadelphia)

CATALOGUE OF COMPOSITIONS

Two of the following items are generally accepted as the standard classifications of Bartók's musical compositions. The numbering system established by Denijs Dille for the youthful works is indicated by DD. The classification employed by András Szőllősy for the remaining body of Bartók's compositions is indicated by Sz. The classification employed by László Somfai in the forthcoming Bartók thematic catalogue is indicated by BB. These numbering systems from the following items are incorporated into the present catalogue of compositions:

(1) Denijs Dille. *Thematisches Verzeichnis der Jugendwerke Béla Bartóks 1890-1904.* Budapest: Akadémiai Kiadó, 1974. 295p. (DD)

(2) András Szőllősy. "Bibliographie des oeuvres musicales et écrits musicologiques de Béla Bartók." In Bence Szabolcsi, ed. *Bartók, sa vie et son oeuvre.* Budapest: Corvina, 1956. pp. 299-345. Slightly revised numbers derive from the English translation of József Ujfalussy. *Bartók Béla.* Budapest: Corvina, 1965; English translation by Ruth Pataki, revised by Elizabeth West. Budapest: Corvina, 1971. pp. 395-430. (Sz)

(3) László Somfai. "Appendix: List of Works and Primary Sources." In *Béla Bartók: Composition, Concepts, and Autograph Sources.* Berkeley and Los Angeles: University of California Press, 1996. pp. 297-320. Classification numbering for the forthcoming Bartók thematic catalogue. (BB)

The following catalogue includes Bartók's published compositions, each given in the language of the original title. English translations are given in brackets. Movements of a work are indicated by Roman numerals, individual pieces within a work by Arabic numerals. Each listing includes some or all of the following: period of composition or its official date of completion (indicated by Date); the person or group to whom dedicated, as referred to by Bartók in the score (indicated by Ded); date, performer(s), and location of the first performance (indicated by Perf); publisher and date of publication (indicated by Pub); and one of the three main catalogues of Bartók's works given above (indicated by Cat). For detailed data on the autograph sources for each work, see item no. 1024.

1. Piano Solo

Youthful Works

1. *Drei Klavierstücke* [Three Piano Pieces] Op. 13
   1. Tavaszi dal [Spring Song]
   2. Valcer [Waltz]
   3. Oláhos [In Wallachian Style]

Date--1896-1897

Pub--No. 1, in Denijs Dille, *Der junge Bartók II*, Zeneműkiadó 1965
Cat--DD 45, BB 8

2. *Scherzo oder Fantasie für das Pianoforte* [Scherzo or Fantasie for Piano] Op. 18

Date--1897
Ded--Gabriella Lator
Pub--in Denijs Dille, *Der junge Bartók II*, Zeneműkiadó 1965
Cat--DD 50, BB 11

3. *Drei Klavierstücke* [Three Piano Pieces] Op. 21
   1. Adagio-Presto
   2. (Without title or tempo indication)
   3. Adagio, sehr düster

Date--1898, Pozsony
Ded--Gabriella Lator
Pub--Nos. 1-2, in Denijs Dille, *Der junge Bartók II*, Zeneműkiadó 1965
Cat--DD 53, BB 14

4. *Változatok F.F. egy témája fölött* [Twelve Variations on a Theme of Felicie Fábián]

Date--1900-1901
Pub--in Denijs Dille, *Der junge Bartók II*, Zeneműkiadó 1965
Cat--DD 64, BB 22

5. *Négy zongoradarab* [Four Piano Pieces]
   1. Tanulmány balkézre [Study for the Left Hand]
   2. I. bránd [Fantasy I]
   3. II. bránd [Fantasy II]
   4. Scherzo

Date--1903
Pub--Bárd Ferenc és Fia 1904 (four pieces published separately);
      Nos. 1-3, Boosey & Hawkes 1950; Zeneműkiadó 1956, 1965;
      Archive 1981
Cat--DD 71, BB 27

6. *Marche funèbre* [Funeral March], arrangement of *Kossuth*, tableau 10

Date--1903
Pub--Kunossy Szilágy és Társa, Budapest 190?, Magyar lant 1905,
      Rozsnyai 1910?, Zeneműkiadó 1950, Archive 1981
Cat--DD 75b, BB 31

Mature Works

7. *Rapszódia* [Rhapsody] Op. 1 (also transcribed for piano and orchestra; and for two pianos)

Date--November 1904
Ded--Emma Gruber
Perf--solo version, November 4, 1906, composer, Pozsony
Pub--Adagio mesto: Rózsavölgyi 1909. Complete: Rózsavölgyi
    1923, Zeneműkiadó 1955, Archive 1981
Cat--Sz 26, Sz 27, BB 36a, BB 36b

8. *Petits morceaux pour piano* [Two Little Pieces for Piano] arrangement and transcription of the following songs:
   1. Add reám csókodat, el kell már búcsúznom [Kiss Me, for I Must Take My Leave]
   2. Őszi szellő [Autumn Breeze], from Four Songs on poems of Lajos Pósa (1902)

Date--1905-1907?
Pub--in Denijs Dille, *Der junge Bartók II,* Zeneműkiadó 1965
Cat--Sz 29/2, DD 67/1, BB 38, BB 24

9. *Három csíkmegyei népdal* [Three Hungarian Folksongs from the Csík District]
   1. Rubato
   2. L'istesso tempo
   3. Poco vivo

Date--1907
Pub--Rozsnyai 1910, Boosey & Hawkes 1950, Zeneműkiadó 1954,
    Archive 1981
Cat--Sz 35a, BB 45b

10. *Tizennégy zongoradarab* [Fourteen Bagatelles] Op. 6
    1. Molto sostenuto
    2. Allegro giocoso
    3. Andante
    4. Grave (arr. of Hungarian folksong "Mikor gulyásbojtár voltam")
    5. Vivo (arr. of Slovak folksong "Ej' po pred naš, po pred naš")
    6. Lento
    7. Allegretto molto capriccioso
    8. Andante sostenuto
    9. Allegretto grazioso
    10. Allegro
    11. Allegretto molto rubato
    12. Rubato
    13. Elle est morte (Lento funebre)
    14. Valse: ma mie qui danse (Presto)

Date--May 1908, Budapest
Perf--June 29, 1908, Vienna (Busoni's piano class)
Pub--Rozsnyai 1908, Boosey & Hawkes 1950, Zeneműkiadó 1953,
    Archive 1981
Cat--Sz 38, BB 50

11. *Tíz könnyű zongoradarab* [Ten Easy Pieces]
    Ajánlás [Dedication]
    1. Paraszti nóta [Peasant Song]
    2. Lassú vergődés [Frustration]
    3. Tót legények tánca [Slovakian Boys' Dance]
    4. Sostenuto
    5. Este a székelyeknél [Evening in Transylvania (Evening with the
       Széklers)]
    6. Gödöllei piactéren leesett a hó [Hungarian Folk Song]
    7. Hajnal (Dawn)
    8. Azt mondják, nem adnak [Slovakian Folk Song]
    9. Ujjgyakorlat [Five-Finger Exercise]
    10. Medvetánc [Bear Dance]

    Date--June 1908, revised 1945
    Perf--No. 10, November 15, 1909, Budapest; No. 5, March 15,
        1910, Budapest
    Pub--Rozsnyai 1909, Zeneműkiadó 1951, Archive 1981
    Cat--Sz 39, BB 51

12. *Két elégia* [Two Elegies] Op. 8b
    1. Grave
    2. Molto adagio, sempre rubato

    Date--No. 1, February 1908; No. 2, December 1909
    Perf--No. 1, April 21, 1919, composer, Budapest
    Pub--Rozsnyai 1910, Boosey & Hawkes 1950, Zeneműkiadó 1955,
        Archive 1981
    Cat--Sz 41, BB 49

13. *Gyermekeknek; Pro dêti* [For Children]
    Eighty-five pieces originally in four volumes. Volumes I and II (I:
    Nos. 1-21, II: Nos. 22-42) are based on Hungarian folk tunes, III and
    IV (III: Nos. I-22, IV: Nos. 23-42) are based on Slovakian folk
    tunes. The revised version (January 1945), which omitted Nos. II/25,
    II/29, IV/27, IV/33, and IV/34 of the original version, contains 79
    pieces in two volumes.
    Vols. I and II
    1. Allegro. Süssünk, süssünk valamit [Let's Bake Something]
    2. Andante. Süss fel nap [Dawn, O Day]
    3. Andante. Elvesztettem páromat [I Lost My Young Couple]

4. Allegro. Elvesztettem zsebkendőmet [I Lost My Handkerchief]
5. Poco allegretto. Cziczkom, Cziczkom [Kitty, Kitty]
6. Allegro. Hej tulipán, tulipán [Hey, Tulip, Tulip]
7. Andante grazioso. Keresd meg a tőt [Look for the Needle]
8. Allegretto. Ej görbénye, görbénye [Hey, Görbénye, Görbénye]
9. Molto adagio. Fehér liliomszál [White Lily]
10. Allegro molto. Az oláhok, az oláhok facipőbe járnak [The Wallachians, the Wallachians Wear Wooden Shoes]
11. Molto sostenuto. Elvesztettem páromat [I Lost My Young Couple]
12. Allegro. Láncz, láncz, este láncz [Chain, Chain, Floral Chain]
13. Andante. Megöltek egy legényt [A Lad was Killed]
14. Allegretto. A csanádi legények [The Poor Lads of Csanád]
15. Allegro. Icike, picike az istvándi ucca [Teeny-Weeny is the Street of Istvánd]
16. Andante rubato. Nem loptam én életembe [I Never Stole in My Whole Life]
17. Adagio. Kis kece lányom [My Little Graceful Girl]
18. Andante con molto. Nagyváradi kikötőbe [In the Harbor of Nagyvárad]
19. Allegretto. Ha bemegyek, ha bemegyek, ha bemegyek a dobozi csárdába [When I Go, When I Go, When I Go into the Inn at Doboz]
20. Poco Allegro. (Drinking Song)
21. Allegro robusto.
22. Allegretto. Debrecenbe kéne menni [One Ought to Go to Debrecen]
23. Allegro grazioso. Így kell járni, úgy kell járni [You Must Walk This Way, That Way]
24. Andante sostenuto. Víz, víz, víz [Water, Water, Water]
25. Allegro. Három alma meg egy fél [Three Apples Plus a Half]
26. Andante. Kerülj rózsám kerülj [Go Round, Sweetheart, Go Round]
27. Allegramente.
28. Parlando. Fehér László lovat lopott [László Fehér Stole a Horse]
29. Allegro. Ej, haj, micsoda [Oh! Hey! What Do You Say]
30. Andante. Felhozták a kakast [They Brought up the Rooster]
31. Allegro scherzando. Anyám édesanyám [Mother, Dear Mother]
32. Allegro ironico. Besüt a nap a templomba [The Sun Shines into the Church]
33. Andante sostenuto. Csillagok, csillagok, szépen ragyogjatok [Stars, Stars, Brightly Shine]

34. Andante. Fehér fuszujkavirág [White Lady's Eardrop]
35. Allegro non troppo. Kertbe virágot szedtem [I Picked Flowers in the Garden]
36. Allegretto. Nem messzi van ide Margitta [Margitta Is Not Far Away]
37. Poco vivace. Ha felmegyek a budai nagy hegyre [When I Go up Buda's Big Mountain]
38. (no tempo indication) Tíz litero bennem van [Ten Liters Are Inside]
39. Allegro. Házasodik a trücsök, szúnyog lányát kéri [The Cricket Marries]
40. Molto vivace. Adjon az úr isten [May the Lord]
41. Allegro moderato. Elmész ruzsám? El bíz én [Do You Go, Darling? I Should Think So]
42. Allegro vivace. Házasodik a trücsök (The Cricket Marries)

Vols. III and IV

1. Allegro. Keby boly čerešne, čerešne, višne, višne [If There Were Cherries, Cherries, Morellos, Morellos]
2. Andante. Kalina, malina [Kite Settled on the Branch]
3. Allegretto. Pod lipko, na lipko edná mala dve [Above the Tree, Under the Tree Two Roses Bloom]
4. Lakodalmas [Wedding Song]. Andante. Ej, Lado, Lado [Hey, Lado, Lado]
5. Változatok [Variations]. Molto andante. Lecela pava, lecela [Flew, the Peacock, Flew]
6. Rondo I [Round Dance I]. Allegro. Stará baba zlá [There Is an Old Witch]
7. Betyárnóta [Sorrow]. Andante.
8. Táncdal [Dance Song]. Allegro. Hej, na prešovskej tudni dva holubky šedza [Hey, Two Pigeons Sit on the Tower of Presov]
9. Rondo II [Round Dance II]. Gyermekdal [Children's Song]. Andante. Zabelej sa, zabelej, zabelej [Unfold Yourself, Blossom, Blossom]
10. Temetésre szól az ének [Mourning Song]. Largo. V mikulásskej kompanii [In the Barracks of Mikulás]
11. Lento. V tej bystrickej bráne [On the Field of Bystrov]
12. Poco andante. Suhajova mati [Mother of My Lover]
13. Allegro. Anička mlynárova [Anička Mlynárova]
14. Moderato. Ore, ore šest volov [Plowing, Plowing Are Six Oxen]
15. Dudanóta [Bagpipe Tune]. Molto tranquillo. Tancuj, dievča, tancuj [Dance, Maiden, Dance]
16. Panasz [Lament]. Lento.
17. Andante. Sluzilo dievča na fare [The Girl Was the Priest's Maidservant]

18. Gúnydal [Teasing Song]. Sostenuto. Mau som ta dievča [Once I Was Your Lover]
19. Románc [Romance]. Assai lento. Daťel na dube, žalostne dube [Bird on the Branch]
20. Kergetőző [Game of Tag]. Prestissimo. Nechocže ty, Hanulienka z rana do trňa [Don't Go at Dawn, Hanulienka, to the Thorny Bush]
21. Tréfa [Pleasantry]. Allegro moderato. Sadla dola, plakala [She Flew Down and Was in Tears]
22. Duhajkodó [Revelry]. Molto allegro. Hnali švarní šuhji kozy do dúbravy [The Lads Caught a Goat]
23. Molto rubato, non troppo lento. Ja som bača velmi starí [I Am Already an Old Shepherd]
24. Poco andante. Koj som išol cez horu [I Passed Through the Forest]
25. Andante. Daťel na dube, žalostne dube [Bird on the Branch]
26. Scherzando   Allegretto.
27. Csúfolódás [Teasing Song]. Allegro
28. Furulyaszó [Peasant's Flute]. Andante molto rubato
29. Még egy tréfa [Another Pleasantry]. Allegro.
30. Andante molto rubato. Dosti som sa nachodil [I Have Wandered a Lot]
31. Kánon [Canon]. Poco vivace.
32. Szól a duda [Bagpipe II]. Vivace. Zahradka, zahradka [Little Garden, Little Garden]
33. Rvagyerek [The Orphan]. Poco andante. Ej, hory, hory, zelené hory [Hey, Forest, Forest, Green Forest]
34. Románc [Romance]. Poco allegretto. Viem ja jeden hájiček [I Know a Little Forest]
35. Nóta egy másik betyárról [The Highway Robber]. Allegro. Bol by ten Jánošik [Jánošik Is a Big Bully]
36. Largo. Kebych ja vedela [If I Knew Where My Darling Mows Hay in the Morning]
37. Molto tranquillo. Pri Prešporku, pri čichom Dunajku [The Danube's Bank Is Green at Bratislava]
38. Búcsú [Farewell]. Adagio. Ešťe sa raz obzrieť mám [I Look Back upon You Once More]
39. Ballada [Ballad]. Poco largo. Pásol Janko dva voly [Janko Drives out Two Oxen]
40-41. Rapszódia [Rhapsody]. Parlando molto rubato-Allegro moderato. Hej! Pofukuj povievaj; Hej! ten stoličny dom [Hey! Blow, You Summer Wind; Hey! What a Beautiful House]
42. Sirató ének [Dirge]. Lento
43. Halotti ének [Funeral Song]. Lento. Dolu dolinami [There in the Deep Valley]

Date--1908-9; revised January 1945
Perf--February 1, 1913, Kecskemét?
Pub--Rozsnyai 1910-1912, Zeneműkiadó 1950; revised Boosey &
    Hawkes 1947, Archive 1981
Cat--Sz 42, BB 53

14. *Két román tánc* [Two Romanian Dances] Op. 8a
    1. Allegro vivace
    2. Poco Allegro

    Date--No. 1, 1909; No. 2, March 1910
    Perf--No. 1, March 12, 1910, composer, Paris
    Pub--Rózsavölgyi 1910, Boosey & Hawkes 1950, Zeneműkiadó
        1951, Archive 1981
    Cat--Sz 43, BB 56

15. *Vázlatok* [Seven Sketches] Op. 9b
    1. Leányi arckép [Portrait of a Young Girl]. Andante (con moto)
    2. Hinta palinta [See-Saw, Dickory Daw]. Comodo
    3. Lento
    4. Non troppo lento
    5. Román népdal [Romanian Folksong]. Andante
    6. Oláhos [In Wallachian Style]. Allegretto
    7. Poco lento

    Date--1908-August 1910; revised January 19, 1945
    Ded--No. 1, Márta Ziegler [Bartók]; No. 3, Emma and Zoltán
        [Kodály]
    Pub--Rozsnyai 1912, Boosey & Hawkes 1950, Zeneműkiadó 1954,
        Archive 1981
    Cat--Sz 44, BB 54

16. *Négy siratóének (Quatre nénies)* [Four Dirges] Op. 9a
    1. Adagio
    2. Andante
    3. Poco lento
    4. Assai andante

    Date--1909-1910; No. 2 transcribed for orchestra 1931
    Perf--in part, October 17, 1917, Ernő Dohnányi, Budapest
    Pub--Rózsavölgyi 1912, Boosey & Hawkes 1950, Zeneműkiadó
        1955, Archive 1981
    Cat--Sz 45, BB 58

17. *Három burleszk* [Three Burlesques] Op. 8c
    1. Perpatvar [Quarrel]
    2. Kicsit ázottan [A Bit Drunk]
    3. Molto vivo capriccioso

Date--No. 1, November 1908; No. 2, May 1911; No. 3, 1910; No. 2
transcribed for orchestra as No. 4 of Hungarian Sketches, 1931
Ded--Márta [Ziegler-Bartók]
Perf--one piece, April 12, 1912, composer, Tîrgu Mureş, Romania;
two pieces, February 1, 1913, composer, Kecskemét; Nos 1 and
2, October 17, 1917, Ernő Dohnányi, Budapest; complete
November 12, 1921, Budapest
Pub--Rózsavölgyi 1912, Boosey & Hawkes 1950, Zeneműkiadó
1954, Archive 1981
Cat--Sz 47, BB 55

18. *Allegro barbaro*

Date--1911
Perf--February 27, 1921, composer, Budapest
Pub--Universal 1918, K.M.P., Kiev 1927, Boosey & Hawkes 1939,
Béla Bartók 1945, Universal (UE 5904, Revision: Péter Bartók)
1992
Cat--Sz 49, BB 63

19. *Kezdők zongoramuzsikája* [The First Term at the Piano]
Eighteen pieces for the piano method of Sándor Reschofsky
1. Moderato
2. Moderato
3. Párbeszéd [Dialogue]. Moderato
4. Párbeszéd [Dialogue]. Moderato
5. Moderato
6. Moderato
7. Népdal [Folk Song]. Moderato
8. Andante
9. Andante
10. Népdal [Folk Song]. Allegro
11. Menüett [Minuet]. Andante
12. Kanásztánc [Swineherd's Dance]. Allegro
13. Népdal [Folk Song]--Hol voltál báránykám? [Where Have You
Been Little Lamb?]. Andante
14. Andante
15. Lakodalmas [Wedding Dance]. Moderato
16. Paraszttánc [Peasant's Dance]. Allegro moderato
17. Allegro deciso
18. Keringő [Waltz]. Tempo di Valse

Date--1913
Pub--Rózsavölgyi 1929, Boosey & Hawkes 1950, Zeneműkiadó
1952, 1955, Archive 1981
Cat--Sz 53, BB 66

20. *Danse orientale*

Date--1913?
Perf--October 23, 1954, Halsey Stevens, Bakersfield, California
Pub--*Pressburger Zeitung,* Christmas issue (1913)

21. *Szonatina*
Three movements based on Romanian folk tunes
   I. Dudások [Bagpipers]
  II. Medvetánc [Bear Dance]
 III. Finale

Date--1915; transcribed for orchestra as Erdélyi táncok
   [Transylvanian Dances], 1931
Perf--March 8, 1920, Berlin?
Pub--Rózsavölgyi 1919, Muzghis (Moscow) 1933, Boosey &
   Hawkes 1950, Zeneműkiadó 1952, Archive 1981
Cat--Sz 55, BB 69

22. *Román népi táncok (Jocuri poporale românești)* [Romanian Folk
Dances]
  1. Jocul cu bâtă [Stick Dance]
  2. Brâul [Sash Dance]
  3. Pe loc [In One Spot]
  4. Buciumeana [Horn Dance]
  5. Poarg· românească [Romanian Polka]
  6. Mărunțelul [Fast Dance]

Date--1915; transcribed for small orchestra as Román népi táncok
[Romanian Folk Dances], 1917
Ded--Professor Ion Bușiția
Pub--Universal 1918, Boosey & Hawkes 1945, Universal (UE 5802,
   Revision: Peter Bartók) 1993
Cat--Sz 56, BB 68

23. *Román kolinda-dallamok* [Romanian Christmas Carols]
Twenty pieces in two series
Series I
   1. Allegro. Pă cel plai de munte
   2. Allegro. Intreabă și'intreabă
   3. Allegro. D-oi roagă sa roagă
   4. Andante. Ciucur verde de mătasă
   5. Allegro moderato. Coborât-o coborât-o
   6. Andante. In patru cornuți de lume
   7. Andante. La lină fântână
   8. Allegretto. Noi umblăm d-a corindare
   9. Allegro. Noi acum ortacilor
  10. Più allegro. Tri crai dela răsăritu
Series II

1. Molto moderato. Colo'n jos la munte'n josu
2. Moderato. Deasupra pa răsăritu
3. Andante. Creşte-mi Doamne creştiu
4. Andante. Sculaţi, sculaţi boieri mari
5. Moderato. Ai, Colo'n josu mai din josu
6. Andante. Si-o luat, luată
7. Variante della precedente. Colo sus, mai susu
8. Allegro. Colo sus pă după lună
9. Allegretto. De ce-i domnul bunu
10. Allegro. Hai cu toţii să suimu

Date--1915
Pub--Universal 1918
Cat--Sz 57, BB 67

24. *Szvit* [Suite] Op. 14
1. Allegretto
2. Scherzo
3. Allegro molto
4. Sostenuto

Date--February 1916, Rákoskeresztúr
Perf--April 21, 1919, composer, Budapest
Pub--Universal 1918, abandoned Andante between first two
movements published in *Új zenei szemle* 5 (1955), Béla
Bartók 1945, Universal (UE 5891, Revision: Peter Bartók)
1992
Cat--Sz 62, BB 70

25. *Három magyar népdal* [Three Hungarian Folk Tunes]
1. Leszállott a páva [The Peacock]
2. Jánoshidi vásártéren [At the Jánoshida Fairground]
3. Fehér liliomszál [White Lily]

Date--1914-1918
Pub--No. 1, in an earlier version, published in *Periszkôp* (Arad,
Romania, June-July 1925); complete in collection "Homage to
Paderewski," revised 1942, Boosey & Hawkes 1942
Cat--Sz 66, BB 80b

26. *Tizenöt magyar parasztdal* [Fifteen Hungarian Peasant Songs]
1-4. Négy régi keserves ének [Four Old Tunes]
5. Scherzo
6. Ballade (Tema con variazioni)
7-15. Régi táncdalok [Old Dance Tunes]

Date--1914-1918; Nos. 6-12, 14-15 transcribed for orchestra as
Hungarian Peasant Songs, 1933

Pub--Universal 1920, Boosey & Hawkes 1948, Universal (UE 6370, Revision: Peter Bartók) 1994
Cat--Sz 71, BB 79

27. *Etüdök* [Three Studies] Op. 18
   1. Allegro molto
   2. Andante sostenuto
   3. Rubato; Tempo giusto, capriccioso

   Date--1918, Rákoskeresztúr
   Perf--April 21, 1919, composer, Budapest
   Pub--Universal 1920, Boosey & Hawkes 1939, Muzghis (Moscow) 1957
   Cat--Sz 72, BB 81

28. *Improvizációk magyar parasztdalokra* [Eight Improvisations on Hungarian Peasant Songs] Op. 20
   I. Molto moderato. Sütött ángyom rétest
   II. Molto capriccioso
   III. Lento rubato. Imhol kerekedik
   IV. Allegretto scherzando. Kályha vállán az ice
   V. Allegro molto
   VI. Allegro moderato, molto capriccioso. Jai istenem, ezt a vént
   VII. Sostenuto, rubato. Beli fiam, beli
   VIII. Allegro. Télen nem jó szántani

   Date--1920
   Ded--No. VII dedicated to the memory of Claude Debussy
   Perf--February 27, 1921, composer, Budapest
   Pub--Universal 1922; No. VII in the *Tombeau de Claude Debussy,* Boosey & Hawkes 1939
   Cat--Sz 74, BB 83

29. *Táncszvit* [Dance Suite], reduction of Suite for Orchestra (1923)
   I. Moderato
   II. Allegro molto
   III. Allegro vivace
   IV. Molto tranquillo
   V. Comodo
   [VI]. Finale

   Date--arranged 1925
   Pub--Universal 1925, Boosey & Hawkes 1952, Universal (UE 8397, Revision: Peter Bartók) 1991
   Cat--Sz 77, BB 86

30. *Szonáta*
   I. Allegro moderato
   II. Sostenuto e pesante

III. Allegro molto

Date--June 1926, Budapest
Ded--Ditta [Pásztory-Bartók]
Perf--December 8, 1926, composer, Budapest
Pub--Universal 1927, Boosey & Hawkes 1939, 1955, Universal (UE
    8772, Revision: Peter Bartók) 1992
Cat--Sz 80, BB 88

31. *Szabadban* [Out of Doors]
    1. Síppal, dobbal [With Drums and Pipes]
    2. Barcarolla
    3. Musettes
    4. Az éjszaka zenéje [The Night's Music]
    5. Hajsza [The Chase]

Date--1926
Ded--No. 4 dedicated to Ditta [Bartók]
Perf--Nos. 1 and 4, December 8, 1926, composer, Budapest
Pub--Universal 1927, Boosey and Hawkes 1954, Universal (UE
    8892a, Revision: Peter Bartók) 1990
Cat--Sz 81, BB 89

32. *Kilenc kis zongoradarab* [Nine Little Piano Pieces]
    Book I (1-4): Négy párbeszéd [Four Dialogues]
    1. Moderato
    2. Andante
    3. Lento
    4. Allegro vivace
    Book II:
    5. Menuetto
    6. Dal [Air]
    7. Marcia delle bestie
    8. Csörgő-tánc [Tambourine]
    Book III:
    9. Preludio, All' ungherese

Date--October 31, 1926
Perf--December 8, 1926, composer, Budapest (one dialogue omitted)
Pub--Universal 1927
Cat--Sz 82, BB 90

33. *Három rondó népi dallamokkal* [Three Rondos on (Slovak) Folk
    Tunes]
    1. Andante
    2. Vivacissimo
    3. Allegro molto

Date--No. 1, 1916; Nos. 2 and 3, 1927

Pub--Universal 1930, Boosey & Hawkes 1957, Universal (UE 9508,
     Revision: Peter Bartók) 1995
Cat--Sz 84, BB 92

34. *Kis szvit* (Petite suite) [Little Suite], transcriptions of Nos. 28, 38,
     43, 16, 36, of Forty-Four Duos for two violins
     1. Lassú [Slow Tune]
     2. Forgatós [Whirling Dance]
     3. Pengetős [Quasi Pizzicato]
     4. Oroszos [Ruthenian Dance]
     5. Dudás [Bagpipes]

     Date--1936
     Pub--Universal 1938; No. 36 unpublished; original version for two
          violins, 1931
     Cat--Sz 105, BB 113

35. *Mikrokosmos,* 153 Progressive Pieces for Piano [English title in
     publication]
     Vol. I
          1-6. Six Unison Melodies
             7. Dotted Notes
             8. Repetition
             9. Syncopation
            10. With Alternate Hands
            11. Parallel Motion
            12. Reflection
            13. Change of Position
            14. Question and Answer
            15. Village Song
            16. Parallel Motion and Change of Position
            17. Contrary Motion
         18-21. Four Unison Melodies
            22. Imitation and Counterpoint
            23. Imitation and Inversion
            24. Pastorale
            25. Imitation and Inversion
            26. Repetition
            27. Syncopation
            28. Canon at the Octave
            29. Imitation Reflected
            30. Canon at the Lower Fifth
            31. Little Dance in Canon Form
            32. In Dorian Mode
            33. Slow Dance
            34. In Phrygian Mode
            35. Chorale
            36. Free Canon

Appendix: Exercises
Vol. II
37. In Lydian Mode
38-39. Staccato and Legato
40. In Yugoslav Mode
41. Melody with Accompaniment
42. Accompaniment in Broken Triads
43. In Hungarian Style, two pianos
44. Contrary Motion
45. Meditation
46. Increasing-Diminishing
47. Big Fair
48. In Mixolydian Mode
49. Crescendo-Diminuendo
50. Minuetto
51. Waves
52. Unison Divided
53. In Transylvanian Style
54. Chromatic
55. Triplets in Lydian Mode, two pianos
56. Melody in Tenths
57. Accents
58. In Oriental Style
59. Major and Minor
60. Canon with Sustained Notes
61. Pentatonic Melody
62. Minor Sixths in Parallel Motion
63. Buzzing
64. Line and Point
65. Dialogue, voice and piano
66. Melody Divided
Appendix: Exercises
Vol. III
67. Thirds Against a Single Voice
68. Hungarian Dance, two pianos
69. Chord Study
70. Melody Against Double Notes
71. Thirds
72. Dragon's Dance
73. Sixths and Triads
74. Hungarian Song, voice and piano
75. Triplets
76. In Three Parts
77. Little Study
78. Five-tone Scale
79. Hommage à J.S.B
80. Hommage à R. Sch.
81. Wandering

127. New Hungarian Folk Song, voice and piano
128. Peasant Dance
129. Alternating Thirds
130. Village Joke
131. Fourths
132. Major Seconds Broken and Together
133. Syncopation
134. Three Studies in Double Notes
135. Perpetuum mobile
136. Whole-tone Scale
137. Unison
138. Bagpipe
139. Merry Andrew
Vol. VI
140. Free Variations
141. Subject and Reflection
142. From the Diary of a Fly
143. Divided Arpeggios
144. Minor Seconds, Major Sevenths
145. Chromatic Invention
146. Ostinato
147. March
148-153. Six Dances in Bulgarian Rhythm

Date--1926, 1932-1939
Ded--Vols. I-II to Peter Bartók; Nos. 148-153 to Harriet Cohen
Pub--Boosey & Hawkes 1940, Zeneműkiadó
Cat--Sz 107, BB 105

36. *Seven Pieces from Mikrokosmos* [Nos. 113, 69, 135, 123, 127, 145, 146] (for two pianos, four hands) [English title in publication]

Date--1940
Pub--Boosey & Hawkes 1947
Cat--Sz 108, BB 120

37. *Suite for Two Pianos* (arrangement of Suite for Orchestra) [English title in publication]

Date--1941
Pub--Boosey & Hawkes 1960
Cat--Sz 34, BB 40

2. Chamber Music

38. *Zongoraötös* [Piano quintet]

Date--1903-1904, revised 1920?

Pub--Zeneműkiadó 1970
Cat--DD 77, BB 33

39. *Gyergyóból. Három csík megyei népdal* [From Gyergyó. Three folk
songs from the Csík District] (for recorder and piano)
1. Rubato
2. L'istesso tempo
3. Poco vivo

Date--1907
Pub--Zeneműkiadó 1961
Cat--Sz 35, BB 45a

40. *I. Vonósnégyes* [String quartet no. 1] Op. 7
  I. Lento
  II. Allegretto
     (Introduzione)
  III. Allegro vivace

Date--1908-January 27, 1909
Perf--March 19, 1910, Waldbauer-Kerpely Quartet, Budapest
Pub--Rózsavölgyi 1910, Boosey & Hawkes 1939, Zeneműkiadó
  1956 and 1964
Cat--Sz 40, BB 52

41. *II. Vonósnégyes* [String quartet no. 2] Op. 17
  I. Moderato
  II. Allegro molto capriccioso
  III. Lento

Date--1915-October 1917, Rákoskeresztúr
Ded--Waldbauer-Kerpely Quartet
Perf--March 3, 1918, Waldbauer-Kerpely Quartet, Budapest
Pub--Universal 1920, Boosey & Hawkes 1939
Cat--Sz 67, BB 75

42. *I. Szonáta* [Sonata No. 1 for Violin and Piano) [MS only: Op. 21]
  I. Allegro appassionato
  II. Adagio
  III. Allegro

Date--October-December 12, 1921, Budapest
Ded--Jelly d'Arányi
Perf--February 8, 1922, Mary Dickenson-Auner and Edward
  Steuermann, Vienna; March 24, 1922, Jelly d'Arányi and
  composer, London
Pub--Universal 1923, Boosey & Hawkes 1950, Universal (UE 7247,
  Revision: Peter Bartók) 1991
Cat--Sz 75, BB 84

43. *II. Szonáta* [Sonata No. 2 for Violin and Piano]
    I. Molto moderato
    II. Allegretto

    Date--July-November 1922, Budapest
    Ded--Jelly d'Arányi
    Perf--February 7, 1923, Imre Waldbauer and composer, Berlin; May
        7, 1923, Jelly d'Arányi and composer, London
    Pub--Universal 1923
    Cat--Sz 76, BB 85

44. *III. Vonósnégyes* [String Quartet No. 3]
    Prima parte. Moderato
    Seconda parte. Allegro
    Ricapitulazione della prima parte. Moderato
    Coda. Allegro molto

    Date--September 1927, Budapest
    Ded--Musical Fund Society of Philadelphia
    Perf--February 12, 1929, Vienna (Kolisch) Quartet, London; February
        19, 1929, Waldbauer-Kerpely Quartet, London; Ferenc Bónis
        indicates a performance on December 30, 1928, Philadelphia
    Pub--Universal 1929, Boosey & Hawkes 1939
    Cat--Sz 85, BB 93

45. *I. Rapszódia* [Rhapsody No. 1 for Violin and Piano] (also versions
    for violoncello and piano, and for violin and orchestra)
    I. Moderato. Lassú
    II. Allegretto moderato. Friss

    Date--1928
    Ded--Joseph Szigeti
    Perf--March 4, 1929, Zoltán Székely and composer, London;
        November 22, 1929, Joseph Szigeti and composer, Budapest;
        orchestrated version, November 1, 1929, Joseph Szigeti with
        unspecified orchestra, cond. Hermann Scherchen, Königsberg
        (Kaliningrad); violoncello and piano version, March 30, 1929,
        Jenő Kerpely and composer, Budapest
    Pub--Universal 1929
    Cat--Sz 86; orchestrated Sz 87; violoncello and piano Sz 88. BB 94

46. *I. Rapszódia* [Rhapsody No. 1 for Violoncello and Piano]
    (transcription of Rhapsody No. 1 for Violin and Piano, Sz 86)
    I. Moderato. Lassú
    II. Allegretto moderato. Friss

    Date--1928
    Perf--March 30, 1929, Jenő Kerpely and composer, Budapest

Pub--Universal 1930
Cat--Sz 88, BB 94

47. *II. Rapszódia* [Rhapsody No. 2 for Violin and Piano] (also for violin and orchestra)
    I. Moderato. Lassú
    II. Allegretto moderato. Friss

Date--1928; revised 1945
Ded--Zoltán Székely
Perf--November 19, 1928, Zoltán Székely and Géza Frid, Amsterdam; for violin and orchestra, November 26, 1929, Zoltán Székely and Philharmonic Society Orchestra (Ernő Dohnányi, conducting), Budapest
Pub--Universal 1929, 1945 revised Boosey & Hawkes 1947
Cat--Sz 90, BB 96

48. *IV. Vonósnégyes* [String Quartet No. 4]
    I. Allegro
    II. Prestissimo, con sordino
    III. Non troppo lento
    IV. Allegretto pizzicato
    V. Allegro molto

Date--July-September 1928, Budapest
Ded--Pro Arte Quartet
Perf--February 22, 1929, Hungarian (Waldbauer) Quartet, London
Pub--Universal 1929, Boosey & Hawkes 1939
Cat--Sz 91, BB 95

49. *Negyvennégy duó* [Forty-Four Duos] (for two violins)
    Vol. I
        1. Párosító [Teasing Song]
        2. Kalamajkó [Dance]
        3. Menuetto
        4. Szentivánéji [Midsummer Night Song]
        5. Tót nóta [Slovak Song]
        6. Magyar nóta [Hungarian Song]
        7. Oláh nóta [Romanian Song]
        8. Tót nóta [Tót Song]
        9. Játék [Play]
        10. Rutén nóta [Ruthenian Song]
        11. Gyermekrengetéskor [Lullaby]
        12. Szénagyűjtéskor [Hay-Harvesting Song]
        13. Lakodalmas [Wedding Song]
        14. Párnás-tánc [Cushion Dance]
    Vol. II
        15. Katonanóta [Soldier's Song]

16. Burleszk
17. Menetelő nóta [Marching Song]
18. Menetelő nóta
19. Mese [Fairy Tale]
20. Dal [Song]
21. Újévköszöntő [New Year's Greeting]
22. Szúnyogtánc [Mosquito Dance]
23. Menyasszony-búcsúztató [Wedding Song]
24. Tréfás nóta [Gay Song]
25. Magyar nóta [Hungarian Song]
Vol. III
26. Ugyan édes komámasszony [Teasing Song]
27. Sántatánc [Limping Dance]
28. Bánkódás [Sorrow]
29. Újévköszöntő [New Year's Greeting]
30. Újévköszöntő
31. Újévköszöntő
32. Máramarosi tánc [Dance from Máramaros]
33. Aratáskor [Harvest Song]
34. Számláló nóta [Counting Song]
35. Rutén kolomejka [Ruthenian Kolomejka]
36. Szól a duda [Bagpipes]
Vol. IV
37. Preludium és kánon
38. Forgatós (Invărtita bâtrănilor) [Romanian Whirling Dance]
39. Szerb tánc (Zaplet) [Serbian Dance]
40. Oláh tánc [Wallachian Dance]
41. Scherzo
42. Arab dal
43. Pizzicato
44. Erdélyi tánc (Ardeleana) [Transylvanian Dance]
Nos. 28, 32, 38, 43, 16, and 36 were transcribed for piano (1936)
as Petite Suite

Date--1931
Perf--in part, January 20, 1932, Imre Waldbauer and György
Hannover, Budapest
Pub--seven pieces, Schott 1932; complete, Universal 1933
Cat--Sz 98, BB 104

50. V. Vonósnégyes [String Quartet No. 5]
I. Allegro
II. Adagio molto
III. Scherzo
IV. Andante
V. Finale

Date--August 6-September 6, 1934, Budapest

Ded--Mrs. Elizabeth Sprague Coolidge
Perf--April 8, 1935, Kolisch Quartet, Washington
Pub--Universal 1936, Boosey & Hawkes 1939
Cat--Sz 102, BB 110

51. *Sonata for Two Pianos and Percussion* [English title in publication]
   I. Assai lento--Allegro molto
   II. Lento ma non troppo
   III. Allegro non troppo

   Date--July-August 1937, Budapest; transcribed as Concerto for Two
   Pianos, Percussion, and Orchestra, December 1940
   Perf--January 16, 1938, Béla and Ditta Bartók, Fritz Schiesser, and
   Philipp Rühlig, Basel; Concerto, January 21, 1943, Béla and
   Ditta Bartók, New York Philharmonic Symphony (Fritz Reiner
   conducting), New York
   Pub--Boosey & Hawkes 1942
   Cat--Sz 110, BB 115

52. *Kontrasztok* [Contrasts] (for violin, clarinet, and piano) [English
   title in publication]
   I. Verbunkos [Recruiting Dance]
   II. Pihenő [Relaxation]
   III. Sebes [Fast Dance]

   Date--September 24, 1938, Budapest
   Ded--Benny Goodman and Joseph Szigeti
   Perf--January 9, 1939, Joseph Szigeti, Benny Goodman, Endre Petri,
   New York
   Pub--Boosey & Hawkes 1942
   Cat--Sz 111, BB 116

53. *VI. Vonósnégyes* [String Quartet No. 6] [English title in
   publication]
   I. Mesto--Più mosso, pesante--Vivace
   II. Mesto--Marcia
   III. Mesto--Burletta
   IV. Mesto

   Date--August-November 1939, Saanen-Budapest
   Ded--Kolisch Quartet
   Perf--January 20, 1941, Kolisch Quartet, New York
   Pub--Boosey & Hawkes 1941
   Cat--Sz 114, BB 119

54. *Sonata for Solo Violin* [English title in publication]
   I. Tempo di ciaccona
   II. Fuga
   III. Melodia

IV. Presto

Date--March 14, 1944, Ashville
Ded--Yehudi Menuhin
Perf--November 26, 1944, Yehudi Menuhin, New York
Pub--Boosey & Hawkes 1947, Urtext Edition (Preface by Peter
   Bartók): Boosey & Hawkes 1994
Cat--Sz 117, BB 124

3. Solo Instruments and Orchestra

55. *Rapszódia* [Rhapsody], Op. 1 (for piano and orchestra), first version
for piano

Date--November 1904; piano and orchestra version 1905
Ded--Emma [Gruber]
Perf--November 15, 1909, composer and Orchestra of the Academy
   of Music (Jenő Hubay), Budapest
Pub--Rózsavölgyi 1910, Zeneműkiadó 1954
Cat--Sz 27, BB 36b

56. *Scherzo* (originally known as *Burlesque*), Op. 2 (for piano and
orchestra)

Date--1904
Perf--September 28, 1961, E. Tusa, Orchestra of Hungarian Radio
   (György Lehel conducting), Budapest
Pub--Zeneműkiadó 1961
Cat--Sz 28, BB 35

57. *Hegedűverseny* [Violin Concerto] (first movement revised as No. 1
of Two Portraits)

Date--July 1, 1907, Jászberényi-February 5, 1908, Budapest
Ded--Stefi Geyer
Perf--May 30, 1958, Hans-Heinz Schneeberger and the Basel
   Chamber Orchestra (Paul Sacher conducting), Basel
Pub--Boosey & Hawkes 1959
Cat--Sz 36, BB 48a

58. *I. Zongoraverseny* [Concerto no. 1 for Piano and Orchestra]
   I. Allegro
   II. Andante
   III. Allegro

Date--August-November 12, 1926, Budapest
Perf--July 1, 1927, composer (Wilhelm Furtwängler conducting),
   Frankfurt am Main

Pub--Universal 1927, 1928; two-piano version Universal 1927
Cat--Sz 83, BB 91

59. *I. Rapszódia* [Rhapsody No. 1 for Violin and Orchestra]
(transcription of Rhapsody No. 1 for Violin and Piano, Sz 86)
　　I. Moderato. Lassú
　　II. Allegretto moderato. Friss

Date--1928
Ded--Joseph Szigeti
Perf--November 1, 1929, Joseph Szigeti (Hermann Scherchen
　　conducting), Königsberg
Pub--Universal 1929
Cat--Sz 87, BB 94

60. *II. Rapszódia* [Rhapsody No. 2 for Violin and Orchestra]
(transcription of Rhapsody No. 2 for Violin and Piano, Sz 89, BB
96)
　　I. Moderato. Lassú
　　II. Allegretto moderato. Friss

Date--1928; revised 1944
Ded--Zoltán Székely
Perf--November 26, 1929, Zoltán Székely (Ernő Dohnányi
　　conducting), Budapest
Pub--Universal 1929, Boosey & Hawkes 1949
Cat--Sz 90, BB 96

61. *II. Zongoraverseny* [Concerto No. 2 for Piano and Orchestra]
　　I. Allegro
　　II. Adagio-Presto-Adagio
　　III. Allegro molto

Date--October 1930-September-October 1931
Perf--January 23, 1933, composer (Hans Rosbaud conducting),
　　Frankfurt am Main
Pub--Universal 1932, 1941, 1955
Cat--Sz 95, BB 101

62. *Hegedűverseny* [Violin Concerto (No. 2)] [English title in
publication]
　　I. Allegro non troppo
　　II. Andante tranquillo
　　III. Allegro molto

Date--August 1937-December 31, 1938, Budapest
Ded--Zoltán Székely
Perf--March 23, 1939, Zoltán Székely and Concertgebouw Orchestra
　　(Willem Mengelberg conducting), Amsterdam

Pub--Boosey & Hawkes 1946, Muzghis (Moscow) 1964
Cat--Sz 112, BB 117

63. *Concerto for Two Pianos, Percussion, and Orchestra* (original version: *Sonata for Two Pianos and Percussion*) [English title in publication]

   Date--transcribed, December 1940
   Perf--January 21, 1943, Béla and Ditta Bartók and the New York Philharmonic Symphony (Fritz Reiner conducting), New York
   Pub--Boosey & Hawkes 1970
   Cat--Sz 115, BB 121

64. *Concerto No. 3 for Piano and Orchestra* [English title in publication]
   I. Allegretto
   II. Adagio religioso--poco più mosso--tempo I
   III. Allegro vivace

   Date--1945, last 17 measures completed by Tibor Serly
   Perf--February 8, 1946, György Sándor and the Philadelphia Orchestra (Eugene Ormandy conducting), Philadelphia
   Pub--Boosey & Hawkes 1946 and 1947
   Cat--Sz 119, BB 127

65. *Viola Concerto* [English title in publication]
   I. Moderato (attacca)
   II. Adagio religioso--allegretto (attacca)
   III. Allegro vivace

   Date--1945, unfinished; reconstructed and orchestrated by Tibor Serly
   Ded--written for William Primrose
   Perf--December 2, 1949, William Primrose and the Minneapolis Symphony Orchestra (Antal Dórati conducting)
   Pub--Boosey & Hawkes 1950, Bartók Records 1995 (facsimile of the autograph manuscript)
   Cat--Sz 120, BB 128

4. Full or Small Orchestra

66. *Scherzo* from *Symphony in E-Flat Major*

   Date--Symphony in piano reduction only, 1902; Scherzo orchestrated1903
   Perf--February 29, 1904, Budapest Opera Orchestra (István Kerner conducting), Budapest; two movements of Symphony orchestrated by Denijs Dille and performed September 28, 1961,

Orchestra of Hungarian Radio (György Lehel conducting),
Budapest
Pub--Symphony unpublished except for recording of the Scherzo,
Bartók Béla, Posztumusz művek [Béla Bartók, Posthumous
Works], ed. Ferenc Bónis, LPX11517.
Cat--DD 68, BB 25

67. *Kossuth szimfoniai költemény* [Kossuth, symphonic poem]
Date--April 2-August 18, 1903
Perf--January 13, 1904, Philharmonic Society (István Kerner),
Budapest
Pub--Zeneműkiadó 1963
Cat--DD 75, BB 31

68. *I. Szvit* [Suite No. 1] Op. 3 (for full orchestra)
Date--1905, Vienna; revised 1920
Perf--three movements only (I, III, V), November 29, 1905,
Gesellschaftkonzerte (Ferdinand Loewe); complete, March 1,
1909 (Jenő Hubay conducting), Budapest
Pub--Rózsavölgyi 1912, revised Zeneműkiadó 1956, 1961
Cat--Sz 31, BB 39

69. *II. Szvit* [Suite No. 2] Op. 4 (for small orchestra; also arranged for
two pianos)
I. Comodo
II. Allegro scherzando
III. Andante
IV. Comodo

Date--Movements I-III, November 1905, Vienna; Movement IV,
September 1, 1907, Rákospalota; rev. 1920 and 1943; version
for two pianos, 1943
Perf--Movement II only (Scherzo), January 2, 1909, composer
conducting, Berlin; complete, November 22, 1909,
Philharmonic Society (István Kerner conducting), Budapest
Pub--Bartók 1907, Universal 1921, Boosey & Hawkes 1939, 1948
Cat--Sz 34, BB 40

70. *Két portré* [Two Portraits] Op. 5
1. Egy ideális [One Ideal]
2. Egy torz [One Grotesque]

Date--1907-1908
Perf--1909, Imre Waldbauer (violin) and Budapest Symphony (László
Kun), Budapest

Pub--Rozsnyai 1914, Boosey & Hawkes 1950, Zeneműkiadó 1953; No. 1 from Movement I of the Violin Concerto, No. 2 also appears as No. 14 ("Ma Mie qui danse") of the Bagatelles, Op. 6
Cat--Sz 37, BB 48b

71. *Két kép* (Deux Images) [Two Pictures] Op. 10 (also arranged for piano)
    1. Virágzás [In Full Flower]
    2. A falu tánca [Village Dance]

    Date--August 1910, Budapest; piano version, c1911
    Perf--February 25, 1913, Philharmonic Society (István Kerner), Budapest
    Pub--Rózsavölgyi 1912, Boosey & Hawkes 1950, Zeneműkiadó 1953; same for piano version
    Cat--Sz 46, BB 59

72. *Négy zenekari darab* [Four Orchestral Pieces] Op. 12
    1. Preludio
    2. Scherzo
    3. Intermezzo
    4. Marcia funebre

    Date--1912, orchestrated 1921
    Perf-January 9, 1922, Philharmonic Society (Ernő Dohnányi conducting), Budapest
    Pub--Universal 1923
    Cat--Sz 51, BB 64

73. *Román népi táncok* [Romanian Folk Dances] (originally for piano)

    Date--transcribed 1917; original piano version, 1915
    Perf--February 11, 1918, E. Lichtenberg conducting, Budapest
    Pub--Universal 1922; Boosey & Hawkes 1945
    Cat--Sz 68, BB 76

74. *A csodálatos mandarin* [The Miraculous Mandarin, Suite]

    Date--1919, 1927
    Perf--October 15, 1928, Philharmonic Society (Ernő Dohnányi conducting), Budapest
    Pub--Universal 1927
    Cat--Sz 73, BB 82

75. *Táncszvit* [Dance Suite]
    I. Moderato
    II. Allegro molto
    III. Allegro vivace
    IV. Molto tranquillo

V. Comodo
(VI). Finale

Date--August 1923, Radvány, North Hungary, composed to celebrate
the fiftieth anniversary of the merging of Pest, Buda, and Obuda
into the city of Budapest
Perf--November 19, 1923, Budapest Philharmonic Society (Ernő
Dohnányi conducting), Budapest
Pub--Universal 1924; piano reduction, Universal 1925
Cat--Sz 77, BB 86

76. A fából faragott királyfi [The Wooden Prince, Suite] Op. 13

Date--three dances from the ballet,1921-1924?
Perf--November 23, 1931, Philharmonic Society (Ernő Dohnányi
conducting), Budapest
Pub-Universal
Cat--Sz 60, BB 74

77. Erdélyi táncok [Transylvanian Dances] (transcription of Sonatina,
for piano)
I. Dudások [Bagpipers]
II. Medvetánc [Bear Dance]
III. Finale

Date--1931
Perf--January 24, 1932, M. Freccia conducting, Budapest
Pub--Rózsavölgyi 1932, Zeneműkiadó 1955
Cat--Sz 96, BB 102b

78. Magyar képek [Hungarian Sketches]
1. Este a székelyeknél [An Evening at the Village]
2. Medvetánc [Bear Dance]
3. Melódia [Air]
4. Kicsit ázottan [A Bit Tipsy]
5. Ürögi kanásztánc [Dance of the Ürög Swineherds]

Date--transcribed from piano works, 1931, Mondsee
Perf--Nos. 1-3, 5, January 24, 1932, Budapest; complete, November
26, 1934, Philharmonic Society (Heinrich Laber conducting),
Budapest
Pub--Rozsnyai-Rózsavölgyi 1932, Zeneműkiadó 1954
Cat--Sz 97, BB 103

79. Magyar parasztdalok [Hungarian Peasant Songs]
I. Ballade (Tema con variazioni)
II. Régi táncdalok [Old Dance Tunes]

Date--transcription of Nos. 6-12, 14, 15 from 15 Hungarian Peasant
Songs for Piano (1914-1917) 1933
Perf--March 18, 1934, Gyula Baranyai conducting, Szombathely
Pub--Universal 1933
Cat--Sz 100, BB 107

80. *Zene húros hangszerekre, ütőkre és celestára* [Music for Strings,
Percussion, and Celesta]
   I. Andante tranquillo
   II. Allegro
   III. Adagio
   IV. Allegro molto

Date--September 7, 1936, Budapest
Ded--commissioned for the tenth anniversary of the Basel Chamber
Orchestra
Perf--January 21, 1937, Basel Chamber Orchestra (Paul Sacher
conducting), Basel
Pub--Universal 1937, Boosey & Hawkes 1939, Muzghis (Leningrad)
1961
Cat--Sz 106, BB 114

81. *Divertimento* (for string orchestra)
   I. Allegro non troppo
   II. Molto adagio
   III. Allegro assai

Date--August 2-17, 1939, Saanen
Ded--Basel Chamber Orchestra
Perf--June 11, 1940, Basel Chamber Orchestra (Paul Sacher
conducting), Basel
Pub--Boosey & Hawkes 1940
Cat--Sz 113, BB 118

82. *Concerto for Orchestra* [English title in publication]
   I. Introduzione
   II. Giuoco delle coppie
   III. Elegia
   IV. Intermezzo interrotto
   V. Finale

Date--August 15-October 8, 1943, Saranac Lake; revised February
1945
Ded--for the Koussevitzky Music Foundation in memory of Mrs.
Natalie Koussevitzky
Perf--December 1, 1944, Boston Symphony Orchestra (Serge
Koussevitzky conducting), Boston
Pub--Boosey & Hawkes 1946
Cat--Sz 116, BB 123

5. *Solo Voice and Piano*

83. *Liebeslieder* [Love Songs]
    2 Diese Rose pflück ich hier [I Pluck this Rose] (Lenau)
    4. Ich fühle deinen Odem [I Feel your Breath] (Lenau)

    Date--1900, Budapest
    Pub--Nos. 2 and 4, in Denijs Dille, *Der junge Bartók I*, Zeneműkiadó
      1963
    Cat--DD 62, BB 20

84. *Négy dal* [Four Songs] (texts by Lajos Pósa)
    1. Őszi szellő [Autumn Breeze]
    2. Még azt vetik a szememre [They are Accusing Me]
    3. Nincs olyan bú [There Is no Greater Sorrow]
    4. Ejnye! Ejnye! [Alas, alas!]

    Date--1902
    Pub--Bárd 1904
    Cat--DD 67, BB 24

85. *Est* [Evening] (text by Kálmán Harsányi)
    Date--April 1903?
    Pub--in Denijs Dille, *Der junge Bartók I*, Zeneműkiadó 1963
    Cat--DD 73, BB 29

86. *Székely népdal* [Székely Folk Song]: "Piros alma leesett a sárba"
    [The Red Apple Has Fallen in the Mud]

    Date--1904
    Pub--in supplement to Magyar lant 1905
    Cat--DD C8, Sz 30, BB 34

87. *Magyar népdalok* [Hungarian Folk Songs]
    First Series, four songs, No. 4 incomplete, only one published
    1. Lekaszálták már a rétet [They Have Mowed the Pasture Already]
    Second Series, ten songs, only four published
    4. Ha bemegyek a csárdába [Down at the Tavern]
    6. Megittam a piros bort [My Glass Is Empty]
    7. Ez a kislány gyöngyöt fűz [This Maiden Threading]
    8. Sej, mikor engem katonának visznek [The Young Soldier]

    Date--First Series 1904-1905; Second Series 1906
    Pub--First Series, No. 1, in Denijs Dille, *Der junge Bartók I*,
      Zeneműkiadó 1963; Second Series, Nos.4, 6, 7, 8, Zeneműkiadó
      1963
    Cat--First Series Sz 29, BB 37, Second Series Sz 33a, BB 43

88. *Magyar népdalok* [Hungarian Folk Songs]
    (Only the first ten set by Bartók, the remaining ten by Kodály)
    1. Elindultam szép hazámbul [I Left My Fair Homeland]
    2. Ital mennék én a Tiszán ladikon [I Would Cross the Tisza in a Boat]
    3. Fehér László lovat lopott [László Fehér Stole a Horse]
    4. A gyulai kert alatt [Behind the Garden of Gyula]
    5. A kertmegi kert alatt [Behind the Garden of Kertmeg] (in the original edition: Ucca, ucca, ég az ucca [The Street Is on Fire])
    6. Ablakomba, ablakomba besütött a holdvilág [In My Window Shone the Moonlight]
    7. Száraz ágtól messze virít a rózsa [From the Withered Branch No Rose Blooms]
    8. Végigmentem a tárkányi sej, haj, nagy uccán [I Walked to the End of the Great Street in Tárkány]
    9. Nem messze van ide kis Margitta [Not Far from Here Is Kismargitta]
    10. Szánt a babám csireg, csörög [My Sweetheart Is Plowing]

    Date--1906; revised 1938
    Pub--Rózsavölgyi 1938, Zeneműkiadó 1953
    Cat--Sz 33, BB 42

89. *Két magyar népdal* [Two Hungarian Folk Songs]
    1. Édesanyám rózsafája [My Mother's Rosebush]
    2. Túl vagy rózsám, túl vagy a málnás erdejin [My Sweetheart, You Are Beyond the Málnás Woods]

    Date--1907
    Pub--No. 1, Zeneműkiadó 1963; No. 2 in *Documenta bartókiana* 4, 1970
    Cat--Sz 33b, BB 44

90. *Négy szlovák népdal* [Four Slovak Folk Songs]
    1. V tej bystrickej bráne [Near the Borders of Bistrita]
    2. Pod lipko nad lipko
    3. Pohřební písen [Dirge]
    4. Priletel pták [Message]

    Date--Nos. 1-3, 1907 (No. 2, lost); No. 4, 1916
    Pub--Nos. 1, 3, and 4, in Denijs Dille, *Der junge Bartók I,* Zeneműkiadó 1963
    Cat--Sz 35b, BB 46

91. *Öt dal* [Five Songs] Op. 15
    1. Tavasz: Az én szerelmem [Spring: My Love] (Klára Gombossy)
    2. Nyár: Szomjasan vágyva [Summer] (Gombossy)
    3. A vágyak éjjele [Night of Desire] (W. Gleiman)
    4. Tél: Színes álomban [Winter: in Vivid Dreams] (Gombossy?)

5. Ősz: Itt lent a völgyben [Autumn: in the Valley] (Gombossy)

Date--1915-1916
Pub--Universal 1961, 1966
Cat--Sz 61, BB 71

92. Öt dal [Five Songs] Op. 16 (texts by Endre Ady)
   1. Három őszi könnycsepp [Three Autumn Tears]
   2. Az őszi lárma [Sounds of Autumn]
   3. Az ágyam hívogat [Lost Content]
   4. Egyedül a tengerrel [Alone with the Sea]
   5. Nem mehetek hozzád [I Cannot Come to You]

Date--1916
Ded--Béla Reinitz 1920
Pub--Universal 1923
Cat--Sz 63, BB 72

93. Szlovák népdal [Slovak folksong]: "Kruti Tono vretana" [Tony Whirls the Spindle]

Date--1916?
Pub--in Denijs Dille, Der junge Bartók I, Zeneműkiadó 1963
Cat--Sz 63a, BB 73

94. Nyolc magyar népdal [Eight Hungarian Folk Songs]
   1. Fekete főd, fehér az én zsebkendőm [Black Is the Earth]
   2. Istenem, istenem, áraszd meg a vizet (My God, My God, Make the River Swell)
   3. Asszonyok, asszonyok [Wives, Let Me Be One of Your Company]
   4. Annyi bánat az szívemen [So Much Sorrow Lies in My Heart]
   5. Ha kimegyek arr' a magos tetőre [If I Climb Yonder Hill]
   6. Töltik a nagyerdő útját [They Are Mending the Great Forest Highway]
   7. Eddig való dolgom a tavaszi szántás [Up to Now My Work Was Plowing in the Springtime]
   8. Olvad a hó, csárdás kis angyalom [The Snow Is Melting]

Date--Nos. 1-5, 1907; Nos. 6-8, 1917
Pub--Universal 1922, Boosey & Hawkes 1939, 1955
Cat--Sz 64, BB 47

95. Falun (Dedinské scény) [Village Scenes]
   (Slovak Folksongs) (also arranged for female voices and chamber orchestra)
   1. Ej! hrabajže len [Haymaking]
   2. Letia pávy, letia [At the Bride's]
   3. A ty Anča krásna [Wedding]

4. Beli žemi, beli [Lullaby]
5. Poza búčky, poza peň [Lad's Dance]

Date--December 1924
Ded--Ditta [Pásztory Bartók]
Pub--Universal 1927, Boosey & Hawkes 1954
Cat--Sz 78, BB 87a

96. *Húsz magyar népdal* [Twenty Hungarian Folk Songs]
Vol. I: Szomorú nóták [Sad Songs]
    1. A tomlöcbën [In Prison]
    2. Régi keserves [Old Lament]
    3. Bujdosó ének [The Fugitive]
    4. Pásztornóta [Herdsman's Song]
Vol II: Táncdalok [Dancing Songs]
    5. Székely "lassú" [Slow Dance]
    6. Székely "friss" [Fast Dance]
    7. Kanásztánc [Swineherd's Dance]
    8. "Hatforintos" nóta (Six-Florin Dance)
Vol III: Vegyes dalok [Diverse Songs]
    9. Juhászcsúfoló [The Shepherd]
    10. Tréfás nóta [Joking Song]
    11. Párosító I [Nuptial Serenade]
    12. Párosító II [Humorous Song]
    13. Pár-ének [Dialogue Song]
    14. Panasz [Complaint]
    15. Bordal [Drinking Song]
Vol. IV: Új dalok [New Style Songs]
    I. Hej, édesanyám [Oh, My Dear Mother]
    II. Érik a ropogós cseresznye [Ripening Cherries]
    III. Már Dobozon régen leesett a hó [Long Ago at Doboz Fell the
         Snow]
    IV. Sárga kukorícaszár [Yellow Cornstalk]
    V. Búza, búza [Wheat, Wheat]

Date--1929; Nos. 1, 2, 14, 11, 12 orchestrated. 1933
Perf--January 30, 1930, Mária Basilides and the composer, Budapest;
    for voice and orchestra, October 23, 1933, Mária Basilides and
    the Philharmonic Society (Ernő Dohnányi conducting), Budapest
Pub--Universal 1932, Boosey & Hawkes 1939
Cat--Sz 92, BB 98

97. *Hungarian folksong: "Debrecennek van egy vize"* (arrangement of
    piano piece from Gyermekeknek I/16)

Date--1937?
Pub--in Béla Paulini, *Gyöngyösbokréta* [Crown of Pearls], Budapest:
    Vajna és Bokor, 1937, p. 10
Cat--Sz 109

98. *Ukrainian folksong:* "A férj keserve" [The Husband's Grief]

Date--February 1945, New York
Ded--Pál Kecskeméti
Pub--in János Demény, ed., *Bartók Béla levelei*, Budapest: Művelt
   Nép, 1951, p. xiv
Cat--Sz 118, BB 125

6. *Chorus, A Cappella and with Piano*

99. *Est* [Evening] (for four-part male chorus) (K. Harsányi)

Date--April 1903
Pub--Denijs Dille: *Documenta bartókiana* I 1964
Cat--DD 74, BB 30

100. *Négy régi magyar népdal* [Four Old Hungarian Folk Songs] (for four-part male chorus, a cappella)
   1. Rég megmondtam bús gerlice [Long Ago I Told You]
   2. Jaj Istenem, kire várok [Oh God, Why Am I Waiting?]
   3. Ángyomasszony kertje [In My Sister-in-Law's Garden]
   4. Béreslegény, jól megrakd a szekeret [Farmboy, Load the Cart Well]

Date--1910, revised 1912
Pub--Universal 1928
Cat--Sz 50, BB 60

101. *Tót népdalok* (Slovácké l'udové piesne) [Slovak Folk Songs] (for four-part male chorus)
   1. Ej, posluchajte málo [Hey, Listen Now My Comrades]
   2. Ked' ja smutny pojdem [If I Must Go to the War]
   3. Kamarádi mojí [Let Us Go, Comrades]
   4. Ej, a ked' mna zabiju [Hey, If Soon I Fall in Battle]
   5. Ked' som šiou na vojnu [To Battle I Went Forth]

Date--1917
Perf--December 15, 1917, Vienna
Pub--Universal 1918, Boosey & Hawkes 1939
Cat--Sz 69, BB 77

102. *Négy tót népdal* (Štyri slovenské piesne) [Four Slovak Folk Songs] (for four-part mixed chorus and piano)
   1. Zadala mamka [Wedding Song]
   2. Naholi, naholi [Song of the Hay-Harvesters]
   3. Rada pila, rada jedla [Song from Medzibrod]
   4. Gajdujte, gajdence [Dancing Song]

Date--1917

Perf--January 5, 1917, Emil Lichtenberg conducting, Budapest
Pub--Universal 1927, Boosey & Hawkes 1939, Zeneműkiadó 1950
Cat--Sz 70, BB 78

103. *Magyar népdalok* [Hungarian Folksongs] (for mixed chorus a cappella)
   1. Elhervadt cidrusfa [The Prisoner]
   2. Ideje bujdosásimnak [The Wanderer]
   3. Adj el, anyám [Finding a Husband]
   4. Sarjut eszik az ökröm [My Ox Is Grazing]
   5. Az én lovam szajkó [Love Song]

   Date--May 1930, Budapest
   Pub--Universal 1932, Boosey & Hawkes 1939
   Cat--Sz 93, BB 99

104. *Székely dalok* [Székely Songs] (for male chorus, a cappella)
   1. Hej de sokszor megbántottál, Túl vagy rózsám [How Often I've Grieved for You, It's All over]
   2. Istenem, életem nem igen gyönyörü [My God, My Life]
   3. Vékony cérna, kemény mag [Slender Thread, Hard Seed]
   4. Kilyénfalvi közeptizbe [Girls Are Gathering in Kilyénfalva]
   5. Vékony cérna, kemény mag [Slender Thread, Hard Seed]
   6. Járjad pap a táncot [Do a Dance, Priest]

   Date--November 1932, Budapest
   Pub--Nos. 1-2, Magyar Kórus 1938; complete Zeneműkiadó 1955
   Cat--Sz 99, BB 106

105. *27 két- és háromszólamú kórus* [Twenty-Seven Choruses] (for two-or three-part children's or women's chorus)
   Vols. I-VI, children's voices; Vols. VII-VIII, women's voices
   Vol. I:
   1. Tavasz [Spring]
   2. Ne hagyj itt! [Only Tell Me]
   3. Jószág-igéző [Enchanting Song]
   Vol. II:
   4. Levél az otthoniakhoz [Letter to Those at Home]
   5. Játék [Candle Song]
   6. Leánynéző [Choosing of a Girl]
   7. Héjja, héjja, karahéjja [Thieving Bird]
   Vol. III:
   8. Ne menj el [Don't Leave Me]
   9. Van egy gyűrüm [The Fickle Girl]
   10. Senkim a világon [Song of Loneliness]
   11. Cipósütés [Breadbaking]
   Vol. IV:
   12. Huszárnóta [Hussar]

13. Resteknek nótája [Loafer]
14. Bolyongás [Lonely Wanderer]
15. Lánycsúfoló [Mocking of Girls]
Vol. V:
16. Legénycsúfoló [Mocking of Youth]
17. Mihálynapi köszöntő [Michaelmas Greeting]
18. Leánykérő [The Wooing of a Girl]
Vol. VI:
19. Keserves [Lament]
20. Madárdal [Song of the Bird]
21. Csujogató [Stamping Feet]
Vol. VII:
22. Bánat [The Sorrow of Love]
23. Ne láttalak volna! [Had I Never Seen You]
24. Elment a madárka [The Song-Bird's Promise]
Vol. VIII:
25. Párnás táncdal [Pillow Dance]
26. Kánon [Canon]
27. Isten veled! [Lover's Farewell]

Date--1935
Perf--Nos. 1, 17, 25, May 7, 1937, conducted by Paula Radnai,
    László Preisinger (Perényi), Mme. Ferenc Barth, Benjamin
    Rajecky, and Adrienne Stojanovics, Budapest
Pub--Magyar Kórus 1937, 1938, Zeneműkiadó 1953; 9 pieces,
    Boosey & Hawkes 1955, remaining 18 pieces, Zeneműkiadó
    1972; Nos. IV/1, III/1, IV/2, IV/3, III/4 arranged with school
    orchestra, Magyar Kórus 1937, Zeneműkiadó 1962, 1963; Nos.
    I/2, V/1 arranged with small orchestra, Boosey & Hawkes 1942
Cat--Sz 103, BB 111

106. *Elmúlt időkből* [From Olden Times] (after old Hungarian folk- and
    art-song texts, for three-part male chorus, a cappella)
    1. Nincs boldogtalanabb [No One's More Unhappy Than the Peasant]
    2. Egy, kettő, három, négy [One, Two, Three, Four]
    3. Nincsen szerencsésebb [No One Is Happier Than the Peasant]

Date--1935
Perf--May 7, 1937, Béla Endre Chamber Chorus (Béla Endre
    conducting), Budapest
Pub--Magyar Kórus 1937
Cat--Sz 104, BB 112

7. Voice and Orchestra

107. *Magyar népdalok* [Hungarian Folk Songs] (arrangement of Nos. 1, 2, 14, 11, 12 from Húsz magyar népdal [Twenty Hungarian Folk Songs] for voice and piano)
     1. Tömlöcben [In Prison]
     2. Régi kerserves [Old Lament]
     3. Párosító I [Nuptial Serenade]
     4. Panasz [Complaint]
     5. Párosító II [Humorous Song]

     Date--1933; original voice and piano version, 1929
     Perf--October 23, 1933, Ernő Dohnányi conducting, Budapest
     Pub--original voice and piano version, Universal 1932
     Cat--Sz 101, BB 108

8. Chorus and Orchestra

108. *Falun* (Tri dedinské scény) [Three Village Scenes]
     (for four or eight women's voices and chamber orchestra; transcription of Nos. 3, 4, and 5 from Five Village Scenes, for voice and piano)
     1. Lakodalom [Wedding]
     2. Bölcsődal [Lullaby]
     3. Legénytánc [Lad's Dance]

     Date--May 1926, Budapest
     Perf--February 1, 1927, Serge Koussevitzky conducting, New York
     Pub--full score, Universal 1927; vocal score, Universal 1927
     Cat--Sz 79, BB 87b

109. *Cantata profana (A kilenc csodaszarvas)* [The Nine Enchanted Stags] (text based on Romanian *colindă*, arrangement and Hungarian translation by the composer; for mixed chorus, tenor and baritone solos, and orchestra)
     I. Molto moderato (attacca)
     II. Andante (attacca)
     III. Moderato

     Date--September 8, 1930, Budapest
     Perf--May 25, 1934, Trefor Jones (tenor), Frank Phillips (baritone), BBC Symphony and Wireless Chorus (Aylmer Buesst conducting), London
     Pub--full score, Universal 1934, 1957; vocal score, Universal 1934, 1951, Boosey & Hawkes 1939, 1955 (English translation copyright)
     Cat--Sz 94, BB 100

9. Stage Works

110. A kékszakállú herceg vára [Duke Bluebeard's Castle] Op. 11; opera
in one act, libretto by Béla Balázs

Date--September 1911, Rákoskeresztúr; revised 1912, 1918
Ded--Márta [Bartók]
Perf--May 24, 1918, Egisto Tango conducting, Olga Haselbeck
[Judith], Oszkar Kálmán [Bluebeard], Budapest
Pub--vocal score, Universal 1922; full score, Universal 1925, 1963
Cat--Sz 48, BB 62

111. A fából faragott királyfi [The Wooden Prince] Op. 13; ballet in one
act, libretto by Béla Balázs

Date--1914-1916, orchestrated 1916-1917; suite, 1932 (unpublished)
Ded--Egisto Tango
Perf--May 12, 1917, Hungarian State Opera House (Egisto Tango
conducting), Budapest
Pub--piano score, Universal 1921; full score, Universal 1924
Cat--Sz 60, BB 74

112. A csodálatos mandarin [The Miraculous Mandarin] Op. 19;
pantomime in one act, libretto by Menyhért Lengyel

Date--October 1918-May 1919, Rákoskeresztúr; also suite
Perf--November 27, 1926, Jenő Szenkár conducting, Cologne
Pub--piano four-hands score, Universal 1925; full score, Universal
1955
Cat--Sz 73, BB 82

10. Bartók's Editions and Transcriptions of Keyboard Works
by Other Composers

For earlier listings, see: Victor Bátor. The Béla Bartók Archives: History
and Catalogue. New York: Bartók Archives publication, 1963. pp. 37-38;
David Yeomans. Bartók for Piano: A Survey of His Solo Literature.
Bloomington and Indianapolis: Indiana University Press, 1988.
Appendix C; and László Somfai/Vera Lampert. "Béla Bartók." The New
Grove Dictionary of Music and Musicians, II., 6th ed. Stanley Sadie.
London: Macmillan Publishers Ltd., 1980, p. 223. Period of
transcription or edition (indicated by Date), where date is available;
publisher and date of publication (indicated by Pub); Publisher's plate
number (indicated by Plate No.); source of original composition
(indicated by Source).

113. Bach, Johann Sebastian. Wohltemperirtes Klavier [Well-tempered
Clavier]

Pub--Rozsnyai Károly, Budapest, Vols. I-IV; Rózsavölgyi, Budapest, Vol. I; Editio Music, Budapest, Vols. I and II
Plate No.--R.K. 246 (Vol. I); R.K. 247 (Vol. II); R.K. 248 (Vol. III); R.K. 249 (Vol. IV)

114. Bach, Johann Sebastian. *Tizenhárom könnyű kis zongoradarab* (Dreizehn Leichte kleine Klavierstücke aus dem "Notenbuchlein für Anna Magdalena Bach") [Thirteen little piano pieces from the "Notebook for Anna Magdalena Bach"]

Pub--Rozsnyai Károlyi, Budapest; Rózsavölgyi és Társa, Budapest, 1917; Zeneműkiadó Vallalat, Budapest, 1950
Plate No.--Z. 30

115. Bach, Johann Sebastian. *Sonata VI,* BWV. 530

Date--arr. c1930
Pub--Rózsavölgyi és Társa, Budapest, 1930
Plate No.--R. & Co. 5172

116. Beethoven, Ludwig van. *Sonatas for Piano* (complete; issued separately; Nos. 15-32 edited by Ernő Dohnányi)

Pub--Rózsavölgyi és Társa, Budapest
Plate No.--R. és Tsa: 3281 (1), 3515 (2), 3318 (3), 3516 (4), 3282 (5), 3319 (6), 3517 (7), 3283 (8), 3320 (9), 3321 (10), 3518 (11), 3377 (12), 3519 (13), 3284 (14), 3520 (15), 3521 (16), 3522 (17), 3523 (18), 3322 (20), 3382 (21), 3378 (23), 3379 (24), 3381 (27)

117. Beethoven, Ludwig van. *Sonata in C-sharp Minor,* Op. 27, No. 2

Pub--Zeneműkiadó Vallalat, Budapest, 1955
Plate No.--Z 2042

118. Beethoven, Ludwig van. *7 Bagatelles,* Op. 33

Pub--Rozsnyai Károly, Budapest

119. Beethoven, Ludwig van. *11 New Bagatelles,* Op. 119

Pub--Rozsnyai Károly, Budapest
Plate No.--R.K. 477

120. Beethoven, Ludwig van. *Polonaise in C,* Op. 89

Pub--Rozsnyai Károly, Budapest
Plate No.--R.K. 493

121. Beethoven, Ludwig van. *6 Variations in F*, Op. 34

    Pub--Rozsnyai Károly, Budapest

122. Beethoven, Ludwig van. *Ecossaises*

    Pub--Rozsnyai Károly, Budapest; Zeneműkiadó Vallalat, Budapest, 1951
    Plate No.--Z. 116

123. Beethoven, Ludwig van. *15 Variations and Fugue*, Op. 35

    Pub--Rozsnyai Károly, Budapest
    Plate No.--R.K. 476

124. Chopin, Frédéric. *Valses*

    Pub--Rozsnyai Károly, Budapest

125. Ciaia, Azzolino Bernardino della. *Sonata (in G Major)*
    I. Toccata
    II. Canzone
    III. Primo tempo
    IV. Secondo tempo

    Date--arr. c1926-1928
    Pub--in Béla Bartók, *XVII and XVIII Century Italian Cembalo and Organ Music Transcribed for Piano*, Carl Fischer, New York, 1930, reprinted 1990 with introduction by László Somfai
    Plate No.--25272-7 P1816 (Toccata), 25272-10 P1817 (Canzone), 25274-4 P1818 (P. Tempo), 25275-4 P1819 (S. Tempo)
    Source--Buonamici, ed., *3 Sonate per Cembalo (op. 4) del Cavaliere Azzolino Bernardino Della Ciaja di Siena* (C. Bratti et Co., 1912)

126. Couperin, François. *Selected Keyboard Works*

    Pub--Editio Musica, Budapest, 1950

127. Couperin, François. *18 Pieces*

    Pub--Rozsnyai Károly, Budapest, October 1924; Zeneműkiadó, Budapest, 1955
    Plate No.--R.K. 1641 (Vol. II), R.K. 1642 (Vol. III); Z. 1769 (1-10) (Vol. II), [see D. Scarlatti for Vol. I]

128. Cramer. *Etudes* (Nos. 29-56 Inc.)

    Pub--Rózsavölgyi és Társa, Budapest
    Plate No.--5387

129. Duvernoy, V.A. *L'école du Mécanisme,* Op. 120

    Pub--Bard Ferenc és Fia, Budapest, 1920
    Plate No.--B.F.F. 2255

130. Frescobaldi, Girolamo. *Fuga (G Minor)*

    Date--arr. c1926-1928
    Pub--in Béla Bartók, *XVII and XVIII Century Italian Cembalo and Organ Music Transcribed for Piano,* Carl Fischer, New York, 1930, reprinted 1990 with introduction by László Somfai
    Plate No.--25277-6 P1821
    Source--Torchi, ed., *L'arte musicale in Italia,* Vol. 3 (Ricordi, n.d.)

131. Frescobaldi, Girolamo. *Toccata (G Major)*

    Date--arr. c1926-1928
    Pub--in Béla Bartók, *XVII and XVIII Century Italian Cembalo and Organ Music Transcribed for Piano,* Carl Fischer, New York, 1930, reprinted 1990 with introduction by László Somfai
    Plate No.--25276-7 P1820
    Source--Torchi, ed., *L'arte musicale in Italia,* Vol. 3 (Ricordi (n.d.)

132. Händel, George Frederic. *Sonatas*

    Pub--Rozsnyai Károly, Budapest

133. Haydn, Franz Joseph. *Deux Sonates*
    Pub--Rózsavölgyi és Társa, Budapest
    Plate No.--4346

134. Haydn, Franz Joseph. *Sonatas,* Vols. I-II (Nos. 1-10; Nos. 11-19)

    Pub--Rozsnyai Károly, Budapest
    Plate Nos.--R.K. 879-888 (Nos. 1-10), R.K. 889-895 (Nos. 11-17), R.K. 1550-1551 (Nos. 18-19)

135. Haydn, Franz Joseph. *Sonata No. 53 in E Minor,* Hob. XVI/34

    Pub--Editio Musica, Budapest

136. Heller, Stephen. *25 Etudes,* Op. 45, Vols. I-III

    Pub--Rózsavölgyi és Társa, Budapest
    Plate No.--R. és Tsa: 3913 (Vol. I), 3914 (Vol. II), 3915 (Vol. III)

137. Heller, Stephen. *30 Etudes,* Op. 46, Vols. I-III

    Pub--Rózsavölgyi és Társa, Budapest
    Plate No.--R. és Tsa: 3926 (Vol. I), 3927 (Vol. II), 3928 (Vol. III)

138. Heller, Stephen. *25 Etudes,* Op. 47, Vols. I-II

    Pub--Rózsavölgyi és Társa, Budapest

139. Heller, Stephen. *Tarantella,* Op. 85, No. 2

    Pub--Rózsavölgyi és Társa, Budapest

140. Heller, Stephen. *24 Etudes,* Op. 125, Vols. I-II

    Pub--Rózsavölgyi és Társa, Budapest

141. Heller, Stephen. *Album,* Vols. I-III

    Pub--Rózsavölgyi és Társa, Budapest

142. Marcello, Benedetto. *Sonata in B-flat Major*

    Date--arr. c1926-1928
    Pub--in Béla Bartók, *XVII and XVIII Century Italian Cembalo and Organ Music Transcribed for Piano,* Carl Fischer, New York, 1930, reprinted 1990 with introduction by László Somfai
    Plate No.--25268-14 P1812
    Source--Pauer, ed., *Alte Meister,* Band V (Breitkopf & Härtel, n.d.)

143. Mendelssohn, Felix. *Scherzo in B Minor*

    Pub--Rozsnyai Károly, Budapest

144. Mendelssohn, Felix. *Prelude and Fugue in E Major*

    Pub--Rozsnyai Károly, Budapest

145. Mozart, Wolfgang Amadeus. "Marcia alla Turka" (published separately from *Sonata in A Major,* K. 331)

    Pub--Zeneműkiadó, Budapest, 1952
    Plate No.--Z. 1102

146. Mozart, Wolfgang Amadeus. *Fantasie in C Minor*

    Pub--Rozsnyai Károly, Budapest

147. Mozart, Wolfgang Amadeus. *Sonatas for Piano* (complete), Vols. I (Nos. 1-10) and II (Nos. 11-20)

    Pub--Rozsnyai Károly, Budapest; Editio Musica, Budapest
    Plate No.--R.K.: 640 (1), 632 (2), 727 (3), 731 (4),732 (5), 733 (6), 686 (7), 734 (8), 550 (9), 735 (10), 736 (11), 737 (12), 738 (13), 739 (14), 740 (15), 551 (16), 741 (17), 435 (18), 872 (19), 873 (20)

148. Mozart, Wolfgang Amadeus. *Twenty Sonatas*

    Pub--Kalmus-Belwin Mills

149. Mozart, Wolfgang Amadeus. *Sonata in G Major, K. 545*

    Pub--Editio Musica, Budapest

150. Purcell, Henry. *Two Preludes* (in G, C)

    Pub--Delkas, Los Angeles

151. Rossi, Michelangelo. *Toccata No. 1 in C Major*

    Date--arr. c1926-1928
    Pub--in Béla Bartók, *XVII and XVIII Century Italian Cembalo and Organ Music Transcribed for Piano,* Carl Fischer, New York, 1930, reprinted 1990 with introduction by László Somfai
    Plate No.--25269-7 P1813
    Source--Torchi, ed., *L'arte musicale in Italia,* Vol. 3 (Ricordi, n.d.), no. 1 of "Dieci Toccate"

152. Rossi, Michelangelo. *Toccata No. 2 in A Minor*

    Date--arr. c1926-1928
    Pub--in Béla Bartók, *XVII and XVIII Century Italian Cembalo and Organ Music Transcribed for Piano,* Carl Fischer, New York, 1930, reprinted 1990 with introduction by László Somfai
    Plate No.--25270-7 P1814
    Source--Torchi, ed., *L'arte musicale in Italia,* Vol. 3 (Ricordi, n.d.), no. 9 of "Dieci Toccate"

153. Rossi, Michelangelo. *Tre correnti*

    Date--arr. c1926-1928
    Pub--in Béla Bartók, *XVII and XVIII Century Italian Cembalo and Organ Music Transcribed for Piano,* Carl Fischer, New York, 1930, reprinted 1990 with introduction by László Somfai
    Plate No.--25271-5 P1815
    Source--Torchi, ed., *L'arte musicale in Italia,* Vol. 3 (Ricordi, n.d.), nos. 5, 1, and 2 of "Dieci Correnti"

154. Scarlatti, Domenico. *Sonatas,* Vols. I and IV

    Pub--Rozsnyai Károly, Budapest, May 1921
    Plate No.--R.K.: 1552 (Vol. I, Nos. 1-5), 1651 (Vol. IV, Nos. 6-10), [see F. Couperin for Vols. II, III]

155. Scarlatti, Domenico. *Selected Sonatas,* Vols. I and II

Pub--Editio Musica, Budapest

156. Scarlatti, Domenico. *Five Pieces*
   Pub--Kalmus-Belwin Mills

157. Scarlatti, Domenico. *Essercizi*
   Pub--Rozsnyai Károlyi, Budapest

158. Schubert, Franz. *Sonata in G Major*
   Pub--Rozsnyai Károlyi, Budapest

159. Schubert, Franz. *Sonata in A Minor,* Op. 143
   Pub--Rozsnyai Károlyi, Budapest

160. Schubert, Franz. *Fantaisie oder Sonate*
   Pub--Rozsnyai Károlyi, Budapest

161. Schubert, Franz. *2 Scherzi*
   Pub--Rozsnyai Károlyi, Budapest
   Plate No.--R.K. 685

162. Schumann, Robert. *Jugend-Album,* Op. 68
   Pub--Rozsnyai Károlyi, Budapest

163. Schumann, Robert. *Phantasiestücke*
   Pub--Univ. Edition, New York

164. Zipoli, Domenico. *Pastorale in C Major*
   Date--arr. c1926-1928
   Pub--in Béla Bartók, *XVII and XVIII Century Italian Cembalo and Organ Music Transcribed for Piano,* Carl Fischer, New York, 1930, reprinted 1990 with introduction by László Somfai
   Plate No.--25278-5 P1822
   Source--Torchi, ed., *L'arte musicale in Italia,* Vol. 3 (Ricordi, n.d.)

II. PRIMARY SOURCES: BARTÓK'S WRITINGS AND OTHER DOCUMENTS

1. Articles by Bartók

1. "Kossuth. Szinfóniai költemény" [*Kossuth:* Symphonic poem]. *Zeneközlöny* (Budapest) 11/6 (January 11, 1904): 82-87. H26.706

    Gives brief history of Kossuth's leadership in the Hungarian revolt of 1848 against Austrian domination, then provides an analysis of the work with musical examples outlining the ten closely related sections of the work, each with an epigraphic description based on the historical events. Also published in *Hallé Concert Society* (Manchester, England) (February 18, 1904): 506-511; *Egyetemi nyomda diáriuma* (Budapest) (1948): 37-38; *Zenei szemle* (Budapest) 8 (December 1948): 427-429; *Bartók Béla levelei*, ed. János Demény. Budapest: Művelt Nép Könyvkiadó, 1951, pp. 54-55; *Documenta bartókiana* (Budapest) 1 (1964):70-73, 80-89; *Bartók Béla összegyűjtött írásai*, ed. András Szőllősy. Budapest: Zeneműkiadó Vállalat, 1966, pp. 767-773, 922-923; Szabolcsi, Bence. *Béla Bartók.* Leipzig: Philipp Reclam, 1968, p. 30; *Béla Bartók Essays,* ed. Benjamin Suchoff. New York: St. Martin's Press, 1976, pp. 399-403.

2. "Strauss: Sinfonia Domestica (Op. 53)." *Zeneközlöny* (Budapest) 3/10 (February 13, 1905): 137-143. H26.706

    Study of Strauss's sketch of the program and his thematic review, with the intention of establishing these aspects by the remarks in the score and the music itself. Shows the work to be divided into four parts. Also published in: *Bartók Béla összegyűjtött írásai,* ed. András Szőllősy. Budapest: Zeneműkiadó Vállalat, 1966, pp. 707-714; *Béla Bartók Essays,* ed. Benjamin Suchoff. New York: St. Martin's Press, 1976, pp. 437-445.

3. "Életrajzi adataim ezek" [My biographical data] (1905, unpublished). In *Sopronvármegye* (Sopron) (May 7, 1922): n.p. H11.421/1073

    Not examined. Also published in: *Bartók Béla (levelek, fényképek, kéziratok, kották),* ed. János Demény. Budapest: Magyar Művészeti Tanács, 1948, p. 69; *Documenta bartókiana* (Budapest) 2 (1965):108-109; *Béla Bartók. Lettere scelte,* ed. János Demény.

Milan: Il Saggiatore di Alberto Mondadori Editore, 1969, p. 78;
Béla Bartók Letters, ed. János Demény. London: Faber & Faber,
1971, p. 54.

4. "Bach-Bartók: Preface and Notes to Well-Tempered Clavier." *J.S.
Bach: Wohltemperiertes Klavier.* Budapest: Rozsnyai Károly, No.
246, 1907, Vol. I: 3, pp. 54-56.

Discusses Bach's aim, which was to point to the enormous
advantages of the tempered tuning. Mentions his necessity of
altering the original order of pieces for pedagogical reasons.
Furthermore, discusses problems of tempo as well as the instrument
for which it was written. Also published by: Budapest: Zeneműkiadó
Vállalat, 1961; and in *Béla Bartók Essays,* ed. Benjamin Suchoff.
New York: St. Martin's Press, 1976, pp. 447-448.

5. "Székely balladák" [Székely Ballads]. *Ethnographia* (Budapest)
19/1,2 (January and March, 1908): 43-52, 105-115.   HB1.743

Represents Bartók's first scholarly effort, in which he
postulates that these old melodies are not closely bound to their
texts and that epic and lyric melodies and texts are interchangeable
within a rhythmic context. Also published in: *Bartók Béla
összegyűjtött írásai,* ed. András Szőllősy. Budapest: Zeneműkiadó
Vállalat, 1966, pp. 15-50. Includes fifteen ballads.

6. "Dunántúli balladák" [Transdanubian Ballads]. *Ethnographia* 20/5
(October 1909): 301-305.   HB1.743

Includes six ballads, but has no commentary by Bartók. Also
published in: *Bartók Béla összegyűjtött írásai,* ed. András Szőllősy.
Budapest: Zeneműkiadó Vállalat, 1966, pp. 51-58.

7. "Függelék a 'Wohltemperiertes Klavier' revideált kiadása I.
füzetéhez" [Appendix to the revised edition of the *Wohltemperiertes
Klavier,* Vol. I]. Budapest: Károly Rozsnyai, c. 1910.

Part of Bartók's editorial work on the keyboard music of Bach
as well as other earlier composers, which he began around 1908.
These have become important pedagogical editions in Hungary.

8. *"Elektra.* Strauss Richard operája" [*Elektra.* Opera by Richard
Strauss]. *A zene* (Budapest) 2/4 (April 1910): 57-58.   H17.962

Essay regarding the first performance of *Elektra* at the Royal
Hungarian Opera House on March 11, 1910. Bartók expresses a
specific dislike for this opera and feels it is especially disappointing
after *Salome.* Expects more from such a gifted composer. Also
published in: *Szimfónia* (1917): n.p.; *Bartók Béla válogatott írásai,*

ed. András Szőllősy. Budapest: Művelt Nép Tudományos és Ismeretterjesztő Kiadó, 1956, p. 261; *Bartók breviárium (levelek, irások, dokumentumok)*, ed. József Ujfalussy. Budapest: Zeneműkiadó Vállalat, 1958, pp. 123-124; *Béla Bartók: Postrehy a názory*, ed. Eva Hykischová. Bratislava: Štátne Hudobné Vydavatel'stvo, 1965, p. 51; *Bartók Béla összegyűjtött írásai*, ed. András Szőllősy. Budapest: Zeneműkiadó Vállalat, 1966, p. 715; *Béla Bartók Essays*, ed. Benjamin Suchoff. New York: St. Martin's Press, 1976, p. 446.

9. "Rhapsodie für Klavier und Orchester (Op. I)" [Rhapsody for Piano and Orchestra, Op. I]. *Signale* (Berlin) 68/21 (May 1910): 809-810. H22.995

    Brief analysis of the thematic organization of what may be considered a sonata form. Says the work is comprised of the "intermutation of two antithetically characterized parts (adagio, allegretto and vivace) which are preceded by an introduction consisting of piano cadenzas." Also published in: *Schweizerische Musikzeitung* (Zurich) 50/17 (May 1910): 184-185; *Die Musik* (Vienna) (1910): 226-228; *Zenetudományi tanulmányok* 3, special issue: *Liszt Ferenc és Bartók Béla emlékére*, ed. Bence Szabolcsi and Dénes Bartha. Budapest: Akadémiai Kiadó, 1955, pp. 448-449; *Bartók Béla összegyűjtött írásai*, ed. András Szőllősy. Budapest: Zeneműkiadó Vállalat, 1966, pp. 774-779; *Béla Bartók Essays*, ed. Benjamin Suchoff. New York: St. Martin's Press, 1976, pp. 404-405.

10. "Bartók Béla. Önéletrajz" [Autobiography]. *Budapesti újságírók egyesülete almanachja.* (Budapest) (1911): 292.

    Not examined. Also published in: *Magyar nemzet* (Budapest) (November 5, 1961): n.p.; *Muzsika* (Budapest) 6/7 (July 1963): 43; *Documenta bartókiana* 2 (Budapest) (1965): 111; *Bartók Béla összegyűjtött írásai*, ed. András Szőllősy. Budapest: Zeneműkiadó Vállalat, 1966. p. 7.

11. "A magyar zenéről" [On Hungarian music]. *Auróra* (Budapest) 1/3 (1911): 126-128.   AP 63.2 A 876

    States that unlike the natural order of things, where practice comes before theory, we see the opposite with Hungarian music. Bartók's previously published scientific works dealt with the characteristic features of Hungarian music, an attempt to define something nonexistent at the time. Discusses the earlier composers who are amateur musicians under the influence of gypsy music. Also published in: *Der Merker* (Vienna) 7/21 (November 1916): 757-758; *Bartók Béla, Önéletrajz, Írások a zenéről*, ed. András Szőllősy. Budapest: Egyetemi Nyomda, 1946, pp. 54-57; *Bartók Béla válogatott zenei írásai,* ed. András Szőllősy. Budapest: Magyar Kórus, 1948, pp. 10-11; *Bartók Béla válogatott írásai,* ed. András Szőllősy. Budapest: Művelt Nép Tudományos és Ismeretterjesztő Kiadó, 1956, pp. 288-290; *Béla Bartók, Scritti sulla musica popolare,* ed. Diego Carpitella. Turin: Edizioni Scientifiche Einaudi, 1955, pp. 108-111; *Ifjúsági könyvkiadó* (Budapest), 1955, 272-274; *La revue musicale* (Paris) 224 (1955): 61-64; *Bartók Béla, Insemnări asupra cîntecului popular,* ed. Zeno Vancea. Bucharest: Editura de Stat Pentru Literatură și Artă, 1956, pp. 108-111; *Béla Bartók: Postrehy a názory,* ed. Eva Hykischová. Bratislava: Štátne Hudobné Vydavatel'stvo, 1965, pp. 69-71; *Bartók Béla összegyűjtött írásai,* ed. András Szőllősy. Budapest: Zeneműkiadó Vállalat, 1966, pp. 609-610; *Béla Bartók Essays,* ed. Benjamin Suchoff. New York: St. Martin's Press, 1976, pp. 301-303.

12. "Delius-bemutató Bécsben." [A Delius premiere in Vienna]. *Zeneközlöny* (Budapest) 9/11 (April 1911): 340-342.   H26.706

    Discusses the performance of *Eine Messe des Lebens* on February 17 by the Vienna Philharmonic Orchestra and Choir. Main point deals with a peculiar musical development that is manifest for the first time in this work: the use of a textless chorus for the sake of tone color. Also published in: *Bartók Béla válogatott zenei írásai,* ed. András Szőllősy. Budapest: Magyar Kórus, 1948, pp. 76-77; *Bartók Béla válogatott írásai,* ed. András Szőllősy. Budapest: Művelt Nép Tudományos és Ismeretterjesztő Kiadó, 1956, pp. 262-264; *Bartók breviárium (levelek, írások, dokumentumok),* ed. József Ujfalussy. Budapest: Zeneműkiadó Vállalat, 1958, pp. 124-126; *Bartók Béla összegyűjtött írásai,* ed. András Szőllősy. Budapest: Zeneműkiadó Vállalat, 1966, pp. 716-717, *Béla Bartók Essays,* ed. Benjamin Suchoff. New York: St. Martin's Press, 1976, pp. 449-450.

13. "Liszt zenéje és a mai közönség" [Liszt's music and today's public]. *Népművelés* (Budapest) 6/17-18 (October 1911): 359-362. H60.629

    States that many musicians have little sympathy with Liszt's music, despite all its originality and greatness. This is perhaps due to his many-sidedness, his eclecticism, etc. Mentions some of the influences on Liszt and gives opinions of some of the works. Also published in: *Zeneközlöny* (Budapest) 9/18 (October 1911): 556-560; *Bartók Béla, Önéletrajz, Írások a zenéről,* ed. András Szőllősy. Budapest: Egyetemi Nyomda, 1946, pp. 58-62; *Bartók Béla válogatott zenei írásai,* ed. András Szőllősy. Budapest: Magyar Kórus, 1948, pp. 68-70; *Monthly Musical Record* (London) 78/899 (1948): 180-183; *Dansk musiktidsskift* (Copenhagen) 26/10 (1951):

212-214; *Liszt Ferenc és Bartók Béla emlékére.* Budapest: Akadémiai Kiadó,1955, pp. 13-15; *Bartók Béla válogatott írásai,* ed. András Szőllősy. Budapest: Művelt Nép Tudományos és Ismeretterjesztő Kiadó, 1956, pp. 215-219; *New Hungarian Quarterly* (Budapest) 11/1 (1961): 5-8; *Béla Bartók: Postrehy a názory,* ed. Eva Hykischová. Bratislava: Štátne Hudobné Vydavatel'stvo, 1965, pp. 58-61; *Bartók Béla összegyűjtött írásai,* ed. András Szőllősy. Budapest: Zeneműkiadó Vállalat, 1966, pp. 687-689; *Nuova rivista musicale italiana* 4/5 (September-October 1970): 913-916; *Béla Bartók Musiksprachen,* ed. Bence Szabolcsi. Leipzig: Philipp Reclam, 1972, pp. 133-137; *Béla Bartók Essays,* ed. Benjamin Suchoff. New York: St. Martin's Press, 1976, pp. 451-454.

14. "A hangszeres zene folkloreja Magyarországon" [Instrumental music folklore in Hungary]. Published as a series in four sections: *Zeneközlöny* (Budapest) 9/5 (January 1911): 141-148; 9/7 (February 1911): 207-213; 9/10 (March 1911): 309-312; 10/19 (April 1912): 601-604.   H26.706

Describes a variety of instruments and gives transcriptions. Mentions that vocal music preceded instrumental and that it plays a greater role in rural folk music. Therefore, instrumental recordings are less available. Better peasant musicians embellish instrumental melodies to a great extent with much improvisation in tempo changes and ornaments. This makes transcription difficult. The phonograph has facilitated transcription. Then, gives a detailed account intended as a description of collecting activities. This is presented in three groups, according to the Hungarian, Slovakian, and Romanian villages where recordings took place. Also published in: *Bartók Béla összegyűjtött írásai,* ed. András Szőllősy. Budapest: Zeneműkiadó Vállalat, 1966, pp. 59-76; *Béla Bartók Essays,* ed. Benjamin Suchoff. New York: St. Martin's Press, 1976, pp. 239-284.

15. "A magyar nép hangszerei" [Hungarian folk instruments]. Published in two parts: I. *A kanásztülök ethnographia* (Budapest) 22/5 (October 1911): 305-310; II. *Duda ethnographia* (Budapest) 23/2 (March 1912): 110-114.

Intended as a series in which only two parts were published. Describes instruments, which are not exclusive to Hungary, and their transcriptions. Main instruments are bagpipe, peasant flute, hurdy-gurdy, natural horn, and home-made zithers in many regions. Also published in: *Bartók Béla összegyűjtött írásai,* ed. András Szőllősy. Budapest: Zeneműkiadó Vállalat, 1966, pp. 818-826; *Béla Bartók Essays,* ed. Benjamin Suchoff. New York: St. Martin's Press, 1976, pp. 239-284.

16. "A clavecinre írt művek előadása" [The performance of works written for the clavecin]. *Zeneközlöny* (Budapest) 10/7 (January 1912): 226-227. H26.706

Opposes the attitude of resurrecting the imperfections of the clavecin when dealing with old keyboard music for performance on the piano. Also protests objections of performing Rameau, Couperin, Scarlatti, and Bach in enlarged modern concert halls on the more perfected piano. Also published in: *Bartók Béla válogatott zenei írásai,* ed. András Szőllősy. Budapest: Magyar Kórus, 1948, pp. 67-68; *Bartók Béla válogatott írásai,* ed. András Szőllősy. Budapest: Művelt Nép Tudományos és Ismeretterjesztő Kiadó, 1956, pp. 257-259; *Béla Bartók: Postrehy a názory,* ed. Eva Hykischová. Bratislava: Štátne Hudobné Vydavatel'stvo, 1965, pp. 64-66; *Bartók Béla összegyűjtött írásai,* ed. András Szőllősy. Budapest: Zeneműkiadó Vállalat, 1966, pp. 685-686; *Béla Bartók Essays,* ed. Benjamin Suchoff. New York: St. Martin's Press, 1976, pp. 285-286.

17. "Az összehasonlító zenefolklore" [Comparative music folklore]. *Új élet népművelés* (Budapest) 1/1-2 (January 1912): 109-114. H60.629

Defines this as a young branch of science on the border between musicology and folklore. Such work is difficult because of an insufficient number of reliable collections. Important work has been done by Finnish ethnologist Ilmari Krohn. Also published in: *Bartók Béla válogatott zenei írásai,* ed. András Szőllősy. Budapest: Magyar Kórus, 1948, pp. 26-28; *Bartók Béla válogatott írásai,* ed. András Szőllősy. Budapest: Művelt Nép Tudományos és Ismeretterjesztő Kiadó, 1956, pp. 58-62; *Béla Bartók, Scritti sulla musica popolare,* ed. Diego Carpitella. Turin: Edizioni Scientifiche Einaudi, 1955, pp. 79-84; *Bartók Béla, Insemnări asupra cîntecului popular,* ed. Zeno Vancea. Bucharest: Editura de Stat Pentru Literatură şi Artă, 1956, pp. 62-66; *Béla Bartók: Postrehy a názory,* ed. Eva Hykischová. Bratislava: Štátne Hudobné Vydavatel'stvo, 1965, pp. 179-183; *Bartók Béla összegyűjtött írásai,* ed. András Szőllősy. Budapest: Zeneműkiadó Vállalat, 1966, pp. 567-570; *Béla Bartók Essays,* ed. Benjamin Suchoff. New York: St. Martin's Press, 1976, pp. 155-158.

18. Bartók, Béla, and Zoltán Kodály. "Az új egyetemes népdalgyűjtemény tervezete" [Draft of the new universal folk song collection]. *Ethnographia* (Budapest) 24/5 (1913): 313-316. HB1.743

Draft, presented to the Kisfaludy Society, proposing a vigorously critical and exact publication of these Hungarian folk songs and musical folk compositions in an edition of a monumental Hungarian *Corpus Musicae Popularis.* Discusses problems with earlier collections and gives a detailed outline of the methodology to be used. Also published in: *Béla Bartók Studies in Ethnomusicology,* ed. Benjamin Suchoff. Lincoln and London: University of Nebraska Press, 1996, pp. 24-28.

19. Bartók, Béla, and Sándor Reschofsky. "Zongoraiskola" [Preface and notes to *Piano School*]. Budapest: Rózsavölgyi és Társa, No. 3635,1913.

   This piano method is intended to comprise the complete material for a first-year course, including all rudiments and elementary aspects of piano technique. Also published in: Budapest: Zeneműkiadó Vállalat, 1954, 1968; London (ed. Leslie Russell): New York: Boosey and Hawkes, 1968.

20. "A hunyadi román nép zenedialektusa" [Folk music dialect of the Hunedoara Romanians]. *Ethnographia* (Budapest) 25/2 (1914):108-115. HB1.743

   Gives some observations regarding the general characteristics of the Romanian people's music. Romanians have preserved the ancient condition of their folk music. Gives division of melodies into five well-defined categories and associates these with Hungarian categories in ancient times. Also published in: *Zeitschrift für Musikwissenschaft* (Leipzig) 2/6 (March 1920): 352-360; *Muzica si poezie* (Bucharest) 1/4 (February 1936): 6-14; Béla Bartók, *Scrieri mărunte despre muzica populară românească,* ed. Constantin Brăiloiu. Bucharest, 1937, pp. 5-13; *Bartók Béla, Insemnări asupra cîntecului popular,* ed. Zeno Vancea. Bucharest: Editura de Stat Pentru Literatură şi Artă, 1956, pp.143-159; See also Júlia Szegő's *Bartók Béla, a népdalkutató.* Bucharest: Ilami Irodalmi és Művészeti Kiadó, 1956, pp. 300-312; *Bartók Béla összegyűjtött írásai,* ed. András Szőllősy. Budapest: Zeneműkiadó Vállalat, 1966, pp. 462-472; and *Béla Bartók Essays,* ed. Benjamin Suchoff. New York: St. Martin's Press, 1976, pp. 103-114.

21. "Observări despre muzica poporală românească [Observations on Romanian folk music]. *Convorbiri literare* (Bucharest) 48/7-8 (July-August 1914): 703-709. H51.515

   Rebuttal of a review of Bartók's collection of Romanian folk music in the ethnographical periodical *Şezătoarea* 14/11-12. Reviewer declares Bartók's collection of being of no value, claiming the notation of the melodies is faulty and other charges. Also

published in: *Muzica şi poezie* (Bucharest) 1/12 (October 1914): 19-
23; *Béla Bartók, Scrieri mărunte despre muzica populară românească,*
ed. Constantin Brăiloiu. Bucharest, 1937, pp. 53-55; *Új zenei
szemle* (Budapest) 7/3 (March, 1956): 9-12; Júlia Szegő. *Bartók
Béla, a népdalkutató.* Bucharest: Ilami Irodalmi és Művészeti Kiadó,
1956, pp. 313-319; *Bartók Béla, Insemnări asupra cîntecului
popular,* ed. Zeno Vancea. Bucharest: Editura de Stat Pentru Literatură
şi Artă, 1956, pp. 219-223; *Bartók Béla összegyűjtött írásai,* ed.
András Szőllősy. Budapest: Zeneműkiadó Vállalat, 1966, pp. 611-
616; *Béla Bartók Essays,* ed. Benjamin Suchoff. New York: St.
Martin's Press, 1976, pp. 195-200.

22. "A Biskra-vidéki arabok népzenéje" [Arab folk music in the Biskra
District]. *Szimfónia* (Budapest) 1/12-13 (September 1917): 308-323.
H17.996

   Discusses travels in June 1913 over the oases of the Biskra
District. States that various Arab music publications are not folk
music but rather music of the urbanized Arabs based on remnants of
old art music. This study deals with the folk music. Reveals
differences between instrumental scales of Eastern Europe (in which
all the notes refer to the steps of the seven-tone scale) and those of
the North Africans (in which additional tones within the octave
cannot be regarded as a chromatic alteration of the diatonic scale).
Also gives outline of the instruments found during his travels and
the problems encountered in recording their scales. The Hungarian
publication comprises only part of the essay. In the complete essay,
discusses wind instruments, stringed instruments, percussion
instruments, range of the melodies, musical form, rhythm,
accompaniment, tempo, peculiarities of performance, relation
between melody and text, and presents a trial classification of the
(instrumental) dance melodies. The complete essay in Bartók's
German translation appears as: "Die Volkmusik der Araber von
Biskra und Umgebung." *Zeitschrift für Musikwissenschaft* (Leipzig)
2/9 (June 1920): 489-522. Also published in: *Annales de l'institut
d'études orientales* 18-19 (1960-1961): 301-359; *Bartók Béla
összegyűjtött írásai,* ed. András Szőllősy. Budapest: Zeneműkiadó
Vállalat, 1966, pp. 518-561 and 849-851; *Béla Bartók Studies in
Ethnomusicology,* ed. Benjamin Suchoff. Lincoln and London:
University of Nebraska Press, 1996, pp. 29-76.

23. "A fából faragott királyfi: II. A zeneszerző a darabjáról" [About *The
Wooden Prince*]. *Magyar színpad* (Budapest) 20/105 (May 1917): 2.
H10.726

   States that *Bluebeard's Castle* prompted the composition of the
Wooden Prince, which Bartók began before the war. Gives a brief
outline of *The Wooden Prince* and speaks of the fondness for both

works and how they can ideally be performed together. Also published in: *Bartók Béla válogatott írásai*, ed. András Szőllősy. Budapest: Művelt Nép Tudományos és Ismeretterjesztő Kiadó, 1956, pp. 278-279; *Béla Bartók: Postrehy a názory*, ed. Eva Hykischová. Bratislava: Štátne Hudobné Vydavatel'stvo, 1965, pp. 39-40; *Bartók Béla összegyűjtött írásai*, ed. András Szőllősy. Budapest: Zeneműkiadó Vállalat, 1966, pp. 777-778; *Béla Bartók Essays*, ed. Benjamin Suchoff. New York: St. Martin's Press, 1976, p. 406.

24. "Primitív népi hangszerek Magyarországon" [Primitive folk instruments in Hungary]. *Zenei szemle* (Budapest) 1/9 (November 1917): 273-275. HA2.398

Talks of the value of transcribing melodies from the phonogram. Bartók and Kodály's interest here is only with music performed on instruments produced by the peasants themselves (i.e., without imitating artificially manufactured instruments, such as the peasant flute or violin). By 1911, discovered certain folk instruments in Hungarian Villages: bagpipe, peasant flute, so-called hurdy-gurdy, natural horn. Says that János Csiky has notated Marosszék dances performed on violin, dulcimer, and clarinet. Thus, no special Hungarian instrument was found, since these instruments are found all over Europe. Discusses instruments and the melodies recorded from them. In Hungary, peasant instrumental music appears to be based on ornamented performance of well-known folk songs with text. Also published in: *Zenei szemle* (Budapest) 1/10 (December 1917): 311-315; *Bartók Béla összegyűjtött írásai*, ed. András Szőllősy. Budapest: Zeneműkiadó Vállalat, 1966, pp. 834-841; *Béla Bartók Essays*, ed. Benjamin Suchoff. New York: St. Martin's Press, 1976, pp. 239-284.

25. "Die Melodien der madjarischen Soldatenlieder" [The melodies of the Hungarian soldiers' songs]. *Programmheft des historischen Konzertes* (Universal Edition, Vienna) (January 12, 1918): 36-42.

Discusses stanza structure, rhythm, scale ambitus, and form in melodies of the old and new styles. Hungarian soldiers' songs, like those of the Hungarian Slovaks and Romanians, belong to a group sung on lyric and epic texts. Young people of the present day sing melodies exclusively of the new style. Also published in: *Bartók Béla összegyűjtött írásai*, ed. András Szőllősy. Budapest: Zeneműkiadó Vállalat, 1966, pp. 834-841; *Béla Bartók Essays*, ed. Benjamin Suchoff. New York: St. Martin's Press, 1976, pp. 50-57.

26. "Selbstbiographie" [Autobiography]. *Musikpädagogische Zeitschrift* (Vienna) 8/11-12 (November-December 1918): 97-99.

Not examined. Also published in: *Rheinische Musik- und Theaterzeitung* (Cöln-Bayrenthal) 20/5-6 (February 1919): 1-2; *Documenta bartókiana* (Budapest) 2 (1965): 113-115; *Bartók Béla összegyűjtött írásai*, ed. András Szőllősy. Budapest: Zeneműkiadó Vállalat, 1966, pp. 816-818; *Béla Bartók Musiksprachen*, ed. Bence Szabolcsi. Leipzig: Philipp Reclam, 1972, pp. 21-26.

27. "A Kékszakállú herceg vára: I szerzők a darabjukról" [About *Duke Bluebeard's Castle*]. *Magyar színpad* (Budapest) 21/143 (May 1918): 1.   H10.726

Gives dates of composition for this "miracle play" (March to September 1911). Simultaneously, Bartók's first stage and vocal work. Talks of early unsuitable conditions for its performance and then about its subsequent first performance only after*The Wooden Prince*. Speaks of first-rate performance by conductor Egisto Tango and singers Olga Haselbeck and Oszkár Kálmán. Also published in: *Bartók Béla összegyűjtött írásai*, ed. András Szőllősy. Budapest: Zeneműkiadó Vállalat, 1966, p. 776; *Béla Bartók Essays*, ed. Benjamin Suchoff. New York: St. Martin's Press, 1976, p. 407.

28. "Musikfolklore" [Music folklore]. *Musikblätter des Anbruch* (Vienna) 1/3-4 (December 1919): 102-106.   H22.955

Comparative music folklore, one of the youngest branches of musicology, was obstructed by the outbreak of World War I. Then, speaks of its development after international traffic is opened. Direction of study is best in the hands of private researchers rather than public institutes. Lists published collections by Poles, Czechs, Slovaks, Yugoslavs, Ukrainians, and Finns (e.g., Ilmari Krohn's system of classification). Most important first step was the introduction of the phonograph. Discusses problems of transcription, outlines those institutes with recording equipment, and finally proposes a brief outline of the framework for recording, transcribing (notating), and classifying as well as an account of practical issues (expenses, etc.) involved with recording equipment. Also published in: Stuckenschmidt, Hans H. *Neue Musik*. Berlin: Suhrkamp Verlag, 1951, pp. 228-296; *Bartók Béla válogatott írásai*, ed. András Szőllősy. Budapest: Művelt Nép Tudományos és Ismeretterjesztő Kiadó, 1956, pp. 63-70; *Bartók breviárium (levelek, írások, dokumentumok)*, ed. József Ujfalussy. Budapest: Zeneműkiadó Vállalat, 1958, pp. 307-309; *Béla Bartók: Postrehy a názory*, ed. Eva Hykischová. Bratislava: Štátne Hudobné vydavatel'stvo, 1965, pp. 184-190; *Bartók Béla összegyűjtött írásai*, ed. András Szőllősy. Budapest: Zeneműkiadó Vállalat, 1966, pp. 571-575; *Béla Bartók Musiksprachen*, ed. Bence Szabolcsi. Leipzig: Philipp Reclam, 1972, pp. 27-34; *Béla Bartók Essays*, ed.

Benjamin Suchoff. New York: St. Martin's Press, 1976, pp. 159-163.

29. "Das Problem der neuen Musik" [The problem of the new music]. *Melos* (Berlin) 1/5 (April 1920): 107-110.   780.5 M492 ISSN 0174-7207

Talks of contemporary music striving toward atonality, which is a gradual development stemming from tonality. Refers to Schoenberg's *Harmonielehre* regarding this development. Says atonality came from the need for the equality of the twelve tones. Gives examples of new types of chords (on fourths and also mixed intervals). Also discusses briefly some principles of organizing atonal material and ends with a statement regarding notation with equal symbolization for the twelve equal tones. Also published in: *Komponisten über Musik*, ed. Sam Morganstern. Munich: Langen-Müller, 1956, pp. 352-356; *Béla Bartók: Eigene Schriften und Erinnerungen der Freunde*, ed. Willi Reich. Basel-Stuttgart: Benno Schwabe & Co., 1958, pp. 23-33; *Bartók breviárium (levelek, írások, dokumentumok)*, ed. József Ujfalussy. Budapest: Zeneműkiadó Vállalat, 1958, pp. 198-204; *Fran Mahler til Ligeti*, ed. Ove Nordwall. Stockholm: Orion/Bonniers, 1965, pp.9-16; *Musikrevy* (Stockholm) 20/2 (1965): 53-56; *Bartók Béla összegyűjtött írásai*, ed. András Szőllősy. Budapest: Zeneműkiadó Vállalat, 1966, pp. 718-722; *Béla Bartók Musiksprachen*, ed. Bence Szabolcsi. Leipzig: Philipp Reclam, 1972, pp. 164-171; *Béla Bartók Essays,* ed. Benjamin Suchoff. New York: St. Martin's Press, 1976, pp. 455-459.

30. "Post-War Musical Life in Budapest to February, 1920." *Musical Courier* (New York) 80/18 (April 1920): 42-43.   780.5 M97

Talks about Hungary "in the throes of reaction," with military dictatorship suppressing intellectual life. Gives some history of this situation in Hungary. Praises Dohnányi for heroically continuing his musical activities. Furthermore, compares pre-war musical activities with this period, speaking of composers, performers, and musical institutions. Also published in: *Béla Bartók Essays,* ed. Benjamin Suchoff. New York: St. Martin's Press, 1976, pp. 460-463.

31. "Rumanian Peasant Music" [Untitled MS, 1920]. *Documenta bartókiana* 4 (Budapest) (1970): 107-111.   ISBN-963-05-1185-1-(Serie)   ML410 B26 D6   ISSN 0134-0131

As a follow-up of his earlier articles on Hungarian and Slovak folk music, Bartók discusses vocal (e.g. *colinde,* or Christmas songs) and instrumental (e.g. dances) music of three million Romanians. Specifies the various Romanian countries regarding the folk music development. Includes facsimiles.

32. "Bartók válasza Hubay Jenőnek" [Reply to Jenő Hubay]. *Szózat* (Budapest) 2/ 125 (1920): 2. H2.132

Public reply to Hubay, who identified himself with charges brought against Bartók by the *Nemzeti újság* publication. Hubay falsely claimed that Bartók intended to trace back all of their Hungarian Transylvanian tunes to Romanian origin, thereby malevolently charging Bartók with unpatriotic conduct. Bartók gives contrary evidence for actually serving the cause of the Hungarian nation. Also published in: *Bartók Béla válogatott zenei írásai*, ed. András Szőllősy. Budapest: Magyar Kórus, 1948, pp. 100-101; *Béla Bartók, Scritti sulla musica popolare*, ed. Diego Carpitella. Turin: Edizioni Scientifiche Einaudi, 1955, pp. 161-164; *Bartók breviárium (levelek, írások, dokumentumok)*, ed. József Ujfalussy. Budapest: Zeneműkiadó Vállalat, 1958, pp. 195-197; *Bartók Béla összegyűjtött írásai*, ed. András Szőllősy. Budapest: Zeneműkiadó Vállalat, 1966, pp. 617-618 and 861-864; *Béla Bartók Essays*, ed. Benjamin Suchoff. New York: St. Martin's Press, 1976, pp. 201-203.

33. "A népzene (paraszt-zene) fejlődési fokai" [The stages in the development of folk music (peasant music) (1920)]. *Documenta bartókiana* 4 (Budapest) (1970): 88-89. ISBN-963-05-1185-1-(Serie) ML410 B26 D6 ISSN 0134-0131

States that the term "folk song" has recently experienced a special sense of fluctuation and that previously the word "folk" had multiple meanings.

34. "Ungarische Bauernmusik" [Hungarian peasant music]. *Musikblätter des Anbruch* (Vienna) 2/11-12 (June 1920): 422-424. H22.955

Distinguishes Hungarian peasant music from the generally known Hungarian national melodies. (The latter are popular art melodies by identifiable composers of the upper classes.) Then, Bartók compares characteristics of the "old" and "new" homogeneous Hungarian peasant styles and also heterogeneous melodies that developed through infiltration of Western European musical culture. While the "old" style is stated as being the most interesting and valuable, many musicians unknowingly acknowledge national art melodies as Hungarian folk music. Gives many transcriptions of folk melodies. Also published in: *Bartók Béla összegyűjtött írásai*, ed. András Szőllősy. Budapest: Zeneműkiadó Vállalat, 1966, pp. 83-90; *Béla Bartók Essays*, ed. Benjamin Suchoff. New York: St. Martin's Press, 1976, pp. 304-315.

35. "Musical Events in Budapest, March-May, 1920." *Musical Courier* (New York) 81/8 (August 19, 1920): 5, 19.   780.5 M97

Letter by Bartók (July 2, 1920) regarding the first performance (April 24) of Kodály's new *Trio* for two violins and viola, a sensational work performed by the Waldbauer-Kerpely combination. Praises this performance, stating that it is Kodály's richest and deepest work, and gives a description of the work. Mentions aspects of Kodály's technical language as well as certain Magyar characteristics. Also discusses the performance of other chamber works of Kodály as strikingly original though tonal. Discussion of performances by the Budapest Philharmonic Society of Norwegian Composers and others are included as well. Ends with a discussion of economic problems as a hindrance to procuring new orchestral material for first performances and of the general poverty of Hungarian musicians. Also published in: *Bartók Béla válogatott írásai,* ed. András Szőllősy. Budapest: Művelt Nép Tudományos és Ismeretterjesztő Kiadó, 1956, pp. 268-269; *Béla Bartók: Postrehy a názory,* ed. Eva Hykischová. Bratislava: Štátne Hudobné vydavatel'stvo, 1965, pp. 62-63; *Bartók Béla összegyűjtött írásai,* ed. András Szőllősy. Budapest: Zeneműkiadó Vállalat, 1966, pp. 737-739; *Béla Bartók Essays,* ed. Benjamin Suchoff. New York: St. Martin's Press, 1976, pp. 464-466.

36. "Der Einfluss der Volksmusik auf die heutige Kunstmusik" [The influence of folk music on the art music of today]. *Melos* (Berlin) 1/17 (October 1920): 384-386.   780.5 M492   ISSN 0174-7207

Gives definition of folk music and surmises that well-known European folk music owes its origin to the influence of some art or popular music. Only in the nineteenth century did folk music begin to exert a significant influence on art music (e.g., Chopin, Liszt, and Slavic composers) but states that it is not so much folk but popular art music here. Then, discusses Debussy and Ravel as the first to be significantly influenced by Eastern European and Eastern Asian folk music, this influence being more decisive in the works of Stravinsky and Kodály. Also published in: *Melos* (Berlin) 2 (February 1930): 66-67; *Melos* (Mainz) (1949): 145-146; *Komponisten über Musik,* ed. Sam Morganstern. Munich: Langen-Müller, 1956, pp. 356-358; *Béla Bartók: Eigene Schriften und Erinnerungen der Freunde,* ed. Willi Reich. Basel-Stuttgart: Benno Schwabe & Co., 1958, pp. 34-40; *Bartók breviárium (levelek, írások, dokumentumok),* ed. József Ujfalussy. Budapest: Zeneműkiadó Vállalat, 1958, pp. 204-209; *Bartók Béla összegyűjtött írásai,* ed. András Szőllősy. Budapest: Zeneműkiadó Vállalat, 1966, pp. 665-667; *Béla Bartók Essays,* ed. Benjamin Suchoff. New York: St. Martin's Press, 1976, pp. 316-319.

37. "Musical Events in Budapest, October-November, 1920." *Musical Courier* (New York) 81/26 (December 1920): 7.   780.5 M97

    Informs us that Dohnányi gives ten Beethoven recitals in Budapest to celebrate the birth of the great Bonn composer. Discusses all the works that Dohnányi will perform in Budapest, e.g., all the piano sonatas, etc. Talks of Dohnányi's educational influence on the public.

38. "Arnold Schönbergs Musik in Ungarn" [Arnold Schoenberg's music in Hungary]. *Musikblätter des Anbruch* (Vienna) 2/20 (December 1920): 647-648.   H22.955

    Bartók's first acquaintance with Schoenberg's music in 1912 was the *Three Piano Pieces,* Op. 11, as yet unpublished, which were brought to Bartók by a pupil. States that "shamefully . . . as yet no Schönberg work has been performed in Budapest." Also published in: *Bartók Béla válogatott írásai,* ed. András Szőllősy. Budapest: Művelt Nép Tudományos és Ismeretterjesztő Kiadó, 1956, pp. 265-267; *Béla Bartók: Postrehy a názory,* ed. Eva Hykischová. Bratislava: Štátne Hudobné vydavateľstvo, 1965, pp. 54-55; *Bartók Béla összegyűjtött írásai,* ed. András Szőllősy. Budapest: Zeneműkiadó Vállalat, 1966, pp. 723-724; *Béla Bartók Musiksprachen,* ed. Bence Szabolcsi. Leipzig: Philipp Reclam, 1972, pp. 155-163; *In Memoriam Igor Stravinsky,* ed. D. Révész. Budapest: Zeneműkiadó Vállalat, 1972, pp. 25-28; *Béla Bartók Essays,* ed. Benjamin Suchoff. New York: St. Martin's Press, 1976, pp. 467-468.

39. "Slovenské ľudové piesne" [Slovak folk songs (1920)]. *Slovenska hudba* 15/3-4 (1971): 118-119.   H50.470

    Bartók originally intended this article for inclusion in the *Musical Courier* (New York), but it remained unpublished.

40. "Die Volksmusik der Völker Ungarns" [The folk music of Hungary's nationalities (1921)]. *Documenta bartókiana* (Budapest) 4 (1970): 112-115.   ISBN-963-05-1185-1-(Serie)   ML410 B26 D6 ISSN 0134-0131

    Discusses the historical interactions of the Hungarian nation with its neighbors and how their changing relations had a bearing upon the development of Hungarian peasant music. Based on this knowledge, several questions are discussed regarding the definition of "folk melody" and how to collect it. Then, it deals with specific sources and characteristics of the old and new styles of Hungarian folk music.

41. "Musical Events in Budapest, December, 1920." *Musical Courier* (New York) 82/8 (February 1921): 7, 51. 780.5 M97

Thankful, at last, for a Schoenberg performance in Budapest on December 8, 1920. Performed by the Viennese Rosés Quartet, who were not intimidated by the scandalous protests in Vienna. Describes the peaceful reaction in Budapest, where Schoenberg and Stravinsky enter "Christian-National" Budapest "without bloodshed."

42. "Kodály Zoltán." *Nyugat* (Budapest) 14/3 (February 1921): 235-236. H23.374

Defense of Kodály's music against "organized persecution" by a large part of the daily press, specifically after the performance on January 10 of Kodály's *Two Songs*. Also published in: *Bartók Béla válogatott zenei írásai*, ed. András Szőllősy. Budapest: Magyar Kórus, 1948, pp. 95-96; *Új zenei szemle* (Budapest) 3/12 (1952): 4-5; *Béla Bartók, Scritti sulla musica popolare*, ed. Diego Carpitella. Turin: Edizioni Scientifiche Einaudi, 1955, pp. 237-240; *Bartók Béla válogatott írásai*, ed. András Szőllősy. Budapest: Művelt Nép Tudományos és Ismeretterjesztő Kiadó, 1956, pp. 335-337; *Bartók breviárium (levelek, írások, dokumentumok)*, ed. József Ujfalussy. Budapest: Zeneműkiadó Vállalat, 1958, pp. 209-211;*Tempo* (London) 63 (Winter 1962-1963): 22-27; *Sovetskaya muzyka* (Moscow) 29/2 (February 1965): 96-98; *Bartók Béla összegyűjtött írásai*, ed. András Szőllősy. Budapest: Zeneműkiadó Vállalat, 1966, pp. 621-622; *Studia musicologica* (Budapest) 13 (1971): 349-353; *Béla Bartók Essays*, ed. Benjamin Suchoff. New York: St. Martin's Press, 1976, pp. 469-470.

43. "Aki nem tud arabusul . . . " [He who knows no Arabic . . .]. *Szózat* (Budapest) 3/32 (February 1921): 4. H2.132

Talks of a (perhaps intentionally) distorted French quote in an article from *Magyar színpad*, suggesting an anti-Kodály and pro-Bartók attitude of the Parisians. States that the article is intended to influence public view. Also published in: *Bartók Béla válogatott zenei írásai*, ed. András Szőllősy. Budapest: Magyar Kórus,1948, pp. 96-97; *Bartók Béla válogatott írásai*, ed. András Szőllősy. Budapest: Művelt Nép Tudományos és Ismeretterjesztő Kiadó, 1956, pp. 340-341; *Bartók Béla összegyűjtött írásai*, ed. András Szőllősy. Budapest: Zeneműkiadó Vállalat, 1966, pp. 619-620; *Béla Bartók Essays*, ed. Benjamin Suchoff. New York: St. Martin's Press, 1976, pp. 204-205.

44. "Selbstbiographie" [Autobiography]. *Musikblätter des Anbruch* (Vienna) 3/5 (March 1921): 87-90. H22.955

Gives history of Bartók's musical studies and focuses on
influences of German composers (Wagner and Strauss), Liszt,
Debussy, and folk-music studies on his compositional development.
Talks of public animosity (in Budapest) toward his new style. Also
published in: *Magyar írás hármaskönyve* (Budapest) 1/2 (May,
1921): 33-36; *Az est hármaskönyve* (Budapest: Az Est Lapkiadó RT
kiadása, 1923): cols. 77-84; *Sovremennya muzyka* (Moscow) 2/7
(1925): 1-6; *Színházi élet* (Budapest) 17/51 (December 1927): 49-
51; *Bartók Béla, Önéletrajz, írások a zenéről,* ed. András Szőllősy.
Budapest: Egyetemi Nyomda, 1946, pp. 47-53; *Bartók Béla
válogatott zenei írásai,* ed. András Szőllősy. Budapest: Magyar
Kórus, 1948, pp. 8-10; *Bartók Béla (levelek, fényképek, kéziratok,
kották),* ed. János Demény. Budapest: Magyar Művészeti Tanács,
1948, pp. 95-100; *Tempo* (London) 13 (1949): 3-6; *Béla Bartók: A
Memorial Review.* New York: Boosey & Hawkes, 1950, pp. 7-10;
Musik der Zeit (Bonn) 3 (1953): 5-7; *Béla Bartók, Scritti sulla
musica popolare,* ed. Diego Carpitella. Turin: Edizioni Scientifiche
Einaudi, 1955, pp. 41-47; *Bartók Béla, Insemnări asupra cîntecului
popular,* ed. Zeno Vancea. Bucharest: Editura de Stat Pentru Literatură
și Artă, 1956, pp. 11-16; *Bartók Béla válogatott írásai,* ed. András
Szőllősy. Budapest: Művelt Nép Tudományos és Ismeretterjesztő
Kiadó, 1956, pp. 7-11; *Bartók, sa vie et son œuvre,* ed. Bence
Szabolcsi. Budapest: Corvina, 1956, pp. 139-143; *Przegląd
kulturalny* (Warsaw) 15 (1956): 10; Béla Bartók, *Weg und Werk,
Schriften und Briefe,* ed. Bence Szabolcsi. Budapest: Corvina, 1957,
pp. 143-147; *Béla Bartók: Eigene Schriften und Erinnerungen der
Freunde,* ed. Willi Reich. Basel-Stuttgart: Benno Schwabe & Co.,
1958, pp. 9-17; *Selections of Bartók's Dissertations and Letters.*
Peking: Music Publishing Society, 1961, pp. 1-6; *Documenta
bartókiana* (Budapest) 2 (1965): 117-119; *Sovetskaya muzyka*
(Moscow) 29/2 (February 1965): 94-96; *Béla Bartók: Postrehy a
názory,* ed. Eva Hykischová. Bratislava: Štátne Hudobné
Vydavatel'stvo, 1965, pp. 9-13; *Bartók Béla összegyűjtött írásai,*
ed. András Szőllősy. Budapest: Zeneműkiadó Vállalat, 1966, pp.
812-816; *Béla Bartók Essays,* ed. Benjamin Suchoff. New York: St.
Martin's Press, 1976, pp. 408-411.

45. "Selbstbiographie." *Documenta bartókiana* (Budapest) 2 (1965):
117-119, 121-123.   ISBN-963-05-1185-1-(Serie)   ML410 B26 D6
ISSN 0134-0131

See item no. 44 for the 1921 version. This edition collates
various versions of 1918, 1921, and 1923 and supplies helpful
notes. The article was originally written in German (1918) for a
Musikpädagogische Zeitschrift and revised for *Musikblätter des
Anbruch* (Vienna) 3 (1921): 87; also in Bence Szabolcsi, ed. *Béla
Bartók, Weg und Werk.* Budapest: Corvina, 1957, pp. 143-147. The

English version in *Tempo* 13 (1949): pp. 3ff., and *Béla Bartók: A Memorial Review.* New York: Boosey & Hawkes, 1950, pp. 7-11.

46. "Musical Events in Budapest, January-February, 1921." *Musical Courier* (New York) 82/13 (March 1921): 6, 12.   780.5 M97

Discusses controversy in the press, in which a storm of criticism was raised over a performance of Kodály's maiden work for orchestra--two orchestral songs for basso. These represent important contributions to modern Hungarian music and are settings of masterpieces of Hungarian literature. Gives details of audience and critics' reactions.

47. "Musical Events in Budapest: October, 1920 to February, 1921 (Lettera da Budapest)." *Il pianoforte* (Turin) 2/5 (May 1921): 153-154.   ML650 C33 P5

Depreciated Hungarian currency due to World War I forces Budapest concert-goers to rely on national rather than international artists. Most prominent is the pianist-composer Dohnányi. Then outlines important works performed by chamber and orchestral groups. Also published in: *Bartók Béla válogatott írásai,* ed. András Szőllősy. Budapest: Művelt Nép Tudományos és Ismeretterjesztő Kiadó, 1956, pp. 270-273; *Bartók Béla összegyűjtött írásai,* ed. András Szőllősy. Budapest: Zeneműkiadó Vállalat, 1966, pp. 740-742; *Béla Bartók Essays,* ed. Benjamin Suchoff. New York: St. Martin's Press, 1976, pp. 471-473.

48. "Musical Events in Budapest, March-April, 1921." *Musical Courier* (New York) 82/21 (May 1921): 47.   780.5 M97

Outstanding event in Budapest's musical life during February and March was the success of Dohnányi in the U.S.A. Points out that concert life in Budapest suffered from his absence and he was sorely missed.

49. "Musical Events in Budapest, May 1921." *Musical Courier* (New York) 83/2 (July 1921): 37.   780.5 M97

Discusses marked enthusiasm that greets pianist in Budapest when he is heard again after his recent American tour. Discusses Dohnányi's performance of Beethoven's E-flat piano concerto and conducting of the D minor symphony.

50. "Lettera da Budapest (No. 2)" (1921). *Documenta bartókiana* (Budapest) 5 (1977): 112f.   ISBN-963-05-1185-1-(Serie) ML410 B26 D6   ISSN 0134-0131

Discusses an extraordinary concert of the Waldbauer-Kerpely Quartet, performing works of Schoenberg and Milhaud. Also discusses performances of works of Debussy, Stravinsky, etc., and the return of Dohnányi from America.

51. "The Relation of Folk-song to the Development of the Art Music of Our Time." *The Sackbut* (London) 2/1 (June 1921): 5-11. H22.977

Refers to some of the manifestations of different folk-music sources on present-day art music and points to Kodály's works as exemplary of all the art music influenced by folk music. Considerable influence begins in the nineteenth century with Chopin, Liszt, Grieg, Smetana, etc. However, these composers had roots in popular art music. Defines peasant music as a natural phenomenon and presents the history of political and social backgrounds to nationalistic developments and orientation toward native folk musics. Sees Musorgsky as the forerunner of this tendency. In parts IV and V of this essay, Bartók also talks of early folk influences on the Viennese classical composers,then about requirements for systematically investigating folk music, and that a uniform plan should be carried out in all countries. Also published in: *Muzyka* (Warsaw) 2/6 (June 1925): 230-233; *Muzyka* (Warsaw) 4/6 (June 1927): 256-259; *The Music Lover's Handbook,* ed. Elie Siegmeister. New York: William Morrow, 1943, pp. 45-47 [extracts]; *Bartók Béla összegyűjtött írásai,* ed. András Szőllősy. Budapest: Zeneműkiadó Vállalat, 1966, pp. 576-578; *Béla Bartók Essays,* ed. Benjamin Suchoff. New York: St. Martin's Press, 1976, pp. 320-330.

52. "Della musica moderna in Ungheria" [On modern music in Hungary]. *Il pianoforte* (Turin) 2/7 (July 1921): 193-197.   ML650 C33 P5

Gives political and geographic reasons for the lack of a true Hungarian composer until the nineteenth century. Then gives history of this development based on folk-music collecting and influences on art music as well as sources in Liszt, the modern French school, and some German composers. Also published in: *The Chesterian* (London) 20 (January 1922): 101-107; *Bartók Béla válogatott zenei írásai,* ed. András Szőllősy. Budapest: Magyar Kórus, 1948, pp. 11-14; *Béla Bartók, Scritti sulla musica popolare,* ed. Diego Carpitella. Turin: Edizioni Scientifiche Einaudi, 1955, pp. 214-221; *Bartók Béla válogatott írásai,* ed. András Szőllősy. Budapest: Művelt Nép Tudományos és Ismeretterjesztő Kiadó, 1956, pp. 235-241; *Béla Bartók: Postrehy a názory,* ed. Eva Hykischová. Bratislava: Štátne Hudobné Vydavatel'stvo, 1965, pp. 72-78; *Bartók Béla összegyűjtött írásai,* ed. András Szőllősy. Budapest: Zeneműkiadó Vállalat, 1966, pp. 745-749 (see also pp. 913-917); *Béla Bartók Essays,* ed. Benjamin Suchoff. New York: St. Martin's Press, 1976, pp. 474-478.

53. "Musical Events in Budapest, March-June, 1921 (Lettera da Budapest)." *Il pianoforte* (Turin) 2/9 (September 1921): 277-278. ML650 C33 P5

     Extraordinary concert by the Waldbauer-Kerpely Quartet of Schoenberg and Milhaud works as well as performances by various ensembles of other new and older works. Also speaks of performance of the Wagner cycle, which raised the level of the Budapest operatic stage. Also published in: *Bartók Béla válogatott írásai,* ed. András Szőllősy. Budapest: Művelt Nép Tudományos és Ismeretterjesztő Kiadó, 1956, pp. 274-275; *Béla Bartók: Postrehy a názory,* ed. Eva Hykischová. Bratislava: Štátne Hudobné Vydavatel'stvo, 1965, pp. 56-57; *Bartók Béla összegyűjtött írásai,* ed. András Szőllősy. Budapest: Zeneműkiadó Vállalat, 1966, pp. 743-744; *Béla Bartók Essays,* ed. Benjamin Suchoff. New York: St. Martin's Press, 1976, pp. 479-480.

54. "Two Unpublished Liszt Letters to Mosonyi." *Musical Quarterly* (New York) 7/4 (October 1921): 520-526. ML1 M725 ISSN 0027-4631

     Has introductory statement to these letters, focusing on Liszt's publicly modest attitude toward public criticism of his works by opponents of the "Neu-deutsche Schule." However, in the first letter, Liszt confides his human signs of impatience, irritation and disgust as well as pride. Second letter deals with Liszt's sense of contribution to modern Hungarian music. Also published in: *Bartók Béla összegyűjtött írásai,* ed. András Szőllősy. Budapest: Zeneműkiadó Vállalat, 1966, pp. 690-696; *Béla Bartók Essays,* ed. Benjamin Suchoff. New York: St. Martin's Press, 1976, pp. 481-487.

55. "La musique populaire hongroise" [Hungarian folk music]. *La revue musicale* (Paris) 2/1 (November 1921): 8-22. 780.5 R328 ISSN 0035-3736

     Discusses variegated folk-music styles of Hungary before 1918. Country made up of inhabitants split into different nationalities (Romanian, Slovak, Yugoslav, and Ruthenian), a basic reason for vigorous research into musical folklore in Hungary. Then, discusses what we must understand by folk music, how to proceed in collecting music examples, and finally the results of research into Hungarian folk music. Gives detailed discussion of the characteristics of the old, new, and mixed Hungarian folk styles. Also published in: *Muzyka* (Warsaw) 6 (1937): 189-191 [extract]; Moreux, Serge, *Béla Bartók.* London: Harvill Press, 1953, pp. 62-67 [extracts]; *Bartók Béla összegyűjtött írásai,* ed. András Szőllősy. Budapest:

Zenemükiadó Vállalat, 1966, pp. 91-100; *Béla Bartók Essays,* ed. Benjamin Suchoff. New York: St. Martin's Press, 1976, pp. 58-70.

56. "The Development of Art Music in Hungary." *Chesterian* 20 (new series) (January 1922): 101-107.

According to David Clegg, in "Select Bibliography of Articles and Interviews by and About Bartók Published in Britain Between 1904 and 1946," *Music Review* 49/4 (November 1988): 296, "Bartók states that Liszt and Erkel were mistaken in believing that they had discovered genuine Hungarian music. What they knew as 'Hungarian' was merely the product of amateur musicians of the gentry class. He expresses the highest regard for Kodály's compositions."

57. "A zongora-irodalom remekművei. Scarlatti--Couperin--Rameau etc." [Masterworks of piano literature. Scarlatti--Couperin--Rameau etc.]. Introduction to *Masterworks of Piano Literature,* Nos. 1552, 1641, and 1642. Budapest: Rozsnyai Károly, 1924, p. 2.

Describes his attempt to remedy the lack of full appreciation for clavecin and clavicembalo works of early masters by publishing several volumes of selected works with editoral markings. Also published in: *Béla Bartók Essays,* ed. Benjamin Suchoff. New York: St. Martin's Press, 1976, p. 488.

58. "Academies, Hungarian; Chamber-Music Players, Hungarian; Hungarian Folk Music; Hungarian Musical Instruments; Hungarian Opera, Pantomime and Ballet; Opera Houses, Hungarian; Orchestras, Hungarian; Publishers, Hungarian; Rumanian Folk Music; Slovak Folk Music." *A Dictionary of Modern Music and Musicians,* ed. A. Eaglefield Hull. London: J. M. Dent & Sons, 1924. pp. 4, 86-87, 243, 243-244, 245, 361, 366, 399, 426-427, 460-461. ML100 D5

In these brief dictionary entries, Bartók provides basic historical and factual information, including names and addresses of early Hungarian publishers, physical structure of certain instruments, categories of folk melodies in terms of ceremonial functions, form, meter and rhythm, syllabic structure, etc. Also published in: *Das Neue Musiklexikon.* Berlin: Max Hesse's Verlàg, 1926; *Muzica şi poezie* (Bucharest) 1/6 (April 1936): 24; *Béla Bartók, Scrieri mărunte despre muzica populară românească,* ed. Constantin Brăiloiu. Bucharest, 1937, p. 22. Also, brief notices of Hungarian composers and musicians: *Bartók Béla összegyüjtött írásai,* ed. András Szőllősy. Budapest: Zeneműkiadó Vállalat, 1966, p. 931; "Slovak Folk Music": *Béla Bartók Essays,* ed. Benjamin Suchoff. New York: St. Martin's Press, 1976, pp. 128-129; "Hungarian Folk Music" and

"Romanian Folk Music": *Béla Bartók Studies in Ethnomusicology,* ed. Benjamin Suchoff. Lincoln and London: University of Nebraska Press, 1996, pp. 135 and 136-137, respectively. Other dictionary entries by Bartók include Hungarian composers and performers, such as Jelly d'Arány, Franz Erkel, Jenő Hubay, Paul Jankó, Zoltán Kodály, László Lajtha, Ödön Mihálovich, Leo Weiner, Nándor Zsolt, and others.

59. "Zum Problem 'Klavier': Rundfragebeantwortung" [About the "piano" problem (answer to a questionnaire)]. *Musikblätter des Anbruch* (Vienna) 9/8-9 (October-November 1927): 390.　H22.955

States that the neutral character of the piano has long been recognized. Its potential to become truly expressive is realized only when the piano is used, as at present, as a percussion instrument. The piano is a universal instrument and has not lost its importance for concert performances. Also published in: *Új zenei szemle* (Budapest) 7/3 (March 1956): 12; *Bartók Béla összegyűjtött írásai,* ed. András Szőllősy. Budapest: Zeneműkiadó Vállalat, 1966, p. 793; *Béla Bartók Essays,* ed. Benjamin Suchoff. New York: St. Martin's Press, 1976, p. 288.

60. "Thomán Istvánról" [About István Thomán]. *Zenei szemle* (Budapest) 2/3 (March 1927): 93-95.　HA2.398

Represents a public expression of gratitude for Bartók's former piano teacher. Joins in Thomán's concert celebration of the fortieth jubilee of his artistic career. Also published in: *Bartók Béla válogatott írásai,* ed. András Szőllősy. Budapest: Művelt Nép Tudományos és Ismeretterjesztő Kiadó, 1956, pp. 344-347; *Béla Bartók Essays,* ed. Benjamin Suchoff. New York: St. Martin's Press, 1976, pp. 489-491.

61. "The Folk Songs of Hungary." *Pro musica* (New York) (1928): 28-35.

Requested by the "Pro Musica Society" to give information regarding contemporary progressive musical aims and trends in Hungary. By turning away from the Romanticists, composers were led toward older music, which included old peasant music (as was the case for Hungarian composers of Bartók's generation and for Stravinsky's work of his Russian period) or a reversion to the older art music of the seventeenth and eighteenth centuries (as can be observed among the neo-classicists). Then discusses his collecting of folk music of different nations, finding the inner spirit of Hungarian peasant music to be entirely distinct. Thus, Hungarian art music has its own characteristics. Folk-music characteristics are discussed as the basis for weakening traditional tonal functions. Also published in: *Zenei szemle* (Budapest) 12/3-4 (March-April

1928): 55-58; *Bartók Béla, Önéletrajz, Írások a zenéről,* ed. András Szőllősy. Budapest: Egyetemi Nyomda, 1946, pp. 63-69; *Bartók Béla válogatott zenei írásai,* ed. András Szőllősy. Budapest: Magyar Kórus, 1948, pp. 14-17; *Bartók Béla válogatott írásai,* ed. András Szőllősy. Budapest: Művelt Nép Tudományos és Ismeretterjesztő Kiadó, 1956, pp. 203-214; *Béla Bartók, Scritti sulla musica popolare,* ed. Diego Carpitella. Turin: Edizioni Scientifiche Einaudi, 1955, pp. 222-228; *Bartók, sa vie et son œuvre,* ed. Bence Szabolcsi. Budapest: Corvina, 1956, pp. 144-148; *Béla Bartók Weg und Werk,* ed. Bence Szabolcsi. Budapest: Corvina, 1957, pp. 148-155; *Selections of Bartók's Dissertations and Letters.* Peking: Music Publishing Society, 1961, pp. 7-12; *Béla Bartók: Postrehy a názory,* ed. Eva Hykischová. Bratislava: Štátne Hudobné Vydavatel'stvo, 1965, pp. 79-89; *Bartók Béla összegyűjtött írásai,* ed. András Szőllősy. Budapest: Zeneműkiadó Vállalat, 1966, pp. 750-757 and 917-920; *Béla Bartók Musiksprachen,* ed. Bence Szabolcsi. Leipzig: Philipp Reclam, 1972, pp. 190-196; *Béla Bartók Essays,* ed. Benjamin Suchoff. New York: St. Martin's Press, 1976, pp. 331-339.

62. "The National Temperament in Music." *Musical Times* 69 (December 1928): 1079. 780.5 M98 ISSN 0027-4666

   Points to the tremendous difficulties one encounters in the collection of folk music.

63. "Zenefolklore-kutatások Magyarországon" [Music folklore research in Hungary]. *Zenei szemle* (Budapest) 13/1 (1929): 13-15. HA2.398

   Speaks of zealous research into folk music by Bartók, Kodály, Lajtha, Molnár and a few others from 1905-1918. From that time on collecting became impossible. Discusses the number of melodies collected in various nations and where the recordings are deposited. Then outlines classification of tunes into three large groups and gives their characteristics. Also published in: *Ethnographia* (Budapest) 40/4 (1929): 3-9; *Magyar tudományos akadémia kiadása* (Budapest) (1929): 44-51; *Art populaire* (Paris) 2 (1931): 127-128; *Musica şi poezie* (Bucharest) 1/12 (October 1936): 18-19; *Béla Bartók, Scrieri mărunte despre muzica populară românească,* ed. Constantin Brăiloiu. Bucharest, 1937, pp. 50-51; *Bartók Béla válogatott zenei írásai,* ed. András Szőllősy. Budapest: Magyar Kórus, 1948, pp. 28-30; *Béla Bartók, Scritti sulla musica popolare,* ed. Diego Carpitella. Turin: Edizioni Scientifiche Einaudi, 1955, pp. 111-117; *Bartók Béla, Insemnări asupra cîntecului popular,* ed. Zeno Vancea. Bucharest: Editura de Stat Pentru Literatură şi Artă, 1956, pp. 68-74; *Bartók Béla kézírása.* Budapest: Editio Musica, 1961, No.

7 [4p. of MS-facsimile]; *Bartók Béla összegyűjtött írásai,* ed. András Szőllősy. Budapest: Zeneműkiadó Vállalat, 1966, pp. 351-353 and pp. 829-834; *Béla Bartók Essays,* ed. Benjamin Suchoff. New York: St. Martin's Press, 1976, pp. 164-172.

64. "Bartók Béla, oroszországi útjáról" [About Béla Bartók's Russian tour]. *Zenei szemle* (Budapest) 3/2 (1929): 10-14.　HA2.398

January trip of three and a half weeks to Leningrad, Kharkov, Odessa, and Moscow. Talks of practical problems regarding concert arrangements (certain cancellations because of disorder and organizational confusion, passport miseries, etc.). Discusses pieces performed, audience reactions, and make-up of audience (not yet "luring" the working class into the concert halls). Speaks of Russian composers as well as certain performances of traditional repertoire. Also published in: *Béla Bartók Essays,* ed. Benjamin Suchoff. New York: St. Martin's Press, 1976, pp. 492-496.

65. "Węgierska muzyka ludowa" [Hungarian folk music]. *Muzyka* (Warsaw) 6/4 (April 1929): 201-202.　ML5 M9917 ISSN 0027-5344

Report on results of Bartók's field research. Deals with questions of folk-music definition and ways of starting a collection of folk music. Also talks of difficulties in collecting. Also published in: *Muzyka* (Warsaw) 1/9 (1950): 60; *Bartók Béla összegyűjtött írásai,* ed. András Szőllősy. Budapest: Zeneműkiadó Vállalat, 1966, pp. 579-580; *Béla Bartók Essays,* ed. Benjamin Suchoff. New York: St. Martin's Press, 1976, pp. 3-4.

66. "Structure of the *Fourth String Quartet.*" Vienna: Universal Edition, No. 9788, W.Ph.V. 166 (1929,1932): ii-iv.

In German, English, and French. States that Movement III is the kernel of the work, IV and II the inner layers around it, and I and V the outer layers. Then, gives a structural thematic outline of each movement. Character of the movements corresponds to classical sonata form. Also published in: *Bartók Béla összegyűjtött írásai,* ed. András Szőllősy. Budapest: Zeneműkiadó Vállalat, 1966, pp. 779-780; *Béla Bartók Essays,* ed. Benjamin Suchoff. New York: St. Martin's Press, 1976, pp. 412-413.

67. "Editor's Note to Seventeenth and Eighteenth Century Italian Cembalo and Organ Music." New York: Carl Fischer, 1930, Nos. 25268-25278, p. 1.

States that only occasionally has the editor (Bartók) suggested minor changes from the original in the transcription of these works. Changes from the original in the transcription are justified by consideration of the specific construction of both instruments. Describes the notational indications for these changes. Also published in: *Béla Bartók Essays*, ed. Benjamin Suchoff. New York: St. Martin's Press, 1976, p. 497.

68. "Magyar népi hangszerek. Román népzene. Szlovák népzene" [Hungarian folk instruments. Romanian folk music. Slovak folk music]. *Zenei lexikon* [Dictionary of music], Vol. II, ed. Bence Szabolcsi and Aladár Tóth. Budapest: Győző Andor, 1931, pp. 58-63, 419-420, 571-572.

Original publication not examined. Also published in: *Musica şi poezie* (Bucharest) 1/6 (April 1931): 21-24; *Béla Bartók, Scrieri mărunte despre muzica populară românească*, ed. Constantin Brăiloiu. Bucharest, 1937, pp. 19-21; *Bartók Béla, Insemnări asupra cîntecului popular*, ed. Zeno Vancea. Bucharest: Editura de Stat Pentru Literatură şi Artă, 1956, pp. 170-175; *Bartók Béla összegyűjtött írásai*, ed. András Szőllősy. Budapest: Zeneműkiadó Vállalat, 1966, pp. 358-365, 473-476, 490-492; *Béla Bartók Essays*, ed. Benjamin Suchoff. New York: St. Martin's Press, 1976, pp. 239-284, 115-118, and 130-133. In the last publication, essay no. 33 describes the difficulty in recording instrumental music because it is less available. Discusses instruments found in Hungarian villages, but none is especially Hungarian. Has photos and transcriptions. Romanian material (essay no. 15) originates mostly from the territories previously belonging to Hungary. Groups material in five classes: *colinde,* laments, other ritual songs, dance songs (chiefly instrumental) and the proper songs. Discusses geographical areas and musical characteristics. Discusses Slovak material (essay no. 18) with much in common with Moravians and Hungarians as well as original Slovak structures. Gives details of structure and rhythm.

69. "Cigányzene? Magyar zene? (Magyar népdalok a német zeneműpiacon)" [Gypsy music or Hungarian music?]. *Ethnographia* (Budapest) 42/2 (1931): 49-62.   HB1.743

Differentiates between gypsy music and Hungarian music, with musical examples in Bartók's own hand. So-called "Gypsy music" is not Gypsy music but Hungarian music; it is not old folk music but a fairly recent type of Hungarian popular art music composed by Hungarians of the upper-middle class. Critical of Heinrich Möller collection, *Ungarische Volkslieder. Das Lied der Völker* (Mainz: B. Schotts Sohne, 1929), especially the twelfth volume devoted to Hungarian folk music. (See also item nos. 76, 77, and 81). Also published as offprint: Berlin-Leipzig: Walter de Gruyter & Co., and Budapest: Rózsavölgyi és Társa, 1931 [offprint], 15p.; *Ungarische Jahrbücher* (Berlin) 11/3 (July 1931): 191-205; *Zeitschrift für Musikwissenschaft* (Leipzig) 13/11-12 (August-September 1931):

580-582 [extracts]; *Musical Quarterly* (New York) 32/2 (April 1931): 240-257; *Bartók Béla válogatott zenei írásai*, ed. András Szőllősy. Budapest: Magyar Kórus, 1948, pp. 78-89; *Béla Bartók, Scritti sulla musica popolare*, ed. Diego Carpitella. Turin: Edizioni Scientifiche Einaudi, 1955, pp. 127-151; *Bartók Béla, Insemnări asupra cîntecului popular*, ed. Zeno Vancea. Bucharest: Editura de Stat Pentru Literatură și Artă, 1956, pp. 114-139; *Bartók Béla válogatott írásai*, ed. András Szőllősy. Budapest: Művelt Nép Tudományos és Ismeretterjesztő Kiadó, 1956, pp. 293-318; *Bartók Béla összegyűjtött írásai*, ed. András Szőllősy. Budapest: Zeneműkiadó Vállalat, 1966, pp. 623-640 and 866-868; *Musical Quarterly* (New York) 30 (1947): 240-257; *Béla Bartók Essays*, ed. Benjamin Suchoff. New York: St. Martin's Press, 1976, pp. 206-223. See also "The Bartók-Möller Polemical Interchange [1931-1932]." Published in: *Béla Bartók Studies in Ethnomusicology*, ed. Benjamin Suchoff. Lincoln and London: University of Nebraska Press, 1996, pp. 142-157.

70. "Mi a népzene?" [What is folk music?]. *Új idők* (Budapest) 37/20 (May 1931): 626-627. H2.101

Distinguishes between "popular art music" (urban folk music) and "rural folk music" (peasant music). Gives some history, styles of performance, and detailed definitions. Also published in: *Magyar Minerva* (Bratislava) 2/7 (September 1931): 193-195; *Mitteilungen der Österreichischen Musiklehrerschaft* (Vienna) 2 (March-April 1932): 6-8; *Revista fundațiilor* (Bucharest) 1/6 (June 1934): 111-113; *Népszava naptár* (Budapest) (1936): 51-54; *Bartók Béla válogatott zenei írásai*, ed. András Szőllősy. Budapest: Magyar Kórus, 1948, pp. 19-21; *Béla Bartók, Scritti sulla musica popolare*, ed. Diego Carpitella. Turin: Edizioni Scientifiche Einaudi, 1955, pp. 74-78; *Bartók Béla, Insemnări asupra cîntecului popular*, ed. Zeno Vancea. Bucharest: Editura de Stat Pentru Literatură și Artă, 1956, pp. 17-22; *Bartók Béla válogatott írásai*, ed. András Szőllősy. Budapest: Művelt Nép Tudományos és Ismeretterjesztő Kiadó, 1956, pp. 184-188 and 120-123 ; *Bartók, sa vie et son œuvre*, ed. Bence Szabolcsi. Budapest: Corvina, 1956, pp. 151-154; *Béla Bartók, Weg und Werk*, ed. Bence Szabolcsi. Budapest: Corvina, 1957, pp. 156-160; *Selections of Bartók's Dissertations and Letters*. Peking: Music Publishing Society, 1961, pp. 13-17; *Bartók Béla összegyűjtött írásai*, ed. András Szőllősy. Budapest: Zeneműkiadó Vállalat, 1966, pp. 672-674, 897-899 and 899-901 ; *Béla Bartók Essays*, ed. Benjamin Suchoff. New York: St. Martin's Press, 1976, pp. 5-8.

71. "A parasztzene hatása az újabb műzenére" [The influence of peasant music on modern music]. *Új idők* (Budapest) 37/23 (May 1931): 718-719. H2.101

Gives some history of earlier folk influences on art music but
states that the beginning of the twentieth century was an historical
turning point, as reaction occurred against the Romanticists.
Gives some history of folk interest by composers of various countries
(e.g., Stravinsky in *Le sacre du printemps* and how the folk elements
are used. Also published in: *Magyar Minerva* (Bratislava) 2/8
(October 1931): 225-228; *Mitteilungen der Österreichischen
Musiklehrerschaft* (Vienna) 2 (March-April 1932): 8-10;
Mitteilungen der Österreichischen Musiklehrerschaft (Vienna) 3
(May-June 1932): 5-8; *Revista fundațiilor* (Bucharest) 1/6 (June
1934): 114-118; Ankara Halkevi (Turkish Institute) No. 8, 1936,
pp. 18-23; *Bartók Béla válogatott zenei írásai*, ed. András Szőllősy.
Budapest: Magyar Kórus, 1948, pp. 21-24; *Tempo* (London) 14
(1949-1950): 19-22; *Béla Bartók: A Memorial Review*. New York:
Boosey & Hawkes, 1950, pp. 71-74; *Dansk musiktidsskift*
(Copenhagen) (1951); *Musik der Zeit* (Bonn) 3 (1953): 18-20;
Moreux, Serge. *Béla Bartók.* London: Harvill Press, 1953, pp. 238-
243; *Új zenei szemle* (Budapest) 5/9 (September 1954): 1-4; *Béla
Bartók, Scritti sulla musica popolare*, ed. Diego Carpitella. Turin:
Edizioni Scientifiche Einaudi, 1955, pp. 101-107; *Bartók Béla,
Insemnări asupra cîntecului popular*, ed. Zeno Vancea. Bucharest:
Editura de Stat Pentru Literatură și Artă, 1956, pp. 54-61; *Bartók
Béla válogatott írásai*, ed. András Szőllősy. Budapest: Művelt Nép
Tudományos és Ismeretterjesztő Kiadó, 1956, pp. 189-195; *Bartók,
sa vie et son œuvre*, ed. Bence Szabolcsi. Budapest: Corvina, 1956,
pp. 154-159; *Composers on Music*, ed. Sam Morganstern. London:
Faber & Faber, 1956, pp. 424-428; Béla Bartók, *Weg und Werk*, ed.
Bence Szabolcsi. Budapest: Corvina, 1957, pp. 160-164; *Selections
of Bartók's Dissertations and Letters*. Peking: Music Publishing
Society, 1961, pp. 17-21 [extracts]; *Musikrevy* (Stockholm) 2
(1965): 74, 79-81; *Bartók Béla összegyűjtött írásai*, ed. András
Szőllősy. Budapest: Zeneműkiadó Vállalat, 1966, pp. 675-679 and
901-904; Schwartz, Elliott and Barney Childs. *Contemporary
Composers on Contemporary Music*. New York: Holt, Rinehart and
Winston, 1967, pp. 72-76; *Béla Bartók Essays*, ed. Benjamin
Suchoff. New York: St. Martin's Press, 1976, pp. 340-344.

72. "A népzene jelentőségéről" [On the significance of folk music]. *Új
idők* (Budapest) 37/26 (June 1931): 818-819.   H2.101

Presents reasons against the idea that it is less of an
achievement to write a composition based on folk melodies than a
composition on "original" themes. Talks of borrowing of sources by
earlier masters, i.e., as seen in compositions by Händel, Bach, and
Shakespeare. Then, points out that folk music will have an immense
transforming influence on music in countries with little or no
musical tradition (e.g., in Southern and Eastern Europe). Quote from

Kodály: "a German musician will be able to find in Bach and Beethoven what we had to search for in our villages: the continuity of a national musical tradition." Also published in: *Magyar Minerva* (Bratislava) 2/9 (November 1931): 257-259; *Mitteilungen der Österreichischen Musiklehrerschaft* (Vienna) 3 (May-June 1932): 8-10; *Revista fundațiilor* (Bucharest) 1/6 (June 1934): 119-121; Ankara Halkevi (Turkish Institute) No. 8, 1936, pp. 23-24; *Bartók Béla válogatott zenei írásai,* ed. András Szőllősy. Budapest: Magyar Kórus, 1948, pp. 24-25; *Tempo* (London) 14 (1949-1950): 22-24; *Béla Bartók: A Memorial Review.* New York: Boosey & Hawkes, 1950, pp. 74-76; *Musik der Zeit* (Bonn) 3 (1953): 20-22; Moreux, Serge. *Béla Bartók.* London: Harvill Press, 1953, pp. 244-247; *Új zenei szemle* (Budapest) 5/9 (September 1954): 4-5; *Béla Bartók, Scritti sulla musica popolare,* ed. Diego Carpitella. Turin: Edizioni Scientifiche Einaudi, 1955, pp. 96-100; *Bartók Béla, Insemnări asupra cîntecului popular,* ed. Zeno Vancea. Bucharest: Editura de Stat Pentru Literatură și Artă, 1956, pp. 23-27; *Bartók Béla válogatott írásai,* ed. András Szőllősy. Budapest: Művelt Nép Tudományos és Ismeretterjesztő Kiadó, 1956, pp. 196-200; *Bartók, sa vie et son œuvre,* ed. Bence Szabolcsi. Budapest: Corvina, 1956, pp. 159-162; *Composers on Music,* ed. Sam Morganstern. London: Faber & Faber, 1956, pp. 428-430; *Béla Bartók, Weg und Werk,* ed. Bence Szabolcsi. Budapest: Corvina, 1957, pp. 165-168; *Selections of Bartók's Dissertations and Letters.* Peking: Music Publishing Society, 1961, pp. 22-25 [extracts]; *Sovetskaya muzyka* (Moscow) 29/2 (February 1965): 98-100; *Bartók Béla összegyűjtött írásai,* ed. András Szőllősy. Budapest: Zeneműkiadó Vállalat, 1966, pp. 679-681 and 904-905; Schwartz, Elliott and Barney Childs. *Contemporary Composers on Contemporary Music.* New York: Holt, Rinehart and Winston, 1967, pp. 76-79; *Béla Bartók Essays,* ed. Benjamin Suchoff. New York: St. Martin's Press, 1976, pp. 345-347.

73. "The Peasant Music of Hungary." *Musical Courier* (New York) 103/11 (September 12, 1931): 6, 22. 780.5 M97

A series of short articles on this subject especially for the *Musical Courier* based on his years spent recording Hungarian, Romanian, and Slovak melodies. Summarizes the basic features of the categories of Hungarian folk music: 1) old style, 2) mixed style, and 3) new style. Also published in: *Bartók Béla összegyűjtött írásai,* ed. András Szőllősy. Budapest: Zeneműkiadó Vállalat, 1966, pp. 354-357; *Documenta bartókiana* (Budapest) 4 (1970): 101-103; *Béla Bartók Studies in Ethnomusicology,* ed. Benjamin Suchoff. Lincoln and London: University of Nebraska Press, 1996, pp. 138-141.

74. "Slovakian Peasant Music." *Musical Courier* (New York) 103/13
    (September 12, 1931): 6.   780.5 M97

    States that in contrast to collecting Hungarian peasant music, it
    is usual to be able to write down 150 to 200 melodies with the help
    of a single Slovak peasant (chiefly a woman). Discusses origins of
    the different types of Slovak songs, with some close connection to
    Hungarian sources. Also published in: *Bartók Béla összegyűjtött
    írásai*, ed. András Szőllősy. Budapest: Zeneműkiadó Vállalat, 1966,
    pp. 487-489; *Documenta bartókiana* (Budapest) 4 (1970): 105-107;
    Béla Bartók Essays, ed. Benjamin Suchoff. New York: St. Martin's
    Press, 1976, pp. 134-136.

75. "Határozati javaslat" [Draft resolution (1931)]. *Új idők* (Budapest)
    6/9 (September 1955): 6.   H2.101

    The UMZE (New Hungarian Music Society) addresses a letter to
    the ISCM asking the drafting of proposals concerning the integrity
    and autonomy of the arts. This came at the news of the grave insult
    suffered by Arturo Toscanini. Also published in: *Bartók Béla
    emlékére*. Budapest: Akadémiai Kiadó, 1962, p. 402; Szigeti,
    Joseph. *With Strings Attached*. New York: Alfred A. Knopf, Second
    Edition, 1967, pp. 347-348; *Béla Bartók Ausgewählte Briefe*, ed.
    János Demény. Budapest: Corvina, 1960, pp. 143-144; *Béla Bartók.
    Lettere scelte*, ed. János Demény. Milan: Il Saggiatore di Alberto
    Mondadori Editore, 1969, pp. 246-247; *Béla Bartók Letters*, ed.
    János Demény. London: Faber & Faber, 1971, pp. 207-208; *Bartók
    Béla levelei (új dokumentumok)*, ed. János Demény. Budapest:
    Zeneműkiadó Vállalat, 1971, p. 61; *Béla Bartók Essays*, ed.
    Benjamin Suchoff. New York: St. Martin's Press, 1976, p. 498.

76. "Möller, Heinrich: *Ungarische Volkslieder. Das Lied der Völker*. Bd.
    XII. Mainz: B. Schotts Sohne, 1929." In: *Zeitschrift für
    Musikwissenschaft* 13/11-12 (August-September 1931): 580-582.

    Critical review of Möller's collection, especially the twelfth
    volume devoted to Hungarian folk music. (See also item nos. 69, 77,
    and 81.) States that "the above publication should have served the
    purpose of presenting to the German public a selection of Hungarian
    folk songs which satisfy musicological as well as aesthetic needs."
    Objects to Möller's lack of a scientific perspective. Also published
    in *Bartók Béla összegyűjtött írásai*, ed. András Szőllősy. Budapest:
    Zeneműkiadó Vállalat, 1966, pp. 866-869. See also "The Bartók-
    Möller Polemical Interchange [1931-1932]." Published in: *Béla
    Bartók Studies in Ethnomusicology*, ed. Benjamin Suchoff. Lincoln
    and London: University of Nebraska Press, 1996, pp. 142-157.

77. "Nochmals: Über die Herausgabe ungarischer Volkslieder" [Again: on the publication of Hungarian folk songs]. *Zeitschrift für Musikwissenschaft* (Leipzig) 14/3 (December 1931): 179.

Continuation of polemical interchange between Bartók and Heinrich Möller. (See also item nos. 69, 76, and 81.) Also published in *Bartók Béla összegyűjtött írásai,* ed. András Szőllősy. Budapest: Zeneműkiadó Vállalat, 1966, pp. 641-642 and 869-871. See also "The Bartók-Möller Polemical Interchange [1931-1932]." Published in: *Béla Bartók Studies in Ethnomusicology,* ed. Benjamin Suchoff. Lincoln and London: University of Nebraska Press, 1996, pp. 142-157.

78. "A hegedű duókról" [About the *Forty-four Duos for Two Violins*]. U.M.Z.E. (New Hungarian Music Society). *Concert Programme* (Budapest), First Concert, January 20, 1932.

Originally appeared without title. Brief statement regarding purpose of composition: to give students in the first years of study the opportunity to perform works based on folk music. Also published in: *Bartók Béla összegyűjtött írásai,* ed. András Szőllősy. Budapest: Zeneműkiadó Vállalat, 1966, p. 786; *Béla Bartók Essays,* ed. Benjamin Suchoff. New York: St. Martin's Press, 1976, pp. vii-ix.

79. "Neue Ergebnisse der Volksliederforschung in Ungarn" [New results of folk-song research in Hungary]. *Musikblätter des Anbruch* (Vienna) 14/2-3 (February-March 1932): 37-42. H22.955

Through his folk-music studies in Hungary, Bartók found that the so-called "Gypsy music," also considerably known in foreign countries, is incorrectly called "Gypsy music," since it is none other than popular Hungarian art music. Thus, it is genuine Hungarian music, which was disseminated by the urban Gypsy bands. Furthermore, the village gypsies have their own folk songs that differ from the repertoire of the city Gypsy bands. This genuine Hungarian music of the village Gypsies has been an impulse for the beginning of contemporary Hungarian high art music. Also published in: Ankara Halkevi (Turkish Institute), No. 8, 1936, pp. 11-17; *Új zenei szemle* (Budapest) 5/7-8 (July-August 1954): 1-4; *Bartók Béla válogatott írásai,* ed. András Szőllősy. Budapest: Művelt Nép Tudományos és Ismeretterjesztő Kiadó, 1956, pp. 112-120; *Bartók Béla összegyűjtött írásai,* ed. András Szőllősy. Budapest: Zeneműkiadó Vállalat, 1966, pp. 366-370 and 841-842; *Béla Bartók Musiksprachen,* ed. Bence Szabolcsi. Leipzig: Philipp Reclam, 1972, pp. 35-42; *Béla Bartók Studies in Ethnomusicology,* ed. Benjamin Suchoff. Lincoln and London: University of Nebraska Press, 1996, pp. 158-162.

80. "Proposals and Commentaries on Arab Folk Music." *Documenta bartókiana* 4 (Budapest) (1970): 117-122.   ISBN-963-05-1185-1- (Serie)   ML410 B26 D6   ISSN 0134-0131

As an outcome of questions raised by the International Congress of Arab Folk Music, held in Cairo in April and May1932, Bartók proposes the inauguration of a general collection of the peasant music of all the Arab countries and its publications. States that an educational program on the history of past and present Arab music is necessary before many essential questions raised by the Congress can be answered. Then, provides a program dealing with Arabic music education in European Countries in both ordinary schools and music schools.

81. "Gegenantwort an Heinrich Möller" [Counter-reply to Heinrich Möller]. *Ungarische Jahrbücher* (Berlin) 12/1-2 (April 1932): 130-131. H23.885

Continuation of polemical interchange between Bartók and Möller. (See also item nos. 69, 76, and 77.) Also published in: *Bartók Béla összegyűjtött írásai,* ed. András Szőllősy. Budapest: Zeneműkiadó Vállalat, 1966, pp. 643-645 and pp. 871-874. See also "The Bartók-Möller Polemical Interchange [1931-1932]." Published in: *Béla Bartók Studies in Ethnomusicology,* ed. Benjamin Suchoff. Lincoln and London: University of Nebraska Press, 1996, pp. 142-157.

82. "Minutes of the Comité permanent des lettres et des ars, deuxième session, convoquée á Francfor du 12 au 14 Mai: *Propositions de M. Béla Bartók concernant les éditions de textes authentiques (Urtextausgaben) des œuvres musicales et les éditions en facsimile des manuscripts d'œuvres musicales.* [in French and German--Motion in the Committee of Intellectual Cooperation of the League of Nations], 1932.

Brings forward the motion that the Institute of Intellectual Cooperation of the League of Nations draw up and publish a list of all authentic editions available for the public, since many modern musical publications are edited without scruple. Published in: *Bartók Béla összegyűjtött írásai,* ed. András Szőllősy. Budapest: Zeneműkiadó Vállalat, 1966, pp. 794-796; *Béla Bartók Essays,* ed. Benjamin Suchoff. New York: St. Martin's Press, 1976, pp. 499-500.

83. "Ungarische Volksmusik" [Hungarian folk music]. *Schweizerische Sänger-Zeitung* (Bern) 23/2 (January 1933): 13-14.

Distinguishes between the folk music of the "educated" or "partly educated" (mostly urban) classes and that of the peasants. Deals here only with the second category. Gives detailed characteristics of the music. Also published in: *Schweizerische Sänger-Zeitung* (Bern) 23/3 (February 1933): 21-22; *Schweizerische Sänger-Zeitung* (Bern) 23/4 (February 1933): 31-32; Bern: Uniondruckerei Genossenschaft [Offprint]; *Emlékkönyv Kodály Zoltán 60. születésnapjára.* Budapest: Magyar Néprajzi Társaság, 1943, pp. 5-8; *Bartók Béla válogatott zenei írásai,* ed. András Szőllősy. Budapest: Magyar Kórus, 1948, pp. 17-19; *Kis újság* (Budapest) (September 17, 1950); *Béla Bartók, Scritti sulla musica popolare,* ed. Diego Carpitella. Turin: Edizioni Scientifiche Einaudi, 1955, pp. 117-123; *Bartók Béla válogatott írásai,* ed. András Szőllősy. Budapest: Művelt Nép Tudományos és Ismeretterjesztő Kiadó, 1956, pp. 47-57; *Béla Bartók: Postrehy a názory,* ed. Eva Hykischová. Bratislava: Štátne Hudobné vydavateľstvo, 1965, pp. 131-139; *Bartók Béla összegyűjtött írásai,* ed. András Szőllősy. Budapest: Zeneműkiadó Vállalat, 1966, pp. 371-377 and 843-845; *Béla Bartók Musiksprachen,* ed. Bence Szabolcsi. Leipzig: Philipp Reclam, 1972, pp. 71-82; *Béla Bartók Essays,* ed. Benjamin Suchoff. New York: St. Martin's Press, 1976, pp. 71-79.

84. "Zum Kongress für Arabische Musik--Cairo 1932" [At the Congress for Arab Music--Cairo 1932]. *Zeitschrift für vergleichende Musikwissenschaft* (Berlin) 1/2 (1933): 46-48.

Bartók's interest was mainly with the recording section of the Congress. Discusses various types of Arab music performed at the Congress, including some urban-type musical compositions and then a more refreshing peasant-bred music. The peak of these performances was a kind of exorcism by people of the lowest class in Cairo (eight or ten melodies with percussion accompaniment). Also published in: *Bartók Béla emlékére.* Budapest: Akadémiai Kiadó, 1962, pp. 426-427; *Bartók Béla összegyűjtött írásai,* ed. András Szőllősy. Budapest: Zeneműkiadó Vállalat, 1966, pp. 562-563; *Béla Bartók Musiksprachen,* ed. Bence Szabolcsi. Leipzig: Philipp Reclam, 1972, pp. 114-116; *Béla Bartók Essays,* ed. Benjamin Suchoff. New York: St. Martin's Press, 1976, pp. 38-39.

85. "Hungarian Peasant Music." *Musical Quarterly* (New York) 19/3 (July 1933): 267-289.   ML1 M725   ISSN 0027-4631

Detailed, scholarly, and authoritative discussion of genuine Hungarian peasant music. Most important essay on the characteristics of the "old," "new," and "mixed" styles of Hungarian peasant music. Speaks of earlier lack of scientific editions of peasant music and the confusion of Hungarian folk music with artistic imitations of it. Then, distinguishes between peasant music and art music in folk style. Also published in: *Bartók Béla válogatott írásai*, ed. András Szőllősy. Budapest: Művelt Nép Tudományos és Ismeretterjesztő Kiadó, 1956, pp. 18-46; *Béla Bartók: Postrehy a názory*, ed. Eva Hykischová. Bratislava: Štátne Hudobné vydavatel'stvo, 1965, pp. 106-130; *Bartók Béla összegyűjtött írásai*, ed. András Szőllősy. Budapest: Zeneműkiadó Vállalat, 1966, pp. 378-396; *Béla Bartók Essays*, ed. Benjamin Suchoff. New York: St. Martin's Press, 1976, pp. 80-102.

86. "Rumänische Volksmusik" [Romanian folk music]. *Schweizerische Sänger-Zeitung* (Bern) 23/17 (September, 1933): 141-142.

General observations, made by Bartók on the folk-styled art song and on the peasant song in the article on "Hungarian Folk Music," in this journal 23/2-4, are applicable to Romanian folk music, except for less importance of urbanized Gypsy music here. Discusses Romanian territories where folk material is still uncontaminated by modern intercommunications with foreign nations. Gives detailed discussion of Romanian folk-song types (e.g., *colinde*). Also published in: *Schweizerische Sänger-Zeitung* (Bern) 23/18 (September 1933): 148-149; *Schweizerische Sänger-Zeitung* (Bern) 23/20 (October 1933): 168-169; *Musica și poezie* (Bucharest) 1/6 (April 1933): 18-22; *Béla Bartók, Scrieri mărunte despre muzica populară românească*, ed. Constantin Brăiloiu. Bucharest, 1937, pp. 14-18; *Bartók Béla válogatott írásai*, ed. András Szőllősy. Budapest: Művelt Nép Tudományos és Ismeretterjesztő Kiadó, 1956, pp. 85-95; *Bartók Béla, Insemnări asupra cîntecului popular*, ed. Zeno Vancea. Bucharest: Editura de Stat Pentru Literatură și Artă, 1956, pp. 160-169; *Béla Bartók: Postrehy a názory*, ed. Eva Hykischová. Bratislava: Štátne Hudobné vydavatel'stvo, 1965, pp. 140-149; *Bartók Béla összegyűjtött írásai*, ed. András Szőllősy. Budapest: Zeneműkiadó Vállalat, 1966, pp. 477-484; *Béla Bartók Musiksprachen*, ed. Bence Szabolcsi. Leipzig: Philipp Reclam, 1972, pp. 83-93; *Béla Bartók Essays*, ed. Benjamin Suchoff. New York: St. Martin's Press, 1976, pp. 119-127.

87. "Béla Bartók Replies to Percy Grainger." *Music News* (Chicago) (Friday, January 19, 1934): 9.

Makes some observations on Grainger's article, "Melody Versus Rhythm." *Music News* (Chicago) (September 29, 1933): 9, Bartók's observations derived from a consideration of the primitive state of music among certain Eastern-European and North-African peoples. Gives basic characteristics: free "parlando" rhythm and strict dance-like rhythm. Also published in: *Bartók Béla levelei. Magyar, román, szlovák dokumentumok,"* ed. János Demény. Budapest: Zeneműkiadó

Vállalat, 1955, pp. 397-398 [MS. in German], 399-400 [in Hungarian]; *Bartók Béla kézírása* (Budapest) 8 (1934) [MS. in German]; *Bartók Béla összegyűjtött írásai*, ed. András Szőllősy. Budapest: Zeneműkiadó Vállalat, 1966, pp. 646-647; *Béla Bartók Musiksprachen*, ed. Bence Szabolcsi. Leipzig: Philipp Reclam, 1972, pp. 131-132; *Béla Bartók Essays*, ed. Benjamin Suchoff. New York: St. Martin's Press, 1976, pp. 224-225.

88. "Népzenénk és a szomszéd népek népzenéje" [Hungarian folk music and the folk music of neighboring peoples]. *Népszerű zenefüzetek* (Budapest: Somló Béla) 3 (1934). 36p.; 32p. music. ML3593.B17 N4

First discusses basic characteristics of Hungarian folk music and of neighboring peoples in terms of form, scale, rhythm, etc., then discusses their reciprocal influences. Comparisons with Hungarian folk music are made with German, Slovak, Ruthenian, Romanian, and Serbo-Croatian music. Also published in: *Ungarische Jahrbücher* (Berlin) 25/2-3 (August 1935): 194-258; *Ungarische Bibliothek.* Berlin-Leipzig: Walter de Gruyter 1/20 (1935); *Archivum Europae Centro-Orientalis* (Budapest) 2/3-4 (1936): 197-232 and I-XXXII [in French]; *Musica și poezie* (Bucharest) 1/9-10 (July-August 1936): 18-44; *Études sur l'Europe Centre-Orientale* (Budapest) 5 (1937): n.p.; *Béla Bartók, Scrieri mărunte despre muzica populară românească*, ed. Constantin Brăiloiu. Bucharest, 1937, pp. 23-49 [extract]; Zeneműkiadó Vállalat (Budapest) (1952); *Bartók Béla, Insemnări asupra cîntecului popular*, ed. Zeno Vancea. Bucharest: Editura de Stat Pentru Literatură și Artă, 1956, pp. 176-214 [extract]; *Muzyka* (Moscow) (1965): n.p.; *Bartók Béla összegyűjtött írásai*, ed. András Szőllősy. Budapest: Zeneműkiadó Vállalat, 1966, pp. 403-461; *Béla Bartók Studies in Ethnomusicology*, ed. Benjamin Suchoff. Lincoln and London: University of Nebraska Press, 1996, pp. 174-240.

89. "Miért gyűjtsünk népzenét?" [Why do we collect folk music?]. *Az Országos Magyar Királyi Liszt Ferenc Zeneművészeti Főiskola Évkönyve az 1934/35-iki tanévről* [Yearbook of the Royal Hungarian State Academy of Music "Ferenc Liszt" from the year 1934/35]. (Budapest) (1935): 3-7.

Gives some history of the awakening of interest in collecting folk songs in Europe and the attempt to uncover the original, "unaltered" form of the folk songs. Talks of gradually changing aims, and speaks of his own experience with music of various nations. Then gives detailed discussion of the means of collecting and what to collect. Ends with discussion of financial obstacles to systematic collecting on a large scale. Also published in: *Válasz*

(Budapest) 2/7-8 (July-August 1935): 397-400; *Magyar dal*
(Budapest) 41/2 (March 1936): 2-4; *Apollo* (Budapest) 2/4 (1936):
31-39; *Bartók Béla összegyűjtött írásai*, ed. András Szőllősy.
Budapest: Zeneműkiadó Vállalat, 1966, pp. 852-856; *Béla Bartók
Essays*, ed. Benjamin Suchoff. New York: St. Martin's Press, 1976,
pp. 9-24.

90. "Magyar népzene. Román népzene. Szlovák népzene" [Hungarian
folk music. Romanian folk music. Slovak folk music.]. *Révai nagy
lexikona*, Vol. 21, A-Z. Budapest: Révai Testvérek Irodalmi Intézet
Rt., 1935, pp. 571-572, 725-726, 776-777.

Distinguishes between the folk music (popular art songs) of the
educated (urban) classes and the folk music of the peasants (village).
Then gives historical origins and the structural principles of the old
and new Hungarian folk-song styles as well as heterogeneous or
mixed materials of foreign influences. Similar discussions are
presented with regard to Slovak and Romanian folk music, in which
various types of melodies are characterized by their musical features
and viewed in their historical and cultural contexts. Also published
in: *Bartók Béla válogatott zenei írásai*, ed. András Szőllősy.
Budapest: Magyar Kórus, 1948, pp. 30-31, 31-32, 32-33; *Béla
Bartók, Scritti sulla musica popolare*, ed. Diego Carpitella. Turin:
Edizioni Scientifiche Einaudi, 1955, pp. 123-126, 152-154, 180-
181; *Bartók Béla, Insemnări asupra cîntecului popular*, ed. Zeno
Vancea. Bucharest: Editura de Stat Pentru Literatură şi Artă, 1956,
pp. 75-78, 140-142, 79-80; *Bartók Béla válogatott írásai*, ed.
András Szőllősy. Budapest: Művelt Nép Tudományos és
Ismeretterjesztő Kiadó, 1956, pp. 83-84 [*Szlovák népzene*]; *Béla
Bartók: Postrehy a názory*, ed. Eva Hykischová. Bratislava: Štátne
Hudobné vydavatel'stvo, 1965, pp. 150-151 [*Slovenská l'udová
hudba*]; *Bartók Béla összegyűjtött írásai*, ed. András Szőllősy.
Budapest: Zeneműkiadó Vállalat, 1966, pp. 397-399, 485-486, and
493; *Béla Bartók Studies in Ethnomusicology*, ed. Benjamin
Suchoff. Lincoln and London: University of Nebraska Press, 1996,
pp. 163-165, 166-167, and 168.

91. *Búzavirág, magyar férfikórus gyűjtemény Bartók Béla előszavával*
[Cornflower, Hungarian men's chorus collection with the preface of
Béla Bartók], ed. Sándor Arany. Tornalja: Kazinczy Könyv- és
Lapkiadó Szövetkezet, 1935, p. 5.

Refers to these 59 folk songs arranged for male chorus as gems
from the treasury of folk music. Praises the people of the Hungarian
villages for preserving this treasure. Also published in: *Bartók Béla
összegyűjtött írásai*, ed. András Szőllősy. Budapest: Zeneműkiadó

Vállalat, 1966, p. 797; *Béla Bartók Essays,* ed. Benjamin Suchoff. New York: St. Martin's Press, 1976, p. ix.

92. "Analyse zum V. Streichquartett" [Analysis for the *Fifth String Quartet*] (MS. includes incomplete French translations of the analysis of the fifth movement), 1935. *Muzsika* (Budapest) 14/12 (December 1971): 26-28. ISSN 0027-5336

  Gives the plan of the tonalities and structure of the work, in which the five movements are shown to be symmetrically related (I/V, II/IV, and III). Also published in *Béla Bartók Essays,* ed. Benjamin Suchoff. New York: St. Martin's Press, 1976, pp. 414-415.

93. "Kisfaludy-levél" [Letter to the Kisfaludy Society]. *Népszava* (Budapest) (January 3, 1936): n.p. H33.180/2133

  Vehement rejection by Bartók of the Greguss Medal received for an early work, *Suite for Orchestra No. 1* (Op. 3), and gives reasons why. Also published in: *Bartók Béla levelei (romániai, csehszlovákiai, magyarországi levelek),* ed. János Demény. Budapest: Zeneműkiadó Vállalat, 1955, pp. 409-410; *Bartók Béla válogatott írásai,* ed. András Szőllősy. Budapest: Művelt Nép Tudományos és Ismeretterjesztő Kiadó, 1956, pp. 348-349; *Béla Bartók, Weg und Werk,* ed. Bence Szabolcsi. Budapest: Corvina, 1957, pp. 280, 283; *Bartók Béla emlékére.* Budapest: Akadémiai Kiadó, 1962, pp. 512-513; *Béla Bartók Ausgewählte Briefe,* ed. János Demény. Budapest: Corvina, 1960, pp. 164-165; Szabolcsi, Bence. *Béla Bartók.* Leipzig: Philipp Reclam, 1968, pp. 152-153; *Béla Bartók. Lettere scelte,* ed. János Demény. Milan: Il Saggiatore di Alberto Mondadori Editore, 1969, pp. 286-287; *Béla Bartók Letters,* ed. János Demény. London: Faber & Faber, 1971, p. 245; *Béla Bartók Essays,* ed. Benjamin Suchoff. New York: St. Martin's Press, 1976, p. 226.

94. "Antwort auf einen rumänischen Angriff" [Answer to the Petranu attack]. *Ungarische Jahrbücher* (Berlin) 26/2-3 (February 1936): 276-284 [Offprint: Walter de Gruyter, Berlin]. H23.885

  Corrects erroneous statements made by Coriolan Petranu, Professor at the University of Cluj, on Bartók's scientific activity. Also published in:*Archivum Europae Centro-Orientalis* (Budapest) 2/3-4 (1936): 233-244 [in French]; *Études sur l'Europe Centre-Orientale* (Budapest) 5 (1937): 37-48; *Szép szó* (Budapest) 4/3 (April-May 1937): 263-272; *La revue internationale de musique* (Brussels) (1938): n.p.; *Bartók Béla válogatott zenei írásai,* ed. András Szőllősy. Budapest: Magyar Kórus, 1948, pp. 89-95; *Béla Bartók, Scritti sulla musica popolare,* ed. Diego Carpitella. Turin: Edizioni Scientifiche Einaudi, 1955, pp. 165-179; *Bartók Béla válogatott írásai,* ed. András Szőllősy. Budapest: Művelt Nép Tudományos és Ismeretterjesztő Kiadó, 1956, pp. 319-332; *Bartók breviárium (levelek, írások, dokumentumok),* ed. József Ujfalussy. Budapest: Zeneműkiadó Vállalat, 1958, pp. 346-347 [extract]; *Bartók Béla összegyűjtött írásai,* ed. András Szőllősy. Budapest: Zeneműkiadó Vállalat, 1966, pp. 653-661 and pp. 878-896; *Béla Bartók Essays,* ed. Benjamin Suchoff. New York: St. Martin's Press, 1976, pp. 227-236.

95. "Liszt Ferenc." *Liszt a miénk!* Budapest: Dante, 1936, pp. 53-67. [Also as offprint]

Deals with four issues regarding Liszt and his life's work: 1) the degree to which the present generation understands Liszt's works, which they like most, and which least; 2) the degree of influence that Liszt's music has had on the general development of the art of music; 3) Liszt's famous book on gypsy music; and 4) with what justification do we regard Liszt as a Hungarian composer? Also published in: *Magyar Tudományos Akadémiai értesítő* (Budapest) 46/462 (January-May 1936): 29-34; *Nyugat* (Budapest) 29/3 (March 1936): 171-179 [does not contain the last paragraph nor the footnotes]; *La revue musicale* (Paris) 17/167 (July-August 1936): 1-4; *Magyar dal* (Budapest) (1936): n.p.; *Monthly Musical Record* (London) 78/900-902 (1948): 199-203, 236-239, 267-269; *Mens en melodie* (Utrecht) 3/11, 12 (1948): 327-330, 366-368; *Bartók Béla válogatott zenei írásai,* ed. András Szőllősy. Budapest: Magyar Kórus, 1948, pp. 70-76; *Musica* (Cassel) (July-August 1953): 309-312; *Bartók Béla levelei (romániai, csehszlovákiai, magyarországi levelek),* ed. János Demény. Budapest: Zeneműkiadó Vállalat, 1955, pp. 410-411 [Abstract]; *Liszt Ferenc és Bartók Béla emlékére.* Budapest: Akadémiai Kiadó, 1955, pp 17-24, 548-549 [Abstract in German, English, and French]; *Béla Bartók, Scritti sulla musica popolare,* ed. Diego Carpitella. Turin: Edizioni Scientifiche Einaudi, 1955, pp. 229-236; *Bartók Béla válogatott írásai,* ed. András Szőllősy. Budapest: Művelt Nép Tudományos és Ismeretterjesztő Kiadó, 1956, pp. 220-234; *Composers on Music,* ed. Sam Morgenstern. London: Faber & Faber, 1956, pp. 418-421 [extract]; *Komponisten über Musik,* ed. Sam Morgenstern. Munich: Lagen-Müller, 1956, pp. 347-351 [extract]; *Muzsika* (Budapest) 4/1 (1961): 1-6; *Bartók Béla emlékére.* Budapest: Akadémiai Kiadó, 1962, pp. 523-524 [Abstract]; *Bartók Béla összegyűjtött írásai,* ed. András Szőllősy. Budapest: Zeneműkiadó Vállalat, 1966, pp. 697-706, 907-910, 910-911 (Abstract); *Béla Bartók Musiksprachen,* ed. Bence Szabolcsi. Leipzig: Philipp Reclam, 1972, pp. 138-154; *Béla Bartók Essays,* ed. Benjamin Suchoff. New York: St. Martin's Press, 1976, pp. 501-510.

96. "Miért és hogyan gyűjtsünk népzenét?" [Why and how do we collect folk music?]. *Népszerű zenefüzetek* 5, ed. Antal Molnár (Budapest) (1936): 3-20. ML248.B285m

   Gives some history of the awakening of interest in collecting folk songs in Europe, and the attempt to uncover the "original," unaltered form of the folk songs. Talks of gradually changing aims, speaks of his own experience with music of various nations, and gives detailed discussion of the means of collecting and what to collect. Ends with discussion of financial obstacles to systematic collecting on a large scale. Also published in: Ankara Halkevi (Turkish Institute), No. 8, 1936, pp. 25-35; *Archives internationales de musique populaire.* Geneva: Albert Kundig, 1948; *Béla Bartók, Scrieri mărunte despre muzica populară românească*, ed. Constantin Brăiloiu. Bucharest, 1937, pp. 45-55; *Új zenei szemle* (Budapest) 5/9 (September 1954): 5-6 [extract]; *Béla Bartók, Scritti sulla musica popolare*, ed. Diego Carpitella. Turin: Edizioni Scientifiche Einaudi, 1955, pp. 48-73; *Bartók Béla, Insemnări asupra cîntecului popular*, ed. Zeno Vancea. Bucharest: Editura de Stat Pentru Literatură şi Artă, 1956, pp. 28-53; *Bartók Béla válogatott írásai*, ed. András Szőllősy. Budapest: Művelt Nép Tudományos és Ismeretterjesztő Kiadó, 1956, pp. 127-150 and 123-126; *Bartók, sa vie et son œuvre*, ed. Bence Szabolcsi. Budapest: Corvina, 1956, pp. 165-185; *Béla Bartók, Weg und Werk*, ed. Bence Szabolcsi. Budapest: Corvina, 1957, pp. 171-193; *Selections of Bartók's Dissertations and Letters.* Peking: Music Publishing Society, 1961, pp. 26-48; *Béla Bartók: Postrehy a názory*, ed. Eva Hykischová. Bratislava: Štátne Hudobné Vydavatel'stvo, 1965, pp. 191-211; *Bartók Béla összegyűjtött írásai*, ed. András Szőllősy. Budapest: Zeneműkiadó Vállalat, 1966, pp. 581-596 and pp. 857-858; *Béla Bartók Musiksprachen*, ed. Bence Szabolcsi. Leipzig: Philipp Reclam, 1972, pp. 43-70; *Béla Bartók Essays*, ed. Benjamin Suchoff. New York: St. Martin's Press, 1976, pp. 9-24.

97. "Népzene és népdalok" [Folk music and folk songs]. *Szép szó* (Budapest) 3/3 (December 1936): 274-278. H50.173

   Gives general observations as well as a detailed critical review of the most recent publication of the Institute International de C.I., the first volume of *Musique et chanson populaire.* Also published as: "A népzenéről" [On folk music]. *Népszava naptár* (1936): 51-54; in French, "Musique et chansons populaires." *Acta musicologica* (Copenhagen) 8/3-4 (July-December 1936): 97-101; *Bartók Béla összegyűjtött írásai*, ed. András Szőllősy. Budapest: Zeneműkiadó Vállalat, 1966, pp. 648-652; *Béla Bartók Studies in Ethnomusicology*, ed. Benjamin Suchoff. Lincoln and London: University of Nebraska Press, 1996, pp. 169-173.

98. "A gépzene" [Mechanical music]. *Szép szó* (Budapest) 4/1 (February 1936): 1-11.   H50.173

Defines mechanical music as that which involves more than only the human body. We are mostly reminded of the piano. Then turns to other instruments and their degrees of relatedness to the human body (air columns, string instruments, etc.). Gives some history and categorizes music machines of the day, with a discussion of the basic characteristics. Includes discussions of manually operated electronic instruments as well as the gramophone, film music, etc. Ends with the comment that mechanical music should not be a substitute for live music. Also published in: *Bartók Béla válogatott zenei írásai,* ed. András Szőllősy. Budapest: Magyar Kórus, 1948, pp. 60-66; *Béla Bartók, Scritti sulla musica popolare,* ed. Diego Carpitella. Turin: Edizioni Scientifiche Einaudi, 1955, pp. 272-287; *Bartók Béla válogatott írásai,* ed. András Szőllősy. Budapest: Művelt Nép Tudományos és Ismeretterjesztő Kiadó, 1956, pp. 242-256; *Bartók breviárium (levelek, írások, dokumentumok),* ed. József Ujfalussy. Budapest: Zeneműkiadó Vállalat, 1958, pp. 338-344; *Bartók Béla összegyűjtött írásai,* ed. András Szőllősy. Budapest: Zeneműkiadó Vállalat, 1966, pp. 725-734; *Béla Bartók Musiksprachen,* ed. Bence Szabolcsi. Leipzig: Philipp Reclam, 1972, pp. 172-189; *Béla Bartók Essays,* ed. Benjamin Suchoff. New York: St. Martin's Press, 1976, pp. 289-298.

99. "Vorschläge für die Errichtung eines Volksmusik Archivs" [Proposal for the establishment of a folk music archive]. *Documenta bartókiana* (Budapest) 4 (1970): 124-127.   ISBN-963-05-1185-1- (Serie)   ML410 B26 D6
ISSN 0134-0131

Detailed outline proposing the absorption of peasant music in the villages themselves by means of the mechanical apparatus of those places--to preserve and absorb the material as accurately as possible by notation and classification. Then lays out the preliminaries, the work plan, approximate annual budget, and budget for material and employees of the archive.

100. "On Music Education for the Turkish People." *Muzsika* (Budapest) 14/4 (April 1937): 1-4.   ISSN 0027-5336

Defines two factors in approaching the music student--active and passive. The former is more important. Speaks of the loss of spontaneity of urban people, so that it is necessary to revive music making in an artificial way, commencing with polyphonic choral singing. Then, deals with the method of how it should be taught and what repertoire should be used. Also published in *Béla Bartók*

Essays, ed. Benjamin Suchoff. New York: St. Martin's Press, 1976, pp. 511-515.

101. "Népdalgyűjtés Törökországban" [Folk song collecting in Turkey]. *Nyugat* (Budapest) 30/3 (March 1937): 173-181.   H23.374

Turkish official circles were interested in developing Turkish national music from Turkish folk music. Therefore, the Ankara branch of the Halkevi, the only authorized Turkish political party, invited Bartók. Gives details of this sojourn in terms of locations of collecting, problems, techniques, and musical characteristics. Official circles determined that systematic collection would benefit both Hungarian and Turkish folk-song research as well as that of international Eastern Europe. Also published in: *The Hungarian Quarterly* (Budapest) 3/2 (Summer 1937): 337-346 [also offprint]; *Bartók Béla válogatott zenei írásai,* ed. András Szőllősy. Budapest: Magyar Kórus, 1948, pp. 33-39; *Tempo* (London) 13 (1949): 15-19; *Béla Bartók: A Memorial Review.* New York: Boosey & Hawkes, 1950, pp. 19-23; *Musik der Zeit* (Bonn) 3 (1953): 23-26; Moreux, Serge. *Béla Bartók.* London: Harvill Press, 1953, pp. 247-256; *Béla Bartók, Scritti sulla musica popolare,* ed. Diego Carpitella. Turin: Edizioni Scientifiche Einaudi, 1955, pp. 182-196; *Bartók Béla válogatott írásai,* ed. András Szőllősy. Budapest: Művelt Nép Tudományos és Ismeretterjesztő Kiadó, 1956, pp. 96-111; *Bartók Béla, Insemnări asupra cîntecului popular,* ed. Zeno Vancea. Bucharest: Editura de Stat Pentru Literatură şi Artă, 1956, pp. 81-96; *Béla Bartók: Postrehy a názory,* ed. Eva Hykischová. Bratislava: Štátne Hudobné Vydavatel'stvo, 1965, pp. 162-175; *Bartók Béla összegyűjtött írásai,* ed. András Szőllősy. Budapest: Zeneműkiadó Vállalat, 1966, pp. 507 and 514; *Béla Bartók Musiksprachen,* ed. Bence Szabolcsi. Leipzig: Philipp Reclam, 1972, pp. 106-113; *Béla Bartók Essays,* ed. Benjamin Suchoff. New York: St. Martin's Press, 1976, pp. 137-147.

102. "Aufbau der Musik für Saiteninstrumente" [Structure of *Music for String Instruments*]. Universal Edition (Vienna), No. 10,888, W. PH. 201, 1937, pp. ii-iii [In German, English, and French].

Gives keys and basic formal outline of the four movements and mentions certain basic procedures: fifth-related fugue entries, stretti, metric changes, diatonic expansions of chromatic themes, etc. Also published in: New York: Boosey & Hawkes, No. 609, 1939, p. iii [In English only]; *Bartók Béla összegyűjtött írásai,* ed. András Szőllősy. Budapest: Zeneműkiadó Vállalat, 1966, p. 787; *Béla Bartók Essays,* ed. Benjamin Suchoff. New York: St. Martin's Press, 1976, p. 416.

103. "Népdalkutatás és nacionalizmus" [Folk song research and nationalism]. *Tükör* (Budapest) 5/3 (March 1937): 166-168.

States that the "impulse to begin folk song research, as well as any folklore science in general, is attributable to the awakening of national feeling." Discusses interactions of neighboring nations as a natural phenomenon and should not be a source of humiliation for one or another nation. Then, discusses diverse questions that show up in folklore research. Folklore researchers should be as objective as possible (in terms of national feelings) when investigating the music of foreign nations. Also published in: *Rytmus* (Prague) 2/9-10 (April-May 1937): 95-96; *La revue internationale de musique* (Brussels) 1/4 (October-November 1938): 608-615 [In French and German]; *Bartók Béla, Önéletrajz, írások a zenéröl*, ed. András Szőllősy. Budapest: Egyetemi Nyomda, 1946, pp. 70-76; *Bartók Béla válogatott zenei írásai*, ed. András Szőllősy. Budapest: Magyar Kórus, 1948, p. 56-58; *Béla Bartók, Scritti sulla musica popolare*, ed. Diego Carpitella. Turin: Edizioni Scientifiche Einaudi, 1955, pp. 85-91; *Bartók Béla válogatott írásai*, ed. András Szőllősy. Budapest: Mővelt Nép Tudományos és Ismeretterjesztő Kiadó, 1956, pp. 178-183; *Bartók, sa vie et son œuvre*, ed. Bence Szabolcsi. Budapest: Corvina, 1956, pp. 188-192; *Béla Bartók, Weg und Werk*, ed. Bence Szabolcsi. Budapest: Corvina, 1957, pp. 194-198; *Béla Bartók: Postrehy a názory*, ed. Eva Hykischová. Bratislava: Štátne Hudobné Vydavatel'stvo, 1965, pp. 96-101; *Bartók Béla összegyűjtött írásai*, ed. András Szőllősy. Budapest: Zeneműkiadó Vállalat, 1966, pp. 597-600; *Béla Bartók Musiksprachen*, ed. Bence Szabolcsi. Leipzig: Philipp Reclam, 1972, pp. 117-123; *Béla Bartók Essays*, ed. Benjamin Suchoff. New York: St. Martin's Press, 1976, pp. 25-28.

104. "Über die Sonate für zwei Klaviere und Schlaginstrumente" [About the *Sonata for Two Pianos and Percussion*]. *National-Zeitung* (Basel) (January 13, 1938): n.p.

Discusses circumstances for its composition, gives the reasons for the instrumentation, which includes the use of two pianos for purposes of balance between piano and percussion, and outlines a tonal, formal, and motivic analysis of the three movements. Also published in: *Alte und Neue Musik, 25 Jahre Basler Kammerorchester*. Zürich: Atlantis-Verlag, 1952, pp. 79-81; *Musik der Zeit* (Bonn) 9 (1954): 47-48; *Bartók Béla válogatott írásai*, ed. András Szőllősy. Budapest: Mővelt Nép Tudományos és Ismeretterjesztő Kiadó, 1956, pp. 280-281; *Béla Bartók: Eigene Schriften und Erinnerungen der Freunde*, ed. Willi Reich. Basel-Stuttgart: Benno Schwabe & Co., 1958, pp. 79-81; *Béla Bartók: Postrehy a názory*, ed. Eva Hykischová. Bratislava: Štátne Hudobné Vydavatel'stvo, 1965, pp. 41-42; *Bartók Béla összegyűjtött írásai*, ed. András Szőllősy. Budapest: Zeneműkiadó Vállalat, 1966, pp. 788-789; *Béla Bartók Essays,* ed. Benjamin Suchoff. New York: St. Martin's Press, 1976, pp. 417-418.

105. "Erklärung" [Declaration (1938)]. *Documenta bartókiana* 4 (Budapest) (1970): 148-151. ISBN-963-05-1185-1-(Serie) ML410 B26 D6 ISSN 0134-0131

Contains Bartók's list of folk-based works. Objection to the decree by STAGMA that his works based on folk-song and folk-dance themes be demoted to arrangements. Thus, no choice for Bartók but to prevent as far as possible the performances of these works in Germany. The list of these works and the examination of the circumstances are then presented in five supplementary letters to the Society of Authors, Composers, and Music Publishers.

106. "Az úgynevezett bolgár ritmus" [The so-called Bulgarian rhythm]. *Énekszó* (Budapest) 5/6 (May 1938): 537-541. H24.379

Gives detailed account of the unequal-beat meters and rhythms of Bulgarian folk music. Presents some history of such occurrences in art music composed of folk influence: Chopin, Tchaikovsky, Stravinsky, and the Hungarians. States that we also find such asymmetrical rhythms in other Eastern-European folk music, but generally such rhythms have been alien to art-music performers and would be educational for them. Gives detailed examples of unequal-beat Bulgarian rhythms and meter. Also published in: *Bartók Béla válogatott zenei írásai,* ed. András Szőllősy. Budapest: Magyar Kórus, 1948, pp. 40-44; *Béla Bartók, Scritti sulla musica popolare,* ed. Diego Carpitella. Turin: Edizioni Scientifiche Einaudi, 1955, pp. 197-207; *Bartók Béla, Insemnări asupra cîntecului popular,* ed. Zeno Vancea. Bucharest: Editura de Stat Pentru Literatură și Artă, 1956, pp. 97-108; *Bartók Béla válogatott írásai,* ed. András Szőllősy. Budapest: Művelt Nép Tudományos és Ismeretterjesztő Kiadó, 1956, pp. 71-82; *Bulgarska muzika* (Sofia) 12/8 (1961): 12-16; *Béla Bartók: Postrehy a názory,* ed. Eva Hykischová. Bratislava: Štátne Hudobné Vydavateľstvo, 1965, pp. 152-161; *Bartók Béla összegyűjtött írásai,* ed. András Szőllősy. Budapest: Zeneműkiadó Vállalat, 1966, pp. 498-506; *Béla Bartók Musiksprachen,* ed. Bence Szabolcsi. Leipzig: Philipp Reclam, 1972, pp. 94-105; *Béla Bartók Essays,* ed. Benjamin Suchoff. New York: St. Martin's Press, 1976, pp. 40-49.

107. "Opinion de M. Béla Bartók (Varsovie) sur l'orientation technique, esthétique et spirituelle de la musique contemporaine" [Béla Bartók's opinion on the technical, aesthetic and spiritual orientation of contemporary music]. *La revue internationale de musique* (Brussels) 1/3 (July-September 1938): 452-453.

Interview questions posed by the editor of this journal. Gives opinions regarding the full use of technical means to express ideas and sentiments. Must direct efforts to search for that which we call "inspired simplicity" and talks of bureaucracy and state control as adversary of a flowering contemporary music. Furthermore, speaks of attitudes toward romanticism. Also published in: *Bartók breviárium (levelek, írások, dokumentumok),* ed. József Ujfalussy. Budapest: Zeneműkiadó Vállalat, 1958, pp. 376-377; *Bartók Béla emlékére.* Budapest: Akadémiai Kiadó, 1962, pp. 671-672; *Bartók Béla összegyűjtött írásai,* ed. András Szőllősy. Budapest: Zeneműkiadó Vállalat, 1966, p. 735; *Béla Bartók Essays,* ed. Benjamin Suchoff. New York: St. Martin's Press, 1976, pp. 516-517.

108. "Hongrie" [The influence of Debussy and Ravel in Hungary]. *La revue musicale* 19/187 (December 1938): 436.   780.5 R328
ISSN 0035-3736

Speaks of the musical dominance of Germany in Europe for several hundred years, but the Hungarian musicians of the present century decisively turned toward France. States that the Latin spirit (especially the French spirit) is nearer to the Hungarian genius than the German. Also published in: *Bartók Béla válogatott írásai,* ed. András Szőllősy. Budapest: Művelt Nép Tudományos és Ismeretterjesztő Kiadó, 1956, pp. 276-277; *Bartók breviárium (levelek, írások, dokumentumok),* ed. József Ujfalussy. Budapest: Zeneműkiadó Vállalat, 1958, pp. 127-128; *Bartók Béla összegyűjtött írásai,* ed. András Szőllősy. Budapest: Zeneműkiadó Vállalat, 1966, p. 736; *Béla Bartók Essays,* ed. Benjamin Suchoff. New York: St. Martin's Press, 1976, p. 518.

109. "Analyse du Deuxième Concerto pour Piano et Orchestre de Béla Bartók par son auteur" [Analysis of the *Second Concerto for Piano and Orchestra*]. *La radio* (Lausanne) (February 17, 1939): 280, 282.

Gives opinion as to the success and degree of difficulty of the *First Piano Concerto.* In writing the *Second Concerto,* the intention was to be more accessible and thematically pleasing. Gives detailed formal and procedural analysis with examples. Outlines basic facts regarding the first performance as well as some following ones. Also published in: *Bartók Béla válogatott írásai,* ed. András Szőllősy. Budapest: Művelt Nép Tudományos és Ismeretterjesztő Kiadó, 1956, pp. 282-287; *Bartók breviárium (levelek, írások, dokumentumok),* ed. József Ujfalussy. Budapest: Zeneműkiadó Vállalat, 195, p. 268; *Tempo* (London) 65 (Summer 1963): 5-7 [program note with examples, written 1939]; *Béla Bartók: Postrehy a názory,* ed. Eva Hykischová. Bratislava: Štátne Hudobné Vydavateľstvo, 1965, pp. 43-47; *Bartók Béla összegyűjtött írásai,* ed. András Szőllősy.

Budapest: Zeneműkiadó Vállalat, 1966, pp. 781-785; American Symphony Orchestra *Bartók Memorial Concert Program.* New York: Carnegie Hall (September 26, 1970); *Béla Bartók Essays,* ed. Benjamin Suchoff. New York: St. Martin's Press, 1976, pp. 419-423.

110. "Preface and Notes to *Mikrokosmos.* " London and New York: Boosey & Hawkes, 1940: Vol. 1 (No. 15196), pp. 3-5, 29-30 [In English, French, and Hungarian]; Vol. 2 (No. 15197), pp. 2, 36; Vol. 3 (No. 15192), pp. 4-6 [In English, French, and Hungarian]; Vol. 4 (No. 15191), pp. 3-5, 52 [In English, French, and Hungarian]; Vol. 5 (No. 15189), p. 44 [Note only, in English, French, and Hungarian]; Vol. 6 (No. 15187), no Preface or Notes.

Discusses the purpose and grade levels as well as more specific technical features regarding practice of the exercises before playing the pieces. Gives certain recommendations for specific practice of certain pieces. Also published in: Benjamin Suchoff. *Guide to the Mikrokosmos of Béla Bartók,* revised ed. London: Boosey & Hawkes, 1970. Also contains Bartók's comments on the pieces, as told to Ann Chenée in July 1944; *Béla Bartók Essays,* ed. Benjamin Suchoff. New York: St. Martin's Press, 1976, pp. 424-425.

111. "Some Problems of Folk Music Research in East Europe." Manuscript of lecture given at Harvard University on April 22 (revised 1941). *Béla Bartók Essays,* ed. Benjamin Suchoff. New York: St. Martin's Press, 1976, pp. 173-192.

Gives some introductory explanations as to what is pure folk music, then speaks about how to begin to study folk music (i.e., with a gramophone). The remaining portion discusses important facts regarding folk styles of various nations and shows some important interrelationships in their historical development. Then enumerates the principal problems in collecting materials.

112. "Contemporary Music in Piano Teaching." Manuscript for lecture-recitals given during the 1940-1941 concert season. *Béla Bartók Essays,* ed. Benjamin Suchoff. New York: St. Martin's Press, 1976, pp. 426-430.   ISBN 0571101208   ML60.B2613 1976b

Always had the idea of writing some easy works for piano students. Felt that the best thing to use would be folk tunes. Then discusses groups of pieces from several of his collections. Suchoff notes: "According to B & H publicity release, this lecture was on the role and importance of contemporary music in the piano teaching of today with explanatory examples on the piano." Presented at various colleges such as Oberlin (December 3, 1940), Mills (February 26, 1941), and the University of Washington (March 3, 1941). Bartók's programs were divided into three parts: 1)

pieces from *For Children;* 2) pieces from *Mikrokosmos;* and 3) four
of his works for piano solo.

113. "The Relation between Contemporary Hungarian Art Music and Folk
Music." Manuscript of lecture given at Columbia University of
Professor Douglas Moore's class in "20th Century Tendencies in
Music" (1941 or 1942). *Béla Bartók Essays,* ed. Benjamin Suchoff.
New York: St. Martin's Press, 1976, p. 348.   ISBN 0571101208
ML60.B2613 1976b

According to Suchoff (*Essays,* p. 348, n.1), the lecture was
given probably sometime during 1941 or 1942 when Bartók was
working at the University on the Parry Collection of Serbo-Croatian
folk songs. Discusses the difference between Bartók's transcriptions
of authentic folk tunes and his own original compositions that only
suggest the folk-music essence in the "general spirit of the style."
Also gives three categories in which transcription is used: 1) where
the folk melody is the more important part of the work; 2) where the
importance of the used melodies and the added parts is almost equal;
and 3) where the added compositional material attains the importance
of an original work, and the used folk melody is only a kind of
motto. Also says that Kodály's musical language is exclusively
based on Hungarian folk music, whereas his own is based on
Hungarian, Slovakian, Romanian, and even Arabic, etc.

114. "Race Purity in Music." *Modern Music* (New York) 19/3-4 (1942):
153-155 [omits p. 6 (partial)-8 of first (corrected) typescript MS
draft]. 780.5 M72

Discussion of the beneficial results of "racial impurity" in
music, showing how art music of an ethnic group can be enriched by
contact with foreign influences. Points out that there is a greater
variety of melodies in Eastern Europe than in North Africa, where
homogeneity has resulted from relatively few changes in population.
Also published in: *Tempo* (London) 8 (September 1944): 2-3;
Horizon (London) 60 (December 1944): 403-406; *Musica* (Cassel)
(1947?); *Mitteilungen des Basler Kammerorchesters* (Basel) (March
22, 1947, No. 9); *Bartók Béla válogatott zenei írásai,* ed. András
Szőllősy. Budapest: Magyar Kórus, 1948, pp. 58-60; *Alte und Neue
Musik. 25 Jahre Basler Kammerorchester.* Zurich: Atlantis Verlag,
1952; *Musik der Zeit* (Bonn) 3 (1953): 27-28; *Österreichische
Musikzeitschrift* (Vienna) 10/9 (1955): 281. *Béla Bartók, Scritti
sulla musica popolare,* ed. Diego Carpitella. Turin: Edizioni
Scientifiche Einaudi, 1955, pp. 92-95. *Bartók Béla, Însemnări
asupra cîntecului popular,* ed. Zeno Vancea. Bucharest: Editura de Stat
Pentru Literatură şi Artă, 1956, pp. 109-112; *Bartók Béla válogatott
írásai,* ed. András Szőllősy. Budapest: Művelt Nép Tudományos és
Ismeretterjesztő Kiadó, 1956, pp. 174-177; *Bartók, sa vie et son*

œuvre, ed. Bence Szabolcsi. Budapest: Corvina, 1956, pp. 195-197; *Composers on Music*, ed. Sam Morgenstern. London: Faber & Faber, 1956, pp. 421-424; *Béla Bartók, Weg und Werk*, ed. Bence Szabolcsi. Budapest: Corvina, 1957, pp. 201-203; *Béla Bartók: Eigene Schriften und Erinnerungen der Freunde*, ed. Willi Reich. Basel-Stuttgart: Benno Schwabe & Co., 1958, pp. 41-46; *Béla Bartók: Postrehy a názory*, ed. Eva Hykischová. Bratislava: Štátne Hudobné Vydavatel'stvo, 1965, pp. 102-105; *Sovetskaya muzyka* (Moscow) 29/2 (February 1965): 101-102; *Bartók Béla összegyűjtött írásai*, ed. András Szőllősy. Budapest: Zeneműkiadó Vállalat, 1966, pp. 601-603; *Béla Bartók Musiksprachen*, ed. Bence Szabolcsi. Leipzig: Philipp Reclam, 1972, pp. 124-127; *Béla Bartók Essays*, ed. Benjamin Suchoff. New York: St. Martin's Press, 1976, pp. 29-32.

115. "On American and British Folk Music Material" [MS dated June 1, 1942]. *Rumanian Folk Music*, ed. Benjamin Suchoff, Vols. 1-3, 4-5. The Hague: Martinus Nijhoff, 1967, 1975; dust cover [extract]. M1718.B3 R7   784.4 B2811

Need for systematic scientific examination of the morphological aspects of the material. Gives procedure for initiating and continuing this work. Also published in *Béla Bartók Essays*, ed. Benjamin Suchoff. New York: St. Martin's Press, 1976, p. 37.

116. "Parry Collection of Yugoslav Folk Music." *The New York Times* (Sunday, June 28, 1942): Music Section.   QAP2 N4884

Gives history of the origin of this important and unique collection of folk music. Bartók heard of this collection when he visited the United States in 1940. Also gives detailed description of the recordings. Also published in: *Bartók Béla válogatott írásai*, ed. András Szőllősy. Budapest: Művelt Nép Tudományos és Ismeretterjesztő Kiadó, 1956, pp. 357-362; Szegő, Júlia. *Bartók Béla a népdalkutató*. Bucharest: Allami Irodalmi és Művészeti Kiadó, 1956, pp. 320-323; *Bartók Béla összegyűjtött írásai*, ed. András Szőllősy. Budapest: Zeneműkiadó Vállalat, 1966, pp. 494-497; *Béla Bartók Essays*, ed. Benjamin Suchoff. New York: St. Martin's Press, 1976, pp. 148-151.

117. "Diversity of Material Yielded up in Profusion in European Meltingpot." *Musical America* (January 10, 1943): 27.   ML1 M97

In the midst of a melting pot of nationalities, Hungarian musicians turned with great interest toward the extraordinary treasury of folk songs. This bore fruit of two different kinds: 1) the scientific research, description, systematic grouping and comparison of Eastern-European folksong types; and 2) the creation of an autochthonous Hungarian musical art. Also discusses some misconceptions that some Western Europeans have regarding the significance of these developments. Speaks with pleasure about the broader artistic aspects of rural life, which unfortunately is doomed to perish. Also published in: *Zenetudományi tanulmányok I,* n.p.; "Le energie musicali." *Il contemporaneo* (Rome) (1955): n.p.; *Bartók Béla válogatott írásai,* ed. András Szőllősy. Budapest: Művelt Nép Tudományos és Ismeretterjesztő Kiadó, 1956, n.p.; *Béla Bartók, Scritti sulla musica popolare,* ed. Diego Carpitella. Turin: Edizioni Scientifiche Einaudi, 1955, n.p.

118. "Folk Song Research in Eastern Europe" [MS title]. *Musical America* (New York) 1 (January 1943): 27.   ML1 M97

Speaks of inexhaustible variety of folk music in Eastern Europe because of close contact between the various national groups. This brought interest for Hungarian musicians in terms of scientific research, description, systematic grouping and comparison of folk song types, which resulted in the science of comparative research. Bartók also relates his experience and perception of the relationship between peasants of different nationalities. Also published in: *Emlékkönyu Kodály Zoltán 70. születésnapjára.* Budapest: Akadémiai Kiadó, 1953, pp. 73-74; *Il contemporaneo* (Rome) (1955[?]): n.p.; *Bartók Béla válogatott írásai,* ed. András Szőllősy. Budapest: Művelt Nép Tudományos és Ismeretterjesztő Kiadó, 1956, pp. 15-17; *Béla Bartók, Scritti sulla musica popolare,* ed. Diego Carpitella. Turin: Edizioni Scientifiche Einaudi, 1955, pp. 208-210; *Bartók, sa vie et son œuvre,* ed. Bence Szabolcsi. Budapest: Corvina, 1956, pp. 186-187; *Béla Bartók, Weg und Werk,* ed. Bence Szabolcsi. Budapest: Corvina, 1957, pp. 204-206; *Béla Bartók: Postrehy a názory,* ed. Eva Hykischová. Bratislava: Štátne Hudobné Vydavatel'stvo, 1965, pp. 93-95; *Sovetskaya muzyka* (Moscow) 29/2 (February 1965): 103-104; *Bartók Béla összegyűjtött írásai,* ed. András Szőllősy. Budapest: Zeneműkiadó Vállalat, 1966, pp. 604-605; *Béla Bartók Musiksprachen,* ed. Bence Szabolcsi. Leipzig: Philipp Reclam, 1972, pp. 128-130; *Béla Bartók Essays,* ed. Benjamin Suchoff. New York: St. Martin's Press, 1976, pp. 33-34.

119. "Harvard Lectures" [MSS of four lectures given during February 1943]. *Journal of the American Musicological Society* (Richmond) 19/2 (Summer 1966): 232-243 [extracts].   780.6 Am3j
ISSN 0003-0139

The titles of the lectures are as follows: 1) Revolution and Evolution in Art; 2) Modes and Polymodality (Polytonality and Atonality or Twelve-tone Music; 3) Chromaticism (very rare in folk music); 4) Rhythm [complete?]. Eight conferences were intended to explain the main characteristics of the "New Hungarian Art Music."

Includes discussion of Bartók's leading contemporaries: Schoenberg, Stravinsky, and Alois Hába. Also published in *Béla Bartók Essays,* ed. Benjamin Suchoff. New York: St. Martin's Press, 1976, pp. 354-392.

120. "Bence Szabolcsi" [MS written in November? 1942]. *The Universal Jewish Encyclopedia,* Vol. 10. New York: Brooklyn, 1943, p. 138 [statistical information added by the editor, Louis Rittenberg].

Brief discussion of Szabolcsi's life and work as musicologist and ethnomusicologist. Also published in: *Bartók Béla összegyűjtött írásai,* ed. András Szőllősy. Budapest: Zeneműkiadó Vállalat, 1966, pp. 762-763; *Béla Bartók Essays,* ed. Benjamin Suchoff. New York: St. Martin's Press, 1976, pp. 519-520.

121. "To Sir Henry Wood" [MS drafted in February? 1944]. *Homage to Sir Henry Wood: A World Symposium.* London: The Performing Right Society, 1944, p. 36.

Discusses Sir Henry Wood's conducting performances of Bartók's works, with Bartók as soloist in two works. The composer expresses deep gratitude toward the conductor. Also published in *Béla Bartók Essays,* ed. Benjamin Suchoff. New York: St. Martin's Press, 1976, p. 521.

122. "Concerto for Orchestra by Béla Bartók." Boston Symphony Orchestra *Concert Program,* No. 8, 1944-1945: 442-444. ML42.B678   780.15

Discusses basic assumptions in terms of the treatment of the single instruments or instrumental groups in a "concertant" or soloistic manner. Then, gives structure of the movements and general mood. Also published in: Boston Symphony Orchestra *Concert Bulletin,* December 1-2, 1944: 606-608; *Bartók Béla összegyűjtött írásai,* ed. András Szőllősy. Budapest: Zeneműkiadó Vállalat, 1966, p. 790; *Béla Bartók Essays,* ed. Benjamin Suchoff. New York: St. Martin's Press, 1976, p. 431.

123. "Hungarian Music." *American Hungarian Observer* (New York) (June 4, 1944): 3, 7.

Discusses certain misunderstandings and misinterpretations regarding the relation between the higher art music of Hungary and the rural music. Makes distinction between this relation with other national composers (e.g., Tchaikovsky, etc.) and the modern Hungarians, especially Kodály and himself. Also published in: *Nuestra música* (Mexico City) 1/1 (March 1946): 14-19 (41); *Magyar zene* (Budapest) 4/3 (June 1963): 294-297; *Bartók Béla összegyűjtött írásai,* ed. András Szőllősy. Budapest: Zeneműkiadó

Vállalat, 1966, pp. 758-761; *Béla Bartók Essays,* ed. Benjamin Suchoff. New York: St. Martin's Press, 1976, pp. 393-396.

124. "Introduction to *Béla Bartók Masterpieces for the Piano.*" [MS drafted in January 1945]. *Seven Sketches Op. 9.* New York: E.B. Marks Music Corp., No. 12726-12, 1950, p. 3 [extract].

   Discusses styles and purposes of these works and the status of this revised edition regarding several editorial changes in fingering and musical text. Gives detailed key outline of the works. Also published in *Béla Bartók Essays,* ed. Benjamin Suchoff. New York: St. Martin's Press, 1976, pp. 432-433.

125. "I Salute the Valiant Belgian People." *Belgium* 5/12 (1945): 563-564.   HA 1399 157 1976

   Discusses his work in the United States as a voluntary refuge since 1940. Also published in: *Bartók Béla összegyűjtött írásai,* ed. András Szőllősy. Budapest: Zeneműkiadó Vállalat, 1966, p. 798; *Béla Bartók. Lettere scelte,* ed. János Demény. Milan: Il Saggiatore di Alberto Mondadori Editore, 1969, pp. 393-394; *Béla Bartók Letters,* ed. János Demény. London: Faber & Faber, 1971, pp. 340-341; *Bartók Béla levelei (új dokumentumok),* ed. János Demény. Budapest: Zeneműkiadó Vállalat, 1971, p. 111; *Béla Bartók Essays,* ed. Benjamin Suchoff. New York: St. Martin's Press, 1976, p. 434.

126. "Autobiography" (September 1945). *The Ten Easy Pieces for Piano.* London: Liber-Southern, Ltd., 1950.

   Short autobiography of the composer reproduced from his own manuscript.   Written shortly before his death on September 26, 1945 in New York. Gives date and place of birth, early education, piano teaching from 1907-1940 (then in New York), outlines main works, latest works, Ph.D. from Columbia University, data on folk-music collecting including related publications.

127. "Some Linguistic Observations." *Tempo* (London) 14 (1946): 5-7.   780.5 T249   ISSN 0040-2982

   Talks of increasing popularity of Russian music and points to problems of consistency in the spelling of Russian composers' names on programs, in catalogues and dictionaries, etc. Suggests the most practical approach to transliteration. Gives brief history of these problems resulting from transcription in Germany, France, and English-speaking countries. Also published in: *Musik der Zeit. Eine Schriftenreihe zur zeitgenössischen Musik.* Heft 9. Bonn: Boosey & Hawkes, 1954, pp. 41-44; *Bartók Béla válogatott írásai,* ed. András Szőllősy. Budapest: Művelt Nép Tudományos és Ismeretterjesztő Kiadó, 1956, p. 260 [extract]; *Bartók Béla összegyűjtött írásai,* ed. András Szőllősy. Budapest: Zeneműkiadó Vállalat, 1966, pp. 799-803; *Béla Bartók Essays,* ed. Benjamin Suchoff. New York: St. Martin's Press, 1976, pp. 522-525.

128. *Cantata Profana. A kilenc csodaszarvas* [*Cantata Profana. The Nine Miraculous Deer*]. Budapest: Zeneműkiadó Vállalat, 1974. 35p.

Facsimile edition of Bartók's autograph of his essay, in Romanian, on the text of the *Cantata Profana.* Also includes the Hungarian text of the work. Contains an introduction by György Kroó and illustrations by László Réber.

2. Essays in Collected Editions

129. *Béla Bartók, Scrieri mărunte despre muzica populară românească* [Béla Bartók, abridged writings on Romanian folk music]. Coll. and trans. Constantin Brăiloiu. Bucureşti: [?], 1937. 55p.

Not examined.

130. *Bartók Béla, Önéletrajz, írások a zenéről* [Béla Bartók, autobiography, writings on music], comp. Lili Almárné-Veszprémi. Introductory study by János Demény. Budapest: Egyetemi Nyomda Kiadása, 1946. 76p.

Contains five studies from five periods of Bartók's life. Includes the composer's autobiography of 1918-1921, an essay written in 1911 on Hungarian folk music and the music of Liszt, a lecture presented in the United States in 1923 on Hungarian folk music and new Hungarian art music, and an essay written in 1937 on the problem of folk-song research and nationalism.

131. *Bartók Béla válogatott zenei írásai* [Selected writings on music], ed. András Szőllősy. Introduction and notes by Bence Szabolcsi. Budapest: Magyar Kórus, 1948. 109p. ML 60.B26; rev. and enlarged as *Bartók Béla válogatott írásai,* ed. András Szőllősy. Budapest: Művelt Nép Tudományos és Ismeretterjesztő Kiadó, 1956. 426p. ML 248.B285 A16 1956

The original 1948 edition contains twenty-eight essays by Bartók. The five chapters include the following topics: 1) Hungarian folk song and old and new Hungarian art music; 2) Bartók's scientific folk-music investigations, the first essay dating from 1912; 3) three articles revealing Bartók's humanism; 4) essays discussing Bartók's musical forebears; and 5) primary source documentation revealing reactionary and chauvinistic attitudes toward Bartók. The revised and enlarged 1956 edition contains forty-seven essays, notes, and bibliography by Szőllősy. See also the Italian translation: *Béla Bartók, Scritti sulla musica popolare*, comp. Diego Carpitella, with preface by Zoltán Kodály. Torino: Edizioni Scientifiche Einaudi, 1955.

132. *Musik der Zeit. Eine Schriftenreihe zur zeitgenössischen Musik*, ed. Lindlar, Heinrich. Heft 3 Béla Bartók. Bonn: Boosey & Hawkes, 1953. 78p.   ML410.B26 B4

Includes the following writings by Bartók: "Autobiographische Skizze" [Autobiographical sketch]; "Unbekannte Bartók-Briefe" [Unknown Bartók letters]; "Vom Einfluss der Bauernmusik auf die Musik unserer Zeit" [The influence of folk music on the art music of today]; "Auf Volkslied-forschungsfahrt in der Türkei" [On folksong investigation in Turkey]; and "Rassenreinheit in der Musik" [Racial purity in music]. Also includes the following articles on Bartók: Zoltán Kodály, "Ungarische Jugend bei Bartók in Schuld" [Hungarian youth indebted to Bartók]; Erich Doflein, "Bartók und die Musikpädagogik" [Bartók and music pedagogy]; Colin Mason,"Bartóks Streichquartette" [Bartók's string quartets]; John Weissmann, "Bartóks Klaviermusik" [Bartók's piano music]; Gustav Oláh, "Bartók und das Musik-Theater" [Bartók and the music theater]; Hans Mersmann, "Der Spätstil Bartóks" [Bartók's late works]; Ferenc Fricsay, "Bartók, Herold des neuen Stils" [Bartók, herald of the new style]; Paul Sacher, "Béla Bartók zum Gedächtnis" [Bartók in recollection]; Ralph Hawkes, "Béla Bartók in der Emigration" [Béla Bartók in emigration]; and Denijs Dille, "Werkverzeichnis" [Worklist]. Contains a complete discography of Bartók's performances of his own compositions.

133. *Bartók, sa vie et son oeuvre* [Bartók, his life and work], ed. Bence Szabolcsi. Budapest: Corvina, 1956. 351p.   ML410.B26 S89; rev. 2nd ed., Budapest: Corvina, 1968. 331p.   ML410.B26 S84; Paris: Boosey & Hawkes, 1968. 332p.   ML410.B37 A3

Collection of essays includes: Bence Szabolcsi on Bartók's life; Zoltán Kodály on *Duke Bluebeard's Castle* (as the first authentic work of the Hungarian opera theater) and on Bartók as folklorist; Szabolcsi on Bartók and folk music, and Ernő Lendvai on Bartók's world of form and harmony (discussing the "polar-axis system" and "Golden Section"). Bartók's own writings include his autobiography, several essays on folk music and its relation to contemporary art music as well as nationalism, and a wide selection of personal letters. Includes bibliography of Bartók's works by András Szőllősy (pp. 299-345). Informed the world for the first time about the state of Bartók research in Hungary and is therefore a pioneering work. See also the German translation: *Béla Bartók, Weg und Werk; Schriften und Briefe*. Budapest: Corvina; Leipzig: Breitkopf und Haertel, 1957, 371p; enlarged 2nd ed., Kassel: Barenreiter; Munich:

Deutsche Taschenbuch, 1972. See the reviews by: Siegfried Borris, in *Musikbildung* 2/7-8 (1970): 340; Erich Kapst, in *Beiträge der Musikwissenschaft* 13/1 (1971): 77-80; Gerard Schuhmacher, in *Musica* 26/6 (1972): 594; Hartmut Fladt, in *Neue Zeitung für Musik* 134/1 (1973): 56-57; Wolfgang Rogge, in *Melos* 40/3 (1973): 152-153; Wolfgang Suppan, in *Jahrbuch Volksliedforschung* 19 (1974): 207; Gunter Weiss-Aigner, in *Musikforschung* 27/1 (1974): 136-137.

134. *Bartók Béla, Insemnări asupra cîntecului popular.* Preface by Zeno Vancea. Bucureşti: Editura de Stat Pentru Literatură şi Artă, 1956.

    Based on *Béla Bartók, Scrieri mărunte despre muzica populară românească* (1937), item no. 129, and *Bartók Béla válogatott zenei írásai* (1948), item no. 131.

135. *Bartók breviárium (levelek, írások, dokumentumok)* [Bartók breviary (correspondence, essays, and documents)], ed. József Ujfalussy. Budapest: Zeneműkiadó Vállalat, 1958, rev. edition by Vera Lampert, 1974. 556p.   ML410.B26 A43

    Extensive collection of letters, essays, and documents with substantial annotations by the editor. Selected documentation significantly reveals the various facets of Bartók's personality and his career as composer, performer, and ethnomusicologist. Chronologically orders Bartók's life in four large chapters: his childhood, student years and early career (1881-1906), the period of his development as man and artist (1906-1919), the years of increasing international recognition (1920-1940), and his emigration (1940-1945). Contains illustrations. See the review by János Breuer in *Magyar zene* 15/3 (September 1974): 330-332.

136. *Béla Bartók: Eigene Schriften und Erinnerungen der Freunde* [Béla Bartók: his own writings and recollections of friends], ed. Willi Reich. Basel-Stuttgart: Benno Schwabe & Co., 1958. 138p. ML410.B28 A39   780.92 B292B1

    Not examined.

137. *Bartók Béla kézírása* [The handwriting of Béla Bartók], ed. Bence Szabolcsi és Benjamin Rajeczky. Budapest: Editio Musica, 1961. 22p. ML410.B26 A3

    A collection of facsimiles of Bartók's letters and writings from different periods of his life. Also contains illustrations and music.

138. *Béla Bartók: Postrehy a názory,* trans. Eva Hykischová. Bratislava: Štátne Hudobné Vydavatel'stvo, 1965. 218p. ML60.B27 8bs

Based on *Bartók Béla válogatott írásai* (1956), item no. 131, and his letters. Contains music, addresses, essays, and lectures.

139. *Bartók Béla összegyűjtött írásai I* [Collected papers of Bartók, Vol. I], ed. András Szőllősy. Budapest: Zeneműkiadó Vállalat, 1966, 1967, 943p.   ML410.B26 A2

    A substantial collection of Bartók's writings, which includes virtually all of his essays in Hungarian. Subjects range from autobiographical to aesthetic and musicological issues, including Bartók's ideas and opinions of other composers. Has illustrations and music (mainly unaccompanied melodies). See the following reviews by: János Kárpáti, in *Élet és irodalom* 11/22 (1967): 8; Béla Hargas, in *Valóság* 10/9 (September 1967): 105-107; John S. Weissmann, in *Ethnomusicology* 12/3 (September 1968): 452-453.

140. *Béla Bartók Musiksprachen. Aufsätze und Vorträge* [Essays on music. Articles and lectures], ed. Bence Szabolcsi, trans. Jörg Buschmann and Mirza Schüching. Reclams Universalbibliothek 353; Leipzig: Philipp Reclam, 1972. 211p.

    Includes Bartók's essays, lectures, and correspondences revealing his opinions on ethnomusicological and contemporary art-music issues. Provides discussions of his own music as well

141. *Béla Bartók Essays,* ed. Benjamin Suchoff. New York Bartók Archive, Studies in Musicology 8. New York: St. Martin's Press; London: Faber & Faber, 1976. xvi, 567p.   ISBN 0-312-07350X ISBN 0571101208   ML60.B2613 1976b; Reprinted Lincoln and London: University of Nebraska Press, 1992.   ISBN 0-8032-6108-X ML410.B26A24   780-dc20

    Main collected edition of Bartók's essays and lectures, all of which are translated into English from various European languages. Included are Bartók's writings on the investigation of musical folklore, book reviews and polemics, discussions of the relation between folk and art music, autobiographical statements, brief analyses of his own music, and discussions of other music and musicians. A thorough listing of other collected editions appears in the bibliography to these essays, pp. 527-528, followed by an extensive listing of the source materials (Bartók's original publications) used by Suchoff for translating and editing. Translations from Hungarian and other languages were made by Richard Toszeghy, Elma Laurvik, Marianne Kethly, and Ida Kohler. The essays on Liszt were translated by Colin Mason. See the reviews by: Anthony Baines in *Music and Letters* 58/2 (April 1977): 217-218; and Halsey Stevens in *Music Library Association Notes* 34/1 (September 1977): 58-61.

142. Somfai, László. "Vierzehn Bartók-Schriften aus den Jahren 1920/21. Aufsätze über die zeitgenössische Musik und Konzertberichte aus Budapest" [Fourteen Bartók writings of 1920/21. Essays on contemporary music and concert reports from Budapest]. *Documenta bartókiana* 5 (Budapest) (1977), pp. 15-141. ISBN-963-05-1185-1- (Serie)   ML410 B26 D6   ISSN 0134-0131

See item no. 1155n. Includes: 1) "Das Problem der neuen Musik" [The problem of new music]; 2) "Hungary in the Throes of Reaction"; 3) "Kodaly's New Trio, a Sensation Abroad"; 4) "Der Einfluss der Volksmusik auf die heutige Kunstmusik" [The influence of folk music on today's art music]; 5) "Arnold Schönbergs Musik in Ungarn" [Arnold Schoenberg's music in Hungary]; 6) "To Celebrate the Birth of the Great Bonn Composer;" 7) "Kodály Zoltán" [Zoltán Kodály]; 8) "Schönberg and Stravinsky Enter 'Christian-National' Budapest Without Bloodshed"; 9) "New Kodály Work Raises Storm of Critical Protest"; 10) "Lettera da Budapest [No. 1]" [Budapest letter (No. 1)]; 11) "Budapest Sorely Misses Dohnányi"; 12) "The Relation of Folk-Song to the Development of the Art Music of Our Time"; 13) "Budapest Welcomes Dohnányi's Return bzw. Lettera da Budapest [No. 2]"; 14) "Della musica moderna in Ungheria bzw. The Development of Art Music in Hungary" [On modern music in Hungary--the development of art music in Hungary]. Appendix includes (see item no. 149): "Vier Briefe Bartóks an Philip Heseltine" [Four Bartók letters to Philip Heseltine].

143. *Béla Bartók Studies in Ethnomusicology,* ed. Benjamin Suchoff. Lincoln and London: University of Nebraska Press, 1996. xxiii, 285p.

According to the editor: "a compilation of those published writings that were intended for *Béla Bartók Essays* but for practical reasons could not be included. They appear here in chronological order of their original publication, and, together with the mentioned edition of essays, the reader is provided with a comprehensive overview of Bartók's development as creator of an extensive body of scientific literature that is unparalleled in ethnomusicology." Editor's Preface includes discussions of musical developments in nineteenth-century Greater Hungary, Bartók and Hungarian folk music, Bartók's investigations of the folk music of the national minorities, Slovaks, Romanians, and Arabs, Post-World War I developments (1920-1929), Pre-World War II events (1930-1939), and Bartók in New York (1940-1945). Essays include: "Preface to *Romanian Folk Songs from Bihor County";* "Draft of the New Universal Collection of Folk Songs"; "Arab Folk Music in the Biskra District"; "Transylvanian Hungarians. Folk Songs"; "Hungarian Folk Music"; "Romanian Folk Music"; "The Peasant Music of Hungary"; "The Bartók-Möller Polemical Interchange"; "New Results of Folk Song Research in Hungary"; "Hungarian Folk Music"; "Romanian Folk

Music"; "Slovak Folk Music"; Folk Music and Folk Songs"; "Hungarian Folk Music and the Folk Music of Neighboring Peoples"; "Introduction to *Slovak Folk Songs.*" Contains folk-music transcriptions, bibliography, index.

3. Letters in Collected Editions

144. *Bartók Béla levelei* [Béla Bartók letters], ed. and annotated by János Demény. Budapest: Magyar Művészeti Tanács, 1948-1971, enlarged 2/1976; German translation, 1960, enlarged 2/1973; English translation, 1971.

   Most comprehensive collection of Bartók's correspondences reflecting his personal life, musical attitudes, compositions, and folk-music research. Originally appeared in four basic volumes. For specific annotations of these volumes, see item nos. 145, 146, 147, and 152.

145. *Bartók Béla levelei I. Családi dokumentumok: Levelek, fényképek, kéziratok, kották* [Béla Bartók's correspondence I. Family documents: letters, photographs, manuscripts, and music scores], ed. János Demény. Budapest: Magyar Művészeti Tanács, 1948. 212p.

   Contains a preface by Demény. Volume contains more than one hundred previously unknown letters of Bartók (Hungarian versions only), with about fifty previously unknown photographs, photostatic copies of many letters (on pp. 157-208), musical scores, and concert programs.

146. *Bartók Béla levelei II: Magyar és külföldi dokumentumok (Az utolsó két év gyűjtése)* [Béla Bartók's correspondence II: Hungarian and foreign documents (material collected during the last two years)], ed. János Demény. Budapest: Művelt Nép Könyvkiadó, 1951. 236p. ML 410.B26 A4

   Preface written by András Mihály. Contains 196 items, including only the Hungarian versions of letters written from Hungary, Switzerland, and the United States. The editor states that "this second volume was presented to participants of the First Bartók Festival in the autumn of 1948. First larger consignment of material for this volume was sent by Mrs. Pál Kecskeméti, a harpsichordist, in New York since 1940. These letters, written in the last years of Bartók's life, reveal Bartók's preservation of his sense of humor even when he was suffering from his fatal illness. Also includes early postcards sent to Etelka Freund, important materials in the hands of Mrs. Müller-Widmann (consisting of sombre letters from Bartók in the 1930s, a letter belonging to Szigeti, etc." Contains sixteen photographic plates.

147. *Bartók Béla levelei III: Magyar, román, szlovák, dokumentumok* [Béla Bartók's correspondence III: Hungarian, Romanian, Slovak, documents], ed. János Demény. Budapest: Zeneműkadó Vállalat, 1955. 504p.

Preface by Demény. Includes the following sections: Part I "Romanian Correspondence," collected by Viorel Cosma, preface by Ferenc Bónis; Part II. "Czechoslovak Correspondence," collected by Ladislav Burlas, preface by Burlas; Part III. "Hungarian Correspondence," collected by János Demény, preface by Demény. Includes 318 items (92 in Hungarian, 124 in Romanian, 72 in Slovak, and 30 more in the Supplement). The editor states that this is a "new volume of correspondence, entirely as the result of the brotherhood stemming from those who made letters available in connection with Bartók's folk-music collections. Plan suggested by Ladislav Burlas, a musicologist of Bratislava, and Viorel Cosma, a Bucharest scholar."

148. *Bartók Béla: Ausgewählte Briefe* [Béla Bartók: selected letters], ed. János Demény. German trans. Mirza Schüching. Budapest: Corvina, 1960. 292p. ML410.B26 A32 1960

Preface by József Ujfalussy. According to the editor, this is the "first volume of Bartók's letters to appear in a foreign language. Collection contains two hundred letters. Preceded by three volumes (though not prepared as a fourth volume of this succession), it was compiled not only of material already published, but also contains fifty new letters." Contains facsimiles, illustrations, ports.

149. Béla Bartók. "Vier unbekannte Briefe" [Four unknown letters], ed. Denijs Dille. *Österreichische Musikzeitschrift* 20 (1965): 449-460. 780.5 Oe8 ISSN 0029-9316

Includes letters written in both French and English to the English composer, Philip Heseltine, between 1920 and 1921. Reveals Bartók's opinions regarding the music of several of his contemporaries, including Debussy, Schoenberg, Stravinsky, and others. See item nos. 142n and 1155n.

150. *Béla Bartók. Lettere scelte* [Béla Bartók. Selected letters], ed. János Demény, trans. Paolo Ruzicska. Milan: Il Saggiatore di Alberto Mondadori Editore, 1969. 510p.

Contains 270 items, including letters from earlier as well as more recent Hungarian volumes.

151. *Bartóks Briefe in die Slowakei* [Bartók's letters to Slovakia], ed. Vladimír Čížik. Bratislava: Slovenské Národné Muzeum, 1971. 179p.   ML410.B26 A455

     Includes introductory material discussing Bartók in connection with Bratislava and Slovakian folksong. The main body provides over 100 chronologically ordered letters by Bartók to people in Slovakia, most of the original Hungarian letters appearing in German translation. Also includes a discussion of the regions in Slovakia where Bartók collected and investigated folksongs. Contains an alphabetical listing of communities, indexes of correspondents, personal names and subjects, bibliography, and map. See reviews by: János Breuer, in *Magyar zene* 13/3 (September 1972): 313-315; and Vladimir Karbusicky in *Musikforschung* 28/3 (1975): 359-360.

152. *Bartók Béla levelei IV: Új dokumentumok* [Béla Bartók's correspondence IV: new documents], ed. János Demény. Budapest: Zeneműkadó Vállalat, 1971. 175p.   ML410.B26 A316

     In addition to newly added documents, contains some illustrations, music, and appendix.

153. *Béla Bartók Letters*, ed. János Demény. New York: St. Martin's Press, 1971. English trans. Peter Balabán and István Farkas. Trans. rev. Elizabeth West and Colin Mason. London: Faber & Faber; Budapest: Corvina Press, 1971. 466p.   ML410.B26 A42 1971b 780.924 B

     Collected, selected, edited, and annotated by János Demény, with preface by Sir Michael Tippett. This English translation includes about 300 letters selected from the four earlier collections (the first three in Hungarian and the fourth in German). Includes letters from Bartók's early years (1899-1905), the years of achievement (1920-1926), at the height of his career (1927-1940), and the years of exile (1940-1945). Contains appendices, notes on the present edition, list of letters, list of correspondents, chronological list of Bartók's compositions, list of places, bibliography, and index. See the review of this English translation by Edmund Rubbra, in *Tempo* 99 (April 1972): 18-20.

154. *Bartók, Béla: Briefe* [Béla Bartók letters], ed. János Demény. Budapest: Corvina, 1973. 2 vols.: 252p. and 264p.   ML410.B26 A45 1973   780.92 4 B

     Includes over 300 annotated letters of Bartók. To this collection of previously published letters are added 34 new ones. Contains illustrations, facsimiles, music examples, bibliography, and index. See the reviews by: Ferenc László, in *Korunk* 33/3 (March 1974):

500-501; Siegfried Borris, in *Musikbildung* 7/11 (1975): 596, in German; and Hartmut Fladt, in *Melos/Neue Zeitung für Musik* 2/1 (1976): 68-69.

155. *Bartók Béla levelei* [Béla Bartók letters], ed. János Demény. Budapest: Zeneműkiadó, 1976. 952p.   780.923 B29 2 19

   Contains almost 1100 annotated letters, which is the largest collection of Bartók's letters published thus far. To the previously published letters are added 170 new ones. Contains illustrations, music, bibliography, index. See review by: Ferenc László, in *A Hét* 8/11 (March 18, 1977): 6.

156. *Béla Bartók: Scrisori* [Béla Bartók: letters], ed. and annot. by Ferenc László. Bucharest: Kriterion. Vol. I, 1976, 294 p., vol. II, 1977, 268p. Foreword by Zeno Vancea, Romanian translation by Gemma Zinveliu.

   The first volume contains 112 selected letters by Bartók, the second volume the complete edition of all of Bartók's letters written to Romanians (185 total).

157. *Béla Bartók. Briefe an Stefi Geyer, 1907-1908,* ed. Paul Sacher. German trans. by von Lajos Nykos. Foreword and Preface by Paul Sacher. Afterword by von Lajos Nykos. Basle: Privatdruck Ltd., 1979. 218p.

   Facsimiles of 27 letters and a poem from Bartók to violinist Stefi Geyer, with whom the composer was in love. Also includes translations of the letters from the original Hungarian into German by von Lajos Nykos. The poem, which appeared on the first page of the *First Violin Concerto* (composed in Jászberényi, 1 July 1907-Budapest, 5 February 1908), is titled "My Confession for Stefi." Contains musical notation engraved from the facsimiles, index of literature, index of names.

158. *Bartók Béla családi levelei* [Family letters of Béla Bartók], ed. Béla Bartók, Jr. Budapest: Zeneműkiadó, 1981. 653p.   ML410.B26 A4

   Comprehensive chronological presentation of 918 of Bartók's letters mostly to members of his family. Includes several drawings and musical sketches by Bartók, as well as a diagram of Bartók's family tree (at the end of the volume). The first letter (dating from 1889) is a birthday poem for his mother, the final letter (dating from 1941) written in the United States. Also includes a final supplementary letter from the composer's younger son, Peter, informing his brother Béla Jr. about their father's death. See review by Ferenc László in *Utunk* 37/34 (August 20, 1982): 6.

4. Letters Published Individually in Other Works

159. Baraczka, István. "Egy ismeretlen Bartók-levél" [An unknown Bartók letter]. *Budapest* 5/2 (February 1967): 11.   Q708.391 B8586TF

   An unknown letter from Bartók (dated March 27, 1938) to Gyula Novágh (Director of the Committee of Adult Education) was found in the Municipal Archives. Also includes Novágh's reply. Bartók's letter reveals his thoughts on an article published in the journal *A Zene* and discusses Bartók's resignation from the awards jury of the National Ferenc Liszt Society.

160. Bartók, Béla. "Letter to Darius Milhaud." In François Lesure. *Exposição Darius Milhaud.* Lisbon: Fundação Calouste Gulbenkian, 1968. Appendix.

   Not examined. According to Lesure, *RILM Abstracts* No. 851 (1968), "An appendix contains ten heretofore unpublished letters written to Milhaud between 1916-1955 by various writers and composers."

161. ----------. "Letter to János Buşiţia 8 May 1921 from No. 2 Gyopár Street in Budapest." *Journal of the American Musicological Society* 20/1 (Spring 1967): 150-151.   780.6 Am3j   ISSN 0003-0139

   The English translation of this letter, first published in *New Hungary* (August 1966): n.p., is reprinted here through the efforts of Irving Lowens. Bartók discusses his financial problems; his cost of living at this time was twice his annual salary. Publication and performance of his music was of no help to him.

162. Čížik, Vladimir. "Neuverejnené listy Bélu Bartóka z korešpondencie Alexandra Albrechta" [The unpublished letters by Béla Bartók from the correspondence of Alexander Albrecht]. *Slovenská hudba* 13/6-7 (1969): 214-220.   H50.470

   Contains four previously unpublished letters from Bartók to the Hungarian composer. Annotations and commentary provide historical and biographical information.

163. Demény, János. "Egy ismeretlen Bartók-levél" [An unknown Bartók letter]. *Zenei szemle* (Budapest) (August 1949): 62-64.   HA2.398

   A previously unknown letter from Bartók to the violinist Joseph Szigeti, dated January 1944.

164. ----------, ed. "Két Bartók-levél Reményi Józsefhez" [Two letters of Béla Bartók to József Reményi]. *Muzsika* (Budapest) 14/5 (May 1971): 1-4. ISSN 0027-5336

> Two previously unknown letters from Bartók to József Reményi in 1942. Includes commentary by the editor.

165. Eősze, László. "Bartók és Kodály levelezése" [The correspondence between Bartók and Kodály]. *Ujhold-Évkönyv* (Budapest: Magvető, 1990): 375-409.

> Contains 34 letters edited by Eősze, 25 of which were previously unpublished. Contains facsimiles, music examples.

166. ----------. "Thirteen Unpublished Letters by Zoltán Kodály to Béla Bartók." *Bulletin of the International Kodály Society* 1 (1991): 3-12.

> In English and Hungarian. According to the author, *RILM Abstracts* No. 4613 (1991), "The four decades of close friendship between Bartók and Kodály are significant for European musicology and ethnomusicology. Living in the same city, they left only a few written records of their relationship, hence the unique importance of editing their correspondence. These 13 letters of Kodály are an addendum to the former 34, edited by the author in the 1990/91 issue of the *Ujhold évkönyv.*"

167. Gál, István. "Bartók Béla levele a népzenénk és a szomszéd népek zenéje francia kiadása ügyében" [A letter of Béla Bartók about the French publishing of "Hungarian Folk Music and the Folk Music of Neighboring Peoples"]. *Forrás* (May-June 1973): 84-85.   H1.056

> Previously unpublished letter by Bartók to Imre Lukinich (1880-1950), editor of the multilingual Budapest periodical *Archivum Europae Centro-Orientalis,* revealing the editor's interest in publishing a French translation of Bartók's article originally appearing in Hungarian in *Népszerű zenefüzetek* 3 (1934). The French translation, "La musique populaire des Hongrois et des peuples voisins," was published in the periodical, 11/3-4 (1936): 197-232 and i-xxxii.

168. ----------. "Bartók és Kodály ismeretlen levelei. Zeneelméleti írásaik angol kiadásáról" [Unknown letters of Bartók and Kodály that concern the English publication of their writings on music theory]. *Tiszatáj* 19/10 (October 1975): 61-71.

> Seven letters between József Balogh, editor of the *Hungarian Quarterly,* and Bartók and Kodály discussing the theoretical ideas of

the two composers as presented in their articles, Bartók's published in 3/2 (1937), Kodály's in 5/2 (1939).

169. Gombocz, Adrienne. "Bartók Bernhard Paumgartnernak írt levelei" [Bartók's letters to Bernhard Paumgartner]. *Zenetudományi dolgozatok* (1989): 147-165.

Six letters by Bartók to Bernhard Paumgartner, the Austrian conductor and musicologist who led the Musikhistorische Zentrale in the Austrian war ministry between 1915 and 1917. These recently discovered documents, which are housed in the Österreichisches Staatsarchiv-Kriegsarchiv in Vienna and the Institut für Musikwissenschaft, Salzburg, address Bartók's collection of soldiers' songs during the First World War, the Historisches Konzert given in Vienna on January 12, 1918, and Bartók's essay on "Die Melodien der magjarischen Soldatenlieder," which was printed in the program notes for the latter musical event.

170. ----------. "Gárdony Zsigmondné, egy pártfogó a fiatal Bartók Béla életében" [Mrs. Zsigmond Gárdony, a patron of the young composer Béla Bartók]. *Magyar zene* (Budapest) 31/1 (March 1990): 86-93. ML5 M14   ISSN 0025-0384

Not examined. According to the author, *RILM Abstracts* No. 4080 (1990), "A survey of the moral and financial support lent by Róza Neumann Gárdony, wife of the ministerial counsellor Zsigmond Gárdony, to the career of the young composer and pianist Béla Bartók. Besides the correspondence between Gárdony and Bartók, eight letters to Gárdony from the composer's mother between 1900 and 1907 are published for the first time."

171. Laki, Peter, trans. "Travel Reports from Three Continents: A Selection of Letters from Béla Bartók." In *Bartók and His World*, ed. Peter Laki. Princeton, New Jersey: Princeton University Press, 1995. pp. 203-227.   ISBN 0-691-00633-4

As summarized by the editor, "In the five letters relating to Bartók's travels in Europe and his emigration to the United States, Bartók describes his current environment to close family members who are far away. The letters from Remete [12 and 13 April 1914] and from the estate of Baron Kohner [24 August 1918] are to his first wife, Márta Ziegler; those from the Swiss Alps [Arolla, 11 July 1930] and Cairo [19 March 1932] are to his second wife, Ditta Pásztory. The Christmas letter from New York [24 December 1940] was addressed to his two sons. The letters to Fritz Reiner [Budapest, 29 October 1928; New York, 17 May 1940, 18 January 1941; Denver, 16 February 1941; Vermont, 28 July 1941, 8 August 1941; New York, 8 October 1941, 27 October 1941, 2 August 1942] are taken from *Bartók Béla levelei* (Béla Bartók's letters), ed. János Demény (Budapest, 1976) [see item no. 155]." States that "Bartók's letters cover a wide array of topics, from ethnomusicology to nature to his American diet. The composer, so reticent about discussing his music, discloses a great deal about himself and his reactions to people and situations. The playful punning tone of the letters is also revealing. These letters add an important dimension to our understanding of a man whose personality has, in spite of an extensive biographical literature, in many ways continued to elude researchers." Contains notes.

172. László, Ferenc. "Bartók Béla és Constantin Brăiloiu tudományos együttműködésének újabb dokumentuma" [A new document on the research collaboration of Béla Bartók and Constantin Brăiloiu]. *Magyar zene* (Budapest) 31/4 (December 1990): 398-402. ML5 M14   ISSN 0025-0384

According to Mária Domokos, *RILM Abstracts* No. 5113 (1990), informs us that "a fragmentary letter by Bartók to Constantin Brăiloiu is published in the original German, with a translation into Hungarian and a commentary. The letter remarks on Brăiloiu's publication *Colinde şi cântece de Stea* (1931), and inquires about a record series devoted to folk music edited by Brăiloiu. Enclosed is a copy of a letter from Universal Edition regarding certification of Bartók's 'Aryan' parentage. The letter published here is dated 'after 13 April 1938,' and is the latest item of the correspondence between the two scholars." Contains musical examples. In Romanian in: *Anuarul arhivei de folclor* 12-14 (1991-1993). Sine loco: Editura Academiei Române 1993. pp. 327-331.

173. ----------. "Kiadatlan Bartók-levél Karl Votterle hagyatékában" [An unpublished Bartók letter in the estate of Karl Votterle]. *Magyar zene* 18/2 (June 1977): 216-217.   ML5 M14   ISSN 0025-0384

Previously unpublished letter (dated April 6,1932) from Bartók to the publisher, Bärenreiter, discussing permission to publish the *Violin Duos*.

174. Ruzicska, Paolo. "Una lettera inedita di Bartók al violinista Vecsey" [An unpublished letter of Bartók to the violinist Vecsey]. *Nuova rivista musicale italiana* 12/2 (April-June 1978): 251-253. 780.5 N928   ISSN 0029-6228

Previously unpublished letter from Bartók to the violinist Ferenc Vecsey (dated January 5, 1907). Provides important insight into Bartók's approach to Hungarian folk-music research.

175. Szepesi, Zsuzsanna. "Bartók-levelek az MTA Zenetudományi Intézet könyvtárának Major-gyűjteményében" [Bartók's letters in the Ervin Major collection in the library of the Magyar Tudományos Akadémia Zenetudományi Intézet, Budapest]. *Zenetudományi dolgozatok* (1988): 323-333.

> Not examined. In Hungarian; summary in German. According to the author, *RILM Abstracts* No. 103 (1988), includes "nine previously unpublished letters of Béla Bartók and transcriptions of three letters previously published in inaccurate versions." Contains facsimiles.

176. Tallián, Tibor. "Bartók levélváltása R. St. Hoffmann-nal" [The exchange of letters between Bartók and R. St. Hoffmann]. *Magyar zene* (Budapest) 14 (1973): 134-185.   781.05 St92
ISSN 0039-3266

> Includes correspondences in 1930 between Bartók and Rudolf Stefan Hoffmann (Viennese physician and musician) as well as letters by Bartók to Universal Edition concerning Hoffmann's German translation and related problems (rhythm of syllables) of *Twenty Hungarian Folk Songs* for voice and piano (1929), and *Four Hungarian Folk Songs,* for mixed chorus, a cappella (1930). Also published in German, in *Studia musicologica* 18/1-4 (1976): 339-365.

177. Weiss-Aigner, Günther. "Zwei unbekannte Briefe von Béla Bartók zu seinem Violinkonzert (op. posth.) 1907-1908 und seinem ersten Streichquartett (op. 7)" [Two previously unknown letters of Béla Bartók on his violin concerto (op. posth.) 1907-1908 and the first string quartet (op. 7)]. *Studia musicologia* 27/1-4 (1985): 379-392.
781.05 St92   ISSN 0039-3266

> According to Márta Szekeres-Farkas, in *RILM Abstracts* No. 3615 (1986), states that "A postcard from the French violinist Henri Marteau to Bartók was previously the only document pointing to correspondence between them. Probably Ernő Dohnányi facilitated a meeting, and Ferruccio Busoni may also have played an important role. Bartók's intention--after the break with Stefi Geyer--was to have his violin concerto played either by Marteau or Jenő Hubay. Marteau returned the materials for the violin concerto and the first string quartet to Bartók. The letters published here are: Bartók to Marteau, 10 May 1908; Marteau to Bartók, 19 May 1909; Bartók to Marteau, 8 June 1909." See also in *Gieseler Festschrift* (1985): 103-111.

5. *Documents, Pictures, Letters and Essays in Collected Editions*

178. Autexier, Philippe A. *Bartók Béla. Musique de la vie.* *Autobiographie, lettres et autres écrits choisis, traduits et présentés par Autexier Philippe A.* [Bartók Béla. Music of his life. Autobiography, letters and other writings selected, translated and presented by Philippe A. Autexier]. Paris: Stock, 1981. 226p. ML410 B26 A25

According to Jean-Michel Nectoux, in *RILM Abstracts* No. 952 (1981), "A translation/re-edition of Bartók's autobiography comprised of various letters and articles and based on the Artisjus edition. Includes a chronological outline of Bartók's life and a chronological catalogue of his œuvre." Includes list of works, discography.

179. Bónis, Ferenc, comp. *Bartók Béla élete képekben és dokumentumokban* [The life of Béla Bartók in pictures and documents]. Introduction by Bence Szabolcsi. Budapest: Zeneműkiadó, 1956, 1958; enlarged 2nd ed., 1972 (in Hungarian and German). 260p. ML410.B26 B66

Includes 105 photographs of Bartók at different times in his life, his family, friends, teachers, and places where he lived. Also includes illustrations, posters, concert programs, music examples, and maps. Other illustrations are added in the 1958 publication. See also the German translation: *Béla Bartóks Leben in Bildern.* Budapest, 1964; English translation by Lili Halápy, rev. by Kenneth McRobbie: *Béla Bartók. His Life in Pictures and Documents.* Budapest: Corvina, 1972. ML410.B26 B663 780.92 4 B; New York: Belwin Mills, 1972; Boosey and Hawkes, 1972; Vienna: Universal, 1973; Budapest: Zeneműkiadó, 1980; Budapest: Corvina, 1981; Budapest: Corvina Kiadó 1982. Foreword by Bónis serves as a guide for the chronological order of the biographical events. See reviews by: János Breuer, in *Magyar zene* 14/1 (March 1973): 101-104; Dale Higbee, in *American Recorder* 14/4 (November 1973): 140, in English; Wolfgang Suppan, in *Jahrbuch für Volksliedforschung* 21 (1976): 221-222; and Ferenc László, in *Korunk* 41/7 (July 1982): 566-568.

180. Helm, Everett. *Béla Bartók in Selbstzeugnissen und Bilddokumenten* [Béla Bartók in his own words and in pictorial documents]. Rowohlts Monographien 107. Reinbeck bei Hamburg: Rowohlt, 1965 and 1977. 156p. ML410.B26 H44

In addition to the primary source materials, contains bibliography of and about Bartók's works. See the review by Helmut Goldmann in *Musikforschung* 21/1 (January-March 1968): 118-119.

181. Liebner, János. "Bartók utolsó amerikai rádióinterjúi" [Bartók's last American radio interviews]. *Új zenei szemle* (Budapest) 6/12 (December 1955): 26-28. HA1.588

    Bartók's statements are heard on Bartók Records, and on "Bartók Record Archives: Bartók Plays and Speaks, 1912-1944," ed. László Somfai. *Hungaroton* LPX 12334-12338. See item no. 1102. Bartók's last two American radio statements were made in 1942, the year of his grave and exasperating financial straits. Includes discussion of his piano works being performed by Mrs. Bartók.

    Bartók breviárium (levelek, írások, dokumentumok) [Bartók breviary (correspondence, essays, documents)], ed. József Ujfalussy. Budapest: Zeneműkiadó, 1958, rev. edition by Vera Lampert, 1974. 556p.

    See item no. 135.

6. Folk Music Collections

182. *Cântece poporale românești din comitatul bihor (Ungaria); Chansons populaires roumanies du département bihar (Hongrie)* [Romanian folksongs from the Bihor district]. București: Academia Română Librăriile Socec & Comp. și C. Sfetea, 1913. xxii, 360p. DR212.A4 vol.14

    Contains 371 Romanian melodies. Represents the first results of Bartók's earliest investigations of Romanian folk music, in which he provides a description of the song types, their special performance characteristics, and the Romanian texts. See the reprint in *Bartók Béla: Ethnomusikologische Schriften, Faksimile-Nachdrucke* [Béla Bartók's writings on ethnomusicology in facsimile], ed. Denijs Dille (Budapest: Editio Musica, 1965-1968). See also "Preface to *Romanian Folk Songs from Bihor County* [1913]." Published in: *Béla Bartók Studies in Ethnomusicology,* ed. Benjamin Suchoff. Lincoln and London: University of Nebraska Press, 1996, pp. 1-23.

183. *Erdélyi Magyarság. Népdalok* [Transylvanian Hungarians. Folk songs.]. Budapest: Népies Irodalmi Társaság, n.d. [1923].

    Collection with Kodály of 150 Hungarian Transylvanian folksongs. Editions in Hungarian, French, and English. See also "Transylvanian Hungarians Folk Songs [1923] [Preface]." Published in: *Béla Bartók Studies in Ethnomusicology,* ed. Benjamin Suchoff. Lincoln and London: University of Nebraska Press, 1996, pp. 77-134.

184. *A magyar népdal* [The Hungarian folk song]. Budapest: Rózsavölgyi es Társa, 1924. Reprinted as *Das ungarische Volkslied*, in *Bartók Béla: Ethnomusikologische Schriften, Faksimile-Nachdrucke I*, ed. Denijs Dille. Budapest: Editio Musica; Mainz: B. Schott's Söhne, 1965. 472p.   ML 3593.B1615 1925a   780.81 B285,JD582e

This basic study of Hungarian folk music by Bartók sets in perspective the basic morphological aspects of Hungarian musical folklore. A large introductory discussion of the Hungarian folksong styles is subdivided into three classes (A, B, and C) based on old, new, and mixed Hungarian styles, which are dealt with in terms of scalar, syllabic, and formal structures as well as social function. This is followed by three Supplements: I. Statistical Data; II. Bibliography; and III. Commentary on Gypsy Musicians. The song texts and translations are followed by the musical examples, which include the transcription of 320 melodies (also organized according to old, new, and mixed Hungarian folk-song styles). This edition includes a facsimile of the original Hungarian version, pp. 341-432. Also contains illustrations and bibliography. See also the German edition: *Das ungarische Volkslied.* Berlin: Walter de Gruyter and Co., 1925. ML3593.B23 1925a; the first English edition: *Hungarian Folk Music.* London: Oxford University Press, 1931, including bibliographies and indexes. ISBN 0883557223   ML 3593.B1613 1979; the second English edition, *The Hungarian Folk Song,* ed. Benjamin Suchoff, trans. M. D. Calvocoressi. Albany: State University of New York Press, 1981. 454p.   ISBN 0873954394 ML3593.B1613 1981b (see item no. 196, below), and the critical edition in Hungarian and German, *A magyar népdal,* ed. Dorrit Révész. *Bartók Béla írásai 5.* Budapest: Musica, 1990. 368p. ISBN 963-330-696-5. See review of the first English edition by Bernard Van Dieren, in *Monthly Musical Record* 61 (November 1931): 330-333.

185. *Volksmusik der Rumänen von Maramureş* [Romanian folk music from Maramureş]. Munich: Drei Masken Verlag, 1923. Reprinted in *Bartók Béla: Ethnomusikologische Schriften, Faksimile-Nachdrucke II*, ed. Denijs Dille. Budapest: Editio Musica; Mainz: B. Schott's Söhne, 1966. xxxvii, 286p.   ML 3608.B37 780.81 B285,JD582e

Contains 365 melodies. Also contains illustrations, tables, and map. Appears in English translation in *Béla Bartók: Rumanian Folk Music,* Vol. V, ed. Benjamin Suchoff, trans. E.C. Teodorescu et al. The Hague: Martinus Nijhoff, 1975.   297p. See item no. 192, below.

186. *Rumänische Volkslieder aus dem Komitat Bihor* [Romanian folk songs from the district of Bihor]. Reprinted in *Bartók Béla:*

Ethnomusikologische Schriften, Faksimile-Nachdrucke III, ed. Denijs Dille. Budapest: Editio Musica; Mainz: B. Schott's Söhne,1967. xxii, 450p.   780.81 B285,JD582e

Not examined. Benjamin Suchoff states, in his review in *Music Library Association Notes* 25/3 (March 1969): 489-490, that this is a "reappearance of Bartók's first Rumanian folk music study as a facsimile reprint. In 1932, however, Bartók incorporated the Bihor material in the three volumes comprising his last and greatest work on Rumanian musical folklore which is included and revised thoroughly on the basis of the phonograph records. This facsimile reprint is therefore obsolete." Contains facsimiles, music, and map. See also the review by Erich Stockmann, in *Beiträge zur Musikwissenschaft* 13/3 (1971): 229-231.

187. *Melodien der rumänischen Colinde (Weihnachtslieder)* [Melodies of the Romanian *colinde* (Christmas songs)]. Vienna: Universal Edition A. G., 1935. xlvip., 1l, 106p.   M1718.B3 M52. Reprinted in *Ethnomusikologische Schriften, Faksimile-Nachdrucke IV* [Bartók's Writings on Ethnomusicology in Facsimile 4], ed. Denijs Dille. Budapest: Editio Musica; Mainz: B. Schott's Söhne, 1968. 538p. 780.81 B285,JD582e

Contains 484 transcriptions of Romanian Christmas songs as well as text material and notes. According to the publisher, *RILM Abstracts* No. 4531 (1969), this reprint appears "in a volume three times larger than the original publication, since the new edition contains also the complete text material, in the original language and in a German translation, as well as the full material of Bartók's notes. Dille's introduction deals with this important piece of Bartók's ethnomusicological activity from the point of view of the history of the work, of reports on the collection of the material, on the scientific and linguistic problems of the notation of folk music, and on Bartók's corrections." Contains music examples and bibliography. Appears in English translation in *Béla Bartók: Rumanian Folk Music,* Vol. IV, ed. Benjamin Suchoff, trans. E.C. Teodorescu et al. The Hague: Martinus Nijhoff, 1975. See the reviews by: Oskár Elschek in *Slovenská hudba* 15/5 (1971): 213-215; and Marius Schneider in *Musikbildung* 2/4 (February 1970): 191-192.

188. *Serbo-Croatian Folk Songs,* ed. Béla Bartók and Albert B. Lord. New York: Columbia University Press, 1951. xvii, 431p. ML3590.B3   784.49497

Appears as Vol. 7 of the Columbia University Studies in Musicology. Foreword by George Herzog. Includes texts and transcriptions of 75 folk songs from the Milman Parry Collection. Part I is by Bartók, Part II by Lord. Bartók's Introduction discusses the method of transcription, setting of bars and choice of values, certain peculiarities appearing in the present publication, pitch of melodies, methods in systematic grouping of folk melodies, the problem of variants, ornaments (grace notes), objectivity and subjectivity in transcribing and grouping folk music, and variability in folk music. The main discussion deals with the morphology of the vocal folk melodies, including stanza structure, scales, etc., followed by the transcriptions of the melodies. Also contains bibliography. Appears also as *Yugoslav Folk Music,* Vol. I, ed. Benjamin Suchoff. Albany: State University of New York Press, 1978.

189. *Corpus musicae popularis hungaricae* [A magyar népzene tára; A Hungarian folk-music thesaurus], ed. Béla Bartók and Zoltán Kodály. Budapest: Akadémiai Kiadó, 1951-1973. 6 vols. 780.821 C815

Comprehensive study containing large collections of folk songs as well as the texts of the songs. Includes: I. *Gyermekjátékok* [children's games], ed. György Kerényi, 1951, xl, 933p.; II. *Jeles napok* [festal days], ed. György Kerényi, 1953, xxiii, 1248p.; III a/b. *Lakodalom* [wedding songs], ed. L. Kiss, 1955 (Vol. IIIA), 1956 (Vol. IIIB), xliv, 1089p. and xii, 701p.; IV. *Párosítók* [pairing songs], ed. György Kerényi, 1959, 905p.; V *Siratók* [laments], ed. Benjamin Rajeczky and L. Kiss, 1966, 1139p.; VI. *Népdaltípusok* [Types of folksongs], ed. Pál Járdányi and Imre Olsvai, 1973, 831p. Contains substantial bibliographies, lists of collectors, notators, localities, music, syllabic numbers, cadences, and rhythmic patterns. Also contains illustrations and maps. See the reviews by: Imre Csanádi, in *Kortárs* 11/5 (May 1967): 696-699; István Halmos, in *Acta ethnographia academiae scientiarum hungaricae* 16/1-2 (1967): 184-185, in English; and Oskár Elschek, in *Musikforschung* 22/2 (April-June 1969): 248-250.

190. *Serbo-Croatian Heroic Songs* I, coll. Milman Parry, ed. and trans. by Albert B. Lord with musical transcriptions and commentary by Béla Bartók. Cambridge, Mass.: Harvard University Press; Belgrade: Serbian Academy of Sciences, 1953 [Vol I, 1954]. 479p. 784.49497 P265s 891.82 P249s v.1

Includes Bartók's musical transcriptions of "The Captivity of Đulić Ibrahim" (pp. 437-462), from the recordings in the Parry Collection. Also, includes extremely detailed notes to the music (pp. 463-467). Contains folding map and ports.

191. *Slovenské l'udové piesne* [Slovak folk songs], ed. Alica and Oskár Elschek. Bratislava: Vydavatel'stvo Slovenskej Akadémie Vied, vol. I, 1959; vol. II, 1970; vol. III, unpublished. 784.49437 B258S

Provides a detailed outline of the arrangement of the materials according to two methods of classification: the first deals with melody-line construction, caesura, syllabic structure, and compass; the second, which is applied after the materials are ordered according to the first method, is based on rhythm and stanza structure. Lists previous publications and discusses classification of variants published elsewhere. Discusses peculiarities of performance, describes instruments and how they are performed, discusses peculiarities in the text, and presents remarks on the texts and performers. Finally, discusses characteristics of genuine Slovak folk melodies, the so-called *Valaská* melodies, and non-autochthonous materials. See also "Introduction to *Slovak Folk Songs* [1959]." Published in: *Béla Bartók Studies in Ethnomusicology,* ed. Benjamin Suchoff. Lincoln and London: University of Nebraska Press, 1996, pp. 241-280.

192. *Rumanian Folk Music,* ed. Benjamin Suchoff, trans. E.C. Teodorescu et al. The Hague: Martinus Nijhoff, 1975. 5 vols.
  ISBN 90-247-0622X   M1718.B3 R7   784.4 B2811

The five volumes appear as volumes 2-6 of the New York Bartók Archive Studies in Musicology series: 2) I. Instrumental Melodies (1967, 704p.); 3) II. Vocal Melodies (1967, 756p); 4) III. Texts (1967, 661p.); 5) IV. Carols and Christmas Songs *(colinde)* (1975, 604p.); 6) V. Maramureş County (1975, 297p.). According to Clemens von Gleich, *RILM Abstracts* No. 4532 (1969), Volumes I-III "contain the Rumanian folk music materials collected by Bartók in 1908-1917, except for the winter solstice melodies *(colinde)* and those from the county of Maramureş; the material from the county of Bihor, published in 1913, is revised. The manuscript of the work--including 2184 hitherto unpublished melodies and 1752 poetic texts--was prepared by Bartók in 1940-1945." According to Bartók, "the work should be of special interest to researchers in music folklore, to ethnologists, and to linguists." Contains illustrations, plates, ports., bibliographies. See the following reviews: of Vols. I-III (1967) by Bálint Sárosi, trans. by Colin Mason, in *Tempo* 84 (Spring 1968): 31-35; John Weissmann in *Music and Letters* 49/4 (October 1968): 377-380; of Vols. I-II (1967) by Paul Henry Lang, in *Musical Quarterly* 54/4 (October 1968): 542-548; Bálint Sárosi, in *Muzsika* (Budapest) 11/8 (August 1968): 15-17; Halsey Stevens, in *Music Library Association Notes* 26/1 (September 1969): 126-127; Wolfgang Suppan, in *Musikforschung* 23/2 (April-June 1970): 225-226; and of Vols. IV-V (1975) by Halsey Stevens, in *Music Library Association Notes* 34/1 (September 1977): 58-61.

193. *Turkish Folk Music from Asia Minor,* ed. Benjamin Suchoff. Princeton and London: The Princeton University Press, 1976. 320p.
  ISBN 0-691-09120-X   ML3757.B37   781.7'561

Appears as Vol. 7 of the New York Bartók Archive Studies in Musicology series. Contains 66 melodies plus variants. Most substantial and thorough musicological analysis of Turkish folk music ever to be published and the first such study in English. Reproduces in facsimile Bartók's autograph record of 87 vocal and instrumental peasant melodies of the Yürük Tribes, a nomadic people in southern Anatolia. Bartók's introduction includes his annotations of the melodies, texts, and translations and establishes a connection between Old Hungarian and Old Turkish folk music. Bartók began the collection in 1936, completing the volume in 1943. Last major folk-music study of Bartók. Editor has provided an historical introduction and a chronology of the various manuscript versions. Afterword by Kurt Reinhard describes recent research in Turkish ethnomusicology and gives a contemporary assessment of Bartók's field work in Turkey. Appendices prepared by the editor include an index of themes compiled by computer. Contains also illustrations, music, bibliography. See the review by Halsey Stevens, in *Music Library Association Notes* 34/2 (December 1977): 342-344.

194. Saygun, A. Adnan. *Béla Bartók's Folk Music Research in Turkey,* ed. László Vikár. Trans. Samira B. Byron. Budapest: Akadémiai Kiadó, 1976. 430p.   ML3757.B368

Includes Bartók's original tabulation of the melodies and all of the original text, beginning with a 41-page facsimile of the autograph of Bartók's introduction. The latter discusses the structure of the melodies, special performance characteristics, the texts and their relation to the melodies. Contains facsimiles, illustrations, music. See reviews by: Vera Lampert in *Muzsika* 19/9 (September 1976): 26-28, and in *Studia musicologica* 18/1-4 (1976): 377-379; Wolfgang Suppan in *Jahrbuch Volksliedforschung* 22 (1977): 198; Halsey Stevens in *Music Library Association Notes* 34/2 (December 1977): 342-344; and Jean Gergely in *Revue de musicologie* 64/2 (1978): 280-284.

195. *Yugoslav Folk Music,* ed. Benjamin Suchoff. Albany: State University of New York Press, 1978. 4 vols.   ML3590.B32

Appears as Vols. 9-12 of the New York Bartók Archive Studies in Musicology series. With foreword by George Herzog. The four volumes include: 9) I. Serbo-Croatian Folk Songs (original publication: Béla Bartók and Albert B. Lord. *Serbo-Croatian Folk Songs.* New York: Columbia University Press, 1951); 10) II. Tabulation of Material; 11) III. Source Melodies: Part One; 12) IV. Source Melodies: Part Two. Includes 3,449 transcribed melodies, their analyses and tabulation, their description and classification, and the conclusions to be drawn from musical folklore as it pertains specifically to the Yugoslav cultural territory. An essential reference for research on musical folklore for ethnomusicologists, linguists,

and specialists in Balkan ethnology or cultural anthropology.
Provides the scholar and student with a general introduction to the
field of ethnomusicological methodology, problems likely to be
encountered, and Bartók's approach to their solution. Contains
illustrations, music.

196. *The Hungarian Folk Song,* ed. Benjamin Suchoff, trans. M.D.
Calvocoressi. Albany: State University of New York Press, 1981.
454p.   ISBN 0873954394   ML3593.B1613 1981b.

See item no. 184 for the original publication. This second
English edition of Bartók's *A magyar népdal,* which appears as Vol.
13 of the New York Bartók Archive Studies in Musicology series,
expands the original volume in many important ways. Suchoff
provides a preface that includes the history of Hungarian
ethnomusicology, a discussion of the Bartók-Kodály relationship, a
comparison of approaches by Bartók and others to the systematic
classification of Hungarian musical folklore, a review of related
literature with emphasis on variant relationships based on data
extracted from source materials published as recently as 1979 and
previously unavailable or new data on Bartók's biography, research
methods, and approach to musical composition. Also contains five
extremely important editorial appendices: I. Addenda and Corrigenda;
II. Provisory List of Variants and Reprints Published Elsewhere; III.
Tabulation of Material; IV. Index of Rhythm Schemata; and V.
Thematic Index of the Tabulated Melodies. In addition are an Index
of First Lines and a General Index. This edition also contains Zoltán
Kodály's annotations of the Bartók texts and the musical examples.
See the reviews by: Anthony Cross in *The Musical Times* 122/1665
(November 1981): 747ff; and Helen Myers in *Folk Music Journal*
(1983): 415-417.

197. *A Magyar népdal* [Hungarian folk song], ed. Dorrit Révész. *Bartók
Béla írásai* 5. Budapest: Musica, 1990. 368p.   ISBN 963-330-696-5

See item no. 184 for the original publication. In Hungarian and
German. According to the editor, *RILM Abstracts* No. 5947 (1991),
this constitutes "a critical edition of Bartók's first book-length work
on Hungarian folk song, based on the first Hungarian edition
(Budapest, 1924) and revised on the basis of all manuscripts and
corrected copies in Hungarian and American archives, including
German and English editions. The appendices of the German and
English editions are provided here, as is the first German-language
draft, with 81 melodies in facsimile. Detailed maps (planned by
Bartók but omitted from all previous editions) and an index of place
names are included." Contains illustrations, facsimiles, music
examples, bibliography, index.

198. *Hungarian Folk Songs: Complete Collection* I, ed. Sándor Kovács and Ferenc Sebő. Budapest: Akadémiai Kiadó, 1993. 1206p. English version of the original Hungarian *Magyar népdalok. Egyetemes gyűjtemény.* Budapest: Akadémiai Kiadó, 1991. ISBN 963-05-6315-0 (Volume I)

Commissioned by the Hungarian Academy of Sciences from 1934 to 1940. The nine projected volumes contain about 13,500 melodies (classified and annotated by Bartók and partly by Kodály), which are systematized and supplied with notes. In the present volume (I), Kovács provides a thorough commentary on the history of the Bartók system of Hungarian folk music, including: I. the evolution of the Bartók system; II. posthumous publication of the collection, types of sources and problems of publication, and principles of the edition; III. Structure of the melody-classification system; IV. Bartók's tabulation of rhythm (facsimile), and explanation of the signs used in the music notation. This is followed by the tune collection (Class AI, Nos. 1-416), including translation of notes. Sebő provides the indexes, including: translation of Hungarian expressions, Bartók-system number index, and indexes of melody types, cadences, rhythm, first lines, sources, collectors, singers, and places. Contains list of places according to counties and list of illustrations. Illustrations include facsimile reproductions of transcriptions and photographs.

7. Facsimiles, Reprints, and Revisions of the Music

199. Bartók, Péter, and Nelson Dellamaggiore, eds. *Béla Bartók, Viola Concerto: Facsimile Edition of the Autograph Draft.* Preface by Peter Bartók, with a Commentary by László Somfai, and Fair Transcription of the Draft with Notes Prepared by Nelson Dellamaggiore. Homosassa, Florida: Bartók Records, 1995. 84p. ISBN 0-9641961-0-7   M2.8 B27 C68

Preface, commentary, and notes are presented in English, Hungarian, German, Chinese, and Spanish. Regarding Tibor Serly's orchestral realization of the original sketch, Peter Bartók states in his Preface that "determinations had to be made by Tibor Serly, who exercised his judgment and discretion in assembling the mosaic and filling the gaps. The question has been asked: how much is Bartók, what details come from Serly? Or, if different solutions to the problems are attempted by others, the same question can be posed regarding their decisions. To provide answers to such questions is the objective of this publication." Somfai's Commentary includes a history of the manuscript, a survey of the paper structure and the contents of the pages, data on the genesis of the *Viola Concerto* (including correspondences between Bartók and William Primrose), and notes on the concept and the survived form of the music (including information on links between the movements, the page written in ink, the elaboration of the texture of the orchestra, and notes about the instrumentation). Dellamaggiore's Notes include a list describing how some of the details were approached while preparing the fair copy (including information on stems, clefs, accidentals, unused data, ambiguities, and ties). Also contains printed musical form of the autograph manuscript.

200. Dille, Denijs, ed. *Béla Bartók and Zoltán Kodály. Hungarian Folksongs for Voice with Piano.* English trans. Ilona L. Lukács. Budapest: Editio Musica, 1970. 54p.

Facsimile edition of the original manuscript with detailed commentary, including description of both Bartók's and Kodály's handwritten notes in ink and pencil. Refers to their corrections, deletions, condition of the leaves, etc.

201. ---------------. *Béla Bartók: Ethnomusikologische Schriften, Faksimile-Nachdrucke* [Béla Bartók: ethnomusicological writings in facsimile]. Budapest: Editio Musica; Mainz: B. Schotts Söhne, 1965-1968. 4v.   780.81 B285,JD582e

The four volumes include: I. *Das ungarische Volkslied,* 1965; II. *Volksmusik der Rumänen von Maramureş,* 1966; III. *Rumänische Volkslieder aus dem Komitat Bihor,* 1967; IV. *Melodien der rumänischen Colinde (Weihnachtslieder),* 1968. Contains bibliography.

202. Somfai László, ed. *Bartók Béla fekete zsebkönyve: Vázlatok 1907-1922* [Béla Bartók, black pocket-book: sketches 1907-1922]. Budapest: Zeneműkiadó (= Editio Musica), 1987. 65p. M2.8 B27 B5

Facsimile edition of the manuscript edited by László Kalmár (34p.), with commentary in Hungarian, English, and German by László Somfai (31p.). This pocket-book is one of many that Bartók used for the first notation of melodies on folk-song collecting trips. Contains sketch excerpts of passages from many of Bartók's compositions from the period between 1907 and 1922. Also includes other handwritten items, such as themes from two of Schubert's symphonies as well as names and addresses.

203. ----------. *Béla Bartók, Andante for Violin and Piano (1902).* Budapest: Zeneműkiadó (= Editio Musica Budapest), 1980. 7p. M221.B273 A55 1980

A reprint of the original manuscript appears here for the first time. Commentary in Hungarian, German, and English provides historical information regarding the origin of the work, including discussion regarding its composition for the eldest of the Arányi daughters. Also states in the commentary that this edition basically adheres to the autograph fair copy with the authenticity of an Urtext edition.

204. ----------------. *Béla Bartók, Két román tánc zongorára. Az eredeti kézirat fakszimile (Bartók Archívum, Budapest).* [*Two Romanian Dances* for piano. Facsimile of the original manuscript (Bartók Archive, Budapest)]. Budapest: Zeneműkiadó (= Editio Musica Budapest), 1974. 38p. ML96.5.B27 no. 2 M30 M1718

Reprint of the original manuscript of Op. 8a, consisting of fourteen pages of music. This is followed by Somfai's commentary in Hungarian, with English translation by Fred Macnicol. First, discusses Bartók's own interest in supporting Urtext and facsimile editions. Then, provides a history of the manuscript, the engraver's workshop notes, Bartók's final notes in the manuscript, discussion of the lost proofs of the first edition, the corrected second edition, the last revision of the *First Romanian Dance,* and marks of the creative process on the manuscript. Contains musical illustrations and appendix.

205. ----------------. *Béla Bartók, Sonata (1926) Piano Solo.* Budapest: Zeneműkiadó (= Editio Musica Budapest), 1980. 150p. 786.4 Bar

Facsimile edition of the manuscript. Represents an intermediary draft stage (NYBA No. 55 PID1) of the work. Contains commentary by Somfai, which gives the chronology of the work. Also provides a useful list with explanations of additions and corrections made in the manuscript by Bartók before he sent the copy to the publisher.

206. Suchoff, Benjamin, ed. *Piano Music of Béla Bartók--The Archive Edition.* New York: Dover Publications, 1981. Series I. 167p. ISBN 0-486-24108-4; Series II. 192p. ISBN 0-486-24109-2

Edition of the early piano music in two volumes: Series I and II. Includes detailed introductory commentary regarding these authentic performing versions as well as discussion of the editorial annotations reflecting musicological scholarship based on primary source materials. Intention is to serve as an intermediary stage in the future preparation of the complete and critical edition of Bartók's works. Also, the annotations are intended to provide an aid for interpretation of the music and for understanding and appreciating the composer. Includes many facsimiles of the autograph manuscripts.

III. BIOGRAPHICAL AND HISTORICAL STUDIES

1. General Studies of Bartók's Life and Music, His Background, Time, and Forebears

207. Antokoletz, Elliott. "Béla Bartók in Eastern Europe and the United States." In Elliott Antokoletz, *Twentieth-Century Music*, pp. 106-140. Englewood Cliffs, N.J.: Prentice Hall, 1992. ISBN 0-13-934126-9   ML 197.A63

   Detailed historical and analytical survey of Bartók's musical development. Outlines the basic sources of Bartók's style, then discusses Bartók's evolution according to the following: Germanic musical influences (1897 to 1902); influence of Liszt, the Magyar nóta, and first contact with authentic Hungarian folk music (1902-1905); Bartók's first folk-music investigations, his discovery of Debussy, and early compositional results (1905 through World War I); expanded folk-music investigations and first mature compositions; move toward synthesis of divergent art- and folk-music sources; activities from end of World War I to mid-1920s; last stylistic period (1926-1945); and final years in the United States (1940-1945). Includes in-depth analyses of No. 1 of the *Eight Hungarian Folksongs* for voice and piano (1907-1917), No. XI of the *Fourteen Bagatelles*, Op. 6, for piano (1908), Nos. VIII and III of the *Eight Improvisations on Hungarian Peasant Songs*, Op. 20 (1920), *Fourth String Quartet* (1928), and some analysis (including Bartók's own commentary) of the *Concerto for Orchestra* (1943). Contains music examples, diagrams, and suggested readings.

208. Ban, Louise G. *Bartók Béla.* Budapest: Zeneműkiadó, 1971. 191p.

   Published in English and Hungarian. Biography commemorates the twenty-fifth anniversary of Bartók's death. Includes discussion of the composer's childhood and apprentice years (1881-1919), the interwar period (1920-1940), and his final years in the United States (1940-1945). Illustrated.

209. *Bartók* (Video). Produced and directed by Curtis W. Davis. Canadian Broadcasting Corporation and Hungarian TV, 1981. 58 minutes.

   Documentary presenting an overview of the composer's life. Includes interviews with Béla Bartók, Jr., Ditta Pásztory, Paul Henry

Lang, Antal Molnár, and readings from Bartók's letters. Presents musical excerpts from *Concerto for Orchestra, Evening in Transylvania* (orchestral version), *Allegro barbaro, The Wooden Prince, The Miraculous Mandarin, First Piano Concerto, Sonata for Two Pianos and Percussion, Violin Concerto* (1938), and *Sixth String Quartet.*

210. Bartók, Béla, Jr. *Apám életének krónikája* [Chronicle of my father's life]. Budapest: Zeneműkiadó, 1981. 473p.　ISBN 9633304040 ML 410 B26 B268

Practically a day-by-day account of the composer's musical life by his son. This chronology is grouped into periods of several years each according to specific activities.

211. Bartók, Béla, Jr. *Bartók Béla műhelyében* [In Béla Bartók's workshop]. Budapest: Szépirodalmi Könyvkiadó, 1982.

Contains much useful information, including listings of acquaintances of the composer and comprehensive lists of his performing locations.

212. Bartók, Béla, Jr. "Mein Vater　Béla Bartók--sein Weg für die moderne Musik" [My father Béla Bartók--his path for modern music]. *Universitas: Zeitschrift für Wissenschaft, Kunst und Literatur* 20/3 (March 1965): 291-297.　AP 4 U57　ISSN 0341-0129 ISSN 0041-9079

Not examined. According to William Austin, *Music in the 20th Century*, New York: W.W. Norton and Co., 1966: 564, this statement by the composer's son is a "touching account of 'an exemplary life that can justly be set beside his epochmaking activity as musician.'"

213. Boys, Henry. "Béla Bartók, 1881-1945." *Musical Times* 86 (October 1945): 41.　780.5 M98　ISSN 0027-4666

Eulogy discusses Bartók as an idealist. Provides the basic history of his career as composer, folk-music collector, and performer. Evaluates the composer's overall stylistic development and speaks of the tragedy of an interrupted career in which the composer still had so much to say, especially at a time when the public was just beginning to understand and appreciate his musical idiom.

214. Chalmers, Kenneth. *Béla Bartók.* London: Phaidon Press, 1995. 239p.　ISBN 0-7148-3164-6

Comprehensive biographical and historical discussion geared to the general reader but also provides significant information on Bartók's life and surrounding political and social events essential for music students and scholars. Key biographical events or features in various periods of Bartók's life serve as chapter titles, which are aimed at accessibility and the interest of the nonspecialist. These include: (1) "Hungary's Future Beethoven 1881-99"; (2) "A Red Apple Drops 1899-1907"; (3) "Portrait of a Girl 1907-9"; (4) Seven Doors All Barred and Bolted 1909-18"; (5) "A Strain of Harsh Asceticism 1918-30"; (6) "The Clearest Springs 1930-39"; and (7) "Two Pale Emigrants 1939-45." Contains no musical analyses, only brief stylistic descriptions for individual works. Musical comments are often in journalese and somewhat subjective. Includes a wealth of pertinent photographs, illustrations, and some autograph facsimiles. Contains classified list of works, basic bibliography indicated as further reading, selective discography, index.

215. Csobádi, Péter. *Bartók*. Budapest: Országos Béketanács, 1955. 62p.

Main aim of this study was apparently to provide simplified and accessible information about the composer's life and work.

216. Demény, János. *Bartók*. Budapest: Egyetemi Nyomda, 1946. 41p.

Provides a view of Bartók's special qualities as a human being. Also surveys Bartók's entire compositional activity. However, omits some rudimentary biographical information and is inadequate in terms of musical analysis.

217. ----------. *Béla Bartók*. Budapest: Magyar-Szovjet Társaság-Kulturkapcsolatok Int., 1955. 37p.

As a result of the interest that developed from the Bartók celebrations held in various cities in the Soviet Union, the author provided a biographical study based on the most recent research by Hungarian Bartók scholars. Also includes new information on the last years of Bartók's life.

218. ----------. *Bartók élete és művei* [Bartók's life and works]. Budapest: Székesfőváros: Irodalmi és Művészeti Intézet, 1948. 119p.
ML 410 B26 D4

Comprehensive documentary biography, which provides an accurate and detailed account of Bartók's career. Adds new information regarding the previously unpublished late works. Also includes chapters on Bartók as ethnomusicologist and pianist.

219. ----------. "Bartók Béla tanulóévei és romantikus korszaka (1899-1905)" [Béla Bartók's student years and romantic period], *Erkel*

Ferenc és Bartók Béla emlékére [*Zenetudományi tanulmányok, 2*], Bence Szabolcsi and Dénes Bartha, eds. Budapest: Akadémiai Kiadó, 1954, pp. 323-487.

First part of Bartók's biography, dealing with the composer's student years at the Royal Academy of Music in Budapest (1899-1903) and the following years (to 1905) in which Bartók turned to the Romantic influence of Liszt. Includes Bartók's nationalistic period, in which he composed *Kossuth* (1903), a symphonic poem on the life of the Hungarian patriot and revolutionary hero.

220. ----------. "Bartók Béla művészi kibontakozásának évei I--Találkozás a népzenével (1906-1914)" [The years of Bartók's artistic evolution (I)--encounter with folk music (1906-1914)], *Liszt Ferenc és Bartók Béla emlékére.* [*Zenetudományi tanulmányok, 3*]. Bence Szabolcsi and Dénes Bartha, eds. Budapest: Akadémiai Kiadó, 1955), pp. 286-459.

Second part of Bartók's biography, in which Bartók entered his first mature period of great compositional originality and moved toward isolation from the Hungarian public (1906-1914). These years also mark his first extensive investigations of Hungarian, Slovak, and Romanian folk music.

221. ----------. "Bartók Béla művészi kibontakozásának évei (II)--Bartók megjelenése az európai zeneéletben (1914-1926)" [The years of Bartók's artistic evolution (II)--Bartók's appearance in European musical life (1914-1926)], *Bartók Béla megjelenése az európai zeneéletben (1914-1926); Liszt ferenc hagyatéka.* [*Zenetudományi tanulmányok, 7*], Bence Szabolcsi and Dénes Bartha, eds. Budapest: Akadémiai Kiadó, 1959, pp. 5-425.

Third part of Bartók's biography, the years in which he found acceptance in the most progressive circles.

222. ----------. "Bartók Béla pályája delelőjén-teremtő évek--Világhódító alkotások (1927-1940)" [Béla Bartók at the height of his career--creative years--world-conquering works (1927-1940)]. *Bartók Béla emlékére (Zenetudományi tanulmányok, 10).* Bence Szabolcsi and Dénes Bartha, eds. Budapest: Akadémiai Kiadó, 1962, pp. 189-727.

Fourth part of Bartók's biography, which includes his last creative period in Europe.

223. ----------. "Béla Bartóks Stellung in der Musikgeschichte des 20. Jahrhunderts" [Bartók's place in the history of music of the twentieth century]. *Studia musicologica* 5 (1963): 403-414. 781.05 St92   ISSN 0039-3266

A general overview of the periods of Bartók's life and works, illustrating the impact and importance of his works for us today.

224. Dille, Denijs. *Béla Bartók.* Mededelingen van de Koninklijke Academie voor Wetenschappen, Letteren en Schone Kunsten 34/3. Bruxelles: Academie voor Wetenschappen, 1972. 15p.

Discusses Bartók as composer, pedagogue, pianist, and ethnomusicologist. Includes illustrations and facsimiles.

225. Gergely, Jean, ed. *Béla Bartók vivant: Souvenirs, études, et témoignages* [Béla Bartók lives: Recollections, studies, and tributes]. *Bibliothèque finno-ougrienne* 2. Paris: Publications Orientalistes de France, 1984. 220 p.

These writings about Bartók by many Hungarian musicians provide insight into various areas of Bartók's life and work. Contains illustrations, facsimiles, music examples.

226. Gergely, Jean, and Vigué, Jean. *Conscience musicale ou conscience humaine? Vie, oeuvre et héritage spirituel de Béla Bartók* [Musical conscience or human conscience? The life, works, and spiritual heritage of Béla Bartók]. *Bibliothéque finno-ougrienne* 7. Paris: Revue Musicale; Budapest: Akadémiai, 1990. 250p.

Study of Bartók's life and works, including discussions of his musical aesthetics, style, and techniques. Provides insight into his personality as well as his work as ethnomusicologist, performer, and pedagogue. Contains illustrations, music examples, bibliography, list of works. See review by Pierre Citron, in *Revue de musicologie* 76/2 (1990): 257-258.

227. Gombocz-Konkoly, Adrienne, and Gillies, Malcolm G.W. "Az első Bartókról szóló könyv terve: Frank Whitaker vázlatai a British Library kézirattárában" [Plan of the first book on Bartók: Frank Whitaker's drafts in the manuscript collection of the British Library]. *Magyar zene* 32/4 (December 1991): 410-424. ML5 M14   ISSN 0025-0384

According to Adrienne Gombocz-Konkoly, *RILM Abstracts* No. 4670 (1991), "The English journalist Frank Whitaker (1893-1962) planned a book on Bartók in the mid 1920s, to be published by Oxford University Press. The work was never finished. The draft manuscript, preserved in the British Library, contains biographical data and analyses of several early works. Gombocz-Konkoly gives an account of Whitaker's research, and Gillies evaluates Whitaker's musical analyses." Contains facsimiles.

228. Griffiths, Paul. *Bartók*. London and Melbourne: J.M. Dent and Sons, Ltd., 1984. [Part of Master Musicians Series] ix, 224p. ISBN 0460-031821   ML 410 B26 G7   780.92/4 B19

Combines biography with some detailed analyses of works from various periods. Deals with Bartók's childhood and youth, folk-song studies, romantic influences, application of folk-song to his compositions, thorough analyses of the stage works, post-war crises, etc. The author asserts that this book profits from the scores, recordings, and documentation that had not been available to earlier general writers on Bartók. The book owes much to the catalogue of works established in *The New Grove* article by László Somfai and Vera Lampert. Has useful biographical calendar (see appendix A). Contains plates, map, illustrations, music, ports., bibliography, index.

229. Haraszti, Emil. *Béla Bartók, His Life and Works*. Paris: Lyrebird Press, 1938. 105p.   780.92 B285 Hts

Gives colorful descriptions of selected works from various genres. Though the analyses reveal little depth, the work contains some interesting historical and biographical discussions. Contains illustrations, port., list of works, bibliography.

230. Helm, Everett. *Bartók*. London: Faber & Faber, 1971. 80p. ISBN 05710091059   ML 410 B26 H4   NBNB 71-17373 780.924ab

Significant reduction of the text of the original German version (Hamburg, 1965). Includes a condensed biographical section and a brief assessment of the music. Not based on in-depth analysis but rather shows the interrelationship of the works in different forms and media. Includes an account of Bartók's folk-music research as well as Bartók's final years in America. See the review by John S. Weissman, in *Tempo* 99 (April 1972): 20-21. Contains illustrations, facsimiles, music, ports., bibliography.

231. Kroó, György. *Bartók kalauz* [A guide to Bartók]. Budapest: Zeneműkiadó; Corvina,1971. English translation by Ruth Pataki and Maria Steiner, Budapest: Corvina, 1974. 248p.; German translation [Bartók Handbuch] Wien: Universal, 1974; Budapest: Zeneműkiadó, 1980.   MT 92 B73 K8

Guide for music lovers. Gives basic information on Bartók's major orchestral, stage, and chamber music, presenting them in chronological order from *Kossuth* to the *Third Piano Concerto*. Includes the means for locating compositions within their genres, and provides brief discussions of the musical characteristics of the works. Also, contains material from both the Budapest and New

York Bartók Archives. Contains bibliography. See reviews of the book by: János Breuer, *Magyar zene* (Budapest) 13/2 (June 1972): 206-207; Ferenc László, *A hét* 3/21 (May 26, 1972): 8; and Wolfgang Suppan, *Jahrbuch Volksliedforschung* 21 (1976): 222. See the reviews of the German translation by: Egon Kraus, *Musikbildung* 7/11 (1975): 596; Wolfram Schwinger, *Muzsica* 29/6 (1975): 528; and Hartmut Fladt, *Melos/Neue Zeitung für Musik* 2/1 (1976): 68-69.

232. Lesznai, Lajos. *Béla Bartók: Sein Leben--seine Werke* [Béla Bartók: his life and works]. Leipzig: Deutscher Verlag für Musik, 1961. 212p. ML 410 B26 L5. English translation by Percy M. Young, in *The Master Musicians Series*. London: Dent, 1973. xii, 219p. ISBN 0460031368   ML 410 B26 L53   780.92/4 B; also New York: Octagon, 1973-1974.

Many biographical details based on special inquiries among those who knew Bartók personally. Attempts to find connections between his life and works and the pattern of the times in which he lived. Also explores Bartók's musicological development. Emphasizes the importance of Hungarian folk music in understanding Bartók's compositions. Contains illustrations, bibliography. See the review by Elizabeth Hiatt Olmsted, in *Choice* 11/5-6 (July-August 1974) : 769.

233. Lindlar, Heinrich. *Lübbes Bartók Lexicon* [Lübbe's Bartók dictionary]. Bergisch Gladbach: Gustav Lübbe, 1984. ML 410 B26 L6

Provides brief, relevant synopses of most issues concerning Bartók biography and analysis. See review by: Ferenc László, in *Magyar zene* 26/3 (September 1985): 331-332.

234. Mari, Pierrette. *Bartók. Clásicos de la música* [Bartók. Classics of music]. Madrid: Espasa-Calpe, 1985. 128p.

Not examined. In *RILM Abstracts* No. 3794 (1987), indicated as a study of Bartók's "life and works."

235. Martynov, Ivan. *Béla Bartók*. Moskva: Sovetskiy Kompozitor, 1968. 288p.   ML 410 B26 M34   USSR 68-13522

According to *RILM Abstracts* No. 708 (1968), this book includes a study of "the life and work of Bartók, with analytical critique of his major works." According to *RILM Abstracts,* No. 3630 (1968): "Bartók's democratic views and his interest in the ancient folk elements in music are due, in part, to the influence of the Russian realists of the nineteenth century. The folk basis of Bartók's works is closely related to his innovative research. His discovery (together with Kodály) of a hitherto-unknown layer of

Hungarian and Rumanian folklore is considered of great aesthetic and scientific importance. The author also discusses Bartók's principal musicological writings (Hungarian folk melodies; Liszt and the modern audience)." Contains illustrations, music, bibliography.

236. ----------. *Béla Bartók. Ocherk zhizni i tvorchestva* [Béla Bartók: sketch of his life and work]. Moscow: Muzgiz, 1956. 168p.

Not examined. According to the listing of the State Lenin Library of the USSR, this study "contains illustrations" and "includes a list of Bartók's works, pp. 164-168."

237. Mihály, András. *Bartók Béla.* Budapest: T.T.I.T., 1955. 41p.

Provides clear and accessible information for the general musical public rather than for those interested in scholarly research.

238. Moreux, Serge. *Béla Bartók , sa vie, ses oeuvres, son langage* [Béla Bartók, his life, his works, his language]. Paris: Richard-Massé, 1949, 1955. 128p., 323p. ML 410 B26 M6. Preface by Arthur Honegger. English trans. G.S. Fraser and Erik de Mauny. London: Harvill Press: 1953. 256p. ML 410 B26 M67. Also New York: Vienna House, 1974. 224p. [Partial reprint of the1953 edition (London: Harvill). German trans. Zürich: Atlantis Verlag, 1950. 165p. Danish trans. by Sven Møller Kristensen. Copenhagen: J. H. Schultz Forlag, 1951. Japanese trans. of the 1955 edition. Tokyo: David Co., Ltd., 1957.

Aside from a number of fundamental errors, the work provides some important basic information. Generally, more sketchy than other studies of Bartók's life and works. Organization tends to be somewhat haphazard, and certain works are discussed at length, while others are omitted altogether. Generally, a superficial study of the music. The 1949 edition contains illustrations, ports., music, catalogue of works by genre. The 1953 edition contains bibliography, recordings of Bartók's works, and appendix with two articles by Bartók.

239. Nest'yev, Izrail. *Béla Bartók 1881-1945: zhizn' i tvorchestvo* [Bartók: life and works]. Moscow: Muzyka, 1969. 797p. ML 410 B26 N5

According to the author, in *RILM Abstracts* No. 1761 (1969), this study contains "analysis of the principal works, evaluation of the composer's world outlook and aesthetic views, and discussion of features of his style. Traces those links that unite Bartók to Hungarian folk music and to the national art and its artistic traditions. Compares his music to Russian and West-European music of the twentieth century." See review by János Marothy in *Muzsika*

(Budapest) 14/1 (January 1971): 41-43. Contains illustrations, music, bibliography, index.

240. Nordwall, Ove. *Béla Bartók. Traditionalist/modernist.* Stockholm: Svenska Musikförlaget, 1972. 128p.   ML 410 B26 N7

Includes biographical and autobiographical materials in addition to a study of a number of Bartók's works in the context of their relationship to traditional and modern features of other composers (including Messiaen, Stravinsky, Berg, Webern, and Ligeti). Also, includes some analysis based on Lendvai's "polar-axis" system (e.g., tonal relations in *Bluebeard).* Contains bibliography of works by and about Bartók.

241. Orbán, László. "Bartók's Message Has Never Been More Topical Than Today." *International Musicological Conference in Commemoration of Béla Bartók 1971,* ed. József Ujfalussy and János Breuer. Budapest: Editio Musica; New York: Belwin Mills, 1972, pp. 9-10.   ML410.B29 I61 [Editio Musica]   ML410.B26 I5 [Belwin Mills]

Statement by the First Deputy Minister of Culture and Education of the Hungarian People's Republic at the opening of the IMC of UNESCO. Organized with the aim of exploring the life and works of Bartók to acquire more knowledge through an international exchange of views on the results of research conducted throughout the world. Discusses the spiritual heritage of Bartók and his significance in the cultural heritage of the twentieth century.

242. Somfai, László, and Vera Lampert. "Béla Bartók." *The New Grove Dictionary of Music and Musicians,* II., 6th ed. Stanley Sadie. London: Macmillan Publishers Ltd., 1980, pp. 197-225. ISBN-0-333-23111-2   ML100.N48   780'.3

Discusses Bartók's biographical development in five categories: childhood and student years; discoveries of Strauss, folk music, and Debussy; neglect and success (1910-1920); concert tours; and his last years (stemming from the threat of fascism). His works are discussed in five categories: early works (1889-1907); establishment of the mature style (1908-1911); years of extension (1911-1924); classical middle period (1926-1937); and his last works (1938-1945). Includes list of works and their data as well as bibliographies of primary and secondary sources. Also published in *Tizennyolc Bartók tanulmány.* Budapest: Editio Musica, 1981, pp. 5-30. See the expanded version in *The New Grove: Modern Masters, Bartók, Stravinsky, Hindemith.* London: Macmillan Limited; New York and London: W.W. Norton & Company, 1984. pp. 1-101. Additions include mention of more recent theoretical studies of Bartók's music and an expanded bibliography.

243. Stevens, Halsey. *The Life and Music of Béla Bartók.* New York: Oxford University Press, 1953; rev. New York University Press, 1964. 364p.   ML 410 B26 S8   780.92. See also the 1967 reprint of the 1953 and 1964 editions, London: Oxford University, 1967; and the Japanese trans. Naosuke Uyama, Tokyo: Kinokuniya Books, 1961. Third edition, prepared by Malcolm Gillies, Oxford: Clarendon Press, 1993.   ISBN 0-19-816349-5

     The first and most important monograph on Bartók in English. Biographical material is derived from several sources: an autobiographical sketch (1921); letters both published and unpublished; a biography of his childhoood and youth (1921-1922) by his mother, Paula Voit; early manuscripts in Hungary and the New York Bartók Archive; and assistance in preparing the later edition of this biography from Victor Bator, former Trustee of the Estate of Béla Bartók, Bence Szabolcsi, and others. Contains illustrations, facsimiles, music, ports., chronological list of works, extensive bibliography of works by and about Bartók, bibliographic footnotes, discography (only in the 1953 edition). See the reviews by: Otto Gombosi, in *Music Library Association Notes* (September 1953): 621-622; Colin Mason, "Bartók and Background," *Musical Times* 106 (1965): 355; and John Vinton, in *Music Library Association Notes* (Summer 1966): 1220-1222.

244. Suchoff, Benjamin. "Béla Bartók, The Master Musician." *Music Educators Journal* (October 1981): 34-57 passim.   780.5 M973 ISSN 0027-4321

     Includes a study of Bartók's life, his Hungarian music dialect, his fusion of national music styles, synthesis of East and West, and his folk-style composition. Many of Bartók's works are referred to in these categories.

245. Szabolcsi, Bence. "Bartók Béla élete" [Bartók's life]. *Csillag* 9 (1955): 18-55.   HA3.437 See the German translation in *Béla Bartók, Weg und Werk, Schriften und Briefe,* ed. Bence Szabolcsi. Budapest: Corvina, 1957, pp. 9-45.   ML410.B28 A32 1957

     Presents a detailed chronological discussion of Bartók's family history and his stylistic musical development (its sources and influences). Begins with some general nineteenth-century history in Europe and its significance in relation to the Hungarian national condition and cultural development. Moves from Bartók's early years in Pozsony, etc., through his last years.

     Bartók, sa vie et son œuvre [Bartók, his life and work], ed. Bence Szabolcsi.

See item no. 133

246. ----------. *Béla Bartók, Leben und Werk* [Béla Bartók, life and work]. Leipzig: Philipp Reclam, 1961. 96p.   ML410.B292 S99be; enlarged 2/Jun 1968. 205p.   ML410.B26 S885 1968

Extensive biography. Includes selected illustrations and commentary by Ferenc Bónis, letters selected and assembled by János Demény, and a complete discography compiled by László Somfai, which includes Bartók's own performances. Also contains lists of compositions.

247. Szabolcsi, Bence, and Ferenc Bónis. *Bartók Béla élete. Bartók élete képekben* [The life of Bartók; Bartók's life in pictures]. Budapest: Zeneműkiadó, 1956. English translation by Sára Karig and Lili Halápy. London, New York: Boosey & Hawkes, 1964. 68p. ML 410.B26 S883

Combines Szabolcsi's revised earlier study (1955), item no. 245, with a selection of pictures, collected and edited by Bónis. Contains 264 illustrations, with maps, facsimiles, music, and ports.

248. Tallián, Tibor. *Bartók Béla.* (Appeared in the series *Szemtől szemben* [Face to face]) Budapest: Gondolat, 1981. 340p. ISBN 963280967X   ML410.B26 T3

A biography discussing Bartók's life, thinking, and music in six chapters, which follow the six periods of his life. Although the book is intended for the general public and therefore contains no footnotes and no detailed musical analyses, it provides in many respects a new insight into Bartók's intellectual world, the social background, and the changes of his musical style. The most up-to-date Bartók biography. Contains pictures, facsimiles, bibliography of works and compositions (pp. 327-337), list of works, and discography (pp. 338-340). See review by Ferenc László in *Korunk* 40/9 (September 1981): 717-720.

249. Uhde, Jürgen. *Béla Bartók.* Collection "Köpfe des XX. Jahrhunderts 2." Berlin: Colloquium Verlag, 1959. 110p.   ML 410 B26 U36

Not examined. According to William Austin, *Music in the 20th Century,* W. W. Norton and Co., 1966: 568, this study was produced "With deep knowledge and love of all Bartók's music, yet also with serious concern for the criticism of the post-Webernites, Uhde presents a beautiful account of Bartók's life and works within 100 pages."

250. Ujfalussy, József. *Bartók Béla. Kis zenei könyvtár* [Béla Bartók. Little music library] 29. Budapest: Gondalat, 1965, rev. 1970 and

1976. 587p. ML 410 B28 U33 1970; English translation by Ruth
Pataki, rev. Elisabeth West. Budapest: Corvina; Boston: Crescendo,
1971. 459p. ISBN 087597077X   ML 410 B26 U383

Comprehensive historical study of Bartók's development
spanning his entire life. Valid comments about the music are mixed
with a broader political and philosophical interpretation of the
material. The revised English version contains more detailed
discussions of the political and social conditions of the time. The
thirteen chapters explore the following: Bartók's childhood and
student years (1881-1898); student years at the Budapest Academy of
Music (1898-1903); the first great works (1903-1905); experience of
folk music (1905-1907); folk music inspiration and its first great
product, *Bluebeard's Castle* (1907-1911); years of silence, folk-music
collections and the anxieties of war, *The Wooden Prince* (1911-
1917); theatre successes, *The Miraculous Mandarin* (1917-1919);
international successes and new creative ideals (1919-1923); pause
in creativity, active concert program, overture to a new period,
journey in the U.S.A. (1923-1928); in the Soviet Union, European
musical fronts and Bartók, choral works, *Cantata Profana* (1928-
1930); oppressive political atmosphere, national attacks at home
and abroad, retreat, collecting tour in Turkey, folk-music studies and
great musical compositions (1931-1936); last years and works in
Europe (1937-1940); in emigration, the end of life and creativity
(1940-1945). Contains significant appendices, including a
chronological survey of the major events in the life of Bartók,
complete list with detailed information of Bartók's works as well as
an extensive listing of Bartók's books, studies, and articles (based
on András Szőllősy's compilation and his numbering system of the
musical compositions), a discography compiled by László Somfai,
and bibliography. Also in Russian (1971) and German (1973). See
reviews by: Jean Gergely, in *Revue de musicologie* 53/1 (1967): 86-
87; Mária Kerényi, in *Muzsika* 14/1 (January 1971): 39; John S.
Weissmann, in *Tempo* 99 (April 1972): 20-21; Benjamin Suchoff, in
Yearbook of the International Folk Music Council 4 (1972): 171-
172; János Breuer, in *Documenta bartókiana* 1/5 (1977): 205-209;
Siegfried Borris, in *Musikbildung* 9/11 (1977): 640-641; and Ferenc
László, in *Utunk* 32/4 (January 28, 1977): 6.

251. ----------. "Bartók Béla--Werk und Biographie" [Béla Bartók--work
and biography]. *Studia musicologica* 23 (1981): 5-16.
781.05 St92   ISSN 0039-3266

Discusses the chronological development of Bartók's works in
connection with the personal and political circumstances surrounding
his own life. These connections include references to R. Strauss,
Wagner, Debussy, and his early studies of Nietzsche's philosophy,
etc.

252. Zielinski, Tadeusz A. *Bartók.* Kraków: Wydawnictwo Muzyczne, 1969. 532p.   ML 410 B26 Z5.

Provides an in-depth chronological study of Bartók's life, supported by extensive documentation based on letters and concert reviews. Also, includes analyses of his entire output, including previously unpublished works, with an emphasis on the early compositions. In addition to the influence of earlier composers, the relation of Bartók's music to that of certain contemporaries is also demonstrated. Furthermore, the ethnomusicological activities of both Bartók and Kodály are explored. Contains illustrations, music, ports., bibliography. German trans. by Bruno Heinrich. Zurich: Atlantis, 1973. See reviews of the book by: Gianfranco Vinay, in *Nuova rivista musicale italiana* 10/1 (January-March 1976): 135-137. See reviews of the translation by: Hartmut Fladt, in *Die neue Zeitung für Musik* 135/5 (May 1974): 331-333; Erich Limmert, in *Melos* 41/3 (1974): 157; Eugen Mayer-Rosa, in *Musikbildung* 6/5 (1974): 335-336; János Breuer, in *Magyar zene* (Budapest) 15/3 (September 1974):326-327; Günter Weiss-Aigner, in *Musikforschung* 29/3 (1976): 366-367.

2. *Discussions of Specific Biographical Events, Aspects, and Details*

253. Abraham, Gerald. "Bartók and England." *The New Hungarian Quarterly* 2/4 (1961): 82-89.   914.39105 N42   ML410 B26 B29

States that the English public has accepted Bartók's music more willingly than most contemporary music from the continent. Then, gives history of Bartók's contact with the English language and his visits to England for performances of his works. Presents criticisms of his works in the *Manchester Guardian* as well as letters by Bartók to his mother regarding his favorable experiences and attitude. Also published in: *Studia musicologica* 5/1-4 (1963): 339-346; *Bartók Studies*, ed. Todd Crow. Detroit: Information Coordinators, 1976, pp. 159-166.

254. *After the Storm: The American Exile of Béla Bartók* (video). Directed by Donald Sturrock. British Broadcasting Corporation and MTC Hungary, 1989. 75 minutes.

Documentary chronicling Bartók's last years, 1940-1945, which were spent in the United States. Includes scenes of Bartók's 1988 re-interment from New York to Budapest and interviews with Peter Bartók, Georg Solti, Yehudi Menuhin, Joseph Szigeti, and neighbors from Saranac Lake. Presents musical excerpts from *Evening in Transylvania* (piano version), *Concerto for Orchestra, Viola Concerto, Allegro barbaro, String Quartets,* and *Sonata for Two Pianos and Percussion.*

255. Bartók, Ditta. "26 September 1945: zum 20. Todestag von Béla Bartók" [September 26, 1945 to the twentieth day after the death of Béla Bartók]. *Österreichische Musikzeitschrift* 20/9 (September 1965): 445-449. 780.5 Oe8 ISSN 0029-9316

     Bartók's wife speaks of the last days of the composer's life, his funeral, and his burial.

256. Baughan, E.A. "A Hungarian Genius?," *Saturday Review* 133 (April 1, 1922): 331-332. AP2 S2794

     Review of Bartók's *Sonata No. 1* for violin and piano, after its first performance by Jelly d'Arányi and the composer at the Aeolian Hall in London on March 24, 1922. The critic found the work convincing, even though he felt that it was unmelodious and difficult to understand.

257. Benkő, Andrei. "Concertele lui Bartók in România" [Bartók's concert tours in Romania]. *Studia musicologica* 14 (1979): 187-221. 781.05 St92 ISSN 0039-3266

     Discusses Bartók's ten concert tours in Romania between 1922-1936. Outlines contents of programs and discusses critical reception.

258. Biba, Otto. "Bartók im Musikverein" [Bartók in the Musikverein]. *Musikblätter der Wiener Philharmoniker* 44/4 (December 1990): 140-144.

     During Bartók's reinterment, in which his remains were transferred from the United States to Hungary in 1988, a memorial service was held at the Gesellschaft der Musikfreunde in Vienna. Points out that on this occasion, in which Bartók's close relationship with the Society was discussed, his elder son, Béla Bartók, Jr., provided a list of all his father's concert performances given at the Society. Contains illustrations.

259. Bónis, Ferenc. "Bartók hat nyilatkozata" [Six statements by Bartók]. *Magyar zene* 29/4 (December 1988): 395-403. ML5 M14 ISSN 0025-0384

     Printed here are five interviews and a statement to the press published after a radio program, all six statements of which were made between 1923 and 1941. These interviews contain essential data on Bartók's life and lend insight into his personal views on a number of scholarly issues.

260. ----------. "Erstes Violinkonzert--Erstes Streichquartett: Ein Wendepunkt in Béla Bartóks kompositorischer Laufbahn" [First violin concerto--first string quartet: A turning point in Béla Bartók's compositional career]. *Musica* 39/3 (1985): 265-273.   780.5 M991 ISSN 0027-4518

The unrequited love affair with violinist Stefi Geyer, which represented a crisis in Bartók's life from 1907 to 1909, is reflected in the first violin concerto, first string quartet, and in his letters. The influence of Wagner's *Tristan* is also explored in connection with his musical thought at this turning point in his career.

261. ----------. "Harminchárom óra ifjabb Bartók Bélával" [Thirty-three hours with Béla Bartók, Jr.]. *Kortárs* 2 (1991): 94-105; 3 (1991): 125-137; 4 (1991): 136-149; 5 (1991): 111-125.   PH3028 L3

According to the author, *RILM Abstracts* No. 4404 (1991), "Transcription of interviews recorded in 1990 with Béla Bartók, Jr., about his father. Béla Bartók, Jr., lived with or near his father for the first thirty years of his life."

262. Botstein, Leon. "Out of Hungary: Bartók, Modernism, and the Cultural Politics of Twentieth-Century Music." *Bartók and His World,* ed. Peter Laki. Princeton, New Jersey: Princeton University Press, 1995. pp. 3-63.   ISBN 0-691-00633-4   ML 410 B26 B272

Proposes a new perspective on Bartók's historical position based on reconsideration in our post-modern era of existing views of the composer's reception. Summarizes the shifting consequences of non-Hungarian perceptions of Bartók as a Hungarian composer and scholar over a long period of changing political and critical developments throughout this century. In his discussion of Bartók and the politics of modernism, points out that Bartók "forged an alternative route for cultural nationalism and modernism." Then discusses the roots of Bartók's modernism in connection with politics and literature in Budapest, 1899-1911, explores early models in late-nineteenth-century Hungarian art and architecture, Bartók's travels abroad, 1904-1905, and discusses Bartók's affinities with the ideas and issues of the young Hungarian intellectual elite of Budapest, 1909-1918. Outlines five phases in Bartók's pursuit of his objectives, spanning his career from *Kossuth* to the *Third Piano Concerto.* Contains illustrations.

263. Breuer, János. "Bartók és a képzőművészet" [Bartók and the Fine Arts]. *Művészet* 16/1 (January 1975): 1-3.

According to an abridged account by Vera Lampert, in *RILM Abstracts* No. 7497 (1976), Breuer's article "documents Bartók's tastes in and understanding of the Fine Arts. Discusses his experiences in the Paris museums in 1905; his furniture, built by a Transylvanian peasant carpenter; his correspondence with his publishers concerning the designs of the title pages of his works; his association with a group of progressive Hungarian painters during the second decade of the twentieth century; his unrealized ideas about the illustrated edition of the Mikrokosmos; etc."

264. ----------. "Die Beziehungen zwischen Bartók und Milhaud" [The relations between Bartók and Milhaud]. *Studia musicologica* 24/3-4 (1982): 283-293.　781.05 St92　ISSN 0039-3266

Discusses various primary source documents, including published articles and correspondences by both composers, providing information on the musical and personal contact that they had with each other since the 1920s. We learn, as one instance, that Bartók initiated the first Milhaud performance in Hungary. An appendix includes several letters from Bartók to Milhaud.

265. Buday, Elizabeth. "Focus on Bartók." *Clavier* 20/8 (October 1981): 21-22.　780.5 C578　ISSN 0009-854-X

A basic biographical sketch of Bartók's early years, with some focus on his professional disappointments during his lifetime and some statements regarding the humanistic elements in his music.

266. Calvocoressi, Michel-Dimitri. "Béla Bartók." *Musical News and Herald* 62 (March 11, 1922): 306.

About the first meeting between Calvocoressi and Bartók at the Rubinstein Prize Competition in Paris in August of 1905. Informs us that at their next meeting in Paris in the spring of 1914, the author was unsuccessful in his attempt to help Bartók publish his transcriptions of Arab melodies, which Bartók had collected in the Biskra district of Algiers in 1913.

267. Demény, János. "Adatok Balázs Béla és Bartók Béla kapcsolatához" [Data on the relationship of Béla Balázs and Béla Bartók]. *Magyar zenetörténeti tanulmányok* 4. Budapest: Zeneműkiadó, 1977, pp. 361-374.　ML55 S992 B6

Gives an account of certain events in the relationship between Bartók and his librettist. Discusses Balázs's unrealized plans in 1913 to have one of his earlier plays set in verse by Endre Ady with music by Bartók. Also, refers to information gained from Balázs's diary regarding the end of their relationship in 1919, when Balázs was forced to leave Hungary. Furthermore, states that Bartók blocked the publication of an article by Balázs for a special Bartók issue in the *Musikblatter des Anbruch*, because it provided some incorrect information about the composer's work.

268. ----------. *Bartók Béla, a zongoraművész* [Béla Bartók the pianist]. Budapest: Zeneműkiadó, 1968,1973. 67p. ML 410 B26 D4

> Presents an historical outline of Bartók's career as a pianist. Includes illustrations, ports. Also published in *Great Hungarian Performers* 5. Budapest: Editio Musica, 1968. 72p.

269. ----------. "Bartók és Balázs Béla kapcsolatáról" [The connection between Bartók and Béla Balázs].*Tiszatáj* 11 (1974): 72-76.

> Gives a history of Bartók's friendship with Balázs, the librettist for his opera *Bluebeard's Castle* (1911) and ballet *The Wooden Prince* (1914-1916). Their relationship began in1906, with their joint folk-song investigations, through 1919, when Balázs was forced to leave Hungary.

270. ----------. "Korrespondenz zwischen Bartók und der holländischen Konzertdirektion 'Kossar.' Bartóks Tourneen in Holland im Spiegel von 104 Briefen aus den Jahren 1935-1939" [Correspondence between Bartók and the Holland conductor 'Kossar.' Bartók's tours in Holland in the light of 104 letters from the years 1935-1939]. *Documenta bartókiana* 6 (1981): 153-229. ISBN-963-05-1185-1- (Serie) ML410 B26 D6 ISSN 0134-0131

> In 1970, the Budapest Bartók Archive acquired, at the auction of Marburger J.A. Stargardt-Antiquariats, documents of the "Kossar-Nachlasses" that included 49 original letters of Bartók and 43 copies from the years of Bartók's last six Holland tours. This material has instigated a new investigation of these tours. These letters as well as commentary are given here.

271. -------------. "The Pianist." *The Bartók Companion*, ed. Malcolm Gillies. London: Faber and Faber, 1993; Portland, Oregon: Amadeus Press (an imprint of Timber Press, Inc.), 1994. pp. 64-78. ISBN 0-931340-74-8 (HB) ISBN 0-931340-75-6 (PB) ML410 B26 B28

> Provides a history of Bartók's career as pianist, beginning with his early piano studies and performances. States that the lack of success during his early years contributed to his increasing focus on composition and folk-music research. Asserts, nevertheless, that Bartók's basic musical personality was oriented toward the piano. Outlines the two formative periods of his life (1908-1911 and 1926-1931) and summarizes the key piano genres and pieces of these periods. Also, evaluates Bartók's performance characteristics as a reflection of those traits found in his personality and compositions,

in which he was "to summon up a monumental strength and demonic vision, perhaps in the finest tradition of Liszt." Provides the attitudes and assessments of important critics, discusses important concerts, and provides a detailed survey of Bartók's piano concert programmes, including a comparison of the frequency of his performances in different countries.

272. ----------. "Zeitgenössische Musik in Bartóks Konzertrepertoire" [Contemporary music in Bartók's concert repertoire]. *Documenta bartókiana* 1/5 (1977): 169-176.   ISBN-963-05-1185-1-(Serie) ML410 B26 D6   ISSN 0134-0131

A listing of compositions by seventeen composers performed by Bartók on his concerts.

273. Dezsényi, Béla. "Bartók és a Nemzeti Könyvtár zenei gyűjteménye" [Bartók and the music collection of the National Library]. *Muzsika* (Budapest) 14/3 (March 1971): 15-17.   ISSN 0027-5336

States that, although the National Széchényi Library of Budapest contained musical materials since the founding of the Library in 1802, a special music collection was established for the first time in 1923. According to the author, it was Bartók who, in 1918, first suggested the establishment of a music division, which would combine instruments from the National Museum with the musical holdings of the Library. This was prevented by the failure of the Revolution in 1919.

274. Dille, Denijs. "Bartók défenseur de Kodály" [Bartók's defense of Kodály]. *Studia musicologica* 13 (1971): 347-353.   781.05 St92 ISSN 0039-3266. See also item no. 1150, Denijs Dille, *Béla Bartók: Regard sur le passé* [Béla Bartók: A look at the past], ed. Yves Lenoir, *Musicologica neolovaniensia* 5; *Études bartokiennes*. Namur: Presses Université de Namur, 1990, pp. 213-228. ML 410 B26 D52

Attempts to clarify vague notions regarding the relations between Bartók and Kodály. Includes Bartók's outspoken attack against the destructive criticism by several Hungarian journals of Kodály's music (two melodies) performed at an evening of the Philharmonic Society on January 10, 1921. Provides an important primary-source document in a fairly literal French translation of Bartók's Hungarian text, which includes Bartók's statement that he could not permit the "systematic persecution" of the great Hungarian composer "without raising his voice." Contains music facsimile.

275. ----------. "Bartók és Kodály első találkozása" [The first meeting of Bartók and Kodály]. *Igaz szó* 1970/1979: 353-357.   HA1.835. See also "La rencontre de Bartók et de Kodály" [1969], in item no.

1150, Denijs Dille, *Béla Bartók: Regard sur le passé* [Béla Bartók: A look at the past], ed. Yves Lenoir, *Musicologica neolovaniensia* 5; *Études bartokiennes*. Namur: Presses Université de Namur, 1990, pp. 199-204. ML 410 B26 D52

Provides documentary evidence, in the form of letters, regarding the first meeting of Bartók and Kodály at the home of Emma Gruber, Kodály's future wife. Discusses Bartók's ethnomusicological interests and the general biographical circumstances surrounding the meeting of the two composers in 1905. Also published in: *Magyar zenetörténeti tanulmányok* (see item no. 1170), pp. 317-322. Contains photos.

276. ----------. "Bartókov pobyt v Grlici a jeho objavenie l'udovej piesne" [Bartók's stay at Grlica and his discovery of folk song]. *Slovenská hudba* 13/3 (1969): 116-121. H50.470

Deals with Bartók's compositional activity as well as his early interests in folk music in the summers of 1904 and 1906 during his visits to this southern Slovakian village.

277. ----------. "Die Beziehungen zwischen Bartók und Schönberg" [The connections between Bartók and Schoenberg]. *Documenta bartókiana* 2 (1965): 53-61. ISBN-963-05-1185-1-(Serie) ML410 B26 D6 ISSN 0134-0131

Discusses the personal connections between the two composers, and the bearing these had on their subsequent exchanges of opinion on artistic issues. Supports this research with documentary evidence, including some letters from Schoenberg to Bartók and two copies of Schoenberg's *Three Piano Pieces,* Op. 11, which had belonged to Bartók. Also published in: *Arnold Schönberg--1874 bis 1951* (see *RILM Abstracts* No. 8797, 1976), pp. 58-64; and item no. 1150, Denijs Dille, *Béla Bartók: Regard sur le passé* [Béla Bartók: A look at the past], ed. Yves Lenoir, *Musicologica neolovaniensia* 5; *Études bartokiennes*. Namur: Presses Université de Namur, 1990, pp. 51-71.

278. ----------. *Généalogie sommaire de la famille Bartók* [Concise genealogy of the Bartók family]. Antwerpen: Metropolis, 1977. 72p. CS 569 B37 929.2/09439 19

Iconographic study of the composer's family history. Includes discussion of his ancestry and early years and provides an outline of his family tree and many family pictures. Contains plates, illustrations, index.

279. Doráti, Antal. "Bartókiana (Some Recollections)." *Tempo* (London) 136 (March 1981): 6-13. 780.5 T249 ISSN 0040-2982

Discusses author's early experience with Bartók's name and music and how this related to the general attitudes toward Bartók in "Germanicized" Hungary. Then discusses his first personal contact with Bartók. Following is a first hand, somewhat chronological account of the musical events surrounding these experiences of the author, with significant information on attitudes and criticisms regarding performances, etc., of the works of Bartók, Kodály, Dohnányi, and Richard Strauss. Doráti's association with Bartók was continued to the last year of Bartók's life.

280. Ellsworth, Ray. "The Shadow of Genius: Béla Bartók and Tibor Serly." *The American Record Guide* 32 (September 1965): 26-33. ML1 A725   789.91   ISSN 0003-0716

Discusses Serly's close relationship with Bartók, especially in Bartók's last years in America. Quotes Serly regarding the conditions that led him to complete the final measures of the master's *Third Piano Concerto.* Refers to Ditta Pásztory Bartók's first performance (for a recording) of the *Concerto* in 1964. Also gives the history of Serly's friendship with Bartók beginning with Serly's student days at the Royal Academy of Music in Budapest in the 1920s. Following is a somewhat detailed chronology of their contact and related concert activities.

281. Fábián, Imre. "Bartók und die Wiener Schule" [Bartók and the Viennese School]. *Österreichische Musikzeitschrift* 19 (1964): 255. 780.5 Oe8   ISSN 0029-9316

Explores the early mutual influences between Bartók and the Vienna Schoenberg Circle about 1912, the year when Bartók first became acquainted with Schoenberg's *Three Piano Pieces,* Op. 11.

282. Fancsali, János. "Bartók Béla Sepsiszentgyörgyi hangversenye" [Béla Bartók's concert in Sepsiszentgyörgy]. *Magyar zene* 31/3 (September 1990): 255-262.   ML5 M14   ISSN 0025-0384

According to the author, *RILM Abstracts* No. 4933 (1990), provides "new information, on the basis of letters, newspaper articles, and other documentary evidence, about Bartók's 1927 concert in Sepsiszentgyörgy (now Sfîntu-Gheorghe in Romania), including exact dating and discussion of his folk music collecting activity in the town."

283. Fassett, Agatha. *The Naked Face of Genius; Béla Bartók's American Years.* Boston and New York: Houghton Mifflin Company; Cambridge: Riverside Press, 1958. 367p.   ISBN 0486225305 ML 410 B26 F3

Based upon Fassett's friendship and close contact with Bartók and his wife since their arrival in the USA in 1940. Serves as an important primary source for insight into Bartók's life and personality in these years of exile. Provides great detail concerning such things as Bartók's everyday little interests--food, cats, house hunting, radios, etc., but also his more serious concerns regarding political developments, for instance, his more optimistic attitude "now that the strength of America has entered the war." However, Bartók's creative activities and compositions are viewed only superficially. Provides insight into Bartók's intensive work habits, despite his illness, and the projects that were most important to him at various times, e.g., completion of the Romanian folk-song collection, work on the Parry Collection at Columbia, etc. Contains illustrations, catalogue of Bartók's works. Reprinted as: *Béla Bartók- -the American Years*. New York: Dover, 1970: 367p.; in Hungarian: *Bartók amerikai évei*. Budapest: Zeneműkiadó, 1960. Japanese trans. [of *The Naked Face of Genius: Béla Bartók's Last Years* (London: Gollancz, 1958)] by Mizuho Nomizu. *Bartók: Bannen no higeki* [Bartók: the tragedy in his last years]. Tokyo: Misuzu-shobo, 1973. 378p. See the review by Halsey Stevens in *Music Library Association Notes* (June 1958): 404.

284. Fuchss, Werner. *Béla Bartók und die Schweiz, eine Dokumentensammlung* [Béla Bartók and Switzerland, a collection of documents]. Bern: Hallway, 1973. 126p.   ML 410 B26 F8

Provides a history of Bartók's varied connections with Switzerland, based on extensive musical, literary, and pictorial documentation. Study includes Bartók's first appearance in Zurich as composer and pianist in 1910, his largely unknown correspondence with Swiss musicians, early performances of his works in Switzerland, his interpretation of his own works as a concert pianist, and his association with the "Volkerbund für Fragen der Kunst und Wissenschaften" in Geneva. Bartók's productive association with Switzerland came to an end after the world premieres of three major works in Basel between 1936 and 1940. Contains illustrations, facsimiles, music, bibliography, index. Appeared also in Hungarian. See also: *Béla Bartók und die Schweiz. Kurze Monographie und Katalog einer Wanderausstellung* [Béla Bartók and Switzerland, a brief monograph and catalogue]. Fribourg: Imprimerie St. Paul, 1970. 80p.; *Béla Bartók en Suisse*. Lausanne: Payot, 1976. See reviews by: János Breuer in *Magyar zene* (Budapest) 15/1 (March 1974): 104-107; Hartmut Fladt in *Die Neue Zeitung für Musik* 135/5 (May 1974): 331-333; Willi Reich in *Melos* 41/5 (1974): 288; István Raics in *Muzsika* (Budapest) 17/6 (June 1974): 40; Volker Scherliess in *Musikforschung* 29/2 (1976): 237-238.

285. Gál, István. "Babits és Bartók" [Babits and Bartók]. *Kortárs* 12/5 (May 1968): 798-808.	PH 3028 L3

Previously unpublished letters from Bartók to Gál provide informative evidence regarding the association, from 1935 to 1936, between Bartók and the Hungarian poet Mihály Babits. At that time, Gál was editor of the journal *Apollo*, to which Babits's literary circle had connections and to which Bartók contributed an article on folk music in 1936.

286. Gáspár, Mária. "The Birthplace of Bartók's Ancestors: A Conversation with Professor Denijs Dille." *Hungarian Music News* 2/3 (1981): 5-6.	ISSN 0441-5973

Traces history of Bartók's ancestry through correspondence with Bartók's younger sister, Elza, and his cousin, Ilonka. Dille then came to Hungary for more research on the subject since 1954. Results of Dille's research appears in Dille's booklet, *Généalogie sommaire de la famille Bartók*. Antwerp: Metropolis, 1977. Dille was also given much help in his work by Mrs. Béla Bartók and Béla Bartók, Jr. as well as Zoltán Kodály and his wife Emma.

287. Gillies, Malcolm. "Bartók in Britain: 1922." *Music and Letters* 63/3-4 (July-October 1982): 213-225.	780.5 M92	ISSN 0027-4224

Discusses Bartók's visits to Britain for concert tours as early as 1904. Includes reactions to his music in the press and the championing of it by composer-critic Philip Heseltine. The first British visit of Bartók's maturity occurred in 1922. Extremely well-documented study (articles, news items, letters, concert programs, etc.), giving us a thorough picture of Bartók's British activities.

288. ----------. *Bartók in Britain. A Guided Tour*. Oxford: Clarendon Press, 1989, 168p.	ISBN 0-19-315262-2	ML410.B26G46 1988

In-depth study of Bartók's many visits to Britain on concert tours between 1904 and 1938. In this book, these short visits are used as "bores" into the bedrock of Bartók's life. The result is a highly detailed account of various aspects of the composer's personality, in particular, his pianism, his views of his own music, and his private opinions. As a second, related theme, Bartók is used as a constant against which the vast changes in British music-making and views of music over this period are depicted. The book concludes with two "in-depth" studies into Bartók's relationships with the British composer-critics Philip Heseltine (Peter Warlock) and Cecil Gray, and with the Arányi sisters. Contains 16 illustrations, bibliography, and index. See reviews by: David Clegg, in *Music Review* 100/3-4 (August-November 1989): 307-308; Sándor

Kovács, in *Hungarian Music Quarterly* 1/3-4 (1989): 55-56; Mike Smith, in *Tempo* 170 (September 1989): 33-34; Douglas Jarman, in *Music and Letters* 71/2 (May 1990): 278; and David Symons, in *Musicology Australia* 13 (1990): 42-43.

289. ----------. "Bartók, Heseltine and Gray: A Documentary Study." *The Music Review* 43/3-4 (August-November 1982): 177-191.
780.5 M9733   ISSN 0027-4445

Interest in Bartók as a composer was fostered in Britain in the early part of the century by two young composer-critics, Philip Heseltine (Peter Warlock) and Cecil Gray. This contributed to his first substantial recognition outside of Hungary. Presents detailed documentation of their writings on Bartók and their views on other contemporary composers throughout the post-World-War-I period. Also discusses their evaluations and connections of his music to Beethoven, etc. Furthermore, includes references to Bartók's letters to Heseltine and Gray and their personal contacts.

290. ----------. *Bartók Remembered.* London: Faber, 1990; New York: W.W. Norton, 1991. xl, 238p.   ISBN 0-571-14243-5
ISBN 0-393-30744-1   ML410 B26 G462

Substantial collection of memoirs ranging from his mother's recollections of his youth to those by other family members (first wife and two sons), folk singers, press writers and publishers, composers (e.g., Milhaud, Honegger, Stravinsky, Grainger), conductors (e.g., Goosens, Dorati, Solti, Ansermet), and performers (e.g., Szigeti, Menuhin, Primrose), among others, all of whom have provided a vivid picture of Bartók during different phases of his life. Detailed and useful chronological outlines of Bartók's life and works and of contemporary personalities and events are followed by almost 100 reminiscences of those who knew Bartók closely in Hungary (1881-1903) during his childhood, youth, and Academy years, earlier professional years clouded by a sense of failure (1903-1920), later professional years of some success (1920-1940), and the final years of exile in America (1940-1945). Obituaries and testimonials (e.g., Krenek, Kodály,) are also included. Brief opinions about Bartók's personality are also presented (Berg, Ady, Britten, Stravinsky, Copland, Lajtha, Graça, Tippett, and Gerson-Kiwi), with a statement from Bartók's own Harvard Lectures on his compositional attitudes. Contains illustrations, photos, facsimiles, a select bibliography, and index. See review by Damjana Bratuz, in *Music Library Association Notes* 49/3 (March 1993): 1031-1033.

291. Gillies, Malcolm; Gombocz-Konkoly, Adrienne. "The *Colindă* Fiasco: Bartók and Oxford University Press." *Music and Letters* 49/4 (October 1988): 482-494.   780.5 M92   ISSN 0027-4224

According to Malcolm Gillies, *RILM Abstracts* No. 11557 (1988), "Béla Bartók experienced great difficulty in securing publication of his folk music collections. Most were not published during his lifetime. His collection of Romanian *colinde* (Christmas songs) was the subject of negotiation and dispute between the London publisher Oxford University Press and Bartók in the decade 1925-35. Original publication plans were complicated by the deaths or inefficiencies of several British translators and the occasional involvement of the Romanian Society of Composers. Principal negotiators with Bartók were Herbert J. Foss (London) and Constantin Brăiloiu (Bucharest). Eventually Bartók abandoned his plans and arranged for publication of part of the collection at his expense through Universal Edition."

292. Gombocz-Konkoly, Adrienne. "Bartók kolinda-könyvének meghiúsult angliai kiadása" [The aborted English publication of Bartók's *colindă* book]. *Zenetudományi dolgozatok* (1986): 19-35.

Documents the problems in connection with the unfulfilled English publication of Bartók's collection of *colinde* (Christmas carols) by Oxford University Press.

293. ----------. "Újabb dokumentumok Bartók és az A.K.M. osztrák jogvédő társaság kapcsolatáról" [Further documents on the relations between Bartók and A.K.M., the Austrian performing rights society]. *Magyar zene* 29/1 (March 1988): 52-112.   ML5 M14 ISSN 0025-0384

In Hungarian, German. According to the author, *RILM Abstracts* No. 4134 (1988), "Supplement to an article by János Breuer (*Magyar zene* 26/3, 1985). Further Bartók documents have been found in the archive of the Austrian Gesellschaft der Autoren, Komponisten, und Musikverleger, in Vienna. Bartók was a member of the society from 1921 until 1938. The documents include announcements of new works (including date of composition, title, publisher, duration, etc.). A list of newly discovered letters is provided, together with the German texts and Hungarian translations of the more important ones." Contains facsimiles, charts, tables.

294. ----------. "With His Publishers." *The Bartók Companion,* ed. Malcolm Gillies. London: Faber and Faber, 1993; Portland, Oregon: Amadeus Press (an imprint of Timber Press, Inc.), 1994. pp. 89-98. ISBN 0-931340-74-8 (HB)   ISBN 0-931340-75-6 (PB) ML410 B26 B28

States that Bartók's most consistent correspondence was with his publishers, due to the wide variety of his materials--musical compositions, folk-music collections, essays, and his editions of early keyboard music--that he intended for publication. States, however, that due to Bartók's own "sensitive and somewhat distrustful character," he did not seem to be aware of the respect his publishers had for him. Provides an overview of Bartók's publishers and Bartók's relations with them, including information on the publication of specific works. Includes quotes by Bartók and his publishers that shed light on their attitudes toward each other and their relations. Also provides insight into the various functions of the publishers.

295. Graça, F. Lopes. "Évocation de Béla Bartók." *La revue musicale* 224 (1955): 112-115.   780.5 R328   ISSN 0035-3736, 0029-9316

Speaks of his personal meeting with Bartók during the winter of 1939. During this season, Bartók was in Paris performing his *Sonata for Two Pianos and Percussion* with his wife. Recounts how Bartók received him with an extreme simplicity, in which his manners, words, and entire person showed no trace of arrogance.

296. Harangozó, Gyula. "Erinnerungen an Béla Bartók" [Reminiscences of Béla Bartók]. *Österreichische Musikzeitschrift* 22/5 (May 1967): 258-261.   780.5 Oe8   ISSN 0029-9316

Reminiscences of Bartók by the first choreographer of his ballets *The Wooden Prince* and *The Miraculous Mandarin*. Originally appeared in Hungarian in a longer version (not examined) in *Táncmũvészet* (1955).

297. Hatvany, Yolan. "An Evening with Thomas Mann and Béla Bartók in Budapest." *The New Hungarian Quarterly* 5/15 (Autumn 1964): 72-75.   914.39105 N42   ML410 B26 B29

As a member of the *Comité permanent des lettres et des arts*, Thomas Mann visited Budapest in 1936. Mann and Bartók were invited to the home of Mrs. Hatvany, who hosted this last meeting between Bartók and Mann. Reprinted in *Bartók Studies,* ed. Todd Crow. Detroit: Information Coordinators, 1976, pp. 173-176.

298. Hawkes, Ralph. "Béla Bartók, A Recollection by His Publisher." *Tempo* (London) 13 (1949): 10-15; reprinted in *Béla Bartók: A Memorial Review*. New York: Boosey & Hawkes, 1950, pp. 14-19. 780.5 T249   ISSN 0040-2982

Discusses happenings during Bartók's last seven years that are closely connected with Ralph Hawkes and the publishing house of Boosey and Hawkes. Gives brief history of the policy of this publisher and the changes that brought contact with and interest in the music of Bartók and Kodály in the 1930s when Universal Edition in Vienna became nazified.

299. Hernádi, Lajos. "Bartók Béla a zongoraművész, a pedagógus, az ember" [Bartók the pianist, the teacher, the man]. *Új zenei szemle* (Budapest) 4/9 (1953): 1ff.   HA1.588

     Outlines Bartók's biographical history as a pianist, discussing his pianistic style, a listing of certain early recital programs, his own compositions, his meticulous approach to playing as well as teaching, and pedagogical compositions such as the *Mikrokosmos*. Also published in French in *La revue musicale* 224 (1955): 77-90. A similar publication appeared in English: "Béla Bartók--Pianist and Teacher," *American Music Teacher* 22/3 (January 1973): 28-31.

300. Heseltine, Philip. "Modern Hungarian Composers." *Musical Times* 63 (1922): 164-167.   780.5 M98   ISSN 0027-4666

     Article anticipating Bartók's visit to England in March 1922, bringing with him a new sonata for violin and piano and other chamber music. Regards London as center of the musical world but refers to a gap in English knowledge of contemporary Hungarian music. Discusses the importance of *Children's Pieces* to piano teachers and the inseparability of the folk material and the attendant harmonies. Praises many other works of Bartók for their freshness, power, and originality (especially the first two quartets, the only ones composed by then). Also, includes reference to an unpublished letter by Bartók to Heseltine dated January 8, 1921 (Quaritch, London, Catalogue 891, 1968, No. 802) confirming Heseltine's comparison of the first movement of Bartók's *First Suite,* op. 3, to Wagner's *Meistersinger* overture. States that Bartók's own countrymen have been as backward in their appreciation of his music as have been the English.

301. Horváth, Béla. "Bartók és a Nyolcak" [Bartók and the Eight]. *Művészettörténeti értesítő* 4 (1974): 328-332.   HB1.202

     Provides information regarding Bartók's connections with a group of avant-garde Hungarian painters in 1911, some with whom he had been associated as early as 1905. One of the members, Robert Berény, published an article, "The Case of Béla Bartók," in *Nyugat* (1911), and in 1913, he painted a portrait of Bartók.

302. Hrcková, Nada. "Nielen chlebom je človek živy. Po stopách Bélu Bartóka" [Man lives not by bread alone. Following the traces of Béla Bartók]. *Hudobný život* 1/9 (June 1969): 3.

     In an interview with Denijs Dille, Director of the Budapest Bartók Archívum, significant information is provided regarding Bartók's stay in Bratislava.

303. Jasionowski, Paul. "An Interview with Saul Goodman About the Bartók Sonata." *Percussive Notes* (April 1994): 53-59. ML1 P3738

Interview with Goodman, on July 13, 1991, at his Lake Placid home in upstate New York, in connection with the United States première of the *Sonata for Two Pianos and Percussion,* performed at Town Hall in New York City in 1940 with Bartók and his wife as the pianists. Summarizes the events leading to Bartók's arrival in the United States and Goodman's performance of the work with the composer. Discusses the problems regarding the proper instruments at the first rehearsal due to Bartók's delayed arrival from Europe, the problems in trying to coordinate rhythmic conceptions during rehearsals, a page-turn error on Bartók's part during the performance, and the generally poor critical reception of the work. Discusses Bartók's personality, his attitude during rehearsal, his inspiration for the work, and his unhappy personal circumstances in the United States (neglect of his works and health problems). Discusses the Sonata's specific musical features and more general issues connected with its performance. Evaluates past and current recordings of the work.

304. Juha, Palne. "Bartók Béla kárpátaljai kapcsolatai" [The connections of Béla Bartók with Ruthenia]. *Szabolcs-szatmári szemle* (May 1974): 120-127.   HA1.528

Provides information on Bartók's life and works, including a discussion of his early studies in Nagyszőllős. Also, discusses the influence of Ruthenian folk music on Bartók's own compositions, two important instances of which are No. 16 of the *Forty-Four Duos* for two violins and No. 128 of the *Mikrokosmos.* Contains illustrations, facsimiles, and music.

305. Juhász, Vilmos. *Bartók Béla amerikai évei* [Béla Bartók's American years]. New York: Kis Magyar Könyvtár VI., A Magyar Nemzeti Bizottmány Vallás és Közoktatásügyi Bizottsága, 1956. 95p. ISBN 0911050515   ML 410 B292 J8

Provides new data on Bartók during his American years, based on a number of interviews with Bartók's friends, pupils, and colleagues. Presents important first-hand information regarding Bartók's philosophy, personality, and attitudes, providing insights that changed certain views about the composer in Hungary since the mid-1950s. See also the English publication: *Bartók's Years in America.* Preface by Yehudi Menuhin and Introduction by Sándor Veress. Washington, D.C.: Occidental Press, 1981. Contains illustrations.

306. Kecskeméti, István. "Bartók Béla Keszthelyen. Egy emlékkiállitás tanulságaiból" [Béla Bartók in Keszthely. The lesson of a commemorative exhibition]. *Magyar zene* (Budapest) 9/3 (1968): 301-308.   ML5 M14   ISSN 0025-0384

The author states, in *RILM Abstracts* No. 4563 (1969), that he has included "Data and comments on and by Bartók relating to the town of Keszthely, on the occasion of a Bartók exhibition (1966) arranged on the sixtieth anniversary of the composer's folklore trip to the town."

307. Kenneson, Claude. *Székely and Bartók: The Story of a Friendship.* Portland, Oregon: Amadeus Press (an imprint of Timber Press, Inc.), 1994. 491p.   ISBN 0-931340-70-5   ML385 K45

States that "for musicians and scholars this book provides a record of Székely's and Bartók's unique insights into the music revealed through their shared history, letters, and discussions of performance practice." In spite of the basically factual description of the events of Székely's life, insight is gained not only into Bartók's influence on the Hungarian violinist (member of the Hungarian String Quartet) but into Bartók's own personality and attitudes, activities, performances of his chamber and other music, its critical reception, Bartók's reactions to reviews, and his interpretative preferences. Includes historical and other information on the *String Quartets,* the two *Violin Rhapsodies, Violin Concerto,* and other works. The actual story of the friendship begins in Chapter 4 and continues through many chapters, though much of the book explores issues outside the sphere of direct Bartók interest. Also contains correspondence from Bartók to the Székelys, including previously unpublished Bartók letters, and appendices including Székely's first performances of Bartók's works. Contains discography, selected bibliography, index, and many photos and illustrations. See review by: László Vikárius, *Hungarian Music Quarterly* 6/1-2 (1995): 42-43.

308. Kiss, Béla. *Bartók Béla művészete* [The art of Bartók]. Cluj: Ifjú Erdély, 1946. 71p.

Concise biographical study, which includes some historical discussion regarding the transformation of Hungarian culture as well as the shift from a romanticized view of folk music to Bartók's discovery of the authentic Hungarian peasant melodies. Also discusses the pedagogical importance of Bartók and his humanistic philosophy.

309. Kodály, Zoltán. "Bartók Béla első operája" [Béla Bartók's first opera]. *Nyugat* (1918): 937-939.   H23.374

On the first performance of *Duke Bluebeard's Castle* in 1918. States that Bartók's stylistic treatment brought with it the development of the Hungarian recitative style and is the first work of the Hungarian opera theater. Also published in French: *Bartók sa vie et son œuvre*, ed. Bence Szabolcsi. Budapest: Corvina, 1956; and in German: *Béla Bartók, Weg und Werk, Schriften und Briefe*, ed. Bence Szabolcsi. Budapest: Corvina, 1957, pp. 60-63.

310. Kristóf, Károly. *Beszélgetések Bartók Bélával* [Conversations with Béla Bartók]. Budapest: Zeneműkiadó, 1957. 192p.

Important primary source, which provides documentary evidence of discussions with Bartók. Provides new data on events relevant to Bartók's life and activities.

311. Kroó, György. "Bartók Béla. 1881-től 1945-ig és tovább" [Béla Bartók. From 1881 to 1945 and later]. *Nagyvilág* 20/9 (September 1975): 1431-1433.   HA1.987   MT 100 B26 K8

Discusses Bartók's position during the fascist era, in which his concern for nature and human causes served as a reminder for his fellow Hungarians. Also, discusses the diminished interest in his music for a brief time following World War II, during the period of revival of those principles stemming from the Viennese School. However, points to the renewed interest in his music, which served as an inspiration for younger generations by providing an alternative to the post-war developments at Darmstadt and other areas in central Europe.

312. ----------. "On the Origin of *The Wooden Prince.*" *International Musicological Conference in Commemoration of Béla Bartók 1971*, ed. József Ujfalussy and János Breuer. Budapest: Editio Musica; New York: Belwin Mills, 1972, pp. 97-101.   ML410.B29 I61

States that, for the origin of this work, certain authors refer to the statements and recollections of the librettist, Béla Balázs. A detailed history of events is also given in connection with its origin. This is followed by a discussion of the sources preserved in the New York Bartók Archive.

313. Laki, Peter. "The Gallows and the Altar: Poetic Criticism and Critical Poetry about Bartók in Hungary." *Bartók and His World*, ed. Peter Laki. Princeton, New Jersey: Princeton University Press, 1995. pp. 79-100.   ISBN 0-691-00633-4   ML 410 B26 B272

Provides a perspective on the general reception of Bartók in Hungary, in which the composer has been viewed according to two extreme positions. Discusses and documents Bartók as a hero figure in Hungary, while his music was often rejected as modernistic and inaccessible. Explores the historical development and interdependence of these contrasting positions, asserting that the polarized reception of Bartók and his music belongs to a larger sphere of political, social, moral, and ethical issues. States that the Hungarian qualities of Bartók's music played a role in promoting favorable responses among critics of extreme nationalistic bent, while his increasing modernism caused a reversal of their attitudes. Provides a history of various Hungarian musicological and psychological studies bearing on the sources of Bartók's artistic and political significance. Documentation ranges from early to present-day scholarly and critical views as well as poetry on Bartók and his music. Includes a wealth of quotations and references.

314. Lampert, Vera. *"The Miraculous Mandarin:* Melchior Lengyel, His Pantomime, and His Connections to Béla Bartók." *Bartók and His World,* ed. Peter Laki. Princeton, New Jersey: Princeton University Press, 1995. pp. 149-171.   ISBN 0-691-00633-4
ML 410 B26 B272

Focuses primarily on the personal studies, development, and international theater/film activities of the librettist of Bartók's *Mandarin* pantomime, Menyhért Lengyel. Career began when the manuscript of his play *A nagy fejedelem* (The great prince) was accepted by Sándor Hevesy, the stage director of the avant-garde Thalia theater in Budapest, and performed there in 1907. Outlines the progress of his career as dramatist, his psychoanalytical treatment with Sigmund Freud, his contributions to the radical literary review *Nyugat* (West), which included his literary critical writings, theater reviews, essays, sketches, plays, excerpts from his diary, and his writings demonstrating his anti-war stance and humanitarian concerns. Interweaves his biographical sketch with the main historical events through the interwar period. Discusses the catalogue of his works and his turn toward the movie industry. The second part of the essay discusses the genesis of his pantomime, *The Miraculous Mandarin,* outlines the plot, analyzes its characteristics, explores its symbolic significance as an expressionist drama, and describes Bartók's attraction to it. Provides critical evaluation (e.g., by Lajos Hatvany in 1916) of the drama, discusses the pantomime in the context of Lengyel's other plays, and describes Lengyel's chief concerns in his dramas. The final part of the essay provides a history of the Lengyel-Bartók connection and how Bartók came to set the work to music. Includes correspondence between Lengyel and Bartók and other substantial documentation.

315. Lang, Paul Henry. "Editorial." *Musical Quarterly* (New York) 32/1 (January 1946): 131-136.   ML1 M725   ISSN 0027-4631

Eulogy written by the editor of the *Musical Quarterly* several months after the composer's death.

316. László, Ferenc. *A százegyedik év. Bartókról, Enescuról, Kodályról* [The 101st year. About Bartók, Enescu and Kodály]. Bucharest: Kriterion, 1984. 212p.

Collection of essays and articles in Hungarian celebrating the centennary in 1991 and 1992 of the births of these composers. A larger article, entitled "Bartók magyarsága és a mi magyarságunk" [Bartók's Hungarianness and our Hungarianness], deals with Bartók's model-consciousness (a consciousness that serves as a model for us) toward the issue of Hungarianness. Includes analytical studies of the following pieces: First movement of *Rhapsody No. 1,* certain themes of *Duke Bluebeard's Castle* and the *Concerto.* Presents a tentative proposal for the reconstruction of the classification of Bartók's folk-song collection from Bánság (Bánát) that had been prepared for publication but was never published. Some articles correct the dating of events in Bartók's life (Bartók's trips in Transylvania, his relationship with Enescu, his broadcast on Romanian folk music on January 22, 1933, at Frankfurt am Main). The author publishes, from his own collection from 1981, hitherto unknown versions of Romanian *colinde* which might have served as the basis for Bartók's *Cantata Profana.* Contains musical examples. See reviews by: János Breuer, in *Élet és irodalom* 38/14 (1984): 10; Elena M. Sorban, in *Muzica* 35/4 (April 1985): 38-39.

317. ----------. "Bartók adalékok egy román könyvújdonságban" [Bartókiana in a new Romanian publication]. *Magyar zene* (Budapest) 16/1 (1975): 102-104.   ML5 M14   ISSN 0025-0384

Discusses the importance of the first volume of the correspondence of Ion Bianu (1856-1935), ed. by Marieta and Petru Croicu, Bucareşti: Editură Minerva, 1974, which contains numerous primary source documents related to Bartók. Gives examples of letters from Bartók and others that provide information on his folk materials, editions of his music, etc.

318. ----------. *Béla Bartók şi lumea noastră. Aşa cum a fost* [Béla Bartók and our world. Such as it was]. Cluj-Napoca: Editura Dacia, 1995. 196p.   ISBN 973-35-0426-2

Compendium of data that has particular interest for the Romanian reader. In 94 chapters, the book provides extensive information about Bartók's collecting trips and concerts that took place in the territory of present-day Romania; it deals with all those compositions which show direct influence of folk music from Transylvania and from the Bánság, all of his ethnomusicological activities concerning the folk musics of these territories, and his relationship with Romanians. Contains tables, selective bibliography, chronological catalogue of Bartók's works. See review by: Mária Kacsír, in *A Hét* 26/31-32 (August 4, 1985): 7-8.

319. ----------. *Béla Bartók. Studii, comunicări și eseuri* [Béla Bartók. Studies, communications, essays]. Bucharest: Kriterion, 1985. 336p.

Twenty-three essays in Romanian, for the most part revised and enlarged versions of the Hungarian writings of item no. 390, *Bartók Béla. Tanulmányok és tanúságok* [Béla Bartók. Studies and testimonies]. Bucharest: Kriterion, 1980. 320p.; and item no. 316, *A százegyedik év. Bartókról, Enescuról, Kodályról* [The 101st year. About Bartók, Enescu and Kodály]. Bucharest: Kriterion, 1984. 212 p. The new articles include essays dealing with Bartók's collection in Csík county in 1907 and Cserbel (Cerbal) in 1913-1914, the *Romanian Folk Dances* (1915) and an essay providing the location of the house where Bartók lived during the academic year 1891/92 in Nagyvárad. Contains 57 photographs, several musical examples. See reviews by: Dan Budiu, in *Steaua* 39/12 (December 1985); Titus Moisescu, in *Karpatenrundschau* 22/36 (September 8, 1989): 4-5.

320. --------------. "Megjegyzesek a Bartók-életrajz Dósa Lidi-epizódjához" [Observations on the Lidi Dósa episode in the life of Bartók]. *Muzsika* (Budapest) 21/2 (February 1978): 1-8. ISSN 0027-5336

Discusses the events and their significance surrounding Bartók's connection with Lidi Dósa, a peasant girl whose tunes he notated in the village of Gerlice puszta in 1904. Points out that this initiated Bartók's folk-music investigations, though the tunes that she sang for Bartók were not actual folk songs and did not represent the oldest Hungarian folk-song style. Also, discusses Bartók's arrangement and publication of her melodies. The same article appeared in English, "Bartók's First Encounter with Folk Music." *The New Hungarian Quarterly* 19/72 (Winter 1978): 67-75. The enlarged version of the article appeared in Hungarian in item no. 390, *Bartók Béla. Tanulmányok és tanúságok* [Béla Bartók. Studies and testimonies]. Bucharest: Kriterion, 1980. 320p.; and in Romanian in item no. 319, *Béla Bartók. Studii, comunicări și eseuri* [Béla Bartók. Studies, communications, essays]. Bucharest: Kriterion, 1985. 336p.

321. Lenoir, Yves. "Béla Bartók et George Herzog: Chronique d'une collaboration exemplaire (1940-1945)" [Béla Bartók and George Herzog: Chronicle of an exemplary collaboration (1940-1945)]. *Revue des archéologues et historiens d'art de Louvain* 21 (1988): 137-145.

Discusses the importance of the unpublished correspondence between Bartók and Dr. George Herzog (1901-84) for information on their personal collaboration. Demonstrates that Bartók's decision to emigrate to the United States owes much to Herzog's influence. Also points to Herzog's academic connections as a major factor in establishing the favorable situation for Bartók's research work (in Herzog's phonograph archive at Columbia University) with the Milman Parry record collection of Yugoslav folk music held at Harvard University. Contains illustrations, port., facsimiles.

322. ----------. "Contributions á l'étude de la Sonate Solo de Béla Bartók (1944)" [Contributions to the study of Bartók's *Solo Sonata*]. *Studia musicologica* 23 (1981): 209-260.   781.05 St92   ISSN 0039-3266

Discusses Bartók's life in his American years (1940-1945) and how he took refuge from his somber existence in his ethnomusicological research and work on transcriptions. Then the style features of this period are outlined. A detailed history of the *Sonata* is given, with letters to Yehudi Menuhin regarding details of the work. An outline of sources (manuscript sketches, letters to Menuhin, etc.) is given regarding the critical study of the edited score, with discussion of corrections for each movement. A detailed analysis is presented for each section within the three movements, in terms of rhythm, polymodal chromaticism, and other stylistic features.

323. ----------. "Le destin des recherches ethnomusicologues de Béla Bartók à la vielle de son séjour aux Etats-Unis" [The fate of Béla Bartók's ethnomusicological research on the eve of his sojourn in the United States]. *Revue belge de musicologie/Belgish tijdschrift voor muziekwetenschap* 42 (1988): 273-283.   780.5 R3269

Discusses the conditions that induced Bartók to emigrate to New York City in October 1940. Informs us that Bartók's decision to settle in the United States was made only after he was assured of the possibility of continuing his ethnomusicological investigations based on access to the Milman Parry collection at Harvard University. Also points to the impact of his emigration on his Slovak, Hungarian, Romanian, and Turkish folk-music collections.

324. Liebner, János. "Unpublished Bartók Documents." *The New Hungarian Quarterly* 3/6 (April-June 1962): 221-224.
914.39105 N42   ML410 B26 B29

The author, a Hungarian cellist and musical critic, was induced by *The New Hungarian Quarterly* to disclose further facts about the life and work of Bartók, including the existence of a fifth movement to the *Piano Suite,* Op. 14, which was hitherto known as consisting of four movements, and to quote the complete text of the last radio interviews in Bartók's life. See also the following publications: "Une œuvre oubliée de Bartók" [A forgotten work of Bartók}. *Schweizerische Musikzeitung* 100 (1960): 357 and 359; "Bartók utolsó amerikai rádióinterjúi" [Bartók's last American radio interview]. *Új zenei szemle* (Budapest) 6/12 (December 1955): 26-28. Reprinted in *Bartók Studies,* ed. Todd Crow. Detroit: Information Coordinators, 1976, pp. 137-140.

325. Lukács, György. "Bartók und die ungarische Kultur" [Bartók and Hungarian culture]. *International Musicological Conference in Commemoration of Béla Bartók 1971.* Budapest: Editio Musica; New York: Belwin Mills, 1972, pp. 11-12. ML410.B29 I61 (Editio Musica)   ML410.B26 I5 (Belwin Mills)

Discusses Bartók's significant role in the history of Hungarian culture. States that Bartók, like other European artists, protested the alienation taking place in modern capitalist society and culture, and this is the essence of his music.

326. ----------. "Béla Bartók. On the Twenty-fifth Anniversary of His Death." *The New Hungarian Quarterly* 12/41 (1971): 42-55. 914.39105 N42   ML410 B26 B29

The author, a major philosopher, discusses the significance of Bartók's work from the point of view of political and cultural history. Asks, "What does it mean to be Hungarian?" Then, states that "Hungarian culture must have the courage and social and moral basis to say: Bartók has opened for us the historical way to true Hungarian culture." Reprinted in *Bartók Studies,* ed. Todd Crow. Detroit: Information Coordinators, 1976, pp. 203-216.

327. Martynov, Ivan. "Quelques pensées sur Bartók" [Some thoughts about Bartók]. *International Musicological Conference in Commemoration of Béla Bartók 1971,* ed. József Ujfalussy and János Breuer. Budapest: Editio Musica; New York: Belwin Mills, 1972, pp. 107-110. ML410.B29 I61 (Editio Musica) ML410.B26 I5 (Belwin Mills)

Activity as composer and folklorist was exemplary in bringing about a synthesis between East and West. Discusses the general significance of Bartók as one of the greatest personalities of our present-day music.

328. Menuhin, Yehudi. "Bartók at 100: A Titan Remembered." *Saturday Review* (March 1981): 39-40.   AP2 S2794

Gives brief history of events that brought Menuhin in contact with Bartók's work and with the composer himself. Describes

Bartók's personality and condition during his last years in New York, as well as focusing on the encounter with Bartók during Menuhin's performance of the *First Sonata* for piano and violin for the composer. Talks of Bartók's final illness.

329. Milne, Hamish. *Bartók, His Life and Times.* Tunbridge Wells: Midas Books, 1982; New York: Hippocrene Books, 1983. 112p. ISBN 0859362736 ML 410 B26 M54

Exclusively a biographical study (without analyses of the music). Includes numerous photos of Bartók with family, friends, composers, folk-music collecting, pictures of old Budapest, villages, some facsimiles, illustrations, index, etc.

330. Molnár, Antal. *Bartók művészete, emlékezésekkel a művész életére* [Bartók's art with recollections of the artist's life]. Budapest: Rózsavölgyi és Társai, 1948. 96p.

An important primary source document, since the author was violist in the Waldbauer-Kerpely String Quartet; the members were friends of Bartók and played the first two quartets when no one else would approach them. Provides significant biographical and cultural data as well as personal insights into the composer's personality and psychology.

331. ----------. *Magamról, másokról* [About me, about others]. Budapest: Gondolat Kiadó, 1974. 309p.

First-hand account of musical activities in Budapest in the early part of the century, including recollections of some of the most prominent Hungarian musical figures, among them Bartók, Kodály, Dohnányi, Hubay, and Mihálovich.

332. Moore, Douglas. "Homage to Bartók." *Modern Music* 23/1 (January 1946): 13-14. 780.5 M72

Discusses Bartók's life in exile in the United States and compares it with the exiles of two other great figures of the post-romantic revolution in music, Stravinsky and Schoenberg. Refers to Bartók's situation in these last years of his life and suggests reasons for his lesser popularity than the other two in the United States. See also the Polish translation in *Ruch muzyczny* (1947).

333. Nest'yev, Izrael. "Béla Bartók v Rossii" [Béla Bartók in Russia]. *Studia musicologica* 5/1-4 (1963): 481-490. 781.05 St92 ISSN 0039-3266

A report on the positive reactions of the Soviet music world to Bartók's visit to Russia. Includes comments of the music critic Boris Asaf'yev on such topics as Bartók's role in the development of the "new music." Also presents contrasting views of another music critic and provides a short comparison of the musical styles of Bartók and Prokofiev as well.

334. Panufnik, Andrzej, Alberto Ginastera, and Iannis Xenakis. "Homage to Béla Bartók." *Tempo* (London) 136 (March 1981): 3-5. 780.5 T249   ISSN 0040-2982

Panufnik feels that Bartók is the greatest composer of the first half of this century, admiring his feeling for the soul of all musical instruments, his humility as a composer, his commitment to education, and devotion in collecting and studying folk music. Ginastera speaks of his first contact with Bartók's music *(Allegro barbaro* played by Rubinstein) and praises his greatness. Xenakis speaks of Bartók's expansion of the musical vision: his exploration of the music of diverse cultures of peoples, the contribution to the harmonic and contrapuntal heritage, and the effort of abstraction which can lead to "une universalité planétaire."

335. Porter, James. "Bartók and Janáček: Contact, Context, and Confluence." *Festschrift für Oskár Elschek.* Bratislava: Slovenská Akademia Vied, 1996.

Points to an important series of contacts between Bartók and Janáček in the period 1924-1927. The two composers met at least three times, and Janáček seems to have been instrumental in helping Bartók solve the issue of his mother's pension (then being denied her by the Czech government). Although they may have met at the ISCM Festival in Prague in 1924, their first documented meeting was in January, 1925 in Prague, where they met again in 1927 on the occasion of Bartók's playing his *Piano Concerto No. 1* in October of that year. Janáček had also invited Bartók to play in his home town of Brno in March, 1925, and they may well have met again at the ISCM Festival in Frankfurt, in June-July 1927, when Janáček's *Concertino* and Bartók's *Piano Concerto No. 1* had their premieres. These contacts suggest a set of converging contexts for their musical interaction, although specific influence or interactivity is hard to document because of their very different personalities, methods, and genre focus. But there seems no doubt that beneath the surface differences, a similar aim was at work, namely to privilege the procedures and textures of folk music in an area of prolonged contact among Hungarian, Moravian, Slovak and Romanian idioms. (Annotation based on the author's own unpublished abstract.)

336. Rácz, Ilona. "Bartók Béla utolsó évei a Magyar Tudományos Akadémián" [Béla Bartók's last years at the Hungarian Academy of Sciences]. *Magyar tudomány* (1961): 383-387.   A119 H8 M268

Author was assistant of Bartók at the Hungarian Academy of Sciences from 1938 until Bartók's departure for America in 1940. Discusses Bartók's means of classifying folk material at the Academy as well as his own capacity and personal way of working.

337. Réz, Pál. "Thomas Mann and Bartók." *The New Hungarian Quarterly* 2/3 (July-September 1961): 89-91.   914.39105 N42
ML410 B26 B29

Based on Mann's correspondence with Hungarian friends, discussing his meetings with Bartók and his personal impressions of him. Reprinted in *Bartók Studies,* ed. Todd Crow. Detroit: Information Coordinators, 1976, pp. 177-178.

338. Rogers, Michael, and Zoltán Oválry. "Bartók in the USSR in 1929." *Music Library Association Notes* 29 (1973): 416-425.
780.6 M971n   ISSN 0027-4380

Provides an account of Bartók's concert tour in the USSR in 1929. Included is a discussion of three letters from Bartók to the Ambassadress. These letters are published here in facsimile as well as in translation.

339. Ruffy, P. "The Dispute over Bartók's Will." *The New Hungarian Quarterly* 7/22 (1966): 206-209.   914.39105 N42
ML410 B26 B29

A will signed and dated October 4, 1940, made because of the uncertainty and risks of Bartók's voyage. A second will was made in the United States. Discusses the history and conditions of these wills and gives the complete Budapest will of 1940. Reprinted in *Bartók Studies,* ed. Todd Crow. Detroit: Information Coordinators, 1976, pp. 141-146.

340. Sárhelyi, Jenő. "Bartók Béla Békés megyében" [Béla Bartók in the County of Békés]." *Békési élet* 9/3 (1974): 557-572.   HA1.525

Outlines Bartók's folk-music collecting and concert activities in Békés County during two periods. From 1906 to 1918 he collected about 500 tunes in Békés, and between 1922 and 1936 he gave five concerts in Békéscsaba. Presents eleven letters from Bartók to Ernő Südy, who made the concert arrangements. Includes illustrations, port., and music.

341. ----------. "Bartók Béla és Kodály Zoltán a Békéscsabai Aurora Körben" [Béla Bartók and Zoltán Kodály and the Békéscsabai Aurora Kör]. *Magyar zene* 30/2 (June 1989): 213-220.   ML5 M14
ISSN 0025-0384

Includes documentation such as programs and critical reviews from concerts with Bartók and Kodály in Békéscsaba in southeastern Hungary. Concerts were arranged by Ernő Südy under the auspices of the Aurora Kör, which was founded in 1913 and reestablished in 1918.

342. Schelken, Pálma. "Levelek Sebestyén Gyulához Bartók és Kodály 'übyben'" [Letters to Gyula Sebestyén about Bartók and Kodály]. *Magyar zene* 25/4 (December 1984): 436-444.   ML5 M14 ISSN 0025-0384

According to Péter Halász, *RILM Abstracts* No. 3866 (1984), discusses "Letters to Gyula Sebestyén, the Hungarian ethnologist who supported Béla Bartók and Zoltán Kodály in their successful effort to initiate *Corpus musicae popularis hungaricae* (1913). In 1934 he urged them to appeal to the Hungarian literary society Kisfaludy Társaság for financial help, but their efforts were unsuccessful." Contains facsimile.

343. Scholz, Gottfried. "Ablösung von Wien, Ein Kommentar zu Bartóks Orchestersuiten" [Commutation from Vienna, a commentary on Bartók's *Suite for Orchestra*]. *Studia musicologica* 24/supplement (1982): 75-80.   781.05 St92   ISSN 0039-3266

Discusses Bartók's appearances (1903-1905) in Vienna as pianist and composer, with reference to critical reviews of the works performed. Places these compositions (with emphasis on style analysis) in the context of the gypsy and Hungarian popular influences seen earlier in Brahms and Liszt to Lehár.

344. Staud, Géza. "Ismeretlen Bartók-levelek" [Unknown letters of Bartók]. *Muzsika* (Budapest) 19/9 (September 1976): 23-26. ISSN 0027-5336

Includes facsimiles of five unknown letters, written by the composer in connection with performances of his stage and other works at the Budapest Opera. The first letter (dated 1916) deals with *The Wooden Prince,* the second and third (1917) with *Duke Bluebeard's Castle,* the fourth (1931) with *The Miraculous Mandarin;* in which Bartók returned the money paid to him in advance, and the fifth (undated), in which Bartók blocked the performance of the *Kossuth Symphony.*

345. Strack, Márta Mohos, ed. *Budapest Történeti Múzeum* [Béla Bartók Memorial House/Budapest History Museum], rev. by László Somfai. Budapest: Budapest Történeti Múzeum, 1981. 69p. ML 410 B26 B85

The house in which Bartók lived from 1932 to 1940, now used as a Bartók museum. Mainly, provides a chronology of Bartók's life with interesting photos. Includes illustrations, a chronological list of all his dwelling places, chronological list of his works, and index.

346. Suchoff, Benjamin. "Bartók in America." *Musical Times* 117/1596 (February 1976): 123-124.   780.5 M98   ISSN-0027-4666

Head of the New York Bartók Archives discusses the lack of acceptance of Bartók's music during his final years of his life in the United States (1940-1945). Also published in Hungarian: "Bartók utolsó évei Amerikában." *Magyar zene* (Budapest) 17/2 (June 1976): 190-193.   ML5 M14   ISSN 0025-0384

347. ----------. "Béla Bartók vid en milstolpe" [Bartók's *Second String Quartet*. Stylistic landmark]. *Nutida musik* (Stockholm) 5-6 (1964/65): 136-139.   ML5 N96   780.904   ISSN 0029-6597

Discusses parallels between earlier masters and Bartók, pointing to architectural, textural (polyphonic), etc., models in Bach, Beethoven, and Debussy. Then, gives a formal-thematic outline of the quartet and a history of the folk sources from 1905 to 1917 as they were absorbed in certain works. Points to the significant position of Bartók's Quartets as a landmark in the line of chamber music since Haydn and Beethoven. Also published in: *The American Music Teacher* 15/2 (November-December 1965).

348. Surrans, Alain. *Bartók és Franciaország. Bartók et la France.* Bilingual Edition. Budapest: Európa--Institut Français, 1993. 142p.

According to László Somfai, in his review entitled "Bartók and France: Aspects of a Relationship," in *Hungarian Musical Quarterly* 35/133 (Spring 1994): 174-178, "Alain Surrans prompts one to reconsider some aspects of the subject of Bartók and France. . . . such as Bartók and French Baroque music [Couperin and Rameau], the extent of Bartók's knowledge of the work of his younger French contemporaries [post-Debussy and Ravel French generation, especially Milhaud and Poulenc], and to what degree a French musician was able to grasp Bartók's real style in order to finally arrive at what really intrigues me: whether ultimately Bartók expected more from France?"

349. Székely, Júlia. *Bartók tanár úr* [Professor Bartók]. Budapest: Dunántúli Magvető, 1957,1978. 243p.   ISBN 9632112369 ML 410 B26 S8977

Student of Bartók at the Academy of Music in Budapest provides important information on Bartók's pedagogical approach. However, gives little information on the man or the music. Contains illustrations, plates.

350. Szentjóbi, Miklós. "Búcsúbeszélgetés Bartók Bélával és Pásztory Dittával amerikai útjuk előtt" [Farewell interview with Béla Bartók and Ditta Pásztory before their American trip]. *Muzsika* (Budapest) 17/5 (May 1974): 33-38.   ISSN 0027-5336

The author, who helped organize a farewell concert for Bartók in Budapest before he left for the United States in 1940, discusses the circumstances surrounding his last interview. Includes the entire text of the interview. See also: "Abschiedsgespräch mit Béla Bartók und Ditta Pásztory vor ihrer Amerika-Reise." *Híd* (Budapest) (October, 1940): 21-22.

351. Szigeti, Joseph. "Bartók Competition, October 1948: A Tribute to Bartók." *Tempo* (London) 10 (Winter 1948-49): 16-21. 780.5 T249   ISSN 0040-2982

Text of a broadcast written by Szigeti for the Budapest Radio. States that this competition is in accordance with the high ideals and uncompromising character of the great artist. Also talks of his last impressions of Bartók during his last days in New York, and mentions his discussions of abuses and unhappy state of affairs as well as activities that concerned him while he was bedridden.

352. ----------. *Beszélő húrok* [Speaking strings]. Budapest: Zeneműkiadó Vállalat, 1965. 74p.   ISBN-9632719565

Includes the violinist's personal recollections of Bartók. Contains bibliography.

353. Takács, Jenő. *Erinnerungen an Béla Bartók.* Vienna, Munich: Doblinger, 1982. 135p.   ISBN 3900035776   ML 410 B26 T28

Includes important primary-source documentation, based on the author's personal connections with Bartók. With the aid of the composer's older son Béla Bartók Jr., the author provides both sides of his correspondence with Bartók between 1925 and 1938. Also, reproduces photographs of Bartók on his Egyptian tour in 1932. Provides essential biographical information, interspersed with the author's own reminiscences as well as quotations by Bartók. In addition, contains discussions of the composer's youth as well as his last years in the United States. Contains illustrations, bibliography, index. See the review by Malcolm Gillies, in *Music and Letters* 66/4 (October 1985): 373-375.

354. Tallián, Tibor. "Bartók és a szavak" [Bartók and words]. *Arion* 13 (1982): 67-72. French trans. Éva Szilágyi (pp. 72-78); English trans. Susan Gray (pp. 78-83). 913.3805 Ar43

States that although Bartók was a prolific writer, he was almost wordless during his piano teaching. Most of his volumes were devoted to folk-song collecting, and his letters were often little more than mere communication of facts. Discusses Bartók's aversion to communication since childhood as being due to illnesses which isolated him. However, since his adulthood Bartók was in various ways connected with poetic and other types of writings. He composed love songs to the texts of the earlier Romantic poets as well as edited and set the texts of contemporary writers. His own writings reflect his stand on art and politics. He also prepared his writings for publication. In this chronological discussion, we are not only provided insights into Bartók's personality but also given an overview of Bartók's articles and their contents.

355. Tóth, Aladár. "Bartók's Foreign Tour. " Trans. David E. Schneider and Klára Móricz. In *Bartók and His World,* ed. Peter Laki. Princeton, New Jersey: Princeton University Press, 1995. pp. 282-289. ISBN 0-691-00633-4. ML 410 B26 B272 Originally published in: *Nyugat* 15, no. 12 (1922): 830-833.

Discusses Bartók's trips to London, Paris, and Frankfurt and his anticipation in determining the degree of popularity and understanding of his music. Also refers to his natural expectations at the opportunity to "provide a genuine picture of himself through his own performance" and to "find allies for his artistic goals." Informs us that Bartók's expectations were entirely met during this tour, documenting many positive critical reviews. Describes Bartók's activities, the music with which he came into contact, and his impressions, observations, and opinions of works by Stravinsky, Milhaud, Ravel, and others. In contrast to London and Paris, he was disappointed with performances of his music and with musical developments (of the young Hindemith, etc.) in Frankfurt. Contains notes. See also: Aladár Tóth. "Bartók külföldi útja" [Bartók's foreign tour]. Vol. 7 *(Bartók Béla művészi kibontakozásának évei II--Bartók megjelenése az európai zeneéletben [1914-1926]* [The years of Bartók's artistic evolution, part 2--Bartók's appearance in European musical life (1914-1926)], ed. János Demény) of *Zenetudományi tanulmányok,* ed. Bence Szabolcsi and Dénes Bartha. Budapest: Zeneműkiadó, 1959. pp. 219-222.

356. Ujfalussy, József, ed. "Béla Bartóks Kinderjahre: aus den Tagebuchblättern seiner Mutter" [Béla Bartók's childhood years: from the diary of his mother]." *Österreichische Musikzeitschrift* 2 0 (1965): 461-466. 780.5 Oe8 ISSN 0029-9316

Provides excerpts from the diary of Bartók's mother, which she had written for Bartók's son. Also published in *Bartók Béla. családi levelei* [Family letters of Béla Bartók], ed. Béla Bartók, Jr. Budapest: Zeneműkiadó, 1981, pp. 315-324.

357. ----------. "1907-1908 in Bartóks Entwicklung" [The years 1907-1908 in Bartók's development]. *Studia musicologica* 24/3-4 (1982): 519-525.   781.05 St92   ISSN 0039-3266

Discusses the risks and yet the necessity in every historical investigation of establishing period divisions in a composer's career. The parameters according to which periods are demarcated are so manifold and overlapping, that valid periodization is difficult to assure. States that the works around 1908-1911 are so new and special that this period can only be compared with the later crucial turning point in Bartók's career in the mid 1920s. Discusses the numerous intersecting influences of the earlier period (Strauss' influence, study of Debussy, first folk-music explorations, etc.) that contributed to Bartók's development at this time. Discusses the stylistic and technical features of the works of this period, as well as certain thematic interrelationships of certain works that developed from Bartók's relationship with the violinist Stefi Geyer. Also discusses Bartók's personal crises in the era of his youth.

358. ----------. "Egy nehéz búcsúzás zenei képlete" [The musical depiction of a sad parting]. *Zenetudományi dolgozatok* (1984): 67-69.

Discusses the biographical connections between the first piece, *Ajánlás* [Dedication], of Bartók's *Tíz könnyű zongoradarab* [Ten easy piano pieces] and the composer's unrequited love for Stefi Geyer. Contains music examples.

359. Valkó, Arisztid. "Adatok Bartók színpadi műveihez" [Data concerning the stage works of Bartók]. *Magyar zene* (Budapest) 18 (1977): 433-439.   ML5 M14   ISSN 0025-0384

Includes several documents held at the Hungarian State Opera archives. These include invitations extended to Bartók and his librettist, Béla Balázs, to attend a preview of *Bluebeard's Castle* and a contract between Bartók and Sándor Bródy (dated 1918) for a performance of a dance setting of *Molnár Anna*.

360. ----------. "Bartók Béla tervezett londoni hangversenyének levéltári háttere" [Archival material concerning one of Bartók's London recitals]. *Magyar zene* (Budapest) 18 (1977): 99-105.   ML5 M14   ISSN 0025-0384

Includes documents (1926-1927) held at the Hungarian foreign office, revealing Bartók's plans to participate in a series of contemporary music concerts by the BBC. However, an illness caused him to postpone his concert until 1929.

361. Vancea, Zeno. "Béla Bartók. Un mare múzicián al veacului nóstru" [Béla Bartók. A great musician of our century]. *Muzica* (Romania) 20/11 (November 1970): 1-3.   ISSN 0580-3713

Discusses Bartók's association with Romanian musicians and presents his views on folk music and aesthetics.

362. Weil, Irving. "Bartók Bows to America in New York Hall." *Musical America* (December 31, 1927): 1, 8.   ML1 M97

Review of Bartók's own performance debut of the *Rhapsody* for piano and orchestra, Op. 1, with the New York Philharmonic, conducted by Mengelberg. The new *Piano Concerto* (No. 1) was abandoned because of insufficient rehearsal, which was disappointing, since it would have shown Bartók as representative of the "extreme left" in Hungary and "presumably summing up the whole current Bartók gospel of dissonance." Also discusses the development of Bartók's style.

3. Specialized Studies of Bartók's Career and Work as Ethnomusicologist

363. Bartók, János. "Bartók, pionnier de la musicologie." *La revue musicale* 224 (1955): 41-57.   780.5 R328   ISSN 0035-3736

Gives historical outline of Bartók's ethnomusicological research and discussion of his publications based on transcriptions of folk melodies from various nations as well as his discussions regarding these investigations. Also mentions briefly Bartók's musicological activities in the area of instructive editions of the works of Bach, Mozart, Haydn, Beethoven, and other composers.

364. Ciolac, Ion. "Béla Bartók şi cîntecul popular bihorean" [Béla Bartók and the folk song of Bihor]. *Ziele folclorului bihorean* (1973): 69-93.

Discusses Bartók's ethnomusicological activities in Bihor County as well as the characteristics of both vocal and instrumental dance tunes.

365. Cosma, Viorel. "Bartók şi inceputurile culegerilor de folclor românesc. Pe marginea unor documente inedite" [Bartók and the first collections of Romanian folklore: marginal notes concerning several unpublished documents]. *Studii şi cercetari de istoria artei. Teatru, muzica, cinematografie* 18/2 (1971): 239-251.

Provides primary-source evidence, including unpublished letters between Bartók and the Romanian ethnomusicologist Tiberiu Brediceanu and other documentation regarding Bartók's early Romanian folk-music investigations, demonstrating the influence of the Romanians on Bartók's folk-song research as well as their own involvement in producing the earliest Romanian folk-music publications.

366. Cvetko, Igor. "Slovenci in terensko delo pri razisk-ovanju glazbenega izročila" [Slovenes and fieldwork in traditional music]. *Zbornik od XIX Kongres na Sojuzot na Združenijata na Folkloristite na Jugoslavija* (Skopje: Združenie na Folkloristite na Macedonia, 1986): 291-295.

In Slovene; summary in English. According to Dimitri Buzarovski, *RILM Abstracts* No. 6484 (1989), "Béla Bartók's methodology and research in traditional music are compared with those of Matija Murko in Slovenia and the Folkjlorni Institut in Ljubljana (now Sekcija za Glasbeno Narodopisje of the Slovenska Akademija Znanosti in Umetnosti). Other perspectives and problems in ethnomusicological research are discussed."

367. Djoudjeff, Stoyan. "Bartók, promoteur de l'ethnomusicologie balkanique et sud-est Européenne" [Bartók, initiator of ethnomusicology in the Balkans and Southeastern Europe]. *International Musicological Conference in Commemoration of Béla Bartók 1971*, ed. József Ujfalussy and János Breuer. Budapest: Editio Musica; New York: Belwin Mills, 1972: 189-195.   ML410.B26 I5 (Editio Musica)   ML410.B29 I61 (Belwin Mills)

Talks of Bartók's inductive and comparative method as a key to recognizing the national styles within musical folklore. Discusses Bartók's desire to transform ethnomusicology into an exact science by introducing quantitative evaluations and demonstrating the significance of this in the development of ethnomusicology in this geographical area.

368. Dobszay, László. "Folksong Classification in Hungary: Some Methodological Conclusions." *Studia musicologica* 30/1-4 (1988): 235-280.   781.05 St92   ISSN 0039-3266

Provides a history of folk-song classification in Hungary based on the methodological techniques of Bartók, Kodály, and Járdányi. Discusses their approaches to the organization of the large quantity of folk sources according to stylistic features. Provides definitions of such terms as *type* and *style* as they are applied in ethnomusicological investigation and presents some methodological conclusions.

369. Domokos, Mária. "Bartóks Systeme zum Ordnen der Volksmusik" [Bartók's system of classification of folk music]. *Studia musicologica* 24/3-4 (1982): 315-325.   781.05 St92
ISSN 0039-3266

Discusses the aim of classifying folk melodies, the method (its sources), Bartók's deviation from Krohn's method, the elements of Bartók's system, the point of view of strophic-song ordering (based on cadential melodic tones, form, mode, strophic structure, rhythmic character, etc.), and the character of Bartók's system.

370. --------------. "Die Volksmusik der Magyaren und der benachbarten Völker" [Folk music of the Hungarians and neighboring peoples]. *Studia musicologica* 23 (1981): 353-362.   781.05 St92
ISSN 0039-3266

Points to the important role that folk music has played in the musical revolution of the early twentieth century and in the creation of modern Hungarian musical culture. Furthermore, Bartók, unlike Kodály, did not stop with Hungarian folk music but expanded his investigations and absorbed Slovak and Romanian folk music also. Well-documented study, referring to primary and secondary sources. Points to the importance of Bartók's philosophical reasons for this involvement, which came not only from his humanism but also his sense of reality.

371. Downey, John William. "La musique populaire dans l'œuvre de Béla Bartók" [Folk music in the work of Béla Bartók]. Ph.D. diss., Paris: University of Paris, 1956. Paris: Centre de Documentation Universitaire, 1966. 565p.   ML410.B26 D7

Divided into two main parts. The first part is an analytical survey primarily dealing with the stylistic and regional traits of those folk music sources investigated by Bartók (Hungarian, Romanian, Slovak, Arabic, Ukrainian, Bulgarian, Serbo-Croatian, and Turkish). Also clarifies Bartók's methodological approach. In-depth analyses of folksong structure, in terms of form, special modal traits, range, contour, and rhythm are provided for the purpose of understanding Bartók's folk-song transformations in his own original compositional idiom. These analyses then serve as the basis for the study in the second part of Bartók's use of these folk-song elements in his own compositions and to what degree they influenced and were transformed in them. Also refers to other, related folk-music studies. Chronological study of Bartók's compositions grouped according to genre. More than 420 musical examples. Contains bibliography. See the review by Jean Gergely, in *Revue de musicologie* 54/1 (1968).

372. Elschek, Oskár. "Bartók ako etnomuzikolog" [Bartók as an ethnomusicologist]. *Musicologica slovaca* 5 (1974): 277-290. ISSN 0581-0558

    Contains a summary in German. Demonstrates the correlation between the development of Bartók's ethnomusicological research and the stylistic evolution of his own compositions.

373. -----------. "Bartóks Beziehung zur Volksmusik und Volksmusikforschung" [The relationship between Bartók and folk music and folk music research]. *International Musicological Conference in Commemoration of Béla Bartók 1971*, ed. József Ujfalussy and János Breuer. Budapest: Editio Music; New York: Belwin Mills, 1972): 197-207.   ML410.B29 I61   ML410.B26 I5

    Divides Bartók's folk-song research into four large periods. Based on letters and essays, the study investigates how Bartók's concept of folk-music research developed, emphasizing the purely musical motives of the research, supported by comprehensive international information, and surpassing the nationalistic limitations of the time.

374. Erdely, Stephen. "Bartók on Southslavic Epic Song." *Bartók in Retrospect,* ed. Elliott Antokoletz, Victoria Fischer, and Benjamin Suchoff. Projected publication of two 1995 conference proceedings.

    Discusses Bartók's appointment during 1941 and 1942 at Columbia University to transcribe and prepare for publication Serbo-Croatian folk and heroic songs collected by Harvard Professor Milman Parry in Yugoslavia during 1934-1935. Bartók made synoptic transcriptions of four of them and decided to concentrate on the recorded "women's songs" of the collection, which he found musically more interesting and more in his line of expertise. Documents emerging from the files of the Parry Collection, however, indicate that Bartók began to change his opinion. Points out that although Bartók never formulated his thoughts in an article, his observations have taken the forms of comparative notes, short remarks, footnotes, intuitive comments, and nonverbal musical sketches which are dispersed within the text of his study, *Serbo-Croatian Folk Songs,* in his letters, and in the aforementioned detailed musical transcriptions. Exploration of Bartók's views reveals that while they remained incomplete and inconclusive, his awakened interest in the musical creativity and personality of epic singers gave Erdelyi the incentive to probe into the musical process unfolding in the singer's mind subconsciously during the performance of a long-narrative oral narrative song. (Annotation based on the author's abstract of the original lecture; see item no. 1139.)

375. ----------. "Folk-Music Research in Hungary Until 1950: The Legacy of Zoltán Kodály and Béla Bartók." *Current Musicology* 43 (1987): 51-61. 780.5 C936

Discusses the pioneering folk-music research by Bartók and Kodály in Hungary during the early part of the century. Demonstrates that both folklorists, in spite of their contrasting backgrounds and methodology, were essential in paving the way for further ethnomusicological investigation by other researchers into the wealth of Hungarian folk-music materials. Also points to the importance of the Hungarian folk-music sources in their own compositions.

376. Fracile, Nice. "In the Wake of Bartók's Recordings: The Changes and Evolutionary Tendencies in the Serbian and Romanian Folklores in Vojvodina, Yugoslavia." *East European Meetings in Ethnomusicology* 2 (1995): 15-23. ISSN 1221-9711

Points to the value of the phonograph recordings of the Serbian and Romanian notation made by Bartók in 1912, especially because of the scarcity of ethnomusicological research in the Balkans in the early twentieth century. Describes these examples and compares Bartók's folklore material with current material. Provides in-depth discussion of melody types, rhythmic schemata, and performance practices. Concludes that Bartók's recordings and transcriptions "are truly challenging for comparative ethnomusicologists--now and in the future." States that the Bartók "source is 'a little, living history' of the Serbian and Romanian folklores." Contains music examples.

377. Gál, István. *Bartóktól Radnótiig. Tanulmányok* [From Bartók to Radnóti. Studies]. Budapest: Magvető, 1973. 184p. PH 3017.G27

In this series of monographs on various twentieth-century Hungarian musicians, information is provided on Bartók's early central-European folk-music investigations. Contains bibliography. See the following reviews: Ferenc Bónis, in *Muzsika* (Budapest) 16/7 (July 1973): 36-37; and János Breuer, in *Magyar zene* (Budapest) 16/4 (December 1975): 428-429.

378. Gerson-Kiwi, Edith. "Béla Bartók--Scholar in Folk Music." *Music and Letters* 38/2 (April 1957): 149-154. 780.5 M92 ISSN 0027-4224

Good survey of Bartók's scholarly achievement. Primarily concerned with that side of Bartók, i.e., as folk-music scholar, that gained him an international reputation at a time when his compositional masterpieces had difficulty in gaining recognition. Does not deal with analysis of folk song as it appeared in his art-music settings. Gives division of Bartók's folk-music research in three main periods, then proceeds with a general description of the geographic areas where he collected, including the type, amount, and means of collecting the material. Also points out Bartók's exactitude in notation by comparison with a Liszt transcription of the same tune as well as the exceptional detail in Bartók's transcription of a Serbo-Croatian tune.

379. Halperson, Maurice. "Béla Bartók Explains Himself." *Musical America* (January 21, 1928): 9.   ML1 M97

Lengthy interview, including references to six musical examples of folk songs.

380. Járdányi, Pál. "Bartók und die Ordnung der Volkslieder" [Bartók and the classification of folk songs]. *Studia musicologica* 5/1-4 (1963): 435-439.   781.05 St92   ISSN 0039-3266

Discusses how Bartók developed his system of classification after first following Krohn's, which compares types and styles of melodies. He developed it further, then developed his own system, which consisted of three categories, differentiating the new style from the old. Compares Bartók's system with that of Kodály.

381. Kerényi, György. "Bartók, a népdal-lejegyző" [Bartók as a notator of folk song]. *Ethnographia* 59 (1948): n.p.   HB1.743

Not examined. As pointed out by Judit Frigyesi, p. 331 of her article (see item no. 891), Kerényi believes that in several of Bartók's publications of folk-tune transcriptions, he was more inclined toward a popular edition than a scholarly ethnomusicological study. Kerényi further suggests that it is for this reason that the edition is uneven in terms of accuracy in transcription.

382. ----------. "The System of Publishing the Collection of Hungarian Folksongs: Corpus Musicae Popularis Hungaricae." *Studia memoriae Béla Bartók sacra.* Budapest: Akadémiai Kiadó, 1956, pp. 453-468. 780.92 B285R

Deals with the question of what, where, and how to arrange, store, and publish the Hungarian folksongs collected by Bartók and Kodály. Discusses principles of classification.

383. Kerényi, György, and Benjamin Rajeczky. "Über Bartóks Volksliedaufzeichnungen" [On Bartók's folk-song transcriptions]. *Studia musicologica* 5 (1963): 441-448.   781.05 St92

ISSN 0039-3266

States that Bartók's first transcriptions are "archetypes," written down after hearing several performances, in which elements may have changed from performance to performance, and even from stanza to stanza.

384. Kneif, Tibor. "Arabische Musik bei Bartók" [Arab music and Bartók]. *Österreichische Musikzeitschrift* 43/7-8 (July-August 1988): 386-390.   780.5 Oe8   ISSN 0029-9316

Dicusses Bartók's early contact with Arab music in 1906 during his visit to the coast of North Africa. He later collected Arab music from the Biskra district in Algiers and was to absorb characteristics of the Arab melodies into his own compositions.

385. Kodály, Zoltán. "A folklorista Bartók" [Bartók, the folklorist]. *Új zenei szemle* (Budapest) 1 (1950): 33.   HA1.588

Outlines Bartók's professional career throughout his life, starting as a pianist, then as a composer in the traditional manner. Only after the age of twenty-four did he turn toward his native folk music. Then discusses the various influences on his development (Liszt, Debussy, etc.) and the gradual expansion of his folk studies outside of Hungary. The latter are given a systematic chronological account. Also published in: *La revue musicale* 212 (April 1952): 31-38; *Musik der Zeit* Heft 9. Bonn: Boosey and Hawkes, 1954, p. 33; and *Visszatekintés* [Retrospection] 2. Budapest: Zeneműkiadó, 1964, p. 450.

386. Kovács, Sándor. "The Ethnomusicologist." *The Bartók Companion,* ed. Malcolm Gillies. London: Faber and Faber, 1993; Portland, Oregon: Amadeus Press (an imprint of Timber Press, Inc.), 1994. pp. 51-63.   ISBN 0-931340-74-8 (HB)   ISBN 0-931340-75-6 (PB)   ML410 B26 B28

Quotes Bartók to reveal his intention "to collect the finest Hungarian folksongs and to raise them, adding the best possible piano accompaniments, to the level of art song." Presents a history from Bartók's first contact with and investigations of the folk sources and his first contact with Kodály, shaping of his attitude toward Hungarian folk song, and development of his ethnomusicological activities and methodology. Points to Bartók's shift from a primarily artistic interest to an increasingly systematic, scientific approach. Follows the expansion of Bartók's research to Slovak, Romanian, Ruthenian, Serbian, Bulgarian, and Arab sources prior to the First World War and his frustrations and curtailment of his investigations during and after the war and his return to its study and classification in the mid 1930s. Presents a survey of Bartók's folk-music publications (including posthumous ones as well as collections that are still unavailable) and some details of his methodological approach to the classification of the materials.

387. Kuckertz, Josef. "Bartóks Volksmusikforschung: Aus der Sicht der vergleichenden Musikwissenschaft" [Bartók's folk-music research: From the viewpoint of comparative musicology]. *Österreichische Musikzeitschrift* 39/2 (February 1984): 78-85.   780.5 Oe8 ISSN 0029-9316

Points to the similarities between Bartók's ethnomusicological methodology in collecting and transcribing folk music and comparative musicology. Discusses Bartók's intuitive absorption of techniques from the latter discipline and addresses the compositional purposes behind his folk-music investigations. Contains illustrations, music examples.

388. Laki, Péter. "Der lange Gesang als Grundtyp in der internationalen Volksmusik" [The long song as basic type in international folk music]. *Studia musicologica* 24/3-4 (1982): 393-400.   781.05 St92 ISSN 0039-3266

States that this type was one of Bartók's greatest discoveries in the area of Romanian folk music. Discusses Bartók's findings and shows parallels with other international folk-music types (e.g., North African Arab) in terms of melodic structure, mode and tonality, and ornamentation. Gives appropriate reference of this type as absorbed by Bartók in the cello melody of the third movement of the *Fourth String Quartet.*

389. Lampert, Vera. *Bartók Béla* (1881-1945). Budapest: Akadémiai Kiadó, 1976. 230p.   ISBN 9630510456   ML 410 B26 L3

Comprehensive study of Bartók's folk-music research from 1904 to 1918, including discussion of his methodological approach in transcribing and classifying thousands of peasant melodies from various countries in Eastern Europe. Also gives an account of his work at the Hungarian Academy of Sciences. Contains illustrations, bibliography.

390. László, Ferenc. *Bartók Béla. Tanulmányok és tanúságok* [Béla Bartók. Studies and testimonies]. Bukarest: Kriterion, 1980. 320p.

Fourteen essays in Hungarian dealing with the following topics: Bartók's first encounter with folk music (1904); persons assisting Bartók on his first collecting trip to Csík (1907); the role of Cornelia Buşiţia, born Nicola, in connection with Bartók's Romanian collections from Belényes (1909); the visit to Bartók of D.G. Kiriac, Romanian composer and folk-music collector from

Bucharest (1912); Konstantin Pavel: Romanian teacher from Belényes, the knowledgeable collaborator with Ioan Bianu, Ioan Bârlea, and Tiberiu Brediceanu in connection with the collection and publication of Romanian folklore from Máramaros (Maramureş) (1912-1923); the "Bucharest Bartók Manuscript" *(Eight Hungarian Folksongs, Nos. II, VI, V, III,* which were notated by Bartók from memory at Marosvásárhely (1922); Bartók, the member of the Societatea Compozitorilor Români of Bucharest (1924); article of Nichifor Crainic about Bartók (1924); 23 letters addressed to Bartók by Brăiloiu (1924-1938); Octavian Beu, the Romanian propagator of Bartók's compositions (1930-1954); an unpublished letter by Bartók in the estate of Karl Vötterle (1932); the history of the composition of *Cantata Profana* (1914-1932); János Demény's editions of Bartók's letters. The five testimonies are interviews with persons who knew Bartók: Iosif Ross, Viktor Dániel, Miklós Fogolyán, Moise Balta, and others. These writings are partly original and partly enlarged and revised versions of earlier publications. Summary in Romanian and German. Contains 37 photographs and several musical examples. See reviews by: János Demény, in *Népszabadság* (March 15, 1981); János Breuer, in *Élet és irodalom* 35/14 (April 1981); Fodor András, in *Magyar hírlap* (May 17, 1981); Lajos Pintér, in *Muzica* 31/4 (April 1981); András Wilheim, in *Muzsika* 24/12 (December 1981); Dénes Zoltai, in *Kritika* (December 1981); János Breuer, in *Magyar zene* 26/4 (October 1985).

391. ----------, ed. *Béla Bartók şi muzica românească* [Béla Bartók and Romanian music]. Bucharest: Editura Muzicală, 1976. 248 p.

Twelve essays in Romanian. Essays discuss Bartók's ethnomusicological work on Romanian folk music (Constantin Brăiloiu, Tiberiu Alexandru, Eugenia Cernea), the issue of Romanian folk-music influence in Bartók's composition (Márta Papp, János Breuer, Tiberiu Olah). Bartók's place in the context of twentieth-century music (Adrian Ratiu, Anatol Vieru, Gheorghe Firca). Aurel Stroe's article deals with the modernity of the *Fourteen Bagatelles,* Op. 6. Publication of documentary material concerning the collaboration of Bartók and the Academia Română, Bartók and Constantin Brăiloiu (Titus Moisescu, Francisc [Ferenc] László). Appendix contains chronological table of the connection between Bartók and Romania. Contains photographs and musical examples.

392. ----------. "Bihar és Máramaros között. Bartók Béla bánsági román gyűjtéséről" [Between Bihor and Maramureş. Béla Bartók's collection of Romanian folk songs in Banat]. *Korunk* 2 (1981): 94-101.

On the basis of the existing evidence, the author concludes that Bartók, after having completed the Bihor volume of Romanian folk music (1913), planned to publish the Banat (Bánsági) volume. He prepared but could not publish this work because of the breakout of the war. On the basis of the numbering of Bartók's "támlap," the author attempts to reconstruct the structure of the volume. He argues that this volume brings numerous new ideas that superseded Bartók's classificatory system in his Bihor volume and anticipated the solutions of the Maramureş volume (1923). Contains two pages of facsimile. The article appeared also in: *Forrás* 7 (1981): 67-73.

393. ----------. "Limba română a lui Béla Bartók" [The Romanian language of Béla Bartók]. *Steaua* 36/10 (October 1985): 51-52.

An account of Bartók's knowledge of the Romanian language.

394. ----------. "Nochmals über die Entstehungsgeschichte der rumänischen Folkloresammlung von Maramuresch" [Once more on the history of the origin and rise of Romanian folklore collection from Maramureş]. *Studia musicologica* 23 (1981): 329-351.
781.05 St92   ISSN 0039-3266

A study of Bartók's Romanian collecting trip to Maramureş (Máramaros). Special attention is given to his collaboration with the pastor Ioan Bârlea and Tiberiu Brediceanu, who had collected folk music in Maramureş before Bartók had done so. There was a plan to publish, together in one volume, the melodies collected both by Bartók and Brediceanu with the texts collected by Bârlea. This plan was wholeheartedly supported by Ioan Bianu of the Academia Română but the outbreak of the war and the following political developments made its realization impossible.

395. Lenoir, Yves. *Folklore et transcendance dans l'œuvre américaine de Béla Bartók (1940-1945): Contributions à l'étude de l'activité scientifique et créatrice du compositeur* [Folklore and transcendence in the American works of Béla Bartók (1940-1945): Contributions to the study of the composer's scholarly and creative activity]. Ph.D. diss., Musicologie, Université Catholique de Louvain, 1984. Louvain-la-Neuve: Institut Supérieur d'Archéologie et d'Histoire de l'Art, 1986. 509p.

In-depth study of the folk-music influences on Bartók's works composed in the United States during his final years, viewed within the context of Bartók's psychological condition related to his illness. Explores and assesses Bartók's ethnomusicological writings on Serbo-Croatian, Romanian, and Turkish music in light of their relevance to the works of this period, i.e., in terms of "compositional mechanisms, internal laws, and modalities of transcendence" and Bartók's contribution to scholarly folk-music research in general. Provides insight into Bartók's overall development as ethnomusicologist. Contains illustrations, music examples, facsimiles, port., bibliography, list of works, index. See Review by Damjana Bratuz in *Music Library Association Notes* 49/2 (December 1992): 581-583.

396. ----------. "Réflexions sur l'activité scientifique de Béla Bartók à la lumière de ses recherches en Amérique" [Reflections on Béla Bartók's scholarly activity in light of his research in the United States]. *Studia musicologica* 29/1-4 (1987): 295-302. 781.05 St92 ISSN 0039-3266

Discusses the importance of ethnomusicological research in Bartók's career and the arduous task that it was for him to master this discipline. Points to the three studies that he completed in the United States in his final years as the most advanced and complex not only in his own academic work but in the history of ethnomusicological transcription.

397. ----------. "The Destiny of Bartók's Ethnomusicological Research Immediately Prior to His Stay in the United States." *Studia musicologica* 24/3-4 (1982): 411-423. 781.05 St92 ISSN 0039-3266

Informative discussion of Bartók's difficulties in realizing his plans for folk-music research in the late 1930s. Lenoir supports his study with some previously unpublished documents.

398. Lükő, Gábor. "Bartók tudományos öröksége" [Bartók's scientific legacy]. *Kortárs* 14/9 (October 1970): 1378-1383. PH 3028 L3

Provides a summary of Bartók's methodological approach and results of his folk-music research.

399. Móži, Alexander. "Po stopach Bélu Bartóka v Dražovciach" [Following traces of Béla Bartók in Dražovce]. *Slovenská hudba* 15/3-4 (1971): 110-117. H50.470

Provides an account of Bartók's folk-song expedition in a Slovak village immediately following World War I.

400. Porter, James. "Bartók and Grainger: Some Correspondences and a Hypothesis." *Studia musicologica* 25 (1983): 223-228. 781.05 St92 ISSN 0039-3266

Contains a letter from Bartók to Delius in 1910 requesting help in making himself known to the Australian composer, pianist, and ethnomusicologist Percy Grainger, and in acquiring Grainger's scores. Suggests that Bartók knew of Grainger's folk-song transcriptions published in the *Journal of the Folk-Song Society* in 1908 and that he recognized their common purpose in providing a detailed record of the singing style. Provides historical background to Grainger's interest in folk music, documents his attitudes and aims in its investigation, and discusses his methodological approach to transcription. Then documents Grainger's subsequent reaction to Bartók's published rebuttal of certain assumptions in Grainger's article "Melody Versus Rhythm" (1933). Bartók's statements provide important insights into "free conversational rhythm" (parlando rubato) and "strict dance-like rhythm" (tempo giusto) as he observed them among certain Eastern European and North African peoples. Also points to certain common traits of personality and philosophy (political, musical, etc.) between Bartók and Grainger, despite their contrasting cultural backgrounds, and points to the importance of their pioneering work in ethnomusicological methodology. Hypothesizes that Grainger may have had some influence on Bartók's techniques and methods.

401. Rácz, Ilona. "Bartók Béla csíkmegyei pentaton gyűjtése 1907-ben" [Béla Bartók's collection of pentatonic tunes in Csík County, 1907]. *Népzene és zenetörténet. I.* Budapest: Zeneműkiadó, 1972, pp. 9-62.

Discusses Bartók's realization of the importance of pentatony during his early collecting tour in the Csík district (1907). Of the 458 melodies he collected from ten villages, 47 were pentatonic. From the studies of both Bartók and Kodály, who was collecting Hungarian peasant melodies in the north during this time, the pentatonic scale was determined to be the basis of the oldest strata of Hungarian folk music. Also, discusses Bartók's methodological approach to classification and how Bartók in 1938 re-classified the pentatonic melodies, which were originally placed in a group by themselves, as part of the larger category of old-style Hungarian melodies ("Class A"). Also includes facsimiles and an index.

402. Rahn, Jay. "Text-tune Relationships in the Hora Lunga Versions Collected by Bartók." *Yearbook of the International Folk Music Council* 8 (1976): 89-96. ML1 1719

Discusses the research done on the Romanian *horă lungă* (long song). Provides information and a methodological approach dealing with the principle of variants (based on recurrent elements) in connection with texts and tunes collected by Bartók. Discusses the basis of phrasal/formal relationships for all the versions, which are variants of a single melody. Includes music examples and bibliography.

403. Saygun, A. Adnan. "Bartók in Turkey." *Musical Quarterly* 37 (1951): 5-9.   ML1 M725   ISSN 0027-4631

   Discusses Bartók's first arrival (1936) at the archives of the conservatory in Istanbul and the author's work with Bartók on Turkish folk tunes on recordings. Then, refers to Bartók's lectures at Ankara and their joint collecting expeditions in the villages. Gives first-hand account of Bartók's collecting methods. Bartók was convinced of the close relationship between Turkish and Hungarian folk music. Ends with reference to their correspondence before Bartók left Hungary for the United States.

404. ----------. "Quelques réflexions sur certaines affinités des musiques folkloriques turque et hongroise" [Some reflections on certain affinities of Turkish and Hungarian musical folklore]. *Studia musicologica* 5/1-4 (1963): 515-524.   781.05 St92 ISSN 0039-3266

   States that it was Bartók who first brought our attention to these affinities. Then gives detailed comparative analyses in terms of scale, rhythm, syllabic structure, etc. This discussion was presented at a conference titled "Bartók and Turkish Music."

405. Schmid, Angeline. "Bartók's Rumanian Christmas Carols." *Clavier* 20/8 (October 1981): 30-31.   780.5 C578   ISSN 0009-854-X

   Deals with Bartók's 20 piano transcriptions of Romanian Christmas melodies. Gives some brief historical information regarding Bartók's explorations of Romanian folk music. Then, some general characteristics of the *colinde* (Christmas carol) melodies and texts are outlined in terms of rhythm, modes, melody sections, and syllabic structure, followed by suggestions for teaching.

   *Somfai, László, ed. *Magyar népzenei hanglemezek Bartók Béla lejegyzéseivel* [Hungarian folk music gramophone records with Béla Bartók's transcriptions].

   See item no. 1118

406. Suchoff, Benjamin. "Bartók, Ethnomusicology and the Computer." *ICRH Newsletter* 4/4 (December 1968): 3-6.

   Gives history of Bartók's ethnomusicological investigations, with Bartók's own comments on the practicality of his scholarly work. Suchoff, as editor of Bartók's folk-music studies, gives evidence that Bartók himself would have welcomed the use of the computer to facilitate the study of the material and his complicated classification system. The author then provides basic features of the method in terms of analysis, transmutation (conversion of the music notation into machine readable graphics), and processing. Includes music and table.

407. ----------. "Bartók and Serbo-Croatian Folk Music." *Musical Quarterly* 58 (1972): 557-571.   ML1 M725   ISSN 0027-4631

Discusses Bartók's collection and publication of Serbo-Croatian folk music. Documentary evidence, obtained from both published and unpublished letters, suggests that Bartók came to the United States in 1940 primarily to transcribe the Serbo-Croatian materials in the Parry collection as well as to work with recorded Yugoslav materials, an area of investigation that had previously been inaccessible to Bartók in Europe. In 1942, Bartók and Albert B. Lord collaborated on a book of Serbo-Croatian folk songs, which was published after Bartók's death.

408. ----------. "Bartók's Rumanian Folk Music Publication." *Ethnomusicology* 15 (1971): 220-230.   781.05 Et38

Discusses the general difficulties Bartók had in trying to have his Romanian folk-song studies published. The author, as editor of the new five-volume edition of Bartók's Romanian folk-music study (beginning in1967), provides a history of Bartók's Romanian publications since his initial investigations in 1908. The contents as well as editorial problems are also described.

409. ----------. "Béla Bartók and Hungarian Folk Song." *The Folk Arts of Hungary* (Pittsburgh: Dusquesne University, Tamburitzans Institute of Folk Arts) (April 1980): 149-159.

Presents a history of the *Volkslied* (popular art songs or urban folk songs), which were eventually propagated by Gypsy bands in Vienna, Budapest, and Hungarian towns. Includes discussion of three major categories of this type, with some reference to their use by art-music composers. Then, a history is given of Bartók's contact with and absorption of the authentic rural musical folklore as well as discussing some of Bartók's transcriptions and his scholarly publication, *The Hungarian Folk Song*. Three categories of this rural folk music is also outlined (old, new, and mixed styles).

410. ----------. "Brief Communications." *Yearbook of the International Folk Music Council* 3 (1971): 141-143.   ML1 1719

Systematic refutation by the author, who served as editor of Bartók's *Rumanian Folk Music* 1-3 (Den Haag: Martinus Nijhoff, 1967) of the criticisms presented in the review by John Weissmann (see *Yearbook of the International Folk Music Council* 1, pp. 251-261). In addition, the author points to erroneous statements in the review regarding Bartók's own work.

411. ----------. "Bartók's Odyssey in Slovak Folk Music." *Bartók in Retrospect*, ed. Elliott Antokoletz, Victoria Fischer, and Benjamin Suchoff. Projected publication of two 1995 conference proceedings.

Reveals that Bartók's odyssey in Slovak folk music was of legendary biblical proportion, spanning forty years since the start of his field work in 1906 until his last thoughts about the fate of his unpublished collection of 1945. Describes the course of events, beginning with Bartók's first visit to Slovakia (at that time part of Hungary), which led to his discovery of a village whose musical repertory represented a Slovak-Hungarian language border. He made other significant findings, such as the determination of autochthonous Slovak folk song, modal peculiarities, and rhythm schemata. His conclusions were based on the recording, transcription, and classification of more than 3,000 vocal and instrumental melodies. Reveals that Bartók's incessant struggles with his Slovak publisher, plagued by adversative editorial problems and disruptive political events, forced him to revoke his contract and leave his manuscript in escrow before he emigrated to the United States in 1940. A flawed and incomplete posthumous edition appeared in Bratislava between 1959 and 1970. (Annotation based on the author's abstract of the original lecture; see item no. 1139.)

412. Szegő, Júlia. *Bartók Béla, a népdalkutató* [Bartók the folk-song researcher]. Bucharest: llami Irodalmi és Művészeti Kiadó, 1956. 335p.

In this clear and accessible biographical study, based largely on Bartók's correspondence, Bartók's study "The Musical Dialect of the Rumanian People of Hunyad" is made available to the public.

413. Vancea, Zeno. "Einige Beiträge über das erste Manuskript der Colindă-Sammlung von Béla Bartók und über seine einschlägigen Briefe an Constantin Brăiloiu" [Some articles about the first manuscript of the *colindă* collection of Béla Bartók and about his letters to Constantin Brăiloiu]. *Studia musicologica* 5/1-4 (1963): 549-556.   781.05 St92   ISSN 0039-3266

Detailed discussion of the preparation and publication of the first manuscript of the *colindă* collection, which contains Bartók's collection of Romanian Christmas songs in his own handwriting as well as Bartók's letter to Brăiloiu concerning the collection. Discusses the songs of the manuscript, concluding with six points of major discrepancies between the manuscript and Universal Edition.

414. Vicol, Adrian. "Premise teoretice la o tipologie muzicală a colindelor românești" [Theoretical premises for a musical typology of the Romanian *colindă*]. *Revista de etnografie și folclor* 15/1 (1970): 63-71.   H49.244

    In Romanian, with summary in French. Reviews Bartók's methodological approach to the classification of the *colinde*. Several categories are suggested: 1) tetrachordal and pentachordal (basically pre-pentatonic); 2) pentatonic and pre-pentatonic "doubles"; 3) Hypodorian; and 4) major-minor constructions.

415. Víg, Rudolf. "Gypsy Folk Songs from the Béla Bartók and Zoltán Kodály Collections." *Studia musicologica* 16 (1974): 89-131.   781.05 St92   ISSN 0039-3266

    Discusses the pioneering research of Bartók and Kodály from 1912 to 1914 and in 1933 in the collection of music of the Hungarian Gypsies. Points to a distinctive folk music of both wandering and settled Gypsies. Also provides information regarding their findings on the ratio of professional musicians to the general Hungarian-Gypsy population. Includes 33 previously unpublished songs, as well as commentaries and facsimiles. Also published in Hungarian: "Cigány népdalok Bartók Béla es Kodály Zoltán gyűjtéséből." *Népzene és zenetörténet* 2 (1974): 149-200.

4. Specialized Discussions of Bartók's Personality, Philosophical Views, Political Attitudes, and/or Philosophy of Composition

416. Bartók, Béla, Jr. "Remembering My Father, Béla Bartók." *The New Hungarian Quarterly* 7/22 (Summer 1966): 201-203.   914.39105 N42   ML410 B26 B29

    Recalls that the most impressive traits of his father's personality were his love of nature, his sense of patriotism and ardor for national freedom, and his diligence and capacity for work. Also speaks of his attitude toward teaching, manner of dress, lack of conventional recreations, reserved manner with strangers but his ease with relatives. Original publication in Hungarian in: *Népművelés* (January 1966). Reprinted in *Bartók Studies,* ed. Todd Crow.   Detroit: Information Coordinators, 1976, pp. 149-151.

417. -----------------. "The Private Man." *The Bartók Companion,* ed. Malcolm Gillies. London: Faber and Faber, 1993; Portland, Oregon: Amadeus Press (an imprint of Timber Press, Inc.), 1994. pp. 18-29.   ISBN 0-931340-74-8 (HB)   ISBN 0-931340-75-6 (PB)   ML410 B26 B28

As time passes and Bartók's contemporaries die, we gradually lose personal contact with the man himself, and the few remaining witnesses who knew him in their youth inevitably provide less reliable personal information. Thus, the recollections of Bartók's older son are all the more important as a source of knowledge about the man and composer. In addition to providing unique information about Bartók as father and family man, the author's aim is to correct misconceptions and errors that have been perpetuated in writings over the years, partly due to Bartók's own reserve. Reveals insight into Bartók's human qualities based also on unpublished written materials. Points to the importance for Bartók of educating children, a concern that was manifested in many musical studies and methods that he composed for children. Also reveals Bartók's wide array of interests, attitudes, meticulous work habits, and activities in both his personal and professional life. Points to Bartók's humanitarian concerns, love for nature, and his uncompromising integrity, which has often been misconstrued to mean that he was "rigid and humourless."

418. Bodnár, György. "Bartók et le mouvement 'Nyugat.'" *Studia musicologica* 5 (1963): 347-354.   781.05 St92   ISSN 0039-3266

Discusses the spiritual connections between Bartók and the great Hungarian writers of his epoch, which had been observed already in the interwar period by Hungarian essayists and critics. Among the spiritual brothers of Bartók, one points above all to Ady and also to that group that surrounded him, the "Nyugat" movement.

419. Bónis, Ferenc. *Igy láttuk Bartókot: Harminchat emlékezés* [Thus appears Bartók: thirty-six memoirs]. Budapest: Zeneműkiadó, 1981. 298p.   ISBN 9633303915   ML 410 B26 I35

Includes memoirs of members of Bartók's family (wife and son), Ernő Balogh, János Demény, Antal Doráti, Pál Gergely, Endre Gertler, Hans W. Heinsheimer, Zoltán Kodály, Antal Molnár, Paul Sacher, György Sándor, Tibor Serly, Bence Szabolcsi, Joseph Szigeti, among many others. Contains illustrations, index. See review by: Ferenc László, in *Művelődés* 36/3 (March 1983): 38-39.

420. ----------. "Quotations in Bartók's Music: A Contribution to Bartók's Psychology of Composition." *Studia musicologica* 5 (1963): 355-382.   781.05 St92   ISSN 0039-3266

First attempt to summarize the topic of quotations in Bartók's music and to clarify their meaning and significance. Paper does not include the influence of folk music on Bartók's art but rather confines itself to examples of Bartók's use of motives or passages from the works of known or unknown composers or examples revealing inspiration from others. Also published in German: "Zitate in Bartók's Musik." *Österreichische Musikzeitschrift* 20/9 (September 1965): 467-482.

421. Breuer, János. "Bartók és Kodály" [Bartók and Kodály]. *Világosság* 15/2 (February 1974): 78-85.   HA1.287

Speaks of Bartók's and Kodály's role in revitalizing Hungarian music in the twentieth century. Outlines common features of the two composers, including their common interest in the collection of Hungarian folk music, the use of folk tunes in their compositions, and their antifascist stance. Also outlines the many differences between them, including Kodály's primary interest in vocal music as well as the limitation of his ethnomusicological activities to Hungarian folk music, while Bartók wrote primarily orchestral music and expanded his ethnomusicological research activities to other Eastern European nations, Turkey, and North Africa. Furthermore, while Kodály's antifascism was based on specific feelings toward the Germans, Bartók's political attitudes were based on a more generalized humanitarianism.

422. ---------. "Theodor Wiesengrund-Adorno: Texte über Béla Bartók" [Theodor Wiesengrund-Adorno: texts on Béla Bartók]. *Studia musicologica* 23 (1981): 397-425.   781.05 St92 ISSN 0039-3266

Series of essays by Adorno, from various journals, revealing his views about Bartók and performances of his works (e.g., Bartók performances in Frankfurt). Discusses Bartók and the reactionary implications of folklorism. However, mentions that the work of Hungary is "only partly known to us, which today stands at the zenith of its artistic power." Editor's preface places Adorno's views in the context of his "Philosophy of new music," in which Bartók stands in the middle of the road between the progressive Schoenberg and the conservative Stravinsky.

423. ----------. "Die zeitgenössische ungarische Musik auf dem Pfade Bartóks" [Contemporary Hungarian music on the path opened up by Bartók]. *International Musicological Conference in Commemoration of Béla Bartók 1971,* ed. József Ujfalussy and János Breuer. Budapest: Editio Musica; New York: Belwin Mills, 1972): 163-167. ML410.B29 I61   ML410.B26 I5

Discusses the increasing impact of Bartók in Hungary in the past fifteen years (1956-1971) and gives evidence that Hungarian musicology has checked the mistaken idea that Bartók's folklorism and modernism are at variance. Talks of the importance of free creative development in the spirit of Bartók in present-day Hungarian composition.

424. Calvocoressi, M.D. "A Conversation with Bartók. The Mandarin Riot." *Daily Telegraph* (March 9, 1929).

 Explores Bartók's thoughts and opinions on several important musical and personal issues. Bartók gives reasons for the riotous demonstrations against the *Mandarin* Pantomime Ballet at its first performance in Cologne on November 27, 1926, and refers to its censorship after an appeal to the Burgomaster. States that having read the plot before the performance, people had already made up their minds that it was objectionable. Then comments on the evolution of his musical technique and other issues. For more detail, see item No. 443.

425. Clegg, David. "Remarks to the Article, 'Quotations in Bartók's Music,' by Ferenc Bónis." *Studia musicologica* 6/3-4 (1964): 380-381. 781.05 St92 ISSN 0039-3266

 Provides additional quotations in certain of Bartók's works from Beethoven as well as from an art song from a popular nineteenth-century Hungarian play.

426. Crawford, Dorothy Lamb. "Love and Anguish: Bartók's Expressionism." *Bartók in Retrospect,* ed. Elliott Antokoletz, Victoria Fischer, and Benjamin Suchoff. Projected publication of two 1995 conference proceedings.

 Reveals that Bartók's expressionist works resulted from psychological and political crises in the years of his early maturity, 1908-1923. Composing provided his only means of transcending devastating rejection and loss and shaped his chaotic and often obsessive emotions into works that in several cases provided him renewed strength to live. His need to taunt and twist his musical subjects into bitterly ironic caricature was, he felt, a characteristic of his times. Bartók wrote in 1909 that his works would manifest his "boundless enthusiasm, regret, fury, revenge, distorting ridicule or sarcasm. . . . A man's works designate the events, the guiding passions of his life more exactly than his biography." The guiding passions of his life between the ages of twenty-seven and forty-two were the truth he found in folk art and the "ideal companion" he sought in young women he hoped would assuage his spiritual loneliness. Bitter disappointments gained for his musical language a unique vocabulary of motives and attitudes deeply rooted in emotion and instinct. (Annotation based on the author's abstract of the original lecture; see item no. 1139.)

427. Dahlhaus, Carl. "Eine latente Kontroverse zwischen Bartók und Schönberg" [A latent controversy between Bartók and Schoenberg]. *Gieseler Festschrift* (1985): 13-17.

According to the author, *RILM Abstracts* No. 5889 (1985), "Bartók's essay *Das Problem der neuen Musik* (1920) may be seen as a reply to Schoenberg's *Harmonielehre* (1911), and certain passages of the latter's treatise *Gesinnung oder Erkenntnis* (1926) may in turn be seen as a response to Bartók's essay of 1920. The discussion centered on the relationship obtaining among free dissonances."

428. Demény, János. "Ady-Gedichtbände in Bartóks Bibliothek" [Ady's poetry in Bartók's library]. *International Musicological Conference in Commemoration of Béla Bartók 1971,* ed. József Ujfalussy and János Breuer. Budapest: Editio Musica; New York: Belwin Mills, 1972): 111-120.	ML410.B29 I61 (Editio Musica) ML410.B26 I5 (Belwin Mills)

   Presents evidence of the importance of Ady's poetry for Bartók, as seen in a former part of Bartók's library now preserved in the Bartók Archives of the Institute for Musicology of the Hungarian Academy of Sciences.

429. --------------. "Ady-tanulmánykötet Bartók könyvtárában" [A volume of Ady's essays in Bartók's library]. *Muzsika* (Budapest) 14/3 (March 1971): 9-11.	ISSN 0027-5336

   Reveals primary-source documentation based on Bartók's marginal annotations, which provide information regarding Bartók's association with the Hungarian poet.

430. Déri, Ottó. "Béla Bartók: A Portrait of His Personality Drawn from his Letters." *Current Musicology* 13 (1972): 90-103.	780.5 C936 ISSN 0011-3735

   Study based on excerpts from Bartók's published correspondence in English translation. From the author's own experience as an emigré from nazified Hungary to the United States, he provides insightful speculation into the wide ramifications (political, cultural, philosophical, personal, etc.) that similar experiences had on Bartók.

431. Dibelius, Ulrich. "Béla Bartók und der Phonograph" [Béla Bartók and the phonograph]. *HiFi-Stereophonie* 15/3 (1976): 245-249.

   Discusses Bartók's attitudes and the circumstances that led him to the investigation and recording of folk music.

432. Dille, Denijs. "Bartók, lecteur de Nietzsche et de La Rochefoucauld" [Bartók, reader of Nietzsche and of La Rochefoucauld]. *Studia musicologica* 10 (1968): 209-228.	781.05 St92	ISSN 0039-3266.	See also item no. 1150, Denijs Dille, *Béla Bartók: Regard*

sur le passé [Béla Bartók: A look at the past], ed. Yves Lenoir, *Musicologica neolovaniensia* 5; *Études bartokiennes*. Namur: Presses Université de Namur, 1990, pp. 87-105.   ML 410 B26 D52

Refers to our lack of knowledge regarding Bartók's intellectual and ideological formation in his early years. Surveys a number of primary source documents providing a perspective of the development of Bartók's political, philosophical and religious (atheistic) views, etc., but attempts to give a proper evaluation of the information. Contains photos.

433. ------------. "Béla Bartók." *Revue musicale* (Brussels) (March 1937): 3ff.

Interview with Bartók on February 2, 1937, in which Bartók answers Dille's questions regarding his attitude toward his own music. This occurred during his sojourn in Brussels, on the occasion of his concert at the broadcasting station of the I.N.R.

434. ----------. "Béla Bartók--seine Persönlichkeit und sein Werk in Kunst und Wissenschaft" [Béla Bartók--his personality and his work in art and science]. *Universitas: Zeitschrift für Wissenschaft, Kunst und Literatur* 22/2 (February 1967): 171-177.   AP4 U57
ISSN 0341-0129   ISSN 0041-9079

A biographical study focusing on Bartók's psychological attitude and its relevance to his musical activities.

435. ----------. "Béla Bartók und Wien" [Béla Bartók and Vienna]. *Österreichische Musikzeitschrift* 19/11 (November 1964): 510-518. 780.5 Oe8   ISSN 0029-9316

Shows that Bartók's relationship to Vienna is possibly more important than his relationship to any other city, including Budapest.

436. ----------. "Le vingtième anniversaire de la mort de Bartók" [The twentieth anniversary of the death of Bartók]. *Studia musicologica* 8 (1966): 3-10.   781.05 St92   ISSN 0039-3266 See also item no. 1150, Denijs Dille, *Béla Bartók: Regard sur le passé* [Béla Bartók: A look at the past], ed. Yves Lenoir, *Musicologica neolovaniensia* 5; *Études bartokiennes*. Namur: Presses Université de Namur, 1990, pp.329-336.   ML 410 B26 D52

Commemoration (September 25, 1965) organized by the Association of Hungarian Musicians and the Bartók Archivum. Reflects upon the great personality of Bartók and the living reality of his work. Despite difficulties he faced during his lifetime, he had never known an intellectual crisis (except for the importance his discovery of folklore held for him), only a crisis of the heart and soul. Refers to some unhappy experiences involving his opposition to political regimes, the lack of public comprehension of his works, and his general style of life determined by some of these factors. Contains photo.

437. ----------. "Interview de Béla Bartók (1937)" [Interview with Béla Bartók (1937)]. *Bulletin of the International Kodály Society* 1 (1991): 12-14. Reprinted from the volume by Denijs Dille, *Béla Bartók: Regard sur le passé* [Béla Bartók: A look at the past]. Ed. Yves Lenoir. *Musicologica neolovaniensia* 5; *Études bartokiennes*. Namur: Presses Université de Namur, 1990, pp. 27-29. ML 410 B26 D52

Provides insight into Bartók's musical language and compositional methodology. Bartók discusses his approach to rhythm, melody, tonality, and harmony in relation to his "national" sources, e.g., pointing out that his harmony is "nationalist" only in its origin. Informs us that the tonal sense of his melodies, folk or original, is very different from that of traditional harmony and the innovations of Schoenberg. Also, states that his techniques are the same for both his original compositions and those based on authentic folk music. Mentions his great affection for thematic variation and transformation. Originally in German, first published in French in *La sirène* (Brussels, March 1937); in Hungarian in *Bartók breviárium* [Bartók breviary], ed. József Ujfalussy, rev. edition by Vera Lampert. Budapest: Zeneműkiadó Vállalat, 1974.

438. Eősze, László. "Aspetti comuni dell'arte poetica di Verdi, Bartók, e Kodály" [Common aspects of the poetic art of Verdi, Bartók, and Kodály]. *Atti del I⁰ congresso internazionale di studi verdiani* (1966): 97-105.

Discussion of the views that the three composers had in common with regard to their art. These include the relation between nationalism and music, musical tradition, reaction to contemporary German musical dominance in their own countries, and their respective attitudes toward "the need for spontaneity and simplicity in musical expression and realism in dramatic works."

439. Fábián, Imre. "Bartók und die Zeitgenossen" [Bartók and his contemporaries]. *Melos* 38 (1971): 456-468.   780.5 M492 ISSN 0174-7207

Discusses the relation of Bartók to his contemporaries, including Richard Strauss, Debussy, Ravel, Stravinsky, Kodály, and members of the Vienna Schoenberg Circle.

440. Fodor, Ilona. "Bartók magyarság-élményének gyökerei" [Origins of Bartók's patriotism]. *Kortárs* 14/9 (October 1970): 1370-1378.

PH 3028 L3

Traces Bartók's nationalism, as represented in such works as his symphonic poem, *Kossuth* (1904), to the nineteenth-century patriotic movements and the struggle for liberation stemming from the Revolution of 1848, led by the patriot Lajos Kossuth. Bartók's nationalism is related to this progressive nationalistic movement rather than the reactionary ruling classes of the Austro-Hungarian Empire.

441. ----------. "A fából faragott királyfi: elidegenedés és művészi teremtmény" [*The Wooden Prince:* alienation and artistic achievement]. *Valóság* 10/4 (1967): 22-23.

According to the author, in *RILM Abstracts* No. 1224 (1967), "the message in Bartók's pantomime is that of the alienated artist whose works turn against him. A juxtaposition of the ideal and the grotesque is also present. Both features are typical of Bartók. The experience of alienation is traced from Nietzsche to the existentialists; from Rousseau's melodrama *Pygmalion* to Stravinsky's *Petruschka;* from 'puppet-maker' Kleist to Kafka and Mann."

442. Frigyesi, Judit. "Béla Bartók and the Concept of Nation and Volk in Modern Hungary." *Musical Quarterly* 78/2 (Summer 1994): 255-287. ML1 M725   ISBN 0-19-508857-3   ISSN 0027-4631

Distinguishes the various notions of "folk," nation," and "nationalism" and evaluates the relevance of these concepts to the Hungarian political position since the nineteenth century in order to establish a context for understanding Bartók's political ideology and humanistic philosophy. Points to several views on the evolution of Bartók's political and cultural attitudes and focuses on the social history of Hungarian nationalism as basis for evaluating Bartók's devotion to the study of peasant music. In particular, addresses "the social radicalism and artistic modernism of Bartók's folklorism" and its reception in polarized Hungarian social life. Discusses the Hungarian nobility as "nation" and "populus," the gentry as the "elite *Volk,"* gypsy music as the symbol of gentry chauvinism, and the "discovery" of peasant music. Provides extensive primary and secondary documentation.

443. Gillies, Malcolm. "A Conversation with Bartók: 1929." *Musical Times* 128/1736 (October 1987): 555-559.   780.5 M98 ISSN 0027-4666

Refers to the frequency of interviews with Bartók during the last 25 years of his life but questions the general reliability of newspaper interviews in terms of accuracy in representing the interviewee's opinions and factual information. Then singles out two interviews with Bartók in the 1920s as exemplary in portraying Bartók's character and the comprehensiveness in reporting his musical thoughts. The second interview (see item no. 424), given by M. D. Calvocoressi, a music critic and loyal supporter of Bartók in Britain in the 1920s and 1930s, delves into several important musical and personal issues. After presenting some historical background on Calvocoressi's connections with Bartók, the complete text of the interview ("A Conversation with Bartók: 'The Mandarin' Riot") is reprinted as published in the *Daily Telegraph,* March 9, 1929. Provides insight into Bartók's thoughts and opinions on a variety of issues. Bartók gives reasons for the riotous demonstrations against his *Mandarin* Pantomime Ballet, then comments on the evolution of his musical technique (including his approach to melody and tonality), his interest in the music of the old Italian masters, the practical problems of young Hungarian composers (Kadosa and Szelényi, especially) in getting their music published, the significance of Liszt's music and its influence on his own. Also, praises the magnificent standard of performance by American orchestras and the activities by the various chapters of *Pro Musica* in promoting contemporary music. Gillies provides a detailed final commentary intended to establish the authenticity of the interviewer's quotations of Bartók.

444. Helm, Everett. *Der Mensch Bartók* [Bartók the man]. *Komponisten des 20. Jahrhunderts in der Paul Sacher Stiftung.* Basel: Paul Sacher Stiftung, 1986. pp. 73-84.   ML141 B22 P4

Provides significant insight into Bartók's personality, attitude, and high moral character. Points to the profound sincerity that had always characterized his personality. Informs us that he never could accept monetary gifts or fees unless he had worked for them, even during his final illness in New York. This attitude as well as his fear of an inability to earn a living during these final years in America spurred him on with great ferver and dedication to work at Columbia University' on the transcription and edition of the Serbo-Croatian folk music recordings in the Milman Parry collection.

445. Hunkemöller, Jürgen. "Kunstwerk, Bauernmusik und Evolution. Bartók's Vision der Moderne" [Artwork, peasant music and evolution. Bartók's vision of modernism]. *Europäischen Musikfest Stuttgart 1995, Sonderheft Béla Bartók* (Stuttgart 1995): 39-52.

Contrasts exaggerated use of the term "modernism" with its actual meaning in Bartók's aesthetics. Points out that Bartók opposed the "modernistic" label as applied to his own music, which is to be understood simply in the context of an evolutionary artistic process based on the synthesis of folk and art music. States that such terms as "modernism," "avant-garde," and "open-mindedness" are conceptual superlatives that expose a morally reprehensible "anti-modernism." According to the author, generations were convinced that to be a modernist was to proceed with responsibility toward the goal of happiness. This conviction took the form of multicolored expressions in speech, which led to the development of many political prescriptions for building a system of happiness either through the evolutionary "long march" toward the goal or through a revolutionary movement. From the latter came, unfortunately, a forced task for the future, with its root in the aesthetics of enlightened genius and its aesthetic postulate of the originality of the work. States that for Bartók, all these skills were interconnected with aesthetic manifestations, based on the correct consciousness contained within religion, politics, knowledge, and art, and the fact that these skills came under the "project" of modernism. Also addresses Adorno's philosophical thought on modern music and Bartók's position in relation to Schoenberg and Stravinsky. Points to the special meaning the study of the folk sources had for Bartók: the possibilities of full emancipation from the major/minor system by means of the modes. Presents Bartók's views on the irreconcilability of folk music and atonality, his opinion about Schoenberg and Stravinsky vis-à-vis modernism, and his own position. Discusses the evolutionary process from Bach, Beethoven, and Debussy as symbolic and real transmissions (motivic, contrapuntal, and thematic) to Bartók, Schoenberg, and Stravinsky as historical synthesis plus folk music.

446. Kecskeméti, István. "An early Bartók-Liszt encounter." *The New Hungarian Quarterly* 9/29 (Spring 1968): 206-210.   914.39105 N42 ML410 B26 B29

Compares the aesthetics and styles of the two composers based on their bagatelles. Deals with Bartók's early mature works primarily between 1905-1908. Reprinted in *Bartók Studies,* ed. Todd Crow. Detroit: Information Coordinators, 1976, pp. 79-83. See also a similar article by Kecskeméti, "Egy korai Bartók--Liszt-találkozás mefisztó jegyében." *Magyar zene* 7/4 (1966): 3-8 (appears as pp. 352-357 in some copies).

447. Klay, Andor C. "Bartók on Liszt." *Journal of the American Liszt Society* 21 (January-June 1987): 26-30.   ML410 L7 A68

According to Jennifer B. Bowen, *RILM Abstracts* No. 5109 (1988), states that "for his inaugural address to the Magyar Tudományos Akadémia in 1936, Bartók spoke of his Hungarian colleague Liszt. The version of this address as published in the Hungarian literary journal *Nyugat* omits five concluding sentences which appear in a later published version of the speech. The missing sentences are highly critical of the pro-axis policies of the Horthy regime, thus prompting the editors of *Nyugat* to omit them to avoid a possible encounter with the State Police."

448. Klein, Sigmund. "Béla Bartók, A Portrait." *Pro Musica* 4 (1925): 4.
     Provides an outline of Bartók's first performances in the United States.

449. Kosztolányi, Dezső. "Béla Bartók: An Interview by Dezső Kosztolányi." Trans. David E. Schneider. In *Bartók and His World,* ed. Peter Laki. Princeton, New Jersey: Princeton University Press, 1995. pp. 228-234.   ISBN 0-691-00633-4   ML 410 B26 B272. Original publication in *Pesti hírlap* (Pest News) (May 31, 1925).

     According to the translator, "The present interview for the *Pesti hírlap* (Pest News) was conducted [by Kosztolányi, a journalist and one of the founders of *Nyugat* (West), Hungary's foremost literary journal (1908-1941)] in Bartók's apartment in Buda (Szilágyi Dezső tér), shortly after Bartók had returned from a meeting of the International Society for Contemporary Music in Prague (15-19 May 1925). It is notable not only for Bartók's recollections of his earliest musical experiences and his views on the musical trends of the early 1920s but also for Kosztolányi's vivid description of the composer." Reprinted in Hungarian in: *Bartók Béla művészi kibontakozásának évei II--Bartók megjelenése az európai zeneéletben (1914-1926)* [The years of Bartók's artistic evolution, part 2-- Bartók's appearance in European musical life (1914-1926)], ed. János Demény, vol. 7 of *Zenetudományi tanulmányok* [Musicological studies], ed. Bence Szabolcsi and Dénes Bartha (Budapest, 1959), pp. 347-349; in Dezső Kosztolányi, *Írók, festők, tudósok* [Writers, painters, scholars] (Budapest, 1958), vol. 2, pp. 244-250; and in *Új hang* [New Voice] (May 1956). An abridged English translation appeared in *Living Age* 340 (March-August 1931): 565-568. Contains notes.

450. Laki, Peter. "Recollections of Béla Bartók." Trans. Peter Laki. In *Bartók and His World,* ed. Peter Laki. Princeton, New Jersey: Princeton University Press, 1995. pp. 243-275.   ISBN 0-691- 00633-4   ML 410 B26 B272. Originally published in Ferenc Bónis, ed. *Így láttuk Bartókot: Harminchat emlékezés* [Thus appears Bartók: thirty-six memoirs]. Budapest: Zeneműkiadó, 1981. ISBN 9633303915   ML 410 B26 I35

     Contains a collection of primary-source documents by a family member, friends, and musicians who were in close contact with Bartók during approximately the last 25 years of his life. These include recollections by Bartók's niece (Mrs. Pál Voit, née Éva Oláh

Tóth), Ivan Engel (who, like Bartók, was a piano student of István Thomán), Géza Frid (piano student of Bartók), Sándor Veress (composition student of Kodály and Bartók), Ernő Balogh (friend, close eyewitness of Bartók's American years, and arranger of his first American tour in the 1920s), letter from Béla Balázs (librettist and friend of Bartók) (originally published in Hungarian in: Béla Balázs. *Válogatott cikkek és tanulmányok* [Selected articles and essays]. Budapest: Zeneműkiado, 1968), and letters to Frid and Balogh from the composer. These documents reveal Bartók's personality, love of nature, practical and professional activities, work habits, political and musical attitudes, approach to performance interpretation, attitude and style as teacher and pianist, specific corrections and choices that he made of certain versions. More generally, also includes a wealth of information on specific events and aspects of his life and career. Contains notes.

451. Lammers, Joseph Edward. "Patterns of Change Under Identity in Shorter Piano Works by Béla Bartók." Ph.D. diss., Florida State University, 1971. 235p.   ML410.B26 L34

According to the author, *RILM Asbstracts* No. 949 (1971), this study "concerns the nature of change in Bartók's shorter piano pieces (1908-1939). Using the initial hypothesis that musical works of value exhibit an epistemic process of 'three-ness,' consisting of a stimulus, a different stimulus or change, and a reidentification of the initial stimulus, the author has used a parametric approach. This study presents the fundamental view that Bartók's music is a reflection of his respect for certain almost truistic 'laws of life,' principles which are felt to be inherent both in his sophisticated art music and in the peasant music that he heard and collected. In essence the study approaches the subject of musical analysis from a philosophical standpoint, rather than from a purely technical theoretical approach." Contains bibliography.

452. László, Ferenc. "Bartók és a kegyelem" [Bartók and mercy]. In: *Erdélyi református naptár 1996* [Transylvanian Protestant Calendar 1996]. Cluj: Erdélyi Református Egyházkerület [Transylvanian Protestant Church District], 1995. pp. 196-199.

Summary of Bartók's religious beliefs and practices. States that after his ardent Catholicism during his childhood years, Bartók distanced himself from the church and later became sceptical about religion as a whole. He became a member of the Unitarian church that denied the Holy Trinity but from the Adagio of his *Third Piano Concerto,* one discerns that--by the grace of God--he crossed the threshold of life as a believer.

453. Lesznai, Lajos. "Realistische Ausdrucksmittel in der Musik Béla Bartóks" [Realistic means of expression in the music of Béla Bartók]. *Studia musicologica* 5/1-4 (1963): 469-479.   781.05 St92 ISSN-0039-3266

   Shows in detail how Bartók, through reference to free and wild nature (piano cycle *Im Freien* and the slow movement of the *Second Piano Concerto*) as well as to folk music, expresses his wish for freedom, his criticism of society, and other concerns of importance to him.

454. Lyle, Watson. "Béla Bartók. A Personal Impression." *Musical News and Herald* 64 (May 19, 1923): 495.

   Describes Bartók as friendly and intelligent, as gleaned from the author's meeting with Bartók in London in May 1923.

455. ----------. "Modern Musicians: III. Béla Bartók. An Interview by Watson Lyle." *Bookman* 32 (April 1932): 67.

   Comments provide insight into Bartók's attitude in setting text to music. Expresses his desire to write a new opera, but the problem lies in finding an appropriate libretto, which would have to be in Hungarian in order to capture the essence of the words.

456. Markowski, Liesel. "Béla Bartók--ein grosser Humanist und Demokrat" [Béla Bartók--a great humanist and democrat]. *Musik und Gesellschaft* 20/9 (September 1970): 577-585.   780.5 M995 ISSN 0027-4755

   Discusses Bartók's humanistic and democratic attitudes and their manifestations in his music. These include his involvement in the patriotic movement for Hungarian independence as well as his interest in and study of Hungarian folk music. Provides an account of Bartók's broad social philosophy based on international brotherhood. Also speaks of the importance of Bartók's compositional and ethnomusicological contributions.

457. Medek, Tilo. "Bartóks 'Mikrokosmos,' eine uneingestandene Kompositionslehre" [Bartók's Mikrokosmos, an unavowed method of composition]. *Béla Bartók: Zu Leben und Werk,* ed. Friedrich Spangemacher. Bonn: Boosey & Hawkes, 1982. 110p. ISBN 3870902027   ML410.B26 B45   780.92/4 2 19

   Discusses the significance of the *Mikrokosmos* in the context of Bartók's life and philosophy. Points out that this collection of pieces was not romantically inspired but was rather a concern for Bartók in terms of producing a didactic piano work.

458. Menuhin, Yehudi. "Bartók--az én szememmel" [Bartók--in my eyes]. *Új zenei szemle* (Budapest) 6 (1955). HA1.588

Reveals the author's knowledge of Bartók's personality, stating that he had a direct and objective approach to the matter at hand, without indication of self-involvement or personal awareness of his genius.

459. Ö, M. "A Conversation with Béla Bartók." Trans. David E. Schneider and Klára Móricz. In *Bartók and His World*, ed. Peter Laki. Princeton, New Jersey: Princeton University Press, 1995. pp. 235-239. ISBN 0-691-00633-4 ML410 B26 B272. Originally published in *Kassai napló* (April 23, 1926).

According to the translators, this "interview was given on 20 April 1926 to a writer for the Hungarian-language *Kassai napló* (Kassa journal) following a concert in Košice, Slovakia (formerly Kassa, Hungary). Only the interviewer's initials, M.Ö., have been identified. The interview is especially noteworthy for the documentation it provides of the audience's sensitivity to the provenance of Bartók's folk sources and Bartók's admission that Stravinsky's concert in Budapest just over a month earlier (15 March 1926) caused Bartók to reevaluate Stravinsky's 'neoclassical' compositions." Reprinted in: *Bartók Béla művészi kibontakozásának évei II--Bartók megjelenése az európai zeneéletben (1914-1926)* [The years of Bartók's artistic evolution, part 2--Bartók's appearance in European musical life (1914-1926)], ed. János Demény, vol. 7 of *Zenetudományi tanulmányok* [Musicological studies], ed. Bence Szabolcsi and Dénes Bartha (Budapest, 1959), pp. 395-396. Contains notes.

460. Parker, Beverly Lewis. "Parallels Between Bartók's Concerto for Orchestra and Kübler-Ross's Theory About the Dying." *Musical Quarterly* 73/4 (1989): 532-556. ML1 M725 ISSN 0027-4631

According to the author, *RILM Abstracts* No. 9651 (1989), "Parallels can be found between the events, patterns, and progressions within Bartók's *Concerto for Orchestra* and the stages described by the psychiatrist Elisabeth Kübler-Ross of the process through which a dying patient moves to acceptance of death. The musical patterns included configurations that William Kimmel describes as 'Phrygian inflections' (see *RILM* [1980] 5655) and associates with the symbolism of death in Western music. Interpreting the concerto in terms of Kübler-Ross's theory sheds light on three aspects of the work that William Austin finds puzzling in his analysis." Contains illustrations, music examples.

461. Pethő, Bertalan. *Bartók rejtekútja* [Bartók's secret path]. Budapest: Gondolat, 1984. 274p.   ISBN-9632813723

Malcolm Gillies, in his review of the "International Bartók Symposium 1981" in *Music and Letters* 66/4 (October 1985): 373-375, states that "Pethő provided a psychological study entitled 'The Meaning of Bartók's Secret Path,' a forerunner to his recent book. In a rather prosaic collection of articles, Pethő's psychological jargon challenges the reader, forcing the question: are these tortuously worded interpretations wild speculative ramblings or uncannily perceptive insights into the complexities of Bartók's real character?"

462. ----------. "Béla Bartók's Personality." *Studia musicologica* 23 (1981): 443-458.   781.05 St92   ISSN 0039-3266

Suggests that the different typologies provide a basis for describing one's personality. Gives a list of characterological features and states that Bartók's physique can also be considered typical. Gives biographical background as evidence that "psychologically, the hidden path originating in the crisis of reaching man's estate was quasi well-known to him from his childhood."

463. ----------. "The Meaning of Bartók's Secret Path." *Studia musicologica* 24/3-4 (1982): 465-473.   781.05 St92 ISSN 0039-3266

Psychological study of Bartók's personality. An attempt to determine the nature of the Bartók mystery. States that Bartók's "ever deepening secret path can be approached in the light of his form of existence and consciousness, manner of life, experience, works, public life and personality," that both his music and life are equally a source of the mystery; they provide no clue to the secret, but rather are manifestations of it. Includes a brief but significant comparison with Thomas Mann. Passing references are made to certain works, e.g., the *Cantata Profana,* a symbol of his withdrawal from humanity with respect to his creative existence.

464. Stehman, Jacques. "Souvenirs sur Béla Bartók by André Gertler" *La revue musicale* 224 (1955): 99-110.   780.5 R328
ISSN 0035-3736

As recalled by the author, the violinist André Gertler talks of his earliest personal interactions with Bartók, recounting details of Bartók's personality as well as his musical advice for performances of his music. As an example, Bartók's metronomic corrections for the *Second String Quartet,* which he gave to Gertler in 1935, are included here. Also discusses Bartók's musical aesthetics, philosophy, and interests.

465. Stern, Karen. "Notes in Passing." *Adirondack Life* 20/2 (1989): 48-51.

    Compares Bartók and Ives in terms of their philosophical thought, influence of folk music, and the significance of their visits to the Adirondack Mountains in upper New York State.

466. Stevens, Denis. "Menuhin: A Symposium, a Concert, a Conversation." *Musical Times* 132/1778 (April 1991): 182-185. 780.5 M98   ISSN 0027-4666

    In this interview, Menuhin provides his reminiscences of Bartók within the context of more general issues of contemporary music.

467. Szabó, Ferenc. "Bartók Béla." *Magyar zene* (Budapest) 18/4 (December 1977): 341-348.   ML5 M14   ISSN 0025-0384

    A lecture, given on September 25, 1950, on the fifth anniversary of the composer's death, defended Bartók when he was criticized in Hungary for the constructivist approach in his compositions. Szabo points to Bartók's loyalty to his nation and his kinship with the Hungarian people, a defense which contributed to a more positive attitude toward Bartók in Hungary.

468. Szabolcsi, Bence. "Bartók and the World Literature." *International Musicological Conference in Commemoration of Béla Bartók 1971*, ed. József Ujfalussy and János Breuer. Budapest: Editio Musica; New York: Belwin Mills, 1972, pp. 103-106.   ML410.B29 I61 ML410.B26 I5

    States that while Bartók did not belong to the "literary" type of composers, literature inspired his work and served as a link to both creative science and creative art. Gives significant quoted evidence from Bartók in chronological order regarding his impressions obtained from his readings.

469. ----------. "Man and Nature in Bartók's World." *The New Hungarian Quarterly* 2/4 (1961): 90-103.   914.39105 N42   ML410 B26 B29

    Provides substantial primary-source documentation, primarily based on Bartók's correspondence, of his deep attachment to nature. Also published in German: "Mensch und Nature in Bartóks Geisteswelt." *Studia musicologica* 5/1-4 (1963): 525-539. Reprinted in *Bartók Studies*, ed. Todd Crow. Detroit: Information Coordinators, 1976, pp. 63-76.

470. ----------. "Two Bartók Obituaries." Trans. Peter Laki. In *Bartók and His World*, ed. Peter Laki. Princeton, New Jersey: Princeton University Press, 1995. pp. 290-295. ISBN 0-691-00633-4 ML 410 B26 B272. Original version of first obituary published as "A hatvanéves Bartók Béla" [Béla Bartók at sixty]. *Nyugat* 34/4 (April 1941): 137-139; original version of second obituary published in *Opera* (Fall 1945): 3-4.

One of the founders of Hungarian musicology, Bence Szabolcsi speaks in the first obituary of Bartók as standing "at the forefront of the aspirations of European music up to the last minute of his life." Describes the youthfulness, vitality, tensions, contrasts, and many other features of Bartók's personality and art, his youthfulness producing the sense that his musical development "seems like a single impulse . . . though it proceeded to its final peak in zigzags and by many strange leaps." Provides an overview of Bartók's works that are emblematic of the latter tendency, describing the aesthetics and moods of these works as they evolved, transformed, and deepened in the course of his lifetime. Discusses Bartók's changing historical positions relative to his contemporaries, e.g., in 1910, Debussy, Ravel, and Strauss were at the height of their fame, while Bartók and Kodály were still in their formative years, which came to full fruition in the 1920s. In the second obituary, Szabolcsi describes the "most painful remoteness" of Bartók's death in a foreign country across the ocean but speaks of his humanistic ideals that separated him from his homeland. Speaks of Bartók as "a poet and a genius, a revolutionary and a creator, a conjuror of demons and a soul-liberating sage, a shaman and a humanist, pioneer of a new world and innovator of the old." Ends with the statement: "let us believe that the nation and society, which have for so long proven unworthy of their greatest sons, will rise to their height one day and become worthy of the work left behind by their prophets--prophets repudiated at first and later accepted in atonement--those pure and shining geniuses." Contains notes. Both obituaries reprinted in: Bence Szabolcsi. *Kodályról és Bartókról* [Of Kodály and Bartók], ed. Ferenc Bónis. Budapest: Zeneműkiadó, 1987. pp. 163-166 and 167-168, respectively.

471. Szinai, Miklós. "Béla Bartók and the Permanent Committee on Literature and Art of the League of Nations." *The New Hungarian Quarterly* 5/15 (Autumn 1964): 143-146.   914.39105 N42 ML410 B26 B29

Based on documents found in the Hungarian National Archive. Bartók was elected to the Committee but accepted his position "without obligation to work." Also co-opted at the session of the Committee was Thomas Mann. Includes letters of Bartók revealing his attitude toward "The Commission for Intellectual Co-operation," expressing misgivings as long as there was little cooperation among nations and foreign exchange restrictions. Thomas Mann also made a speech against the fascist murderers of freedom. Reprinted in *Bartók Studies,* ed. Todd Crow. Detroit: Information Coordinators, 1976. pp. 167-171.

472. Vámos, Magda. "Une heure avec Bartók" [An hour with Bartók]. *Nouvelle revue de hongrie* (1932); reprinted in "A 1932 Interview with Bartók." *The New Hungarian Quarterly* 14/50 (Summer 1973): 141-151. 914.39105 N42 ML410 B26 B29

    The author visited Bartók and engaged him in what seems to be the longest interview Bartók ever gave. Discussion seems to have been confined to musical questions. In addition to the interview itself, in which Bartók appears to have discussed primary issues related to the history and characteristics of Eastern European folk music, the author gives a detailed account of the political and social environment before World War II, during which the interview took place. Also discusses Bartók's role on the Committee in Geneva, in the Palace of the League of Nations, as well as the immediate circumstances that led the author to the interview with Bartók. States that Bartók probably would not have allowed this interview if he had not thought it important "that outstanding European artists and writers should build a bridge over an abyss in which hatred was eddying dangerously--in the interests of intellectual cooperation." Reprinted in *Bartók Studies,* ed. Todd Crow. Detroit: Information Coordinators, 1976, pp. 179-189.

473. Vinton, John. "Bartók on His Own Music." *Journal of the American Musicological Society* 19 (1966): 232-243. 780.6 Am3j ISSN 0003-0139

    States that Bartók's remarks on folk music were a product of scholarly research and systematic analysis, while on his own music his comments were based on informal thinking. Then gives many quoted statements in several categories: 1) melodic economy; 2) melodic and rhythmic variability; 3) tonality and modality; 4) harmonic mannerisms; and 5) the use of percussion instruments.

474. Whitaker, Frank. "A Visit to Béla Bartók." *Musical Times* 67 (1926): 220-223. 780.5 M98 ISSN 0027-4666

    Discusses the sharp contrasts in Bartók's living environment in Budapest and how this is symbolic of Bartók himself as not one man but two: the adventurous self and the one with an enthusiasm for the simple songs of the people. The author discusses Bartók's personality based on his personal contact with the composer, who told him about his work and his plans. Also, reveals Bartók's views on the music of Stravinsky and Schoenberg and provides an account of Bartók's ethnomusicological research, including Bartók's call for making a distinction between Gypsy and Hungarian folk music.

475. ----------. "The Most Original Mind in Modern Music." *Radio Times* 34 (February 26, 1932): 504.

Compares Bartók's originality with that of Sibelius, whom he considers perhaps the most original of contemporary composers.

5. Discussions Dealing with the State of Bartók Research or Performance

476. Antokoletz, Elliott. "The State of Bartók Research in the Centennial Year." *Music Library Association-Texas Quarter-Notes Newsletter* 11 (Spring 1981): 2-3.

Mentions division of the Bartók sources between the two Archives (in New York and Budapest) as well as language barriers that have contributed to difficulties in producing a complete critical edition of Bartók's works and the general facilitation of research and analysis. Refers to stages of the compositional process, basic catalogue and essay sources, and publishers. Also points to the opportunity to elucidate scholarly issues through many international festivals and conferences devoted to Bartók studies in the centennial year.

477. Bátor, Victor. "Bartók's Executor Speaks." *Musical Courier* (January 1, 1951): 8-9.   780.5 M97

Describes the "situation of the modern composer, not surrounded by institutions that help him." Discusses financial issues, in which the publishers have benefited far more than the estate of the composer, and the executor's struggle to change this situation.

478. Chao, Feng. "Bartók and Chinese Music Culture." *Studia musicologica* 5 (1963): 393-401.   781.05 St92   ISSN 0039-3266

Discusses the increasing importance of Bartók's music in China only since the founding of the People's Republic. Refers to a number of Bartók's works, with some description of technical characteristics, to illustrate how Bartók contributed to the enrichment of musical expression and set a shining example for the Chinese people in musical folklore research for the study of their own fine tradition of musical culture dating back several thousand years. Also outlines Bartók's creative periods with reference to influences by his predecessors.

479. Demarquez, Suzanne. "Souvenirs et réflexions" [Memories and reflections]. *La revue musicale* 224 (1955): 91-97.   780.5 R328 ISSN 0035-3736

Talks of Bartók's devotion to his work, which reflects both a nation and all of humanity. Mentions the slow recognition of his work especially in the West. Gives a survey of certain performances of his works during and after his lifetime and refers to the diverse reactions to them. Also refers to various stylistic influences or relations of his musical language to other sources.

480. Demény, János. "A Bartók-kultusz tévedései" [Errors of the Bartók cult]. *Kortárs* 11/4 (April 1967): 637-643.   PH 3028 L3

Speaks of the problems that come with the popularization of Bartók's music in Hungary, in which erroneous interpretations are often the results. Short popular publications often include irrelevant and trite statements that have nothing to do with the true nature of his music. Personal recollections of performances of Bartók's music also produce factual distortions and incorrect information.

481. ----------. "The Results and Problems of Bartók Research in Hungary." *The New Hungarian Quarterly* 2/1 (1961): 9-31. 914.39105 N42   ML410 B26 B29

As the stream of literature is growing ever broader and because only a fragment of the Hungarian Bartók literature is known abroad, the editors of *The New Hungarian Quarterly* have asked János Demény to give an account of the Bartók literature of Hungary. His study discusses this literature in chronological order from 1945 to the date of this issue and outlines the problems and results of Bartók research. Includes a comprehensive survey of selected volumes of Bartók's writings as well as of secondary sources. Contains facsimiles, photographs, and an extensive bibliography. Also appeared in *Beiträge zur Musikwissenschaft* 3/4 (1961): 49-61. Reprinted in *Bartók Studies*, ed. Todd Crow. Detroit: Information Coordinators, 1976, pp. 221-248.

482. Dent, Edward Joseph. "A Hungarian Bluebeard." *Nation and Athenaeum* 31/10 (June 3, 1922): 354 and 356.   052 N21 V31

Refers to the production of Bartók's *Bluebeard* opera conducted by Jenő Szenkar at Frankfurt on May 13, 1922.

483. Dille, Denijs. "Les problèmes des recherches sur Bartók." *Studia musicologica* 5 (1963): 415-423.   781.05 St92   ISSN 0039-3266

States that problems of Bartók research are not a subject of musicology per se but ones of information, either false or insufficient. Proposes a more precise classification of areas for a methodological approach to the study of the complexities of Bartók (genesis, history, nature, aesthetics and style, etc.). From this method we can gain insight into Bartók's personality from a three-fold point of view, historical, scientific, and aesthetic, and only then will it be possible to make a synthesis approaching his psychological as well as historical reality. We have a serious hope to accomplish this task since the research material and its organization have been provided by the Bartók family and the Academy of Sciences.

484. Fábián, Imre. "Bartók im Wandel der Zeiturteile" [Fluctuating judgment on Bartók over the years]. *Österreichische Musikzeitschrift* 26/3 (March 1971): 127-134.   780.5 Oe8   ISSN 0029-9316

Speaks of a basic problem in Bartók research, which has been the result of fluctuating biased judgments both for and against his music in the divergent attitudes between East and West.

485. Franck, Georges. "Report from Budapest: Third Annual Bartók Conference." *Current Musicology* 10 (1970): 53-56.   780.5 C936 ISSN 0011-3735

The author, from Brussels, provides an evaluation of the Conference, which took place from July 22 to August 6, 1969, in terms of its intentions and problems.

486. Gillies, Malcolm. "Bartók and His Music in the 1990s." *The Bartók Companion*, ed. Malcolm Gillies. London: Faber and Faber, 1993; Portland, Oregon: Amadeus Press (an imprint of Timber Press, Inc.), 1994. pp. 3-17.   ISBN 0-931340-74-8 (HB) ISBN 0-931340-75-6 (PB)   ML410 B26 B28

Assesses Bartók's status at the end of our century by comparing his prominent public recognition in the 1990s with the earlier sudden rise of interest in his music just after his death in 1945. Based on the fewer number of pages devoted to Bartók (than to Debussy, Schoenberg, and Stravinsky) in scholarly writings on twentieth-century music, assumes that scholars have a somewhat less primary opinion of Bartók as a leading innovator, in contrast to his "first tier" public reputation. Then, provides a concise biographical overview of Bartók's key personal and musical developments as well as an assessment of his personality. Cites Bartók's letters and essays as important sources for insight into Bartók as man and musician. States, however, that "the Bartók debate is by no means over," and that basic assumptions about Bartók's personal image, political convictions, and musical contributions are problematic and need a more candid reappraisal within both the Hungarian and broader contemporary historical contexts. Also addresses the problems and issues pertaining to the influences of Bartók's folk-music research and Western art music on his own stylistic development.

487. Hawkes, Ralph. "Béla Bartók in der Emigration" [Béla Bartók in emigration]. *Musikblätter der Wiener Philharmoniker* 41/9 (1986-1987): 265-267.

    While Bartók's music publisher at Boosey and Hawkes attests to the composer's severe financial straits in the United States, he also informs us that Bartók was entirely neglected there as a composer during these final years of his life.

488. Helm, Everett. "Bartók on Stage: Fresh Light on a Long Undervalued Dramatic Trilogy." *High Fidelity* 14/11 (November 1964): 74. ML1 H45 789.91 ISSN 0018-1455

    Refers to the enthusiastic reception of Bartók's three stage works--*Duke Bluebeard's Castle, The Wooden Prince*, and *The Miraculous Mandarin*--in Budapest in 1964.

489. Jones, Robert. "A Feast of Piano Music by Bartók." *The American Record Guide* 32 (September 1965): 22-25, 33. ML1 A725 789.91 ISSN 0003-0716

    Begins with a list of recorded performances of Bartók's piano music (including *Mikrokosmos, For Children, Piano Concerto No. 3, Fifteen Hungarian Peasant Songs, Dance Suite*, and *Sonata for Two Pianos and Percussion*). Then, discusses the performances, degree of difficulty of some of the works, and the extent to which certain record companies have ignored some of the smaller pieces. Speaks of the pleasing situation in the sudden deluge of Bartókian pianists, and especially of the presumably definitive performances by the composer's widow.

490. Kárpáti, János. "Nemzetközi Bartók szeminárium" [International lectures on Bartók]. *Élet és irodalom* 11/26 (1967): 9. HC1.285

    Not examined. According to Iván Pethes, *RILM Abstracts* No. 1876 (1967), the author presents a report of the lectures.

491. Klemm, Eberhardt. "Bemerkungen zur Rezeption Béla Bartók" [Remarks on the reception of Béla Bartók]. *Jahrbuch Peters* (1985): 76-84. ML5 J16

    Refers to the critical roles of music journals such as the *Musikblätter des Anbruch* and *Melos* since the 1920s and Theodor Adorno, Pierre Boulez, and East German critics during the 1950s as factors hindering the reception of Bartók's music.

492. Körtvélyes, Géza. *A modern táncművészet útján* [Concerning the modern art of dance]. Budapest: Zeneműkiadó, 1970. 200p.

   Includes a first-hand account, following a brief historical study of twentieth-century ballet, of the performances of Bartók's *The Miraculous Mandarin*. Contains illustrations, bibliography.

493. Kuttner, Fritz A. "Das Bartók-Archiv in New York--ein Nachtrag" [The Bartók Archive in New York--An addendum]. *Die Musikforschung* 22/1 (March 1969): 75-76.　780.5 M9921 ISSN 0027-4801

   Provides a follow-up of the report published in *Musikforschung* 21/1 (1968): 61-63, including discussion of recent developments in the management of the Archive, with speculation as to its future course.

494. ----------. "Der Katalog des Bartók-Archivs in New York City" [Catalogue of the Bartók Archives in N.Y.C.]. *Die Musikforschung* 21/1 (January-March 1968): 61-63.　780.5 M9921 ISSN 0027-4801

   Discusses the criticism and legal questions concerning the catalogue of the New York Bartók Archive and questions the extent of their relevance to musicologists.

495. László, Ferenc. "A Bartók Összkiadás órája" [The hour of the Bartók Complete Edition]. *Muzsika* 38/5 (May 1995): 39-40. ISSN 0027-5336

   A summary of the history of the Bartók estate up to the point when, after the death of Ditta Pásztory in 1982, Peter Bartók became the proprietor of the Bartók estate. He sent photographed copies of the entire material to the Budapest Bartók Archive, and Somfai was able to study the original manuscripts. Already in 1971, when Somfai became the Director of the Bartók Archive, his intention was to realize the complete critical edition. Nevertheless, today we are still at the stage of preliminary work, even though Somfai, the only scholar able to coordinate such a complete edition, is over sixty years old and such work could take more than twenty years. States that we are in need of an editor of the caliber of Somfai.

496. Lenoir, Yves. "Réflexions critiques sur une édition posthume: B. Bartók, *Rumanian Folk Music*. Ed. Benjamin Suchoff" [Critical reflections on a posthumous edition: Bartók's *Rumanian Folk Music*. Ed. Benjamin Suchoff]. *Revue musicale de Suisse romande* 40/2 (June 1987): 79-88.　780.5 R3281

Calls for a new edition of Bartók's *Rumanian Folk Music* collection, based on a more authentic and scientific approach. Contains illustrations, port., facsimiles, bibliography.

497. Lindlar, Heinrich. "Viermal Bartók Musik für Saiteninstrumente: Notizen zu einem Interpretationsvergleich" [Four times Bartók's *Music for String Instruments:* notes to a comparison of interpretation]. In S. Borris et al. *Vergleichende Interpretationskunde.* Berlin: Merseburger, 1965. p. 35. 780.904 D25V

Provides a detailed comparison of recordings of this work by four conductors: Herbert von Karajan, Günter Wand, Sir Georg Solti, and Ferenc Fricsay.

498. Mason, Colin. "Bartók Festival in Budapest." *Musical Times* (December 1948): 376.   780.5 M98   ISSN 0027-4666

Outlines the format and works performed at the first International Bartók Festival of Modern Music in Budapest (October 10 and 31, 1948). Discusses the competitions as the most important part of the Festival and reviews performances.

499. ----------. "Bartók's Scherzo for Piano and Orchestra." *Tempo* (London) 65 (1963): 10-13.   780.5 T249   ISSN 0040-2982

Talks of the re-discovery of the Scherzo in Budapest and its first performance on September 28, 1961. Then, discusses problems regarding the lack of documentation and finally gives an analysis of the work.

500. McCredie, Andrew Delgarno. "Karl Amadeus Hartmann and the Hungarian Music of the Early Twentieth Century." *Studia musicologica* 33/1-4 (1991): 151-193.   781.05 St92 ISSN 0039-3266

According to Márta Szekeres-Farkas, *RILM Abstracts* No. 4944 (1991), McCredie demonstrates that "Hartmann's commitment to Hungarian music can be seen in his activities as a concert organizer, *Programmgestalter,* and composer. His enthusiasm focused on Bartók, Kodály, Mátyás Seiber, and Sándor Jemnitz. . . . Hartmann's reception of Bartók can be studied in his early Juryfreien concerts (keyboard works and string quartets) and in the Munich Musica Viva concerts (concertos and string quartets)." Contains facsimiles, music, charts, tables.

501. Mila, Massimo, and Fred K. Prieberg. "Bartók--Webern 25 Years Later: Their Place in Today's Music." *The World of Music* 12/3 (1970): 32-48.   780.5 W893   ISSN 0043-8774

Speaks of the return of Bartók's music from America to devastated Europe after World War II as one of the most conspicuous events. Questions the significance of the fluctuations in the posthumous evaluation of Bartók, at a time in that delicate phase in the destiny of a composer at which he passes from modernity to history. Specifies the various musical aspects of Bartók's compositions which were selected and absorbed by composers of different nations, e.g., folk-song features into the technique of certain Italian composers, and the expressionist component of timbral phenomena into the music of certain Polish composers.

502. Nagy, Alpár. "Bartók Béla Soproni kapcsolatai" [Béla Bartók's relationship to Sopron]. *Életünk* 5/9-10 (1975): 455-470.

Based on an account of the articles and reviews of Bartók's concerts in Sopron, the author shows that Bartók's music was not properly evaluated or appreciated until after his death.

503. Oláh, Gustáv. "Bartók and the Theatre." *Tempo* (London) 13-14 (1949-50): 4-8; reprinted in *Béla Bartók: A Memorial Review*. New York: Boosey & Hawkes, 1950, pp. 54-60.　　780.5 T249 ISSN 0040-2982

First-hand account of Bartók's theater works, discussed here from the point of view of Oláh's profession, which included the design and production of a number of performances of Bartók's stage works. Also includes synopses as well as some history of their production.

504. Percival, John. "Bartók's Ballets." In: *The Stage Works of Béla Bartók*, ed. Nicholas John. Sponsor: Martini. *Operaguide* 44. New York: Riverrun; London: Calder, 1991. pp. 103-108. ISBN 0-7145-4194-X　　ML410 B26 S78

Discusses the neglect by dance companies and choreographers of Bartók's ballets, *The Wooden Prince* and *The Miraculous Mandarin*. States that failure of these dance works during Bartók's lifetime in contrast to the relative success of his *Bluebeard* opera and Stravinsky's ballets may be attributed to the nature of their plots, the practical limitations of ballet companies in financing the large orchestral forces, and the lack of specific choreographic guidelines from the librettist. Provides a reception history of the ballets in their time, including comparison with the reception of the Diaghilev productions. Describes the staging, scenery, and costumes of both ballets of various productions and evaluates the intentions of the designers. In contrast, discusses the attraction of choreographers to other works of Bartók not originally conceived as ballets, most notably *Music for Strings, Percussion, and Celesta* and the *Bluebeard* opera.

505. Pernye, András. "New Records." *The New Hungarian Quarterly* 11/38
(Summer 1970): 211-215.   914.39105 N42   ML410 B26 B29

Includes, among other composers' works, a review of recordings
of several of Bartók's compositions: *Music for Strings, Percussion
and Celesta, The Miraculous Mandarin Suite* (Hungaroton SLPX
1301); *The Miraculous Mandarin, Dance Suite, Hungarian Peasant
Songs* (1918-1933) (Hungaroton SLPX 11319); and the early *Violin
Concerto* (1907-1908), *The Wooden Prince Suite*, and *Romanian
Dance no. 1* (Orchestral version) (Hungaroton SLPX 11314).

506. Sharp, Goeffrey. "Bartók's Violin Concerto." *The Music Review* 5/4
(1944): 260.   780.5 M9733   ISSN 0027-4445

Review of the first English performance of this work on
September 20, 1944, given by Yehudi Menuhin and the B.B.C.
Symphony Orchestra conducted by Sir Adrian Boult.

507. Stephan, Rudolf. "Zur Bartók-Rezeption in den zwanziger Jahren"
[The reception of Bartók's music in the 1920s]. *Österreichische
Musikzeitschrift* 39/2 (February 1984): 86-93.   780.5 Oe8
ISSN 0029-9316

Discusses the performance of Bartók's works as well as his own
concerts in Frankfurt in 1922. Points to Adorno's critique as one of
the earliest German writings on Bartók. Contains port.

508. Tallián, Tibor. "Bartók fogadtatása Amerikában 1940-1945"
[Bartók's reception in America 1940-1945]. *Zenetudományi
dolgozatok* (1985): 7-21.

A new perception of Bartók during his American years is
revealed in a wealth of documentation. Includes concert reviews,
interviews, and other documentation to provide evidence for the
increasingly favorable reception of Bartók after 1943 among
informed musicians but not the general public.

509. ----------. *Bartók fogadtatása Amerikában 1940-1945* [Bartók's
reception in America 1940-1945]. Budapest: Zeneműkiadó, 1988.
271p.   ISBN 963-330657-4

The main points of this book are summarized in item no. 510.
See review by András Fodor in *Magyar zene* (Budapest) 30/4
(December 1989): 441-444.

510. ----------. "Bartók's Reception in America, 1940-1945" (translated by Peter Laki). *Bartók and His World,* ed. Peter Laki. Princeton, New Jersey: Princeton University Press, 1995. pp. 101-118. ISBN 0-691-00633-4   ML 410 B26B272

Originally, a lecture given at the Musicological Institute of the Hungarian Academy of Sciences (April 11, 1985). Documents Bartók's reception in America between 1940 and 1945, based on all concert, record, and score reviews as well as newspaper and magazine articles available to the author during his research in the United States in 1984. Intention is to add a modest amount of information to our knowledge of Bartók's last years and the compositions resulting from his conditions during this period. Considers this research the duty of Hungarian musicology. Discusses the different political, social, and cultural conditions that Bartók encountered in his new environment, in contrast to the nondemocratic country of Hungary, where Bartók did not have to take the press seriously since 1920. Discusses Bartók's lack of success during his American years in light of his expectations. Provides a detailed account of Bartók's concert activities at this time, addressing the frequency of his concerts and the often-negative critical reception of his music, his interest in marketing his music, his intention to record, and most importantly his concerns regarding the possibility of having his scholarly work published. Speculates on the reasons for Bartók's fate during his American years, one of which was the lack of understanding of his native Hungarian folk music. However, points to the orchestral concerts as the highpoint of his American concert career. Provides substantial critical documentation. This essay summarizes the main points of Tallián's book (see item No. 509), *Bartók fogadtatása Amerikában 1940-1945* [Bartók's reception in America 1940-1945]. Budapest: Zeneműkiadó, 1988. 271p. ISBN 963-330657-4

511. ----------. "Vier Bartók-Dissertationen aus der BRD" [Four Bartók dissertations from the BRD]. *Documenta bartókiana* 6 (Budapest): 279-288.   ISBN-963-05-1185-1-(Serie)   ML410 B26 D6 ISSN 0134-0131

Evaluates four dissertations on Bartók by Werner Pütz, Günter Weiss-Aigner, Peter Petersen, and Helmut Fladt.

512. Vikár, László. "Bartók Libretti in English Translation." Trans. Thomas Land. *The New Hungarian Quarterly* 120 (1990): 158-171. 914.39105 N42   ML410 B26 B29

According to the author, *RILM Abstracts* No.10261 (1990), the article serves as "an introduction to Land's translation of the texts of two of Bartók's works: the libretto of *Kékszakállú herceg vára,* based on Béla Balázs's mystery play, and Bartók's own verse rendering of the Romanian *colindă* texts used for the *Cantata profana*. Various translations of the works are compared."

513. Vitányi, Iván. "Bartók and the Public." *The New Hungarian Quarterly* 2/2 (1961): 175-179.   914.39105 N42
ML410 B26 B29

Discusses the attitudes of different generations toward Bartók's music, including the author's own changing views since the death of the composer.

514. Weissmann, John. "On Some Problems of Bartók Research in Connection with Bartók's Biography." *Studia musicologica* 5/1-4 (1963): 587-596.   781.05 St92   ISSN 0039-3266

States that the collection and publication of relevant sources, documents, and factual data constitute the task of biographical research. Then, criticizes the Trustee (Victor Bátor) of the New York Bartók Archive for hampering the research of Demény and others. Thereby, proposes to establish an International Bartók Society to collect documents relating to Bartók.

515. Zoltai, Dénes. "Bartók in Sicht der Frankfurter Schule" [The Bartók image of the Frankfurt School]. *International Musicological Conference in Commemoration of Béla Bartók 1971*, ed. József Ujfalussy and János Breuer. Budapest: Editio Musica; New York: Belwin Mills, 1972: 13-17.   ML410.B29 I61 (Editio Musica)
ML410.B26 I5 (Belwin Mills)

Discusses Adorno's attitudes toward Bartók and folklorism, pointing out Adorno's misunderstanding of Bartók's art, which he branded as a compromise.

516. ----------. "Bartók nem alkuszik" [Bartók does not compromise]. *Világosság* 11/11 (November 1970): 663-668.   HA1.287

Provides a rebuttal against Adorno's opinion regarding the supposed compromise of Bartók and his folk-music orientation. States that Bartók's philosophy regarding his use of folk sources differs from other contemporary folkloristic trends; Bartók's is directly related to his humanism.

IV. STUDIES OF BARTÓK'S MUSICAL COMPOSITIONS

1. Analytical and Theoretical Studies of Bartók's Works

517. Abraham, Gerald. "Bartók: String Quartet No. 6." *The Music Review* 3/1 (1942): 72-73.   780.5 M9733   ISSN 0027-4445

> In review of the score, states that *String Quartet No. 6* is the latest of the most important series of string quartets since Beethoven. Gives brief summary of quartet composers since Beethoven and then discusses the significance of this quartet in terms of Bartók's evolution. Presents brief analysis of its form and texture as well as certain technical devices.

518. Agawu, V. Kofi. "Analytical Issues Raised by Bartók's Improvisations for Piano, Op. 20." *Journal of Musicological Research* 5 (1984): 131-163.   ML5 M6415   780.7 ISSN 0141-1896

> Study of pitch organization in Bartók's music. Emphasis is not on the compositions themselves but rather on the analytical issues that result from their study. Prefers a historically based approach, with a balance between the historical information and the theoretical discussions.

519. Albrecht, Jan. "Das Variations- und Imitationsprinzip in der Tektonik von Bartóks Bratschenkonzert" [The variation- and imitation principle in the construction of Bartók's *Viola Concerto*]. *Studia musicologica* 14 (1972): 317-327.   781.05 St92 ISSN 0039-3266

> Detailed discussion of how Bartók applies the variation principle to the whole structural system of the piece, emphasizing the system in the inversion of the facture.

520. Antokoletz, Elliott. "'At last something truly new': Bagatelles." *The Bartók Companion,* ed. Malcolm Gillies. London: Faber and Faber, 1993; Portland, Oregon: Amadeus Press (an imprint of Timber Press, Inc.), 1994. pp. 110-123.   ISBN 0-931340-74-8 (HB) ISBN 0-931340-75-6 (PB)   ML410 B26 B28

Discusses the history and reception of these early pieces and how they represent Bartók's first major attempt to absorb and transform both Eastern European folk sources and elements of Debussy's music into a new, anti-Romantic idiom. Outlines the basic principles of Bartók's musical language as contained in these early pieces of 1908. Study of the individual pieces reflects in microcosm the various stages of Bartók's entire evolution. Includes exploration of harmonic and linear derivations from authentic folk songs and original modal constructions, fusion of traditional and symmetrical concepts of tonal centricity, diatonic, octatonic, and whole-tone interactions, and generation of the interval cycles from intervallic cells.

521. ----------. "Concerto for Orchestra." *The Bartók Companion*, ed. Malcolm Gillies. London: Faber and Faber, 1993; Portland, Oregon: Amadeus Press (an imprint of Timber Press, Inc.), 1994. pp. 526-537. ISBN 0-931340-74-8 (HB) ISBN 0-931340-75-6 (PB) ML410 B26 B28

Discusses the political, professional, and unhappy personal circumstances surrounding the composition of the *Concerto* during Bartók's final residence in the United States. Refers to Bartók's performance reception during this period and discusses the culminating position of the *Concerto* in Bartók's oeuvre as part of the tendency toward synthesis of divergent Eastern European folk-music sources and abstract contemporary art-music techniques, which are set within the five-movement framework of traditional Classical forms and procedures as outlined by the composer himself. Provides in-depth analysis of the traditional folk-like themes and overall harmonic fabric based on the interaction and transformations between traditional (diatonic) and non-traditional (octatonic, whole-tone, and other cyclic-interval) pitch formations.

522. ----------. "Middle-period String Quartets." *The Bartók Companion*, ed. Malcolm Gillies. London: Faber and Faber, 1993; Portland, Oregon: Amadeus Press (an imprint of Timber Press, Inc.), 1994. pp. 257-277. ISBN 0-931340-74-8 (HB) ISBN 0-931340-75-6 (PB) ML410 B26 B28

Points to the Third and Fourth String Quartets as the most intensive stage of Bartók's evolution toward increasing synthesis of divergent folk-music and art-music sources. Provides a brief history of the political and cultural circumstances as well as Bartók's own professional activities in the 1920s that contributed to the expansion of the basic principles of pitch organization, texture, and instrumental writing in these two middle-period quartets. After discussing the new sources of influence on Bartók's style during this period and the events leading to the composition of these quartets, in-depth analyses are provided to reveal insight into Bartók's aesthetic bases, theoretical principles, and musical language in terms of both pitch and rhythmic organization. Structural principles of these quartets are shown to be based on the infusion of traditional forms with Bartók's own notion of expansions and contractions between diatonic and chromatic themes. Focuses on generation of the larger structure and design by means of special transformational links between Eastern European folk modes (diatonic and non-diatonic) and abstract symmetrical, or cyclic-interval constructions. In the *Fourth Quartet,* especially, shows how the interaction of symmetrical cells underlies a new concept of tonal centricity based on "axes of symmetry."

523. ----------. "Modal Transformation and Musical Symbolism in Bartók's *Cantata Profana." Bartók in Retrospect,* ed. Elliott Antokoletz, Victoria Fischer, and Benjamin Suchoff. Projected publication of two 1995 conference proceedings.

Discusses the *Cantata Profana* (1930) as the most explicit embodiment of Bartók's philosophy, based on the composer's ideal concerning the brotherhood of neighboring nations--Romania, Slovakia, and Hungary. Demonstrates that the conjoining of Bartók's social concerns during the period of increasing political repression in the 1930s with his lifelong musical endeavors to synthesize divergent Eastern folk modalities and Western art-music sources came to full fruition in the *Cantata.* Analyzes the work as an exemplar of Bartók's ability to transform both diatonic and nondiatonic folk modes into octatonic, whole-tone, and other abstract pitch constructions of contemporary art music in correspondence with dramatic symbolization of the text. The music paraphrase from the opening of Bach's *St. Matthew Passion* is pivotal in these transformations and appears to serve a deeper level of symbolization in the manifestation of Bartók's philosophical statement. Contains music examples. (Annotation based on the author's abstract of the original lecture; see item no. 1139.)

524. ----------. "The Music of Bartók: Some Theoretical Approaches in the U.S.A." *Studia musicologica* 24/4 (1982): 67-74.   781.05 St92 ISSN 0039-3266

Lecture given at the IMC of UNESCO Conference on Bartók in Budapest (1981). Illustrates the diversity of analytical/theoretical approaches to Bartók's music in the U.S.A., discussing the concepts of such theorists as Roy Travis (Schenkerian), Allen Forte (serial scheme), Tibor and Peter Bachmann and Hilda Gervers (as followers of Ernő Lendvai's "Golden Section" and "Fibonacci" principles), George Perle (concepts of the interval cycle and inversional symmetry), and Elliott Antokoletz (transformation of the folk modes to the system of the interval cycles and inversional symmetry).

Explores these varied approaches by moving from the more traditional concepts to those that can only belong to the present century. This high degree of individuality and divergence among theorists, which is particularly prominent in the United States, may partly be due to the versatility and complexity of Bartók's musical language.

525. ----------. *The Music of Béla Bartók: A Study of Tonality and Progression in Twentieth-Century Music.* Berkeley and Los Angeles: University of California Press, 1984. xviii, 342p.
ISBN 0520046048   ML 410.B26A8   780.92 4

In-depth study of Bartók's musical language, showing stages of transformation from the folk-music sources to a highly abstract set of art-music principles. These stages include the harmonization of authentic folk tunes, symmetrical transformation of the diatonic folk modes, the construction, development, and interaction of intervallic cells, tonal centricity based on axes of symmetry and traditional modal-tonal centers, interactions of diatonic, octatonic, and whole-tone formations, and generation of the interval cycles. Many compositions spanning Bartók's lifetime are explored and placed in the historical context of the musical developments and activities of Bartók's contemporaries. Bartók's own activities in connection with his folk-music investigations and compositions are explored in-depth to shed light on the development of his own personal musical language. Includes discussion of a number of Bartók's sketches to support the theoretical conclusions. Conclusion introduces a study of the use of folk-music sources and symmetrical pitch relations in music of the nineteenth century. Contains 390 music examples, 14 holographic excerpts, 3 indexes, and a bibliography. See reviews by: Arnold Whittall in *The Times Literary Supplement* (London) (August 16, 1985): 904; Péter Halász in *Magyar zene* 26/3 (September 1985): 327-330; Jim Samson in *Tempo* 155 (December 1985): 54-55; Mitchell Morris in *Current Musicology* 47 (1986): 71-76; Paul Wilson in *Journal of Music Theory* 30/1 (Spring 1986): 113-121; Douglas Jarman in *Music and Letters* 67/3 (July 1986): 321-322; Pieter C. van den Toorn in *Music Theory Spectrum* 9 (1987): 215-222.

526. ----------. "The Musical Language of Bartók's 14 Bagatelles for Piano." *Tempo* 137 (June 1981): 8-16.   780.5 T249
ISSN 0040-2982

Demonstrates the fundamental principles of pitch organization of Bartók's musical language as already contained in these early pieces of 1908. Reflects stages of transformation from harmonization of authentic folk tunes to symmetrical reordering of their modal intervals. Further development is seen in the interactions of diatonic (traditional) with whole-tone and octatonic (nontraditional) pitch sets as well as in more abstract concepts of pitch organization based on interactions of intervallic cells, generation of the interval cycles, and a new concept of tonal centricity based on "axes of symmetry." Also published in Spanish translation by Victoria López Meseguer. "El Lenguaje musical en las 14 Bagatelas para Piano de Bartók." *Quodlibet* (Madrid) 1 (February 1995): 76-90.

527. ----------. *Musical Symbolism in the Operas of Debussy and Bartók.* New York and Oxford: Oxford University Press, forthcoming. ca. 300p.

Explores the means by which these two early twentieth-century operas transform the harmonic structures of the traditional major/minor scale system into a new musical language and how this language reflects the psycho-dramatic symbolism of the Franco-Belgian poet, Maurice Maeterlinck, and his Hungarian disciple, Béla Balázs. In reaction to the realism of nineteenth-century theater, many authors began to develop a new interest in psychological motivation and a level of consciousness manifested in metaphor, ambiguity, and symbol. In his plays, Maeterlinck was to transform the internal concept of subconscious motivation into an external one, in which human emotions and actions are controlled by fate. These two operas represent the first significant attempts to establish more profound correspondences between the symbolist dramatic conception and the new musical language. Demonstrates that the new musical language is based almost exclusively on interactions between pentatonic/diatonic folk modalities and their more abstract symmetrical transformations, the opposition of these two harmonic extremes serving as the basis for dramatic polarity between the characters as real-life beings and as symbols of fate. Also explores the new musico-dramatic relations within their larger historical, social, and aesthetic contexts. Provides a formulation of the new theoretic-analytical principles and shows how these principles serve to conjoin various historical and cultural as well as philosophical and psychological issues within the operatic milieu. Based on internal (analytical) and external (primary source) evidence, also explores direct historical, philosophical, and compositional connections between the two operas.

528. ----------. "Organic Development and the Interval Cycles in Bartók's Three Studies, Op. 18." *Studia musicologica* 36/3-4 (1995): 249-261.   781.05 St92   ISSN 0039-3266

Lecture given at the International Bartók Colloquium 1995. Held at Szombathely, Hungary (July 3-5, 1995). Points to the *Three Studies,* Op. 18, for piano (1918) as a significant stage in Bartók's evolution toward a new kind of harmonic construction and new means of progression during the decade following World War I. Shows that while the work is founded upon a kind of twelve-tone language, the concept of a *set* or *series* in Bartók's music is fundamentally different from that of Schoenberg's twelve-tone system. Bartók's special twelve-tone set is analogous to the precompositional assumptions of the major and minor scales in traditional tonal music. States that the concept of the interval cycle appears to lie at the core of Bartók's evolution, tracing it back to the nineteenth century. Then provides an analysis of the work based on systematic interlocking of the interval cycles, the combinations of which outline expanding interval ratios between semitones (interval-ratios 1:1, 1:2, 1:3, etc.). Demonstrates that interaction between cyclic-interval constructions and the pentatonic/modal elements of Eastern European folk music is fundamental to the organic development of Bartók's music. In light of Bartók's own stated premise regarding diatonic "extension in range" of chromatic material, or the reverse, "chromatic compression," shows how structural relationships in Op. 18 support cyclic-interval expansion from the abstract symmetrical construction of chromatic (cell X), whole-tone (cell Y), and double-tritone (cell Z) tetrachords to increasingly diatonic collections. Other Bartók works are also cited as examples. Contains music examples, diagrams.

529. ----------. "Organic Expansion and Classical Structure in Bartók's *Sonata for Two Pianos and Percussion." Bartók in Retrospect*, ed. Elliott Antokoletz, Victoria Fischer, and Benjamin Suchoff. Projected publication of two 1995 conference proceedings.

Explores the means by which Bartók could generate an entirely organic fabric within the rigorous Classical structures of this work, composed in the mid-1930s during a new stage in the development of his aesthetic approach. First, points to the historical precedents in two opposing sources for the development of the organizational principles: the ultrachromaticism of German late Romantic music and the pentatonic-diatonic modalities of peasant music of Eastern Europe. Includes primary source reference in Bartók's own comments on the principle of diatonic "extension in range" of chromatic themes and the reverse, chromatic "compression" of diatonic themes, and his indication as to the exact moment in his evolution (mid-1920s) when he moved toward abstract chromaticism. Then focuses on transformations between modal and chromatic extremes by means of systematic intervallic expansions and contractions in the *Sonata.* Also shows that in spite of the more abstract medium of much of the *Sonata,* in which pure chromatic constructions and polymodal chromatic combinations expand to the larger intervals of the folk modes and the interval cycles, rhythmic and structural features of folk music (Hungarian, Slovak, Romanian, Bulgarian, and other sources) are still very much in evidence. Contains examples and diagrams.

530. -----------. "Pitch-Set Derivations from the Folk Modes in Bartók's Music." *Studia musicologica* 24/3 (1982): 265-274.   781.05 St92 ISSN 0039-3266

Lecture given at the International Bartók Symposium in Budapest (1981). Discusses the derivation of abstract intervallic pitch collections from the folk modes as a means of integration and progression in Bartók's *Eight Improvisations*, Op. 20, for piano, the *Fourth String Quartet*, and *Fifth String Quartet*. Use of intervallic sets or cells compensates for the disappearance of the traditional triad and harmonic functions. Includes some discussion of Bartók's sketches. Also published in Spanish translation by Victoria López Meseguer. "Derivación de sets a partir de los modos folklóricos en la música de Bartók." *Quodlibet* (Madrid) 3 (October 1995): 113-123.

531. ----------. "Principles of Pitch Organization in Bartók's *Fourth String Quartet.*" Ph.D. diss. City University of New York, 1975. 152p. MT145.B25 A5M

An in-depth study of uni-intervallic cycles, symmetrical pitch-cells, and a new means of establishing tonal centricity. The system of pitch relations in Bartók's *Fourth String Quartet* is associated with a larger system, which has been referred to by George Perle as "12-tone tonality." The system in the quartet is primarily based on the principle of equally subdividing the octave into the total complex of interval cycles. A subsystem can be derived by selecting tetrachordal segments from each of these cycles. The four-note symmetries (designated as cells X, Y, and Z)--C-C#-D-Eb, Bb-C-D-E, and G#-C#-D-G--are basic in the generation of the interval cycles. Principles include the construction and interaction of the three cells according to the equal-divisions of the octave, generation of the two complementary whole-tone cycles, generation and partitioning of the interval-5/7 (perfect fourth/perfect fifth) cycle into two complementary collections. Tonality, modality, and the traditional diatonic system are viewed according to the methodized approaches of Colin Mason, Roy Travis, and Ernő Lendvai, and a serial approach to tonality by Allen Forte. An analysis of the quartet's special rhythmic properties is included as an appendix. Contains illustrations, bibliography. An extract is published in *In Theory Only* 3/6 (September 1977): 3-22.

532. ----------. "Rhythmic Form in Three of Bartók's String Quartets." Master's thesis. Hunter College of the City University of New York, 1970. 132p.

Bartók's *Third, Fourth,* and *Sixth Quartets* (1927, 1928, 1939) are the basis for this study. Rhythmic tension and release, essential to rhythmic form, are derived from several sources: tempo changes; metric changes; rhythmic grouping; rhythmic consonance and dissonance; and recurrence and modification of rhythmic motives. Patterns in tempo changes determine tension and release. Cross meters, metric displacement, and metric change increase tension. Rhythmic grouping determines which sections are accented and released from the non-accented anacrustic sections. Rhythmic dissonance results from the conflict between metric and rhythmic groupings. The *Third* and *Fourth Quartets* have cumulative rhythmic forms; the rhythmic elements build to their peaks of tension in the last movements. The *Sixth Quartet* has a rhythmic arch-form; the highest peaks of tension occur in the two middle movements.

533. ----------. "Transformations of a Special Non-Diatonic Mode in Twentieth-Century Music: Bartók, Stravinsky, Scriabin and Albrecht." *Music Analysis* 12/1 (March 1993): 25-45.   ML5 M68 ISSN 0262 5245

Shows how Bartók and Stravinsky absorbed and utilized basic elements from their folk music idioms to develop their new musical languages, while Scriabin derived his compositional materials from more abstract sources. Albrecht's approach belongs to both categories. In spite of the different sources, all of these composers are shown to exploit a special non-diatonic mode (C-D-E-F#-G-A-Bb and its rotations) commonly found in both spheres: Eastern European folk music and (as explicitly described by Albrecht and circumstantially by writers about Scriabin's music) the "overtone series." Bartók's *Cantata Profana* and No. 3 of the *Eight Improvisations on Hungarian Peasant Tunes,* Op. 20, for piano, are discussed to demonstrate how more abstract symmetrical sets (whole-tone and octatonic) as well as diatonic forms are generated by means of special transformations, including modal variation by rotation, extension, and symmetrical reinterpretation.

534. Austin, William. "Bartók's Concerto for Orchestra." *The Music Review* 18/1 (February 1957): 21-47.   780.5 M9733 ISSN 0027-4445

Mentions the popularity of the work and gives a detailed measure-by-measure analysis of the entire work in a somewhat romanticized descriptive language. Deals with motivic-thematic, rhythmic, tonal, contrapuntal, and textural parameters within the context of the structure and design. Gives occasional references to folk sources.

535. Avasi, Béla. "Tonsysteme aus Intervallpermutationen" [Tone system from interval permutations]. *Studia memoriae Bélae Bartók sacra* (55/16): 249-300. Budapest: Aedes Academiae Scientiarium Hungaricae, 1956, 2nd ed., 1957; 3rd ed., 1959.   780.92 B285R

Devises charts and classification systems for various possible pitch combinations. As one instance, according to this scheme, the fugue subject of *Music for Strings, Percussion, and Celesta* is graduated in nine stages.

536. Babbitt, Milton. "The String Quartets of Bartók." *Musical Quarterly* 35 (July 1949): 377-385.   ML1 M725   ISSN 0027-4631

States that the "idiomatic differences between the first two quartets and the later four are secondary to the basic unity of purpose that invested all six." Shows some significant functions of intervallic structures with analogical references in traditional tonal functions. However, points out that Bartók was "aware of the hazards inherent in the use of a language overladen with connotations, in which the scarcely suggested is perceived as the explicitly stated."

537. Bachmann, Tibor, and Maria Bachmann. *Studies in Bartók's Music,* 3rd ed. N.p.: Russell P. Getz, Tibor and Maria Bachmann, 1983. 100p.   ML 410.B26 B215.

Includes: analyses of Bartók's works, based on diatonic modality, hexatony, and octatony. In the first category, he explores concepts of simultaneous scaling, unconventional types of scales, acoustic scales, axis-major and axis-minor scales, the Fibonacci scale, etc. The second category explores cyclic expansion of hexachords and other general concepts of hexachordal extensions of the medieval Guidonian hexachordal scale to the twelve-tone limit. The third category deals with an eight-note scale system derived from the hexachordal cycle as a means of bridging the gulf between seven-note Diatony and the twelve-tone Duodecatony.

538. Bachmann, Tibor, and Peter J. Bachmann. "An Analysis of Béla Bartók's Music Through Fibonaccian Numbers and the Golden Mean." *Musical Quarterly* 65 (1979): 72-82.   ML1 M725 ISSN 0027-4631

Application of Lendvai's theories. Explains the Golden Mean and its relation to Fibonacci numbers and relates these to Bartók's interest in nature. Shows the relation of Fibonacci numbers to the anhemitonic scale (containing interval of 2 or 3) and the "pentatonic chord," a minor triad with a minor 7th, specifically in second inversion showing the numbers 2, 3, 5, and 8. Also gives examples from *Bluebeard* and *String Quartets Nos. 2* and *4* and shows patterns of durational values with these relations. Cites the end of

Music for Strings, I, as "the most convincing Fibonacci structure presented," showing the correlation between important notes in the mirrored inversion and their placement in relation to the Golden Section and the G.S. reversed.

539. Balanchivadze, E. "Bartók's The Miraculous Mandarin." *Collected Articles from the Tbilisi Conservatory, V.*, ed. Aleksandr Saverzasvili. Tbilisi: Tbilisskaya Gosudarstvennaya Konservatoriya (1977). 296p.

   Not examined. Only the English translation of the title is given in *RILM Abstracts* No. 2276 (1977). According to *RILM*, this study is part of a collection of articles in Russian, dealing with "theoretical and historical problems of contemporary foreign and Soviet music."

540. Balázs, Béla. "A fából faragott királyfi," [The Wooden Prince]. *Nyugat* (1912): 879-888. H23.374

   Describes the staging and then the story with its action in each of the eight dances. Also published in English in *The New Hungarian Quarterly* 4/11 (July-September 1963): 36-45. Trans. István Farkas. Reprinted in *Bartók Studies,* ed. Todd Crow. Detroit: Information Coordinators, 1976, pp. 101-110.

541. Bartha, Dénes. "La musique de Bartók." In: *La résonance dans les échelles musicales,* ed. Edith Weber. Paris: Centre National de la Recherche Scientifique, 1963, pp. 279-90.   781.22 F844R

   Discusses Lendvai's theories in connection with Bartók's harmonic language, applications of its principles to folk-music research and jazz as well as the connections with other theories.

542. Bates, Karen Anne. "The Fifth String Quartet of Béla Bartók: An Analysis Based on the Theories of Ernő Lendvai." Ph.D. diss., University of Arizona, 1986. 261p.   DA 8613806

   Discusses Ernő Lendvai's theoretical principles and provides an in-depth analytical study of Bartók's *Fifth String Quartet*. Attempts to demonstrate that Lendvai's theories, because of their reliance on the intervallic constructions found in folk music, can provide a degree of insight into the various types of harmonic constructions, both tertian and nontertian, in Bartók's work.

543. Benary, Peter. "Der zweistimmige kontrapunkt in Bartóks 'Mikrokosmos'" [Two-part counterpoint in Bartók's *Mikrokosmos*]. *Archiv für Musikwissenschaft* 15 (1958): 198-206.   780.5 Ar252 ISSN 0003-9292

Examines most of the 30 two-part pieces in counterpoint in the *Mikrokosmos*, listing nine of the most common characteristics pertaining to all of these.

544. Bernard, Jonathan W. "Space and Symmetry in Bartók." *Journal of Music Theory* 30/2 (Fall 1986): 185-201.   781.05 J826 ISSN 0022-2909

Individualized approach to the study of symmetry in several of Bartók's works--*Mikrokosmos*, piano concertos nos. 1 and 2, *Music for strings, percussion, and celesta*, and *Sonata for two pianos and percussion*--based on a literal spatial conception without reliance on the principles of octave or inversional equivalence.

545. Berry, Wallace. "Symmetrical Interval Sets and Derivative Pitch Materials in Bartók's String Quartet No. 3." *Perspectives of New Music* 18 (1979-1980): 287-380.   780.5 P432

First establishes the importance of "tonal" implications of linear and vertical pitch affiliations, then devotes the discussion to extracts from the quartet in demonstration of the applicability of certain interval sets as "sources" of pitch structures. These "sources" and quasi-tonal functions are not mutually exclusive. Discusses generative processes in the music based on the symmetrical, "major" hexachord as the overall progenitor material. Principles involve relations of the material through juxtaposition, overlap, transposition, etc., of the basic interval structures.

546. Bigelow, Ralph. "Music for Strings, Percussion, and Celesta." Masters thesis. Eastman School of Music, 1953. 52p.

Almost exclusively confined to a discussion of thematic relations and developments in an approach directly adopted from Rudolf Réti. Contains bibliography.

547. Breuer, János. "Egy Bartók-dallam nyomában" [The tracing of a Bartók melody]. *Muzsika* (Budapest) 14/8 (August 1971): 26-29. ISSN 0027-5336

Study of one of the themes from the *Concerto for Orchestra*. See also the following publications: "I. Szerkezet" [Structure] and "II. Dramaturgiája" [Dramaturgy]. *Muzsika* 14/9 (September 1971): 37-39; "III. Interpretáció" [Interpretation]. *Muzsika* 14/10 (October 1971): 25-27; "IV. Tradició" [Tradition]. *Muzsika* 14/11 (November 1971): 31-32.

548. Brinkmann, Reinhold. "Einige Aspekte der Bartók-Analyse." *Studia musicologica* 24 (1982): 57-66.   781.05 St92   ISSN 0039-3266

First, discusses the methodological approach to Bartók's music, in three parts: premises-investigative situation, and analytical evidence. Well-documented study expressing concern for Bartók's aesthetics of composition in addition to the analysis in the larger theoretical design. The final part presents a detailed analysis of *Music for Strings, Percussion, and Celesta* in order to understand the significant moments and meaning of the work.

549. Campfield, Donald John. "A Study of Interval Configuration and Related Parameters in Selected Chromatic Melodies of Béla Bartók." D.M.A. treatise. Cornell University, 1985. 74p.

Demonstrates the priority of the melodic line in the analysis of Bartók's music. First divides Bartók's melodies into diatonic and chromatic categories, then explores Bartók's use of polymodal chromaticism, using supporting primary-source documentation. Provides a descriptive analysis of nineteen chromatic melodies in compositions written between 1923 and 1944, focusing on their "intervallic content and configuration, tonality, contour, stepline structure, and patterning of various kinds."

550. Carner, Mosco. "Béla Bartók." *Chamber Music,* ed. Alec Robertson. London and Tonbridge: The White Friars Press, 1957, pp. 220-252. MT140 R6   785.7 R545C

First presents a general outline of the style of the quartets and how they reflect the composer's development over a period of 31 years. Then provides brief general analyses of the six quartets, exploring basic aspects of form, theme or motive, harmony, texture, and contrapuntal devices.

551. Chailley, Jacques. "Essai d'analyse du Mandarin merveilleux" [Analytical essay on the *Miraculous Mandarin*]. *Studia musicologica* 8 (1966): 11-39.   781.05 St92   ISSN 0039-3326

Praises Lendvai for his Golden Section and Acoustic systems as applied to Bartók's music but rejects the image of Bartók as exclusively calculated and mathematical. Feels this to be incompatible with his human warmth. Suggests different sources for certain structures that Lendvai derived from the overtone series, rather suggesting the work of Downey (i.e., "La musique populaire dans l'œuvre de B. Bartók"). Points to harmonic sources in Bartók's discovery of Debussy and Ravel, revealing new concepts of consonance and the whole-tone scale derived from ninth-chords, etc., as well as discussing the relationship between the whole-tone scale and a special non-diatonic mode common in Bartók and folk sources. Then proceeds to a detailed discussion of scalar and harmonic structures and their variants in each section of the *Miraculous Mandarin*.

552. Chapman, Roger E. "The *Fifth Quartet* of Béla Bartók." *The Music Review* 12 (November 1951): 296-303.   780.5 M9733 ISSN 0027-4445

Discusses thematic, motivic, tonal, contrapuntal, and textural devices in the context of the five-movement arch form. Largely descriptive analysis of what at first promises to be a discussion of the quartet in the context of Bartók's period of "synthesis." Shows concern for the linear writing and structural considerations, emphasizing the importance of contrapuntal devices, especially inversion, and the disposition of tonal centers.

553. Chazelle, Thierry. *"En plein air,* suite pour piano de Béla Bartók: L'imbrication d'une forme ternaire" [Béla Bartók's suite for piano *Szabadban:* Overlapping ternary form]. *Analyse musicale* 7 (April 1987): 56-61.

Discusses the ternary form of the work and its more general significance in Bartók's music. Describes and explores the various parameters, including thematic, harmonic, rhythmic, and dynamic levels as well as tempo relations in the overall formal organization. Contains music examples.

554. ----------. "La *Cantate profane* de Béla Bartók" [The *Cantata profana* of Béla Bartók]. *Analyse musicale* 2 (February 1986): 70-76.

Contains summary in English. Provides a formal analysis and considers the perceptual difficulties that arise in connection with its organizational complexity. Contains music examples.

555. Chigareva, Yevgeniy. "Ladogarmonicheskaya sistema v 4-m kvartete Bély Bartóka i yeye formoobrazuyushchiye funktsii" [The modal harmonic system in Bartók's *Fourth Quartet*]. *Teoreticheskiye problemy muzyki XX veka,* 2nd ed. Yu.N. Tyulin. Moskva: Izdatel'stvo Muzyka, 1978, pp. 69-102.   ML197.T35

Detailed analysis of various thematic and harmonic structures, dealing with their intervallic connections, scalar features, and traditional harmonic functions. Also compares with themes of *Music for Strings, Percussion, and Celesta.* Includes illustrations and music.

556. Child, Peter. "Structural Unities in a Work of Bartók: 'Boating' from *Mikrokosmos,* Vol. 5." *College Music Symposium* 30/1 (Spring 1990): 103-114.   ISSN 0069-5696   780.5 C686

Demonstrates that many of the pieces of this cycle serve not only as technical sources for the keyboard teacher but also as structural models for the teacher of analysis in conveying much about Bartók's mature compositional technique. Explores three independent and self-contained musical systems in this piece--phrase structure and grouping, pitch-class set structure (not associated with the set-theoretic models developed by Allen Forte), and pitch function--and shows how they are interrelated and complementary. Refers to certain analogies with tonal music in terms of certain aspects of phrase structure, while exploration of pitch "function" is based on idiosyncratic contextual considerations. Provides a detailed analysis of various parameters as determinants of the larger structure. Includes the score of the entire piece, music examples, and diagrams.

557. Chittum, Donald. "The Synthesis of Material and Devices in Non-serial Counterpoint." *Music Review* 31/2 (May 1970): 124-135. 780.5 M9733   ISSN 0027-4445

Study of two contemporary compositions, including a detailed analysis of the first movement of Bartók's *Music for Strings, Percussion, and Celesta,* to show the means by which various levels are integrated in a non-serial contrapuntal style. Points out that the chordal structures and their relations are based upon a variety of intervallic arrangements, without recourse to the principles of the major-minor tonal system. These intervallic arrangements pervade the entire organization, thereby permitting perhaps even a greater unity than in the traditional tonal system. First discusses Beethoven's *String Quartet,* Op. 59, no. 3 as a means of comparison with the earlier principles. Concludes that, in the Bartók work, "the subject contains intervallic material [cells] and suggests certain devices which influence all aspects of the fugue's organization and development."

558. Clegg, David. "Bartók's 'Kossuth Symphony.'" *Music Review* 23 (1962): 215-220.   780.5 M9733   ISSN 0027-4445

Study supported by Bartók's own analysis of the work.

559. Cohn, Richard. "Bartók's Octatonic Strategies: A Motivic Approach." *Journal of the American Musicological Society* 44/2 (Summer 1991): 262-300.   780.6 AM3J   ISSN 0003 0139

According to the author, *RILM Abstracts* No. 9313 (1991), this study "presents an alternative to the diatonic interaction model to explain Bartók's interest in the octatonic collection. The special ability of the octatonic collection to be partitioned into alternative sets of transpositionally related subsets is revealed through an abstract study. Exploitation of this potential through the interaction of the subsets is seen in two compositions from *Mikrokosmos* and in the first movement of the sonata for two pianos and percussion."

560. ----------. "Inversional Symmetry and Transpositional Combination in Bartók." *Music Theory Spectrum* (1988): 19-42.   ML1 M855

Approach to transpositional processes using Allen Forte's principles of atonal pitch-class sets and terminology. Acknowledges that the principle of *inversional symmetry* (IS), proposed by other theorists, plays some role in Bartók's music but asserts that the "IS" principle can also be interpreted according to what he calls *Transpositional Combination* (TC). This method (TC) refers to pitch-class sets of two or more elements that may be combined and recombined to produce larger, transpositionally related pitch-class sets. His argument in favor of the competing "TC" principle is based on the notion that the explicit surface manifestation (that is, in local texture and contour) of a literal inversional design is necessary for validating the "IS" interpretation of a given pitch or pitch-class phenomenon. Analyzes excerpts from Bartók's *Music for Strings, Percussion, and Celesta, Mikrokosmos* Nos. 109, 136, and 143, *Sonata for Two Pianos and Percussion,* and *Third* and *Fourth String Quartets.* See also Richard Lawrence Cohn, "Transpositional Combination in Twentieth-Century Music," Ph.D. diss., University of Rochester, 1987.

561. Collins, Malvina Yerger. "Béla Bartók's Major Piano Compositions: Analytical and Critical Study." Master's thesis. University of Texas at Austin, 1954. 141p.

Presents a traditional analysis of each movement, with musical examples and a formal diagram of each movement. Examines several major piano compositions, including both solo works and the three concertos. Both a formal analysis and an estimate of the idea behind each work is given. Schoenberg's concept of "developing variation" from his book *Style and Idea* is used as the basis of many of Collins' analyses.

562. Debruyn, Randall Keith. "Contrapuntal Structure in Contemporary Tonal Music: A Preliminary Study of Tonality in the Twentieth Century."   D.M.A. diss.   University of Illinois, 1975. 263p. ML197 D4

Includes an analysis of the second movement of Bartók's *Third Piano Concerto,* based on the Schenkerian analytical approach to structure and prolongation.

563. Donahue, Robert L. "Part II: A Comparative Analysis of Phrase Structure in Selected Movements of the String Quartets of Béla Bartók and Walter Piston." D.M.A. treatise. Cornell University, 1964. 161p.

Comparison of the phraseological structure in the corresponding (slow and fast) movements of the string quartets of Bartók and Piston. The first movement of Bartók's *Second Quartet* was analyzed and compared with the second movement of Piston's *Second Quartet,* and the fourth movement of Piston's *Fourth Quartet* was analyzed and compared with the exposition of the first movement of Bartók's *Fifth Quartet.* The study was conducted with a view to how these forms have evolved since the Classical era, using certain traditional sonata-form phrase types as a model. Considers thematic and non-thematic types, from which were established four basic categories: vocal thematic phrases; figurational thematic phrases; vocal non-thematic phrases; and figurational non-thematic phrases. Contrapuntal phrases are also considered in connection with these types. The results show strong ties with tradition. Contains bibliography.

564. Dustin, William Dale. "Two-Voiced Textures in the *Mikrokosmos* of Béla Bartók." Ph.D. diss. Cornell University, 1959. 355p. ML410.B26 D8M

Examination of the pieces organized according to their textural identities: homophonic with parallel voices; unequal voices with the secondary lines based on pedal point, ostinato, etc.; and equal voices. Concerned with density (number and tessitura of voices) and rhythmic as well as pitch activity of individual voices, all as the basis of texture. Also, concern with tonality to the extent that it creates a particular texture, e.g., separate scalar content in two voices, or the partitioning of a single mode between the two hands. Contains music, bibliography.

565. Evans, Edwin. "Béla Bartók." *Cyclopedic Survey of Chamber Music,* ed. by W.W. Cobbett. Oxford: Oxford University Press, 1929. pp. 60-65. ML1100 C7

Entry on the main chamber works of Bartók composed at the time the article was written. Descriptive analyses of the first two *String Quartets* and the two *Sonatas* for violin and piano. Contains music examples.

566. Ferguson, Donald N. "Béla Bartók." *Image and Structure in Chamber Music.* Minneapolis: University of Minnesota Press, 1964, pp. 273-292. 785.7 F381I

Analyses of the six quartets. Primarily discusses thematic and contrapuntal designs and tonality in the context of the formal plans. Fairly detailed descriptions permit a good systematic introduction to the basic organization of the quartets. Contains music examples.

567. Folio, Cynthia J. "Analysis and Performance: A Study in *Contrasts.*" *Intégral* 7 (1993): 1-37.

Analytical approach, which focuses on the first movement, is intended to distinguish between theorists and performers in the application of analysis to performance. Coming from the performer's analytical perspective, the author draws upon historical information, primary sources (Bartók's autographs of the first sketch and final copy), and recordings (including the earliest one by Bartók, Goodman, and Szigeti) for guidance in performance interpretation. Analytical discussion explores the meaning of the title in purely musical (non-programmatic) terms. Explores the interrelation of the performers' individual personalities and addresses contrasts of style (e.g., folk *versus* art music) as well as conflicts and narratives on various musical levels--structural, motivic, intervallic (especially the A/D# polarity), tonal, harmonic, sonic, etc.--which are viewed together as basis for determining the large-scale organic shaping of the work. Contains music examples, diagrammatic reductions, and autograph excerpts.

568. Forner, Johannes. "Zum Sonatenform-Problem bei Béla Bartók: Eine vergleichende Studie" [Sonata-form in Béla Bartók: A comparative study]. *Jahrbuch Peters* (1981/82; publ. 1985): 62-75. ML5 J16

In consideration of Bartók's own comments, provides a comparative analytical study of the *Piano Sonata* and the *Sonata for Two Pianos and Percussion* to elucidate Bartók's evolutionary approach to sonata form within the larger context of changes in the form in early twentieth century composition. Points to the changing functions and relations of the sections of the sonata form (exposition, development, and recapitulation), in which the development section acquires the role of a bridge.

569. Forte, Allen. "Bartók's 'Serial' Composition." *Musical Quarterly* 46/2 (April 1960): 233-245. ML1 M725 ISSN 0027-4631

Attempts to show that tonal centricity in Movement III of the *Fourth Quartet* is produced through the use of a unique system resembling a "serial schema." Various pairings of mutually exclusive whole-tone trichords may generate anyone of three species of hexachords (whole tone, diatonic, chromatic). The specific diatonic hexachord (A G F E D C) unfolds as a cantus firmus, permitting its two whole-tone trichords to have maximal association with other trichords in the system. Also published in *Problems of Modern Music,* ed. P.H. Lang. New York, 1962, p. 95.

570. ----------. "Béla Bartók Number VIII from Fourteen Bagatelles, Op. 6." *Contemporary Tone-Structures*. New York: Columbia University, 1955, pp. 74-90, 167-170.   ML197.F7

Detailed analysis (measure-by-measure) of various levels and techniques to reveal a rigorous structure, including: major structural events based on "unfolding;" recurrent motions; techniques based on elision, interruption, qualifying tones, register transfer, referents; linear generation including simpler duplication of parts; linear continuity and discontinuity; structural background including functional relationships, basic grouping, homogeneity of texture, and register. Deals also with the problematic nature of the basic structure. Also includes six aspects of the foreground: direction, rests, phrasing, accents, rhythm, and notation. Compares the importance of this work with Stravinsky's *Petrushka* and Schoenberg's Op. 11.

571. Frank, Oszkár. *Bevezető Bartók Mikrokozmoszának világába* [Introduction to the world of Bartók's *Mikrokosmos*]. Budapest: Zeneműkiadó, 1977. 205p.   ISBN-9633301696   MT-145.B25 F7

Explores principles in connection with various pieces in terms of rhythm (including, e.g., tempo, syncopation, etc.), tonality and melody (e.g., pentachord, diatony, pentatony, distance scales, tonal centers, bitonality, and polytonality, etc.), voice textures (e.g., unison-, two-, three-, and four-part polyphony, and chordal homophonic texture), formal principles (including folk form, period form, two- and three-part form, as well as formal principles based on the Golden Section of Lendvai). Also included are discussions of principles developed by Ernő Lendvai, such as "alpha" chords, Fibonacci numbers defining pitch structures, etc., and principles of Lajos Bárdos, including "heptatonia secunda" scalar concepts, etc. Contains music, bibliography, index.

572. Gaburo, Kenneth Louis. "Studies in Pitch Symmetry in Twentieth Century Music." D.M.A treatise. University of Illinois, 1962. 307p. ML3809 G3

Chapter II presents a detailed discussion of *Mikrokosmos No. 101*, "Diminished Fifth," in which he focuses on the tetrachord, 3 (4) in this work. Includes some general remarks about tetrachords, general compositional observations with respect to the Bartók "tetrachord" (e.g., linear, aggregate set forms) and a detailed analysis of symmetrical content: diads, aggregates, the basic tetrachord, permutations, other tetrad types, subset symmetry (e.g., trichords), tetrad aggregates, trichord aggregates, aggregates within the phrase, aggregates between phrases, misc. symmetries, and macro-symmetry. Chapter IV provides further analysis of these partitions as well as

2(6), 4(3), 2(5), including use of Bartók works for this demonstration. Contains illustrations, bibliography.

573. Gervers, Hilda. "Béla Bartók's Five Songs (Öt dal), Op. 15." *The Music Review* 30/4 (November 1969): 291-299.   780.5 M9733 ISSN 0027-4445

Discusses this cycle of songs in the context of Bartók's small output of solo songs, providing some history of its copyright and publication problems. Analyzes the formal and tonal properties of the songs and points to the expressionistic style of the texts. The analyses are based on Ernő Lendvai's "polar-axis" system as a compensation for the loss of Classical key relations. Considers these songs, in terms of their synthesis of structural elements, with a view to Bartók's later stylistic development.

574. Gillies, Malcolm. "Analyzing Bartók's Works of 1918-1922: Motives, Tone Patches, and Tonal Mosaics." *Bartók in Retrospect,* ed. Elliott Antokoletz, Victoria Fischer, and Benjamin Suchoff. Projected publication of two 1995 conference proceedings.

Investigates the different "horizontal," "vertical," and "oblique" configurations of Bartók's tonal structure as defined by his use of pitch notations. Reconsiders the meaning of tonality, modality, polymodal chromaticism, "new" chromaticism, and atonality in Bartók's music through a comparison of selected Bartók scores, concentrating on the works of the early 1920s. Assesses how instrument, genre, and chronology affect Bartók's tonal configurations and outlines important areas of his repertory where further investigation of his tonal thinking is needed. (Annotation based on the author's abstract of the original lecture; see item no. 1161.)

575. ----------. "Bartók's Last Works: A Theory of Tonality and Modality." *Musicology* 7 (1982): 120-130.   ML5 M897

Presents a theory of Bartók's tonality and modality based on the composer's "Harvard Lectures," the principles of which are especially applicable to the late works. Notational spellings are essential to the tonal and modal concepts and are especially relevant to the issues of modulation and tonal hierarchy. Categories of analysis include tonality and modality, notation, the theory based on "encirclement," "half-encirclement (or leading-tone motions)," range, other means based on modulation and levels of tonal activity, and a statement of analytical procedures.

576. ----------. "Final Chamber Works." *The Bartók Companion,* ed. Malcolm Gillies. London: Faber and Faber, 1993; Portland, Oregon:

Amadeus Press (an imprint of Timber Press, Inc.), 1994. pp. 331-345. ISBN 0-931340-74-8 (HB)   ISBN 0-931340-75-6 (PB) ML410 B26 B28

Provides historical information on the genesis (commissions, inspirations, etc.) of *Contrasts, Divertimento,* and the *Sonata* for solo violin, Bartók's intentions for specific performers, and the conditions under which these works were composed. Analyses of the three works include comparison of their differences and similarities in their overall formal outlines and approaches to the individual movements. Points to Bartók's pervasive use of variation technique (in texture, rhythm, mode, and theme), in which Bartók exploits transformational procedures within unified contexts based on thematic/motivic economy. Addresses issues of scalar construction ranging from pentatonic through diatonic to chromatic materials, simple and complex rhythmic relations and their sources (e.g., Bulgarian), thematic and phrasal structure, and contrapuntal (imitative) procedures that reveal Bartók's most skillful exploitation of variation techniques. The most detailed analysis of Bartók's use of contrapuntal variation is presented in the discussion of the Fugue from the *Sonata.* Points to analogies in tonal relations between the Fugue and the finale of the *Fifth String Quartet.*

577. ----------. "Masterworks (I): Music for Strings, Percussion and Celesta." *The Bartók Companion,* ed. Malcolm Gillies. London: Faber and Faber, 1993; Portland, Oregon: Amadeus Press (an imprint of Timber Press, Inc.), 1994. pp. 303-314.   ISBN 0-931340-74-8 (HB)   ISBN 0-931340-75-6 (PB)   ML410 B26 B28

Points to this work of 1936 as a culmination of Bartók's increasing concerns since the mid-1920s for counterpoint and symmetry in pitch, rhythm, and form. Also asserts that this highly original work exemplifies Bartók's move toward integration of his styles drawn from folk- and art-music sources. Analysis indicates a synthesis of opposites ranging from Bartók's "new" chromaticism in the opening fugue movement, nevertheless based on a strong tonal orientation, to diatonic modality and the "acoustic" scale in the finale. Discussion of this process includes systematic coverage of the formal and tonal designs of each movement as well as basic thematic interconnections and transformations between movements. Touches upon special structural aspects, including Ernő Lendvai's theory of Golden Section (and Fibonacci) proportions. Also includes basic historical data on the commission, premiere, reception, and later performances of the work.

578. ---------------. "Notation and Tonal Structure in Bartók's Later Works." Ph.D. diss. University of London, 1986; New York and London: Garland Publishing, Inc., 1989. 299p. ISBN 0-8240-8420-9 ML 410.B26G48 1989   781.2'6092-dc20

Explores the changing role of pitch notations in the course of Bartók's compositional development. The early works reveal a notation oriented toward a late-Romantic chordal role. Between 1908 and the early 1920s, a competition and gradual shift occurs in the role of Bartók's notation from a vertical to a horizontal emphasis. Since 1926, these pitch notations became primarily horizontal, the consistency of this role permitting notation to serve as a useful tool for tonal analysis. Volume I (128p.), "Theory," outlines eight hypotheses regarding the relevance of notation in the tonal analysis of Bartók's later works as follows: "1. that the notes of a tonal music belong to a tonal structure, in which at least one note acts as a tonal centre; 2. that Bartók's music is tonal; 3. that Bartók strove to represent the tonal structures of his music in his pitch notations; 4. that Bartók's pitch notations provide a key for the analyst in identifying the tonal structures of his music; 5. that in a number of situations pitch notations are insufficiently pure to be used as the overriding criterion in the identification of tonal structures; 6. that in many situations pitch notations are insufficiently exclusive to be the sole criterion of identification of tonal structures; 7. that differences in pitch spellings between sections or parts of the music normally reflect differences in tonal structure; 8. that, working from a foundation of pitch notations, it is possible to provide a comprehensive account of tonal structures in works by Bartók, and, by using Bartók's analyses of his own works as models, to propose a structural hierarchy." Volume II (171p), "Analyses," is intended to support these hypotheses by analyzing *Music for Strings, Percussion, and Celesta,* the *Violin Concerto, Sixth String Quartet, Sonata for Solo Violin,* pieces from the *Forty-Four Duos, Twenty-Seven Choruses, Mikrokosmos,* and the first movement of the *Fifth String Quartet.* Contains bibliography, 2 appendices, 80 musical examples (35 in Vol. I, 45 in Vol. II), facsimile reproductions of pages of the *Sonata for Solo Violin* sketches in Vol. II, and chronological list of cited works by Bartók.

579. ----------. "Violin Duos and Late String Quartets." *The Bartók Companion,* ed. Malcolm Gillies. London: Faber and Faber, 1993; Portland, Oregon: Amadeus Press (an imprint of Timber Press, Inc.), 1994. pp. 285-302.   ISBN 0-931340-74-8 (HB)
ISBN 0-931340-75-6 (PB)   ML410 B26 B28

Points to the intervening years between the *Fourth* (1928) and *Fifth String Quartets* (1934), in which Bartók produced many new folk-song settings. The most significant of these were the *Forty-Four Duos* for violins (1931), which were intended for pedagogical purposes. Provides a brief history of the genesis of the work and points to the use of a broader spectrum of authentic folk sources. Identifies the stylistic influences of the *Duos* and analyzes selected pieces in terms of melodic and phrasal outline, harmonic (modal/chromatic) intervallic construction, and textural devices. Points to the important lessons Bartók learned about idiomatic string writing at this time. Then analyzes the *Fifth* and *Six String Quartets*, emphasizing the importance in the *Fifth Quartet* of symmetry in the five-movement formal plan and some aspects of symmetry in the thematic and tonal relations. Also points to the importance of the variation process. The *Sixth Quartet* is shown to be exemplary of "integration rather than innovation," where the variation process is, again, prominent. Discusses external factors that may have influenced certain decisions in the compositional process of the quartet and provides an analytical overview of its structure and tonal organization.

580. Gorczycka, Monika. "Neue Merkmale der Klangtechnik in Bartóks Streichquartetten" [New characteristics of sound technique in Bartók's string quartets]. *Studia musicologica* 5 (1963): (In: *Bericht über die [. . .] Konferenz Liszt-Bartók): 425-433.   781.05 St92 ISSN 0039-3266

Analysis of the reactivation of the conflict between dynamics (i.e., rhythm, agogics) and statics (i.e., internal structure of harmony, their saturation and closed form) in Bartók and an examination of their influence on the form of his string quartets.

581. Gow, David. "Tonality and Structure in Bartók's First Two String Quartets." *The Music Review* 34 (August-November 1973): 259-271. 780.5 M9733   ISSN 0027-4445

States that Bartók is still working within the traditional tonal structure to some extent in these two quartets. Most important contribution of the analyses is the concept of "emergent tonality" rather than "progressive" or shifting tonalities. Combines traditional tonal concepts (dominant-tonic) with ambiguous chromatically related keys, e.g., concerned with establishing tensions between keys a major-third apart (first below, then above A: F, A, C#) in the *First Quartet.*

582. Hartzell, Lawrence William. "Contrapuntal-Harmonic Factors in Selected Works of Béla Bartók." Ph.D. diss. University of Kansas, 1970. 225p.

An introductory chapter covers important literature relating to the composer and the specific interests of the dissertation procedure. Successive chapters move from studies of the single melodic line to textures of two, three, and four parts, respectively. Shows connections between Bartók's treatment of contrapuntal and homophonic principles based on both traditional and non-traditional procedures.

583. Haun, Errol Eugene. "Modal and Symmetrical Pitch Constructions in Béla Bartók's *Sonata for Two Pianos and Percussion.*" D.M.A. treatise. The University of Texas at Austin, 1982. 106p.

Related to principles discussed by Elliott Antokoletz in item no. 531. Demonstrates that the materials are organized according to the system of "interval cycles," from which are derived various symmetrical pitch collections that move around tonal centers, or "axes of symmetry." Both symmetrical and nonsymmetrical "cells" are basic in the expansion through the work to the larger interval cycles, and serve as invariant links between the latter and traditional modal formations. Bimodal and hybrid-modal constructions, which are based on combinations of the traditional folk modes, are a part of the larger abstract system as they are integrated with symmetrical scales and their cellular segments. Such integration occurs not only through these cellular links but also by means of cyclic, or symmetrical, transformations of the modal (or bimodal) materials themselves. The ultimate fusion and significance of these pitch-set relations are found in a hierarchy of axes, in which secondary ones complementarily define a primary one. These principles of construction and progression within the system of interval cycles are relevant to Bartók's larger compositional output as well as to a larger body of "post-tonal" music in general. Contains bibliography.

584. Hawthorne, Robin. "The Fugal Technique of Béla Bartók." *The Music Review* 10 (1949): 277-285. 780.5 M9733 ISSN 0027-4445

Compares the fugue of the last movement of the *Fifth String Quartet* and that of the last movement of the *Third Piano Concerto.* Discusses the tonal answer as Bartók used it in the *Third Concerto.* Also, presents some comparisons with certain fugal techniques of Bach and Beethoven.

585. Helm, Everett. "Bartók's Musik für Saiteninstrumente" [Bartók's *Music for String Instruments*]. *Melos* 20 (1953): 245-249. 780.5 M492 ISSN 0174-7207

Discusses thematic relations and gives a brief overview of the movements. Discusses the presence of tonality but concludes that it is not present in the usual sense of tonic, dominant, and subdominant functions. Instead, single notes function as poles with which the other materials form specific relationships.

586. Howat, Roy. "Bartók, Lendvai and the Principles of Proportional Analysis." *Music Analysis* 2/1 (March 1983): 69-95. ML1 M68 ISSN 0262-5245

Review article. Concentrates on proportion in Bartók's music and on Lendvai's claim that Bartók organized many pieces around the ratio known as "golden section." States that this theory attempts to link together intervallic structures in harmony, tonality and melody, the use of rhythm and meter, and the organization of forms in terms of large- and small-scale proportion. In view of critical challenges to Lendvai's methods, Howat evaluates the musical relevance of proportional analysis and aims at a wider-ranging examination of the technical issues involved. Presents detailed analyses of a number of Bartók's compositions. Provides some reference to primary-source material (sketch drafts) for evidence. See Lendvai's response (item no. 612), "Remarks on Roy Howat's 'Principles of Proportional Analysis,'" *Music Analysis* 3/3 (October 1984): 255-264.

587. ----------. "Debussy, Ravel and Bartók: Towards Some New Concepts of Form." *Music and Letters* 58/3 (July 1977): 285-293.   780.5 M92 ISSN 0027-4224

Explores proportional relations in the musical forms of these three composers, based on an expansion of the principles of the Golden Section ratios established by Ernő Lendvai in his studies of Bartók's music. Formal symmetry is also discussed. Compares Debussy's *Reflets dans l'eau*, Ravel's *Oiseaux tristes,* and Bartók's *Music for Strings, Percussion and Celesta.*

588. ----------. "Masterworks (II): Sonata for Two Pianos and Percussion." *The Bartók Companion,* ed. Malcolm Gillies. London: Faber and Faber, 1993; Portland, Oregon: Amadeus Press (an imprint of Timber Press, Inc.), 1994. pp. 315-330.   ISBN 0-931340-74-8 (HB) ISBN 0-931340-75-6 (PB)   ML410 B26 B28

Discusses the emergence of Bartók's idea for the *Sonata* (1937) prior to the Basle commission, the instrumental combination foreshadowed in certain movements of the *First* and *Second Piano Concertos* and *Music for Strings, Percussion, and Celesta.* Compares certain basic tonal (tritone) relations of the *Sonata* with those in the last work. Analysis explores timbre, instrumentation, tempo fluctuations, and chromatic/modal processes (documenting Bartók's own writings) in relation to the larger organic formal design of the three movements. Compares certain devices and stylistic elements with those of other composers, including Bach, Schubert, Schumann, Liszt, Chopin, Ravel, and Debussy, as well as those of other Bartók works. Includes analysis of certain geometric formal relations based on Ernő Lendvai's theory of Golden Section (and Fibonacci) proportions and also those defined by the "Lucas" sequence. Also, points to Lendvai's speculation that the non-diatonic (hybrid Lydian-Mixolydian) mode of the finale is related to the open overtone series based on C, and may have served for Bartók as an antithesis to modal chromaticism. Includes some historical information and brief comparison of the *Sonata* with its *Concerto* transcription.

589. Hwang, Hae-Joung. "Transformation of Rumanian Folk Sources into Abstract Pitch Formations in Bartók's Violin Rhapsodies." D.M.A. treatise, The University of Texas at Austin, 1995. 136p.

Focuses on the interactions and relations between the authentic Romanian folk dance tunes and their accompaniments and how they function within the tonal and formal schemata of the *Two Rhapsodies*. Provides historical background and genesis of the *Rhapsodies*, discusses the peasant violin music, explores the characteristics of the original folk-music sources in terms of structure, mode, rhythm, and influence of neighboring peoples, and examines the modal/tonal structure of the diatonic and non-diatonic Romanian folk tunes and polymodal-chromatic accompaniments as developed compositionally by Bartók. Demonstrates that a kind of twelve-tone chromaticism is produced by polymodal chromatic combinations, which result from the vertical projection of conflicting second, third, sixth, and seventh degrees of a given folk tune, as well as by the unfolding of the cycle of fifths. Varying degrees of polymodal combination and transformation also underlie the process of intervallic expansion and contraction, a principle basic to the organic formal development of the *Rhapsodies*. Contains music examples, two appendices containing a map of Bartók's folk-song collection area in Romania and the authentic folk tunes employed in the *Rhapsodies*, and bibliography.

590. Jagamas, János. "*Mikrokosmos* books I-II. Despre sisteme tonale in *Mikrokosmos* de Béla Bartók" [Tonal systems in Bartók's *Mikrokosmos*]. *Lucrări de muzicologie* (Romania) 2 (1966-1967): 99-122.

Explores the diverse tonal uses of chromatic, pentatonic, and polytonal formations in analyses of pieces from the first two books of Bartók's *Mikrokosmos*.

591. Kárpáti, János. "Alternatív struktúrák Bartók Kontrasztok című művében" [Alternative structures in Bartók's *Contrasts*]. *Zeneelmélet, stíluselemzés*. Budapest: Zeneműkiadó, 1977, pp. 103-108.

Demonstrates that Bartók, without intending to follow a dodecaphonic series, has arrived at a structure closely approximating it in principle (explores systematic chains of fifths with common third). Discusses triads with major-minor third structures as "dual" or "alternative" structures, which means they still can be justified separately, and, while appearing together, preserve their original modal content. Discusses the meaning of this structure also in the context of Nüll's as well as Lendvai's theoretical concepts (i.e.,

Lendvai's 1:3 scale model). Also explains that if the two equivalent kinds of third can appear within the stable frame of a fifth, then one arrives logically at the dual root and fifth situated around the stable third. In *Contrasts,* the motif of the Lydian fourth becomes equivalent to the dual third-structure of sound. The author also refers to his own concepts of "mistuning." Also published in English in *Studia musicologica* 23 (1981): 201-207.

592. ----------. "Piano Works of the War Years." *The Bartók Companion,* ed. Malcolm Gillies. London: Faber and Faber, 1993; Portland, Oregon: Amadeus Press (an imprint of Timber Press, Inc.), 1994. pp. 146-161. ISBN 0-931340-74-8 (HB)   ISBN 0-931340-75-6 (PB) ML410 B26 B28

Speaks of Bartók's creative crisis following rejection of his music prior to the First World War, his withdrawal from public life, and consolation in his scientific studies of folk music. His return to composition in 1915 brought new arrangements of his recently collected folk songs for piano and other genres. Provides a historical overview of the works of the period, identification of the folk sources, and comparative analyses of the various sources (Romanian, Hungarian, and other sources) as employed compositionally. Points to Bartók's techniques of variation and transformation, including the author's concept of "mistuning" as an important means for modal/scalar transformations. Places the discussion of the piano music within the larger context of Bartók's compositions in general. Provides quotations from Bartók's essays.

593. Karpinski, Gary S. "The Interval Cycles in the Music of Bartók and Debussy Through 1918." Ph.D. diss. The City University of New York, 1991. 204p.

Study of Bartók's and Debussy's common musical language and the larger system of the interval cycles to which their compositions belong. Provides a perspective dealing with contextually "controlling" factors in the interaction of the interval cycles and hybrid collections. States that the interval cycles already play an important role in Bartók's works during the early part of his career. Draws parallels between the types of pitch collections used by these two composers and the compositional contexts themselves. Also asserts that the notions of "planing" and "pantonality" that have been applied to many passages can be shown to be generated from the interval cycles by examination of how the cycles function on various structural levels and how they interact with diatonic collections. Analyses of piano works of Bartók include excerpts from the *Four Piano Pieces* (1903), "Funeral March" arrangement from *Kossuth* (1903), *Fourteen Bagatelles,* Op. 6 (1908), *Suite,* Op. 14 (1916), and *Three Rondos* (1916; 1927). Contains music examples and bibliography.

594. Katz, Robert. "Symmetrical Balancing of Local Axes of Symmetry in Bartók's 'Divided Arpeggios.'" *International Journal of Musicology* 2 (1993): 333-347. ISBN 3-631-46907-1 ML5 15787 ISSN 0941-9535

Employs an analytical method based on principles of inversional symmetry to demonstrate the means by which Bartók establishes a hierarchy of structural levels within the overall form of this piece from Vol. VI of the *Mikrokosmos*. The concept of an "axis of symmetry" replaces the traditional notion of a tonal center, which had been established in traditional tonal music by the hierarchy of functional triadic relations and harmonic modulations within the major-minor scale system. In this piece by Bartók, the primary axis of symmetry is established by means of symmetrical organization of subsidiary axes around it (that is, the construction of an "axis of axes") within the larger symmetrical formal outline. Supports his conclusions by documenting this procedure in other works of Bartók, including the *Fourth String Quartet* and *Music for Strings, Percussion, and Celesta*. Compares this analytical approach with two other contrasting approaches to this piece: Ivan Waldbauer's notion of the superimposition of an "intellectual construct" upon an essentially traditional tonal-harmonic framework (see item no.669); and Richard Cohn's concept of transpositional processes related to Allen Forte's principles of atonal pitch-class set analysis (see item no. 560).

595. Kessler, Richard Carner. "Béla Bartók's Etudes Op. 18: An Analysis for Performers." Mus. A. D. Boston University, 1984. 177p.

According to the author, this study "seeks to identify those elements which substantially contribute to the extraordinary character of the music. Begins with a brief chapter placing the etudes in biographical context. Sources are then discussed, including a comparison of manuscript facsimile and published editions. Each etude is then considered individually with a survey of general impressions and a formal discussion, followed by specific comments focusing on those events which most significantly contribute to its musical organization. The analysis reveals the multiplicity of ideas in these compact pieces, including: cell permutation, avoidance of pitch duplication, symmetrical relationships, serial implications, and whole-tone application. The concluding chapter deals with performance considerations. Problems associated with fingering, pedalling, dynamics and tempo are addressed with specific suggestions based on personal interpretation of the score." Contains music, illustrations, bibliography.

596. Kramer, Jonathan. "The Fibonacci Series in Twentieth-Century Music." *Journal of Music Theory* 17 (1973): 110-148.

781.05 J826   ISSN 0022-2909

Includes a brief discussion of Bartók's *Music for Strings, Percussion and Celesta* (third and first movements), offering some corrections of Lendvai's findings but generally accepting them as true if one concedes that they are approximations.

597. Kramolisch, Walter. "Das Leitthema des VI. Streichquartetts von B. Bartók" [The principal theme of B. Bartók's *Sixth String Quartet*]. *Becking Gedenkschrift* (Gottingen) (1976): 437-482.

Detailed analysis of the various means by which a basic theme in Bartók's *Sixth String Quartet* is developed. Deals with the principles of thematic return, derivation, and motivic relations. Also, explores Bartók's use of the arch-form based on the principle of a formal axis as a primary means for large-scale organization of all the material.

598. Kreter, Leo Edward. "Part Two: Motivic and Textural Delineation of the Formal Design in the First Three Bartók Quartets." D.M.A. treatise. Cornell University, 1960. 308p.

Detailed analysis which aims to establish basic principles for systematic analysis based on the role of motivic construction and texture in the articulation of the form.

599. Kroó, György. *Bartók Béla színpadi művei* [Bartók's stage works]. Budapest: Zeneműkiadó, 1962. 294p.   MT100.B26 K8

An important study of the three stage works analyzing the relationship between dramatic action and musical structure. Historical documentation and thorough musical analysis are combined with a profound discussion of the stage characters' psyche. Contains music examples.

600. ----------. "Monothematik und Dramaturgie in Bartóks Bühnenwerken" [Monothematicism and dramaturgy in the stage works of Béla Bartók]. *Studia musicologica* 5/1-4 (1963): 449-467. 781.05 St92   ISSN 0039-3266

Discusses the relationship between monothematicism and dramaturgy in Bartók's opera *Duke Bluebeard's Castle*, his ballet *The Wooden Prince,* and the pantomime *The Miraculous Mandarin,* by way of a detailed summary of analyses of the musical and dramatic structure, of the thoughts behind the works, and of the characters.

601. ----------. "Pantomime: *The Miraculous Mandarin.*" *The Bartók Companion,* ed. Malcolm Gillies. London: Faber and Faber, 1993; Portland, Oregon: Amadeus Press (an imprint of Timber Press, Inc.), 1994. pp. 372-384.   ISBN 0-931340-74-8 (HB)

ISBN 0-931340-75-6 (PB)   ML410 B26 B28

Provides historical information on the circumstances, inspiration, libretto by Melchior Lengyel, and compositional process (sketches, drafts, and versions) of Bartók's pantomime. Presents Bartók's synopsis of the plot, his intentions as to type of work (pantomime rather than ballet), and Kroó's own interpretation of its dramatic symbolism. Analysis points to the various musical techniques (among them instrumental and orchestrational devices) used to reflect the psychology and dramatic gestures of the characters, and the importance of the rhythmic-metric patterns as well as melodic and motivic relations in the interpretation of the text. Also discusses the basic elements of the harmonic language, in which all twelve tones are exploited in a context which, while still tonal, borders on atonality. Quotes Bartók on the nature of his non-traditional harmonic constructions and points to their aesthetic associations in the work.

602. László, Ferenc. "Béla Bartóks neun Violinduos über rumänische Volksweisen" [Béla Bartók's nine Violinduos on Romanian folksongs]. In: Andreas Traub, editor. *Sándor Veress. Festschrift zum 80. Geburtstag.* Berlin: Haseloff, 1986. pp. 129-156. ML55 V374 S218

Provides a detailed exploration of the pitch organization and scalar construction in a selection of nine pieces, based on Romanian folk melodies, from Bartók's Forty-Four Violin Duos. Points to the origin of the entire set of duos in Erich Doflein's instigation of Bartók to compose them. Also cites Veress's analysis of the pieces. Contains musical examples.

603. László, Zsigmond. "A prozódiától a dramaturgiáig: Bartók Béla" [From prosody to dramaturgy: Béla Bartók]. In *Költészet és zeneiség.* Budapest: Akadémiai, 1985. pp. 100-129.

Explores rhythmic and melodic prosody in Bartók's opera, *Duke Bluebeard's Castle,* and demonstrates that prosody is essential to its dramaturgy. Compares the opera with Debussy's *Pelléas et Mélisande.* Contains music examples.

604. Leafstedt, Carl S. "Structure in the Fifth Door Scene of Bartók's *Duke Bluebeard's Castle:* An Alternative Viewpoint." *College Music Symposium* 30/1 (Spring 1990): 96-102.   780.5 C686 ISSN 0069-5696

Provides a response to a reading of a pre-publication copy of Elliott Antokoletz's article, "Bartók's *Bluebeard:* The Sources of Its 'Modernism,'" published in the same issue of this journal. The author

Studies of Bartók's Musical Compositions

presents an alternative to Antokoletz's structural interpretation of the Fifth Door Scene. Intends to show that while Antokoletz interprets the line structure of the scene (in conjunction with the symbolic dramatic meaning) as part of a progressively irregular, extended musical departure from the underlying quaternary structure of the octosyllabic Hungarian text, this ambiguity can actually be reduced by grouping the text into subsections based on either four or two lines, similarly to the previous two sections.

605. Lendvai, Ernő. "Allegro barbaro. Az új magyar zene bölcsőjénél" [Allegro barbaro. At the cradle of the new Hungarian music]. *Magyar zenetörténeti tanulmányok 3. Mosonyi Mihály és Bartók Béla emlékére.* Budapest: Zeneműkiadó, 1974, pp. 257-278. ML55 S992 B6

Detailed analysis of the *Allegro barbaro* (1911) according to the author's principles of the "polar-axis" system. Demonstrates the derivation of these principles from pentatonic folk-music sources. In Hungarian with summaries in English and German. Contains illustrations and music.

606. ----------. *Bartók and Kodály*, Vols. 1-3. Budapest: Népművelési Intézet [Institute for culture], 1979. 240p., 247p., 215p.; Vol. 4, 1980. 100p. ISBN 9636510512 MT92.B37 L48 780.92/2 2 19

Comprehensive study of selected works based on Lendvai's well-known theories, in which he attempts to show the "organic synthesis" of the music of East and West in Bartók's and Kodály's music. Uses the terms "bartókian chromaticism" and "bartókian diatony" to denote this dual way of thinking, naming the former the *Pentatonic* and the latter the *Acoustic/Overtone* system. Presents his axis system, harmonic principles (based on the pentatonic-chromatic system, alpha chords, scale-interval models, equidistant scales, the diatonic-overtone system, authentic and plagal way of thinking) and nature symbolism. Also discusses modality, atonality, function, and Bartók's conception of form as well as polymodal chromaticism. Contains illustrations, many musical examples.

607. ----------. "Bartók und der Goldene Schnitt" [Bartók and the Golden Section]. *Österreichische Musikzeitschrift* 21 (1966): 607-614. 780.5 Oe8 ISSN 0029-9316

Evaluates Bartók's use of the "Golden Section" principle and explains how its use brings about the fusion of Bartók's two-fold view of life: a fusion of the continuity of the biological being with the intellectual power of logic.

608. ----------. *Béla Bartók, An Analysis of His Music.* London: Kahn and Averill, 1971. 115p. ISBN 900707 04-6 MT92 B37 L5

Represents the most comprehensive English-language presentation of Lendvai's theories of Bartók's music. Intended to demonstrate that the various levels of the music are integrated by means of several interlocking systems, including tonal principles based on the "polar-axis" system, formal principles based on the Golden Section and Fibonacci Series, the use of chords and intervals derived from the Golden Section or "chromatic system" and its inversion, the acoustic (overtone scale) or "diatonic system." Also, includes some historical reference to ancient Greek, Gothic, and Renaissance mathematical models and presents some discussion of the philosophical significance of the principles. Contains an Introduction by Alan Bush, numerous diagrams and examples, and three appendices. See reviews by: Todd Crow, in *Notes* 29/4 (June 1973): 722-724; and Brian Fennelly, in *Journal of Music Theory* 17/2 (Fall 1973): 330-334 .

609. ----------. "Duality and Synthesis in the Music of Béla Bartók." *The New Hungarian Quarterly* 3/7 (1962): 91-114.   914.39105 N42
ML410 B26 B29

Provides a concise view of Lendvai's basic theoretical ideas. Discusses his ideas on the Golden Section, "polar-axis" system, Bartók's diatonic and chromatic scale systems, and the relationships these ideas share with traditional and folk-music idioms, Impressionistic music, and twelve-tone technique. Reprinted in *Bartók Studies,* ed. Todd Crow. Detroit: Information Coordinators, 1976, pp. 39-62.

610. ----------. "Einführung in die Formen- und Harmoniewelt Bartóks" [Introduction to Bartók's world of form and harmony]. In *Béla Bartók, Weg und Werk, Schriften und Briefe,* ed. Bence Szabolcsi. Leipzig: Breitkopf und Haertel, 1957, pp. 91-137.   ML410.B28 A32

Contains an exposition of Lendvai's theories relating to Bartók's music. The section on the "polar-axis" system contains two examples from *Music for Strings, Percussion and Celesta* as well as a chart showing the formal middle point of the movement (according to Golden Section proportions), where the tonality has moved from the opening key (which also closes the movement) to its polarized area at the tritone .

611. ----------. "Modalitás--atonalitás--funkció. (Utóhang egy Bartók-Kodály könyvhöz.)" [Modality--atonality--function. Epilogue to a book on Bartók and Kodály]. *Magyar zenetörténeti tanulmányok 4. Kodály Zoltán emlékére.* Budapest: Zeneműkiadó, 1977, pp. 57-112. ML55 S992 B6

Relates the author's polar-axis ideas to Kodály's solmization system, which contains a movable Do (major scales represented by

Do through Ti and minor scales by La through Sol), using an example from Bartók's *Music for Strings, Percussion and Celesta* IV. Refers to examples contained in the author's *Bartók és Kodály harmóniavilága* (The harmonic realm of Bartók and Kodály). In Hungarian with summaries in English and German.

612. ----------. "Remarks on Roy Howat's 'Principles of Proportional Analysis,'" *Music Analysis* 3/3 (October 1984): 255-264. ML1 M386   ISSN 0262-5245

   Response to Howat's critical challenges to Lendvai's methods. See item no. 586, Roy Howat, "Bartók, Lendvai and the Principles of Proportional Analysis." *Music Analysis* 2/1 (March 1983): 69-95.

613. Lengyel, Menyhért. "The Miraculous Mandarin." *The New Hungarian Quarterly* 4/11 (July-September 1963): 30-35. English translation by István Farkas.   914.39105 N42   ML410 B26 B29

   Provides an in-depth description as well as a setting of the tale. The Hungarian original was first published in the literary magazine, *Nyugat* (West) (1917): 87-93. Reprinted in *Bartok Studies*, ed. Todd Crow. Detroit: Information Coordinators, 1976, pp. 111-116.

614. Ligeti, György. "Analyse des V. Streichquartetts von Béla Bartók" [Analysis of the *Fifth String Quartet* of Béla Bartók]. *Philharmonia-Partituren Nr. 167* (= U.E. 10734), no date; also reprinted in Boosey and Hawkes pocket score 9044.

   Detailed, measure-by-measure thematic-formal analysis of each of the five movements. Commentary in German, English, and French.

615. Lowman, Edward A. "Some Striking Propositions in the Music of Béla Bartók." *Fibonacci Quarterly* 9/5 (December 1971): 527-528, 536-537.   QA1 F5

   Discusses some Fibonacci relations in terms of form and lengths of movements. Gives examples in Movements I and III of *Music for Strings, Percussion and Celesta.*

616. Locke, Derek. "Numerical Aspects of Bartók's String Quartets." *Musical Times* 128/1732 (June 1987): 322-325.   780.5 M98 ISSN 0027-4666

   Intention is to identify a rigorous framework in several of Bartók's works, including the last three string quartets and other works, based on an exploration of the principles of Golden Section proportions and the Fibonacci series, which were first identified in Bartók's music by Ernő Lendvai.

617. Mancini, David. "Teaching Set Theory in the Undergraduate Core Curriculum." *Journal of Music Theory Pedagogy* 5/1 (Spring 1991): 95-107.　MT10 J85

　　Intention is to demonstrate, by means of analyses of passages from the music of Webern and Bartók, how new developments in *set theory* (including principles of integer notation, transposition, inversion, and inclusion) can serve the pedagogical interests of the undergraduate musical curriculum. Contains music examples, charts, tables.

618. Mason, Colin. "An Essay in Analysis: Tonality, Symmetry, and Latent Serialism in Bartók's Fourth Quartet." *The Music Review* 18/7 (August 1957): 189-201.　780.5 M9733　ISSN 0027-4445

　　Asserts through detailed analysis that polymodality, based on simultaneous modes on a common tonic (opening on C), is supplementary to symmetrical formations in the pitch organization. Tonal implications are gradually fulfilled in the course of the work, which gradually grows into the key of C. States that polymodality was Bartók's final solution of the problem of total chromaticism. See also the German translation by Gerhard Schuhmacher, in *Zur musikalischen Analyse* (1974): 241-260.

619. Maxwell, Judith Shepherd. "An Investigation of Axis-Based Symmetrical Structures in Two Compositions of Béla Bartók." D.M.Ed. thesis. University of Oklahoma, 1975. 312p.

　　Detailed account of various factors, including metronomic relationships, dynamics, orchestration, etc., that contribute to the formation of formal and structural relations. Relies somewhat on Lendvai for orientation. Study based on recognition of axis-based symmetrical structure as a recurrent, thus important, feature of Bartók's compositional style. Subjects two mature works to analysis: *Music for Strings, Percussion and Celesta* and *Cantata Profana*. Considers seven categories: pitch, duration, timbre, texture, dynamics, structure, and text. Contains illustrations, diagrams, frequency tables, bibliography.

620. McCabe, John. *Bartók's Orchestral Music.* London: BBC, 1974. 64p.　ISBN-0563126744　MT-130.B34 M2

　　Brief descriptive analysis commenting on the principal themes, forms, and some special effects. Contains illustrations, music, index.

621. McCandless, William Edgar. "Cantus Firmus Techniques in Selected Instrumental Compositions, 1910-1960." Ph.D. diss. Music Theory: Indiana University, 1974. 309p.   ML446.M33C3

   Includes a discussion of Bartók's *Eight Improvisations on Hungarian Peasant Songs,* Op. 20, as one of ten twentieth-century compositions based on the use of a pre-existing cantus firmus. Analyzes the melodies in the context of tonality, rhythm, and texture. Contains illustrations, bibliography.

622. Michael, Frank. "Analytische Anmerkungen zu Bartóks 2. Klavierkonzert" [Analytical observations on Bartók's *Second Piano Concerto*]. *Studia musicologica* 24/3-4 (1982): 425-437.
   781.05 St92   ISSN 0039-3266

   A study of thematic structure and relations, in which the entire work is developed from a basic motive. Unity is created through variation technique and metamorphosis. However, these observations are not intended to replace a detailed analysis.

623. Monelle, Raymond. "Bartók's Imagination in the Later Quartets." *The Music Review* 31 (1970): 70-81.   780.5 M9733
   ISSN 0027-4445

   Descriptive analysis of various passages of these quartets, illustrating those features that are classically derived with those that are "radical and astringent." Discusses scales, motives, textures, and harmonies in terms of their relations to tradition and territories removed from Western art music. Shows that they blend in an imaginative process.

624. Morrison, Charles Douglas. "Prolongation in the Final Movement of Bartók's String Quartet No. 4." *Music Theory Spectrum* 13/2 (Fall 1991): 179-196.   ML1 M855

   According to the author, *RILM Abstracts* No. 9571 (1991), "Post-tonal prolongations require flexibility concerning acceptable patterns and processes. Analysis of the first 148 measures of the final movement of Bartók's string quartet no. 4 identifies a departure-return pattern as the vehicle for foreground prolongation, and the nesting of that pattern--to span the entire passage--as the means for large-scale prolongation. The so-called Lydian-Phrygian polymode is shown to hierarchize components in the departure-return pattern. Oscillation-reiteration of the foreground pattern at three different scale degrees connects constituents of the large-scale pattern. This process is defined as a non-Schenkerian (but nonetheless viable) prolongation technique."

625. Nelson, Mark. "Folk Music and the 'Free and Equal Treatment of the Twelve Tones': Aspects of Béla Bartók's Synthetic Methods." *College Music Symposium* 27 (1987): 59-116.   ISSN 0069-5696 780.5 C686

    Points to the work of two groups of scholars, one of which has explored the significance of Bartók's folk-music research in the composer's own compositional development, the other of which has explored Western art-music sources in Bartók's development, thereby pointing to the great variety of musical languages influencing Bartók's work. In the context of both folk- and art-music influences, explores Bartók's melodic construction, chord structures derived from pentatonic folk songs, chromatic variation, polymodal chromaticism, semitone transformations of peasant-music prototypes, and coherence based on developing variation and pitch-cell arrangements. These discussions are based on principles established by other scholars, as documented by the author. Includes examples from *String Quartets Nos. 3-6, Piano Concerto No. 3,* the *Piano Sonata, Dance Suite, Two Portraits, Fourteen Bagatelles,* Op. 6, *Suite,* Op. 14, *Improvisations,* Op. 20, and *Mikrokosmos.*

626. Nordwall, Ove. "Béla Bartók och den moderna musiken" [Béla Bartók and modern music]. *Nutida musik* 7/2 (1964): 1-9. ML5 N96   ISSN 0029-6597

    Presents a broad analytical coverage of Bartók's compositions, including the *Sonata for Two Pianos and Percussion* and its concerto version, the *Quartets,* and the *Concertos,* and other works. Also published in *Studia musicologica* 9/3-4 (1967): 265-80.

627. Novak, John. "The Benefits of 'Relaxation': The Role of the 'Pihenő' Movement in Bartók's *Contrasts.*" *Bartók in Retrospect,* ed. Elliott Antokoletz, Victoria Fischer, and Benjamin Suchoff. Projected publication of two 1995 conference proceedings.

    States that the two movements that Bartók completed for the composition which he later named *Contrasts* had already significantly exceeded the performance timings that its commissioner, Benny Goodman, had intended; nevertheless, the composer believed that the work required a slow middle movement in order to be complete. Although a mere 51 measures in length, the "Relaxation" movement appears to contain great diversity of harmonic language and pitch collections. Much of this movement's harmonic materials, however, are developed from the principal compositional ideas and pitch collections of the surrounding two movements. These materials include octatonic and whole-tone collections and formations, the prevalent [016] unordered pitch class interval set (and extensions to this collection), and the composer's characteristic juxtaposition of major and minor thirds within tertian harmony. Through much of the movement, Bartók employs two types of inversional symmetry, strict and "free," for distinct purposes. In addition, the symmetrical Locrian pentachord on B is featured both on a melodic and structural level. Shows that the role of the movement as a transition between the outer movements is especially evident at its opening and closing, where common pitch collections form a segue between adjacent movements. Finally, considers the significance of the titles "Contrasts" and "Relaxation." (Annotation based on the author's abstract of the original lecture; see item no. 1161.)

628. Oramo, Ilkka. "Modale Symmetrie bei Bartók" [Modal symmetry in Bartók]. *Die Musikforschung* 33 (1980): 450-464.   780.5 M9921
ISSN 0027-4801

Uses Bartók's definition of bimodality and polymodality as given in the Harvard Lectures. These lectures serve as the bases for a discussion of polymodality in his music. Focuses on symmetrical combinations.

629. ----------. "Tonaalisuudesta Bartókin bagatellissa Op. 6 No. 1" [Tonality in Bartók's *Bagatelle* Op. 6, No. 1]. *Festskrift till Erik Tawaststjerna,* ed. Erkki Salmenhaara (October 10, 1976), *Acta musicologica fennica* 9 (Helsinki) (1976): 198-220.

In Finnish and Swedish. Presents a detailed and thorough analysis of this work.

630. Orvis, Joan. "Technical and Stylistic Features of the Piano Etudes of Stravinsky, Bartók, and Prokofiev." Mus. D. diss. Piano Pedagogy and Literature: Indiana University, 1974. 90p.

Includes a discussion of Bartók's *Three Etudes,* Op. 18 for piano (1918). Speaks of the technical difficulty of the Bartók Etudes, which are cited as containing atonal principles and complex rhythms. Explores these pieces in terms of harmony, tonality, rhythm, meter, and formal characteristics, and describes their pianistic and pedagogical significance as well.

631. Perle, George. "Berg's Master Array of the Interval Cycles." *Musical Quarterly* (New York) 63/1 (January 1977): 1-30.   ML1 M725
ISSN 0027-4631

Includes a brief discussion of inversional symmetry as the basis of Bartók's use of interval cycles in his *Fourth String Quartet.* States that this principle can be traced back as early as the second of Bartók's *Fourteen Bagatelles* (1908). Demonstrates some basic properties of three cyclically derived symmetrical cells in the quartet. Includes a facsimile of a letter that Berg sent to Schoenberg in 1920, which contains a complete chart of the interval cycles. Contains facsimile and musical examples.

632. ----------. "The String Quartets of Béla Bartók." *Béla Bartók.* New York: Dover Publications, Inc., 1967. pp. 2-8. Program notes for the recordings performed by the Tátrai String Quartet. HCR-ST-7272-7273-7274 HCR-ST-5272-5273-5274. Reprinted in *A Musical Offering: Essays in Honor of Martin Bernstein,* ed. Claire Brook and E. H. Clinkscale. New York: Pendragon Press, 1977. 301p. ISBN 0-918728-03-7

States that the quartets are representative of each phase of Bartók's career. Provides concise, original analyses of each of the quartets in the context of Bartók's historical and stylistic development. Analyses of all six quartets include a focus on motivic and pitch-set functions in relation to the large-scale structure and design, revealing some analogies to traditional structural functions. The historical discussion also includes some reference to Bartók's own writings. Contains photograph, musical examples, and a brief bibliography.

633. ----------. "Symmetrical Formations in the String Quartets of Béla Bartók." *Music Review* 16 (November 1955): 300-312. 780.5 M9733 ISSN 0027-4445

Pioneering article giving a brief history of symmetrical pitch collections in the late nineteenth and early twentieth centuries (in Debussy and Russian composers). Then presents a significant discussion of the equal subdivisions of the octave into the interval cycles and the use of inversionally symmetrical relations that define axes as a new concept of tonal focus in the *Fifth, Second* and *Fourth Quartets.* Also establishes the concept of symmetrical sets (x and y in the *Fourth String Quartet,* as one instance) as the basis of progression or "modulation." According to the author, these relations define only part of the context otherwise based on "a curious amalgam of various elements."

634. Persichetti, Vincent. "Current Chronicle." *Musical Quarterly* 35/1 (January 1949): 122-126. ML1 M725 ISSN 0027-4631

Refers to Bartók's concern for intricate detail in his stage works and provides an analysis of the melodic, harmonic, and rhythmic elements in *The Miraculous Mandarin.*

635. Petersen, Peter. *Die Tonalität im Instrumentalschaffen von Béla Bartók* [Tonality in the instrumental works of Béla Bartók]. Hamburger Beiträge zur Musikwissenschaft, no. 6. Hamburg: Wagner, 1971. 244p. ML410.B26 P5

According to the author, in *RILM Abstracts* No. 3841 (1973), "Bartók recognized two components in tonality: a controlling pitch and a system of relationships. The latter could be predetermined (as in the case of modes, pentatonic structures, etc.) or constructed from the available twelve pitches. In purely chromatic pieces, Bartók sometimes created tonality through mirror images (as in *Mikrokosmos*, no. 144) or by the use of pitch groups (as in the *Sonata for Two Pianos and Percussion,* where twelve-tone fields are repeated in ostinato fashion). Individual pitches emphasized linearly, dynamically, or by means of register, are often used to support the structurally constituted primary key of the themes, sections, movements, or cyclic works. The function of the tonic with regard to the form of Bartók's instrumental works corresponds, in principle, to that in older music." Contains list of Bartók's compositions (pp. 191-226) and bibliography (pp. 227-244). See *Musikforschung* 26/1 (1973): 105, for a summary of the author's dissertation. See reviews by: Friedrich Neumann, in *Musikforschung* 27/2 (1974): 246-248; Hartmut Fladt, in *Neue Zeitung für Musik* 133/8 (1972): 484-485.

636. Pütz, Werner. "Studien zum Streichquartettschaffen bei Hindemith, Bartók, Schönberg und Webern" [Studies of the string quartets of Hindemith, Bartók, Schoenberg and Webern]. Ph.D. diss. University of Köln, 1968. 217p.   MT-140 P84

Comprehensive study based on stylistic and structural analyses of these works. Relates Bartók's use of motivic development to that of Beethoven and points to the setting of folk-like materials within the contrapuntal contexts as the basis for expanding the sonority of the medium. Also shows the predominance of the organic process, rather than traditional concepts, as the basis of structural organization. Contains music, illustrations. Published in *Kölner Beiträge zur Musikforschung* 36. Regensburg: Bosse, 1968. 217p. See review by Wolfgang Rogge in *Melos* 36/9 (1969): 375-376.

637. Réti, Rudolf. *Tonality--Atonality--Pantonality: A Study of Some Trends in Twentieth Century Music.* London: Rockliffe; New York: Macmillan, 1958, pp. 73-78.   MT 40.R394 T6

Discusses these principles in connection with *Music for Strings, Percussion and Celesta* in particular. Contains illustrations.

638. Rosenbloom, Paul David. "Part II: A Study of Phrase Rhythm in Late Bartók." D.M.A. treatise. Cornell University, 1979. 322p.

Presents a detailed analytic-theoretic study of each movement of several late chamber works, including the *Fifth* and *Sixth String Quartets,* the *Sonata for Two Pianos and Percussion,* and the *Sonata for Solo Violin.* Discusses phraseological structure, based on the interrelation of harmonic, melodic, formal, and textural parameters in these works but suggests a more generalized application of the principles to all of Bartók's works. Also suggests the relevance of these findings to the performance of these works. Contains graphs of the analytical results.

639. Rosse, Carolyn Walton. "An Analysis of *Improvisations,* Op. 20 by Béla Bartók." M.A. diss. San Diego State College, 1968. 122p.

Stylistic analysis based on the interrelationship of the various technical procedures (involving melodic contour and cadences, harmonic construction, and rhythmic structure) with the peasant melodies. Focuses on harmonic constructions in terms of their intervallic properties, and suggests the secondary importance of traditional functional concepts. Also explores segmental inversion, bitonality, bimodality, and canonic imitation.

640. Russ, Michael. "Atonality, Modality, Symmetry, and Tonal Hierarchy in Bartók's Improvisation, Op. 20, No. 8." *Musicology in Ireland.* Dublin: Irish Academic, 1990. pp. 278-294.

Compares contrasting theoretic-analytical approaches by Elliott Antokoletz, Ernő Lendvai, and Paul Wilson to pitch organization in Bartók's *Improvisations on Hungarian Peasant Songs,* op. 20, no. 8. States that these analysts rely on divergent theoretical models and differ in their definitions of tonality. Offers a new approach based on synthesis and extension of these analyses. Contains music examples, bibliography, charts, tables.

641. Sabin, Robert. "Revolution and Tradition in the Music of Bartók." *Musical America* 49/3 (February 1949): 7, 140.   ML1 M97

Provides detailed descriptive technical and stylistic analyses of several late works, e.g., the last three quartets and *Music for Strings, Percussion and Celesta,* with the aim of showing how Bartók pursued a course of self-development and creative evolution that were misunderstood during his life-time and, paradoxically, revealing him as one of the preservers of tradition--not of the rigid rules and regulations, but of the principles of expression and self-discipline.

642. Sabo, Anica. "Palindromična simetrija u koncertima Bele Bartoka: Rezultat transformacije motivsko-tematskog sadržaja/The Palindromic Symmetry in Béla Bartók's Concertos: The Result of the Motive-Thematic Contents Transformation." *Folklor i njegova umetnička transpozicija* III. Beograd: Fakultet Muzičke Umetnosti, 1991. pp. 349-360; 361-383.

Not examined. In Serbian and English. *RILM Abstracts* No 9585 (1991); See *RILM* [91]1009. Contains music, charts, tables.

643. Schwinger, Wolfram. "Béla Bartóks Streichquartette." *Muzsika* (Budapest) 27 (1973): 13-18, 133-137, 245-252, 350-355, 445-451, 569-574. ISSN 0027-5336

Discusses the evolution of Bartók's compositional techniques based on an analysis of the six string quartets. Compares these works with string quartets of Schoenberg and other twentieth-century composers.

644. Seiber, Mátyás. *The String Quartets of Béla Bartók.* London: Boosey and Hawkes, 1945. 22p. MT-145.B25 S43

Approaches Bartók's string quartets as his most representative works and evaluates them as the most important music of our time, suggesting an analogy to Beethoven's development in his quartets. Gives precise descriptive analysis of the thematic-formal scheme of each quartet, presented in a somewhat subjective, romanticized language. Contains illustrations, music.

645. Sergienko, Raisa. *Iz nablyudeniy nad tematizmom v proizvedeniya Bély Bartóka* [Observations concerning thematic structure in the works of Béla Bartók]. Minsk: Vyseysaya skola, 1977. 51p.

Not examined. According to Svetlana Sigida, *RILM Abstracts* No. 5762 (1977), the author "formulates basic principles for the study of thematic structure in Bartók's works. Examines not only simple structural forms but also complex multi-element structures, e.g., the complex timbral idioms such as are found in contemporary music by B. Asaf'yev."

646. ----------. "Problema tonal'nosti v pozdnem tvorchestve Bély Bartóka" [Tonality in the late works of Béla Bartók]. Ph.D. diss. Belorusskaya Conservatoriya, Kiev, 1978.

Not examined. A 26 page summary of the dissertation, in Russian, according to *RILM Abstracts* No. 1866 (1978), "discusses the question of tonality as seen in the late works of Bartók. His use of sound texture and pitch arrangement in the monophonic and polyphonic works is analyzed for formal structural principles."

647. Smith, Don Davis. "Béla Bartók's Bluebeard's Castle." Master's thesis. University of Texas at Austin, 1961. 90p.

Presents a study of structure, scales, motivic technique, harmony, rhythm, vocal and orchestral style, symbolism and dramatic content. Contains bibliography and music.

648. Smith, Robert. "Béla Bartók's Music for Strings, Percussion, and Celesta." *Music Review* 20/3,4 (August-November 1959): 264-276. 780.5 M9733   ISSN 0027-4445

Comprehensive article, discussing the forms of the movements, thematic material, and orchestration. Also includes a chart showing the recommended placement of the performers. Thematic development and interrelationships of the movements are stressed. Also presents a comparison with other works of Bartók and works of Bach. See also the German translation by Gerhard Schuhmacher, in *Zur musikalischen Analyse* (1974): 261-181.

649. Solomon, Larry Joseph. "Symmetry as a Determinant of Musical Composition." Ph.D. diss. West Virginia University, 1973. 227p. MT-58.S65

Provides a method of analysis based on principles of symmetry in works of several composers, including movements of Bartók's *Music for Strings, Percussion and Celesta.* Gives a definition of symmetry (involving "operations of reflection, rotation, and translation," as well as developing a concept of "quadrates"), presents a detailed analysis of the work, and speculates on the psychological implications. Contains illustrations, music, bibliography.

650. Somfai, László. *Cantata Profana,* preface to the score. Vienna: Universal Edition (UE 12760 W. Ph. V. 359), 1934. New York: Boosey and Hawkes, 1955.   M1530.B37 C3

In German, English, and French. States that the *Cantata* appears to be the most distinguished and direct musical manifestation of Béla Bartók's philosophy. Gives the history of the text and of the composition of the cantata as well as a discussion of the musical language, which includes a formal and tonal analysis. Also, includes a brief reference to one of Ernő Lendvai's concepts, showing that the interval structure of the closing scale (an intervallic inversion of the opening scale) is based on proportions of the Golden Section principle. Contains facsimile excerpt.

651. ----------. "Strategics of Variation in the Second Movement of Bartók's Violin Concerto 1937-1938." *Studia musicologica* 19 (1977): 161-202.   781.05 St92   ISSN 0039-3266

Assumes that the middle variation movement of the *Concerto* was considered by Bartók to be of the greatest importance. A thoroughly documented history of its composition is given, followed by an exhaustive analysis of several factors of the numerous variation phenomena: 1) study of the "melodic theme" and its sketches; 2) the variation of tonal structure (including melodic modification of the theme); 3) the variation of phrase structure (including modification of meter and rhythm); 4) the variation of instrumental groups (including modification of timbre); and 5) the variation of register formations (including density of tone space, modification and motion of tone-bands).

652. Starr, Lawrence. "Melody-Accompaniment Textures in the Music of Bartók, as Seen in his Mikrokosmos." *The Journal of Musicology* 4/1 (Winter 1985-1986): 91-104.   780.5 J826   ISSN 0277-9269

An adaptation of material in a chapter on texture in Bartók's music from the author's manuscript study *Mikrokosmos: The Tonal Universe of Béla Bartók*. States that in "such a texture, one predominant voice is the determining factor in establishing the tonal direction and coherence of the piece." Bartók's main starting point was the tonally self-sufficient monophonic folk tune, around which Bartók freely developed a wide span of textural possibilities. Moves from the least complex examples (e.g., No. 68, based on an ostinato derived from important tones from the melody) to more complex relations (e.g., Nos. 100 and 125).

653. ----------. "Mikrokosmos: The Tonal Universe of Béla Bartók." Ph.D. diss.   University of California at Berkeley, 1973. 2 vols. 189p., 66p.

Attempts to join certain features of "structure and prolongation" from the familiar methodological approach of Schenker-Salzer-Travis with more recently established concepts of structure based on "axes of symmetry," rather than the traditional structural harmonic nomenclature based on I-IV (or II, III, VI) - V - I of Schenkerian analysis. Primarily deals with *Mikrokosmos* Nos. 1, 103, and 144, moving from unison melodies to tone clusters. Also explores concepts of polymodal chromaticism, scale systems, textures, etc.

654. Stefani, Gino. "Tritono e forma-arco nel 5° quartetto di Bartók" [Tritone and arch-form in Bartók's Quartet No. 5]. *Nuova rivista musicale italiana* 5/5 (September-October 1971): 847-860. 780.5 N928   ISSN 0029-6228

Demonstrates the structural primacy of the tritone in the first, third, and fifth movements of the arch-form of Bartók's *Fifth String Quartet*. Also discusses motivic construction and its relation to the tritone.

655. Szabó, Miklós. *Bartók Béla kórusművei* [Béla Bartók's choral works]. Budapest: Zeneműkiadó, 1985. 300p.   ISBN-963-330-554-3

Part I presents a brief survey of all of Bartók's choral works. Then, Part II provides a detailed analysis of each of the *Twenty-*

Seven Choruses for children and women's voices, followed by a summary of principles. Much of the analysis is prominently based on Ernő Lendvai's theoretical concepts, including discussions of the "polar-axis" system, principles of the Golden Section and Fibonacci series, scalar "models," polymodality, etc. Provides some insight into interpretative issues. Contains music examples.

656. Szentkirályi, András. "Bartók's Second Sonata for Violin and Piano (1922)." Ph.D. diss. Princeton University, 1976. 236p. ML410.B262 S9

Presents an analysis of the work based on the theoretical principles established by Ernő Lendvai. The dissertation is divided into two parts, based on a study of the formal structure and the tonal structure. Includes a discussion of the "polar-axis" system, the Golden Section ratios and Fibonacci series, and the principle of duality and synthesis. Explores the tonal structure in terms of "alpha" formations (comprising axes separated by a major second), "distance models" (involving periodic repetitions of two intervals), "acoustic scale" (C-D-E-F#G-A-Bb, derived from the natural overtone series), and the pentatonic scale. Demonstrates the structural relation of these tonal structures to the Fibonacci numbers. Contains illustrations, music, bibliography.

657. ----------. "Some Aspects of Béla Bartók's Compositional Techniques." *Studia musicologica* 20 (1978): 157-182. 781.05 St92 ISSN 0039-3266

Asserts that Bartók's compositional techniques cannot only be the result of intuition (though Bartók suggested its role) but rather of conscious, systematic, and logical thinking. Outlines a conglomerate of diverse principles (based on folk modes, romantic chromaticism leading to equal divisions of the octave, etc.) then focuses on Lendvai's principles of the Golden Section, Fibonacci, and polar-axis systems as the basis of an analysis of the first twenty measures of the *Second Sonata for Violin and Piano* (1922). Also outlines three main categories of the literature dealing with Bartók's life, music, and scientific work.

658. Taylor, Vernon H. "Contrapuntal Techniques in the Music of Béla Bartók." Ph.D. diss. Northwestern University, 1950. 318p.

Not examined. Contains music examples, bibliography.

659. Thayer, Fred Martin. "Part II: The Choral Music of Béla Bartók." D.M.A. treatise. Cornell University, 1976. 228p.

Provides basic information derived from primary-source materials held at the Budapest and New York Bartók Archives, and presents detailed analyses of several major choral works of Bartók. These include the *Four Slovak Folk Songs* (1917) for mixed voices and piano, *Four Hungarian Folk Songs* (1917) for mixed voices, and the *Cantata Profana* (1930) for double chorus and orchestra. More general analyses of later works are then given. These include *Twenty-seven Choruses* (1935) for two- and three-part children's or women's chorus, and *From Olden Times* (1935) for male voices.

660. Thomason, Leta Nelle. "Structural Significance of the Motive in the String Quartets of Béla Bartók." Ph.D. diss. Michigan State University, 1965. 395p.

Analyses based on the construction and transformation of melodic-rhythmic motives in the individual movements of all the quartets.

661. Thyne, Stuart. "Bartók's 'Improvisations': An Essay in Technical Analysis." *Music and Letters* 31/1 (January 1950): 30-45. 780.5 M92   ISSN 0027-4224

Includes a line-by-line analysis of the *Improvisations,* which are among the most significant of Bartók's middle period works in terms of the extended treatment of actual folk-song material. Claims that the *Improvisations* represent a meeting point between Bartók's interpretation of Impressionism, formalism, and folk-song harmonies. Most of the analysis of pitch organization is in terms of traditional triadic structures, which seem to have little relevance here.

662. Traimer, Roswitha. *Béla Bartóks Kompositionstechnik, dargestellt an seinen sechs Streichquartetten* [Béla Bartók's technique of composition as shown by his six string quartets]. 3rd edition. Regensburg: Gustav Bosse Verlag, 1956, 1964. 91p. ML410.B 26 T17   ML410.B 292 T7   785.74 B285yt

Detailed but concise analytical study of the basic elements of Bartók's musical language as shown in the string quartets. First discusses the fundamental materials of construction. These include I) the motive, its interval sequence, contour, and rhythmic character, as well as its horizontal and vertical relations, spinning-out technique, imitative treatment, harmonic summary, and formal connection; and II) the constructive interval, its imitative and harmonic treatment, and function in the formal organization. Second, discusses the harmonic disposition, and principles of polyphony, timbre, harmony, and tone modification. Furthermore, provides analytical discussion based on rhythmic and metric character, formal construction, and influences of folklore. Contains music and bibliography. Issued originally as a dissertation, Universität München, 1953.

663. Travis, Roy. "Tonal Coherence in the First Movement of Bartók's Fourth String Quartet." *The Music Forum* 2 (1970): 298-371. ML55 M49

   Attempts to explain tonal centricity and progression according to traditional tonal principles, i.e., Schenkerian methodized approach based on principles of contrapuntal prolongation of and harmonic focus on the chordal (I, IV, V, I) structural areas. However, replaces the concept of "tonic triad" with "dissonant tonic sonority." Presents Schenkerian voice-leading graphs of foreground, midground, and background levels.

664. Treitler, Leo. "Harmonic Procedure in the *Fourth Quartet* of Béla Bartók." *Journal of Music Theory* 3 (November 1959): 292-297. 781.05 J826   ISSN 0022-2909

   Provides "observations about the ways in which the music is located around specific pitch-areas, and about the relationships that are imposed upon the pitch-groups which assume this central role." Study deals with the dual approach to harmonic organization in the work, including traditional tonal concepts and new concepts of pitch-set relations, which introduce a new cell ("z") as a follow-up to George Perle's "sets x and y" (See Perle, "Symmetrical Formations") in this quartet.

665. Ujfalussy, József. "A hídszerkezetek néhány tartalmi kérdése Bartók mǔvészetében" [Some inherent questions of arch symmetry in Bartók's works]. *Zenetudományi tanulmányok* 10 (1962): 15-30.

   Analyses of formal symmetry with respect to certain genres of Bartók's works, i.e., slow movements and scherzos as well as folk music. The German translation by the author is in *Studia musicologica* 5 (1963): 541-547.

666. ----------. "Az Allegro barbaro harmóniai alapgondolata és Bartók hangsorai" [The basic harmonic concept of the *Allegro barbaro* and the scales used by Bartók]. *Magyar zenetörténeti tanulmányok: Szabolcsi Bence 70. születésnapjára* [Studies in Hungarian musical history dedicated to Bence Szabolcsi on his 70th birthday], ed. Ferenc Bónis. Budapest: Zenemǔkiadó Vállalat, 1969, pp. 323-332. ML55 S992 B6

   In Hungarian with summaries in German and English. Discusses the importance, in the development of Bartók's polymodal system, of the simultaneous use of two chords (one major the other minor) a half-step apart (bitonal), in which a common third degree is shared between them. This is shown to occur as early as the *Allegro barbaro* (1911). States that this relation has its roots in the preceding century.

667. ----------. "Bartók Béla: Kontrasztok . . . (1938)" [Béla Bartók: *Contrasts* . . . (1938)]. *Magyar zene* 9 (1968): n.p.   ML5 M14 ISSN 0025-0384

Based on the concept that the "hexaphonic" system of the first rondo theme of the finale is built upon a "mistuned" chain of fifths, which is initially presented by the retuned violin. See the related discussion by János Kárpáti, in "Alternative Structures in Bartók's *Contrasts.*" *Studia musicologica* 23 (1981): 201-207.

668. Volek, Jaroslav. "Über einige interessante Beziehungen zwischen thematischer Arbeit und Instrumentation in Bartóks Werk: 'Concerto für Orchester'" [About some interesting relationships between the thematic work and the instrumentation in Bartók's work: 'Concerto for Orchestra.']. *Studia musicologica* 5/1-4 (1963): 557-586. 781.05 St92   ISSN 0039-3266

Detailed analysis of each movement of Barók's *Concerto for Orchestra,* establishing a strong relationship between the formal structure and instrumentation. Analysis includes distribution of themes to groups of instruments, instrumental transformations, and standardizing the presentation of intonation for the instruments.

669. Waldbauer, Ivan. "Intellectual Construct and Tonal Direction in Bartók's 'Divided Arpeggios.'" *Studia musicologica* 24/3-4 (1982): 527-536.   781.05 St92   ISSN 0039-3266

Study based on a traditional Schenkerian graphic analysis, with the intention of revealing the mechanical construction as well as tonal structure of the work. Views the main major-minor symmetrical motif, identified as "the intellectual construct," primarily within the context of traditional tonal-harmonic functions. In connection with his notion of a conflict between the "construct" and the tonal-harmonic framework, the author invokes the Schenkerian principle of prolongation of a background-level I-V-I harmonic structure in C to illustrate the resolution of this conflict, which is achieved through the final disintegration of the motif.

670. ----------. "Interplay of Tonality and Nontonal Constructs in Three Pieces from the *Mikrokosmos* of Bartók." [*Ward Festschrift*] *Music and Context: Essays for John M. Ward,* ed. Anne Dhu Shapiro and Phyllis Benjamin. Cambridge, Mass: Department of Music, Harvard University, 1985. pp. 418-440.   ISBN 0-674-58888-6

According to the author, *RILM Abstracts* No. 5919 (1985), "Voice-leading charts show how Bartók establishes the primacy of tonal goals over abstract, nontonal constructs in nos. 140, 144, and 143 of his *Mikrokosmos.* To render the inversionally symmetrical, nontonal sets and the nontonal methods of their operation compatible with traditional tonal expectation, he (1) modifies both sets and operations as needed, or (2) adds controlling bass notes to establish tonal meaning where there would otherwise be none, and (3) by these manipulations often creates parallelisms between the disparate tonal and nontonal expectations. The resulting synthesis, or illusion of synthesis, is unique to each piece." Contains music, charts, tables.

671. ----------. "Polymodal Chromaticism and Tonal Plan in the First of Bartók's 'Six Dances in Bulgarian Rhythm.'" *Studia musicologica* 32/1-4 (1990): 241-262.   781.05 St92   ISSN 0039-3266

Intention is to show that Bartók's systematic use of compositional techniques in the first of the "Six Dances in Bulgarian Rhythm" *(Mikrokosmos* no. 148) is a reflection of his more comprehensive approach to structure that can be traced to constructional methods belonging to the traditional tonal era rather than to the sphere of abstract speculation. Contains music examples, charts, tables.

672. Walker, Mark Fesler. "Thematic, Formal, and Tonal Structure of the Bartók String Quartets." Ph.D. diss. Indiana University, 1955. 387p.

Identifies and discusses the structural properties of the themes, establishes the formal schemes of the quartets, and analyzes the tonal plan and relationships.

673. Whittall, Arnold. "Bartók's Second String Quartet." *The Music Review* 32/3 (August 1971): 265-270.   780.5 M9733 ISSN 0027-4445

Analysis illustrating a close but creative relationship with traditional procedures. States that there is the presence of a tonal center without emphasis on diatonic scales and major/minor triads. States that although the composer employs components from the equal-division system (symmetries), links with hierarchical practices are preserved. Includes discussion of motivic transformations, melodic types, and tonal relationships in a context of structural tensions and relaxations.

674. Wilson, Paul. "Approaching Atonality: Studies and Improvisations." *The Bartók Companion,* ed. Malcolm Gillies. London: Faber and Faber, 1993; Portland, Oregon: Amadeus Press (an imprint of Timber Press, Inc.), 1994. pp. 162-172. ISBN 0-931340-74-8 (HB)   ISBN 0-931340-75-6 (PB)

ML410 B26 B28

Explores various reasons for the separation of Bartók's works composed between 1918 and 1922 from his main compositional development. From these works of "crisis," which include *The Miraculous Mandarin, Three Studies* Op. 18, *Eight Improvisations on Hungarian Peasant Songs* Op. 20, and the *First* and *Second Violin Sonatas,* the two sets of piano pieces (Op. 18 and Op. 20) are selected to demonstrate what the author considers to be an "approaching atonality." Provides a brief history of their composition, performance, and a dscription of their aesthetic and technical characteristics in comparison with certain earlier piano works of Bartók. Then presents an analysis of these two "experimental" works based on the structural functions of specific chordal constructions. In certain cases where such chords have no inherent tonal implications, Bartók induces cadential shaping by means of texture, tempo, rhythm, and dynamics. Invokes Bartók's own comments on the *Improvisations* to demonstrate the new relation between folk tune and accompaniment, which according to a quote from Bartók, "reached, I believe, the extreme limit in adding most daring accompaniments to simple folk tunes," as part of his new style. Points to varying degrees of relatedness and separation between the folk tunes and their harmonic settings.

675. ----------. "Atonality and Structure in Works of Béla Bartók's Middle Period." Ph.D. diss. Yale University, 1982. 255p. MT-145.B25 W3555

Analyzes three works of Bartók composed between 1917 and 1922, in order to illustrate Bartók's use of atonal procedures. Chapter I introduces certain basic premises, including discussion of Bartók's use of "tonal configurations to create analogues of hierarchical structure and the interaction of Bartók's atonality with his continuing use of tonal or pitch centric organization." Chapters II and III include detailed analyses of the *Eight Improvisations on Hungarian Peasant Songs,* Op. 20, and the *Three Etudes for Piano,* Op. 18, providing both theoretical information as well as to elucidate the organizational principles specific to each work. Chapter IV then explores atonal principles in the *Second Sonata for Violin and Piano* (1922). Also deals with techniques based on the interaction of both tonal and atonal structures in Bartók's music. Contains illustrations, bibliography.

676. ----------. "Concepts of Prolongation and Bartók's Op. 20." *Music Theory Spectrum* 6 (1984): 79-89.   ML1 M855

Analytical study of three pieces from Bartók's *Eight Improvisations on Hungarian Peasant Songs,* op. 20, based on a twentieth-century application of Schenker's theoretical concept of prolongation, in which prolongational gestures are shown to be contextually determined. In place of a traditional tonal hierarchy, points to recurrences of melodic and intervallic gestures as the basis for large-scale structural integration. Contains music examples.

677. ----------. "Function and Pitch Hierarchy in Movement II of Bartók's Fifth Quartet." *Theory and Practice* 14-15 (1989-1990): 179-186.

Points to an analogy between pitch-class and harmonic progression in the second movement of Bartók's *Fifth String Quartet* and traditional tonal functions although asserts that there is no consistent relation between Bartók's harmonic relations and a priori intervallic assumptions. Outlines several functions of tones in this analysis.

678. ----------. *The Music of Béla Bartók.* New Haven and London: Yale University Press, 1992. ix, 222p. ISBN 0-300-05111-5 ML 410.B25W5 780'.92--dc20

Detailed theoretic-analytical study of five works of Bartók, including the *Sonata for Piano, Third String Quartet, Fifth String Quartet* (Movs. II and IV), *Sonata for Two Pianos and Percussion* (Movs. I and II) and *Concerto for Orchestra* (Mov. I). First, provides an introductory outline of the basic "steps toward a theory," including a general overview of Bartók's sources, style, and tonality, and a synopsis of contrasting theoretical views of the music (Ernő Lendvai, The Hungarian Circle, Babbitt and his successors, Elliott Antokoletz, Felix Salzer and Roy Travis, and other recent work). The first part of the book contains the theory in abstract terms, the second the series of analyses based on application of the theoretical ideas. Wilson's theory adopts the notion of a diverse amalgam of elements as the basis for his analyses, in which he admits traditional harmonic principles based on contextual considerations along with the concepts and terminology derived from Allen Forte's "atonal set theory." Fundamentals of the latter include a catalogue of set types, projected sets, and large set types as potential context. Also refers to symmetry as a structural element, harmonic function, privileged pattern, and context and presents a model of hierarchical structure. Concludes by pointing to the "philosophical similarities between his theory and the work of David Lewin and Charles Taylor in the related fields of perception and hermeneutics." Includes many reductive analytical diagrams and figures, Appendix ("Ernő Lendvai and the Axis System"), bibliography, and index. See reviews by: David Cooper, in *Music Analysis* 13/2-3 (July-October 1994): 319-325; László Somfai, in *Music Library Association Notes* 50/1 (September 1993): 151-153.

679. ----------. "Violin Sonatas." *The Bartók Companion,* ed. Malcolm Gillies. London: Faber and Faber, 1993; Portland, Oregon: Amadeus Press (an imprint of Timber Press, Inc.), 1994. pp. 243-256. ISBN 0-931340-74-8 (HB)   ISBN 0-931340-75-6 (PB) ML410 B26 B28

Places the *First* and *Second Violin Sonatas* (1921-1922) within the broader context of Bartók's works immediately following the First World War. Presents historical information concerning the early performances of these *Sonatas* which, like the preceding piano works, Op. 18 and Op. 20, were intended for his own concert performances. Then, points to the two *Sonatas* and their two companion piano compositions as "problem" works, generally assumed as such because of the composer's increasing isolation from the Hungarian folk-music sources. However, analyses of these works are intended to show rather that Bartók was absorbing the folk sources into a "wider frame of reference." Explores issues of musical coherence within a compositional context assumed, controversially (as noted by the author), to be tending toward a "temporary and incomplete" atonality. Relates the external structure to the Classical model (especially in the *First Sonata)* and the pattern of the rhapsody (in the two-movement *Second Sonata)* but reveals how the internal content (harmonic, thematic, etc.) marks a radical change in Bartók's evolution. Shows how complex chord constructions and their recurrences replace discreet tonal centers as the means for structural articulation and integration. Also points to the importance of Bartók's variation technique and thematic transformation. Contains pertinent structural tables and harmonic examples.

680. Winrow, Barbara. "Allegretto con indifferenza. A Study of the 'Barrel Organ' Episode in Bartók's Fifth String Quartet." *The Music Review* 32 (1971): 102-106.   780.5 M9733   ISSN 0027-4445

States that some attempts have been made by other writers to explain the derivation of this episode from the inherent structure of the quartet, but it generally is seen as an "alien intrusion." Detailed analysis shows that the A and B-flat tonalities are gradually built up from the opening of the quartet and traced through basic thematic and tonal structural points. Suggests that there is increasing evidence that for the listener and analyst, one might "work backwards" to understand Bartók's work.

681. Wittlich, Gary E. "An Examination of Some Set-theoretic Applications in the Analysis of Non-serial Music." Ph.D. diss. University of Iowa, 1969. 153p.

Includes detailed analyses of Bartók's *Mikrokosmos,* Nos. 91 and 109, among works of other early twentieth-century composers, based on principles of Allen Forte's set-complex theory. Contains illustrations, bibliography.

682. Zuilenburg, Paul Enea Loeb van. "A Study of Béla Bartók's *Mikrokosmos* with Respect to Formal Analysis, Compositional Techniques, Piano-technical and Piano-pedagogical Aspects." Ph.D. diss. University Witwaterstrand at Johannesburg,1969. 934p.

According to the author, *RILM Abstracts* No. 4194 (1969), this study is based on "a phenomenological investigation in two parts: 1) an analytical section, containing analyses of 153 works, and 2) a pedagogical section, concerned with piano-technical matters, interpretation, and general teaching principles. The pieces show no marked preference for ternary over binary forms. The main unit of design is the symmetrical sentence of 4 + 4 bars. The varied repetition of motifs is more frequent than motif transformation. The perfect fourth is a more characteristic interval than the augmented fourth. Bitonality is not a marked feature of the music and atonality is virtually absent. The lateral shifting of the arm is the basic idiomatic technique required of the performer." Contains illustrations, music, bibliography and index.

2. Studies of Bartók's Style and Aesthetics

683. Adorno, Theodor. "Béla Bartóks Drittes Streichquartett" (1929) [Béla Bartók's Third String Quartet]. Trans. Susan Gillespie. In *Bartók and His World,* ed. Peter Laki. Princeton, New Jersey: Princeton University Press, 1995. pp. 278-281. ISBN 0-691-00633-4   ML 410 B26 B272. Originally published in Theodor W. Adorno, *Gesammelte Schriften,* vol. 18. Frankfurt am Main, 1978.

Considers the *Third String Quartet* (1927) to be Bartók's best achievement to date. Contrasts Bartók's approach to the developmental process in this work with that of Schoenberg and Stravinsky, stating that "it moves as a spiral in faithful repetition of the tasks of its origin, in a process that is at the same time continuous rejuvenation." Discusses Bartók's individual orientation to movement models, the work also revealing his ability to maintain the vitality of Hungarian folklore without "retreating into romantic security." Discusses the quartet within the larger context of his works, evaluating his development of three basic formal types. Then explores the means by which he was able to transform the traditional structures, including those of his native folk music and the sonata, for instance, into a fresh conception. Also provides a lucid description of Bartók's approach to thematic/motivic material, contrapuntal texture, and instrumental color. Argues that the quartet freed him from his temporary seduction by the neoclassical Stravinsky and from his own past as well.

684. Agárdi, Péter. "Révai József Bartók Béláról, Kiadatlan levelek" [József Révai on Béla Bartók. Unpublished letters]. *Kritika* (January 1972): 13. HB1.244

Provides previously unpublished correspondence (dating from 1955) between the communist politician József Révai and the Hungarian composer András Mihály, who view Bartók's constructivistic music as pessimistic.

685. Antokoletz, Elliott. "Bartók's *Bluebeard:* The Sources of Its 'Modernism.'" *College Music Symposium* 30/1 (Spring 1990): 75-95. ISSN 0069-5696 780.5 C686

Discusses the historical sources of the opera's modernistic musical language, which is based on a radical departure from the basic premises of the traditional tonal system. Also addresses aspects of its reception history, including early rejection due to the conservative tastes of the Hungarian public and its pioneering position as the first genuinely Hungarian opera. Also provides a brief overview of its subsequent performances. Explores its historical, aesthetic, and musical connections with Debussy's symbolist opera, *Pelléas et Mélisande,* its fusion of impressionist musical techniques with the modal structures of Hungarian folk music, transformation of the latter into more abstract, symmetrical (e.g., whole-tone) pitch relations, and the interaction of discrete pitch collections as the basis for symbolic representation. In-depth analysis focuses primarily on the new musical language itself, its relation to the larger structure and design of the scenes, and how Bartók exploited the musical principles to reflect the new dramatic symbolism that began to emerge in literature in the late nineteenth century. Contains music examples, diagram.

686. Arthuys, Philippe. "Béla Bartók, expression du phénomène contemporain" [Béla Bartók, expression of a contemporary phenomenon]. *La revue musicale* 224 (1955): 117-125. 780.5 R328 ISSN 0035-3736

Attempts to resolve certain philosophical issues regarding Bartók's position as a contemporary phenomenon: "Is he renovator or innovator, well bred or common, or better yet . . .?" Speaks of the ambiguities and paradoxes in trying to determine or define this master in the context of the contemporary idea.

687. Banks, Paul. "Images of the Self: 'Duke Bluebeard's Castle.'" In: *The Stage Works of Béla Bartók,* ed. Nicholas John. Sponsor: Martini. *Operaguide* 44. New York: Riverrun; London: Calder, 1991. pp. 7-12. ISBN 0-7145-4194-X ML410 B26 S78

Refers to the reception of the opera and its libretto by Hungarian critics at the first performance on May 24, 1918, in which Bartók's music was praised while the symbolist libretto by Béla Balázs was rejected. Discusses the issue of personal identity that lies below the surface of the opera, not only in connection with the characters but with the librettist himself in his sense of isolation from his cultural background. States that this feeling is embodied in Bartók's operatic setting based on a libretto that portrays a "bleak, fatalistic vision of a world in which significant relationships between men and women are impossible." Balázs's new dramatic idiom represents a reaction against realism, rather looking inward to "the silent visionlike images of the self." Also, discusses relations between the dramatic structure of the libretto and Bartók's musical setting, stating that Bartók was primarily concerned with characterization and organic development, the librettist with the large-scale arch structure. States that Balázs and Bartók both achieved the fusion of the archaic and the modern. Several brief analytical interspersions identify musical features with dramatic processes.

688. Batta, András. "Gemeinsames Nietzsche-Symbol bei Bartók und bei R. Strauss" [Common Nietzsche symbols in Bartók and R. Strauss]. *Studia musicologica* 24/3-4 (1982): 275-282. 781.05 St92 ISSN 0039-3266

States that the Straussian enchantment from Nietzsche's delirium is strengthened in the aesthetic view of life of the young Bartók. Thus, the result is complete and consistent, since this dual experience based on common symbols is outwardly preserved in Bartók's dramatic conception in durable and perceptible form. Discusses the influence of Strauss's music (e.g., *Also sprach Zarathustra*) on the musical language of Bartók.

689. Blom, Eric. "The String Quartets of Béla Bartók." *Musical Opinion* 45 (May 1922): 696-697. 780.5 M974 Reprinted in Eric Blom. *Stepchildren of Music* (London: G.T. Foulis, 1925), pp. 239-246. 780.4 B622S

Points to the originality of Bartók's first two string quartets but considers the harmonic idiom agitating and less accessible than that of his piano music.

690. Bónis, Ferenc. "*The Miraculous Mandarin:* The Birth and Vicissitudes of a Masterpiece." In: *The Stage Works of Béla Bartók,* ed. Nicholas John. Sponsor: Martini. *Operaguide* 44. New York: Riverrun; London: Calder, 1991. pp. 81-93. ISBN 0-7145-4194-X ML410 B26 S78

Refers to the mystery surrounding the conception of the work and the confusion revealed by recent scholarly research on the data and interpretation. Points to contradictions between statements by Elza Galafrés (wife of Ernő Dohnányi) regarding musical correspondence to geographical setting and the actual musical evidence. By means of substantial primary-source documentation, presents historical background to Menyhért Lengyel's libretto and Bartók's circumstances surrounding his musical setting of the pantomime. Outlines the musico-dramatic structure and the plot and provides a brief analysis of the score, including reference to musical symbols and the dramatic meaning underlying both thematic interconnections and harmonic and pentatonic associations. Contains music examples, illustrations.

691. ----------. *"The Wooden Prince:* A Tale for Adults." In: *The Stage Works of Béla Bartók,* ed. Nicholas John. Sponsor: Martini. *Operaguide* 44. New York: Riverrun; London: Calder, 1991. pp. 61-67.   ISBN 0-7145-4194-X   ML410 B26 S78

Explores the means by which Bartók's three stage works are closely bound together in spite of their differences, referring to Kodály's statement that "the strength of the way the music is constructed is even more evident if we listen to *The Wooden Prince* after *Duke Bluebeard's Castle.* " Points out that all three stage works (including *The Miraculous Mandarin)* explore the mysteries of the relationship between men and women. Provides information on the origins of *The Wooden Prince* and gives some historical background on the circumstances surrounding its composition. Includes reference to Balázs's intentions to please Bartók and gives some chronology regarding the compositional process (sketches and orchestration), rehearsals, and performance (as documented by comments from Bartók and Balázs). Summarizes the plot and outlines the basic musical themes of the ballet, with explanations of their dramatic associations. Contains illustrations, music examples.

692. Brelet, Gisèle. "L'esthétique de Béla Bartók." *La revue musicale* 224 (1955): 21-39.   780.5 R328   ISSN 0035-3736

Emphasizes the importance of folk music as the basis of Bartók's aesthetics, which also developed from such divergent sources as the music of Beethoven, Liszt, Brahms, and others. States that while folklorism is not new, Bartók's approach to it contrasts with its usage in preceding eras. Discusses various aspects of folk music (forms, rhythms, melodic structure, etc.) and their absorption in works of Bartók. States that Bartók's originality, in terms of form, is the fruit of evolution rather than revolution. Also in Hungarian, in *Új zenei szemle* (1955).

693. Breuer, János. "Adorno und die ungarische Musik" [Adorno and Hungarian music]. *Zeitschrift für Musiktheorie* 5/2 (1974): 23-28. ML5 Z155

   Discusses Adorno's change of opinion of Bartók's music, based on documentation in *Die Musik,* in which he became more critical in his later writings. States that this new appraisal had its source in cultural and social differences between Germany and Hungary.

694. ----------. "Népzene és modern zene. Adorno és a magyar zene" [Folk music and modern music. Adorno and Hungarian music]. *Világosság* 14/7 (July 1973): 418-424. HA1.287

   Refers to Adorno as the originator of the idea that Bartók's music is distinctly divided into folk music and "modern" music, a view no longer held in Hungary. Also discusses other Hungarian composers, including the unfortunate reference to Kodály's music as the result of fascism.

695. Browne, Arthur G. "Béla Bartók." *Music and Letters* 12/1 (1931): 35-45. 780.5 M92 ISSN 0027-4224

   Discusses Bartók's economy of means and force of his developmental power. In this way his use of development is unique in "ultra-modern" music. As antithesis to Stravinsky, Hindemith, Honegger, etc., he is in line of descent from Beethoven and Brahms. Refers to Bartók's general technical and stylistic features in this context of individual approach, in which he is free to adapt his different genres according to the musical matter at hand.

696. Bukovin, A. "Cherty stilya" [Style characteristics]. *Sovetskaya muzyka* 31/12 (December 1967): 117-128. ISSN 0038-5085

   In this issue dealing with a study of Bartók's heritage, the author discusses analyses by Roswitha Traimer of Bartók's quartets (see item no. 662) and the theories of Ernő Lendvai to demonstrate their efforts in defining Bartók's stylistic characteristics. The author infers that the organic connections of Bartók's music with Hungarian folk sources are more essential to the characteristics of his style than the influence of European art music.

697. Calvocoressi, Michel-Dimitri. "Bartók and His Piano Concertos." *Listener* 10 (November 8, 1933): 714.

   Discusses the style of Bartók's first two piano concertos. Deals with the approach to texture based on the relation of piano and orchestra, in which solo and orchestra are well integrated.

698. ----------. "Bluebeard's Castle." *Radio Times* 55 (April 9, 1937): 12.

Points to the organic and integrated musico-dramatic whole, which results from the close correspondences and interconnections between music and libretto.

699. ----------. "More About Bartók and Kodály." *Monthly Musical Record* 52 (August 1922): 181-183.　780.5 M767

Provides a concise stylistic evaluation of the music of Bartók and Kodály.

700. Carner, Mosco. "Bartók's Viola Concerto." *Musical Times* 91 (August 1950): 301-303.　780.5 M98　ISSN 0027-4666

Author discusses the concerto in preparation for performance of the work in England. First gives history of its composition as a work that is not pure Bartók but reconstructed and completed by Tibor Serly. Provides some analytic comments to demonstrate its greater emotional expression, so unusual for Bartók's more marked intellectual bent.

701. ----------. "Béla Bartók." *The New Oxford History of Music, Vol. X: The Modern Age 1890-1960*. London: The Oxford University Press, 1974, pp. 274-299.　ML160 N44

Presents a detailed historical and analytical survey of Bartók's major works in terms of formal features, style, rhythm, and texture, etc. Begins with an in-depth discussion of folk-music characteristics (form, syllabic structure, rhythm, and modal and pentatonic bases) that Bartók uncovered in his investigations since 1905. Provides many examples of folk tunes in both the "old" and "new" Hungarian folk styles as well as those of the "mixed" type. States that in Bartók's total achievement, "he succeeded in an organic fusion of Western art-music with Eastern folk music, bringing all the technical resources of the West to bear upon his native material." Also refers to earlier art-music sources in Liszt, Brahms and Bach.

702. Chalupka, Lubomír. "Slácikové kvartetá Bélu Bartóka" [String quartets of Béla Bartók]. *Slovenská hudba* 12/1 (January1968): 18-22.　H50.470

Provides a concise discussion of certain fundamental aesthetic and stylistic issues encountered in Bartók's string quartets.

703. Chapman, Ernest. "Béla Bartók; An Estimate and Appreciation." *Tempo* 13 (December 1945): 2-6.　780.5 T249　ISSN 0040-2982

Evaluation of Bartók's musical aesthetics, in which the author criticizes the works of his middle period (between 1921 and 1931) for their dearth of expressiveness, while the later works such as the

Sixth String Quartet and *Concerto for Orchestra* are praised as "a triumphant assertion of faith." Believes that Bartók's music will become increasingly understood and appreciated.

704. Citron, Pierre. *Bartók.* Collection 'Solfège.' Paris: Les Éditions du Seuil, 1963. 185p.   ML410.B29 C5

Provides an overview of Bartók's music based on somewhat subjective evaluations of the works. Also views Bartók's music in a broader contemporary context. Contains bibliography, discography. Also in Japanese translation by Masakuni Kitazawa and Miyoko Hachimura. Tokyo: Hakusui-sha, 1969. 262p.

705. Clyne, Anthony. "Béla Bartók and Magyar Music." *Bookman* 62 (June 1922): 145-146.

Contrasts Bartók's stylistic approach with what the author considers the aggressiveness found in many contemporary compositions.

706. Danchenka, Gary. "Diatonic Pitch-Class Sets in Bartók's Night Music." *Indiana Theory Review* 8/1 (Spring 1987): 15-55. MT6 1645   ISSN 0271-8055

According to the author, *RILM Abstracts* No. 7340 (1987), "*Night Music* refers to those contexts, from brief passages to complete works, in which Bartók conveys the sounds of nature at night. Various theories on the night music's origin, and a succession of musical excerpts regarded collectively to be generally emblematic of the style are offered. Those events that relate through similarity of configuration for the purpose of determining the most frequently recurring diatonic pitch-class sets out of which these configurations are generated are excerpted." Contains music examples, list of works, charts, tables.

707. Dawson, George Clarence. "Bartók's Development as Orchestrator." Ph.D. diss. University of Southern California, 1970. 2 vols. 397p., 523p.

As summarized by the author, *RILM Abstracts* No. 709 (1970), the dissertation provides "an historical and analytical study of the development of Bartók's orchestration (1903-45) in 31 works. His historical position, style periods and styles, influences, and the various instrumentations are reviewed. The orchestration of each of his four major style periods is analyzed for treatment of unisons, homophonic and contrapuntal textures, part-writing, tuttis, complex textures, and instrumental groupings. A chart gives the instrumentation of every published orchestral work. All important trends of the first two decades of the century influenced Bartók: Strauss, Impressionism, and neo-Classicism as well as folk instrumental practices. An important contribution to the modern orchestra is his use of the percussion as a complete self-contained choir of instruments. This figures prominently in his unique 'night music,' with sounds of nature produced by standard orchestral instruments. Bartók's very progressive compositional techniques, which are not serial, are wedded to conservative yet most imaginative orchestration practices."

708. Dent, Edward Joseph. "Béla Bartók." *Nation and Athenaeum* 31/1 (April 1, 1922): 30 and 32.   052 N21 V31

Refers to Bartók's piano works as most representative of his style and points to the significance of Bartók's use of bitonality within the broader context of twentieth-century music.

709. Detelbach, Hans von. *Breviarium musicae*. Graz: Stiasny, 1967. 479p.

In German. This collection of writings on composers from Bach through the twentieth century includes a study of Bartók's musical style, forms, and aesthetics. Contains illustrations.

710. Dille, Denijs. "Bartókov hudobný prejav a folklór" [Bartók's musical language and folklore]. *Slovenská hudba* 12/5 (June 1968): 216-221.   H50.470

Explores Bartók's aesthetics and style as influenced by folk music and the evolution of his musical language.

711. Dinkel, Philippe. "La tentation atonale de Béla Bartók: Les études op. 18 et les Improvisations op. 20 pour piano (1918-1920)" [Béla Bartók's attraction to atonality: The *Etudes* Op. 18 and the *Improvisations on Hungarian Peasant Songs* Op. 20 for Piano (1918-1920)]. *Revue musicale de Suisse romande* 36/3 (September 1983): 119-126.   780.5 R3281

According to the author, *RILM Abstracts* No. 6038 (1984), "The works of Bartók before 1920 followed two paths: one from the Classic-Romantic German tradition, the other from East European folk music. These merged by means of a third influence: Schoenberg. Bartók's études op. 18 are the extreme evolutionary point in the direction of free atonality, while, in the *Improvisations,* the popular melodies serve as a type of harmonic barrier, inhibiting a freer tonality and determining a classical form that is reflected as well as in his later works." Contains music examples, bibliography.

712. Doflein, Erich. "Herzog Blaubarts Burg" [*Duke Bluebeard's Castle*]. *Neue Zeitschrift für Musik* 12 (1961): 511-514.   ML5 N315 780.5 Z37   ISSN 0170-8791

Discusses Bartók's opera fifty years after it was composed, concentrating on the history of its origin, thematic contents, symbolism, musical contents, and the importance of the work as a whole.

713. Eisikovits, Max. "Contribuţii la geneza unor elemente de stil ale creaţiei lui Béla Bartók" [The genesis of some stylistic elements in Béla Bartók's work]. *Muzica* (Romania) 25/9-10 (September-October 1975): 20-27, 19-27.   ISSN 0580-3713

Reveals the influence of Romanian folk sources on Bartók's music, describing their manifestations in the melodic and harmonic structure of his compositions and how this folk idiom contributed to the development of his personal style.

714. Eller, Rudolf. "Über Gestalt und Funktion des Themas bei Bartók" [Regarding the form and function of the theme in the works of Bartók]. *Festschrift für Ernst Hermann Meyer zum sechzigsten Geburtstag.* Leipzig: DVfM, 1973, pp. 281-285.   ML55 M44 K5

Points to the thematic source, which undergoes constant transformation and variation, as the basis of Bartók's personality and aesthetics. Discusses thematic structure and function and contrasts the composer's own personal treatment with traditional usage.

715. Fine, Irving G. "Bartók's New Koussevitzky Number." *Modern Music* 22/2 (January-February 1945): 115-117.   780.5 M72

This composer gives a brief statement regarding the first performance of Bartók's *Concerto for Orchestra,* with a somewhat subjective description of its themes and orchestration.

716. Finger, Hildegard. "Béla Bartók: *Konzert für Orchester*" [Concerto for orchestra]. *Werkanalyse in Beispielen* [Music analysis in examples], ed. Siegmund Helms and Helmuth Hopf. Regensburg: Gustav Bosse Verlag, 1986. pp. 277-296.   ISBN 3 7649 2276 1

Provides descriptive analyses of the five movements in terms of traditional sonata and ABA forms, based on motivic development, thematic shape, instrumental timbre, and interval priority. Contrasts the movements according to different sonic qualities, in which diatonic-modal and whole-tone material is combined in a context ranging from triads to clusters. Refers to the composer's own commentary as the basis for analysis and further understanding. States that Bartók's program note for the first performance in

Boston brings the listener into the general mood of the work. It also reveals how Bartók conceived of the work as a concerto. Furthermore, points out that while Bartók used Italian headings for the movements, they were not conceived according to a unified aesthetic but have cosmopolitan significance. Includes some reference to critical reception of the work.

717. Fischer, John Frederic. "Cyclic Procedures in the String Quartet from Beethoven to Bartók." Ph.D. diss. The University of Iowa, 1981. 235p.

Includes a discussion of the importance in Bartók's quartets of the cyclic use of themes, which is demonstrated in connection with the large-scale organization of the movements. Deals with the continuous one-movement plan of the *Third Quartet,* the five-movement arch-form constructions of the *Fourth* and *Fifth Quartets* (in which the symmetrical formal relations between corresponding movements rely on thematic connections), and the motto principle that underlies the four movements of the *Sixth Quartet.*

718. Fladt, Hartmut. "Zur Problematik traditioneller Formtypen in der Musik des frühen zwanzigsten Jahrhunderts. Dargestellt an Sonatensätzen in den Streichquartetten Béla Bartóks" [Concerning the ambiguity of traditional formal types in the music of the early twentieth century. Illustrated with sonata movements in the string quartets of Béla Bartók]. Ph.D. diss. Technische Universität Berlin, 1973. Published in Berliner musikwissenschaftliche Arbeiten 6. Munich: Katzbichler, 1974. 182p.

According to the author, in *RILM Abstracts* No. 930 (1976), "axioms of recent theory of form show justifiable skepticism toward preconceived schemas and structural principles: form at any given time unfolds specifically out of the musical events. This postulate, however, fails to recognize that at least from Beethoven to Eisler pre-existing formulas were repeatedly subjected to elements of ambiguity, that schemas were not filled; rather, they served as the basis for meaningful processes that grew out of the specific content. If Bartók or Schönberg reverted to traditional formal types, even though they did away with various fundamentals (such as major-minor tonality), there resulted a conscious onward propulsion--a surmounting of norms, not blind acceptance of them. If and how sonata-form principles were taken over in the string quartet, abandoned, or reactivated depended on concrete historical, social, ideological, and subjective phases of the composer's development." Summary of *RILM* No. 930 (1976) in *Musikforschung* 28/4 (1975): 445-446. See the review of the dissertation by Klaus Stahmer, in *Musikforschung* 30/3 (1977): 368-369.

719. French, Gilbert G. "Continuity and Discontinuity in Bartók's Concerto for Orchestra." *The Music Review* 28/1-2 (February, May 1967): 122-134.   780.5 M9733   ISSN 0027-4445

Deals with a psychological orientation to the analysis of the work, based on the dynamic, organic process of the form rather than the mechanical details of descriptive analysis. Feels that the work is structurally weak according to this approach.

720. Frigyesi, Judit. *The Birth of Hungarian Modernism: Béla Bartók and Turn of the Century Budapest.* Berkeley and Los Angeles: University of California Press, forthcoming. ca. 400p.

Discusses the role of Hungarian culture in the development of European modern intellectual and artistic currents, provides a broad perspective of European cultural issues in order to elucidate the circumstances surrounding the Hungarian intellectual milieu at the turn of the century, and explores Bartók's aesthetics as an outgrowth of these circumstances. States that an understanding of Hungarian modernism and the centrality of Bartók's music to that development relies on a multitude of interactive issues that transcend any isolated view of the composer's life and work. Opposes the notion that Bartók's genius emerged from a culture that is at best peripheral and inferior to those of Western Europe, pointing out that the sources of Hungarian modernism are similar to those of Viennese modernism. Focuses on the "organicist theory" of art, exploring its broad connections to both Romanticism and the modernist aesthetics of the Vienna Schoenberg circle as well as its relevance to Hungarian modernism and Bartók's folklorism; addresses the anti-nationalist significance of "organicist folklorism." Substantiates the historical and aesthetic arguments by documenting Bartók's philosophical inclinations and stylistic development during the early years of the century. Provides information on Bartók's connections with the inner circles of Hungarian intellectuals, exploring the relation of Bartók's aesthetics to the poetry of such Hungarian figures as Endre Ady. Several key musical works of Bartók are studied primarily to reflect modernist Hungarian thought rather than to explain the "system" of Bartók's modern musical style per se.

721. ----------. "The *Verbunkos* and Bartók's Modern Style: The Case of *Bluebeard's Castle.*" *Bartók in Retrospect,* ed. Elliott Antokoletz, Victoria Fischer, and Benjamin Suchoff. Projected publication of two 1995 conference proceedings.

Points to the close connection of the *Bluebeard* music with Hungarian Romantic symphonic style rather than the old folk-song style claimed by Bartók as his inspiration. Then addresses the question as to how the Hungarian instrumental tradition could function as the modernist breakthrough for Bartók and Hungarian music. Points to the apparent contradiction between Bartók's written statements and his compositions regarding his turn against Hungarian instrumental styles, especially Gypsy music. Deals with the relation of "real" folk music and "Gypsy" music, placing the issue in the context of Bartók's broader musical environment. Explores "traditional Hungarian instrumental musics and their 'Hungarianness,'" "the technique of *verbunkos*/Gypsy improvisation and Bartók's system of rhythmic variation," and "the development of *verbunkos*-like rhythmic variation as a source of Bartók's modern style in *Bluebeard's Castle*." Contains music examples.

722. Gergely, Jean. "Les choeurs à cappella de Béla Bartók" [The a cappella choruses of Bartók]. *La revue musicale* (1955): 127-169. 780.5 R328   ISSN 0035-3736

   Speaks of the paradox of Bartók as a vocal composer, since he is considered by most musicians to be essentially an instrumental composer, while Kodály is vocally oriented. Yet it is necessary to study these choral works of Bartók to penetrate into his art. Then presents a thorough thematic and textual catalogue and encyclopedic description of the choral works.

723. Gillies, Malcolm. "Dance Suite." *The Bartók Companion,* ed. Malcolm Gillies. London: Faber and Faber, 1993; Portland, Oregon: Amadeus Press (an imprint of Timber Press, Inc.), 1994. pp. 487-497. ISBN 0-931340-74-8 (HB)   ISBN 0-931340-75-6 (PB) ML410 B26 B28

   Presents a concise history of the political and geographical changes that led to an extreme post-war Hungarian nationalism and chauvinism in the early 1920s. In this context, refers to the commission by the new conservative municipal authorities in 1923 of Dohnányi, Kodály, and Bartók, which was surprising in view of the association of these three composers with the former Communist government and especially Bartók's expanded research into Romanian and Slovak folk music. From this commission came Bartók's orchestral *Dance Suite,* a work which continued to reveal Bartók's humanistic inclinations toward cultural pluralism based on the synthesis of divergent folk-music styles. Then provides a structural analysis, focusing on tonal, modal, and other pitch relations, instrumental usage, and stylistic derivations from the different folk-music sources. Places discussion of the work within a broader historical context that includes reference to its performance and audience reception as well as Bartók's personal circumstances.

724. ----------. "Portraits, Pictures and Pieces." *The Bartók Companion,* ed. Malcolm Gillies. London: Faber and Faber, 1993; Portland,

Oregon: Amadeus Press (an imprint of Timber Press, Inc.), 1994. pp.
477-486. ISBN 0-931340-74-8 (HB) ISBN 0-931340-75-6 (PB)
ML410 B26 B28

Discusses Bartók's efforts to synthesize divergent stylistic
strands in his pre-war orchestral works, the *Two Pictures* Op. 10
(1910) and *Four Orchestral Pieces* Op. 12 (1912), at a time when he
had already made substantial investigations into Hungarian, Slovak,
and Romanian folk music and had been studying Debussy's music
thoroughly since 1907. However, states that these two works, unlike
his *Bluebeard* opera (1911), are less successful in this regard. Then,
discusses the genesis of the *Two Portraits* Op. 5 (1911) as derived
from the *Violin Concerto* (1907-1908), which was inspired by his
love for the violinist Stefi Geyer, and also points to their special
programmatic and musical connections with the last of the
Bagatelles Op. 6 (1908). Summarizes some of the basic differences
between the *Portraits* and their original forms, showing instrumental
changes intended to heighten the sense of the grotesque, which
resembles certain passages of Strauss and Berlioz. Ensuing
discussion of the three Bartók works explores structural, motivic,
tonal, harmonic/melodic, orchestrational, and other parameters, and
points to their stylistic influences and/or associations with works of
other composers, including Debussy, Stravinsky, and Schoenberg.
Places this study within the broader context of Bartók's own
development according to different chronological frames.

725. ----------. "Two Orchestral Suites." *The Bartók Companion,* ed.
Malcolm Gillies. London: Faber and Faber, 1993; Portland, Oregon:
Amadeus Press (an imprint of Timber Press, Inc.), 1994. pp. 454-
467. ISBN 0-931340-74-8 (HB) ISBN 0-931340-75-6 (PB)
ML410 B26 B28

Refers to the diversity of stylistic characteristics in the two
orchestral *Suites* Op. 3 (1905) and Op. 4 (1905-1907) so common to
Bartók's works since 1902. Points to the infusion into their
essentially Brahmsian style of aspects from Strauss, Liszt,
Dohnányi, Romantic Hungarian patriotic composers (Liszt,
Mosonyi, and Erkel), *verbunkos* and *csárdás* dances, popular and
gypsy elements. The two suites, together with his other orchestral
works between Op. 1 and Op. 5, were considered by Bartók in 1918
to be of no real significance, but changed his opinion about the
Second Suite later. Discusses Bartók's approach to form,
thematic/motivic connections, orchestration, rhythm and tempo.
Also, points to the tendency in these works toward a new
conception of intervallic "consonance" and "dissonance," as in the
more consonant conception of the minor-seventh chord, and an
increasing prominence in his use of interval cycles. Analysis points
to certain structural deficiencies that concerned Bartók in the later
revisions of these works, and then focuses on tonal and thematic

construction. Provides some reference to the performance and reception of these works.

726. Gombosi, Otto. "Béla Bartók: Third Piano Concerto." *Music Library Association Notes* 4/4 (September 1947): 479-480.　　780.6 M971m ISSN 0027-4380

Review of this work which gives brief history of the composition in the context of Bartók's late personal circumstances, outlines some basic stylistic features, and gives opinions about the greatness of the work as a manifestation of Bartók's personality and career.

727. Grant, Julian. "A Foot in Bluebeard's Door." In: *The Stage Works of Béla Bartók,* ed. Nicholas John. Sponsor: Martini. *Operaguide* 44. New York: Riverrun; London: Calder, 1991. pp. 25-34. ISBN 0-7145-4194-X　　ML410 B26 S78

Mentions the slow development of musical nationalism in Hungary in the nineteenth century and that the Hungarian music that spread over Europe was based on a romanticized Gypsy music rather than the authentic folk music that Bartók and Kodály were to collect later. States that nationalism was only one of the sources for *Duke Bluebeard's Castle,* the opera representing a synthesis of the various influences that he had absorbed thus far. Provides some historical data on Bartók's absorption and transformation of both art-music (Richard Strauss and Debussy) and folk-music sources into a personal idiom based on increasing technical mastery in the works of the period. Discusses the common expressive intentions of the librettist (Béla Balázs) and the composer but asserts that the musical setting does not focus on the dramatic formal structure of the seven doors but rather on the psychological development of the two characters. Demonstrates that the libretto outlines an arch form, which is reflected in the tonal scheme of the music. Also points to the lack of Wagnerian leitmotifs, stating that Bartók's approach to motivic transformation is derived rather from Liszt. Then provides a descriptive survey of the musico-dramatic events of the opera, including references to color projection, tonality, modality, harmony, and instrumentation in connection with dramatic events. Expresses regret that the initial rejection of *Bluebeard* and the *Mandarin* discouraged a "potentially great opera composer" from contributing further to the stage.

728. Gray, Cecil. "Béla Bartók." *Sackbut* 1/7 (November 1920): 301-312. Reprinted in Cecil Gray. *A Survey of Contemporary Music.* London: Oxford University Press, 1924. pp. 194-207; second edition, 1927.　　780.904 G791S

Points to the historical importance of Bartók's *First String Quartet* and *Four Dirges* for piano, both of which the author considers landmark works in their respective genres. Includes a list of Bartók's compositions.

729. Gray, Steven Earl. "Tempo Indication in the Piano Music of Béla Bartók: Notation and Performance." D.M.A. diss. Stanford University, 1990. 67p.   DA9024307

According to the author, *RILM Abstracts* No. 8371 (1990), "Recordings of Bartók's piano works with the composer as pianist were made between 1912 and 1945 and are commercially available as the *Bartók record archive* collection (Hungaroton 12334/8). In his general performance style, music that is directly related to a folk tradition is most likely to vary from the notated tempo, while the movements that show the least deviation are those that are shorter and simpler in tempo design. Also, music of a narrative character, which the composer termed *parlando-rubato*, requires the notation to be interpreted through the rhythmic inflections of speech, whereas music related to bodily motion (dancing or marching) requires a stricter regulation of the pulse ("tempo-giusto").

730. Grey, Michael. "Bartók's 'Cantata Profana.'" *Radio Times* 43 (May 18, 1934): 518.

Points to the special position of Bartók's *Cantata Profana* within the broader spectrum of choral literature in general.

731. Groth, Clause Robert, Jr. "A Study of the Technical and Interpretative Problems Inherent in Bartók's Violin Sonatas." D.M.A. treatise. University of Oregon, 1971. 147p. ML410.B26 G76

Intended mainly as a guide for the performer. Discusses the style of these sonatas based on melodic, harmonic, rhythmic, and textural analysis, provides a detailed discussion of form, and deals with problems related to performance, which includes both technical and interpretative issues. Contains illustrations, music, bibliography.

732. Guerry, Jack Edwin. "Bartók's Concertos for Solo Piano: A Stylistic and Formal Analysis." Ph.D. diss. Michigan State University, 1964. 216p.

Explores the history of their composition, including various reactions to them, evaluates their relative status in the composer's output, and provides discussions of their individual stylistic characteristics as well as how they reflect the general evolution of Bartók's style.

733. Hamvas, Béla. *Bartók. Mousseion. A Magyar Esztétikai Társaság Évkönyve* [Yearbook of the Hungarian Aesthetics Society] (1946): 23-27.

   Attack on Bartók by this Hungarian critic, who states, from the point of view of abstract art, that Bartók retreated from the more progressive approach by Stravinsky, Picasso, and Joyce to the dissolution of classical form.

734. Händel, Günter. "Dynamik und Energetik in der Klangwelt von Rondo I und Improvisation II" [Dynamics and energetics in the sound world of *Rondo I* and *Improvisation II*]. *Studia musicologica* 24/3-4 (1982): 339-350.   781.05 St92   ISSN 0039-3266

   Deals with concepts of form in these two works based on analysis of the various parameters (tonal and harmonic organization, dynamics, rhythm, etc.) and their associations. Refers to historical sources in Bach, Beethoven, Debussy, and others regarding these principles.

735. Haraszti, Emil. "La musique de chambre de Béla Bartók." *La revue musicale* 107 (August-September 1930): 114-125.   780.5 R328 ISSN 0035-3736

   States that Bartók's evolution is influenced by all the main trends of the twentieth century. In his work, we discover all the problems from Debussy to Schoenberg. Outlines the various phases of Bartók's development, with reference to the works of each period. Based on the importance of Bartók's chamber music in terms of the sources of his language and style development, various chamber works (including his sonatas for violin and piano and his first four string quartets) are given floridly descriptive analyses in terms of general form, with references to characteristics of themes, rhythm, texture and general style features.

736. Heath, Mary Joanne Renner. "A Comparative Analysis of Dukas's *Ariane et Barbe-bleu* and Bartók's *Duke Bluebeard's Castle.*" Ph.D. diss., Musicology. University of Rochester, Eastman School of Music, 1988. 219p.   DA 8814817

   Justifies a comparative analysis of these two operas--that by Dukas (1907) a setting of Maeterlinck's play *Ariane et Barbe-bleu,* that by Bartók (1911) a setting of Béla Balázs's *Kékszakállú herceg vára,* inspired by Maeterlinck--on the basis of their chronological proximity, common influence of Debussy, and composition of both operas during a period in which the symbolist movement was prominent in Europe.

737. Henry, Leigh. "Béla Bartók." *Chesterian* 22 (new series) (April 1922): 161-167.   780.5 C426

   English composer and music critic indicates that in his stylistic evolution, Bartók became increasingly removed from the conscious influence of the folk sources. This observation is entirely accurate considering the highly original developments of Bartók's compositional style at the time this article was published in the early 1920s.

738. ----------. "Contemporaries--Béla Bartók." *Musical Opinion* 44 (October 1920): 53-54.   ISSN 0027-4623

   English composer and music critic discusses several of Bartók's early piano pieces, including the *Two Elegies, Fourteen Bagatelles, Ten Easy Pieces,* and *For Children.*

739. Herbage, Julian. "Bartók's Violin Concerto." *The Music Review* 6/2 (May 1945): 85-88.   780.5 M9733   ISSN 0027-4445

   States that "musical cross-breeding" is basic to Bartók's creative work, giving reference to Bartók's own views regarding racial purity or impurity in folk music. After a brief outline of his absorption of elements from various twentieth-century musical sources, an analysis of the *Violin Concerto* is given to demonstrate Bartók's constant artistic process at his full maturity.

740. Horn, Herbert Alvin. "Idiomatic Writing of the Piano Music of Béla Bartók." D.M.A. treatise. University of Southern California, 1963. xv, 221p.   ML410.B26 H6 1978

   Explores the sources, innovations, and applications of Bartók's piano idiom. Deals with the idiomatic aspects of the piano music in two general categories: absorption and transformation of traditional pianistic materials and idioms and the creation of new idioms based on Bartók's experience and kinesthetic sensitivity as a pianist. Also deals with specific aspects of piano technique, including scales, arpeggios, chords, double notes, octaves, repeated notes, and ornamentation. Provides some reference to the source of these innovations in the development of Bartók's approach to the keyboard. Contains illustrations, music, bibliography.

741. Howat, Roy. "Debussy, Bartók et les formes de la nature" [Debussy, Bartók and the forms of nature]. *Revue musicale de Suisse romande* 3 (1986): 128-141.   780.5 R3281

   Demonstrates the use of Golden Section proportions in Debussy's *Spleen* and *Images* and discusses Debussy's influence on Bartók, referring to Ernő Lendvai's application of these principles to

Bartók's *Music for Strings, Percussion and Celesta.* Deals with the question of the degree of consciousness on the part of the composers regarding their use of these proportions. Also published in *Nombre d'or et musique* (Frankfurt am Main: Peter Lang, 1988): 125-138, and in Hungarian as "Debussy, Bartók és a természeti formák," in *Spirál a tudományban és a művészétben* [The spiral in science and art] (Budapest: INTART, 1988): 84-107.

742. Hundt, Theodor. "Bartóks Satztechnik in den Klavierwerken" [Bartók's technique of composition in the piano works]. Ph.D. diss. University of Köln, 1971. 278p.   ISBN-376492067
ML410.B26 H85   786.1'6924

Discusses the shift in Bartók's music from the late Romantic style of his early piano works to a more economical approach due to the influence of his Balkan folk-music research. Deals with Bartók's development from traditional harmonic settings of the folk melodies to a more abstract and personal harmonic idiom in more contrapuntal textures and progressive forms in the middle period. States that these new piano works are based on a more percussive style, strong rhythmic definition, asymmetrical motives, and cacophonous effects as well as polymodality, bitonality, chromaticism, dissonance, and new types of intervallic chordal construction, etc. The *Mikrokosmos,* as representative of the late style, shows further developments. Contains music, bibliography. Published in *Kölner Beitrage zur Musikforschung* 63. Regensburg: Gustav Bosse, 1971. See the review by Gunter Weiss-Aigner, in *Musikforschung* 27/4 (1974): 492-493.

743. Hunkemöller, Jürgen. "Bartóks Urteil über den Jazz" [Bartók's judgment of jazz]. *Die Musikforschung* 38/1 (January-March 1985): 27-36.   780.5 M9921   ISSN 0027-4801

Investigates relationships between Bartók and jazz. Poses a set of questions and provides documentary evidence regarding Bartók's knowledge, recognition, and opinion of jazz. Addresses the kind of jazz Bartók knew, in what circumstances and where he encountered it, and which interpretational and compositional reflexes drew him to it. Searches for evidence in Bartók's personal collections of recordings, books, and scores, and his piano performances (of jazz-influenced works by Debussy, Ravel, and Stravinsky), compositions, and attendance of concerts. Provides primary-source documentation, including Bartók's own statements on the phenomenon of jazz and its influences on his compositions, and gives accounts by his relatives, students, and friends. Points to jazz features in *Contrasts* (stemming from his collaboration with swing-clarinetist Benny Goodman), several *Mikrokosmos* pieces, and *Concerto for Orchestra* (fugato theme in the finale suggesting Gershwin). Also, documents Bartók's own comparison of jazz (as foreign musical language) and Hungarian folk music (as native musical language).

744. ----------. "Choral-Kompositionen von Béla Bartók" [Choral compositions of Béla Bartók]. *Studien zur Musikgeschichte. Eine Festschrift für Ludwig Finscher*, hg. von Annegrit Laubenthal. Kassel usw.: Bärenreiter Verlag, 1995, pp. 697-707. ISBN 3-7618-1222-1

Explores the meaning of "chorale" in Bartók's compositions. States that to talk about chorale composition in Bartók's music can be surprising and perhaps irritating. For the author, chorale style in Bartók is not convincing in general but believes that at least *Mikrokosmos* No. 35, which contains the composer's own "Chorale" indication, can be titled thus. People in Hungary today are convinced that Bartók's indication refers to a broader "chorale"-complex. To this "chorale"-complex belong three primary works, which Bartók himself indicated: *Concerto for Orchestra* (Mov. 2), *Piano Concerto No. 3* (Mov. 2), and *Mikrokosmos* (No. 35). States that these examples can be supported by other pieces, which create the illusion of the "chorale"-complex, for instance, both slow movements (2 and 4) of the *Fifth String Quartet*. Addresses the following questions: What does "chorale" mean for Bartók the composer and the person? In which compositional perception should we place Bartók the chorale-composer, and to what degree does it belong to his compositional context? How far can one work out and interpret the definition? Exploration of the topic in historical context provides a picture of Hungary as a mosaic comprised of liturgical music, Catholic church reform in Hungary, Jewish tradition, etc., all of which served as direct sources for Bartók's chorale writing. States that Bartók's experience as ethnomusicologist and his Catholic background permitted him to absorb and go more deeply into these sources. Points to the lack of sacred music in Bartók's output in contrast to Kodály and Dohnányi but asserts that the church influence is felt. Provides some documentation on Bartók's views of religion.

745. Ito, Nobuhiro. "Some Problems Concerning the Study of Folksong Arrangements: No. 28 from *44 Duos for Two Violins* by Béla Bartók." *Tradition and Its Future in Music*. Osaka: Mita, 1991. pp. 49-54. ML36 1677

Shows that Bartók's different arrangements of an authentic folk song (which he recorded on wax cylinder in 1907) in two of his own compositions--no. 28 *(Bánkódás)* of his *Forty-Four Duos* for two violins and the first movement of the *Petite Suite* for piano solo--transform the stylistic essence of the original folk source into music belonging primarily to the sphere of Western art music. As seen in Bartók's own performance of the *Petite Suite* arrangement (which he recorded in 1941), his use of rubato is characteristic of traditional Western virtuoso performance rather than the *parlando-rubato* style of folk music. States that Bartók's intention was to create an independent piece of music rather than an arrangement that simply imitates the rhythmic style of the original folk-music source. Contains music examples, charts, tables.

746. Kalotaszegi, Tünde B. "Béla Bartóks Einakter *Herzog Blaubarts Burg* und seine Zeichenhaftigkeit" [Béla Bartók's one-acter *Kékszakállú herceg vára* and its symbolist tendencies]. *Geschichte und Dramaturgie des Opereinakters.* Laaber: Laaber Verlag, 1991. pp. 323-336.

Points to the transformation of the one-act opera around the turn of the century. This new conception of the genre provided the new aesthetic context for Béla Balázs's *Bluebeard* libretto, which paved the way for Bartók's symbolist aesthetic in his operatic setting. Contains music examples.

747. Kapst, Erich. "Bartóks Anmerkungen zum Mikrokosmos" [Bartók's remarks on the *Mikrokosmos*]. *Musik und Gesellschaft* 20/9 (September 1970): 585-595.   780.5 M995   ISSN 0027-4755

Discusses technical, stylistic, and expressive characteristics in these piano pieces and the composer's absorption of folk sources or styles as well.

748. ----------. "Stilkriterien der polymodal-kromatischen Gestaltungsweise im Werk Béla Bartóks" [Stylistic criteria for polymodal-chromatic structural processes in the works of Béla Bartók]. *Beiträge zur Musikwissenschaft* 21/1 (1970): 1-28. 780.5 B397

Discusses the importance of Bartók's own comments as a primary source for analyzing his music. Provides certain technical criteria for the analyst, including a study of melodic, rhythmic, tonal, and structural features of motives, characteristics of folk-like themes and their harmonizations, the use of polymodal chromaticism in folksong style, structural processes, and timbre. Contains music examples.

749. ----------. "Zum Tonalitätsbegriff bei Bartók" [Bartók's concept of tonality]. *International Musicological Conference in Commemoration of Béla Bartók 1971,* ed. József Ujfalussy and János Breuer. Budapest: Editio Musica; New York: Belwin Mills, 1972, pp. 31-40.   ML410.B29 I61   ML 410. B26 I5

Discusses the primacy that tonality had for Bartók in understanding the various parameters (melodic, rhythmic, harmonic, and structural) of his compositions. Also, discusses the vocal source of Bartók's chromaticism based on various types of scalar structures--pentatonic, modal, whole-tone, chromatic, and especially the use of polymodal-chromatic coordination.

750. Kárpáti, János. "Bartók és Schönberg" [Bartók and Schoenberg]. *Magyar zene* 4-5 (1963-1964): 563;15,130. ML5 M14 ISSN 0025-0384

Not examined. William Austin states, in *Music in the 20th Century,* New York: W.W. Norton and Co., Inc., 1966, p. 566, that this is a "promising by-product of a book in progress on Bartók's quartets."

751. ---------. *Bartók kamarazenéje* [Bartók's chamber music]. Budapest: Zeneműkiadó, 1976. 361p. ISBN-9633301467 ML410.B26 K4. See also the enlarged and revised American edition, Eng. trans. Fred Macnicol and Mária Steiner, trans. rev. by Paul Merrick, Stuyvesant, N.Y.: Pendragon Press, 1994. 508p. ISBN 0-945193-19-X ML410.B26K413 785'.0092-dc20

Revises and enlarges the author's study of the string quartets (see item no. 753) by adding discussions of the developments of the forms and styles of Bartók's other major chamber works and places the chamber music in the larger context of Bartók's oeuvre. The first part deals with Bartók's "musical idiom and style," including discussions of the legacy of Beethoven, forerunners and contemporaries, the folk music influence, monothematicism and variation, "polymodal chromaticism," and tonality and polytonality--the phenomenon of mistuning. The enlargement and revision concerns mainly the second part, "analyses," which adds discussions of selected early chamber works composed between 1895 and 1904, two *Sonatas for Violin and Piano* (1921, 1922), the *Sonata for Two Pianos and Percussion* (1937) and *Contrasts for Violin, Clarinet, and Piano* (1938). Contains music examples, appendix (source list of the works quoted), bibliography, and index. See review by László Somfai, "A Classic on Bartók Revised," in *The Hungarian Quarterly* 36 (Spring 1995): 141-143.

752. ----------. "Bartók, Schoenberg, Stravinsky." *The New Hungarian Quarterly* (Budapest) 7/24 (Winter 1966): 211-216. 914.39105 N42 ML410 B26 B29

Relates Bartók's harmonic language to the twelve-tone idiom and to some of Stravinsky's techniques, concluding that Bartók provided a synthesis of these divergent trends. Contains some remarks on Lendvai and Bartók's variation technique. Cites several people in the text, including Adorno, Boulez, Moreux, and Bartók. Reprinted in *Bartók Studies,* ed. Todd Crow. Detroit: Information Coordinators, 1976, pp. 93-98.

753. ----------. *Bartók vonósnégyesei* [Bartók's string quartets]. Budapest: Zeneműkiadó, 1967. 252p.   MT-145.B25 K4

　　Provides an in-depth discussion of fundamental theoretical principles underlying Bartók's general musical language in the first part (I: Musical Idiom and Style), including information regarding the sources of Bartók's compositional tools: folk influences, monothematicism and variation, polymodal chromaticism, tonality, the "phenomenon of mistuning," and polytonality. This part also includes a significant and detailed chronological chart of the historical interrelations of Bartók's various musical activities (folk, compositional, etc.) with the evolution of his string quartets as well as a discussion of Bartók's forerunners and contemporaries. Then, chronologically explores thematic, motivic, tonal, scalar, phrasal, and structural details of the quartets themselves in the second part (II: Analyses), each discussion introduced by specific historical information. Also explores basic information investigated by other scholars. These include the special theories of pitch organization set forth by Ernő Lendvai, in which the author points out the aims and limitations of the latter. Contains numerous music examples, charts, bibliography, and source list of works quoted. English trans. Fred Macnicol, *Bartók's String Quartets,* Budapest: Corvina Press, 1975, ISBN 963 13 3655 7; revised as *Bartók kamarazenéje* [Bartók's chamber music], Budapest: Zeneműkiadó, 1976, further revised and enlarged as *Bartók's Chamber Music,* trans. Fred Macnicol and Mária Steiner, trans. rev. by Paul Merrick, Stuyvesant, N.Y.: Pendragon Press, 1994 (see item no. 751). See reviews by: László Somfai. "Egy jelentős új Bartók-könyvről" [An outstanding new book on Bartók], in *Magyar zene* 8/6 (December 1967): 592-598; and János Breuer, in*Valóság* 11/3 (March 1968): 100-101. See the reviews of the English translation by: Peter Evans, in *Music and Letters* 58/1 (January 1977): 78-80; and Halsey Stevens, in *Notes* 33/3 (March 1977): 593-595.

754. ----------. "Early String Quartets." *The Bartók Companion,* ed. Malcolm Gillies. London: Faber and Faber, 1993; Portland, Oregon: Amadeus Press (an imprint of Timber Press, Inc.), 1994. pp. 226-242. ISBN 0-931340-74-8 (HB)   ISBN 0-931340-75-6 (PB) ML410 B26 B28

　　Points to the historical and musical connections between the *First String Quartet* and *First Violin Concerto.* Informs us that the personal mood, philosophy, and musical tone of these works stem from Bartók's relationship with the violinist Stefi Geyer, his readings of Nietzsche and Schopenhauer, and his enthusiasm for the *Tristan* idiom of Wagner. Then provides analyses of the *First* and *Second String Quartets,* including discussion of their formal outlines, tonal/harmonic structures, and thematic/motivic, rhythmic, and textural features. In connection with the technical analyses, also provides references to the varied art- and folk-music influences that Bartók absorbed into an original style beyond "mere quotation or adaptation," summarizes the stylistic affinities of these quartets with other Bartók works of the period and those of other composers and gives data on early performances.

755. ----------. "Le désaccordage dans la technique de composition de Bartók" [The mistuning phenomenon in Bartók's compositional technique]. *International Musicological Conference in Commemoration of Béla Bartók 1971,* ed. József Ujfalussy and János Breuer. Budapest: Editio Musica; New York: Belwin Mills, 1972, pp. 41-51.   ML410.B29 I61 (Editio Musica)
ML410.B26 I5 (Belwin Mills)

Refers to the "extension of the 'scordatura' phenomenon," which comes about through partial modification of the familiar "normal" (fifth-octave framework) structures. Discusses its origins and gives examples in Bartók's works.

756. ----------. "The First Two Piano Concertos." *The Bartók Companion,* ed. Malcolm Gillies. London: Faber and Faber, 1993; Portland, Oregon: Amadeus Press (an imprint of Timber Press, Inc.), 1994. pp. 498-514.   ISBN 0-931340-74-8 (HB)   ISBN 0-931340-75-6 (PB)
ML410 B26 B28

Refers to the importance of Bartók's piano music in his compositional evolution, pointing especially to the period beginning in 1926 with the *Sonata, Out of Doors, Nine Little Piano Pieces,* and the *First Piano Concerto.* Outlines Bartók's extensive international activities as pianist during this time, which accounts for this production, and provides a detailed performance history of the *First Concerto* with Bartók as soloist. Quotes Bartók as to the reasons for composing the contrasting *Second Concerto* (1931), based on his experiences with the *First Concerto.* Provides a performance history of this *Concerto* as well. Documents Bartók's aesthetic intentions and compares this inclination toward contrasting pairs of works also in his other genres. Explores stylistic sources in folk music and Baroque and Classical forms, asserting that Bartók reveals a particular affinity to Stravinsky's approach to these sources. Then, provides detailed analyses focusing on thematic/motivic generation of the large-scale structure. The analysis of the *First Concerto* points to generation from a percussive, hammering "proto-motif," the *Second Concerto* based on a more refined usage of this idea within a more flexible and melodic style. The differences between these two works reflect Bartók's broader stylistic evolution in the 1920s and 1930s.

757. ----------. "Tonal Divergences of Melody and Harmony: A Characteristic Device in Bartók's Musical Language." *Studia musicologica* 24 (1982): 373-380.   781.05 St92   ISSN 0039-3266

Analysis focusing on the first *Sonata for Violin and Piano*, examining the new use of structures built on thirds and a new conception of tonality. Discussion of chains of thirds or fifths and the concept of "mistuning" in his investigation of bitonality.

758. ----------. "A Typical *Jugendstil* Composition: Bartók's String Quartet No. 1." *The Hungarian Quarterly* 36 (Spring 1995): 130-140.   914.39105 H893

Defines *Jugendstil,* or Art Nouveau, in the context of a broad current in art in Europe at the turn of the century, pointing to this movement (known elsewhere as *Sezession*) as a special link between two styles, Impressionism and Expressionism. States that this movement included artists who reacted to petty bourgeois naturalism and were drawn to folk art or to the art of the East, the Hungarian *Szecesszió* in art being based on the need to escape from the Austrian and German influence. Discusses Bartók's shift from the Wagner-Strauss influence to that of Hungarian national style, an interest similar to that of the Budapest architect Ödön Lechner. Points to various influences on the *First String Quartet* and examines the work from the point of view of "what musical devices, structures and effects might be linked to the style and idiom of Art Nouveau and what might constitute a musical translation, as it were, of the ideas that typify Art Nouveau." Analysis of the quartet, which also includes references to stylistic sources, deals with (1) line (as a structure and a melodic principle) and ornaments, (2) folk art and some history of Bartók's ethnomusicological investigations and (3) the grotesque, including humor and sarcasm, and its biographical significance in the work. Concludes that the *First String Quartet* is a typical example of Art Nouveau and points to other Bartók works as well. Contains music examples and illustrations.

759. Kecskeméti, István. "A Chopin-Bartók-Kodály Analogy." *The Musical Times* (March 1981): 163-166.   780.5 M98   ISSN 0027-4666

Study reveals a perhaps surprising resemblance among three "second pieces" found in the three piano cycles--*Preludes* Op. 28 of Chopin, *Ten Easy Piano Pieces* of Bartók, and *Ten Pieces for Piano* Op. 3 by Kodály. Explores similarities in terms of length, use of introduction, ostinato accompaniment and soloistic use, monothematicism, tendency to transposition, complements, mode, bitonality (different key at the beginning and end of a work), descending basses, unaccompanied melody, melodic sections with iambic endings, tempo marks, meter, use of "espressivo," dynamics, and decelerating ending.

760. Keszi, Imre. "A vitatott Bartók" [Bartók the debated]. *Új írás* (Budapest) 11/3 (March 1971): 75-83.   H1.582

Discusses Bartók's music in relation to the music of his contemporaries, including comparison with the music of Falla, Milhaud, Stravinsky, Schoenberg, Berg, Webern, and others.

761. Kincaid, Desmond. "Béla Bartók: 'Out of Doors:' a Lecture Recital." D.M.A. treatise. North Texas State University, 1971. 44p.

Includes a stylistic analysis of Bartók's *Out of Doors* suite. Also provides some information on his life and works in general. Contains music, bibliography.

762. Klimo, Stefan. "Bartókove klavírne koncerty" [Bartók's piano concertos]. *Slovenská hudba* 15/3-4 (1971): 103-109.   H50.470

Presents brief, but useful analyses of the three piano concertos.

763. Kneif, Tibor. "Zur Enstehung und Kompositionstechnik von Bartóks Konzert für Orchester" [The origin and compositional technique of Bartók's *Concerto for Orchestra*]. *Die Musikforschung* 26 (1973): 36-51.   780.5 M9921   ISSN 0027-4801

Demonstrates that the thematic concept is subordinate to the principle of variation technique. Discusses motivic relationships between movements based on the principle of differentiation and synthesis. Also refers to a philosophical basis for these processes in Bartók's music.

764. Kovács, János. "'Heiliger Dankgesang' in der lydischen Tonart und 'Adagio religioso.'" *International Musicological Conference in Commemoration of Béla Bartók 1971,* ed. József Ujfalussy and János Breuer. Budapest: Editio Musica; New York: Belwin Mills, 1972, pp. 25-30.   ML410.B29 I61 (Editio Musica)   ML410.B26 I5 (Belwin Mills)

Endeavors to draw conclusions from the generally known parallel between the "Lydian Thanksgiving Song" in Beethoven's *String Quartet* Op. 132 and the "Adagio religioso" in Bartók's *Concerto No. 3* for Piano and Orchestra. Focuses on structure with some style references in certain sections.

765. Kovács, Sándor. "Final Concertos." _The Bartók Companion,_ ed. Malcolm Gillies. London: Faber and Faber, 1993; Portland, Oregon: Amadeus Press (an imprint of Timber Press, Inc.), 1994. pp. 538-554. ISBN 0-931340-74-8 (HB)   ISBN 0-931340-75-6 (PB) ML410 B26 B28

Discusses the relatively more favorable personal (financial and health) and professional conditions in 1944-1945 under which Bartók was to compose his last two works--the _Viola Concerto_ and _Third Piano Concerto._ Provides basic historical data on practical and other concerns associated with Bartók's compositional and performance plans for these works. Discusses Bartók's general procedures in the compositional process from draft to full score and completion of both works by Tibor Serly. Refers to the contrasting attitudes after Bartók's death toward the _Piano Concerto_ in different countries and addresses its position in Bartók's output. Analysis deals with formal structure, tonality, modality, polymodal chromaticism, and thematic connections, identifies a wide range of stylistic sources and connections, and points to the apparent biographical significance of the work, especially the slow movement. Study of the _Viola Concerto_ focuses primarily on the history and problems of its reconstruction by Serly.

766. Kozak, Hanna Barbara. "Koncerty fortepianowe Béli Bartóka" [Piano concertos of Béla Bartók]. M.A. thesis. University of Warszawa, 1969. 97p.

Not examined. According to Danuta Idaszak, _RILM Abstracts_ No. 939 (1971), the thesis provides "a discussion of the piano concertos in relation to Bartók's activity as a composer, pianist, and scholar. Deals specifically with the orchestration, the instrumentation, the role of the piano as a percussion instrument (its function in producing rhythmic, dynamic, and coloristic effects), problems of form, and the influences of folk music."

767. Krones, Hartmut. "Stilkundliche Betrachtungen auf soziologischer Basis, insbesondere dargestellt am Beispiel Béla Bartóks" [Stylistic issues based on sociology demonstrated on the example of Béla Bartók]. _International Musicological Conference in Commemoration of Béla Bartók 1971,_ ed. József Ujfalussy and János Breuer. Budapest: Editio Musica; New York: Belwin Mills, 1972, pp. 83-88. ML410.B29 I61 (Editio Musica)   ML410.B26 I5 (Belwin Mills)

Gives sociological examinations for understanding two mainstreams of the early twentieth century: 1) breaking away from traditions (second Viennese School); and 2) based on socially broader foundations (folklorist groups). Mentions relationships of stylistic elements of folk music to Bartók's world of melody, tonality, and rhythm.

768. Kroó, György. "Ballet: *The Wooden Prince.*" *The Bartók Companion,* ed. Malcolm Gillies. London: Faber and Faber, 1993; Portland, Oregon: Amadeus Press (an imprint of Timber Press, Inc.), 1994. pp. 360-371. ISBN 0-931340-74-8 (HB) ISBN 0-931340-75-6 (PB) ML410 B26 B28

Bartók's ballet (1916), based on Béla Balázs's libretto, is identified as the work that brought Bartók back to his creative mold after a series of crises and growing personal depression since 1907. Provides historical data on its composition and first performance and points to the close affinity between the scores of the ballet and the *Bluebeard* opera. Presents a thorough synopsis of the drama and a systematic overview of the musical structure stemming from Bartók's own analysis. Explores the "symphonic" conception of the work, including analysis of thematic structural functions and transformations, and their role in the spiritual process of the work, expression of moods and emotions, and portrayal of human character. Also, presents views of contemporary critics and Bartók's own concerns regarding his approach to the relation between the music and drama.

769. ----------. "Cantata profana." *The Bartók Companion,* ed. Malcolm Gillies. London: Faber and Faber, 1993; Portland, Oregon: Amadeus Press (an imprint of Timber Press, Inc.), 1994. pp. 424-437. ISBN 0-931340-74-8 (HB) ISBN 0-931340-75-6 (PB) ML410 B26 B28

Places Bartók's *Cantata profana* (1930) in the context of a larger body of works that emerged as manifestations of conscience on the eve of fascism. As an instrumental composer, Bartók's difficulty in approaching works with text is traced to the time of his *Bluebeard* setting and the Five "Ady" Songs, Op. 16. Outlines the chronological development of Bartók's vocal works that prepared the way for the *Cantata.* Discusses Bartók's international and humanistic intentions as basis for his choice of text during a critical phase in his philosophical development. Provides a history of Bartók's activities and the basic data on the folk texts in connection with the genesis of the *Cantata.* Also addresses Bartók's political and musical concerns regarding feasibility of performance. Then, provides a synopsis of the plot, assessment of the formal musical construction according to different scholarly views, analysis of tonality, relations between the basic scalar constructions, and motivic integration. Addresses the message contained in the symbolism of the Romanian *colindă* myth and the ethnological roots in Bartók's references to Bach's *St. Matthew Passion.* Then, provides a chronological analytical survey of the musical structure and its dramatic meaning.

770. ----------. "Duke Bluebeard's Castle." *Studia musicologica* 1 (1961): 251-340.   781.05 St92   ISSN 0039-3266

    Well-documented, comprehensive, and detailed duscussion of all aspects of the opera, providing historical and compositional background information as well.

771. ----------. "Opera: *Duke Bluebeard's Castle.*" *The Bartók Companion,* ed. Malcolm Gillies. London: Faber and Faber, 1993; Portland, Oregon: Amadeus Press (an imprint of Timber Press, Inc.), 1994. pp. 349-359.   ISBN 0-931340-74-8 (HB)   ISBN 0-931340-75-6 (PB) ML410 B26 B28

    Provides a brief historical overview of the Bluebeard tale, research by folklorists, studies of its symbolic connotations, and summarizes the literary, dramatic, and operatic arrangements of the story. Presents basic historical information on performances of the *Bluebeard* "mystery play" by Béla Balázs (a disciple of the symbolist poet Maurice Maeterlinck and friend of the Bartók-Kodály circle) and the circumstances leading to Bartók's operatic setting of it. Also provides historical information on the early rejection of the opera and its revisions (especially of the ending). Presents symbolic and dramaturgical interpretations as part of the author's thorough synopsis of the Balázs libretto. Then, discusses Bartók's musical interpretation based on links with nineteenth-century opera (especially of Wagner), philosophy and literature, and the direct musico-dramatic influence of Debussy's *Pelléas et Mélisande.* Analysis of the opera includes an account of the tonalities of the scenes, harmonic construction derived from various folk- and art-music sources, motivic recurrence and development as a significant source of the opera's "symphonic" organic unity, and discussion of the orchestral and vocal styles, the latter of which grows out of the inflections of Hungarian folksong.

772. Laberge, Mary Jane. "The Formal Structure in Debussy's *Reflects dans l'eau* and Bartók's *Allegro barbaro.*" M.A. thesis. Piano: Chicago Conservatory Col., 1974. 25p.

    Provides a comparison of the forms and styles of these two contrasting compositions.

773. Lampert, Vera. "Second Violin Concerto." *The Bartók Companion,* ed. Malcolm Gillies. London: Faber and Faber, 1993; Portland, Oregon: Amadeus Press (an imprint of Timber Press, Inc.), 1994. pp. 515-525.   ISBN 0-931340-74-8 (HB)   ISBN 0-931340-75-6 (PB) ML410 B26 B28

    Discusses the genesis of the *Concerto* (1938) beginning in the mid-1930s and outlines Bartók's busy professional activities, commissions, compositional work, and scholarly folk-music research during that time. Discusses the emergence of the formal conception, and provides a chronology from the first thematic sketches to the final draft and orchestration. While some stylistic comparison with Classical composers is documented, points especially to the deep roots of the melodies in folk-music tradition, including Transylvanian folk dances of peasant violinists and *verbunkos* style. Then, provides a chronological analysis of the Classical formal outline, exploring the thematic characteristics (including twelve-tone tendency in a tonal context and quaternary melodic structure influenced by "new"-style Hungarian melodies), modal coloring, instrumentation, and more general stylistic features. Also, gives data on main performances and refers to the recording of the première by Zoltán Székely as an important primary source in understanding the composer's intentions.

774. ----------. "Works for Solo Voice with Piano." *The Bartók Companion,* ed. Malcolm Gillies. London: Faber and Faber, 1993; Portland, Oregon: Amadeus Press (an imprint of Timber Press, Inc.), 1994. pp. 387-412. ISBN 0-931340-74-8 (HB) ISBN 0-931340-75-6 (PB) ML410 B26 B28

Compares the limited output of Bartók's song settings to poetic texts--these include the mature song cycles (Op. 15 and Op. 16) and those few collections dating from his youth modelled on the German *Lied*--with his large production of folk-song arrangements for voice and piano (about eighty songs in four collections). Follows Bartók's evolution from simple chordal accompaniments to more complex settings in a chronological survey of these four collections of folk-song settings: the twenty *Hungarian Folksongs* (1906), *Eight Hungarian Folksongs* (1907-1917), *Village Scenes* (1924), and *Twenty Hungarian Folksongs* (1929), with preliminary discussion of the *Four Songs* (1902) on Pósa texts. Discusses the genesis of these works in the context of the political and social influences on Bartók's attitudes. Explores the circumstances in which he collected the tunes, his compositional intentions, and provides some information on publication and early performances. Describes the structural and stylistic (melodic, harmonic, and rhythmic) features of the songs and surveys their musical sources and influences. Then, focuses on the historical circumstances, aesthetic intentions, compositional form and style, and musico-poetic expression in the two highly original collections (Op. 15 and Op. 16) based on poetic texts.

775. László, Ferenc. "Major-Minor Encounters. . . and under the Sign of the Kalindra." In: *Enesciana IV. Georges Enesco, compositeur roumain.* Bucharest: Editura Muzicală, 1985. pp. 59-73.

Analytical study of the common or related stylistic aspects of certain pieces by Bartók and Enescu. Contains musical examples.

776. Leafstedt, Carl. *"Bluebeard* as Theater: The Influence of Maeterlinck and Hebbel on Balázs's Bluebeard Drama." *Bartók and His World,* ed. Peter Laki. Princeton, New Jersey: Princeton University Press, 1995. pp. 119-148.   ISBN 0-691-00633-4   ML 410 B26 B272

Explores the sources of Béla Balázs' symbolist dramatic ideas for the *Bluebeard* libretto. Draws together a wide array of historical data that provide insight into Balázs' dramaturgical thought. Initially discusses the opera in the context of Bartók's career, alludes to influences of Strauss, Debussy, and Liszt and describes the importance of the work in Bartók's stylistic development. Then, explores the relatively little-known factors that contributed to Balázs's dramatic style. Describes the mood of the *Bluebeard* play, its absorption of elements from both East and West, and its textual features exhibiting ancient folk characteristics of the Transylvanian Magyars. Discusses sources of influence and the genesis of the Balázs play, including the primary impact of the French symbolist techniques of Maurice Maeterlinck and the theories of tragedy of the German Friedrich Hebbel as well as the technological advances in stage lighting around the turn of the century. Provides some biographical background to Balázs's development and then focuses on the dramaturgy of the libretto. The following discussions include the nature of Balázs's interest in Maeterlinck, a comparison of Balázs's *Bluebeard* with Maeterlinck's *Ariane,* Balázs's personal interest in Hebbel and German Romantic drama, and Hebbel's dramatic theories and their effect on the *Bluebeard* drama.

777. ----------. "Music and Drama in Béla Bartók's Opera *Duke Bluebeard's Castle."* Ph.D. diss. Harvard University, 1994. 345p.

Well-documented study of the history and dramaturgy of the opera, focusing on the sources of Béla Balázs' symbolist dramatic ideas for the *Bluebeard* setting. Draws together a wide array of historical data that provide insight into Balázs' dramaturgical thought, while less emphasis is placed on the investigation into the central issues of the musical language of Bartók's operatic setting itself. The first chapter, on "Bartók, Balázs, and the History of *Bluebeard's Castle,"* explores Balázs's life and contribution (partly through his recollections) to the understanding of the attitudes, concerns, and interests of his era, while it is shown that Bartók's own written summary of the opera is meager. Also discusses Bartók's personal and professional relation with Balázs, their common interest in the folk sources, and the genesis of the play. The second chapter, on "Dramatic and Aesthetic Influences on Balázs's *Bluebeard*

Drama," explores the social, political, and artistic environment in which the libretto emerged, discussing in detail Maeterlinck's dramas in particular but also those of other turn-of-the-century dramatists as significant influences on Balázs's literary style. Chapter 3, on "The Figure of Judith in Early Twentieth-Century Art and Culture: The Significance of a Name," provides an account of the sources and changing meaning of the Judith character in literary history since the Bible, after which Chapter 4 presents a general overview of the "Music and Drama in *Bluebeard's Castle:* The Opera and Its Individual Scenes." Chapter 5 explores "Bartók's Revisions to *Bluebeard's Castle,* 1911-21." Contains appendices, bibliography, musical examples, and illustrations.

778. Leibowitz, René. "Béla Bartók or the Possibility of Compromise in Contemporary Music." *Transition* 48/3 (1948): 92-122.

Evaluates Bartók's contributions to the radical innovations that were revolutionizing music in the early twentieth century. First, outlines several independent strands of development in France (Debussy), Vienna (Schoenberg, Berg, and Webern), and Russia (Scriabin and Stravinsky), in which the pioneers of that "terrifying modern music," while hardly aware of each other, reveal certain common tendencies in facing the crisis in the evolution of polyphony. Places Bartók's *First String Quartet* (1908) favorably within this revolution, stating that the Bartók of this chamber work already showed promise for a great future. Bartók's expansion of the tonal and structural possibilities of pure counterpoint in the quartet provided, like Schoenberg's first quartets, "new and radical answers to the problems raised by [the late quartets of] Beethoven." Then, surveys the development of Bartók's awareness of these issues. Assesses Bartók's genuine interest in Eastern European folk music, but views as naive the conception that borrowings from folk music can enrich musical language. According to the author, the qualities that Bartók supposedly drew from the folk sources were really based on the experience through which he had already passed as a composer. While the author considers such works as the *Sonatas for Violin and Piano* of the early 1920s as front-rank developments in the "genuinely radical approach to most of the problems of contemporary polyphony," he sees Bartók's "folklorizing" intentions as producing "stiffness and poverty in the musical thought," a *path of compromise* which he traces through Bartók's later works, especially after the revolutionary contrapuntal achievement of the *Fourth String Quartet* (1928).

779. Leichtentritt, Hugo. "On the Art of Béla Bartók." *Modern Music* 6/3 (March-April 1929): 3-11.   780.5 M72

States that the racial character of Bartók's music has been a barrier to the proper appreciation and understanding of his music.

Gives a brief history prior to Bartók's discovery of the authentic Hungarian peasant music and then discusses these problems of intelligibility to the general listener by giving some detailed analyses in several works. These include *Allegro barbaro, Dance Suite for Orchestra,* and the *Second Violin Sonata.* However, ends by stating that certain features of Bartók's art (such as tonality) serve as a strong argument against the concept of atonality. Includes use of pitch notations as an aid in understanding Bartók's tonality. For instance, in the *Second Violin Sonata,* shows direct correspondences between chromatically altered tones of two descending scales, the combination of which adds up to all twelve tones in a kind of "mixed tonality."

780. Lendvai, Ernő. "Bartók Húrosütöhangszeres zenéjének néhány értelmezési problémájáról" [Some problems in the interpretation of Bartók's *Music for Strings, Percussion and Celesta*]. *Muzsika* (Budapest) 11/7 (July 1968): 24-28.   ISSN 0027-5336

Explores spatial sound relations in connection with certain impressionistic and expressionistic style features of the work.

781. ----------. *Bartók stílusa a "Szonáta két zongorára és ütőhangszerekre" és a "Zene húros-ütő-és celestára" tükrében* [Bartók's style as reflected in *Sonata for Two Pianos and Percussion* and *Music for Strings, Percussion and Celesta*]. Budapest: Zeneműkiadó, 1955. 155p.   ML410.B26 L45

Expansion of Lendvai's article on the *Sonata,* in *Zenei Szemle* (December 1948). Introductory chapters present discussions on key relationships, form, and intervals, referring to many of Bartók's works. Then provides a detailed study of the *Sonata,* dealing further with rhythm, form, content, and polarity. *Music for Strings, Percussion and Celesta* is also explored according to these features with an emphasis on its form in the summary. Contains illustrations, music. See Halsey Steven's review, in *Music Library Association-Notes* (March 1956): 292-293.

782. ----------. *The Workshop of Bartók and Kodály.* Budapest: Editio Musica, 1983. 762p.   ISBN-9633303826   ML410.B26 L47 1983

Provides detailed analyses of many of Bartók's major works based on the author's theories, which have been established in his earlier writings. The essential theoretical thread that runs throughout his discussions is the principle of duality, as represented in the chromatic (Golden Section) versus acoustic (diatonic) systems and the principles of the "polar-axis" system as well as more musically abstract juxtapositions (instinctive/intellectual, masculine/feminine, emotional/sensuous, etc.). Lendvai's ultimate aim is to demonstrate by means of analysis how these opposing principles are integrated in Bartók's music. Contains illustrations, music. See reviews by: Jim Samson in *Tempo* 151 (December 1984): 39-41; and Malcolm Gillies in *Music Analysis* 5/2-3 (1986): 285-295.

783. Little, Jean. "Architectonic Levels of Rhythmic Organization in Selected Twentieth-Century Music." Ph.D. diss. Indiana University, 1971. xviii, 405p.

Compares the rhythmic styles based on rhythmic density or number of articulations per minute in violin compositions by Bartók, Berg, Stravinsky, and Webern. Includes a study of Bartók's 1938 *Violin Concerto*. Outlines five steps in the analytical process: morphological lengths and perception (the relation of static structural lengths); rhythmic form (the microrhythm of rhythmic groupings at superior and primary levels); rhythmic species (types of rhythmic impulse-initial, medial, terminal); rhythmic structure (the macrorhythm of metric, multimetric, and non-metric organizations); and rhythmic patterns and accentuation. Contains bibliography.

784. Maegaard, Jan. "Béla Bartók und das Atonale" [Béla Bartók and his "turn to the atonal"]. *Jahrbuch Peters* (!981-82; publ. 1985): 30-42. ML5 J16

Addresses Bartók's use of the term "atonal" in his 1920 article "Das Problem der neuen Musik" (see item no. 29) and the relevance of his definition to his aesthetic and compositional approach around that time. In that article, Bartók had pointed to atonality as deriving from the need for the equality of the twelve tones. Provides an analysis of Bartók's *Etude* Op. 18, No. 2 (1918) to reveal Bartók's inclination toward atonality but points to his subsequent withdrawal from the Schoenbergian conception. Contains music examples.

785. Mason, Colin. "Bartók's Early Violin Concerto." *Tempo* (London) 49 (1958): 11-16.   780.5 T249   ISSN 0040-2982

Discusses the extra-musical significance of the *Concerto* in Bartók's love for the violinist Stefi Geyer, which is also seen in its musical connections with the *First String Quartet* and *Two Portraits*. Gives a brief descriptive outline of formal and thematic relations. Mentions Lisztian and Straussian influences on these works.

786. Meister, Christopher Dale. "Textural Analyses and 'Concerto for Piano and Orchestra' (Original Composition)." Ph.D. diss. Washington University, 1983. 216p.

Presents textural analyses in works of several composers, based on the use of pitch-set, pitch-class-set, pitch-space, intervallic, timbral, articulatory, durational, figural, and mapping procedures.

Bartók's *String Quartets* and *Music for Strings, Percussion and Celesta* are selected for this study. Contains illustrations, bibliography.

787. Menasce, Jacques De. "Berg and Bartók." *Modern Music* 21/2 (January-February 1944): 76-81.   780.5 M72

Calls attention to many affinities existing between Berg and Bartók, who have generally been separately "classified" and "pigeonholed" through ignorance. Also shows how they diverge for reasons other than those generally attributed. Gives historical data to present his arguments and focuses on the period from 1920 on. States that the most apparent parallelisms are in the years of Bartók's two *Violin Sonatas* and Berg's *Lyric Suite* and later in the violin concertos, etc., of both composers. Also compares other works from their earlier periods.

788. ----------. "The Classicism of Béla Bartók." *Modern Music* 23/2 (Spring 1946): 83-88.   780.5 M72

Brief comparison of the *Third Piano Concerto* and the *Concerto for Orchestra,* particularly mentioning the extraordinary serenity they have in common. Suggests that the essential classical element in the *Third Concerto* is its obvious tonality and quality of restraint.

789. Mersmann, Hans. "Der Spätstil Bartóks" [The late style of Bartók]. *Musik der Zeit* (Bonn) 3 (1953): 60-64.   ML410.B26 B4

Contrasts Bartók's late works, beginning with the *Fifth String Quartet,* with the earlier ones to demonstrate the results of Bartók's style evolution.

790. Meyer, John A. "Bartók and Popularity." *Studia musicologica* 3 (1969): 70-73.   781.05 St92   ISSN 0039-3266

Compares the concerto with other of Bartók's works to provide intrinsic evidence for the popularity of the *Third Piano Concerto.* Intended to dismiss certain aesthetic assumptions on the part of critics that the concerto's popularity resulted from the composer's concession to public taste.

791. Michael, Frank. *Béla Bartóks Variationstechnik. Dargestellt im Rahmen einer Analyse seines 2. Violinkonzert* [Béla Bartók's variation technique. An illustrative analysis of his *Second Violin Concerto*]. *Forschungsbeiträge zur Musikwissenschaft* 27. Regensburg: Gustav Bosse, 1976. 48p.   ISBN-3764921374 ML410.B26 M5

Points to continual motivic transformation in the *Concerto* as the basis of the formal construction. Demonstrates the common motivic basis for the contrasting themes of the movements, a factor contributing to the variational connections between the outer movements. Also discusses the importance of tonal and harmonic relations in the construction of the form. Furthermore, explores principles of symmetry in the overall form, melodic structure, harmony, rhythm, and orchestration.

792. Milloss, Aurel von. "L'importanza dell'opera di Béla Bartók per l'evoluzione dell'estetica del balletto novecentesco" [The importance of Béla Bartók's works in the evolution of the aesthetic of 20th-century ballet]. *Chigiana* 38/18 (1982; publ. 1987): 185-198. 780.5 C435

Provides a substantive study of the relation of Bartók's music to the choreography for *Csodálatos mandarin*. In particular, addresses the function of Bartók's music in the choreography of the abstract rather than narrative thematic materials of the libretto. Also explores relevant aspects of Bartók's career and aesthetic development that drew him to set this work.

793. Molnár, Antal. "Die Bedeutung der neuen osteuropäischen Musik" [The significance of new East-European music]. *International Musicological Conference in Commemoration of Béla Bartók 1971*, ed. József Ujfalussy and János Breuer. Budapest: Editio Musica; New York: Belwin Mills, 1972, pp. 159-161. ML410.B29 I61 ML410.B26 I5

Suggests that we no longer can explain traditional European culture because of new musical phenomena in the twentieth century. Speaks of the freshness of Eastern European music as opposed to the "fatigue" of Western music. Discusses the development of independent and authentic national musical works (Enescu, Janáček, and Bartók) in the creation of new schools. Relates the discussion to the entire history of Hungarian culture.

794. ----------. "Hat írás Bartókról" [Six talks on Bartók]. Ed. Ferenc Bónis. *Magyar zene* 27/2 (June 1986): 169-184. ML5 M14 ISSN 0025-0384

Lectures given in the 1970s for Magyar Rádió, including personal recollections of the premiere of Bartók's *First String Quartet*, a discussion of Bartók's artistic development, and a somewhat subjective account of Bartók's stage works and the *Sonata for Two Pianos and Percussion*.

795. Monelle, Raymond. "Notes on Bartók's Fourth Quartet." *Music Review* 29/2 (May 1968): 123-129. 780.5 M9733 ISSN 0027-4445

Discusses the connections of the quartet with traditional formal characteristics but suggests that the older forms are not basic to Bartók's aesthetics. Rather, stresses the importance of the organic process based on the principle of variation or thematic transformation. Refers to the progressive clarification of the material through the emergence of the main idea in its primary form in the finale, the melodic and rhythmic components of this idea of which represent a synthesis of all the material of the work.

796. Morgan, Robert P. "Bartók's Extraordinary Quartets." *High Fidelity* 20/9 (September 1970): 58-61.   ML1 H45   789.91 ISSN 0018-1455

Evaluates the quartets and their importance in terms of their historical position. Contains a discography.

797. Nest'yev, Izrael. "Prokofiev and Bartók: Some Parallels." *International Musicological Conference in Commemoration of Béla Bartók 1971,* ed. József Ujfalussy and János Breuer. Budapest: Editio Musica; New York: Belwin Mills, 1972, pp. 137-143. ML410.B29 I61 (Editio Musica)   ML410.B26 I5 (Belwin Mills)

States that the musical legacy of the early twentieth century is not limited to the output of the leaders of atonality. Points to the significance also of those masters that have preserved ties with the musical past: Prokofiev, Shostakovich, Ravel, Honegger, Bartók, Kodály, etc. Yet, like Bartók and Stravinsky, Prokofiev, too, blazed new trails. Then gives parallels between Prokofiev and Bartók in terms of the "graphic" trend, their independence from Schoenberg's twelve-tone technique and neo-classical stylizations. Then elaborates their ideological and aesthetic closeness.

798. Newlin, Dika. "Four Revolutionaries." *Choral Music,* ed. Arthur Jacobs. Harmondsworth and Baltimore: Penguin Books, 1963. 444p. ML1500.J3

Discusses mainly Bartók's *Cantata Profana* (pp. 320-323). Subjective description of music and text, using terms as "floating harmonies," "harsh note-clusters," and "tonal vagueness." Not analytical but useful in its general descriptiveness. Contains illustrations, bibliography, discography.

799. Nüll, Edwin von der. "Stilwende" [A Change in Style]. Trans. Susan Gillespie. In *Bartók and His World,* ed. Peter Laki. Princeton, New Jersey: Princeton University Press, 1995. pp. 276-277.   ISBN 0-691-00633-4   ML 410 B26 B272. Original publication in: Edwin von der Nüll. *Béla Bartók. Ein Beitrag zur Morphologie der neuen Musik.* Halle [Saale]: Mitteldeutsche Verlags A.G., 1930. ML 410.B26 N8   780.81

See item no. 1131. Discusses Bartók's evolution from the predominantly harmonic conception underlying a single dominant melody in his piano works from the *Bagatelles*, Op. 6 (1908), to the *Etudes*, Op. 18 (1918). Points to this as one of the distinctions between Bartók and Schoenberg. States that contrapoint begins to appear in a more important structural capacity for the first time in the *Improvisations*, Op. 20 (1920), and later, in the 1926 *Sonata*. Yet, in both works, in which intermittent contrapuntal elements serve to articulate tonal shifts, the harmonic conception still prevails. Then cites the 1926 *Nine Little Piano Pieces* and *Out of Doors* as landmarks in Bartók's stylistic transformation from the predominantly harmonic to contrapuntal conception, equating this transformation with the shift of Bartók's influence from Beethoven to Bach.

800. ----------. *Béla Bartók. Ein Beitrag zur Morphologie der neuen Musik* [Béla Bartók. A contribution to the morphology of the new music]. Halle: Mitteldeutsche Verlags A.G., 1930. viii, 120p. ML 410.B26 N8   780.81

One of the earliest major studies of Bartók, which includes an attempt to deal with his own original means of tonal organization. Contains illustrations and music.

801. Oramo, Ilkka. "Marcia und Burletta. Zur Tradition der Rhapsodie in zwei Quartettsatzen Bartóks" [Marcia and Burletta. On the tradition of Rhapsody in two of Bartók's quartet movements]. *Die Musikforschung* 30/1 (1977): 14-25.   780.5 M9921 ISSN 0027-4801

Explores the stylistic and formal characteristics of the verbunkos (lassu and friss) style in late works of Bartók, stemming from the two Rhapsodies for violin (1928). Presents a comparison of the Marcia and Burletta of the *Sixth Quartet* with the verbunkos and Sebes of *Contrasts*.

802. ----------. "Die notierte, die wahrgenommene und die gedachte Struktur bei Bartók" [The notated, the perceived, and the intended structure of Bartók]. *Studia musicologica* 24/3-4 (1982): 439-449. 781.05 St92   ISSN 0039-3266

Discusses the evolution of Bartók's polymodal chromaticism, exploring the corresponding trend toward a structural synthesis of the divergent tendencies inherent in his early works. Refers to Bartók's polymodal thinking as early as the first of the *Fourteen Bagatelles*, Op. 14 (1908). Initially discusses the linear modal divergence indicated by the bitonal key signature, including a comparison with the polytonal thinking of Milhaud. Then explores

Bartók's development of these principles in the *First String Quartet, Second Violin Concerto, Third String Quartet,* and *Divertimento.* Provides a thorough and well-documented investigation based on both primary and secondary source studies.

803. Pap, Gábor. *"Csak tiszta forrásból": Adalékok Bartók* Cantata profanájának *értelmezéséhez* ["But from the clearest springs"; A contribution to the interpretation of Bartók's *Cantata profana*]. Budapest: Kós Károly Egyesülés, 1990. 304p. ISBN 963-04-0227-0

According to László Vikárius, *RILM Abstracts* No. 4424 (1990), "Bartók's *Cantata profana* is based on *colinde* texts associated with the winter solstice. Documentation is offered concerning folk traditions and visual representation connected with the ecliptic and the zodiac, and especially those elements that appear in the text of *Cantata profana.* Much of this musical interpretation is derived from Ernő Lendvai's work." Contains illustrations.

804. Petersen, Peter. "Bartók--Lutosławski--Ligeti: Einige Bemerkungen zu ihrer Kompositionstechnik unter dem Aspekt der Tonhöhe" [Bartók, Lutosławski, Ligeti: Comments on their compositional techniques as regards pitch]. *Hamburger Jahrbuch für Musikwissenschaft* 11 (1991): 289-309.   ML5 H5355

According to the author, *RILM Abstracts* No. 9363 (1991), "Although the composers belong to different generations and are stylistically distinct, their compositional techniques have parallels. These include the practice of creating diatonic fields within twelve-tone contexts (so-called inherent diatonicism), in which the pentatonic cell of the minor third and major second plays a special role. In his work with microintervals, Lutosławski continues what Bartók began. For both composers, microintervals are linked to the principle of equidistance. Ligeti, on the other hand, always uses microintervallic digressions to bring a moment of uncertainty into the compositional structure." Contains music examples.

805. Pleasants, Henry, and Tibor Serly. "Bartók's Historic Contribution." *Modern Music* 17/3 (April 1940): 131-140.   780.5 M72

Explores the phenomenon of unresolved passing tones as the fundamental concept in the evolution of Bartók's idiom.

806. Pollatsek, Ladislaus. "Béla Bartók and His Work: On the Occasion of His Fiftieth Birthday." *Musical Times* 72/1059 (May 1931): 411-413; (June 1931): 506-510; (July): 600-602; (August): 697-699. 780.5 M98   ISSN 0027-4666

Provides a broad overview of Bartók's music, discussing his stylistic development in terms of sources and the harmonic system of his compositions. Contains music examples.

807. Porter, James. "Bartók's Concerto for Orchestra (1943) and Janáček's Sinfonietta (1926): Conceptual and Structural Parallels." *Bartók in Retrospect*, ed. Elliott Antokoletz, Victoria Fischer and Benjamin Suchoff. Projected publication of two 1995 conference proceedings.

Given the converging contexts around Bartók and Janáček in the period 1924-1927, states that it would not be surprising if the source material used by both composers gave rise to similar procedures in their compositions. Despite the differences in personality and style, both were captivated by the folk music of East-Central Europe, both were acquainted with modernist trends in the 1920s, and both experienced similar difficulties in having their music accepted. They met at least three times and exchanged publications. Two masterworks, composed towards the end of the composer's life, invite comparison to demonstrate these similarities and differences: Janáček's *Sinfonietta* (1926) and Bartók's *Concerto for Orchestra* (1943). Points out that both works draw upon folk idioms, among other techniques, for their power and appeal. But where Bartók's style is eclectic and attempts to fuse very disparate influences, Janáček's is based on the dance, music and speech rhythms of East Moravia. Shows that the two works demonstrate related ways of transcending the crisis of modernism in the first half of the twentieth century. (Annotation based on the author's abstract of the original lecture; see item no. 1139.)

808. Prime, Dennis Gordon. "The Clarinet in Selected Works of Béla Bartók and Igor Stravinsky." D.M.A. treatise. The University of Wisconsin-Madison, 1984. 214p.

Includes a study of Bartók's *Contrasts* for clarinet, violin, and piano, providing an analysis from the point of view of the clarinetist. Presents performance problems and their solutions as well as a study of Bartók's own recording. Discusses formal proportions in terms of time periods, including a discussion of the use of the Fibonacci series, and points to the important structural use of the tritone. Contains music, bibliography.

809. Purswell, Joan. "Bartók's Early Music: Forecasting the Future." *Clavier* 20/8 (October 1981): 23-27.   780.5 C578
ISSN 0009-854-X

The appearance of Bartók's *Bagatelles, Burlesques,* and *Sketches* in 1908-1910 represents the influences of folk sources and music of

Debussy as well as a new approach to harmony and melody. These works are described briefly in terms of basic musical and performance techniques. An entire reprint of *Bagatelle* No 5 is given.

810. Racek, J. "Leoš Janáčeks und Béla Bartóks Bedeutung in der Weltmusik" [Leoš Janáček's and Béla Bartók's significance in world music]. *Studia musicologica* 5 (1963): 501-513.   781.05 St92 ISSN 0039-3266

Comparison of the two composers with respect to their sources of inspiration and their relationship to folk music; includes a detailed analysis of the style of their musical language.

811. Rands, Bernard. "The Use of Canon in Bartók's Quartets." *Music Review* 18/3 (August 1957): 183-188.   780.5 M9733 ISSN 0027-4445

Demonstrates that Bartók, like Bach, Palestrina, and Byrd, uses canon as part of an organic whole. Also states that in Bartók's music, the horizontal movement is of prime importance, while vertical analysis seems irrelevant. Bartók's use of "short canons, possessing little significance in themselves, are of the utmost value as an intrinsic part of the whole."

812. Reaves, Florence Ann. "Bartók's approach to Consonance and Dissonance in Selected Late Instrumental Works." Ph.D. diss. University of Kentucky, 1983. 511p.

Explores parts of the *Fifth* and *Sixth String Quartets, Divertimento for String Orchestra, Violin Concerto No. 2,* and *Concerto for Orchestra,* with the aim of demonstrating a theory of consonance and dissonance (tension and relaxation) in Bartók's music based on evidence obtained through aural perception. Study of his tonality is supported by discussions of rhythm as a determinant of the consonant or dissonant functions of specific intervallic constructions. On the basis of the investigations, the study provides a classification of types of sonorities. Contains bibliography.

813. Rhodes, Sally Ann. "A Music-Dramatic Analysis of the Opera *Duke Bluebeard's Castle* by Béla Bartók." M.A. thesis. Eastman School of Music, 1974. 2 vols. 201, 70p.

According to the author, *RILM Abstracts* No. 2916 (1974), the study "demonstrates how Bartók's music makes an intensely dramatic opera from a libretto that is almost devoid of dramatic action. Reveals the symbolism of the play and various literary motives such as the recurrence of blood and the role of light. Discusses problems which arise in using the play in an unaltered form as a libretto: the lack of characterization, the small number of characters, the lack of dramatic action, and the unvarying metric structure of the Hungarian verse. Examines the various ways in which the dramatic impact is effected through the music. Analyzes musical motives, the form and tonal structure of each door-scene, and the solutions to the problems inherent in using the play as a libretto. Discusses the form of the opera as a whole: the arch created by the tonalities of each scene, the leitmotiv, and the return of the opening material at the end of the opera."

814. Rothe, Friede F. "The Language of the Composer. An Interview with Béla Bartók, Eminent Hungarian Composer." *The Etude* 59 (February 1941): 83, 130.   780.5 Et81

Interview focusing on the meaning of national music and discusses Bartók's own varied activities as a Hungarian composer, folklorist, and musicologist (involving both contemporary issues as well as in presenting his own findings). Gives some history regarding the development of a true Hungarian national art music. Also outlines Bartók's compositions using folk materials.

815. Rubbra, Edmund. "Béla Bartók's Second Piano Concerto." *Monthly Musical Record* 63 (November 1933): 199-200.   780.5 M767

Reprinted in the program notes for the première of the *Concerto* on November 8, 1933, with Bartók as the soloist. Discusses the different sonic (percussive, etc.) characteristics of the piano as exploited in this work.

816. Rummenhöller, Peter. "Zum Spätwerk Béla Bartóks im Verhältnis zum Gesamtwerk" [The late works of Béla Bartók in relation to his œuvre as a whole]. *Musik als Schöpfung und Geschichte: Festschrift Karl Michael Komma zum 75. Geburtstag* (Laaber: Laaber Verlag, 1989): 205-210.

Considers the common assignment of a tripartite division to the creative career of a composer, such as Beethoven, to be entirely appropriate to Bartók's stylistic development. Contrasts Bartók's late style with his early and middle periods and suggests that the classical serenity of Bartók's late style is in accord with what one expects during the final phase of a creative artist's development. Contains illustrations.

817. Sabin, Robert. "Béla Bartók and the Dance." *Dance Magazine* 35 (April 1961): 46.   GV 1580 D246

The author, who is editor of *Musical America,* discusses the importance of Bartók's music to the dance.

818. Saminsky, Lazare. "Bartók and the Graphic Current in the World Music." *Musical Quarterly* 10/3 (1924): 400-404.   ML1 M725 ISSN 0027-4631

Refs to Bartók, in company with Milhaud, Casella, Prokofiev, and others, as a leader of the reaction against "Debussyism" as well as the cult of Schoenberg and Stravinsky to invent new conventions. Rather, Bartók and the other composers of this reaction refer to the eighteenth-century principles of linear clarity and concision in design, the "purely linear" element of which may be termed the "graphic" one. States that the "Graphic Group" is an offshoot of a well-known historic current in the general stream of musical development.

819. Sándor, György. "Béla Bartók: Extending the Piano's Vocabulary." *Contemporary Keyboard* (September/October 1975): 16-18, 32. ML1 C9153

Attempts to list some of Bartók's pianistic contributions in terms of new techniques and sonorities that he evolved. Gives some reference to connections between these devices and his compositional patterns. Contains numerous musical examples.

820. Schloezer, Boris De. "Béla Bartók (History vs. Esthetics)." Translated by Michael Dixon. *Transition* 48/3 (1948): 123-128.

Finds Bartók's personal art and source of its originality elusive. Assumes that unlike Schoenberg and Stravinsky he founded no school because his music is not reducible to a system. Considers this lack defective and assumes that because his compositional solutions were not generalized but rather realized only within each individual context, his art assumes no significant historical role in contrast to that of Schoenberg. However, defends Bartók's art on aesthetic grounds, criticizing René Leibowitz's primarily historical considerations (see item no. 778), the latter regarding musical evolution "as a process which unfolds purely on the plane of technique (more especially of polyphony)." While pointing to the diverse ancestry of Bartók's art in Richard Strauss, Brahms, late Beethoven, and Debussy, on the one hand, and Hungarian folk music, on the other, the author disagrees with Leibowitz's criticism of Bartók's lack of purity (that is, his tendency to compromise) on the basis that "purity and rigour can be demanded by logic, but by a relentless pursuit of them the artist is in danger of sterilizing his creative activity."

821. Schmid, Angeline. "Bartók's Music for Small Hands." *Clavier* 20/8 (October 1981): 22.   780.5 C578   ISSN 0009-854-X

Short statement regarding the degree of stretch of Bartók's hands. Lists works according to the amount of stretch required.

822. Schollum, Robert. "Stilkundliche Bermerkungen zu Werken Bartóks und die 2. Wiener Schule" [Stylistic comments on works of Bartók and the Second Viennese School]. *International Musicological Conference in Commemoration of Béla Bartók 1971*, ed. József Ujfalussy and János Breuer. Budapest: Editio Musica; New York: Belwin Mills, 1972, pp. 77-82.   ML410.B29 I61 (Editio Musica) ML410.B26 I5 (Belwin Mills)

A stylistic comparison of the melodic, rhythmic, harmonic, and timbral characteristics of Bartók's idiom, which stylistically refers back to Beethoven's classicism and to folk-music sources, with the aesthetics of the Vienna Schoenberg School, which has its roots in German late Romantic sources.

823. Schroder, Charles Frederick. "Final Periods of Mozart, Beethoven, and Bartók." Ph.D. diss. State University of Iowa, 1965. 531p. ML410.M9 S385

Discusses primarily the late works of these composers as a focus for an understanding of how their earlier divergent stylistic tendencies are developed and transformed and their earlier goals finally realized. Contains music, bibliography.

824. Seiber, Mátyás. "Béla Bartók." *The Monthly Musical Record* 75/871 (November 1945): 195-199.   780.5 M767

Talks of the great master as the Beethoven of our era and, at the same time, discusses his scientific approach as folklorist. Briefly mentions Bartók's contributions to rhythm and harmony.

825. ----------. "Béla Bartók's Chamber Music." *Tempo* (London) 13 (1949): 19-31.   780.5 T249   ISSN 0040-2982

Chooses to discuss Bartók's chamber music as an expression of the essence of his creation, especially the string quartets. Gives a brief history of Bartók's earliest chamber works, followed by analyses of form, themes, rhythm, and general style features. Also includes some basic historical comments on the *String Quartets*, two *Violin and Piano Sonatas, Contrasts*, and the *Solo Violin Sonata*. Reprinted in *Béla Bartók: A Memorial Review*. New York: Boosey & Hawkes, 1950, pp. 23-35.

826. Sidoti, Raymond Benjamin. "The Violin Sonatas of Béla Bartók: An Epitome of the Composer's Development." D.M.A. treatise. Music: Ohio State University, 1972. 55p.

Provides analyses of the *First Sonata* (1921), *Second Sonata* (1922), and the *Solo Sonata* (1944), including a discussion of their stylistic sources in Strauss , Debussy, Stravinsky, and Schoenberg as well as his absorption of Eastern European and Arab folk elements. Also refers to the Germanic influence in an early *Violin Sonata* (1903). These sonatas are landmarks in the developmental stages of Bartók's compositional and stylistic evolution. Contains bibliography.

827. Skarbowski, Jerzy. "O problemach interpretacyjnych utworów Béli Bartóka" [The problem of interpretation in the works of Béla Bartók]. *Ruch muzyczny* (Poland) 7 (April 1968): 5-7. ISSN 0035-9610

Explores characteristics of Bartók's aesthetics and style based on the study of dynamism, rubato style, movement, and expression, with the aim of clarifying issues of interpretation in his music.

828. Sólyom, György. "'De mi nem megyünk....'. Bartók: *Cantata profana*--részletes elemzés--esztétikai problémák" ["We shall never return...". Bartók: An analysis of Bartók's *Cantata profana*--some aesthetic problems]. *Magyar zene* 32/1 (March 1991): 3-51. ML5 M14   ISSN 0025-0384

According to the author, *RILM Abstracts* No. 9807 (1991), "Bartók's middle creative period, 1926-37, saw a broadening of the composer's social range through use of folklore sources as well as historical deepening through his interest in Renaissance polyphony, Bach's fugal technique, and the Classic sonata concept. His middle-period music shows no recourse to 'stylizations,' but makes reference instead to the greatest achievements of European historical emancipation. The *Cantata profana* is analyzed." Contains music examples.

829. Somfai, László. "Analytical Notes on Bartók's Piano Year of 1926." *Studia musicologica* 26/1-4 (1984): 5-59.   781.05 St92 ISSN 0039-3266

Includes ten short analytical essays of highly varied subjects, which together provide a comprehensive view of the aesthetics, styles, and techniques in Bartók's piano music of this year. Topics deal with the construction of nature's noises (discussing musical symbols of the objective world, the individual poetry, and the art of the folk community), the stratagem in creating inarticulation (involving motivic development), the dialectics of compressed and extended themes, contrast form with "explosion coda," folk-music genre form, metre-breaking rhythmic patterns, theme with long notes, thematic contrast and organic construct in a sonata exposition, layout of a development section, and sonata-form revision. Includes many detailed diagrams and music examples.

830. ----------. "Bartók--saját műveinek interpretátora" [Bartók as an interpreter of his own works]. *Magyar zene* (December 1968): 354-360. ML5 M14 ISSN 0025-0384

Compares characteristics of Bartók's pianistic style with his compositional style. In connection with his career as a performer, a survey of his repertoire is outlined, including the keyboard works of Frescobaldi, Scarlatti, Bach, Mozart, Beethoven, Liszt, Debussy, Stravinsky, Kodály, etc. Contains a discography. Also published as "Bartók als Interpret." *Beiträge* 1968/69 (1969): 41-45.

831. ----------. "Egy sajátos kulminációs pont Bartók hangszeres formáiban" [A characteristic culmination point in Bartók's instrumental forms]. *Magyar zene* (June 1971): 132-143. ML5 M14 ISSN 0025-0384

States that through the extensive research that now exists on Bartók's music, a re-examination can be conducted of certain decisive characteristics of Bartók's style, including the "dramaturgy" of certain form models as well as some structural characteristics. Examines characteristic and emphatically "Hungarian" culmination points located in the penultimate form sections of movements. Provides analyses of excerpts from several works, including the *Divertimento* (1939), *Music for Strings, Percussion and Celesta* (1936), *First String Quartet* (1908-1909), *Second String Quartet* (1915-1917), *The Wooden Prince* (1916), and the *First Piano Concerto* (1926). Refers to two specific analytical systems that have led to new observations concerning the influence of folk music on Bartók's style; these include 1) Ernő Lendvai's study of the pentatonic sources for Bartók's melodic and harmonic use of Golden Section principles, and 2) János Kárpáti's discussion of folk sources as the basis of Bartók's use of polymodality. Also published in English, in *International Musicological Conference in Commemoration of Béla Bartók 1971,* ed. József Ujfalussy and János Breuer. Budapest: Editio Musica; New York: Belwin Mills, 1972, pp. 53-64; and in *Tizennyolc Bartók tanulmány* No. 13. Budapest: Editio Musica, 1981, pp. 270-278.

832. ----------. "'Per finire': Some Aspects of the Finale in Bartók's Cyclic Form." *Studia musicologica* 11 (1969): 391-408. 781.05 St92 ISSN 0039-3266

Explores the purpose and function of the finale, which the author concludes, "should be a solution of a higher moral character, a conclusion eliciting the feeling of catharsis," and not "just an antithesis to what has been expressed by the preceding movements."

As one instance, the last four pages are devoted to *Music for Strings, Percussion and Celesta* IV, dealing with the relationship of structure and previously stated material to performance problems of tempo and character. Also published as "'Per Finire'--Gondolatok Bartók finálé-problematikájáról." *Magyar zene* (December 1970): 3-15; and in *Tizennyolc Bartók tanulmány* No. 13. Budapest: Editio Musica, 1981, pp. 255-264.

833. ----------. "The 'Piano Year' of 1926." *The Bartók Companion*, ed. Malcolm Gillies. London: Faber and Faber, 1993; Portland, Oregon: Amadeus Press (an imprint of Timber Press, Inc.), 1994. pp. 173-188.   ISBN 0-931340-74-8 (HB)   ISBN 0-931340-75-6 (PB) ML410 B26 B28

Points to Bartók's "piano year" of 1926 as a landmark in his stylistic development. Discusses Bartók's return to intensive composition at this time after a lull of three years. Based on evidence in the sketches and other compositional stages, outlines the compositional chronology (including the order of movements) of the *Piano Sonata, Out of Doors*, the *First Piano Concerto*, and the *Nine Little Piano Pieces*. Presents some historical discussion of Bartók's early performances of these works, points to stylistic influences (folk-music sources, though without direct quotations, and both traditional and contemporary art-music sources), and provides concentrated structural analyses of these piano works based on thematic, modal/tonal, and rhythmic construction and interaction within the larger formal designs. Also discusses Bartók's aesthetic and structural intentions in these works and relates them to a broader body of his music.

834. ----------. *Tizennyolc Bartók-tanulmány* [Eighteen Bartók studies]. Budapest: Editio Musica, 1981. 323p.   ISBN-9633303702 ML410.B26 1981

Includes comprehensive and varied collections of studies by Somfai from his previously published articles. Topics range from an overall history of Bartók's style development to detailed studies of the primary sources and in-depth analyses of form, scale, etc., in his music. Contains illustrations, music, bibliography. See reviews by: Ferenc László, in *A hét* 13/3 (January 15, 1982): 7; and János Kárpáti, in *Studia musicologica* 25/1-4 (1983): 239-242, and *Muzsika* 26/2 (February 1983): 45-46.

835. Spinosa, Frank. "Beethoven and Bartók: A Comparative Study of Motivic Techniques in the Later Beethoven Quartets and the Six String Quartets of Béla Bartók." D.M.A. diss. University of Illinois, 1969. 214p. MT-140.S65 1969a

Comparative study of motivic construction and transformation in the six quartets of Bartók and the last six quartets of Beethoven (Op. 95-135). Analyses include a study of motivic procedures in connection with variation in melodic contour, intervallic structure, and rhythm. Contains illustrations, bibliography.

836. Stenzl, Jürg. "Béla Bartók--'Repräsentant der alten Welt'?" [Béla Bartók--"a representative of the old world"?]. *Studia musicologica* 24/supplement (1982): 31-45.   781.05 St92   ISSN 0039-3266

Argues that Bartók is a representative of the Old World, though this opinion is not shared by every composer who was in his youth during the 1950s. Illustrates this point by using Jacques Wildberger, Klaus Huber, and Constantin Regamey as examples.

837. Stern, Gershon. "Semiotic Levels in Performances of Bartók's *Music for Strings, Percussion and Celesta.*" D.M. diss. Indiana University, 1989. 154p.

According to the author, *RILM Abstracts* No. 12670 (1989), "Various layers of symbolism (semiotic levels) are followed through the score for Bartók's *Music for Strings, Percussion and Celesta,* then through 13 recordings. The performers' deviations from written indications are discussed. The process of symbolic thinking as applied in daily musical practice should be incorporated into aesthetic studies of a more comprehensive scope, as potentially valid contributions to the understanding of the subjective reality of music." Contains illustrations, music examples, bibliography, discography.

838. Stevens, Halsey. "Some 'Unknown' Works of Bartók." *Musical Quarterly* 52 (1966): 37-55.   ML1 M725   ISSN 0027-4631

States that many of Bartók's works only became known to the listening public after his death. Surveys a number of works, providing some historical information on their recorded performances, publications, and basic stylistic and technical characteristics. Discussed to some extent from the point of view of subjective critical evaluation. Also talks of certain works that were either lost or overlooked and are not listed in Bartók's catalogue of his own music.

839. Stockhausen, Karlheinz. "Bartók's *Sonata for Two Pianos and Percussion.*" *The New Hungarian Quarterly* 11/40 (1970): 49-53. 914.39105 N42   ML410 B26 B29

Provides an analysis of the work to demonstrate Bartók's progressive rhythmic style.

840. Streller, Friedbert. "Musikalische Sprachmittel in Werken der zeitgenössischen Musik (Bartók, Chatschaturjan)" [Musical speech in contemporary music (Bartók, Khatchaturian)]. *Bericht über den Internationalen Musikwissenschaftlichen Kongress, Leipzig 1966,* hrsg. von Carl Dahlhaus et al. Kassel: Bärenreiter, 1970. pp. 362-371.   ML36 I628

Provides a thematic and figural analysis in works of Bartók and Khatchaturian, with the aim of establishing a means of studying principles of musical "speech."

841. Suchoff, Benjamin. *Bartók: Concerto for Orchestra, Understanding Bartók's World.* New York: G. Schirmer, 1995. 200p. ISBN 0-02-872495   ML410.B26S83   784.2'186-dc20

Demonstrates that the *Concerto for Orchestra* is based on a comprehensive synthesis of Eastern European folk-music sources and Western art-music techniques, and is a kind of index to the multiplicity of musical sources that the composer absorbed and transformed throughout his evolution. The author's organizational approach in three large parts and the individual topics subsumed under them forms a comprehensive and coherent view of Bartók's varied musical life and compositional activity. The overall development of Bartók's musical language and style is traced in *Part 1--Bartók's Musical Language:* (1) Childhood and Youth; (2) Summary of Hungarian Musical Dialect: 1900-1905; (3) Fusion of National Musical Styles: 1906-1925 (including: Discovery of the Romanian Folkloric Mother Lode, The Turn toward Musicological Ethnography, Approaching Musical Synthesis: *Duke Bluebeard's Castle,* Op. 11); (4) Synthesis of East and West: 1925-1945 (including: *Mikrokosmos,* an Introduction to Bartók's System of Composition, Bartók in America). A systematic analytical survey follows in *Part 2--Concerto for Orchestra--*analysis: (5) I. Introduzione--Allegro Vivace, which draws together the folk and art-music sources; (6) Second Movement (Presentando le Coppie); (7) Third Movement (Elegia); (8) Fourth Movement (Intermezzo Interroto); (9) Fifth Movement (Finale). *Part 3--Bartók's Legacy:* (1) The Influence of Bartók's Music on Latter-Day Composition (including: Alberto Ginastera, Benjamin Britten, György Ligeti, George Crumb, Witold Lutosław ski, Olivier Messiaen, Béla Bartók's Stylistic Development: An Overview). Contains music examples, chronological list of cited Bartók compositions, notes, bibliography, and index.

842. ----------. "Bartók's Musical Microcosm." *Clavier* 16/5 (May-June 1977): 18-25.   780.5 C578   ISSN 0009-854-X

Provides an historical outline of Bartók's piano music of the 1920s, including the *Mikrokosmos* (1926-1939). After a brief definition of this work as well as a summation of its pedagogical aims, its "stylistic cosmos" (based on influences or parallels from Bach to Debussy, Schoenberg, and Gershwin) and its "folkloristic cosmos" (including that of American, Arabic, Balkan, Hungarian, etc.) are outlined.

843. ----------. "Synthesis of East and West: *Mikrokosmos.*" *The Bartók Companion,* ed. Malcolm Gillies. London: Faber and Faber, 1993; Portland, Oregon: Amadeus Press (an imprint of Timber Press, Inc.), 1994. pp. 189-211. ISBN 0-931340-74-8 (HB) ISBN 0-931340-75-6 (PB) ML410 B26 B28

Examines the textural and other stylistic aspects of selected pieces from Bartók's *Mikrokosmos.* Begins with an outline of the varied art-music sources that influenced Bartók's stylistic development during the third period of his career (1926-1945). Points especially to the decisive impact of Bach's Italian predecessors and contemporaries--Frescobaldi, della Ciaia, and others--who, as the author informs us, were curiously omitted from Bartók's own references that included Bach, Beethoven, and Debussy. Provides an historical overview of the events and "many-sided" musical concerns which led to the publication of the *Mikrokosmos.* In accordance with Bartók's own stated interests concerning a synthesis of musical and technical problems in piano playing, the author shows how these technical exercises were actually intended to introduce the student to the compositional principles themselves. Discusses the synthesis of stanzaic structures from Eastern and Western sources, rhythmic and syllabic schemata, and transformation of Eastern European folk modes into chromatic polymodes and more abstract scale and pitch-cell constructions. Also points to certain analogies between Bartók's contrapuntal devices and those of the Baroque, and addresses technical issues concerning piano touch and special tone-colour symbols that Bartók developed as early as 1907 while preparing an edition of Bach's keyboard music.

844. ----------. "The Genesis of Bartók's Musical Language." *Bartók in Retrospect,* ed. Elliott Antokoletz, Victoria Fischer, and Benjamin Suchoff. Projected publication of two 1995 conference proceedings.

Discusses the conditions and events that contributed to Bartók's compositional development between 1900 and 1910, focusing on the folk and art music sources that he absorbed during this period. Refers to Bartók's interest in creating a specifically Hungarian style of composition, originally seeking inspiration in the Gypsy-disseminated Hungarian popular art music which was then considered to be indigenous Hungarian folk music. Discusses the influence of Richard Strauss and Liszt, which led to his symphonic poem *Kossuth*

(1903), his first encounter with the rural song repertory, including pentatonic specimens and modally-transformed popular art songs, and his collaboration with Kodály in the collection of folk music in the rural areas of then-Greater Hungary. Points out that Bartók's transcription and comparative analysis of the collected materials disclosed unique structural characteristics which became foundational attributes of his musical language. Also refers to the influence of Debussy's innovative use of nonfunctional harmony, which Bartók adapted as a solution to the homophonic treatment of monodic folk music. Informs us that Bartók's compositions for piano, from the *First Elegy* (1908) to the *Three Burlesques* (1910-1911), illustrate his fusion of national styles, that is, the methodical articulation of Hungarian peasant music with that of the national minority peoples in the Slovak and Romanian linguistic areas under the fertilizing effect of Liszt and Debussy. (Annotation based on the author's abstract of the original lecture; see item no. 1160.)

845. Sulikowski, Jerzy. "Béla Bartók: 'Im Freien.' Wpływ faktury na problematykę wykonawcza" [Béla Bartók's *Out of Doors:* the influence of piano texture on problems of execution]. *Zeszyty naukowe. Państwowa wyższa szkoła muzyczna w Gdańsku* (Poland) 11 (1972): 224-245.

A performer's view of the technical problems in Bartók's piano suite, *Out of Doors* (1926), presenting an analysis to show that the work is more pianistic than previously suggested.

846. Sung, Stella Cheng-Yu. "Absorption of Divergent Musical Sources and Compositional Techniques into Béla Bartók's *Third Piano Concerto.*" D.M.A. diss. University of Texas, Austin, 1991. 95p. DA9128134

Analyzes the *Third Piano Concerto* to demonstrate how Bartók moved in his late works toward a thorough synthesis of divergent traditional and contemporary elements. The work is based on complete absorption and synthesis of techniques, procedures, and forms from Baroque, Classic, and impressionist idioms with characteristics of his native Hungarian folk music, including pentatonic/diatonic modality, thematic contour, and rhythmic patterns. Furthermore, transformational processes are revealed between the folk modalities and more abstract symmetrical (octatonic and whole-tone) collections within the Classic structure. These processes are further drawn into the sphere of symmetrical pitch construction through the structural use of axes of symmetry as a new means of establishing tonal centricity and articulating the traditional form. Summarizes Bartók's compositional evolution and also discusses the influence of the Italian Baroque and other contrapuntal sources in the second and third movements. Contains music examples, bibliography.

847. Szabó, Csaba. "Jelleg és prozódia: Szöveg és zene a *Cantata profanában*" [Character and prosody: Text and music in *Cantata profana*]. *Társadalomtudomány* (1990): 171-196.

According to the author, *RILM Abstracts* No. 4646 (1990),"The Hungarian prosody in Bartók's *Cantata profana* is investigated in relation to all compositional elements of the work, with emphasis on the connections between musical language and Hungarian word-stress and vowel length." Contains music examples.

848. Szabó, Miklós. "Choral Works." *The Bartók Companion*, ed. Malcolm Gillies. London: Faber and Faber, 1993; Portland, Oregon: Amadeus Press (an imprint of Timber Press, Inc.), 1994. pp. 413-423.   ISBN 0-931340-74-8 (HB)   ISBN 0-931340-75-6 (PB) ML410 B26 B28

Discusses Bartók's choral works based on folk texts and, with two exceptions, folk melodies from Hungarian, Slovak, and Romanian sources. Provides a list of the choral works explored (including scoring and dates of composition and premières). Addresses the question of Bartók's motives and intentions for composing choral works, provides some stylistic comparisons of these works with others by Bartók (and Kodály). Considers the chronology and style (texture, modal structure, etc.) of the eight choral works under discussion in three categories and compares the level of performing difficulty in the cycles of the different periods. Then, provides more specific analytical discussions of the individual works, addressing techniques (harmonic, modal, tonal, formal, and textural) of arranging the folk tune. Contains some reference to Bartók's more characteristic use of "instrumental" style in these choral works.

849. Szentkirályi, András. "Bartók and the Twentieth Century." *Studia musicologica* 24/3-4 (1982): 475-481.   781.05 St92 ISSN 0039-3266

Author reveals a bias against avant-garde music, showing favor for Bartók's change of direction in his late period toward use of more traditional procedures.

850. Tawaststjerna, Erik. "Sibelius und Bartók: einige Parallelen" [Sibelius and Bartók: a parallel]. *International Musicological Conference in Commemoration of Béla Bartók 1971*, ed. József Ujfalussy and János Breuer. Budapest: Editio Musica; New York:

Belwin Mills, 1972, pp. 121-135.   ML410.B29 I61 (Editio Musica)
ML410.B26 I5 (Belwin Mills)

Discusses the question of Sibelius's national style on the basis
of the three categories of folk-music influence defined by Bartók.
Mentions the status of Sibelius's interest in folk music as compared
with Bartók's and his main contributions in this area.

851. Tusa, Erzsébet. "Bartók und die Naturformen: Der Goldene Schnitt"
     [Bartók and natural forms: The Golden Section]. *Polyaisthesis* 4/1
     (1989): 78-87.

     Explores the relations between the structural proportions of
     Bartók's music, the organic structures of nature, and the Golden
     Section and Fibonacci series. Includes summary in English. Contains
     illustrations, music examples.

852. Twittenhoff, Wilhelm. "Zur Struktur und Thematik des
     Violinkonzerts von Béla Bartók" [On the structure and thematic of
     Béla Bartók's *Violin Concerto*]. *Musikerkenntnis und*
     Musikerziehung, Dankesgaben für Hans Mersmann zu seinem 65.
     Geburtstage, ed. W. Wiora. Kassel: Bärenreiter, 1957: 143-157.
     780.4 W741M

     Structural and thematic analysis comparing the technical
     mastery and aesthetic principles of Bartók with those of Beethoven.

853. Ujfalussy, József. "Béla Bartóks Entwicklung vor dem ersten
     Streichquartett" [Béla Bartók's development before the first string
     quartet]. *Gesellschaft für Musikforschung, Report, Bayreuth 1981*
     (1984): xii-xvi.

     According to Günther Rötter, *RILM Abstracts* No. 6164 (1984),
     states that "Bartók sought to combine two different stylistic realms--
     Hungarian folklore and the modern--by using melodic material from
     Hungarian peasant songs, but not orienting this material
     harmonically on the major-minor system. The first string quartet
     contains structural and stylistic innovations and stands at the
     beginning of a new creative period."

854. ----------. "Egy nehéz búcsúzas zeneu képlete" [The musical depiction
     of a sad parting]. *Zenetudományi dolgozatok* (1984): 67-69.

     Discusses "Dedication," which is the first of the *Ten Easy*
     Pieces, as an expression of Bartók's unrequited love for the violinist
     Stefi Geyer.

855. Vauclain, Constant. "Bartók: Beyond Bi-Modality." *Music Review* 42/3-4 (August-November 1981): 243-251. 780.5 M9733 ISSN 0027-4445

Quotes Bartók's 1943 Harvard lectures dealing with "bi-" or "poly-modality." However, the author shows various places in Bartók's music from 1926 on, where non-modal analysis can be made of his simultaneous use of two scales (e.g. slow movement of the *Piano Sonata*, opening of *Music for Strings, Percussion and Celesta*, and *Sixth String Quartet*, especially the last movement). States that such intermingling goes back to the *Bagatelles* of 1908. States that a fusion of combined scales produces a new and different perceptible surface with its own melodies and harmonies.

856. Veress, Sándor. "Béla Bartóks 44 Duos für zwei Violinen" [Béla Bartók's *44 Duos for Two Violins*]. *Erich Doflein: Festschrift zum 70. Geburtstag.* (August 7, 1970). Mainz: Schott, 1972. pp. 31-57. ML55 D63

Comprehensive study of the *Duos*. Includes an historical discussion in terms of origin, chronology of composition, and folk sources. Also presents a stylistic investigation based on a harmonic, melodic, and rhythmic study. Compares their musical and pedagogical significance to the *Mikrokosmos*.

857. -------------. "Bluebeard's Castle." *Tempo* (London) 13 (1949): 32-38; reprinted in *Béla Bartók: A Memorial Review*. New York: Boosey & Hawkes,1950, pp. 36-53. 780.5 T249   ISSN 0040-2982

Presents an in-depth discussion of the drama in terms of its asceticism as well as the psychological and spiritual process of the two characters. States that Bartók faithfully follows this dramatic-psychological process in the vocal styles and musical construction of the opera. Then provides a detailed analytical outline dealing with motif- and harmonic-symbolism, tonalities characterizing the door-scenes, musical expression, harmonic construction, melodic style, and musical form. Includes illustrations and music examples.

858. ----------. "Einführung in die Streichquartette Béla Bartóks" [Introduction to the string quartets of Béla Bartók]. *Schweizerische Musikzeitung* (Zürich) 90 (1950): 437-443.   ML5 S413

Introductory remarks given on the three evenings the Végh Quartet performed Bartók's six string quartets in Basel, February 1950. Briefly points out characteristics of each quartet.

859. Volek, Jaroslav. "Bartók--Determination of a Period." *International Musicological Conference in Commemoration of Béla Bartók 1971*, ed. József Ujfalussy and János Breuer. Budapest: Editio Musica; New

York: Belwin Mills, 1972, pp. 19-24.   ML410.B29 I61 (Editio
Musica)   ML410.B26 I5 (Belwin Mills)

Discussion of Bartók's use of folk elements and his exploitation
of each of the twelve notes of our chromatically tempered scale.
Aims at tracing the impulses which Bartók's lifework and the
significance of his compositions offer as lessons towards the
solution of the problem of qualifying and defining an entire period
of music. Points out that Bartók, like Beethoven, lived at the
meeting point of two periods in music history.

860. Walsh, Stephen. *Bartók's Chamber Music.* (BBC Music Guide).
London, 1982. 88p. ISBN-0563124652   785.700924 B285Z,W168
MT145.B292 W227. See also the French trans. by Virginie Bauzou.
Musique. Paris: Actes Sud, 1991. 133p.

Includes discussion of the *Six String Quartets,* the *Sonatas* and
Rhapsodies for violin and piano, *Contrasts,* and the *Sonata for Two
Pianos and Percussion.* Provides biographical information
surrounding the specific compositions dealt with in the study. Also,
explores the works in terms of emotional interpretation as well as
various influences. In addition, provides reference to basic
theoretical studies of Bartók, including those of Lendvai and Kárpáti.
Contains illustrations, music, index. See the review by Paul
Griffiths, in *The Musical Times* (October 1982): 764.

861. Weber, Horst. "Material und Komposition in Bartóks Concerto for
Orchestra" [Material and composition in Bartók's *Concerto for
Orchestra*]. *Neue Zeitung für Musik* 134/12 (1973): 767-773.

Presents an outline of Bartók's stylistic evolution with a focus
on the *Concerto for Orchestra.*

862. Weiss-Aigner, Günter. "Béla Bartók: Musik für Saiteninstrumente,
Schlagzeug und Celesta" [Béla Bartók: *Music for Strings, Percussion
and Celesta*]. *Musik und Bildung* 7/9 (1975): 440-448.

Explores principles of differentiation, repetition and variation
and their role in the process of synthesis, which is so essential to
Bartók's aesthetics.

863. ----------. "Die frühe Schaffensentwicklung Béla Bartóks im Lichte
westliches und östliches Traditionen" [Béla Bartók's early creative
development in light of Western and Eastern traditions]. Diss.
Friedrich-Alexander Universität, Erlangen-Nuremberg, 1970. vii,
562p.   MT 92.B36 W4 1970a

First part explores rhythm, form types, orchestration, melody,
and tonality in western art-music of the nineteenth century,
including developments with R. Strauss, Schumann, Brahms,

Schubert, Liszt, and Beethoven. Also includes some discussion of folk melody in this tradition. Second part deals with the Eastern tradition, including political factors and its ethnological consequences, cultural history and its musical consequences, and Hungarian peasant music, its structural characteristics and its relation to Romantic national music. Third part is a study of Bartók's early development in light of the influences and the stylistic concentration in his later works. Contains music, bibliography. Published: Kommissionsverlag, Musikverlag Emil Katzbichler, 1974. vii, 562p.   ML410.B292 W42 1974z

864. ----------. "Der Spätstil Bartóks in seiner Violinmusik" [Bartók's late style in his violin music]. *Studia musicologica* 23 (1981): 261-293. 781.05 St92   ISSN 0039-3266

Discusses the stylistic manifestations and developments of string technique in those works of Bartók that include the instrument since 1934 (beginning with the *Fifth String Quartet* to the *Viola Concerto* of 1945). Gives a detailed discussion of thematic or figural structure in terms of scales (modal or chromatic) and intervals in connection with problems of fingering and various devices (pizzicato, etc.).

865. ----------. "The 'Lost' Violin Concerto." *The Bartók Companion,* ed. Malcolm Gillies. London: Faber and Faber, 1993; Portland, Oregon: Amadeus Press (an imprint of Timber Press, Inc.), 1994. pp. 468-476. ISBN 0-931340-74-8 (HB)   ISBN 0-931340-75-6 (PB) ML410 B26 B28

Refers to the critical change in Bartók's career and compositional attitudes between the creation of his *Kossuth* symphony (1903) and *Violin Concerto* (1907-1908) and the decline in public interest in Budapest toward his new artistic inclinations. Points to his espousal of Nietzsche's philosophy during his growing depression and isolation and his rejection of urban society in connection with his discovery of folk music. Provides essential biographical, psychological, and philosophical information in connection with the genesis of the *Concerto*. Focuses on Bartók's unrequited love for the violinist Stefi Geyer and its bearing on his Romantic musical expression of a programmatic bent. Provides an analytical study of the basic major-seventh (D-F#-A-C#) leitmotif, its transformations (and uses in his other works at this time), and tonal relations within the overall structure and design. Points especially to the influence of Liszt and Strauss during this period.

866. ----------. "Youthful Chamber Works." *The Bartók Companion,* ed. Malcolm Gillies. London: Faber and Faber, 1993; Portland, Oregon: Amadeus Press (an imprint of Timber Press, Inc.), 1994. pp. 215-

225.   ISBN 0-931340-74-8 (HB)   ISBN 0-931340-75-6 (PB)
ML410 B26 B28

Survey and analysis of Bartók's early chamber works, demonstrating the evolution of his style around the turn of the century. Points to the stimulating musical climate and the predominating Germanic influence in Bartók's home town of Pozsony (now Bratislava). More specifically, refers to the influence of Beethoven on his *Piano Sonata in G Minor* (1894). In the early *Violin Sonata* (1895), Bartók began to show a more concise and dynamic approach to the Classical model. Analyses of his next chamber works reveal Bartók's absorption of influences from other German Romantics, demonstrate his marked development and "growing boldness" especially beginning with his extant *Violin Sonata in A Major* (1897), and show increasing juxtapositions of elements from Eastern and Western styles. Also presents background information on Bartók's circumstances and activities in connection with the stylistic discussions of the individual works.

867. ----------. "Youthful Orchestral Works." *The Bartók Companion*, ed. Malcolm Gillies. London: Faber and Faber, 1993; Portland, Oregon: Amadeus Press (an imprint of Timber Press, Inc.), 1994. pp. 441-453.   ISBN 0-931340-74-8 (HB)   ISBN 0-931340-75-6 (PB)
ML410 B26 B28

Survey and analyses of Bartók's early orchestral works, including the Eb major Symphony (1902), *Kossuth* symphonic poem (1903), and other works, which reveal the decisive influence of Strauss and other late-Romantic composers and also contain Hungarian themes, motives, and rhythmic formulas. Includes discussion of the historical and personal circumstances in which these works developed. This includes Bartók's increasing concerns for the creation of a national Hungarian music as part of his growing anti-Habsburg sentiment. Also, points to stylistic and technical connections with his works of the period in other genres.

868. ----------. "Youthful Piano Works." *The Bartók Companion*, ed. Malcolm Gillies. London: Faber and Faber, 1993; Portland, Oregon: Amadeus Press (an imprint of Timber Press, Inc.), 1994. pp. 101-109.   ISBN 0-931340-74-8 (HB)   ISBN 0-931340-75-6 (PB)
ML410 B26 B28

Provides a brief history surrounding the composition of Bartók's earliest piano compositions, all of which have remained unpublished. Discusses his early piano studies at the Budapest Academy of Music, the negative impact of his compositional studies there on his creativity, and a new phase of inspiration stemming from his initial contact with Richard Strauss's symphonic poem, *Also sprach Zarathustra*. Primarily presents an overview of Bartók's early piano works, including description of their forms, procedures, and influences, and some analysis of his tonal idiom. Ends with a brief analysis of the work that initiated his mature opus numbering, the *Rhapsody* Op. 1 (1904). Also relates these piano works to his other genres of this period. Contains music examples.

869. Weissmann, John S. "Bartók's Piano Music." *Tempo* (London) 13-14 (Winter 1949-1950): 60-71.   780.5 T249   ISSN 0040-2982

Discusses the "different world" of the *Third Piano Concerto* in comparison with the *First* and *Second*. Explores the textural writing for the piano, for the orchestra, and their combination. Discusses stylistic aspects that set the *Third* apart (e.g., lack of percussion and the minimizing of the competitive principle) and the influence of Bartók's fatal illness on the character of the work. Reprinted in *Béla Bartók: A Memorial Review*. New York: Boosey & Hawkes, 1950, pp. 60-71.

870. ----------. "Béla Bartók: An Estimate." *Music Review* 7/4 (November 1946): 221-241.   780.5 M9733   ISSN 0027-4445

Traces the development of Bartók's artistic career and creative evolution by observing various tendencies of contemporary musical expression assembled in his style. Also, discusses his mastery of possibilities stemming from the early historical transitional period in which he began to assimilate ancient folk music. Places this development in historical context.

871. ----------. "La musique de piano de Bartók: L'evolution d'une écriture" [The piano music of Bartók: the evolution of a writing]. *La revue musicale* 224 (1955): 171-222.   780.5 R328   ISSN 0035-3736

States that Bartók's pianistic talent was always a stimulus for his compositional talent. Since most of his early compositions were for piano, in which he looked for solutions to problems of technique and language, we can study his piano works as a source for understanding the development of his style. Then, discusses various piano works in terms of stylistic features and their historical sources in Liszt, Schumann, Debussy, folk music, etc. States that Bartók's evolution moved from a pianistic style to a more universal one to express his vision of the world, characterized by a novel humanism and renaissance of musical values.

872. -----------. "Notes Concerning Bartók's Solo Vocal Music I." *Tempo* 36 (1955-1956): 16-25.   780.5 T249   ISSN 0040-2982

States that while Bartók's instrumental music is enjoying popularity, the vocal music is neglected in the recording catalogues, especially the *Cantata Profana* and *Village Scenes*. Asserts that

Bartók resorted to the human voice, with its "concrete verbal responses to creative experience," and this is a "distinct guide to the psychological constitution of his creative personality." Focuses on the two sets of songs, Op. 15 and Op. 16, providing some discussion of the poets, historical background, and detailed musical analyses. Also relates materials of the songs to other works of Bartók.

873. Wightman, Alistair. "Szymanowski, Bartók and the Violin." *The Musical Times* (March 1981): 159-163.   780.5 M98
ISSN 0027-4666

States that there is abundant internal evidence in certain works of Bartók regarding his admiration for Szymanowski's violin and piano writing. However, similarities of texture and idiom are superficial and their fundamental styles and approaches differ significantly. While Bartók admired Szymanowski, he did not express this publicly.

874. Winking, Hans. "Klangflächen bei Bartók bis 1911. Zu einigen stilistischen Beziehungen in den Orchesterwerken Béla Bartóks zur Orchestermusik des späten 19. und frühen 20. Jahrhunderts" [Tonal planes of Bartók to 1911. On unified stylistic relations of the orchestral works of Bartók to the orchestral music of the late-nineteenth and early twentieth centuries]. *Studia musicologica* 24/3-4 (1982): 549-564.   781.05 St92   ISSN 0039-3266

Explores special stylistic thematic, and tonal principles as they evolved in Bartók's early works (to 1911), moving from the conscious influences of Brahms, Dohnányi, Wagner, Liszt, and Strauss, to Debussy. Points to Bartók's evolution of "Klangflächen" from the concept to its realization in *Duke Bluebeard's Castle* of 1911.

875. Wolff, Hellmuth Christian. "Béla Bartók und die Musik der Gegenwart" [Béla Bartók and the music of the present day]. *Melos* 8 (1952): 209-217.   780.5 M492   ISSN 0174-7207

Outlines Bartók's development as a composer, stressing the importance of his folk-music collecting, and argues that he went through all stages of the new European music from Impressionism to Expressionism, and Classicism to a new "optimism" in his late works. Provides analytical descriptions of several works, with the aim of elucidating Bartók's style in relation to other contemporary developments.

876. ----------. *Ordnung und Gestalt. Die Musik von 1900 bis 1950* [Order and form. Music from 1900 to 1950]. Bonn-Bad Godesberg: Verlag

für Systematisches Musikwissenschaft, 1978. 294p.   ML197.W73
780.904

Includes analyses of the forms and genres of several composers, significantly including compositions by Bartók. Presents a new concept of "ordo-style," dealing with technical materials based on sonority, melody, and rhythm, and their distinction as well as relationship with spiritual tendencies. Contains music examples, illustrations, bibliography, index.

3. Folk-Music Influences on Bartók's Compositions

877. Andraschke, Peter. "Folklora in kompozicija" [Folklore and composition]. *Ljudska in umetna glasba v 20. stoletju v Evropi* (Ljubljana: Festival Ljubljana, 1990): 28-34.

Explores the compositional use of folk sources by three composers, Béla Bartók, Hans Werner Henze, and Karlheinz Stockhausen.

878. Arauco, Ingrid. "Bartók's Romanian Christmas Carols: Changes from the Folk Sources and Their Significance." *The Journal of Musicology* 5/2 (Spring 1987): 191-225.   780.5 J826
ISSN 0277-9269

According to the author, *RILM Abstracts* No. 3351 (1987), "An attempt to define the criteria underlying Béla Bartók's compositional choices in a single work: the *Róman Kolinda-dallamok* of 1915 for piano. Examined are the often slight but telling changes made in the melodies from their folk-song sources to Bartók's final arrangement. Types of change fall into three categories: (1) the removal of incidental tones and ornaments, (2) the repositioning of barlines, and (3) the alteration of notes and rhythms. The effect of these changes is to enhance the structural clarity of the melodies in accordance with certain norms of Western art music. Also evident, however, is the composer's desire to preserve the integrity of the original melodies to the greatest extent possible in the concert hall." Contains music examples.

879. ----------. "Methods of Translation in Bartók's Twenty Hungarian Folksongs." *Journal of Musicological Research* 12/3 (1992): 189-211.   ML5 M6415   780.7   ISSN 0141-1896

Asserts that it is possible to study Bartók's music entirely by means of the interaction of folk and art traditions. Applies this approach to a detailed analytical exploration of this final set of folk-song transcriptions for voice and piano (1929). First, provides a brief history of Bartók's compositions for voice and piano, pointing to the predominance of folk-song arrangements over an art-song conception in his output, and refers to Bartók's task in relating folk song to an urban audience. Then discusses the composer's considerations of the relation between folk tune and piano accompaniment in view of text translation, stating that the "synthesis of musical characteristics [folk and art] makes apparent the compromise that must lie at the heart of any translation." The author's main focus is on the exploration of tonal and motivic processes as articulative means toward Bartók's creation of architectonic (rounded) structure in his transcriptions, a structural feature found only in the new Hungarian folk-song style and Western (primarily German) art music. However, asserts that the rounded structural concept is manifested even in Bartók's settings of folk tunes in the old Hungarian folk-song style, which is characterized exclusively by the nonrounded stanzaic principle (e.g., ABCD), in order to produce a sense of higher-level structure.

880. Bahk, Junsang. "Die Auswirkungen der Volksliedforschung auf das kompositorische Schaffen von Béla Bartók" [Effects of folk-song research on Béla Bartók's compositional production]. Ph.D. diss. Musikwissenschaft: Universität Wien, 1991. 214p.   DAC320886

Points to Bartók's folk-music research and its significance as manifested in his music during different phases of compositional absorption of the folk sources. Discusses the changing status of the folk tunes in his works according to the composer's varied approaches to their use. Spans the gamut from arrangement of authentic folk tunes, in which the folk tune is pre-eminent and the accompaniment serves simply as a setting for it, and the imitation of the folk sources in a more abstract context, to the complete assimilation of the folk-music essence into a highly original art-music idiom in which the material is entirely removed from the original folk source. Contains music examples, bibliography.

881. Balas, Edith. "Brâncuşi and Bartók: A Parallel." *Imago musicae* 6 (1989): 165-192.   ML85 142

Outlines the three essential ways in which Bartók employed traditional folk-music sources in his art-music compositions. The first is based on the arrangement of an unchanged authentic folk tune by means of adding an accompaniment to it, the second based on imitation of the folk-music sources, the third by absorption of the essence of folk music without quotation or imitation of the original folk-tune source. Then, points to an intermedia parallel between Bartók's approach to folk-music absorption and the methodology of the Romanian sculptor Constantin Brâncuşi (1876-1957), who employed these three approaches to folk-music absorption in his sculptures in a strikingly similar manner to Bartók. Contains music examples, illustrations.

882. Bárdos, Lajos. "Bartók dallamvilágából" [Bartók's melodies]. *Tíz újabb írás, 1969-1974* [Ten recent essays, 1969-1974]. Budapest: Zeneműkiadó, 1974, pp. 107-114.

Presents twelve melodies by Bartók in imitation of folk-song style. These examples demonstrate the principal four-line type of folk melody in closed form, with descending or stationary cadences at the first, second, and fourth caesuras, and an ascending one at the third caesura.

883. Bónis, Ferenc. "Bartók und der Verbunkos" [Bartók and the *verbunkos*]. *International Musicological Conference in Commemoration of Béla Bartók 1971*, ed. József Ujfalussy and János Breuer. Budapest: Editio Musica; New York: Belwin Mills, 1972, pp. 145-153. ML410.B29 I61 (Editio Musica) ML410.B26 I5 (Belwin Mills)

Provides a brief history of the *verbunkos* (the Hungarian national dance) as it developed since the latter part of the eighteenth century and discusses its influence on the development of Hungarian art music in the nineteenth century. Then, investigates Bartók's relationship with the *verbunkos* style, based on an analysis of its influence in his early compositions and its structural manifestations as it evolved in his later works. Also published in *Österreichische Musikzeitschrift* 27/11 (November 1972): 588-595. See also "Bartók und der *verbunkos:* Ausgangspunkt, Konfrontation, Synthese" [Bartók and the Verbunkos: Point of origin, confrontation, Synthesis]. *Volks- und Kunstmusik in Südosteuropa* (Regensburg: Bosse, 1989): 37-49.

884. Breuer, János. "Kolinde Rhythm in the Music of Bartók." *Studia musicologica* 17 (1975): 39-58.   781.05 St92   ISSN 0039-3266

Asserts that investigation of rhythmic-metric roots are treated too lightly in Bartók's music. While the frequent changes of meter and the complicated rhythmic structures are typical of *colindă* melodies, the author only deals with a single type of the above phenomena employed by Bartók in his composed works, which are constructed of at least three changes in meter, symmetrical and asymmetrical measures, and where there is a change in the time signature. Very detailed study with many examples from Bartók's music. The variable *colindă* rhythm is examined in the *First* and *Second Sonatas* for violin and piano (1921-22), *Dance Suite* (1923), *Village Scenes* (1924, *First Piano Concerto* (1926), *Nine Little*

Pieces for piano (1926), *Piano Sonata* (1926), *Music for Strings, Percussion, and Celesta* (1936), *Third String Quartet* (1927), and several pieces from the *Mikrokosmos.* See also: "Kolinda-ritmika Bartók zenéjében," in *Zeneelmélet, stíluselemzés.* Budapest: Zeneműkiadó, 1977, pp. 84-102.

885. Broughton, Simon. "Bartók and 'World Music.'" In: *The Stage Works of Béla Bartók,* ed. Nicholas John. Sponsor: Martini. *Operaguide* 44. New York: Riverrun; London: Calder, 1991. pp. 13-22.   ISBN 0-7145-4194-X   ML410 B26 S78

Describes Bartók's folk-music collecting activities in Transylvania and speaks of the riches in the ethnic synthesis of the folk sources and Bartók's own varied background. Points out that because of the separation between the middle class to which Bartók belonged and the peasant class, he did not encounter authentic folk music until 1904. Provides a detailed biographical sketch of Bartók's early years leading to the influence of the cultural climate of Budapest on him when he came to study there in 1899, the Hungarian musical movement drawing him to study the "folk music" (actually *verbunkos* tunes) available there at the time. Discusses the events leading to Bartók's absorption, for instance, of the ancient pentatonic melodies among the Székelys in Transylvania in 1907, which became essential to his musical style. Points to the connections between peasant and urban music, Bartók's rejection of the latter, and summarizes Bartók's collections of the different folk sources by 1918 (Hungarian, Slovak, Romanian, Bulgarian, Ruthenian, and others). Then refers to *Duke Bluebeard's Castle* (1911) as the most significant work to that date to benefit from his folk-music investigations but also points to the Symbolist and Impressionist movements as basic sources for the opera. States that *Bluebeard* and *The Wooden Prince* (1916) are essentially Hungarian, whereas *The Miraculous Mandarin* (1919) is a synthesis of all the folk sources he investigated. Contains illustrations.

886. Burlas, Ladislav. "The Influence of Slovakian Folk Music on Bartók's Musical Idiom." *International Musicological Conference in Commemoration of Béla Bartók 1971,* eds. József Ujfalussy and János Breuer. Budapest: Editio Musica; New York: Belwin Mills,1972, pp. 181-187.   ML410.B29 I61 (Editio Musica) ML410.B26 I5 (Belwin Mills)

Gives a detailed outline of Bartók's interest in Slovakian folk songs, providing dates, places, and number of tunes collected. Also, presents the results of Bartók's research, a list of his Slovakian folk-song arrangements, and a detailed modal and harmonic analysis of these arrangements. Through specific examples, shows how Bartók treated material derived from Slovak folk music, e.g., showing harmonizations for tritones in Lydian melodies by using parallel motion. Also mentions a "tonal fourth structure," containing the fourth, tritone, and fifth, as transmutations rather than chromatic alterations that caused Bartók to make "specific alterations of the tonal system."

887. ----------. "Neuerertum und Tradition in Bartóks Formenwelt" [Innovation and tradition in Bartók's world of forms]. *Studia musicologica* 5 (1963): 383-391. 781.05 St92 ISSN 0039-3266

Concentrating on his smaller piano pieces, the author discusses such influences as folk music on Bartók's form, their fusion, and his creation of a new compact symmetrical form.

888. Dille, Denijs. *Béla Bartók.* Antwerpen: Metropolis, 1974. 180p.

Points to the significance of the folk sources in connection with Bartók's compositions.

889. Dobszay, László. "The Absorption of Folksong in Bartók's Composition." *Studia musicologica* 24/3-4 (1982): 303-313. 781.05 St92 ISSN 0039-3266

Poses the question: "If Bartók and Kodály derived their composing styles from Hungarian folk music, why do their styles in their developed form differ so widely from one another?" Intention here is to present only some remarks about the role of folk song in Bartók's composition. Only one of a large number of items is referred to for clarity's sake: the *Forty-Four Violin Duos* can serve as a guide to the understanding of other simple compositions and works that go beyond the direct use of folk song. The folk song chosen is from Transylvania, which is thoroughly analyzed in terms of pitch structure and Bartók's bitonal integration of its details.

890. Forner, Johannes. "Die Sonatenform im Schaffen Béla Bartóks" [Sonata form in the works of Béla Bartók]. Ph.D. diss. in Musicology-Music Aesthetics. Wilhelm-Pieck-U., Rostock, 1975. 158p.

According to the author, *RILM Abstracts* No. 6025 (1976), the dissertation "presents conceptual and historical considerations; analyzes Bartók's works up to 1917, his experiments, attainment of formal clarity, and his late style. Discusses the 'process' character of the sonata-form idea and Bartók's tendencies toward synthesis, placing emphasis on the relationship between art music and folklore. In the late works the increasing integration of folkloristic tonal elements leads to a change in the content of sonata form. This is characterized by the removal of the secondary material and the simultaneous striving toward inner unity and formal balance. Bartók retained tonality and recapitulations."

891. Frigyesi, Judit. "Between Rubato and Rigid Rhythm: A Particular Type of Rhythmical Asymmetry as Reflected in Bartók's Writings on Folk Music." *Studia musicologica* 24 (1982): 327-337. 781.05 St92 ISSN 0039-3266

    Deals with a special problem of ethnomusicology as treated by Bartók, i.e., while trying to give an interpretation of rhythmical asymmetry in Bartók's music, the author's point of departure was not the folk music itself. Points out that "folk performances employ an infinite variety of transitional stages between rigid rhythm and free rubato. There are examples of partly rubato performance in a basically giusto melody, while . . . a series of fixed elements can be discovered in the rhythm of parlando melodies. It is in this ambiguous sphere of performance that free rhythm often becomes fixed in asymmetrical forms." Well-documented study, including many folk-song examples from Bartók's essays. Presents analyses of passages from the *First* and *Third Piano Concertos*.

892. Gergely, Jean. "Béla Bartók compositeur hongrois" [Béla Bartók, Hungarian composer]. Institut National des Langues et Civilisations Orientales, Paris. Doctorat d'etat, Musicology--Hungarian civilization. University of Strasbourg II, 1975. Paris: La Revue musicale, 1980. 546p.   ML5.R613 no. 328-335

    According to the author, *RILM Abstracts* No. 1467 (1975), the dissertation provides "an examination of Hungarian history and art as an influence on music of the past and present. The new Hungarian school, formed in the first half of the twentieth century by Zoltan Kodály, and his disciples, represents the greatest intellectual synthesis realized in Hungary thus far. Bartók, in his own personal style, created a historical, ethnic, and sociological synthesis in transferring elements of the musical language, style, and variety of popular music to the realm of art music. From the Hungarian point of view his music is composed of a historical part, which is the heritage of the style of verbunkos, and a part modeled on folklore. The parlando rhythms give his music an unlimited dimension which, like its folk models, is shaped by the Hungarian language." Contains facsimiles, illustrations, music, ports., bibliography, index.

893. Helm, Everett. "Béla Bartók und die Volksmusik--zur 20. Wiederkehr von Bartók's Todestag" [Béla Bartók and folk music--to the 20th anniversary of Bartók's death day]. *Neue Zeitung für Musik* 126 (1965): 330.

Examines the human aspect of Bartók's folk music usage in his music and its influence on his compositional process. Also discusses Bartók's ethnomusicological investigations.

894. Hirashima, Naeko. "Barutóko no ongaku no tokushitsu nikansuru ichi kosatsu" [A consideration of the character of Béla Bartók's music]. *Ongaku gakkei ongakugaku* 15/1 (1969): 53-65. ML5 05

Contains a summary in English. States that folk-song sources are more significant than traditional art-music influences of Bach, Beethoven, and Debussy in the construction of the melodies and the developmental process of the material in the string quartets. Contains illustrations and music examples.

895. Kapst, Erich. "Die 'polymodale Chromatik' Béla Bartóks: ein Beitrag zur stilkritischen Analyse" [Béla Bartók's "polymodal chromaticism": a contribution to style-critical analysis]. Ph.D. diss. Karl-Marx University of Leipzig, 1969. 2 vols. 413p.

According to the author, *RILM Abstracts* No. 1677 (1969), "the written statements of the composer were used as primary sources for the musical analysis. An introductory chapter on the folk song is followed by investigations into 1) folk-song arrangement and motivic construction, 2) transformation of the folk song and thematic configuration, 3) melody and tonality, and 4) formal variations and determination of sonority. Harmony, chromatic tonality, form, structural and temporal organization, and the folk-like character of Bartók's themes are dealt with. A new approach to style criticism for Bartók's music is proposed: the investigation of the relationship between the folk model and the emerging new musical system." Abridged in *Beiträge zur Musikwissenschaft* 12 (1970): 1.

896. Kárpáti, János. "Bartók in North Africa: A Unique Fieldwork and Its Impact on His Music." *Bartók in Retrospect,* ed. Elliott Antokoletz, Victoria Fischer, and Benjamin Suchoff. Projected publication of two 1995 conference proceedings.

Describes how the impressions of a short excursion from Spain to the North African coast in 1906 led Bartók to undertake a well-prepared folk-music collecting trip to the Algerian Biskra and three surrounding oases in 1913. A major part of the recorded Arab peasant music was transcribed and published in German in 1920. Like other folk music material, the Arab peasant music significantly influenced Bartók's music. In some cases, he declared he deliberately used tunes and rhythms taken from Arab sources. Similar uses can be observed in other compositions not referred to by Bartók. Intention is to illustrate, by a sequence of the original phonograph recordings, Bartók's notations, some modern recorded reconstructions, and finally the composed works influenced by Arab folk music. (Annotation based on the author's abstract of the original lecture; see item no. 1139.)

897. ----------. *Bartók korai melódia világa az első és második vonósnégyes tükrében* [Bartók's early world of melody as reflected in his *First* and *Second String Quartets*]. Budapest: [in mimeograph], 1956. 76p.

Provides analyses demonstrating Bartók's absorption of elements from the melodic structure of Arab folk music.

898. ----------. "Béla Bartók and the East" (Contribution to the History of the Influence of Eastern Elements on European Music). *Studia musicologica* 6 (1964): 179-194.   781.05 St92   ISSN 0039-3266

Lecture, given at the East-West '64 Music Conference in New Delhi, discusses Bartók's use in his compositions of Arab and Javanese folk-music sources, with reference to the model in Debussy. Also published in *Magyar zene* (Budapest) 5/6 (December 1964): 581-593.

899. ----------. "Les gammes populaires et le système chromatique dans l'œuvre de Béla Bartók" [Folk scales and the chromatic system in the music of Béla Bartók]. *Studia musicologica* 11 (1969): 227-240. 781.05 St92   ISSN 0039-3266

Discusses the synthesis of European (Romantic) musical tradition and the secular folk tradition in Bartók's works. Analytical focus is on bimodal or polymodal chromaticism in the *String Quartets,* with an example from No. 33 of the *Forty-Four Duos* (for two violins).

900. Knapp, Calvin Horace. "A Study, Analysis and Performance of Representative Piano Works of Various Periods of Béla Bartók." Ed.D. thesis. Columbia University, 1973. 209p.

For purposes of performance, traces Bartók's development from the post-Romantic style to his own original idiom, based on the analysis of works from five of Bartók's style periods. Study includes the *Fantasy in A Minor* (1903), *Three Popular Hungarian Songs* (1907), *Fifteen Hungarian Peasant Songs* (1914-1917), *Improvisations on Hungarian Peasant Songs,* Op. 20 (1920), and the *Out of Doors Suite* (1926). Demonstrates the importance of the folk-music sources in Bartók's stylistic evolution, discussing use of the folk modes, rhythmic and metric characteristics, and the imitation of folk instruments as well as natural sounds.

901. Kristiansen, Lidia. "Cherty edinstva v interpretatsii fol'klora Bartókoy--teoretikom i tvortsom" [The unity of interpretation of folklore by Bartók--theorist and creator]. *Studia musicologica* 24/3-4 (1982): 351-360.   781.05 St92   ISSN 0039-3266

Discussion of Bartók's theoretical works on folk music. Also provides a detailed analysis of the influence of folk music on his works, focusing on melody, modality, rhythm, and harmony.

902. Kuss, Malena. "The Structural Role of Folk Elements in 20th-Century Art Music." *Atti del XIV congresso della Società Internazionale di Musicologia, Bologna, 1987: Trasmissione e recezione delle forme di cultura musicale* 3. Torino: Edizioni di Torino, 1990. pp. 99-119.

Points to Ginastera's opera *Don Rodrigo* (1964) and Bartók's *Fourth String Quartet* (1928) as analytical models to demonstrate how post-tonal composers transform a folk-derived pitch formation into a structural element. Traces the evolution of a special symmetrical tetrachord commonly referred to as "cell Z" not only in the music of these two composers but also in the music of non-folk-oriented composers (Berg, Schoenberg, Webern, Dallapiccola, and others), who have exploited this construction for its symmetrical properties.

903. Lampert, Vera. "Bartók's Choice of Theme for Folksong Arrangement: Some Lessons of the Folk-Music Sources of Bartók's Works." *Studia musicologica* 24/3-4 (1982): 401-409.   781.05 St92 ISSN 0039-3266

A compilation of the folk melodies used by Bartók for his compositions. Deals with three categories of inquiry: 1) why Bartók chose the 313 melodies that he did out of several thousand possibilities for arrangement; 2) whether or not his choice of theme changed during his career; and 3) examination of Bartók's method of folk-song use. Contains music examples as well as graphs, which are intended to show the degree to which the melodies arranged by Bartók reflect the proportions of the various styles of Hungarian folk music based on Bartók's classifications. Provides a summary of the statistics as chronologically reflected in Bartók's stylistic development.

904. ----------. "Violin Rhapsodies." *The Bartók Companion,* ed. Malcolm Gillies. London: Faber and Faber, 1993; Portland, Oregon: Amadeus Press (an imprint of Timber Press, Inc.), 1994. pp. 278-284. ISBN 0-931340-74-8 (HB)   ISBN 0-931340-75-6 (PB) ML410 B26 B28

Points to the practical performance intentions of the two *Violin Rhapsodies* during a period (1920s) of Bartók's more extensive international concertizing, which provided him the opportunity to bring his music to the public. Presents some historical background regarding the Hungarian violinists with whom Bartók performed his own music and gives information on publication of the different versions of the *Rhapsodies*. Also addresses the question of Bartók's less specific identification of the folk sources used in these pieces in contrast to the numerous other works in which he had used folk songs, provides some speculation as to the reasons for his vague references, and informs us that all the sources in these *Rhapsodies* have now been identified. Presents a history of Bartók's use of the *verbunkos* style and summarizes its characteristics. Then provides a structural and thematic analysis of the two works and identifies the various characteristics with the appropriate folk-music types (Romanian or Hungarian).

905. László, Ferenc. "A szarvasokká lett vadászfiak nyomában" [In the footsteps of the sons of the hunter who were metamorphosed into stags]. *Igaz Szó* 2 (1981): 170-178.

The article presents and analyzes the newly collected version of the folk text that might have served as the basis for Bartók's *Cantata profana*. Contains musical examples. In Romanian in item no. 319: Ferenc László. *Béla Bartók. Studii, comunicări și eseuri* [Béla Bartók. Studies, communications, essays]. Bucharest: Kriterion, 1985. 336 p.

906. ----------. "Két 'Bartók-népdal'-ról" [About two "folk songs by Bartók"]. *Művelődés* 3 (1981): 25-27.

Analysis of the first melodies of *Bluebeard's Castle* and the *Concerto* in relation to the old-style Hungarian folk songs. Contains music examples.

907. ----------. "Muzica românească a lui Béla Bartók" [Romanian music of Béla Bartók]. *Studii de muzicologie* 19. Bucharest: Editura Muzicală, 1985. pp. 39-73.

Analytical study of all those pieces of Bartók where direct influence of Romanian folk music could be found: *Oláhos* (In Walachian style) DD 6, *Vázlatok/5,6* (Sketches), *Két román tánc* (Two Romanian dances), "A falu tánca" (Village dance) from *Két kép/2* (Two pictures/2), *Szonatina, Román népi táncok* (Romanian Folk Dances), *Román kolinda-dallamok* (Romanian Christmas carols), *Tánc-szvit* (Dance suite), *1. Rapszódia* (Rhapsody No. 1), *2.*

Rapszódia (Rhapsody No. 2), *Duók/7, 21, 29, 30, 31, 32, 38, 40, 44.* Contains music examples.

908. Leichtentritt, Hugo. "Bartók and the Hungarian Folksong." *Modern Music* 10/3 (March-April 1933): 130-139.   780.5 M72

Describes Bartók's treatment of folk-song material, using examples primarily from the *20 Hungarian Folk Songs* for voice and piano. Refers to the ultra-modern harmonic devices in the piano part as a probable detriment to making these peasant songs popular but nevertheless speaks of "a strange fascination in his arrangements." Then follows a fairly detailed discussion of each of the songs.

909. Lenoir, Yves. "Béla Bartók et le folklore: Le cas de la période américaine (1940-1945)" [Béla Bartók and folklore: His American period (1940-1945)]. *Bulletin de la Société Liégeoise de Musicologie* 70 (July 1990): 19-31.

Discusses Bartók's folkloristic research during his residence in New York City and his absorption of the folk-music sources into the compositions of his American period. Study includes the *Concerto for Orchestra, Sonata for Solo Violin, Third Piano Concerto,* and *Viola Concerto.*

910. Mason, Colin. "Bartók and Folksong." *The Music Review* 11/4 (November 1950): 292-302.   780.5 M9733   ISSN 0027-4445

Discusses several of Bartók's folk-song settings in terms of the development of his musical language. Analysis focuses on pentatony and the modes as well as concepts of harmonic consonance and dissonance. Gives some reference to rhythmic and other features of certain national folk-song types (e.g., Hungarian and Slovak).

911. Mirza, Traian. "Citeva date şi observaţii privind folclorul muzical bihorean" [Some dates and observations concerning the folk music of Bihor]. *Ziele folclorului bihorean* (1973): 69-93.

Discusses the characteristics of the melodies from Bihor. Presents Bartók's observations regarding this area of Romanian folksong and his changing views as influenced by the research of Romanian ethnomusicologists.

912. Ng-Quinn, David. "Improvisations on Hungarian Peasant Songs, Op, 20 for Solo Piano by Béla Bartók: Analysis, and Study of Bartók's Recordings." D.M.A. treatise. Stanford University, 1984. 161p.

Discusses the *Eight Improvisations* (1920), in which the characteristics of the folk-song sources are studied according to

Bartók's classification of the Hungarian peasant melodies. Also, provides an analysis of each of the pieces and explores the means by which the folk melodies are absorbed. Furthermore, Bartók's recordings of the pieces (on Hungaroton,1981) are explored in-depth as a primary source for a better understanding of the work. Contains illustrations.

913. Nicola, R. Ioan. "Colindă vînatorilor metamorfozati în cerbi" [The Christmas carol of the hunters transformed into stags]. *Lucrări de muzicologie* 4 (1968): 59-86.   780

Provides some historical data on this old-style carol, determined by an examination of both text and melody. The symbolic text was used as the basis of Bartók's *Cantata Profana*, expressing Bartók's own philosophy involving the relation of man to nature as well as his ideals of freedom.

914. Olsvai, Imre. "West-Hungarian (Trans-Danubian) Characteristic Features in Bartók's works." *Studia musicologica* 11/1-4 (1969): 333-347.   781.05 St92   ISSN 0039-3266

Cites examples of Bartók's Hungarian peasant song settings, in which the composer alters the accidentals of succeeding statements to reveal a concept of pitch organization that does not correspond to semitonal scale divisions. Also relates many specific features in examples of Bartók's later compositions to Transdanubian sources.

915. Papp, Márta. "Bartók hegedűrapszódiái és a román népi hegedűs játékmód hatása Bartók műveire" [Bartók's *Rhapsodies* for violin and the impact of Romanian folk fiddling on Bartók's work]. *Magyar zene* (Budapest) 14/3 (September 1973): 299-308.   ML5 M14 ISSN 0025-0384

Discusses the technical sources of Bartók's *Two Rhapsodies for Violin* found in the fiddle styles of Romanian and Ruthenian folk music. Points to characteristics of the folk dance and discusses rhythmic style in connection with the technical details of the instrument in terms of bowing, dynamics, etc. Refers to the use of open strings for bagpipe effects in the second movement of the *First Rhapsody,* the second movement of the *Second String Quartet,* the second movement of the *Second Sonata for Violin and Piano, Contrasts,* the *Violin Concerto,* and the *Sonata for Solo Violin.* Also, points to the structural functions of these techniques.

916. Pernecky, John Martin. "The Historical and Musico-Ethnological Approach to the Instrumental Compositions of Béla Bartók." Ph.D. diss. Northwestern University, 1956. 193p.   ML410.B26 P46 1956a

Investigation of the origins and characteristics of the folk sources as well as the art-music sources that influenced Bartók's compositional style. Mainly explores the Asiatic-Semitic-Oriental as found in Balkan folk music. Discusses Bartók's absorption and employment of the ancient folk elements, leading to his own personal compositional use of the modal and pentatonic scales, harmonic intervallic constructions, special rhythmic devices, and special contrapuntal treatment. Also compares the extent of Bartók's ethnomusicological activities and influences with those of some of his contemporaries. Contains illustrations, bibliography.

917. Petrov, S. "Béla Bartók o bolgarskaya musikal'naya kultura" [Béla Bartók and the Bulgarian music culture]. *Studia musicologica* 5/1-4 (1963): 491-499.   781.05 St92   ISSN 0039-3266

Detailed analysis of Bartók's studies of Bulgarian folk music and their influence on his pedagogical, theoretical, and compositional works. Emphasis is placed on the importance to Bartók of discovering and explaining Bulgarian rhythms as well as his use of them in his compositions.

918. Pfrogner, Hermann. "Hat Diatonik Zukunft?" [Does diatonicism have a future?]. *Musica* 17 (1963): 146-155.   ML100 M895

Discusses Bartók's harmonic idiom and its relation to folk-music sources.

919. Rice, Timothy. "Béla Bartók and Bulgarian Rhythm." *Bartók in Retrospect,* ed. Elliott Antokoletz, Victoria Fischer, and Benjamin Suchoff. Projected publication of two 1995 conference proceedings.

Discusses Bartók's fascination with the asymmetrical meters of the Balkans, and his apparent view of the Bulgarian versions as archetypal. Explores Bartók's understanding of what he termed "Bulgarian Rhythm" in two senses: his ethnomusicological understanding and his compositional understanding. First explores Bartók's musicological understandings of these rhythms in relation to the sources he had at his command and in relation to those of his generation of musical folklorists. It reconstructs his knowledge of Bulgarian sources and his contacts with Bulgarian scholars. Extends our understanding of these rhythms based on the author's own field research in Bulgaria and on the work of Bulgarian scholars working since Bartók's day. Then analyzes those of Bartók's compositions that use Bulgarian rhythm prominently in order to show how he translated his musicological understanding into music. Analyzes the following pieces: "Six Dances in Bulgarian Rhythms" from *Mikrokosmos,* vol. 6; the *Sonata for Two Pianos and Percussion,* first movement; and the "Scherzo" from *String Quartet No. 5.* Various performances of these pieces are critiqued for the effectiveness with which they transmit Bartók's understanding of Bulgarian meters. Contributes to our understanding of Bartók as both musical folklorist and composer and to one important way Bulgarian folk traditions have found their way into the classical canon. (Annotation based on the author's abstract of the original lecture; see item no. 1139.)

920. Ritchie, Anthony Damian. "The Influence of Folk Music in Three Works by Béla Bartók: Sonata No. 1 for Violin and Piano, Sonata (1926) for Piano, and *Contrasts* for Violin, Clarinet, and Piano." Ph.D. diss., University of Canterbury, New Zealand, 1986. 2 v. 626p.

Selects three representative works from different periods of Bartók's life as basis for a study of direct folk-music influence. Sources of influence include Bartók's imitation of folk styles from both vocal and instrumental genres, regional sources, and indirect influences. Also addresses non-folk sources and other theoretical approaches to these works. Contains music examples, bibliography, discography.

921. Somfai, László. "Az 'Árvátfalvi kesergő' Bartók 1. rapszódiájában" [The "Lament from Árvatfalva" in Bartók's *Rhapsody No. 1*]. *Muzsika* (Budapest) 20/5 (May 1977): 9-11.   ISSN 0027-5336

Traces the source of the melody in the trio of the slow movement of the *Rhapsody No. 1* for violin and orchestra to a Hungarian folk song played by a Gypsy violinist recorded by Béla Vikár. Also discusses the discovery of a manuscript of the folk song in the hand of Bartók's wife as well as the history of the tune as it came to be used in Bartók's composition.

922. ----------. "Bartók 2. hegedűrapszódiájának rutén epizódja" [A Ruthenian episode in Bartók's *Second Rhapsody for Violin*]. *Muzsika* (Budapest) 14/3 (March 1971): 1-3.   ISSN 0027-5336

Compares this passage in the *Rhapsody* with an unpublished Ruthenian fiddle dance tune, which was recorded by Bartók between 1912 and 1914. Contains facsimile and music.

923. ----------. "Bartók egynemű kórusainak szövegforrásáról" [Text sources for Bartók's *27 Choruses* for children's or women's voices and for the work *From Ancient Times*]. *Magyar zenetörténeti tanulmányok: Szabolcsi Bence 70. születésnapjára* [Studies in Hungarian musical history dedicated to Bence Szabolcsi on his 70th birthday], ed. Ferenc Bónis. Budapest: Zeneműkiadó Vállalat. pp. 359-376.   ML55 S992 B6

In Hungarian, with summaries in German and English. States that the text sources of these and other works were established through research by the author at Bartók's ethnomusicological library. A collection of Hungarian folk texts, entitled *Magyar népköltési gyűjtemény* (published between 1846 and 1906), was found to be a basic source. Contains illustrations.

924. ----------. "The Influence of Peasant Music on the Finale of Bartók's Piano Sonata: An Assignment for Musicological Analysis." *Studies in Musical Sources and Styles: Essays in Honor of Jan LaRue.* Madison: A-R, 1990. pp. 535-554.   M55 L217

According to the author, *RILM Abstracts* No. 8945 (1990), "After a discussion of Bartók's relation to folk music that emphasizes ideological motivations and chronological aspects, the finale of the piano sonata (1926) is studied. The following elements of the structural influence of folk music are analyzed: the stanza-form rondo theme considered as an imaginary folk song; the long and revised form of the movement; folk music genres serving as a variation principle in the monothematic rondo form; the pianistic variations (mostly discarded during the revision of the form); special strategies in rhythmic variation; and opened-up variant forms of so-called stanzas. This focus on unorthodox analytic approaches is more relevant to Bartók's music than traditional analytic methodology."

925. Stevens, Halsey. "The Sources of Bartók's Rhapsody for Violoncello and Piano." *International Musicological Conference in Commemoration of Béla Bartók 1971,* ed. József Ujfalussy and János Breuer. Budapest: Editio Musica; New York: Belwin Mills, 1972, pp. 65-76.   ML410.B29 I61 (Editio Musica) ML410.B26 I5 (Belwin Mills)

States that Bartók's monumental study of Romanian folk music points to the sources of many of his transcriptions of both vocal and instrumental Romanian material. Based on a well-documented study of various scholars and performers who gave information on the *Rhapsody.*

926. Suchoff, Benjamin. "Ethnomusicological Roots of Béla Bartók's Musical Language." *The World of Music* (1987): 43-64. 780.5 W893 ISSN 0043-8774

Presents a brief history of the development of Bartók's musical language in his early years, beginning with late-nineteenth-century Romantic influences, through a period of imitation of Liszt's Hungarianisms in *Kossuth* and other works between 1902 and 1905 (a period referred to as Bartók's summary of urban-Hungarian musical dialect), to the use of authentic folk-music sources from various nations. Then provides detailed but concise information on the melodic organization and rhythmic structure of Hungarian, Slovak, Romanian, Ruthenian, Bulgarian, Yugoslav, Arab, and Turkish folk materials. In each case, examples from Bartók's compositions are provided as demonstration of his absorption of the folk-music characteristics. Contains facsimiles, photographs, music examples.

927. ----------. "Folk Music Sources in Bartók Works." *Reinhard Gedenkschrift,* ed. Christian Ahrens, Rudolf Maria Brandl, and Felix Hoerburger. Laaber: Laaber Verlag, 1984. pp. 197-218.

Outlines several stages in Bartók's transformation of folk-music sources into art music as determined by a study of Bartók's writings and music. Provides analysis of Bartók's *Concerto for Orchestra* to illustrate these stages and to reveal the folk-music sources the composer absorbed from different Eastern European countries.

928. ----------. "Fusion of National Styles: Piano Literature, 1908-11." *The Bartók Companion,* ed. Malcolm Gillies. London: Faber and Faber, 1993; Portland, Oregon: Amadeus Press (an imprint of Timber Press, Inc.), 1994. pp. 124-145.   ISBN 0-931340-74-8 (HB) ISBN 0-931340-75-6 (PB)   ML410 B26 B28

Discussion of the second stage in Bartók's stylistic development, which developed from Bartók's systematic approach to the investigation and classification of the authentic folk music of Hungary and the national minorities, and the absorption of their essence and characteristics into his art-music compositions. Includes a concise summary of the basic structural, rhythmic, and modal features of Eastern European rural music and indicates Bartók's specific piano compositions in which the various characteristics are manifested. Points to tone color as an important stylistic element in Bartók's piano writing, in which notation served as an important vehicle for indicating the performance style. Outlines five innovative levels of complexity in Bartók's evolution based on the ways in which Bartók absorbed and employed musical folklore. Then analyzes specific piano works to identify the various modal folk characteristics and how they interact with abstract, symmetrical pitch cells derived from the modal folk sources and polymodal chromatic combinations. The study includes selections from *Ten Easy Pieces, For Children, Two Elegies,* Op. 8b, *Two Romanian Dances,* Op. 8a, *Three Burlesques,* Op. 8c, *Four Dirges,* Op. 9a, *Seven Sketches,* Op. 9b, and *Allegro barbaro.* Points to connections with other works by Bartók as well as those of other composers, including Liszt and Debussy.

929. Szabolcsi, Bence. "Bartók Béla kompozíciós elvei, egy nyilatkozata tükrében" [Bartók's principles of composition in the light of an interview]. *Új zenei szemle* (Budapest) 7/9 (September 1956): 14-15. HA1.588

Statement by Bartók to his first important biographer, Denijs Dille, in 1937, explaining the means by which folk elements are manifested in his art-music compositions. Discusses how there is the impulse to follow the trend of folk music, on the one hand, and the impulse that counter balances that trend, on the other, both trends of which are manifested in his art. Also published in: *The New Hungarian Quarterly* 11/39 (Autumn 1970): 10-12, which is reprinted in *Bartók Studies*, ed. Todd Crow. Detroit: Information Coordinators, 1976, pp. 19-21.

930. -----------. "Bartók und die Volksmusik." *Béla Bartók, Weg und Werk, Schriften und Briefe*, ed. Bence Szabolcsi. Budapest: Corvina, 1957, pp. 76-88. ML410.B28 A32 1957

Quotes Bartók extensively to document Bartók's relationship to folk-music material. Comments on melody, rhythm, harmony, and forms derived from folk music manifested in Bartók's later works. For example, cites a theme from the second movement of *Music for Strings, Percussion and Celesta*, comparing it with no. 130 of the *Mikrokosmos* and a Hungarian folk tune.

931. Szelényi, István. "Bartók und die Modalität" [Bartók and modality]. *International Musicological Conference in Commemoration of Béla Bartók 1971*, ed. József Ujfalussy and János Breuer. Budapest: Editio Musica; New York: Belwin Mills, 1972, pp. 169-180. ML410.B29 I61 (Editio Musica)   ML410. B26 I5 (Belwin Mills)

Talks of Bartók's folk-collecting tours as the source of his harmonies as a means of rejecting the constructions of classical harmony. Gives several examples from Bartók's compositions to demonstrate his harmonic solutions for modal folk tunes, which marked the path of development of twentieth-century music. Refers to the relation of folk music to Bartók's abstract compositional materials.

932. Tallián, Tibor. *Cantata profana--az átmenet mítosza* [Cantata Profana--myth of transition]. Budapest: Magvető, 1983. 273 p.

Presents an in-depth anthropological (ethnomusicological) study of the symbolic meaning of the original *colinde* texts on which Bartók's *Cantata profana* is based. Explores the meaning of the text in its relationship to rites of separation, initiation, and transition. See also item no. 933, "Die Cantata profana--ein 'Mythos des

Übergangs,'" the author's earlier version published as an article in *Studia musicologica* 23 (1981): 135-200.

933. ----------. "Die Cantata profana--ein 'Mythos des Übergangs'" [The Cantata profana--a "myth of transition"]. *Studia musicologica* 23 (1981): 135-200.   781.05 St92   ISSN 0039-3266

See item no. 932, *Cantata profana--az átmenet mítosza* [Cantata Profana--myth of transition]. Budapest: Magvető, 1983.

934. ----------. "'Um 1900 nachweisbar': Skizze zu einem Gruppenbild mit Musikern" [Around 1900 authenticated: sketch for a group portrait with musicians]. *Studia musicologica* 24/3-4 (1982): 497-503. 781.05 St92   ISSN 0039-3266

States that Bartók's path led through all types of national music but already in the direction of the esoterics. Folklore for the young Bartók was above all a symbol of something new and foreign. A perspective of a new musical democracy was first foreshadowed by Bartók's music at a time when the figures of the "group portrait" around 1900 had already fallen into oblivion.

935. Tóth, Anna. "Der Dudelsack-Effekt in Bartóks Werk" [The bagpipe effect in Bartók's work]. *Studia musicologica* 24/3-4 (1982): 505-517.   781.05 St92   ISSN 0039-3266

Presents an historical survey of Bartók's works employing instrumental devices and techniques that are reminiscent of this folk instrument. Effect first used in 1908 in his piano cycle *For Children,* in the first Slovakian volume, through 1943 in the finale of the *Concerto for Orchestra.* Gives three categories of works where this instrument always appears: 1) in authentic rural songs; 2) in works that are based on imitations of peasant melodies; and 3) in works based only on the atmosphere of peasant music.

936. Tsirikus, Irina. "Lado-funktsionalnost' v narodnoy pesne i yeyë otrazenie v professionalnoy muzyke" [Modal function in folk song and its reflection in art music]. Ph.D. diss. Kievskaya Konservatoriya, 1975. 23p.

Explores Bartók's use of folk-music sources within the highly systematic structural organization of his compositions. Deals with the relation between the elements of modal construction in Hungarian folk music and Bartók's modal idiom. Also includes a comparison of structurally related Hungarian and Ukrainian folk songs.

937. Vargyas, Lajos. "Bartók's Melodies in the Style of Folk songs." *Journal of the International Folk Music Council* 16 (January 1964): 30-34.   780.6 In 82j

In reference to several compositions of Bartók, e.g., from *Ten Easy Piano Pieces* and the *Mikrokosmos,* shows what folk songs meant to Bartók, how he translated their characteristic features into his own language, and how folk songs can become the means of expression in the highly intellectual type of modern art.

938. Weissmann, John S. "Bartók and Folk Music." *The Monthly Musical Record* 87/981 (1957): 92-95.   780.5 M767

Suggests that the symmetrical patterns of Bartók's later works came from the influence of folk tunes. First distinguishes authentic Hungarian peasant music from the "urban" type used by Brahms, Liszt, and others, and then gives Bartók's definition.

939. Westphal, Kurt. "Béla Bartók und die moderne ungarische Musik" [Béla Bartók and the modern Hungarian music]. *Die Musik* (Stuttgart-Berlin) 20 (October 1927): 188-191.   780.5 M992

Argues that Bartók's efforts to make Hungarian folk music prominent were mostly successful because of the introduction of Impressionistic harmony, which made it possible to convey the Hungarian folk-music style and at the same time to preserve its true character.

940. Yeomans, David. "Background and Analysis of Bartók's Romanian Christmas Carols for Piano." *Bartók in Retrospect,* ed. Elliott Antokoletz, Victoria Fischer, and Benjamin Suchoff. Projected publication of two 1995 conference proceedings.

Informs us that Bartók's *Romanian Christmas Carols* are adaptations for piano of *colinde* which he began collecting in 1908 in the Transylvania sector of Romania. *Colinde* were traditionally sung on Christmas Eve by young peasant men and women who would serenade households and receive gifts. Although most of the original texts are liturgical in nature, many of them draw upon purely pagan subject matter. Almost all of the texts are interspersed with refrains of a laudatory nature, explaining to some extent the rhythmic peculiarities of the melodies. Includes a discussion of *colinde,* their melodic, rhythmic, ornamental, and variational characteristics; their adaptations by Bartók in the *Romanian Christmas Carols;* the poetic structures and subject matter of the original text material; Bartók's detailed editing of the original melodies; and his own elaborations, for concert use, of some of the pieces in the collection. (Annotation based on the author's abstract of the original lecture; see item no. 1139.)

941. Zieliński, Tadeusz A. "Die modalen Strukturen im Werk Bartóks" [Modal structures in the works of Bartók]. *Jahrbuch Peters* (1981-1982; publ. 1985): 18-29.   ML5 J16

    Discusses the importance of the folk modes for Bartók as a means of freeing his music from the functional confines of the traditional major-minor scale system. Points to the sources of his diverse modalities (including pentatonic, diatonic, and Arab-Persian constructions) in his early folk-song investigations, and to the more abstract basis of the twelve-tone scale. Also, addresses the aesthetic role of the folk modes in his compositional contexts.

4. Art-Music Influences on Bartók's Compositions

942. Bónis, Ferenc. "Bartók und Wagner. Paul Sacher zum 75. Geburtstag" [Bartók and Wagner. For Paul Sacher's seventy-fifth birthday]. *Österreichische Musikzeitschrift* 36 (1981): 134-147. 780.5 Oe8   ISSN 0029-9316

    Discusses Bartók's first encounters with Wagner's music and the future musical relations Bartók had with it. In Bartók's development, a synthesis emerged as the result of the conflict between image and rejection (which came early as Bartók found greater possibilities in Liszt's influence for the further development of music, although the references to Wagner occur in his own music. Also published in *The New Hungarian Quarterly* 10/34 (Summer 1969): 201-209.

943. ----------. "Idézetek Bartók zenéjeben" [Bartók's musical quotations]. *Magyar zene* 3 (1962): 105.   ML5 M14   ISSN 0025-0384

    Includes Bartók's musical quotations from Bach, Beethoven, Debussy, Ravel, and Stravinsky.

944. Boronkay, Antal. "Béla Bartók's Baroque Transcriptions." *Hungarian Music Quarterly* 1/3-4 (1989): 35-37.   914.39105 H893 ISSN 0238-9401

    Provides historical information on the publication (by Carl Fischer of New York in 1930 and the subsequent extension of rights to Bartók's Hungarian publishers) of Bartók's transcriptions of seventeenth- and eighteenth-century Italian cembalo and organ music. Transcriptions include works by B. Marcello, B. Rossi, A.B. della Ciaia, G. Frescobaldi, and D. Zipoli. Evaluates the relevance of Bartók's transcriptions in the context of changing contemporary attitudes to the interpretation of early music. Then, traces the historical events in and around Bartók's life that contributed to his attraction to Baroque music. Demonstrates how Bartók's approach, as exemplified in his transcription of Frescobaldi's Toccata in G major, hardly differs from modern principles of early music practice but also reveals his originality as a subjective musician. Also, addresses Bartók's intentions and thinking behind the transcriptions. Informs us that "in accordance with the rules of the genre, instructions and phrasing indications concerning the analysis and clarification of the polyphonic texture play a major role."

945. Breuer, János. "Bach és Bartók" [Bach and Bartók]. *Muzsika* 18/9 (September 1975): 20-24.   ISSN 0027-5336

Discusses Bartók's early systematic studies of Bach's music and demonstrates the compositional (e.g., use of dissonance) as well as the pedagogical influence on him. Also, compares Bach's and Bartók's varied approaches in their compositions to the use of folk music. Also published in *Bericht über die Wissenschaftliche Konferenz zum III. Internationalen Bach-Fest der DDR*, ed. Werner Felix, et al. 1977, pp. 307-313.

946. Cross, Anthony. "Debussy and Bartók." *Musical Times* 108 (1967): 125-131.   780.5 M98   ISSN 0027-4666

Part of a series of articles building a composite portrait of Debussy through the study of impressions he made on other composers. Discusses Bartók's turn toward France and Debussy as a replacement of the German influence. Gives this history in the first decade of the century and presents documentation regarding sources in Bartók's library at the Budapest Bartók Archivum (Debussy scores purchased between 1907 and 1911, etc.). Points to features both composers have in common in terms of influence but illustrates how they used them in individual ways.

947. Demény, János. "A szecesszió zenében" [Secession in music]. *Filológiai közlöny* 13/1-2 (1967): 221-226.   PB 5 F5

Refers to Bartók's musical connections with Strauss and Debussy as well as to Busoni, Reger, and Delius. Also points to sources of some of Bartók's innovations in the late works of Liszt. Includes a discussion of Bartók's *Valse* (1908) and *For Children*. Contains bibliography.

948. Fábián, Imre. "Debussy und die Meister der ungarischen Musik" [Debussy and the master of Hungarian music]. *Österreichische Musikzeitschrift* 18/1 (January 1963): 23-28.   780.5 Oe8 ISSN 0029-9316

Examination of the intellectual and stylistic influence of Debussy on Bartók and Kodály, using five musical examples of each Hungarian composer.

949. Falvy, Zoltán. "Franz Liszt e Béla Bartók (Béla Bartók su Franz Liszt)" [Franz Liszt and Béla Bartók (Béla Bartók about Franz Liszt)]. *Nuova rivista musicale italiana* 3/4 (July-August 1969): 664-671.   780.5 N928   ISSN 0029-6228

Primary-source evidence, provided by Bartók's writings about Liszt, revealing similarities in the development of the two composers. Contains no musical examples.

950. Frobenius, Wolf. "Bartók und Bach" [Bartók and Bach]. *Archiv für Musikwissenschaft* 41/1 (1984): 54-67.   780.5 Ar252   ISSN 0003-9292

According to the author, *RILM Abstracts* No. 2906 (1984), "Bartók's editions of Bach's works and his compositional involvement with Bach, particularly his new chromaticism, betray a late Romantic conception of the Baroque composer. Bartók's conclusions about form in this new chromaticism parallel the serialists' use of Bach as a model. The author touches on neobaroque style, Bartók's compositional development, and Bartók's reception of Liszt's music."

951. Gombosi, Otto. "Béla Bartók (1881-1945)." *Musical Quarterly* 32/1 (January 1946): 1-11.   ML1 M725   ISSN 0027-4631

Begins with an account of Bartók's last years of suffering through disease and exile. An account is then given of the sources of Bartók's style and language, including Richard Strauss, Debussy, and the folk music of various nations. Also refers to some influences by Schoenberg, Stravinsky, Beethoven, and the Italian Baroque. Briefly discusses parallel approaches to arranging folk songs and his own original compositions, with references to many of Bartók's works. Ends with discussion of Bartók's personality.

952. Hundt, Theodor. "Barocke Formelemente im Kompositionsstil Béla Bartóks" [Baroque form elements in the compositional style of Béla Bartók]. *Studia musicologica* 24/3-4 (1982): 361-372.   781.05 St92   ISSN 0039-3266

Discusses Bartók's turn toward Baroque composers and techniques since the mid-1920s. His letter to Null expresses these neo-Baroque concerns, though not following in Stravinsky's footsteps. This represented a turning away from the expressionism of his *Violin Sonatas* of the early 1920s. States that Bartók's classicism ultimately depends on the synthesis of distinct stimuli rather than the external compositional memory of the Baroque.

953. Hunkemöller, Jürgen. "Bartók und Mozart" [Bartók and Mozart]. *Archiv für Musikwissenschaft* 43/4 (1986): 261-277.   780.5 Ar252 ISSN 0003-9292

Examines Bartók's knowledge and opinion of Mozart to determine whether or not the formula "Bartók and Mozart" could be added to the documented list of conjunctions: "Bartók and Bach," "Bartók and Beethoven," "Bartók and Debussy," "Bartók and Schoenberg." Compares this list to numerous mosaic stones, which have to be pieced together to create a picture of the "context-bond" of the individuals. States that this investigation brings insight into a dark as well as sensitive network of traditions and relationships. In connection with Bartók's role as pupil, teacher, pianist, and composer, outlines a history of Bartók's contact with and performances of Mozart's music, his possession of Mozart's and other composers' scores, and his edition of Mozart's piano sonatas (published in one volume by Rozsnyai in 1911) to serve the pedagogical needs of the Budapest Academy. Also, evaluates Bartók's performance interpretation of Mozart's piano music. Concludes that the personalities of Bartók and Mozart were not compatible and that essentially Bartók did not take anything from the Mozart world, especially after 1912.

954. Iwaki, Hajimu. "Utam Bartók világához" [My road to Bartók]. *The New Hungarian Quarterly* 15 (1974): 211-218.   914.39105 N42 ML410 B26 B29

Provides personal recollections of his teacher and his relationship with him during a period of study in Hungary. Iwaki has translated Bartók's collected writings into Japanese.

955. Jellinek, George. "First and Only." *Opera News* 39 (New York) (February 22, 1975): 11-17.   782.05 Op2   ISSN 0030-3607

Discusses influences of Wagner, Strauss, Debussy, and Bartók's own musical nationalism on his opera, *Bluebeard's Castle*. Describes both the psychological and musical characteristics. Describes the style of the vocal line, which is based on the speech-like pattern of the parlando-rubato style of ancient Hungarian folksongs (a path established by Debussy in his setting of the French language to music), discusses the musico-dramatic structure of the work, and gives a description of the motives. Also provides a detailed history of the *Bluebeard* story, outlines the story itself, and presents information on the historical background of the opera. Contains music examples, photographs, and illustrations.

956. Káldor, János. "Common Sources of Liszt's and Bartók's Music." *Hungarian Musical Guide* 18 (1981-1982): 23.   ML21 H86

ISSN 0441-4446

States that Bartók, as a student, was brought up on Brahms's music, but intuitively or consciously was linked with the form world of Liszt. What Liszt heard in the works of the Russians (e.g., Musorgsky) matured in the art of Bartók and Kodály. This had serious political significance for Bartók.

957. Kodály, Zoltán. "Béla Bartók." *La revue musicale* 2/5 (1921): 205-218.   780.5 R328   ISSN 0035-3736

Outlines a history leading to the rebirth of the Hungarian spirit and the creation of contemporary Hungarian intellectual culture. Then provides a history of influences and sources of Bartók's works in Bach, Debussy, and others, as basic to the Hungarian developments.

958. Meyer, John A. "Beethoven and Bartók. A Structural Parallel." *Music Review* 31/4 (December 1970): 315-321.   780.5 M9733 ISSN 0027-4445

Suggests that the style of the slow movements of Bartók's *First* and *Second Piano Concertos* were influenced by the slow movement of Beethoven's *Fourth Piano Concerto,* based on the interaction of the solo piano and orchestra.

959. Radice, Mark A. "Bartók's Parodies of Beethoven." *Music Review* 42/3-4 (August-November 1981): 252-260.   780.5 M9733 ISSN 0027-4445

Discusses Beethoven's influence (Op. 131-133 *String Quartets)* on Bartók's *Sixth String Quartet* and *Third Piano Concerto.* Gives evidence based on the repertoire studied by Bartók in his formative years. Provides analyses based on formal outlines as well as technical string articulations and other parameters. Also quotes Bartók as evidence.

960. Schneider, David E. "Bartók and Stravinsky: Respect, Competition, Influence, and the Hungarian Reaction to Modernism in the 1920s." *Bartók and His World,* ed. Peter Laki. Princeton, New Jersey: Princeton University Press, 1995. pp. 172-199. ISBN 0-691-00633-4   ML 410 B26 B272

Deals with Bartók's reception in Hungary in the 1920s and the question of Bartók's inspiration from and competition with Stravinsky. In this unreciprocated attitude, Bartók saw Stravinsky as "an emblem of modernity and sophistication." Provides a compositional list of suggested Stravinsky influences on Bartók which include, for instance, *The Firebird* (1909), *Petrouchka* (1911), and *Le Rossignol* (1914) on *The Wooden Prince* (1914-17). First, explores Bartók's relationship to Stravinsky before 1926, Bartók's early isolation from musical developments in Western Europe during his folk-music expeditions, and his increasing awareness of Stravinsky and other composers in the 1920s. Includes some performance history and reception of Stravinsky's music in Budapest, compares several works of the two composers, and then focuses primarily on the stylistic connections between Bartók's *First* and *Second Piano Concertos* (1926) and Stravinsky's *Concerto for Piano and Winds* (1924). Concludes that Stravinsky was "one of Bartók's most inspirational models," while asserting that Bartók's originality manifests itself, nevertheless, because of the Hungarian folk-music background of the *First Piano Concerto*. Discusses the subsequent reaction by Bartók and Hungarian critics in the mid 1920s against Stravinsky's neoclassical objectivity, and documents the negative reception of Bartók's *First Concerto* in Budapest. Points to the *Second Concerto* as representing a new and more obvious stage of influence from Stravinsky.

961. Siegmund-Schultze, W. "Tradition und Neuertum in Bartóks Streichquartetten" [Tradition and innovation in Bartók's string quartets]. *Studia musicologica* 3 (1962): 317-328. 781.05 St92 ISSN 0039-3266

Discusses Beethoven's influence on Bartók as apparent in the *First String Quartet,* his turn to radical innovation by the time he composed the *Third Quartet,* and his return to Beethoven's model by the *Sixth Quartet.* Also compares the values and historical circumstances of the two composers.

962. Somfai, László. "Bartók és a Liszt-hatás: Adatok, időrendi összefüggések, hipotézisek" [Liszt's influence on Bartók: Data, chronology, hypotheses]. *Magyar zene* 27/4 (December 1986): 335-351. ML5 M14 ISSN 0025-0384

Suggests that because of contemporary critical assumptions placing Bartók within the historical line of Strauss and Schoenberg, Bartók exaggerated his case in his autobiography regarding the importance of Liszt over Wagner and Strauss for future musical developments and for the influence of Liszt on his own stylistic development. See a similar article by Somfai, "Liszt's Influence on Bartók Reconsidered," *The New Hungarian Quarterly* 27/102 (Summer 1986): 210-219.

963. Suchoff, Benjamin. "The Impact of Italian Baroque Music on Bartók's Music." *Bartók and Kodály Revisited,* ed. György Ránki. Budapest: Akadémiai Kiadó, 1987, pp. 183-197. ISBN 963 05 4510 1

Discusses various art-music influences on Bartók's music during different stages of his career, with emphasis on seventeenth- and eighteenth-century Italian Baroque sources. Divides Bartók's compositions into three stages of stylistic development and provides historical information regarding Bartók's activities as folklorist, composer, and pianist as well. The first stage of Bartók's development, to 1905, represents a summary of Hungarian musical dialect, in which Gypsy-styled popular art song served as a source for his compositions. During the second stage, to 1925, his compositions developed from his investigations of authentic Hungarian folk music, which led to a complex fusion of national music styles in his compositions. In the third stage, from 1926 to 1945, he achieved a synthesis of Eastern European folk music sources and Western art-music techniques. It was in the early 1920s that Bartók turned to the contrapuntal styles of Italian Baroque composers, including keyboard works of Benedetto Marcello, Michelangelo Rossi, Azzolino Bernardino della Ciaia, Girolamo Frescobaldi, and Domenico Zipoli. Prominent evidence of these sources was first manifested in 1926 in the *Piano Sonata, Out of Doors Suite* for piano, the *Nine Little Piano Pieces,* and what the author refers to as Bartók's "great 'toccata cromatica'"--the *First Piano Concerto* (1926). Also, provides musical examples, which illustrate structural and contrapuntal as well as modal elements in a *Toccata* by Frescobaldi and della Ciaia *Canzona* as the basis for comparing aspects of Bartók's musical language in the *Piano Concerto.* Also discusses Bartók's works from his other style periods, in which he points to sources in the music of Strauss and Liszt.

964. Szabolcsi, Bence. "Liszt és Bartók" [Liszt and Bartók]. *Élet és irodalom* 4/51-52 (1960): 9.　　HC1.285

For the preparation of the 1961 commemoration of their common anniversaries (150th of Liszt, 80th of Bartók). Discusses the fraternal homage of one great master to another and the decisive impact Liszt's music had not only on Bartók as performer, composer, thinker, and humanist but also on the contemporary public. Also published in *The New Hungarian Quarterly* 2/1 (January 1961): 3-4, which is reprinted in *Bartók Studies,* ed. Todd Crow. Detroit: Information Coordinators, 1976, pp. 119-120.

965. Traimer, Roswitha. "Béla Bartók und die Tondichtungen von Richard Strauss" [Béla Bartók and the tone poems of Richard Strauss]. *Österreichische Musikzeitschrift* 36 (1981): 311-318.　　780.5 Oe8 ISSN 0029-9316

Analyzes the influence of Strauss and his tone poem *Also sprach Zarathustra* on Bartók's development as a composer, comparing Strauss' work with Bartók's symphonic poem, *Kossuth.*

966. Ujfalussy, József. "Debussy et Bartók" [Debussy and Bartók]. *Silences.* 4 (May 1987): 165-170.   ML197 S57

Discusses the influence of Debussy's music on that of Bartók after Bartók's original encounter with it in 1907. Contains illustrations.

967. ----------. "Gemeinsame Stilschicht in Bartóks und Kodálys Kunst" [Common layer in the art of Bartók and Kodály]. *International Musicological Conference in Commemoration of Béla Bartók 1971,* ed. József Ujfalussy and János Breuer. Budapest: Editio Musica; New York: Belwin Mills, 1972, pp. 155-157.   ML410.B29 I61 (Editio Musica)   ML410.B26 I5 (Belwin Mills)

Reveals differences between Bartók's and Kodály's works but states that it is easy to detect certain stimuli and inspiration from works of Kodály in Bartók's music. However, points out that while there are hardly any preserved documents regarding the influence of their relationship in their compositions, Bartók's works show common elements of both their musical activities. States that the inspiration from Kodály's *Psalmus Hungaricus* is evident in Bartók's *Cantata Profana.* Also, discusses common stylistic features stemming from the Hungarian folk-music idiom.

968. Véber, Gyula. "De Hongaarse opera na Erkel: Een historische schets tot ca. 1970" [The Hungarian opera after Erkel: A historical sketch up to ca. 1970]. *Harmonie en perspectief: Zevenendertig bijdragen van Utrechtse musicologen voor Eduard Reeser.* Deventer: Sub Rosa, 1988. pp. 229-235.

In Dutch. According to the author, *RILM Abstracts* No. 11122 (1991), "Hungarian folk music and Western art music traditions have influenced the stage works of Hungarian composers. Among the composers discussed are Ernő Dohnányi, Ede Poldini (1869-1957), Bartók, Kodály, György Ránki (b. 1907), Ferenc Farkas (b. 1905), and Ferenc Erkel (1810-1893). Erkel was the chief conductor of the National Theater from 1837-1884, exerting a powerful influence over the development of Hungarian opera." Contains music examples.

969. Weiss-Aigner, Günter. "Tonale Perspektiven des jungen Bartók" [Tonal perspectives of the young Bartók]. *Studia musicologica* 24/3-4 (1982): 537-548.   781.05 St92   ISSN 0039-3266

Detailed study of the elements of Bartók's early works in terms of their Classical and Romantic sources, especially in Beethoven and Liszt. As one instance, the octatonic scale already appears in such works as Liszt's Symphonic Poem *Tasso.*

5. Bartók's Influences on Others

970. Borio, Gianmario. "L'eredità Bartokiana nel secondo quartetto di G. Ligeti: Sul concetto di tradizione nella musica contemporanea" [Bartók's legacy in Ligeti's second string quartet: The concept of tradition in contemporary music]. *Studia musicologica* 13/2 (1984): 289-307. 781.05 St92 ISSN 0039-3266

According to Pinuccia Carrer, *RILM Abstracts* No. 6016 (1984), states that "György Ligeti's second string quartet shows a connection to the formal and tonal procedures of Bartók's chamber music. The concept of tradition, in relation to *Rezeptionsgeschichte* and *Wirkungsgeschichte*, plays an important role in this study." Contains music examples.

971. Hsu, Madeleine. *Olivier Messiaen, the Musical Mediator: A Study of the Influence of Liszt, Debussy, and Bartók*. London: Associated University Presses, 1996. 183p. ISBN 0-8386-3595-4

Analytical insights into Messiaen's works complement the key issues of stylistic genesis and influence which the author traces back to Liszt, Debussy, and Bartók (see especially Chapter 4, "Bartók: Messiaen's Master of Thought?"). Uses Messiaen's own comments about Bartók's folksong research to substantiate Bartók's influence on Messiaen's use of birdsongs, which he collected, and his own native folk music as sources of inspiration for his compositions. Shows that Messiaen's concern with new rhythmic techniques, derived from his knowledge of Bulgarian rhythm in particular, came from Bartók, whose influences are also evident in Messiaen's percussive use of the piano in certain works. (Annotation derived from the Foreword by Elliott Antokoletz.)

972. ----------. "Olivier Messiaen, The Musical Mediator, and His Major Influences Liszt, Debussy and Bartók." Ph.D. diss. New York University, 1984. 270p.

Intention is to determine the degree of influence of Bartók on Messiaen. States that evidence is provided by Messiaen's comments regarding Bartók's folk-song research as a source of inspiration for his own interest in collecting birdsongs as well as acquiring an interest in his own folk music. Furthermore, Messiaen's concern with new rhythmic techniques, particularly his knowledge of Bulgarian rhythm, came from Bartók. Influences can also be seen in Messiaen's percussive use of the piano in certain works. Contains illustrations.

973. Juhász, Előd. "Beszélgetés Sárai Tiborral" [An interview with Tibor Sárai]. *Kritika* (January 1975): 10-11. HB1.244

Interview discussing Bartók and Kodály as models for a simplified style that became important among Hungarian composers in the early 1950s.

974. Láng, István. "Bartók's Heritage. A Composer's View." *The New Hungarian Quarterly* 11/39 (Fall 1970): 13-16.   914.39105 N42 ML410 B26 B29

Talks of the influence of Bartók on his contemporaries, especially evident in those composers of lesser stature. Reprinted in *Bartók Studies,* ed. Todd Crow. Detroit: Information Coordinators, 1976, pp. 198-201.

975. Nováček, Zdenko. "Frano Dostalik--propagator Bartóka" [Frano Dostalik--Bartók's champion]. *Hudzivot* 7/2 (1975): 3.

In commemoration of the thirtieth anniversary of Dostalik's death, the author points to the special importance that Bartók's original musical language had for this Slovak composer.

976. Petersen, Peter. "Bartók und Lutosławski: Ein Vergleich" [Bartók and Lutosławski: a comparison]. *Studia musicologica* 24/3-4 (1982): 451-463.   781.05 St92   ISSN 0039-3266

Shows Bartók's technical influence on Lutosławski. The latter gave Bartók's music an extraordinarily high appraisal, stating that he reached Beethoven's loftiness of human thought and feeling. Bartók's and Lutosławski's works are equally intensive. Above all, Lutosławski has further developed Bartók's principles of pitch organization. He has extended Bartók's "modal chromaticism" to a diatonically based twelve-tone style as well as continuing Bartók's well-known diatonic-chromatic duality. Lutosławski transforms the latter in many works into a semitone-quartertone relation.

977. Sanina, Nina. "Music Full of Cordiality and Humanity." *Sovetskaya muzyka* 8 (August 1973): 117-124.   ISSN 0038-5085

Not examined. Only the English translation of the Russian title is given in *RILM Abstracts* No. 2231 (1973). According to *RILM,* the author discusses the symphonic style and aesthetics of the Hungarian composer, Pál Kadosa, and "considers the considerable influence of Hungarian folk music and of Béla Bartók upon the compositions of Kadosa." Contains illustrations.

978. Sarkisova, Svetlana. "Bartók Béla és az új örmény zene" [Béla Bartók and the new Armenian music]. *Magyar zene* 26/3 (September 1985): 271-284.   ML5 M14   ISSN 0025-0384

Points to Bartók's influence on the new music of Armenian composers in their tendency toward synthesis of folk- and art-music sources. Also points to Bartók's influence on these composers as seen in their use of the principles of monothematicism, variation, tonal serialism, formal symmetry, and the concerto form.

979. Satory, Stephen. "String Quartet Composition in Hungary, 1958-1981." Ph.D. diss. Musicology: University of Toronto, 1991. 300p. DANN69165

According to the author, *RILM Abstracts* No. 5200 (1991), "After an easing of ideological pressure in the mid-1950s, Hungarian music underwent a series of profound stylistic changes, influenced by trends in world music. The state-sanctioned style of the early 1950s, known as the Kodály School, had been characterized by tonality, diatonicism, and triadic harmony, with a strong reliance on folk songs and folk dances. The first new influence arrived in 1955-56 with the rehabilitation of all of Bartók's music for public use, after almost a decade of banishment. His work was eagerly emulated, with a number of string quartets composed between 1958 and 1960 seeming to follow Bartókian models closely. . . . During the 1960s Hungarian composers forged the New Hungarian Style in quartet composition, inspired by Bartók and several types of folk music (laments and *verbunkos* music). This style is characterized by a micropolyphony that is tight, busy, highly accented and sharply rhythmicized." Contains music examples, bibliography, discography.

980. Seefried, Irmgard. "Meine Wege zu Hindemith und Bartók" [My paths to Hindemith and Bartók]. *Österreichische Musikzeitschrift* 4 (1954): 113-118.   780.5 Oe8   ISSN 0029-9316

Brief essay on how Irmgard Seefried learned to love Hindemith and Bartók, especially through Hindemith's "Christmas Motets," available only in manuscript, and Bartók's cycle, *Dorfszenen*. Refers to the "magic" of folk melody and discusses stylistic features of both voice and piano accompaniment.

6. Studies of Bartók's Compositional Process (Sketches, Manuscript Drafts, Editions, Versions, His Own Recordings) and/or History of the Works

981. Ashman, Mike. "Around the Bluebeard Myth." In: *The Stage Works of Béla Bartók*, ed. Nicholas John. Sponsor: Martini. *Operaguide* 44. New York: Riverrun; London: Calder, 1991. pp. 35-38. ISBN 0-7145-4194-X   ML410 B26 S78

Traces the history of the Bluebeard myth through its various literary manifestations, looking as far back as *Genesis II* and *III* and ancient classical and medieval sources. Points to Charles Perrault's 1697 *Histoires ou contes du temps passé* as the main source in which the myth first became widely known. Outlines historical variants stemming from the Perrault story through the Symbolist settings by Maurice Maeterlinck and Béla Balázs (as basis for Bartók's opera) in the early twentieth century. Provides insight into the metaphorical associations, meanings, and reinterpretations among the various manifestations of the myth. Contains illustration.

982. Barna, István. "Bartók II. vonósnégyesének módosított metronóm jelzései" [The altered metronome indications in Bartók's *Second Quartet*]. *Zenei szemle* (1948). HA2.398

Discusses discrepancies in the metronome markings between editions of the score and parts for the first two string quartets. Metronome indications in the original U.E. score (1920) of the *Second String Quartet* were subsequently revised by Bartók; the list of corrections was sent to André Gertler in 1935, and published, with the latter's permission, by Barna.

983. Bartók, Peter. "Correcting Printed Editions of Béla Bartók's Viola Concerto and Other Compositions." *Bartók in Retrospect,* ed. Elliott Antokoletz, Victoria Fischer, and Benjamin Suchoff. Projected publication of two 1995 conference proceedings.

Lecture originally given in combination with Nelson Dellamaggiore, "Deciphering Béla Bartók's Viola Concerto Sketch" (see item no. 1161). States that the published editions of Béla Bartók's works have been known to contain some minor errors, not serious enough to interfere with their successful performance or even to be detected in most cases. The accessibility of his manuscripts or copies thereof since 1985 enabled comparison of the printed editions with the corresponding manuscript sources and the preparation of new editions with much fewer errors. Points out that the task is not always straightforward, owing to inconsistencies among different sources for the same work, illustrated by a specific example. The most complex correction project has been that of the posthumous *Viola Concerto,* which was not even orchestrated by the composer. Revision of the score, prepared first by Tibor Serly, could rely on only the composer's sketches and involved a varying degree of analysis, conjecture and reference to the composer's other, completed, works. Examples, the solution of a clear-cut detail and of a number of puzzling features, illustrate the varying relative roles of direct and indirect interpretation that had to be employed so as to produce a performable score that may come close to, although can never claim to be exactly, what the composer had intended. (Annotation based on the author's abstract of the original lecture; see item no. 1161.)

984. Beach, Marcia. "Bartók's Fifth String Quartet: Studies in Genesis and Structure." Ph.D. diss., Musicology. Eastman School of Music, University of Rochester, 1988. 3v. 334p.   DA 8822218

Points to the manuscripts as an essential source for understanding Bartók's compositional methodology. Discusses Bartók's changing conception of the structural organization in his music during the compositional process, asserting that aesthetic or expressive demands are a significant force in the process of revision. Demonstrates that the study of Bartók's revisions of the first, third, and fifth movements of the *Fifth String Quartet* entails the move toward systematic use of symmetrical pitch constructions derived from the cycle of fourths/fifths.

985. Breuer, János. "Adatok a Két arckép keletkezéséhez" [Data on the origin of *Two Portraits*]. *Magyar zenetörténeti tanulmányok Mosonyi Mihály és Bartók Béla emlékére* 3. Budapest: Zeneműkiadó, 1973, pp. 279-288.   ML55 S992 B6

In Hungarian; summaries in English and German. Discusses the origin of the second movement of the *Two Portraits,* Op. 5, which is an orchestration of the last of the *Fourteen Bagatelles,* Op. 6, for piano. According to information obtained from a review in *A Zene* (1912), Bartók made this orchestration between February 12 and March 27, 1911.

986. ----------. "Béla Bartók: Der wunderbare Mandarin. Dokumente zur Geschichte der Kölner Uraufführung" [Béla Bartók: *The Miraculous Mandarin.* Documents on the history of the Cologne premiere]. *Jahrbuch Peters* (1985): 43-61.   ML5 J16

Addresses the scandal at the *Mandarin's* first performance at Cologne in 1926 and the censorship of the work in Hungary during Bartók's lifetime. Attributes the scandal mainly to the naturalistic staging by Hans Strobach and the attitude of the press.

987. ----------. "On the Three Posthumous Editions of Works by Bartók." *Studia musicologica* 13/1-4 (1971): 357-362.   781.05 St92 ISSN 0039-3266

Deals with problems of editions concerning three vocal works of Bartók: *Bluebeard's Castle,* the *Cantata Profana,* and the *Five Songs,* Op. 16. Some problems involve rhythmic changes by adapting rhythms to the German translation in *Bluebeard,* omitting the original Hungarian text in a new edition by Universal Edition, and omitting the translator's name as well as other details in different editions of the Op. 16.

988. ----------. "Újabb adatok a Két arckép keletkezéséhez" [Additional data on the origin of the *Two Portraits*]. *Magyar zenetörténeti tanulmányok Kodály Zoltán emlékére* 4. Budapest: Zeneműkiadó, 1977, pp. 359-360.   ML55 S992 B6

In Hungarian, with summaries in English and German. Provides a correction of earlier information, now stating that the orchestration of the last of the *Bagatelles, Op.* 6, as the second movement of the *Two Portraits* was finished in the fall of 1910. However, problems still remain regarding the date in which the two movements were joined as part of the same opus.

989. Conrad, Márta. "Eine dritte Autorenaufnahme von 'Abende am Lande'" [A third survey by the composer of *Evening in Transylvania*]. *Studia musicologica* 24/3-4 (1982): 295-302. 781.05 St92   ISSN 0039-3266

Points to problems of making correct evaluations of a work based on a comparative study of the sketches, especially when the composer himself has made subsequent corrections to the work. The first printing of "Evening," made in 1908 in accordance with Bartók's autograph, was published by Rozsnyai in that year as a movement in the cycle *Ten Easy Piano Pieces*. It was published by Rózsavölgyi in 1936 with Bartók's corrections.

990. Dalton, David. "I. Genesis and Synthesis of the Bartók Viola Concerto. II. A Performer's Perspective of Hindemith's *Die Serenaden.*" D.M. diss. in viola performance. Indiana University, 1970. 143p.

According to the author, *RILM Abstracts* No. 705 (1970), "the reconstruction and performance of the Bartók viola concerto is closely examined in interviews by the author with the two persons most intimately associated with the work. Tibor Serly comments on his friendship with the composer and the painstaking task of preparing the posthumous work for publication. William Primrose elaborates on his contributions toward the editing of the concerto. The author's own formal analysis plus considerations of performance are included." Contains music examples and bibliography. Also see the publication in *Music and Letters* 57/2 (April 1976): 117-129.

991. De Varon, Lorna Cooke. "Béla Bartók: Enchanting Song; Mocking Youth; Spring; The Wooing of a Girl." *Music Library Association Notes* (June 1954): 437-438.   780.6 M971n   ISSN 0027-4380

Review of these four songs for women's voices. Discusses their editions and general stylistic features.

992. Dellamaggiore, Nelson. "Deciphering Béla Bartók's Viola Concerto Sketch." *Bartók in Retrospect,* ed. Elliott Antokoletz, Victoria Fischer and Benjamin Suchoff. Projected publication of two 1995 conference proceedings.

Originally given as a joint lecture with Peter Bartók (see item no. 1161). (See annotation in item no. 983: Peter Bartók, "Correcting Printed Editions of Béla Bartók's Viola Concerto and Other Compositions").

993. Dille, Denijs. "Ein unbekanntes Bartók-Manuskript" [An unknown Bartók manuscript]. *Österreichische Musikzeitschrift* 22/5 (May 1967): 283-284. 780.5 Oe8 ISSN 0029-9316. See also "Un manuscrit inconnu de Bartók" [1966], in item no. 1150, Denijs Dille, *Béla Bartók: Regard sur le passé* [Béla Bartók: A look at the past], ed. Yves Lenoir, *Musicologica neolovaniensia* 5; *Études bartokiennes.* Namur: Presses Université de Namur, 1990, pp. 73-86. ML 410 B26 D52

Refers to the discovery by Mark E. Johnson, Music Department at the University of Illinois at Urbana-Champaign, of a previously unknown manuscript in which Bartók had orchestrated Beethoven's *Erlkönig.* Alexander L. Ringer's approximate dating of the manuscript has led to 1905 supposedly as the exact date. Dille disagrees with the conclusions that Ringer draws from Bartók's writing and the music paper used, stating that documentation at the Budapest Bartók Archívum provides evidence that this manuscript already existed in 1898. Also presents documentation refuting Ringer's contention that this manuscript was hitherto unknown to Bartók scholars. Contains letters, photo, and complete holograph manuscript of Bartók's orchestration of Beethoven's song.

994. ----------. "En relisant quelques œuvres éditées de Bartók" [In realizing some edited works of Bartók]. *Studia musicologica* 18 (1976): 3-18. 781.05 St92 ISSN 0039-3266. See also item no. 1150, Denijs Dille, *Béla Bartók: Regard sur le passé* [Béla Bartók: A look at the past], ed. Yves Lenoir, *Musicologica neolovaniensia* 5; *Études bartokiennes.* Namur: Presses Université de Namur, 1990, pp. 239-256. ML 410 B26 D52

Proposes to communicate some information received directly from Bartók or from the composer's papers and scores. Discusses and compares different editions or versions of a number of Bartók's works, including changes or corrections in instrumentation, metronome indications, etc. Regarding errors and contradictions in the editions, the author states that his intention is to inform rather than accuse, but if we continue to endure this state of affairs, we are all more or less responsible.   Contains illustrations, music examples.

995. Garst, Marilyn M. "How Bartók Performed His Own Compositions." *Tempo* 155 (December 1985): 15-21.   780.5 T249 ISSN 0040-2982

Analyzes recordings of Bartók's own performances of his piano compositions, relating the performances to relevant writings and to the notation for enhancement of the interpreter's understanding. Considers 1) duration timings, 2) rhythmic fluctuations, 3) variation of repeated sections and interpretation of "ossia" passages, 4) the use of different touches, 5) articulation, 6) ornamentation, 7) dynamics, and 8) pedalling techniques.   Performances of Bartók's works from five different recordings include *Bagatelle*, Op. 6, No. 2, *Rondo* No. 1, *Petite Suite*, *Preludio-All' Ungherese* from *Nine Little Piano Pieces*, pieces from the *Mikrokosmos*, Nos. 1, 2, 6, and 7 from *Eight Improvisations*, Op. 20, *Three Hungarian Folk Tunes*, *Contrasts* for clarinet, violin, and piano, *Romanian Folk Dances*, *Evening in the Country* from *Ten Easy Pieces*, *Sonatina*, and Nos. 6-10, 12, 14 and 15 from *Fifteen Hungarian Peasant Songs*. Also includes performances of other composers' works. Concludes that details of interpretation should be based on a study of the individual character of each work rather than a general set of recommendations for all the works.

996. Gillies, Malcolm. "Bartók's Notation: Tonality and Modality." *Tempo* (London) 145 (June 1983): 4-9.   780.5 T249 ISSN 0040-2982

Study of the sketches of the *Sonata for Solo Violin* suggests that new insights into Bartók's use of tonality and modality are to be gained from three sources: the ethnomusicological writings; writings on wider musical issues; and the compositional process from sketch to revised published score. Sketches provide evidence in terms of notation as a clue to tonal centering based on the principle of "encirclement," as shown in Bartók's folk music transcriptions. Deals with varying scalar bases. States that the evidence is most clear in the later works.

997. Hunkemöller, Jürgen. "Bartók analysiert seine 'Musik für Saiteninstrumente, Schlagzeug und Celesta'" [Bartók analyzes his *Music for Strings, Percussion, and Celesta*]. *Archiv für Musikwissenschaft* 40 (1983): 147-163. 780.5 Ar252   ISSN 0003-9292

States that the analysis of *Music for Strings, Percussion, and Celesta* directs itself to the specific and typical of Bartók. It searches for answers regarding Bartók's historical position, the source of his style, development of the idea while composing, his compositional understanding in a concrete case, his degree of consciousness of what guided him, and the degree of reflection within himself. The author provides a history of Bartók's own three analyses of the work requested by Universal Edition for the pocket scores, then interprets and evaluates Bartók's analysis and that of László Somfai. The work is viewed according to Arnold Gehlen's theory of modern painting, worked out on the basis of sociological-aesthetic research and flanked by philosophical-historical thought. Aside from the controversies regarding its application to the fine arts, Hunkemöller states that it is directly relevant to music but evokes a question about it. Looking for the truth about art, Gehlen discovered in the painting of many centuries "the subjectivity of man" and, even more, its "reflexivity." Consequently, the reflexive form in twentieth-century art comes from certain emotions, which are then ordered, examined, colored, compared, and clarified, all as a process of train of thought of which keenness and relationships are dependent upon each other. While this art is conceptual, its essence stems from an intuitive level that creates the substantial part of it, manifesting itself in two streams: visual and verbal. Hunkemöller points to Schoenberg, Bartók, Stravinsky, Messiaen, Cage, Boulez, Stockhausen, etc., who seek evidence and enlightenment for the compositional work.

998. ----------. "Béla Bartók. Musik für Saiteninstrumente" [Béla Bartók. "Music for String Instruments"]. *Meisterwerke der Musik. Werkmonographien zur Musikgeschichte,* Heft 36. hg. von Stefan Kunze. München: Wilhelm Fink Verlag, 1982; 86 S. zuzüglich Tafelbeispiele.   ISBN 3-7705-2109-9   MT 130 B34 H8

Provides a history of the genesis of the work, analyzes its structure, musical language, and character, addresses compositional issues between folk music and dodecaphony, and discusses documents. Points to the *Music for Strings, Percussion, and Celesta* (1936) as the first of three works commissioned by Paul Sacher and discusses Bartók's association with Sacher since 1929. Focuses on Bartók's challenge in finalizing the title, the original one, "Music for String Instruments," of which was changed to "Music for Strings, Percussion, and Celesta" in connection with the evolution toward the final conception of the orchestration itself. Provides evidence in Bartók letters to the Secretary of the Basel Orchestra and to his publisher Universal Edition, Vienna, regarding the size of the orchestra, its symmetrical division into two instrumental groups, disagreement about the title, and other matters. Also, Bartók's own periodization of his stylistic development serves as background for Hunkemöller's analysis of the work. Provides detailed descriptive analyses of each of the four movements. Shows how the character effects the genre, in which Bartók's search for new solutions to the shape of the work led him to the use of palindrome and his concern for cyclic balance and proportional lengths of the movements. The chapter "To Compose Between Folk Music and Dodecaphony" outlines the history of Bartók's folk-music research, its roots in the nationalist ideal of the nineteenth century, and its significance for Bartók in the development of a genuine contemporary Hungarian idiom based on the synthesis of folk-music sources with art-music techniques.

999. Kovács, Sándor. "A Bartók-rend hátlapjai" [Versos of the *Bartók-rend* autograph]. *Magyar zene* 28/1 (March 1987): 53-60. ML5 M14 ISSN 0025-0384

Points to Bartók's writing on the versos of the page proofs of his folk-music collection as an important primary source for biographical information as well as insight into the development of his folk-music classification system. Contains facsimiles.

1000. ----------. "Formprobleme beim Violakonzert von Bartók/Serly" [Formal problems in the Bartók/Serly *Viola Concerto*]. *Studia musicologica* 24/3-4 (1982): 381-391.   781.05 St92 ISSN 0039-3266

Based on the author's study of the sketch copies of the work given by Serly to the Budapest Bartók Archive in 1963, he questions the three-movement "attacca" form in Serly's reconstruction and completion of the work.

1001. ----------. "Reexamining the Bartók/Serly Viola Concerto." *Studia musicologica* 23 (1981): 295-322.   781.05 St92 ISSN 0039-3266

Detailed discussion of the history of Serly's completion of the *Concerto,* the difficult reconstruction problems he had to face, an outline of the compositional stages (dealing with thematic memo sketches, corrections, first, continuity drafts, scoring, etc.). Includes a study of the formal construction, Serly's misreadings and misinterpretations, minor deliberate changes, amplifications and additions, and orchestration. Concludes that modern Bartók scholarship could help to create a more "Bartókian" version of the *Concerto,* with a new structure and new orchestration based on the example of Bartók's other orchestral works. However, states that history will be grateful to Serly for his efforts.

1002. Kroó, György. "Adatok 'A kekszakállú herceg vára' keletkezéstörténetéhez" [Some data on the genesis of *Duke*

Bluebeard's Castle]. *Magyar zenetörténeti tanulmányok: Szabolcsi Bence 70. születésnapjára* (1969): 333ff.   ML55 S992 B6

In Hungarian, with summaries in German and English. Comparison of different versions of the opera. Using source materials held in Hungary and the United States, the author compares various endings of the opera, which provides insight into Bartók's approach to composition and dramaturgy. Establishes dates for Bartók's revisions and presents his revised vocal parts written after publication of the work. Also deals with Bartók's compositional problems in his setting of the Hungarian text. See the English translation in *Studia musicologica* 23 (1981): 79-123.

1003. Lampert, Vera. "Contribution to the Dating of Some Bartók Folk Song Arrangements." *Studia musicologica* 23 (1981): 323-327. 781.05 St92   ISSN 0039-3266

Discusses erroneous dating of *Three Hungarian Folk Tunes* (B&H 17679), *Fifteen Hungarian Peasant Songs,* and other arrangements. Gives detailed historical and source discussions involving evidence of problems in catalogues (e.g., that of Dille). Outlines certain considerations that suggest a more exact dating of certain pieces of the *Three Hungarian Folk Tunes,* referring to sources in Bartók's book, *A magyar népdal* (1924), autographs at the Institute for Musicology of the Hungarian Academy of Sciences, and Bartók's letters and other writings.

1004. László, Ferenc. "A *Cantata profana* szövegének ismeretlen változata: A 'műhelypéldány'" [An unknown version of the *Cantata profana* text: The "workshop copy"]. *Magyar zene* (Budapest) 29/2 (June 1988): 191-196.   ML5 M14   ISSN 0025-0384

Discusses the text sources of Bartók's *Cantata profana* based on two versions of a Romanian *colindă* text that Bartók recorded in 1914. Bartók later outlined a new version of the ballad in Romanian by combining and rewriting the two original folk ballads. The author reveals that Bartók sent an early version of the compilation to Constantin Brăiloiu (1893-1958), who made corrections to it. The present article contains this early version, Bartók's rough Hungarian translation of the text, and the relevant correspondences between Bartók and Brăiloiu, all of this documentation of which belongs to the Péter Bartók Collection in Homosassa, Florida (former New York Bartók Archive).

1005. ----------. "A kicsi 'tót.' Bartók műve a műjegyzék és az összkiadás között" [The little "tot": Bartók's piece in between the list of works and the complete edition]. *A Hét* 25/34-35 (September 2, 1994): 6-7. Also in: *Forrás* 27/1 (January 1995): 54-58.

Critical remarks concerning the five pieces for children that Bartók composed on December 20, 1905, and dedicated to his sister's newborn son. The manuscript, in the collection of the family, is unfinished, but it appears to be likely that Bartók later returned to this composition.

1006. ----------. "Széljegyzetek egy Bartók-kéziratra" [Marginal notes on a Bartók manuscript]. *Bartók-dolgozatok*. Bukarest: Kriterion, 1974, pp. 29-39.   ML410.B26 B275

Description of the "Bukarest Bartók Manuscript." In 1922 at Marosvásárhely, Bartók notated four songs from memory before a concert (*Eight Hungarian Folksongs*, Nos. II, VI, V, III). The study analyzes the differences between this notation and that of the printed score. Contains seven facsimile pages. The same article appeared in Romanian in item no. 319: Ferenc László. *Béla Bartók. Studii, comunicări și eseuri* [Béla Bartók. Studies, communications, essays]. Bucharest: Kriterion, 1985.

1007. Leafstedt, Carl. *"Pélleas* Revealed: The Original Ending of Bartók's Opera, *Duke Bluebeard's Castle." Bartók in Retrospect,* ed. Elliott Antokoletz, Victoria Fischer, and Benjamin Suchoff. Projected publication of two 1995 conference proceedings.

Points out that the first of Bartók's three stage works, *Bluebeard's Castle* (1911), was a milestone in his musical development, for with this work he was able successfully to synthesize the modal and stylistic elements of Eastern European folk music with his own personal style for the first time on a larger scale. Ten years lapsed from the time of its composition to its publication in 1921. During this period Bartók took advantage of the opportunity to revise the opera. The concluding scene, where Judith submits to her fate of entombment within Bluebeard's castle, was the area most heavily affected by the composer's revision process. Demonstrates that the original ending of the opera can be reconstructed from surviving manuscripts, and how extensively Bartók's conception of the opera's final moments had changed upon later reflection. States that the original ending reveals an obvious debt to the music of Debussy, and that Bartók's interest especially in the *parlando* style of *Pelléas* soon translated into the uniquely Hungarian, folk-like declamatory style of his own opera. In the process of revising, Bartók obscured the Debussy influence. At the same time, and perhaps deliberately, he covered over the musico-dramatic symbolism he had so carefully composed into the original ending. (Annotation based on the author's abstract of the original lecture; see item no. 1139.)

1008. Liebner, János. "Une œuvre oubliée de Bartók" [A forgotten work of Bartók]. *Schweizerische Musikzeitung* 100 (1960): 357-359. ML5 S413

States that the original manuscript of the *Piano Suite,* Op. 14, contained a second-movement "Andante" to form a five- rather than four-movement plan. Discusses the influence on this work of Arab peasant music, which Bartók absorbed during his visit to the Biskra district of Algiers. Describes basic style features of the "Andante." The score of the "Andante" is published in *Új zenei szemle* (Budapest) 6/10 (October 1955): 3-4. Also published in: *The New Hungarian Quarterly* 3/6 (April-June 1962): 221-224; *Gesellschaft für Musikforschung.* Kassel: Bärenreiter 1963, pp. 315-317; *Beiträge zur Musikwissenschaft* 6/3 (1964): 243-244.

1009. Lipman, Samuel. "Bartók at the Piano." *Commentary* 77 (May 1984): 54-58.

Explores Bartók's recorded performances of his own music and that of other composers.

1010. Mason, Colin. "Bartók's Rhapsodies." *Music and Letters* 30/1 (January 1949): 26-36.   780.5 M92   ISSN 0027-4224

Discusses the *Three Rhapsodies* from different periods of Bartók's life in terms of their different versions, the history of their publications (with an attempt at chronology of composition), Bartók's approach to their form in the compositional process, and a comparative analytical study of the *Rhapsodies* primarily in terms of form, with some reference also to tonal and stylistic features. See also the letter "containing an important amendment to this article," *Music and Letters* 30/2 (April 1949): 199.

1011. Móricz, Klára. "New Aspects of the Genesis of Béla Bartók's Concerto for Orchestra: Concepts of 'Finality' and 'Intention.'" *Studia musicologica* 35/1-3 (1993-94): 181-219.   781.05 St92 ISSN 0039-3266

Draws upon documentary evidence, including correspondence with publisher, sketches, and continuity draft (the most important source of the latter is Bartók's Turkish field book from 1936), as basis for revising some established biographical assertions made by Hans Heinsheimer (American manager of Boosey and Hawkes) regarding the genesis of the work. In correcting the myth of the genesis, contends that Bartók's plans to compose the *Concerto* can be traced back before 1943 to his early American years during the time of a compositional hiatus in his creative work when he was making practical transcriptions of some of his compositions and preparing several folk music collections for publication. From a detailed study of the documentary sources (thematic memos, sketches, and continuity draft, including ink, pencil, and notational comparisons, etc.), the author proposes a "hypothetical micro-chronology" of the compositional process. Also addresses Bartók's personal condition and mood during this period, pointing to some discrepancy in his depressed attitude toward composition and his actual compositional activity by 1943. Contains Appendix outlining the *Chain of Sources,* detailed description of the sources, music examples, and facsimiles.

1012. Nirschy, A. "Varianten zu Bartóks Pantomime Der wunderbare Mandarin" [Variations of Bartók's pantomime, *The Miraculous Mandarin*]. *Studia musicologica* 2 (1962): 189-223. 781.05 St92 ISSN 0039-3266

Traces the development of this work through a number of different versions as found in Bartók's manuscript.

1013. Nordwall, Ove. "The Original Version of Bartók's Sonata for Solo Violin." *Tempo* (London) 74 (1965): 2-4. 780.5 T249 ISSN 0040-2982

Mentions significant differences between the original version and the published edition of the *Sonata,* the finale's original text providing the most obvious example in all of Bartók's music of the use of microtones. Gives analysis of these uses and other details as well as their changes, some of the information already having been provided by Bartók for Menuhin in an appendix of "alternatives."

1014. Ringbom, Nils-Eric. "Skrev Bartók en eller tva violinkonserter?" [Did Bartók write one or two violin concertos?]. *Finsk tidskrift* 72/10 (1972): 480-485.

Discusses authenticity regarding the posthumous publication of Bartók's early two-movement *Violin Concerto,* composed between 1907 and 1908. Presents Bartók's own views as to its status as a violin concerto based on his correspondence of 1943 with violinist Tossy Spivakovsky. Evidence shows that Bartók considered the Second Violin Concerto (1938) to be the only one of concerto status. Bartók also discussed with Spivakovsky the combined performance of the first of the *Deux Portraits* (Op. 5) with the first movement of this early concerto and the second *Violin Rhapsody,* the last in place of the second movement of the concerto. Includes a facsimile of a page of the letter.

1015. Serly, Tibor. "A Belated Account of the Reconstruction of a Twentieth-Century Masterpiece." *College Music Symposium* 15 (Spring 1975): 7-25. 780.5 C686 ISSN 0069-5696

Provides a history and detailed description of the author's reconstruction of Bartók's *Viola Concerto*. See also the author's related discussion, "Story of a Concerto, Bartók's Last Work." *The New York Times* (December 11, 1949): II-x-7.

1016. Somfai, László. "A rondó-jellegű szonáta-expozíció Bartók 2. zongoraversenyében. Széljegyzetek egy sajtóhibáról és egy kifejtetlen Bartók autoanalízisről" [The sonata exposition in rondo character in Bartók's *Second Piano Concerto*. Marginal notes on a misprint and on an unexamined analysis by Bartók himself]. *Muzsika* (Budapest) 20/8 (August 1977): 16-20.   ISSN 0027-5336

Based on Bartók's original manuscript draft of the *Second Piano Concerto*, the author corrects several errors that appeared in Benjamin Suchoff's edition of *Béla Bartók Essays* (New York: St. Martin's Press, 1976), which resulted from a broadcast on February 17, 1939 by La Radio de Lausanne. The broadcast was based on Bartók's own analysis of the work (in French), which he himself sent for this event. These corrections deal with a formal misconception, a wrong placement of an example, and an incorrect reference to a retrograde-inversion instead of a proper retrograde form. Includes a facsimile of the original draft.

1017. ----------. "Die 'Allegro barbaro'--Aufnahme von Bartók textkritisch bewertet" [The *Allegro barbaro*--textual source value of the recording by Bartók]. *Documenta bartókiana* (Budapest-Mainz) 5 (1981): 259-275.   ISBN-963-05-1185-1-(Serie)   ML410 B26 D6 ISSN 0134-0131

Discusses the textual source value of Bartók's recordings, with the intention of establishing a methodological approach to the study of this source for interpretation. Provides a detailed discussion of thematic, metric/rhythmic, and other functions. Contains many diagrams and examples.

1018. ----------. "A 4. vonósnégyes genezise: Bartók és a kottapapírok" [The genesis of String Quartet No. 4: Bartók and the music papers]. *Magyar zene* 3 (1988): 324-332 (1988): 324-332.   ML5 M14 ISSN 0025-0384

States that the study of the actual manuscript-paper has proven to be a major source of information concerning authenticity and dating in Bartók's music as well as chronology in the compositional process. Asserts that this is an important investigative method for scholars at a time of preparatory work on the thematic index and the *Béla Bartók Complete Critical Edition,* and that the value of this method can become apparent from a study of the manuscripts of the *Fourth String Quartet.* Presents a detailed, well-documented study based on this method proving that the five-movement symmetrical arch-form conception of the quartet came very late in the compositional process (i.e., as an "afterthought"), the overall form of which was originally conceived in four movements, even as late as writing out the fair copy. Also discusses Bartók's new habits of saving documentation (sketches, etc.) in the 1920s, the type of score sheets used, problems in reconstructing the original bifolios, and Bartók's methods in working with the music-paper. Also refers to different stages of Bartók's notation in the compositional process, and explores the order of composition of the movements, thematic materials, etc. Concludes that knowledge of Bartók's original intentions in the genesis of a work will also contribute to a fuller understanding of his compositional approach in general. Contains manuscript facsimiles, structural charts, tables. See also Somfai, "Bartók and the Paper Studies: The Case of String Quartet No. 4." *Hungarian Music Quarterly* 30/1 (1989): 6-13. 914.39105 H893 ISSN 0238-9401

1019. ----------. *Bartók műhelyében / Bartók's Workshop. Sketches, Manuscripts, Versions: the Compositional Process.* Budapest: Bartók Archives, 1987. 68p. ML141 B9 B37

Exhibition of the Budapest Bartók Archives in the Museum of Music History of the Institute for Musicology of the Hungarian Academy of Sciences. Both the exhibition and text are by László Somfai. Does not deal with Bartók's life, artistic and ethnomusicological activities, general influences, nor stylistic development but is rather intended to represent Bartók's creative process as far as can be done by sketches, manuscripts, and other sources. Includes a discussion of the nature of Bartók's workshop, including the conditions under which he worked as well as his approach and attitude toward the compositional process. First, the wall displays, as discussed by Somfai, deal with the following: 1) a chronological survey of Bartók's works from 1890 to 1945 (with publication information and routine in the compositional process); 2) autobiography, influences, and contemporaries; 3) source types and source chains in Bartók's method of composition; 4) the plan of a new work: *Sonata for Violin and Piano No. 2;* 5) arithmetic calculations in Bartók's manuscripts; 6) versions of juvenile works; 7) compositional studies and early works. Then, discussion of the upright showcases includes the following: 8) genealogy of the versions of *Rhapsody,* Op. 1; 9) Béla Bartók, the copyist; 10) copyists of Bartók's drafts; 11) from sketch to print: *For Children, String Quartet No. 1;* 12) corrected proof sheets; 13) lithography of Bartók's handwriting; 14) concert copies; 15) corrected copies; 16) unfinished works, unrealized works; 17) unusual manuscripts and fragments; 18) orchestration; 19) significance and limits of facsimile reprints: *Two Romanian Dances;* 20) genesis of a piece: *Sonata 1926,* Finale; 21) from manuscript to author's performance:

Evening in Transylvania, Allegro barbaro; 22) *Bagatelles* (1908); 23) revised versions: *Suite No. 2, Violin Rhapsody No. 2.* Discussion of the horizontal showcases includes the following: 24-26) the stage works; 27) drafts of essays and lectures; 28) *The Hungarian Folk Song:* genesis of a book; 29) *Carols and Christmas Songs (Colinde):* 30-31) folksong transcriptions, folksong arrangements, and studies. Contains video programs, bibliography, illustrations, and facsimile pages.

1020. ----------. "Bartók rubato játékstílusáról" [Rubato style in Bartók's own interpretation]. *Magyar zenetörténeti tanulmányok 3. Mosonyi Mihály és Bartók Béla emlékére* (1973): 225-235.   ML55 S992 B6

In Hungarian; summaries in German and English. According to *RILM Abstracts* No. 3834 (1974), "two recorded performances by Bartók of *Az este a Székelyeknél,* made by the composer dating from 1930 and 1940, reveal continual casual deviations from the printed score. Several of the revisions in the 1936 Rózsavölgyi edition of the work, which was first published in 1908 by Rozsnyai, may be attributed to the experience gained from performances. The characteristic divergences of the performance from the score occur in sections employing lento or rubato rhythms. All of the differences between the recorded performances by Bartók and the score are shown in tables based on a precise transcription of the recordings. Bartók's tempo giusto style of performance is displayed in the sections marked 'vivo.'" Contains illustrations, music examples, and a discography. Also published as "Über Bartóks Rubato-Stil. Vergleichende Studie der zwei Aufnahmen 'Abend am Lande' des Komponisten." *Documenta bartókiana* (Budapest) 1/5 (1977): 193-201.

1021. ----------. "Bartók-vázlatok". I: Témafeljegyzések a Zongoraszonáta I. tételéhez" [Bartók sketches. I: Thematic notes for the first movement of the sonata for piano]. *Zenetudományi dolgozatok* (Budapest) (1984): 71-81.

According to Melinda Berléasz, in *RILM Abstracts* No. 6147 (1984), states that "The bequest of Bartók's wife, Ditta Pásztory, produced a single-sheet sketch for the first movement of the sonata for piano. The sketch (64 bars) is compared to related sources." Contains facsimiles, charts, tables.

1022. ----------. "Bartók-vázlatok". III: A 'fekete zsebkönyv' kidolgozatlan témefeljegyzései" [Bartók sketches. III: Fragments in the "black note-book"]. *Zenetudományi dolgozatok* (Budapest) (1986): 7-19.

Provides transcription, with commentary, of six fragments of piano pieces composed by Bartók around 1908-1909 and a fugato sketch based on the Stefi Geyer motif, these fragments of which are taken from Bartók's "black note-book." This sketchbook, used by Bartók between 1907 and 1922, contains sketch excerpts of passages from many of Bartók's compositions from this period (see item no. 202: facsimile edition published in 1987 by Zeneműkiadó).

1023. ----------. "Bartók's Notations in Composition and Transcriptions." *Bartók in Retrospect,* ed. Elliott Antokoletz, Victoria Fischer, and Benjamin Suchoff. Projected publication of two 1995 conference proceedings.

Shows that the three activities of Béla Bartók--composer, ethnomusicologist, and pianist--present an extremely interesting case in studying the phenomenon of "perfect notation." Does a composer aim at writing down a new composition in the notation of Western music unambiguously? Can ultimate perfection be reached in transcribing recorded traditional (folk) music in normal musical notation? In most cases, the full source chain of the composition--everything but the preliminary improvisation at the piano--survived and shows the maturation of the notation from sketch, through several manuscript stages, to the authorized print and revised edition(s). In addition, some ten hours of gramophone recording exists of Bartók's piano playing, occasionally four different recordings of the same piece, demonstrating how he understood the performance of the written text. Similarly, the original folk music recordings can be compared with the draft notation and revised form of the transcription. Suggests that while in folk music transcription constant maturation of the notational concept prevails, in composition--depending on the genre or the intended user--Bartók employed distinctly different notational systems for different purposes. (Annotation based on the author's abstract of the original lecture; see item no. 1139.)

1024. ----------. *Béla Bartók: Composition, Concepts, and Autograph Sources.* Berkeley and Los Angeles: University of California Press, 1996. 334p. ISBN 0-520-08485-3   ML410.B26S59   780'.92-dc20

Extended form of six public lectures by the Director of the Budapest Bartók Archives delivered in the Ernest Bloch Lecture Series from September 18 to October 23, 1989, at the University of California at Berkeley. Comprehensive study of Bartók's compositional process based on all of the extant primary sources. Conclusions are based on the analysis of about 3,600 pages of sketches, drafts, and autograph manuscripts as well as numerous documents that include corrections preserved on recordings of Bartók's performances of his own compositions. Chapters present documentation pertaining to the following: (2) Bartók on composition, his concepts, and works; a survey of the sources, including a study of the existing sources, the function of different types of manuscripts, and reconstruction of the chain of sources; sketches and the plan of a work in successive stages of development; fragments and unrealized plans; paper studies and the micro-chronology of the composition; the draft as key manuscript; final copy, orchestration, reduction, arrangement; editing and correcting process; and a study of Bartók's notation and performing style. Contains facsimiles, list of works and primary sources, index of basic terms, index of Bartók's compositions, general index.

1025. ----------. "Béla Bartók Thematic Catalogue: Sample of Work in Progress." *Studia musicologica* 35/1-3 (1993-1994): 229-241. 781.05 St92   ISSN 0039-3266

With the recent availability in Budapest of the complete source material of the former "Béla Bartók Estate," the Director of the Budapest Bartók Archívum discusses his task of extending the work of Denijs Dille's thematic catalogue of Bartók's juvenile compositions to the entire Bartók œuvre. States that work on the thematic index of compositions began immediately because of its importance to the editors in preparation of the *Béla Bartók Complete Critical Edition* (BBCCE). Documents several of his published essays written in anticipation of issues and problems relevant to the editorial plans (e.g., the chronological organization of the thematic index), and outlines editorial principles guiding the decisions in such problematic areas of the catalogue as languages, proportions, handling hypotheses, etc. Uses the *Four Pieces for Orchestra* as a typical example for the structure and style of the individual entries in the catalogue. Categories include original title, ensemble, duration, composition (date, etc.), premiere, primary sources (sketches, autograph draft, autograph full score, MS copy of the full score, MS parts), printed editions (first edition, corrected copy, printed parts, posthumous edition), arrangement, dedication, correspondence, literature, notes, and worklist numbers.

1026. ----------. "Definitive Authorized Version vs. Authentic Variant Forms in Bartók's Music." *International Musicological Society Madrid Congress 1992.* (Kassel: forthcoming).

Discusses aspects of Bartók's notations (genre notations and chronological aspects), the maturation process of the definitive version (prematurely printed scores, temporary editions, and the ramification of his European and American revisions), the source value of Bartók's own gramophone recordings, and the significance of variant endings and alternative versions. The author's extensive source analysis in connection with the *Béla Bartók Complete Critical Edition* (in preparation) is gradually revealing the facts about Bartók's lifelong struggle for the definitive version and the perfect edition of his works. However, it also reveals that there are still a great many unsettled and controversial cases or ramifications among authorized versions. Demonstrates that Bartók's musicianship within the context of creating the definitive notation of a new piece was derived from the interaction of three phenomena: (1) believing in intuition in composition; (2) being a professional performer; and (3) being a master of transcriptions of recorded folk music.

1027. ----------. "Drei Themenentwürfe zu dem Violinkonzert aus den Jahren 1936/37" [Three thematic sketches for the *Violin Concerto* of the years 1936/37]. *Documenta bartókiana* (Budapest) 6 (1981): 247-255. ISBN-963-05-1185-1-(Serie) ML410 B26 D6 ISSN 0134-0131

Bartók sent his first sketches of the concerto, including the first and second themes of Movement I and the first theme of Movement II, to Tossy Spivakovsky as a souvenir of his performances in 1943. States that the sketches are necessary for the correction of errors. Then discusses rhythmic structure, form, melody type, and style category of the themes as well as the tonal structure as it evolved in different phases of the compositional process.

1028. --------------. "In his 'Compositional Workshop.'" *The Bartók Companion,* ed. Malcolm Gillies. London: Faber and Faber, 1993; Portland, Oregon: Amadeus Press (an imprint of Timber Press, Inc.), 1994. pp. 30-50. ISBN 0-931340-74-8 (HB) ISBN 0-931340-75-6 (PB) ML410 B26 B28

Discusses Bartók's practice of composing in great privacy, which prevented those around him from gaining insight into his compositional process until a work was completed. This has led to some misconceptions regarding the nature of that process. Bartók did provide some limited answers on several occasions to questions about his work habits, but he himself was generally adverse to analyzing his creative processes. Scholars have had to rely, therefore, on a "deductive method" for a true understanding of Bartók's "compositional workshop," based on comparison of extant sources and other such means. However, states that genuine source studies have lagged behind analyses of the published music until the 1980s, and publication of the primary sources was limited because of the separation of materials between the Hungarian and American archival holdings. Then presents a historical and technical survey based on the author's thorough acquaintance with all the sources. Discusses the existing sources, source types and source chains, sketches relating to the plan of a new work, exploration of the draft which represents the key manuscript and most valuable link in Bartók's source chain, study of the orchestration, reduction, arrangement, and fair copy, study of the edition, revision, and author's performance, and discussion of fragments and unrealized compositions. Addresses these issues in connection with many works from various periods of Bartók's lifetime. Extensively documented study.

1029. ----------. "Kompositionsprozess und Quellenlage bei Bartók" [Bartók's compositional process and source situation]. *Österreichische Musikzeitschrift* 39/2 (February 1984): 65-77. 780.5 Oe8   ISSN 0029-9316

Discusses the many types of primary sources (generally unknown) belonging to Bartók's compositional process. Summarizes the chains of source materials in connection with a given stage in Bartók's development, his working methods, and his relationships with publishers. Contains illustrations, music examples.

1030. ----------. "Manuscript Versus Urtext: The Primary Sources of Bartók's Works." *Studia musicologica* 23 (1981): 17-66. 781.05 St92   ISSN 0039-3266

Aim is to provide analysts of Bartók's style and interpreters of his music a theoretical knowledge of "the multiplicity and variety of the sources, and to make clear to general musical opinion why all the information, most of it locked away, needs to be made public through a complete critical edition." Outlines the following categories: 1) a catalogue-form listing of the source types and the principal chains of sources; 2) a more detailed presentation of the various kinds of sources; 3) some specific problems (dual-function particella/piano score; printer's copy; composer's concert copy); and 4) an outline of the basic musical and philological requirements for a future Béla Bartók Complete Critical Edition. Fully documented, exhaustive study of each category is given.

1031. ----------. "Nineteenth-Century Ideas Developed in Bartók's Piano Notation in the Years 1907-14." *19th-century Music* 11/1 (Summer 1987): 73-91.   ML5 N56

According to the author, *RILM Abstracts* No. 6855 (1987), "Bartók, who edited some 2,000 pages of piano music ranging from Bach to Chopin, was influenced in his own notational practice by such work. His notes explaining the performance indications in historical editions are thus equally indispensable to the interpreters of his own music. The present study focuses on Bartók's bagatelles of 1908 and their notation as compared with that of his edition of Bach's *Wohltemperiertes Clavier,* prepared in 1907-08. A special triangle of related sources is examined: (1) the various versions of Bartók's works; (2) his recorded performances; and (3) his performing editions." Contains facsimiles, music examples. Also published in: *Music at the Turn of Century,* ed. Joseph Kerman.

Berkeley and Los Angeles: University of California Press, 1990, pp. 181-199; and in Spanish translation by Luis Carlos Gago, in *Quodlibet* (Madrid) 3 (October 1995): 60-87.

1032. Suchoff, Benjamin. "Errata in the *Mikrokosmos* Publication." *Piano Quarterly Newsletter* 16 (1956).   ML1 P66

Outlines more than twenty typographical errors as evidenced by the comparison of the published edition with the manuscripts on file at the New York Bartók Archive. Some were discovered by the composer and the others by the author. Also published in *Zenei szemle* (Budapest) (October 1956).

1033. ----------. "History of Béla Bartók's *Mikrokosmos.*" *Journal of Research in Music Education* 7/2 (Fall 1959): 185-196. 780.705 J826   ISSN 0022-4294

From the author's dissertation (New York University, 1956), we are provided a well-documented study regarding primary source evidence for the chronological order of composition of the pieces (i.e., based on description of the manuscript sketches, Bartók's numerical cataloging of his manuscripts, etc.). Includes a discussion of correspondence between Bartók and his publisher. Also discusses classifications of the *Mikrokosmos* manuscripts on file at the New York Bartók Archive with a detailed description of the manuscripts.

1034. ----------. "Interpreting Bartók's Piano Works." *Piano Quarterly Newsletter* 20 (Summer 1957): 15-18.   ML1 P66

States that the primary sources of Bartók, including an elementary piano method, edited piano works from the standard repertory, lectures, and his own recordings, point toward the composer's preoccupation with aspects of piano playing: touch, dynamics, phrasing, and rhythm. These sources provide data for interpretation and technique in performing Bartók's piano works.

1035. ----------. "Some Observations on Bartók's *Third Piano Concerto.*" *Tempo* (London) 65 (Summer 1963): 8-10.   780.5 T249 ISSN 0040-2982

Gives historical information on the work based on corrrespondence between Bartók and his publisher, Ralph Hawkes. Discusses the fair copy left by Bartók and Serly's reconstruction and completion of the ending based on this primary source. Also speaks of Seiber's reduction for two pianos for publication as well as errors in both publications. Gives brief characteristics of the work. Suggests parallels between the dirge from the third movement and the *Four Dirges,* Op. 9a (1909-1910) as well as the *Mikrokosmos* No. 35, Vol. I.

1036. ----------. "Structure and Concept in Bartók's Sixth String Quartet."
Tempo (London) 83 (Winter 1967-1968): 2-11.   780.5 T249
ISSN 0040-2982

> Discusses Bartók's sketches for the *Sixth String Quartet* in light
> of the final version. Points to certain formal principles not apparent
> in the early sketches. Also compares folk-like material in the
> sketches for the finale with the authentic folk tunes in Bartók's own
> collection. Also published in *Muzica* 9 (Bucharest) (September
> 1970).

1037. Sulyok, Imre. "Béla Bartóks Handschrift im Liszt-Material in
Weimar" [Béla Bartók's handwriting on a Liszt manuscript in
Weimar]. *Studia musicologica* 29/1-4 (1987): 353-354.   781.05 St92
ISSN 0039-3266

> Points to Bartók's handwritten instructions (in Hungarian) on
> the manuscript of Liszt's *Czárdás macabre* in the Goethe-Schiller-
> Archiv, Weimar, *D-WRgs,* MS I 83, as evidence that Bartók intended
> to edit the piece for the Breitkopf and Härtel complete edition of
> Liszt's music. Bartók's editorial project was not published.

1038. Szabolcsi, Bence. "A csodálatos mandarin" [*The Miraculous
Mandarin*]. *Zenetudományi tanulmányok* 3 (1955): 519-535.

> Gives a history of the composition, orchestration, publication,
> and first (etc.) performances of the work. Also discusses the story
> and its significance as well as providing a descriptive and stylistic
> analysis of the music. For a list of its publications in various
> languages, see "Bence Szabolcsi's Works." *Studia musicologica*
> 11/1-4 (1969): 18.

1039. Szelényi, István. "Bartók opusz-számozásának kérdéséhez" [On the
problem of Bartók's opus numbering]. *Muzsika* (Budapest) 17/9
(September 1975): 17-20.   ISSN 0027-5336

> States that Bartók's autographs and page proofs establish that
> Bartók's opus numbers were assigned at a later date. Therefore, this
> information provides criteria for the numbering by the publishers.

1040. ----------. "Bartók Zongoraszonátájának kialakulása" [The evolution
of Bartók's *Piano Sonata*]. *Zenei szemle* (Budapest) (October 1954):
20-24.   HA2.398

> Complex analysis of Bartók's drafts. Arrives at several
> important conclusions that should revise the traditional picture of
> Bartók's music.

1041. Tallián, Tibor. "Quellenschichten der Tanz-Suite Bartóks" [Layers of sources for Bartók's *Táncszvit*]. *Studia musicologica* 25/1-4 (1983): 211-219.   781.05St92   ISSN 0039-3266

Provides a history of the *Táncszvit* and Bartók's own commentary on the work. Also, explores folk-music influences on the work and Bartók's compositional sketches.

1042. Thyne, Stuart. "Bartók's *Mikrokosmos*. A Reexamination." *The Piano Quarterly* 27/107 (1979): 43-46.   786.405 P573 ISSN 0031-9554

Discusses a published list of errata in the *Mikrokosmos* in the Summer 1956 issue of *The Piano Quarterly Newsletter,* compiled by Benjamin Suchoff after comparison of the printed text with the composer's autograph. Then points to a number of self-evident errors that seem to have escaped the composer, the publisher, and Suchoff. Author deals with several categories in detail: a) self-evident errors; b) probable errors; c) possible errors; d) discrepancies between metronome figures and timings; and e) discrepancies between text and composer's recording. States that we must strive for the establishment of an authentic text.

1043. Townsend, Douglas. "Béla Bartók: Suite for Two Pianos." *Music Library Association Notes* (June 1962): 526-527.   780.6 M971n ISSN 0027-4380

Review of this composition dealing with a comparison of the two-piano setting with a miniature score of the orchestral version. States that by comparing the two versions one can learn first hand how a modern master transfers a work from one medium to another.

1044. Ujfalussy, József. "Is Bartók's Concerto for Violin Really His Second?" *Studia musicologica* 13/1-4 (1971): 355-356.   781.05 St92 ISSN 0039-3266

States that the renumbering of the 1938 *Violin Concerto* as his "second" upon the discovery of the earlier 1907-1908 work should not be a simple question of chronology. Bartók himself had annulled the earlier *Concerto* by omitting it from his list of mature works and denying its existence in various ways. Gives a history of its rediscovery and publication. Thus, the renumbering of the later *Concerto* is entirely against Bartók's own judgment and intentions.

1045. Vinton, John. "The Case of *The Miraculous Mandarin.*" *Musical Quarterly* 50 (1964): 1-17.   ML1 M725   ISSN 0027-4631

Provides new information on the history of the composition of the work, including its revisions, publication, and performance. Also discusses the causes of its lack of success.

1046. ----------. "Hints to the Printers from Bartók." *Music and Letters* 49/3 (July 1968): 224-230.   780.5 M92   ISSN 0027-4224

States that Bartók was precise in his instructions to his publisher, Universal Edition, since their personnel seemed to have exercised the prerogative of making changes in the music. After World War II, reprintings by Boosey and Hawkes continued to contribute to faulty scores. Points to the need for a complete edition of Bartók's music.

1047. ----------. "New Light on Bartók's *Sixth String Quartet.*" *Music Review* 25 (1964): 224-238.   780.5 M9733   ISSN 0027-4445

Provides new insights into the work based on a detailed study of manuscript draft and sketches.

1048. ----------. "Towards a Chronology of the *Mikrokosmos.*" *Studia musicologica* 8/1-4 (1966): 41-69.   781.05 St92   ISSN 0039-3266

States that Bartók was vague regarding the chronology of the *Mikrokosmos,* but by combining his remarks and comparing them with the manuscripts, deductions can be made. Categories of investigation are: documentary evidence (letters, concert programs, etc.); manuscript sources (drafts for *Nine Little Piano Pieces* and *Mikrokosmos);* and dating based on the first two categories. A summary is then given, followed by reproductions of Bartók's drafts and fair copies of the *Mikrokosmos.*

1049. Waldbauer, Ivan. "Bartók's First Piano Concerto: A Publication History." *Musical Quarterly* 51 (1965): 336-344.   ML1 M725   ISSN 0027-4631

Deals with certain historical issues involving the first appearance of the full score. Also, provides a study of the manuscripts, editions, and correspondences as the basis for establishing correct tempo indications.

1050. ----------. "Bartók's 'Four Pieces' for Two Pianos." *Tempo* (London) 53-54 (1960): 17-22.   780.5 T249   ISSN 0040-2982

Study based on the primary sources held at the New York Bartók Archive.

1051. Wangenheim, Annette von. *Béla Bartók:* Der wunderbare Mandarin- *-Von der Pantomime zum Tanztheater* [Béla Bartók: *The Miraculous Mandarin*--From pantomime to dance theater]. (Ph.D. diss.,

Musicology, University of Köln, 1984). *Die Tanzarchiv-Reihe: Beiträge zur Musik- und Tanzgeschichte* 21. Overath bei Köln: Ulrich Steiner Verlag, 1985. 210p.   ISBN-3924953015
MT100.B26 W3 1985   782.9/5/0924 2 19

Provides a history of the productions of Bartók's pantomime, including the scandalous first performance of the work at Cologne in 1926 and the first choreographed production directed by Aurel von Milloss at Milan in 1942. Discusses the significance of the *Mandarin* for modern dance. Contains appendix (with unpublished letters by Bartók, commentary by Milloss, and documents on the reception), illustrations, bibliography.

1052. Welch, Allison. "Approaches to Bartók's Source Materials with a Focus on the Facsimile Edition of the *Piano Sonata* (1926)." Master's thesis. The University of Texas at Austin, 1985. 139p.

Detailed discussion of the various scholarly approaches to the study of Bartók's manuscript sources, theoretical approaches to analyzing the music, and a thorough analysis of the musical language of the *Sonata* as supported and understood in light of the autograph facsimile edition. Contains many facsimile illustrations, music examples, and bibliography.

1053. Wilheim, András. "Bartók's Exercises in Composition." *Studia musicologica* 23 (1981): 67-78.   781.05 St92   ISSN 0039-3266

Discusses the creative basis of composition in general, a history of Bartók's compositional studies (including documentation of his exercises in counterpoint, fugue, choral setting, and studies of musical form), pedagogical principles of his teacher, János Koessler, and analysis of Bartók's compositional exercises.

1054. ----------. "Egy Bartók-kottarészletről" [A manuscript fragment of Bartók]. *Muzsika* (Budapest) 20/4 (April 1977): 33-35.
ISSN 0027-5336

Establishes a fragment of a musical inscription by Bartók as coming from his *Five Lieder*, Op. 15. States that the Op. 15 appeared only after the publication of the fragment in a journal on February 1, 1917. Contains facsimile and music.

1055. ----------. "Két Bartók-vázlat" [Two sketches by Bartók]. *Magyar zene* (Budapest) 19 (1978): 401-412.   ML5 M14   ISSN 0025-0384

Hungarian version of item no. 1056. Presents a complex analysis of Bartók's sketch drafts. Arrives at important conclusions for the revision of the traditional picture of Bartók's music. Discusses the importance of the study of these sketches for contributing to a better interpretation of the works as well as establishing a theoretical basis for works on style history and criticism. Then gives some historical and analytical information on both pieces as well as examples comparing stages of the compositional process.

1056. ----------. "Skizzen zu 'Mikrokosmos' Nr. 135 und Nr. 57" [Sketches for *Mikrokosmos* Nos. 135 and 57]. *Documenta bartókiana* (Budapest) 6 (1981): 235-246. ISBN-963-05-1185-1-(Serie) ML410 B26 D6 ISSN 0134-0131

German version of item no. 1055.

1057. ----------. "Zu einem Handschriften-Faksimile aus dem Jahre 1917" [On a handwritten facsimile of the year 1917]. *Documenta bartókiana* (Budapest) 6 (1981): 233-234.-05-1185-1-(Serie) ML410 B26 D6 ISSN 0134-0131

Discusses the autobiographical significance of an eleven-measure fragment found on the title page of a journal under the title "Béla Bartók: A Musical Fragment" and the motivic parallels of this material to certain works of Bartók of this period.

1058. Worbs, Hans Christoph. *Welterfolge der modernen Oper* [International successes of modern opera]. Berlin: Rembrandt, 1967. 190p. ML1705.W67

Includes a discussion of Bartók's *Duke Bluebeard's Castle* and other twentieth-century operas, with critical reviews of their premières as well as stage photographs. Contains illustrations, bibliography, and discography.

7. Bartók's Orientation Toward Pedagogy and/or Performance Interpretation

1059. Baróthy, Zoltán. "Bartók Béla Mikrokozmosza az általános iskolai zenehallgatásban" [Béla Bartók's *Mikrokosmos* in the music-listening curriculum of the general school]. *Az ének-zene tanítása* 18/5 (October 1975): 209-212.

Discusses the pedagogical value of the *Mikrokosmos* for use in the music-listening curriculum of the schools because of the graded organization of these 153 progressive pieces.

1060. Brandon, Ann. "An Afternoon of Bartók." *Clavier* 20/8 (October 1981): 28-29. 780.5 C578 ISSN 0009-854-X

An unusual plan for a student recital of Bartók's music during Bartók's centennial year. Program included a long preparation by each student of a piece by Bartók and the awarding of competitive prizes (including recordings of Bartók's music). Also involved use of a worksheet for study of his life and music. Ann Brandon is a private piano teacher in New York State and President of the Albany Chapter of the New York State Music Teachers Association.

1061. Bratuz, Damiana. "On Bartók's Improvisations and the 'Pippa Principle.'" *Studia musicologica* 2 (1977): 8-14.   781.05 St92 ISSN 0039-3266

Discusses the accentual linguistic problems in the performance interpretation of those Bartók works based on non-Western folk idioms, performed by those coming from the background of the Indo-European languages.

1062. Dobai, Tamásné. "Tapasztalataim a kortárs zene tanításában (elfogadtatásában)" [My experiences with the teaching of the new music (and its acceptance)]. *Parlando* 17/1 (January 1975): 12-14. HB1.429

States that, based on the experience of pedagogical use of the *Mikrokosmos,* children are capable of accepting sounds other than the diatonic ones found in popular music.

1063. Doflein, Erich. "A propos des '44 Duos pour deux violons' de Bartók" [On the purpose of the *Forty-Four Duos* for two violins of Bartók]. *La revue musicale* 224 (1955): 110-112.   780.5 R328 ISSN 0035-3736

States that Bartók's *Duos* were composed with the pedagogical purpose of writing for the Doflein violin method.

1064. ----------. "Bartók und die Musikpädagogik" [Bartók and music pedagogy]. *Musik der Zeit* (Bonn) 3 (1953): 32.   ML410.B26 B4

Shows how, for Bartók, the didactic and artistic values are mutually interdependent, how the *Mikrokosmos* is related to the rest of Bartók's work as composer, performer, scholar, and teacher and how his achievement compares with those of Bach and Schumann.

1065. Edwards, Lorraine. "The Great Animating Stream of Music." *Music Educators Journal* 57/6 (February 1971): 38-40.   780.5 M973 ISSN 0027-4321

Praises the Hungarian system of music education developed by Bartók and Kodály as superior to that of other countries, refers to statistical evidence in their academic records. Talks of the important role of music in contributing to the development of the national culture.

1066. Fischer, Victoria. "Articulation Notation in Bartók's Piano Music: Sources and Evolution." *Bartók in Retrospect,* ed. Elliott Antokoletz, Victoria Fischer and Benjamin Suchoff. Projected publication of two 1995 conference proceedings.

States that Béla Bartók created one of the richest and largest bodies of piano music in the twentieth century, yet his works are not performed or taught in proportion to that legacy. His highly detailed attempts to communicate his new approaches to piano playing can be confusing, even intimidating. He used traditional articulation marks--staccato, tenuto, slurs, accents--in great profusion to indicate new ideas of sonority, articulation and rhythmic inflection. Traces the development of Bartók's language of piano notation as it parallels the evolution of his musical language in general. Focusing on the early piano works of 1907-1909, the sources of this notational language are explored and identified, and principles of interpretation suggested. (Annotation based on the author's abstract of the original lecture; see item no. 1161.)

1067. ----------. "Béla Bartók's *Fourteen Bagatelles,* Op. 6: Determining Performance Authenticity." D.M.A. diss., University of Texas at Austin, 1989. 163p.

Points to the *Bagatelles* as a landmark in the emergence of Bartók's personal musical idiom and that a study of the influences upon them is essential to an understanding of the broader body of his piano music. Reveals that both the historical background of the *Bagatelles*--Bartók's folk-song collecting tours, his feelings of nationalism, and his activities in Budapest as well as the countryside--and Bartók's own markings have a direct bearing on an authentic performance interpretation of his works composed during this period. Addresses autobiographical aspects of the *Bagatelles* (Nos. 13 and 14 directly related to the end of Bartók's love affair with Stefi Geyer). Discusses problems for the performer due to some confusing markings in Bartók's didactic notation, especially in the area of articulation, in spite of the many editions and recordings. Points out that he had an unorthodox approach to piano technique and attempted to communicate this through these markings. Tempo indications are also problematic, due to discrepancies between various primary sources and editions as well as Bartók's use of a faulty metronome during these early years. Contains music examples, appendix (analytical notes), bibliography, brief discography, brief list of primary sources.

1068. ----------. "Béla Bartók's *Fourteen Bagatelles,* Op. 6, for Piano: Towards Performance Authenticity." *Bartók in Retrospect,* ed. Elliott

Antokoletz, Victoria Fischer, and Benjamin Suchoff. Projected publication of two 1995 conference proceedings.

Demonstrates that Bartók's pivotal *Fourteen Bagatelles* of 1908 can be seen to contain in microcosm all that was to come in the development of his musical language. In particular, his original piano style is established with this work and the other piano works of about the same time. A study of the folk elements, new ideas in piano articulation and sonority, and the composer's personal issues at the time reveals their role in the inspiration for this work and contributes to the understanding of an authentic piano style, which can to some degree be applied to his piano works in general. Bartók was attempting in the *Bagatelles* to communicate a very new approach to piano playing and notation, and it is the intention of this paper to shed some light on its significance and interpretation. (Annotation based on the author's abstract of the original lecture; see item no. 1139.)

1069. Földes, Andor. "Béla Bartók." *Tempo* (London) 43 (1957): 22. 780.5 T249   ISSN 0040-2982

Pupil of Bartók provides a first-hand account of both Bartók's teaching and piano playing.

1070. Foss, Hubert James. "An Approach to Bartók." *Musical Opinion* 67 (April 1944): 218-219.   780.5 M974

Points to the six volumes of Bartók's *Mikrokosmos* as the most practical way to acquire an understanding and appreciation for what the author considers to be a difficult musical idiom.

1071. Gakkel', L. "Béla Bartók's *Mikrokosmos.*" *Voprosy fortepiannoy pedagogiki* 4 [Problems in piano pedagogy 4], ed. Vladimir Natanson. Moskva: Muzyka, 1976. 272p.

Not examined. Only the English title is given in *RILM Abstracts* No. 6966 (1976). It is suggested in *RILM* that Bartók's pedagogical and pianistic methods are evaluated as part of the larger school curriculum, which includes both Soviet and foreign composers, and provides an analysis of Bartók's *Mikrokosmos.*

1072. Genovefa, Sister M. "The Pedagogical Significance of the Bartók Duos." *American String Teacher* 12/2 (1961): 22-29.   780.7 ISSN 0003-1313

Presents a detailed discussion of the *Forty-Four Duos* for two violins, demonstrating their relevance to advanced violin study and pedagogy.

1073. Gillies, Malcolm. "Bartók as Pedagogue." *Studies in Music* 24 (1990): 64-86. ML5 S9255

    Refers to Bartók's extensive pedagogical activities throughout his life, beginning in the 1890s, and provides an account of his various works based on pedagogical intention. Points to the *Mikrokosmos* for piano as his most prominent pedagogical work but discusses his compositions intended not only for the education of pianists but other performers as well. Included are his *Twenty-Seven Choruses* (for two- or three-part children's or women's chorus) and the *Forty-Four Duos* (for two violins). Provides insight not only into Bartók's attitudes toward teaching of both piano and composition but also documents the opinions of his students. Furthermore, discusses Bartók's editorial work on piano music of the standard repertory, addressing his edition of Mozart's *Piano Sonata in D Major,* K. 311 (K. 284c) in particular.

1074. ----------. "The Teacher." *The Bartók Companion,* ed. Malcolm Gillies. London: Faber and Faber, 1993; Portland, Oregon: Amadeus Press (an imprint of Timber Press, Inc.), 1994. pp. 79-88. ISBN 0-931340-74-8 (HB)   ISBN 0-931340-75-6 (PB) ML410 B26 B28

    Documents Bartók's negative attitude toward teaching based on information derived from his correspondence, conversations, and essays. Yet shows that he accomplished much as a teacher, pointing to his works with pedagogic aims and his editions of much of the piano literature from various historical periods. Provides a chronological history of Bartók's teaching career and discusses his philosophy and manner of teaching as well as his classroom procedure. Includes significant quotations by his students as evidence for his attitudes and teaching techniques. Points to Bartók's wider educational influence through his compositions rather than his teaching. Provides a systematic overview of those works, significantly based on authentic folk tunes, intended to have pedagogical value for various levels of students. Also summarizes Bartók's editions of piano music from different eras for his Hungarian piano students and assesses their pedagogical aims.

1075. Hodges, Janice Kay Gray. "The Teaching Aspects of Bartók's *Mikrokosmos.* " D.M.A. treatise. The University of Texas at Austin, 1974. 97p.

    Discusses the pedagogical use of these progressive pieces, in which the composer gradually introduces advanced and complex contemporary rhythmic and harmonic principles to the student. Shows that each piece reveals a special feature of Bartók's pedagogical approach. Contains bibliography.

1076. Huang, Fung-Yin. "Bartók's Contributions to Piano Pedagogy; His Edition of Bach's *Well-Tempered Clavier* and Impressions of Former Students." D.M.A. diss., Ohio State University, 1994.

A study of Bartók's approach to teaching through his writings, editorial comments, and interviews with two former students.

1077. Malinkovskaya, Avgusta. "Pedagogicheskaya kontseptsiya Bartóka i yeeznachenie dlya sovremennoy muzykal'noy pedagogiki" [Bartók's pedagogical concepts and their place in contemporary music education]. Ph.D. diss. Muzykal'no-pedagogicheskiy Institut im. Gnesinyh, Moskva, 1975. 24p.

Discusses the historical position of the *Mikrokosmos,* describing the work as a complete methodological system that serves as a link between pianistic education and musical understanding.

1078. Meyer, Heinz. "Bartók's Mikrokosmos nur ein Klavierwerk?" [Bartók's *Mikrokosmos:* only a piano work?]. *Musikbildung* 2/4 (April 1970): 176-178.

Points to Bartók's own suggestion of arranging pieces from the first three volumes of the *Mikrokosmos* for group performance. Outlines the following categories of arrangement: 1) strict adaptation (transposition, abridgement, repetition, change in instrumentation, 2) free adaptation (changes in accompaniment pattern and rhythm), 3) improvisation studies (exercises in completion, variation, and structuring of rondos).

1079. Novik, Ylda. "Teaching with 'Mikrokosmos.'" *Tempo* (London) 83 (Winter 1967-1968): 12-15.   780.5 T249   ISSN 0040-2982

Points to the young student's accessibility to and acceptance of modern pianistic and musical problems through the *Mikrokosmos.* See the summary of this article in *American Music Teacher* 18/1 (1968): 38-39.

1080. Parker, Mary Elizabeth. "Bartók's Mikrokosmos: A Survey of Pedagogical and Compositional Techniques." D.M.A. diss. The University of Texas at Austin, 1987. 143p.

States that the importance of the *Mikrokosmos* lies in its comprehensive and systematic organization of both keyboard and compositional techniques. Provides both pedagogical and theoretical analyses of selected pieces from all six volumes. Following an Introduction, Chapter II discusses the historical background of the work and the development of Bartók's career in connection with it. Chapters III-V then illustrate the pedagogical value of each volume, using examples to show Bartók's approach in developing technical facility and basic musical skills. The remaining Chapters (VI-XI) provide theoretical analyses dealing with new principles of pitch organization based on the equalization of the twelve tones. These principles include analyses of pentatony and modality, which reflect the influence of folk music, post-Romantic and polymodal chromaticism, whole-tone and other uni-intervallic cycles, the octatonic scale, and inversional symmetry, in which axes of symmetry interact with traditional modal centers. These theoretical principles are related to those discussed by Elliott Antokoletz, in *The Music of Béla Bartók: A Study of Tonality and Progression in Twentieth-Century Music.* Berkeley and Los Angeles: University of California Press, 1984. The author attempts to provide musical examples of the various keyboard techniques according to progressive difficulty in correspondence with the increasing complexity of the compositional techniques. The conclusion deals with a comparison of the pedagogical value of this work with others of the twentieth century. Contains a selected bibliography.

1081. Suchoff, Benjamin. "Béla Bartók and a Guide to the 'Mikrokosmos' Vols. I and II." Ed.D. diss. New York University, 1956. 389p.

Intended as a pedagogical guide to the *Mikrokosmos* in terms of both the technical and musical principles involved in piano playing. The study of these principles is combined with the composer's own attitudes regarding piano playing and pedagogy. Furthermore, the author, as curator of the newly formed New York Bartók Archive, provides historical information based on a study of unpublished primary-source materials held at that institution as well as acquired from Bartók's former pupils and friends. The 153 pieces are discussed in numerical order, each in terms of technique, musicianship, Bartók's comments, and suggestions. Contains illustrations, music, diagrams, tables, bibliography.

1082. ----------. "Bartók's Contributions to Music Education." *Music Teaching Methods and Techniques.* Washington, D.C.: Catholic University Press, 1961, pp. 35-44.

Gives a brief history of influences on Bartók's compositional development. Then, focusing on Bartók's *Mikrokosmos,* the author examines briefly two important contributions to music education: a) the introduction of the "simple and non-romantic beauties of folk music"; and b) presentation of aspects of musicianship, technique, and style requisite for the performance of twentieth-century keyboard music, all in the form of transcriptions or teaching pieces for the piano. Also published in *The Journal of Research in Music Education* 9/1 (Spring 1961): 3-9; and *Tempo* (London) 60 (Winter 1961-1962): 37-43.

1083. ----------. *Guide to Bartók's Mikrokosmos*. London: Boosey and Hawkes, 1957, rev. 2/1971. 152p. Reprint (of the rev. 1971 edition) New York: Da Capo Press, 1983.   ISBN 0-306-76159-9. MT145.B25S89 1983   786.4'041'0924

Provides an historical overview of Bartók's career as a pianist, composer, folklorist and linguist, author of books and articles on music and musicians, and pedagogue. Then surveys basic compositional principles in the pieces, including rhythm and polyrhythm, tonality and polytonality, harmonic principles, and structure. Also refers to Bartók's intentions regarding pedagogy, technique, and musicianship, including the relationship of the *Mikrokosmos* to general education theory, its relation to trends in piano teaching, and Bartók's principles of piano teaching as well as his ideas concerning piano playing. Each piece, presented in numerical order, is then explored in terms of technique, musicianship, Bartók's comments (prepared for his pupil, Ann Chenée, in 1944), and suggestions. Contains illustrations, music, bibliography. The reprint (1983) contains a new introduction by György Sandor, a selected bibliography, and index. See also the original publication: *Guide to the "Mikrokosmos" of Béla Bartók*. Silver Spring, Maryland: Music Services Corporation of America, 1956, 1962. See reviews by: John Ogden, in *Tempo* (London) 65 (1963): 2-4; János Breuer, in *Magyar zene* (Budapest) 13/3 (September 1972): 315-316; and János Breuer, in *Documenta bartókiana* (Budapest) 1/5 (1977): 209-212, in German.

1084. Sueyoshi, Yasuo. "Kodomo no tameno ongaku to Bartók" [Bartók's compositions for pedagogical use]. *Ensemble* (1971-1973). PN 6034 E5

Series of analytical essays on Bartók's pedagogical compositions, significantly including a study of several pieces from the *Mikrokosmos* (1926), nos. 32-39. Primary consideration is given to the relationship between Bartók's art-music techniques and Hungarian folk-music sources. Contains illustrations, music, and list of works.

1085. Szabó, Csaba. "A romániai magyar zeneszerzők zenepedagógiai művei" [Teaching pieces by Hungarian composers resident in Romania]. *Az ének-zene tanítása* 20/1 (January 1977): 35-41.

Using Bartók's *Mikrokosmos* as an example, the author points not only to the plausibility but also the importance of teaching asymmetrical meters to children. States that this metric characteristic is shared among various Hungarian composers living in Romania and is found in popular music of Eastern Europe.

1086. Uhde, Jürgen. *Bartóks Mikrokosmos: Spielenweisungen und Erläuterungen: Einführung in das Werk und seine pädagogischen Absichten* [Bartók's *Mikrokosmos:* playing instructions and explanations: introduction to the work and his pedagogical intentions]. Regensburg: Gustave Bosse, 1952. 120p. ML410.B26 U2

> Not examined. According to William Austin, *Music in the 20th Century,* New York: W.W. Norton & Company, Inc., 1966, p. 568, this study provides an "exemplary balance of detail and general interpretation." Malcolm Gillies, *Notation and Tonal Structure in Bartók's Later Works,* New York and London: Garland Publishing, Inc., 1989, p. 34, cites this study as one of several in the 1950s that "fostered a greater interest in correctly-spelled scales, often as the basis for identification of bimodal or bitonal formations."

1087. ----------. "Zur Neubewertung von Béla Bartóks Mikrokosmos" [About the re-evaluation of Béla Bartók's *Mikrokosmos*]. *Studia musicologica* 24 (1982): 9-20.   781.05 St92   ISSN 0039-3266

> Argues that Bartók's *Mikrokosmos* is sometimes underestimated in its value for teaching piano. Concludes that a re-evaluation is desirable, which would mean a detailed analysis of each piece. Reprinted in *Musik Bildung* 16/7-8 (1984): 493-498.

1088. Veszprémi, Lili Almárné. "Közreadta: Bartók Béla" [Edited by Béla Bartók]. *Magyar zene* (Budapest) 18/1 (March 1977): 75-81. ML5 M14   ISSN 0025-0384

> Discusses Bartók's edition of ten sonatas by Scarlatti, which he used for pedagogical purposes. While relying upon the Longo edition, Bartók also referred in some cases to the Urtext. Points to differences between the two editions in terms of ornamentation, tempo, and degree of general performance indications.

1089. Yeomans, David. *Bartók for Piano: A Survey of His Solo Literature.* Bloomington and Indianapolis: Indiana University Press, 1988. 163p.   ISBN 0-253-31006-7   ML134.B18Y4   786.1'092'4

> Comprehensive survey of the entire solo piano literature of Bartók and a useful guide to the vast array of reference materials relevant to all factual aspects as well as understanding of the music. Provides introductory discussion of Bartók as pianist and piano teacher, including Bartók's own performance directives for interpretation, and outlines specific aspects of Bartók's pianism: touch; dynamics, accents; rhythm, tempo, metronome; phrasing, musicianship; fingering; and pedals. Also, contains basic introductory commentary on using the survey which, among other data, includes information on folk origin (includes a list of modal

types as well). Then, provides a chronological survey of more than four hundred piano works, ranging from the early Funeral March from *Kossuth* through the *Mikrokosmos*. The commentary on each work includes: publication data; brief historical commentary with occasional quotations by the composer; outline of movements and their basic characteristics (tempo, key, form, as well as dedication, folk text of original melodic source, etc.). Contains four appendices, selected bibliography, and index. See review by László Somfai, in *Hungarian Music Quarterly* 3/1 (Budapest) (1992): 32-34.

1090. Zimmerschied, Dieter, ed. *Perspektiven neuer Musik. Materialien und didaktische Information* [Perspectives of new music. Materials and didactic information]. Mainz: Schott, 1974. 333p.
ISBN-3795729513   ML197.253

Among the twentieth-century works explored, this study includes a discussion of Bartók's *Violin Concerto,* providing historical information, analysis, didactic and learning goals, etc. Contains illustrations, bibliography, index.

1091. Zuilenburg, Paul Enea Loeb van. "Why the *Mikrokosmos?*" *Opus* 2-3 (May-June 1971): 6-9.   ML156.9 0688

Demonstrates both the pianistic and compositional importance of the *Mikrokosmos* in the pedagogical situation, and suggests a classification of the volumes for the purpose of music examinations. Provides a descriptive use of examples showing principles of variation, melodic construction, and textural characteristics.

V. DISCUSSIONS OF INSTITUTIONAL SOURCES FOR BARTÓK RESEARCH AND ESSAYS IN COLLECTED VOLUMES

1. Archives, Special Libraries, Societies, Organizations, and Institutes Devoted to Bartók

1092. Lampert, Vera. "Zeitgenössische Musik in Bartóks Notensammlung" [Contemporary music in Bartók's score collection]. *Documenta bartókiana,* ed. László Somfai. (Mainz) 5 (1977): 142-168. ISBN-963-05-1185-1-(Serie)   ML410 B26 D6 ISSN 0134-0131

Summarizes and describes the contents of part of Bartók's score collection held at the Bartók Archívum and in the possession of Bartók's widow. States that of the approximately 1,200 items, 569 are works by contemporary composers. Also provides certain historical information regarding Bartók's acquisition and use of the scores. Contains facsimiles.

1093. Somfai, László. "The Budapest Bartók Archives." *Fontes artis musicae* 29/1-2 (January-June 1982): 59-65.   780.5 F737

Gives a history and outline of the contents of the Archive. Also discusses problems based on the division of the source materials between the two existing Archives in New York and Budapest and the hindrance of this separation in producing a complete critical edition of Bartók's music.

1094. Suchoff, Benjamin. "The Musical Present as History to Be: Sources and Documents (Béla Bartók)." *Proceedings of the American Society of University Composers, April, 1970* 5 (1972): 124-128. ISSN 0066-0701

Discusses the present state of the New York Bartók Archive.

1095. ----------------. "The New York Bartók Archive Resources and Contributions." *Musical Times* (March 1981): 156-159.   780.5 M98 ISSN 0027-4666

Gives a brief history of the New York Bartók Archive and an outline of the resources placed in sixteen categories: compositions;

folk-music collections; letters; printed music; essays; books, monographs, offprints; journal articles; cuttings; concert programs; iconography; records and tapes; documents; legal documents; other material; scholarly apparatus; and the New York Bartók Archive papers. Also outlines publications in the New York Bartók Archive Studies in Musicology series as well as other outstanding studies of Bartók.

2. Bibliographies, Discographies, and Catalogues

1096. Austin, William. *Music in the 20th Century: From Debussy through Stravinsky.* New York: W.W. Norton & Company, Inc., 1966, pp. 564-568.   ISBN-0-393-09704-8   ML197 A9

Includes a lengthy bibliography of more than 100 entries on Bartók with concise and often highly generalized annotations.

1097. Bátor, Victor. *The Béla Bartók Archives: History and Catalogue.* New York: Bartók Archives publication, 1963. 39p. ML410 B26 B3 780.92 B285ym

The first volume in the New York Bartók Archive Studies in Musicology Series written by the original Trustee of the Estate of Béla Bartók. States the aim of the Archive, which is to aid in the study of Bartók's life, his compositions, and his ethnomusicological work. Also suggests possible interest for those involved in library, museum, or archive activities. Provides an in-depth discussion of the origin of the Archive and a detailed listing and description of its holdings. Categories include an inventory of autograph and non-autograph manuscripts of Bartók's compositions listed in chronological order, works of Bartók's youth, list of his compositions of which the Archive has neither autograph nor other manuscript, ethnomusicological works, letters, books, magazine articles, original and photostatic copies of newspaper clippings, concert programs, printed music, photographs, phonograph records and tapes, and miscellany. Includes facsimiles of musical drafts, illustrations of a program and autographed title page of a first edition, and other memorabilia.

1098. *Béla Bartók: A Celebration.* Book of the Month Records. New York: Book of the Month Club, Inc., 1981. 24p. brochure.

Special issue of a three-record set, prepared in collaboration with Dr. Benjamin Suchoff, Trustee of the Estate of Béla Bartók. Contains a detailed set of program notes by Suchoff as well as introductory notes by Harold Schonberg. Contains rare photos and extracts from Bartók's original scores, which are held at the New York Bartók Archive.

1099. *Béla Bartók: A Complete Catalogue of his Published Works.* London: Boosey and Hawkes; Budapest: Editio Musica, 1970. 40p. ISBN 0-913932-37-X

A chronological index and a listing of Bartók's musical compositions according to genre. Also includes an alphabetical index of titles. This catalogue includes all of Bartók's compositions published by Boosey & Hawkes (London and New York), Universal Edition (Vienna and London), and Zeneműkiadó Vállalat (= Editio Musica Budapest). In English, German, and French.

1100. *Béla Bartók: Complete Piano Music.* New York: Vox, 1961. SVBX 5425

Performed by György Sándor, with program notes by Christiane de Lisle.

1101. *Béla Bartók: Összkiadós* [Complete edition on 39 records]. Budapest: Hungaroton, 1968.　SLPX 11480

In several series organized according to genre (Series 5 includes posthumous works), performed by various soloists, instrumentalists, orchestras, and conductors. According to the brochure published by the distributor, Kultúra (H-1389 Budapest, P.O.B. 149), "It is for the first time that all Bartók works were recorded in authentic performance under the control of the Bartók Committee. In seven years the Bartók complete edition has been prepared in the interpretation of the most outstanding Hungarian and Foreign performers. Each record is accompanied by an illustrated booklet in four languages (Hungarian, English, German, and Russian) containing also Bartók photographs. The complete series was awarded the 'Grand Prix de l'Academie Français.'" See also: Qualiton Records, Ltd. 39-28 Crescent Street, Long Island City, N.Y. 11101. Complete recorded edition of Bartók's works, as produced by Hungaroton on 39 long-playing records. Each record in the Qualiton edition is also accompanied by an illustrated booklet containing extensive notes on the works performed.

1102. *Centenary Edition of Bartók's Records (Complete).* Ed. László Somfai, Zoltán Kocsis, János Sebestyén. Budapest: Hungaroton, 1981. 2 vols.: LPX 12326-33 Mono and LPX 12334-38 Mono.

Critical edition of the recordings. Vol. I: "Bartók at the Piano 1920-1945." Vol. 2 (ed. László Somfai, János Sebestyén, and Zoltán Kocsis): "Bartók Record Archives--Bartók Plays and Talks 1912-1944." Detailed commentary, in Hungarian, English, French, German, and Russian, dealing with various issues such as (in Vol. I) the quality of the recordings, collecting the material (Péter Bartók's issues, collections on LPs, etc.), new collections (Hungarian research, phono-cylinders in the Budapest Bartók Archives, etc.), types of sources of sound, chronological order and variants, the principles of compilation governing volume I and (in Vol. II) the story of the recordings in the Bartók Record Archives and marginal notes to the piano recordings in the Bartók Archives. Volume 1 includes gramophone records, piano rolls, and live recordings, volume 2 private and family recordings (fragments). Also available on six CDs.

1103. Clegg, David. "Select Bibliography of Articles and Interviews by and About Bartók Published in Britain Between 1904 and 1946." *Music Review* 49/4 (November 1988): 295-307.   780.5 M9733 ISSN 0027-4445

   Annotated bibliography, which provides a thorough investigation of all the musical and non-musical periodical literature about Bartók published in Great Britain during these years. Shows the increasing interest in Bartók's music in Great Britain, especially between 1922 and 1934 when Bartók made a number of visits there. States that the bibliography mentions some writers, including M.D. Calvocoressi, Philip Heseltine, Cecil Gray, E.J. Dent, Frank Whitaker, Edwin Evans, Ladislaus Pollatsek, and Henry Cowell, who knew Bartók and wrote first hand about his works. Also, includes what the author considers to be some of the best music writers of the period, such as Leigh Henry, Gerald Abraham, Mosco Carner, Colin Mason, and John S. Weissmann. Includes some of Bartók's own writings published in Great Britain, ranging from analytical notes on the early *Kossuth* symphonic poem and *Sonata for Two Pianos and Percussion* to articles on folk music and other subjects. From his entries in the *Dictionary of Modern Music and Musicians* (1924), edited by Eaglefield Hull, the most important are those on Kodály, Hungarian Musical Instruments, Romanian Folk Music, and Slovak Folk Music.

1104. Clough, Francis F., and G.J. Cuming. "The Music of Béla Bartók on Records." *Tempo* (London) 13 (Autumn 1949): 39-41. 780.5 T249   ISSN 0040-2982

   Provides a brief history of Bartók's own recordings of various dates and sources with some reference to re-issues as well. After a list of abbreviations of the recording companies, a list of recordings by various artists is organized according to genre. Also published as "Bartók on Records." *Béla Bartók: A Memorial Review.* New York: Boosey & Hawkes, 1950, pp. 77-82.

1105. Demény, János. "Zeitgenössische Musik in Bartóks Konzertrepertoire" [Contemporary music in Bartók's concert

repertory]. *Documenta bartókiana* (Budapest) 1/5 (1977): 169-176.
ISBN-963-05-1185-1-(Serie)   ML410 B26 D6   ISSN 0134-0131

Provides a listing of those contemporary composers and their
compositions that Bartók performed as pianist. Includes names of
those who performed with him as well as the dates and location of
the performances as well. Contains illustration and facsimile.

1106. Dille, Denijs. *Thematisches Verzeichnis der Jugendwerke Béla
Bartóks 1890-1904* [Thematic catalogue of Béla Bartók's youthful
works 1890-1904]. Budapest: Akadémiai Kiadó, 1974. 295p.
ISBN-9630500809   Z6817.B29 D585

The classification employed in this Bartók catalogue is widely
accepted for the early works and is indicated by the abbreviation DD.
Contains illustrations, facsimiles, ports., bibliography. See reviews
by: Tibor Tallián, in *Studia musicologica* 17 (1975): 427-438, with
errata; and Ferenc László, in *A Hét* 6/38 (September 19, 1975): 6.

1107. Doflein, Erich. "Béla Bartóks Werk" [Béla Bartók's work]. *Melos*
5-6 (May-June 1949): 153-155.   780.5 M492   ISSN 0174-7207

Catalogue of Bartók's compositions, arrangements, and
scholarly publications. Revised by György Ligeti.

1108. Douglas, John R. "The Composer and His Music on Record."
Library Journal 92/6 (March 15, 1967): 1117-1121.   020.5 L61

According to Guy A. Marco, *RILM Abstracts* No. 532 (1967),
the author provides "a discography of 115 composers conducting or
performing their own works."

1109. Goodfriend, James. *Bartók. Six String Quartets.* Columbia D3L-
317.

Notes by the literary editor of the Columbia Recordings of
Bartók's *Six String Quartets* performed by the Juilliard String
Quartet. Provides some rudimentary comments on the history of the
quartets regarding composition and performance, and briefly
discusses their influences (folk sources, Debussy, Ravel, Beethoven,
etc.) as well as their forms and unifying stylistic elements based on
thematic, textural, and instrumental treatment.

1110. Kiss, Gábor. "A Bartók Bibliography, 1980-1989." *Studia
musicologica* 35/4 (1993-1994): 435-453.   781.05 St92
ISSN 0039-3266

Extensive year-by-year listing of sources and scores, books,
records, studies and articles, each of these categories of which is
organized alphabetically. Includes most European-language

publications. Items not annotated. Also contains Hungarian-language journals published outside of Hungary, index of names.

1111. Lampert, Vera. *Bartók népdalfeldolgozásainak forrásjegyzéke* [Source catalogue of Bartók's folksong arrangements]. Budapest: Zeneműkiadó, 1980. 152p.   ISBN 963-330-369-9
ML128.F74 L35 1980

Includes lists of Bartók's arrangements, source types, variants of source types, and a comprehensive thematic catalogue of Hungarian, Romanian, Serbian, and Arab folksongs and dances. Illustrations, map, music, bibliography. Also published in German as "Quellenkatalog der Volksliedbearbeitungen von Bartók. Ungarische, slowakische, rumänische, ruthenische, serbische und arabische Volkslieder und Tänze." *Documenta bartókiana* (Budapest) 6 (1981): 15-149. See review by Ferenc László, in *Muzsika* 24/11 (November 1981): 37-39.

1112. Lenoir, Yves. "Bibliographie de Denijs Dille Sur Béla Bartók" [Bibliography of Denijs Dille on Béla Bartók]. In Denijs Dille. *Béla Bartók: Regard sur le passé* [Béla Bartók: A look at the past]. Ed. Yves Lenoir. *Musicologica neolovaniensia* 5; *Études bartokiennes*. Namur: Presses Université de Namur, 1990. pp. 387-402.
ML 410 B26 D52

Comprehensive bibliography on Bartók by Denijs Dille, the original director (from 1961 to his retirement in 1971) of the Budapest Bartók Archives. Bibliographic categories include: "I. Ouvrages publiés sous la forme de livres" [works published in the form of books]; "II. Travaux d'édition" [editorial works]; "III. Articles, études, mémoires, notices et interviews" [articles, studies, recollections, accounts and interviews]; "IV. Éditions de partitions et de fac-similés" [editions of scores and facsimiles]; "V. Conférences, allocutions, cours et exposé" [lectures, speeches, courses and reports]; "VI. Orchestrations" [orchestrations]; "VII. Traductions" [translations]; "VIII. Conférences pour la radio" [lectures for radio]; "IX. Interviews et conférences pour la télévision" [Interviews and lectures for television]; "X. Programmes" [program notes]; "XI. Recensions" [reviews]; "XII. Pochette de disque" [record notes]; "XIII. Préface" [preface].

1113. Martynov, Ivan. *Béla Bartók.* Moskva: Gos. Filarmoniya, 1956. 20p.   ML410.B26 M36

Not a scholarly study but rather a practical and useful guide to Bartók's music for general concert audiences.

1114. McCabe, Rachel Ann. "Five Programs of Piano Music. (Musical Performance)." A.Mus.D. The University of Michigan, 1984.

Lecture-recital discussing the *Sonata for Two Pianos and Percussion* according to the theories of Ernő Lendvai.

1115. Nordwall, Ove. "Förteckning over av Bartók inspelade grammofonskivor" [A list of records made by Bartók]. *Musik-kultur* 32/7 (1968): 6-7.

Discography of Bartók's piano performances of his own compositions and those of other composers.

1116. Novik, Ylda. "Publisher Re-visited." *Piano Quarterly* 83 (Fall 1973): 29-33.   786.405 P573   ISSN 0031-9554

Surveys some of Bartók's piano compositions in the Boosey and Hawkes catalogue, including many music examples from Bartók as well as other composers.

1117. Somfai, László. "Bartók Discography." In József Ujfalussy. *Béla Bartók*. Budapest: Corvina, 1971; Boston: Crescendo, 1972, pp. 446-447.   ISBN 087597077X   ML410.B26 U383

Includes a complete listing of Bartók's voice on phonodiscs.

1118. -------------, ed. *Magyar népzenei hanglemezek Bartók Béla lejegyzéseivel* [Hungarian folk music: gramophone records with Bartók's transcriptions]. Budapest: Hungaroton, 1981. LPX 18058-60.

Critical edition of the recordings. Includes three discs, transcriptions, and extensive commentary in Hungarian, English, French, German, and Russian. Provides a history of the recording, including discussion of the preliminaries: the first four records of 1936. In the discussion of the recordings of 1937/38, both the number of the recording and date are given, as well as the performer and record F-number of the recording and parallel events in Bartók's biography. Also describes the characteristics of transcription accompanying the records, the drafts and fair copies of Bartók's transcriptions, melodies which were transcribed twice, and general information on Bartók's folk-song transcriptions (pitch level, tempo and metronome indication, meter and rhythm, notation of the ornaments, and recording of the text pronunciation). Also includes performers' data.

1119. ----------. "Why Is a Bartók Thematic Catalog Sorely Needed?" *Bartók and His World*, ed. Peter Laki. Princeton, New Jersey: Princeton University Press, 1995. pp. 64-78.   ISBN 0-691-00633-4   ML 410 B26 B272

Discusses current progress with the thematic catalog of Bartók's music, pointing especially to the urgent need for its completion because of the lack of a complete critical edition. States that until the latter is completed, the conflicting versions and editions of many of Bartók's works that currently exist will continue to produce serious obstacles and confusion for the performer, music librarian, and musicologist. Points out, for instance, that many pianists are either unaware that different "versions" exist or that they are hampered in making the proper choice from the myriad of publications of a given work. Provides a history of Bartók's changes of publishers, the problems the composer encountered upon seeing reprints for the first time, and his attempts to make corrections. Outlines the practical problems in beginning the actual production of the BBCCE. Discusses some of the most significant accomplishments and lacunae in Bartók research. Also, outlines the editorial principles guiding the decisions in the most problematic aspects of the cataloging, including proportions, languages, and hypotheses. Uses the *Allegro barbaro* as a typical example of the content, style, and format of the individual entries in the catalogue. Categories include duration, composition, premiere, primary sources (a. autograph, b. MS copy), printed editions (a. preliminary editions, b. first edition, c. corrected reprint, d. Boosey & Hawkes reprint edition, e. new edition), recordings, arrangements, dedication, correspondence, literature, and work list numbers.

1120. Stevens, Halsey. "A Bartók Bibliography." *Tempo* (London) 13-14 (1949-1950): 39-47.   780.5 T249   ISSN 0040-2982

Issue devoted to Bartók. Contains biographical and analytical material and a comprehensive bibliography. Bibliographic categories include: 1) books by Bartók; 2) articles by Bartók; and 3) books and articles about Bartók. Reprinted in *Béla Bartók: A Memorial Review.* New York: Boosey & Hawkes, 1950, pp. 83-91.

1121. Suchoff, Benjamin. "Béla Bartók." *Proceedings of the American Society of University Composers* (1972): 124-128. ISSN 0066-0701

The successor-trustee of the Bartók Estate provides an account of the current status of the New York Bartók Archive. Then presents an historical overview as well as an inventory of the holdings of the estate, originally referred to as the Béla Bartók Archives of New York. Discusses the establishment of the Archive under the trusteeship of Victor Bator, its research functions, and general activities (acquisition, publication, etc.). After Bator's death in 1967, its research services were interrupted when the source materials were placed in storage as a result of litigation against the original trustee by Bartók's heirs. Contains bibliography.

1122. ----------. "Béla Bartók: Man of Letters." *International Musicological Conference in Commemoration of Béla Bartók 1971*, ed. József Ujfalussy and János Breuer. Budapest: Editio Musica; New York: Belwin Mills, 1972, pp. 89-96. ML410.B29 I61 (Editio Musica) ML410.B26 I5 (Belwin Mills)

Paper read at the International Conference of Musicologists, Budapest, March 25, 1971, and published in the Report of the Conference. Talks of Bartók as transcendental Hungarian musician as Leonardo da Vinci was a transcendental Italian artist. Bartók's numerous accomplishments in varied areas of music are discussed in the context of his historical development with a focus on the literary efforts. Also includes a descriptive survey of Bartók's books, monographs, and essays on his folk-music research, the international scope of these investigations, comparison of the various melodies for reciprocal influences, reviews or polemical responses to criticisms of his ethnomusicological work, musical instruments, the relation between folk music and art music, his life as well as his commentaries and analyses of his compositions, and his discussions of music and musicians. Also published in: *Magyar zene* (Budapest) 12/4 (December 1971); and *Tempo* (London) 102 (1972): 10-16.

1123. Szepesi, Zsuzsanna. "A Bartók Discography: Records Published in Hungary 1971-1980." *Studia musicologica* 23 (1981): 493-499. 781.05 St92 ISSN 0039-3266

Comprehensive coverage of Bartók's works organized according to genre (stage works, choral works, songs for voice and piano or other accompaniment, orchestral works, concertos, solo instrument and orchestra, chamber music, and piano compositions. Includes 86 items, with basic factual information as well as reference to authors of program notes.

1124. Szerző, Katalin. "Bartóks Scarlatti-Repertoire" [Bartók's Scarlatti repertoire]. *Studia musicologica* 24/3-4 (1982): 483-495. 781.05 St92 ISSN 0039-3266

Discusses Bartók's encounter with Scarlatti's music, expansion of the Scarlatti repertoire in the 1920s, the reconstruction by János Demény of Bartók's Scarlatti repertoire from his programs, and Bartók's principal selections.

1125. Szőllősy, András. "Bibliographie des oeuvres musicales et écrits musicologiques de Béla Bartók" [Bibliography of musical works and musicological writings of Béla Bartók]. In Bence Szabolcsi, ed. *Bartók, sa vie et son oeuvre*. Budapest: Corvina, 1956. pp. 299-345. ML410.B28 A32 1957 780.92 B285B1

Brief history of the origin of Bartók's bibliography and eight points of instruction for its use. Also provides a list of Bartók's compositions with information on publishers, first performances with dates, etc. Then lists Bartók's folk music books and essays published in collections and individually. Also in German translation as "Bibliographie der Werke Béla Bartóks" [Bibliography of Bartók's works]. In Bence Szabolcsi, ed. *Béla Bartók, Weg und Werk Schriften und Briefe.* Budapest: Corvina, 1957, pp. 317-367. ML410.B28 A32 1957

1126. Walsh, Connie, and Joseph Szeplaki. "Bibliography on Béla Bartók, Available in the Ohio University Main and Music Library, Athens, Ohio." Athens: Ohio University, c. 1970.

Not examined. According to Todd Crow, *Bartók Studies.* Detroit: Information Coordinators, Inc., 1976, p. 288, this is a "mimeograph item from the Ohio University Music Librarian. Includes 'Bartók the Teacher,' a personal experience by Christine Ahrendt."

1127. Weissmann, John S. "Bartókiana." *Tempo* (London) 55-56 (1960): 34. 780.5 T249 ISSN 0040-2982

Presents a critical review of the literature on Bartók.

1128. Wilheim, András. "A Bartók Bibliography, 1970-1979." *Studia musicologica* 23 (1981): 477-491. 781.05 St92 ISSN 0039-3266

Extensive listing of books, studies, and articles, each area organized chronologically. Includes most European-language publications. Items not annotated.

3. Conferences, Festivals, Journals, Newsletters, and Special Issues Devoted or Relevant to Bartók

1129. *Arion* 13, ed. György Somlyó. Budapest: Corvina, 1982. 270p. 913.3805 Ar43

International Almanac of Poetry, or Yearbook, with a special issue devoted to the centennial of Bartók's birth. Presents a well-rounded picture of the literature that developed around Bartók's music, about what he himself wrote and what others wrote about him, as well as the literary texts of his vocal compositions. Categories include: poetry; unpublished writings on Bartók; Bartók and words (from Bartók's writings and librettos); and tributes, recollections, and critiques. Contains illustrations.

1130. The Bard Music Festival Rediscoveries: Béla Bartók and His World. Held at Bard College, Annandale-on-Hudson, New York (August 11-13, 18-20, 1995).

Organized and directed by the president of Bard College, Leon Botstein. Featured panels, pre-concert lectures, and performances of Bartók's orchestral (American Symphony Orchestra, conducted by Leon Botstein), chamber, piano, and vocal works, and works by other composers. For lectures, see publication, item no. 1131: *Bartók and His World*, ed. Peter Laki. Princeton, New Jersey: Princeton University Press, 1995. 314p. Programs included the following topics and works: (Aug. 11) *Béla Bartók's Life and Works:* Bartók, *Five Songs, Fourteen Bagatelles, Violin Sonata No. 2, Sixth String Quartet.* (Aug. 12) Panel/Performance--*Music Pedagogy in 20th Century for Young Musicians;* (Aug. 12) *Influences and Contemporaries:* Liszt, selections; Bartók, *Improvisations,* Op. 20, *Violin Sonata No. 1;* Debussy, selected preludes; Dohnányi, *Piano Quintet No. 2;* (Aug. 12) *Bartók: The Early Years:* Liszt, *Rhapsodie Espagnol;* Strauss, *Also sprach Zarathustra;* Bartók, *Two Portraits, Suite No. 1,* Op. 3. (Aug. 13) Panel--*The Development of the String Quartet: Haydn to Bartók;* (Aug. 13) *Bartók and the String Quartet:* Lajtha, *String Quartet No. 10;* Bartók, *First* and *Fourth String Quartets;* (Aug. 13) *Bartók and the Piano: Piano Sonata, Dance Suite, Piano Quintet.* (Aug. 18) *Hungarian Folk Music:* Special performance by Muzsikás Folk Ensemble from Budapest. (Aug. 19) Panel/Performance--*Evolution of Violin Technique in the 20th Century;* (Aug. 19) Bartók and the Violin: Weiner, *Sonata No. 2;* Kodály, *Serenade;* Bartók, *Sonata for solo violin, Rhapsody No. 2;* (Aug. 19) *Budapest Renaissance, 1900:* Erkel, Festival Overture; Kodály, *Summer Evening;* Dohnányi, *Konzertstück for cello,* Op. 12; Bartók, *Four Orchestra Pieces, Cantata profana.* (Aug. 20) Panel--*Folk Influences: Nationalism and Modernism;* (Aug. 20) *The Folk Element in Bartók's Music:* Bartók, *Third String Quartet;* A cappella choral works; (Aug. 20) *Bartók and the Theater:* Bartók, *Bluebeard's Castle,* and *The Miraculous Mandarin.* For pre-festival commentary, see: Edward Rothstein, "The Sounds of Cultures Clashing," under "Classical View" in *The New York Times* (Sunday, August 6, 1995): H (26); See review by: Anthony Tommasini, "Casting an Ear on Béla Bartók," under "The Living Arts" in *The New York Times* (Tuesday, August 22, 1995): B1 (p. 1).

1131. *Bartók and His World*, ed. Peter Laki. Princeton, New Jersey: Princeton University Press, 1995. 314p.   ISBN 0-691-00633-4 ML 410 B26 B272

The editor's intention in this book (published in conjunction with the Bard Music Festival, Annandale-on-Hudson, N.Y., August, 1995) is to close the gap in Bartók scholarship that has resulted from socio-cultural and linguistic barriers to Western scholars. The editor suggests that because of the advantageous position of Hungarian scholars in relation to Bartók's native culture and language, this collection of essays should contribute to new insights and a more well-rounded perspective of the composer by providing information that has been isolated from the international audience. States that there is a Bartók "hidden" from readers of English, and that the integration of Bartók's socio-cultural context into the musical discourse on the composer "has often been left to specialists working in Hungary." The editor points in particular to the lack of integration of historical information into the primarily analytical orientation of Western scholars due to the unavailability of many historical sources outside the Hungarian language. *Part I, Essays,* which explores both general socio-cultural issues and more specific background materials to several of Bartók's works, includes: Leon Botstein, "Out of Hungary: Bartók, Modernism, and the Cultural Politics of Twentieth-Century Music"; László Somfai, "Why Is a Bartók Thematic Catalog Sorely Needed?"; Peter Laki, "The Gallows and the Altar: Poetic Criticism and Critical Poetry about Bartók in Hungary"; Tibor Tallián, "Bartók's Reception in America, 1940-1945"; Carl Leafstedt, *"Bluebeard* as Theater: The Influence of Maeterlinck and Hebbel on Balázs's Bluebeard Drama"; Vera Lampert, *"The Miraculous Mandarin:* Melchior Lengyel, His Pantomime, and His Connections to Béla Bartók"; and David E. Schneider, "Bartók and Stravinsky: Respect, Competition, Influence, and the Hungarian Reaction to Modernism in the 1920s." *Part II, Writings by Bartók,* includes: "Travel Reports from Three Continents: A Selection of Letters from Béla Bartók" (trans. Peter Laki); "Béla Bartók: An Interview by Dezső Kosztolányi" (trans. David E. Schneider); and "A Conversation with Béla Bartók" (trans. David E. Schneider and Klára Móricz). *Part III, Writings About Bartók,* includes: "Recollections of Béla Bartók" (trans. Peter Laki and Balázs Dibuz); Edwin von der Nüll, "A Change in Style" (trans. Susan Gillespie); Theodor Adorno, "Bartók's Third String Quartet" (trans. Susan Gillespie); Aladár Tóth, "Bartók's Foreign Tour" (trans. David E. Schneider and Klára Móricz); Bence Szabolcsi, "Two Bartók Obituaries" (trans. Peter Laki); and "A Selection of Poems Inspired by Béla Bartók" (trans. Peter Laki and Claire Lashley). Contains illustrations and index.

1132. *Bartók and Kodály Revisited,* ed. György Ránki. Budapest: Akadémiai Kiadó, 1987. 229p.   ISBN 963-05-4510-1

Publication of some of the lectures given at the *Bartók-Kodály Symposium,* held at the University of Indiana at Bloomington (April 5-7, 1982). See item no. 1141. Some titles of the lectures that have been included in this publication are slightly altered. Includes the following: Foreword by György Sebők; Mary Gluck, "The Intellectual and Cultural Background of Bartók's Work"; Miklós Lackó, "The Intellectual Environment of Bartók and Kodály with Special Regard to the Period between the Two World Wars"; Ivan Sanders, "Three Literary Bartók Portraits"; Marianna Birnbaum, "Bartók, Kodály and the *Nyugat";* Ferenc Glatz, "Music, Political Thinking, National Ideas. The Social and Cultural Background of the *Kossuth Symphony";* Stephen Erdely, "Complementary Aspects of Bartók's and Kodály's Folk Song Researches"; László Vikár, "On the Folk Music Arrangements of Bartók and Kodály"; Linda Dégh, "Bartók as Folklorist: His Place in the History of Research"; Robert Layton, "Some Reflections on Bartók and Sibelius"; György Kroó, "Bartók and Hungarian Music (1945-1981)"; János Kárpáti, "Béla Bartók: The Possibility of Musical Integration in the Danube Basin"; Tibor Tallián, "Bartók and His Contemporaries"; Benjamin Suchoff, "The Impact of Italian Baroque Music on Bartók's Music"; Ivan Waldbauer, "Conflict of Tonal and Non-Tonal Elements in Bartók's 'Free Variations'"; George Jellinek, "Bartók the Humanist"; Bálint Vázsonyi, "Bartók and the Twenty-First Century. Some Personal Remarks to the Discussion." Contains music examples.

1133. *Bartók and the Piano. Tempo* (London) 65 (Summer 1963). pp. 1-13.   780.5 T249

Most of this short issue is based on four articles devoted to several of Bartók's piano works. These articles include: John Ogden, "Mikrokosmos" (pp. 2-4); Béla Bartók, "The Second Piano Concerto" (pp. 5-7); Benjamin Suchoff, "Some Observations on Bartók's Third Piano Concerto" (pp. 8-10); and Colin Mason, "Bartók's Scherzo for Piano and Orchestra" (pp. 10-13). Contains music examples as well as a supplementary section of facsimiles and photographs.

1134. *Bartók-dolgozatok 1974* [Bartók studies 1974], ed. Ferenc László. Bucharest: Kriterion, 1974. 261p.   ML410.B26 B275

Includes articles by: István Almási, István Angi, András Benkő, Viorel Cosma, János Demény, János Jagamas, Ferenc László, Traian Mirza, György Orbán, and Ilona Szenik. See the review by János Breuer, in *Magyar zene* (Budapest) 15/3 (September 1974): 327-328.

1135. *Bartók-dolgozatok 1981* [Bartók studies 1981], ed. Ferenc László. Bucharest: Kriterion, 1982. 375p.   ML410.B26 B277

A sequel to the previous volume with the same title. Articles include: János Szekernyés, "Újabb adalékok Bartók bánsági kapcsolataihoz" [Additional data on Bartók's connections in the Banat], 7-58; Ovidiu Bîrlea, "Bartók Béla példája" [The example of

Béla Bartók], 59-64; Titus Moisescu, "Bartók Béla és a román folklór. Újabb tanúságok" [Béla Bartók and Romanian folklore. Additional evidence], 65-126; János Jagamas, "Bartók Béla: A magyar népdal--hatvan esztendő távlatából" [Béla Bartók: The Hungarian folk song--from the perspective of sixty years], 127-146; Ilona Szenik, "Kutatás és módszer II. A hangszeres zenéről" [Research and method II. Concerning instrumental music], 147-174; János Breuer, "Bartók román népzenegyűjtése Kodály kezén" [Bartók's Romanian folk-song collection in the care of Kodály], 175-181; István Almási, "Bartók és Brăiloiu elvei a népzenegyűjtés módszereiről" [Bartók's and Brăiloiu's principles of method of collecting folk music], 182-189; Péter Laki, "Ismeretlen Bartók-fénykép 1934-ből" [An unknown photograph of Bartók from 1934], 362-363 ; Ferenc László, "Találkozások. Bartók és Enescu" [Meetings. Bartók and Enescu], 197-208; Hans Peter Türk, "Részleges hangköz-szimmetria Bartók műveiben" [Partial symmetry of intervals in Bartók's works], 209-218; Adám Rónai, "Akusztikus-pentatonikus. Rendszeralkotási kérdések Lendvai Ernő Dualitás-elméletében" [Acoustic-pentatonic. Questions of systematization in Ernő Lendvai's theory of Duality], 219-235; István Angi, "Polifónia és poliszémia. Két tanulmány" [Polyphony and polysemy. Two studies], 236-271; and András Benkő "Romániában megjelent Bartók-interjúk" [Interviews with Bartók published in Romania], 272-361. The articles are all in Hungarian, with abstracts in Romanian and German. Most of them explore Bartók's Romanian connections in terms of his ethnomusicological and personal contacts. Three articles (by Türk, Rónai, and Angi) are analytical. Contains music examples, facsimiles, and photographs.

1136. Bartók Festival. Held at the University of Washington (April 29-May 7, 1981).

Guest lecturers included Dénes R. Bartha (worked with Bartók on the first Hungarian peasant music recording program), Albert Lord (co-author with Bartók on *Serbo-Croatian Folk Songs and Yugoslav Folk Music),* László Somfai (Head of the Budapest Bartók Archívum), Lawrence Starr, Michael Steinberg, and Roy Travis, all of whom have contributed to the literature on Bartók.

1137. Bartók Festival. Held at Westminster Choir College in Princeton (November 19-22, 1981).

Featured lectures and performances of Bartók's music. Keynote speaker was Benjamin Suchoff (Trustee of the Estate of Béla Bartók and Head of the New York Bartók Archive). Focused on a broad spectrum of the composer's lesser-known works, including choral and piano pieces, folk songs, and chamber works. Four of the six string quartets were performed by the Chester String Quartet of

Indiana University. In addition to other invited guest artists (e.g., violist Paul Doktor), the festival utilized the entire Westminster force in recitals, concerts, lectures, and lecture-recitals.

1138. *Bartók in Retrospect*, ed. Elliott Antokoletz, Victoria Fischer, and Benjamin Suchoff. Projected publication of two 1995 conference proceedings.

Selected from two international conferences on Bartók in 1995, held at Radford University, Virginia, and the University of California, Los Angeles (see item nos. 1161 and 1139). Studies of Bartók's life, career as ethnomusicologist, and folk music materials with respect to his fieldwork, transcription techniques, classification methodology, and influences on his compositions. Also, analyses of his music with respect to compositional technique, style, aesthetics, compositional process, and performance authenticity. *Part I. The Folklorist and His Transcriptions* includes: Stephen Erdely, "Bartók on Southslavic Epic Song"; János Kárpáti, "Bartók in North Africa: A Unique Fieldwork and Its Impact on His Music"; James Porter, "Bartók's *Concerto for Orchestra* (1943) and Janáček's *Sinfonietta* (1926): Conceptual and Structural Parallels"; Timothy Rice, "Béla Bartók and Bulgarian Rhythm"; László Somfai, "Bartók's Notations in Composition and Transcriptions"; Benjamin Suchoff, "Bartók's Odyssey in Slovak Folk Music"; David Yeomans, "Background and Analysis of Bartók's *Romanian Christmas Carols for Piano*." *Part II. The Man and His Compositions* includes: Elliott Antokoletz, "Modal Transformation and Musical Symbolism in Bartók's *Cantata profana*"; Elliott Antokoletz, "Organic Expansion and Classical Structure in Bartók's *Sonata for Two Pianos and Percussion*"; Peter Bartók, "Correcting Printed Editions of Béla Bartók's *Viola Concerto* and Other Compositions"; Dorothy Lamb Crawford, "Love and Anguish: Bartók's Expressionism"; Nelson Dellamaggiore, "Deciphering Béla Bartók's *Viola Concerto* Sketch"; Victoria Fischer, "Béla Bartók's *Fourteen Bagatelles* Op. 6, for Piano: Towards Performance Authenticity"; Victoria Fischer, "Articulation Notation in Bartók's Piano Music: Sources and Evolution"; Judit Frigyesi, "The *Verbunkos* and Bartók's Modern Style: The Case of *Bluebeard's Castle*"; Malcolm Gillies, "Analyzing Bartók's Works of 1918-1922: Motives, Tone Patches, and Tonal Mosaics"; Carl Leafsteadt,"*Pelléas* Revealed: The Original Ending of Bartók's Opera, *Duke Bluebeard's Castle*"; John Novak, "The Benefits of 'Relaxation': The Role of the 'Pihenő' Movement in Bartók's *Contrasts*"; Benjamin Suchoff, "The Genesis of Bartók's Musical Language."

1139. Bartók in Retrospect: A Pre-Conference International Symposium of the Society for Ethnomusicology. Held at the University of California, Los Angeles (October 17-18, 1995).

International conference in commemoration of the fiftieth anniversary of Bartók's death. Lectures included: Elliott Antokoletz, "Modal Transformation and Musical Symbolism in Bartók's *Cantata profana"*; Dorothy Lamb Crawford, "Love and Anguish: Bartók's Expressionism"; Stephen Erdely, "Bartók on Southslavic Epic Song"; Victoria Fischer, "Béla Bartók's *Fourteen Bagatelles* for Piano, Op. 6: Determining Performance Authenticity"; Judit Frigyesi, "Gypsy Music and Béla Bartók's Musical Style"; Malcolm Gillies, "The Canonisation of Béla Bartók"; János Kárpáti, "Bartók in North Africa: A Unique Fieldwork and Its Impact on His Music"; Carl Leafsteadt, *"Pelléas* Revealed: The Original Ending of *Bluebeard's Castle"*; James Porter, "Bartók's *Concerto for Orchestra* (1943) and Janáček's *Sinfonietta* (1926): Conceptual and Structural Parallels"; Timothy Rice, "Bartók and Bulgarian Rhythm"; László Somfai, "Bartók's Notations in Composition and Transcriptions"; Benjamin Suchoff, "The Course of Bartók's Odyssey in Slovak Folk Music"; and David Yeomans, "Background and Analysis of Bartók's *Romanian Christmas Songs* for Piano (1915)."

1140. Bartók-Kabalevsky International Competition. Held at Radford University (April 6-9, 1995).

Fifteenth annual piano competition, György Sándor, guest pianist and judge. Held in conjunction with the International Bartók Conference (see item no. 1161). Included master class and recital by Sándor.

1141. Bartók-Kodály Symposium. Held at the University of Indiana at Bloomington (April 5-7, 1982).

Chaired by Hungarian Professor György Ránki. Sponsored by the Hungarian Chair in the Department of Uralic and Altaic Studies and the School of Music. Main topic I: *The Intellectual and Cultural Life of Hungary and the Works of Bartók and Kodály Between the Two Wars*. Lectures included: Mary Gluck, "The Intellectual and Cultural Background of Bartók's and Kodály's Work"; and Miklós Lackó, "The Intellectual Environment of Bartók and Kodály in Hungary Between the Two World Wars." Short papers included: Ivan Sanders, "Three Literary Bartók Portraits"; Ferenc Glatz, "Musicology, Cultural Superiority, Ethnical Research"; Marianna Birnbaum, "Bartók-Kodály and the Nyugat"; Thomas Szendrey, "The Significance of the Work of Bartók and Kodály for Musical Education in Hungary." Main Topic II: *Folk Music in the Lives and Works of Bartók and Kodály and the Folk Music of East-Central*

Europe. Lectures included: Stephen Erdely, "Complementary Aspects of Zoltán Kodály's and Béla Bartók's Folksong Researches"; László Vikár, "Folk Music in the Lives of Bartók and Kodály and the Folk Music of East-Central Europe"; Benjamin Suchoff, "The Impact of Italian Baroque Music on Bartók's Music." Short papers included: Linda Dégh, "Bartók and Research in Folklore;" Albert B. Lord, "Bartók and the Milman Parry Collection"; Robert Layton, "Some Reflections on Bartók and Sibelius"; Jean Sinor, "The Application of Kodály's Pedagogical Principles in the United States." Main Topic III: *Bartók's Place and Influence in the Music of the Twentieth Century.* Lectures included: Tibor Tallián, "Bartók and His Contemporaries: Twentieth-Century Musical Poetics"; György Kroó, "Bartók and Hungarian Music, 1945-1982"; János Kárpáti, "The Possibility of a Musical Integration in the Danube Valley"; Bálint Vázsonyi, "Bartók and the Twenty-First Century"; Damiana Bratuz, "Bartók and Brâncuşi"; George Jellinek, "Bartók the Humanist." Performances included: *Duke Bluebeard's Castle* (Hungarian Television Film); *Violin Concerto* (1938); and the *Piano Concerto No. 3* (1945). See item no. 1132.

1142. *Bartók Könyv 1970-1971. Az 1970-1971--es romániai Bartók--megemlékezések* [Bartók book 1970-1971. The 1970-1971 Bartók Commemorations in Romania], ed. Ferenc László. Bucharest: Kriterion, 1971. 151p.   ML 410.B26 B28

For the 1970-1971 Romanian Bartók Commemoration, Romanian and Hungarian writers contributed articles, poems, recollections, and other information relevant to Bartók. Contains illustrations.

1143. Bartók Seminar-Conference. Held at the University of Pittsburgh (October 14-16, 1975).

Participation by Hungarian and American scholars. Basic topics included: style-analytic problems; recent research into Bartók's creative process based on his sketches; authenticity in Bartók performance; and Bartók and ethnomusicology. Lectures included: George Perle, "Bartók and the Twelve-Tone Modal System"; Elliott Antokoletz, "Principles of Pitch Organization in Bartók's *Fourth Quartet";* John Vinton, Peter Petersen and Denes Bartha, "Bartók's View on Tonality"; László Somfai, "Analysis of *Piano Concerto No. 2";* Denes Bartha, "Quatrain, a Classical Thematic Structure, Demonstrated in Bartók's Piano Music"; Halsey Stevens, "The Evolution of *Piano Rondo No. 2* in Bartók's Sketches"; László Somfai, "The Development of Thematic Materials in Selected Works by Bartók"; László Somfai, "An Analysis of Authenticity in Bartók Performance, Demonstrated in Piano Works and *Violin Concerto* (1938)"; Benjamin Suchoff, "Materials and Research Facilities in the New York Bartók Archive at Cedarhurst, with Special Emphasis on his Folk Music Collections and Computerized Data Analysis"; Theodore Grame, "The Relevancy of Bartók's Folk Music Research Methods for Current Modern U.S. Ethnomusicology"; Denes Bartha, "The Use of Pre-Existent Folk Music Materials in Selected Bartók Works"; and John Vinton, "Bartók's Place in History."

1144. Bartók Session. Held in Oakland, California (Fall 1990).

Held at a joint meeting of the American Musicological Society, Society for Ethnomusicology, and Society for Music Theory. Entitled "Béla Bartók: Synthesis of Eastern Folk-Music Sources and Contemporary Western Art-Music Techniques," the session included the following lectures: Elliott Antokoletz, "A Discrepancy Between Editions of Bartók's *Fifth String Quartet:* Resolved by a Comparative Study of Primary Sources and Analysis"; Ingrid Arauco, "Methods of Translation in Bartók's Twenty Hungarian Folksongs"; Malcolm Gillies, "Clues for the Analyst and the Performer in Bartók's Correspondence"; Benjamin Suchoff, "The Genesis of Bartók's Musical Language: Art Music and Folk Music Sources, 1900-1910"; and Paul Wilson, "Function and Pitch Hierarchy in Movement II of Bartók's Fifth Quartet."

1145. *Bartók Studies.* Comp. and ed. Todd Crow. Detroit: Information Coordinators, 1976. 299p. ISBN 0-911772-78-2 ML410.B26 B29

Collection of articles, documents, and letters relating to Bartók's life and music, all 27 items of which are reprinted from *The New Hungarian Quarterly,* except for the addition by Todd Crow of source notes, partially annotated bibliography, and two indexes. Includes studies of Bartók's musical style, his precursors and contemporaries, libretti for two dramatic works, documents (Bartók's essays and letters, etc.), Bartók as musician and humanist, and views of Bartók today. Contains facsimiles, illustrations, music, bibliography, index. See also the reviews by: Halsey Stevens, in *Music Library Association Notes* 33/3 (March 1977): 593-595; and László Somfai, in *Music and Letters* 58/4 (October 1977): 459-460.

1146. *Béla Bartók.* Comp. Yevgeniy Chigareva. Moskva: Muzyka, 1977. 262p.

According to *RILM Abstracts* No. 4885 (1977), this volume, in Russian, includes a discussion of theoretical problems relative to Bartók's style and includes three essays by Bartók on Hungarian music. Authors' names and translated titles of their essays are provided in this abstract: Y. Chigareva, "Béla Bartók's Musical Idiom as Discussed in the Works of Foreign Musicologists"; I. Nest'yev, "Bartók and Prokofiev;" M. Tarakanov, "Variant Development in Bartók's *Music for Strings, Percussion and Celesta";*

J. Paisov, "Polytonality in Bartók's Music"; J. Kan, "Observations Concerning the Harmony in Bartók's Piano Sonata"; N. Fin, "The Cultivation of Hungarian Folk Song in the Works of Bartók"; E. Kuteva, "Links Between the Modal Structure of Bartók's Music for the Ballet *A csodálatos mandarin* [*The Miraculous Mandarin*] and Modal Forms of East-European Folk Music"; V. Tsytovich, "Two Studies on Bartók"; E. Denisov, "Bartók's Use of Percussion Instruments"; N. Piskunova, "Bartók, The Interpreter, as Seen in Hungarian Music Criticism"; G. Rozhdestvensky, "A Conductor's Notes on Some Bartók Works"; and B. Bartók, "Influence of Peasant Music on Today's Music," "Hungarian Folk Music and the New Music," and "The Influence of Folk Music on Contemporary Art Music." Contains music examples.

1147. *Béla Bartók: A Memorial Review*. New York: Boosey & Hawkes, 1950. 95p. 780.5 T249 ISSN 0040-2982

Reprinted from two issues of *Tempo* (London) 13-14 (special issue) (1949-1950): 47p., 47p., a quarterly review of contemporary music. Contains articles on Bartók's life and works, Bartók on records, a Bartók bibliography, and chronological list of his works. Articles include an autobiographical sketch of 1921, fragments of letters, abridgments of Bartók's articles on collecting folk songs in Turkey (1937) and on the influence of peasant music on art music (1920, 1931), discussions of his chamber music, piano music, and opera, a recount of Bartók's publisher's relationship with him, and Bartók and the theater. See the review by Halsey Stevens in *Music Library Association Notes* (September 1952): 616.

1148. *Clavier* 20/8 (October 1981): 21-31. 780.5 C578 ISSN 0009-854-X

Includes "Special Feature on Bartók." In celebration of the Bartók Centennial, this issue of *Clavier* offers a variety of perspectives on Bartók. Articles include: Elizabeth Buday, "Focus on Bartók"; Angeline Schmid, "Bartók's Music for Small Hands"; Joan Purswell, "Bartók's Early Music: Forecasting the Future"; Ann Brandon, "An Afternoon of Bartók"; and Angeline Schmid, "Bartók's Rumanian Christmas Carols."

1149. *Contribuţii la cunoaşterea legaturilor lui Béla Bartók cu viata noastră muzicală. Volum editat cu prilejul comemorăii unui sfert de veac de la moartea* [Contributions to the knowledge of the relation between Béla Bartók and our musical life. A volume published on the commemoration of the anniversary of his death], ed. I.D. Smântânescu Chira et al. Oradea: Comitetul de Cultura şi Educaţie Socialista al Judeţulŭi Bihor, 1971.

Series of articles dealing with Bartók's folk-music research in Romania.

1150. Dille, Denijs. *Béla Bartók: Regard sur le passé* [Béla Bartók: A look at the past]. Ed. Yves Lenoir. *Musicologica neolovaniensia* 5; *Études bartokiennes.* Namur: Presses Université de Namur, 1990. 448p.   ML 410 B26 D52

A collection of studies, essays, interviews, and speeches published between 1937 and 1980 encompassing diverse topics on the man and his music. Preliminary material includes a Preface by the editor, Dille's essay "Regard sur le passé" and "Interview de Béla Bartók" (1937). Part One (studies and articles) includes: "Les relations Busoni-Bartók" (1963); "Les relations entre Bartók et Schönberg" (1965); "Un manuscrit inconnu de Bartók" (1966); "Bartók, lecteur de Nietzsche et de La Rochefoucault" (1967); "Gerlice puszta" (1967); "Bartók et le concert historique du 12 janvier 1918" (1968); "Notes complémentaires concernant l'édition de 'Die Melodien der rumänischen Colinde'" (1968); "La rencontre de Bartók et de Kodály" (1969); "L'Allegro barbaro de Bartók" (1969); "Bartók défenseur de Kodály" (1970); "Bartók et Szymanowski" (1974); "En relisant quelques œuvres éditées de Bartók" (1975); "L'Opus 15 de Béla Bartók" (1978); "Quelques remarques biographiques" (1980); "Bartók et Ady" (1980). Part Two (lectures and speeches) includes: "Bartók et Kodály" (1962); "Bartók, l'homme et l'artiste" (1964); "Trois œuvres de musique de chambre du jeune Bartók" (1964); "Le vingtième anniversaire de la mort de Bartók" (1965); "Bartók, folklore et langage" (1967); "De l'exècution de l'œuvre de Bartók" (1967). Also includes a memoir by Ditta Bartók, " Le 26 septembre 1945" (1965), a bibliography of Dille's writings on Bartók, illustrations, port., facsimiles, music examples, list of works, indexes, tables.

1151. *Documenta bartókiana* [Bartók documents]. Heft 1., ed. Denijs Dille. Budapest: Akadémiai Kiadó; Mainz: B. Schotts Söhne, 1964. 136p., 41p. music.   ISBN-963-05-1185-1-(Serie)   ML410 B26 D6 ISSN 0134-0131

Published under the editorship of the Director of the Budapest Bartók Archívum. Contains items in Hungarian and German on aspects of Bartók's life and works, including articles, news items, letters, recollections, photographs, and music. See reviews by: John Vinton, in *Music Library Association Notes* 23/3 (March 1967): 520-521; and Rudolf Stephan, in *Musikforschung* 20/1 (January-March 1967): 95-97.

1152. *Documenta bartókiana.* Heft 2., ed. Denijs Dille. Budapest: Akadémiai Kiadó; Mainz: B. Schotts Söhne, 1965. 200p. ISBN-963-05-1185-1-(Serie)   ML410 B26 D6   ISSN 0134-0131

Includes the following articles: Márta Ziegler, "Bartóks Reise nach Biskra" [Bartók's trip to Biskra]; G.V. Zágon, "Briefe an Bartók" [Letters to Bartók]; László Somfai, "Nichtvertonte Libretti im Nachlass und andere Bühnenpläne Bartóks" [Libretti and other stage plans of Bartók]; Denijs Dille, "Die Beziehungen zwischen Bartók und Schönberg" [The relations between Bartók and Schoenberg]; Denijs Dille, "Dokumente über Bartóks Beziehungen zu Busoni" [Documents on Bartók's relations to Busoni]; János Demény, "Das Konzert vom 12. Februar 1911 (Pressestimmen)" [The concert of February 12, 1911 (Press reviews)]; Denijs Dille, "Angaben zum Violinkonzert 1907, den Deux portraits, dem Quartett Op. 7 und den Zwei rumänischen Tänzen" [Statements on the 1907 *Violin Concerto, Two Portraits, First String Quartet, Two Romanian Dances*]; János Demény, "Veröffentlichte Briefe Bartóks, die vom Concerto, den Deux portraits und vom Quartett Op. 7 handeln oder auf diese Werke hinweisen" (Published Bartók letters treating or alluding to the *Violin Concerto, Two Portraits* and the *First String Quartet*]; Denijs Dille, "Über ein Konzert (3. März 1906)" [About a concert of March 3, 1906]; János Demény, "Bartóks Selbstbiographie aus dem Jahre 1905" [Bartók's autobiography of 1905]; László Somfai, "Bartóks Selbstbiographie aus dem Jahre 1911"; Denijs Dille, "Bartóks Selbstbiographie aus dem Jahre 1918, 1921, 1923"; Denijs Dille, "Bartóks Briefe an Ravel" [Bartók's letters to Ravel]; Denijs Dille, "Bartóks Briefe an Dr. E. Latzko" [Bartók's letters to Dr. E. Latzko]; D. Clegg, "Ein unveröffentlicher Brief Bartóks an E.J. Dent" [An unpublished Bartók letter to Edward J. Dent]; Viorel Cosma, "Ein Brief Bartóks in den rumänischen Archiven" [A Bartók letter to the Romanian Archives]; R. C., "Mr. Béla Bartók's bombardment]; and Denijs Dille, "Nachtrag zu Documenta bartókiana I" [Postscript to *Documenta bartókiana 1*]. Contains additional materials, e.g., photographs and facsimiles, etc. See reviews by: John Vinton, in *Music Library Association Notes* 23/3 (March 1967): 520-521; and Rudolf Stephan, in *Musikforschung* 20/1 (January-March 1967): 95-97.

1153. *Documenta bartókiana.* Heft 3., ed. Denijs Dille. Budapest: Akadémiai Kiadó, 1968. 315p.; Budapest-Mainz: B. Schotts Söhne, 1968. 325p.   ISBN-963-05-1185-1-(Serie)   ML410 B26 D6 ISSN 0134-0131

Includes 175 letters in many languages, written to Bartók between 1902 and 1945. Also contains unknown letters written by Bartók to various musical personalities, including Alfredo Casella, Otto Erich Deutsch, Erich Doflein, Ernő Dohnányi, Alfred Einstein, Manuel de Falla, Wilhelm Furtwängler, Erich M. von Hornbostel, Leoš Janáček, Yehudi Menuhin, Darius Milhaud, Francis Poulenc, Géza Révész, Hans Rosbaud, Hermann Scherchen, Edgard Varèse, and Egon Wellesz. Includes appendix with materials relevant to

references in the letters. Some of the letters (1910-1945) published
in the German edition of *Documenta bartókiana* 3 are reprinted in
The New Hungarian Quarterly 11/40 (Winter 1970): 37-48. See
reviews by: Ferenc Bónis, in *Muzsika* (Budapest) 11/9 (September
1968): 31; Massimo Mila, in *Nuova rivista musicale italiana* 3/6
(November-December 1969): 1189-1191; Walter Salmen, in
Musikforschung 25/1 (January-March 1972): 116.

1154. *Documenta bartókiana*. Heft 4., ed. Denijs Dille. Budapest:
Akadémiai Kiadó, 1970; Mainz: B. Schotts Söhne,1970. 244p.
ISBN-963-05-1185-1-(Serie)   ML410 B26 D6   ISSN 0134-0131

Contains contributions in German by several authors.
Contributions by Denijs Dille include: "Gerlice puszta: May to
November 1904"; "Street Sounds of Paris by Béla Bartók"; "Bartók
and the Historical Concert of 12 January 1918"; "Bartók and Folk
Music" (also includes four letters from Kodály to Bartók); "Bartók's
Correspondence with Frau R. Katzarova"; "Several Remarks on the
Edition of *Der Melodien der rumänischen Colinde";* "Concerning the
history of the origin of *Volksmusik der Rumänen von Maramureş";*
"Bartók's text for the *Cantata Profana";* "Supplement to *Documenta
bartókiana* 1"; "Supplement to *Documenta bartókiana* 3." Also
includes: László Somfai, "A Declaration by Bartók from the Year
1938"; and Márta Ziegler, "Concerning Béla Bartók." See the review
by Erich Kapst in *Musikgesellschaft* 23/6 (June 1973): 370-372.

1155. *Documenta bartókiana*. Heft 5., ed. László Somfai. Budapest:
Akadémiai Kiadó, 1977. 224p.   ISBN-963-05-1185-1-(Serie)
ML410 B26 D6   ISSN 0134-0131

Includes a compilation by Somfai of fourteen writings of Bartók
from 1920 to 1921 on contemporary music and concert reports in
Budapest. Also included are the following: "Vier Briefe Bartóks an
Philip Heseltine" [Four letters from Bartók to Philip Heseltine]; Vera
Lampert, "Zeitgenössische Musik in Bartóks Notensammlung"
[Contemporary Music in Bartók's Music Collection]; János Demény,
"Zeitgenössische Musik in Bartóks Konzertrepertoire"
[Contemporary Music in Bartók's Concert Repertoire]; Vera Lampert,
"Bartóks Skizzen zum III. Satz des Streichquartetts Nr. 2" [Bartók's
Sketches to the Third Movement of the *Second String Quartet*];
László Somfai, "Über Bartóks Rubato-Stil. Vergleichende Studie der
zwei Aufnahmen 'Abend am Lande' des Komponisten" [About
Bartók's Rubato Style. Comparative study of two arrangements
'Abend am Lande' of the composer]; János Breuer, "Drei Bartók-
Bücher" [Three Bartók books]; and Denijs Dille, "Nachtrag zu
Documenta bartókiana 2" [Supplement to *Documenta bartókiana* 2].
Contains facsimiles and photographs. See review by: Ferenc László,
in *Korunk* 37/4 (April 1978): 343-344.

1156. *Documenta Bartókiana.* Heft 6., ed. László Somfai. Budapest: Akadémiai Kiadó; Mainz: Schott, 1981. 296p. ISBN-963-05-1185-1- (Serie) ML410 B26 D6 ISSN 0134-0131

Includes a large study by Vera Lampert, "Quellenkatalog der Volksliedbearbeitungen von Bartók. Ungarische, slowakische, rumänische, ruthenische, serbische und arabische Volkslieder und Tänze" [Source catalogue of folk-song arrangements by Bartók], which is a German translation of her book originally in Hungarian. Also includes: János Demény, "Korrespondenz zwischen Bartók und der holländischen Konzertdirektion 'Kossar.' Bartóks Tourneen in Holland im Spiegel von 104 Briefen aus den Jahren 1935-1939" [Correspondence between Bartók and the Holland conductor "Kossar." Bartók's tours in Holland in reflection of 104 letters from the years 1935-1939]; two studies by András Wilheim, "Zu einem Handschriften-Faksimile aus dem Jahre 1917" [On a handwritten facsimile from the year 1917] and "Skizzen zu 'Mikrokosmos' Nr. 135 und Nr. 57" [Sketches to "Mikrokosmos" No. 137 and No. 57]; and two studies by László Somfai, "Drei Themenentwürfe zu dem Violinkonzert aus den Jahren 1936-1937" [Three thematic sketches for the *Violin Concerto* from the years 1936-1937] and "Die 'Allegro barbaro'--Aufnahme von Bartók textkritisch bewertet" [*The Allegro barbaro*--textual source value of the recording by Bartók]. Under *Neue Bartókiana,* is an article by Tibor Tallián, "Vier Bartók-Dissertationen aus der BRD" [Four Bartók dissertations from the BRD]. Contains music, facsimiles, photographs, index. See Reviews by: Ferenc László in *Muzsika* 25/4 (April 1982): 38-39; and Brigitte Burkhardt in *Beiträge zur Musikwissenschaft* 28/3 (1986): 243-244.

1157. Focus on Piano Literature: Bartók. Held at the University of North Carolina, Greensboro (June 15-17, 1995).

For its sixth annual focus on piano literature, the UNCG School of Music commemorated the fiftieth anniversary of Bartók's death with a three-day symposium of concerts and lectures devoted to the study of the life, times, and music of the composer. Concerts included full-length recitals and other performances by the Hungarian pianist, Imre Rohmann, and members of the UNCG faculty. Lectures included the following: Andrew Willis, "Overview of Bartók's Piano Music: Styles, Genres, Sources"; Victoria Fischer, "Articulating Bartók's Piano Music: Legato, Portato, Staccato"; Elliott Antokoletz, "Bartók's Improvisations, Op. 20: From 'Folksong Arrangement' to 'Composing with Folk Tunes'"; J. Kent Williams, "Post-Tonal Theory in Bartók's *Mikrokosmos:* Pitch Sets, Other Analytical Techniques"; Paul Stewart (assisted by students from the Greensboro Academy), "Bartók's *Mikrokosmos* and Other Memorable, Miniature Masterpieces: A Pedagogical Survey"; Andrew Willis, "Bartók's Three Etudes, Op. 18: Romantic Technique in a Brave, New World"; and Elliott Antokoletz, "Bartók's Humanistic

Philosophy as Reflected in His Musical Aesthetics: The Fusion of Divergent Folk- and Art-Music Sources." Also included were two filmed documentaries about the composer and a discussion between audience and panelists, Antokoletz and Rohmann.

1158. Gillies, Malcolm, ed. *The Bartók Companion.* London: Faber and Faber, 1993; Portland, Oregon: Amadeus Press (an imprint of Timber Press, Inc.), 1994. xviii, 586p.   ISBN 0-931340-74-8 (HB) ISBN 0-931340-75-6 (PB)   ML410 B26 B28

Fifteen international scholars discuss Bartók's aesthetics, style, musical language, and compositional processes, his activities as pianist, teacher, and ethnomusicologist, and basic issues regarding interpretation of his life and work. Includes biographical, historical, philosophical, folkloristic, compositional, theoretical, and analytical studies. Under *Perspectives,* includes: Malcolm Gillies, "Bartók and His Music in the 1990s"; Béla Bartók, Jun., "The Private Man"; László Somfai, "In his 'Compositional Workshop'"; Sándor Kovács, "The Ethnomusicologist"; János Demény, "The Pianist"; Malcolm Gillies, "The Teacher"; and Adrienne Gombocz, "With His Publishers." Under *Piano Music,* includes: Günter Weiss-Aigner, "Youthful Piano Works"; Elliott Antokoletz, "'At last something truly new': *Bagatelles";* Benjamin Suchoff, "Fusion of National Styles: Piano Literature, 1908-11"; János Kárpáti, "Piano Works of the War Years"; Paul Wilson, "Approaching Atonality: Studies and Improvisations"; László Somfai, "The 'Piano Year' of 1926"; and Benjamin Suchoff, "Synthesis of East and West: *Mikrokosmos."* Under *Chamber Music,* includes: Günter Weiss-Aigner, "Youthful Chamber Works"; János Kárpáti, "Early String Quartets"; Paul Wilson, "Violin Sonatas"; Elliott Antokoletz, "Middle-period String Quartets"; Vera Lampert, "Violin Rhapsodies"; Malcolm Gillies, "Violin Duos and Late String Quartets"; Malcolm Gillies, "Masterworks (I): *Music for Strings, Percussion and Celesta";* Roy Howat, "Masterworks (II): *Sonata for Two Pianos and Percussion";* and Malcolm Gillies, "Final Chamber Works." Under *Music for Stage,* includes: György Kroó, "Opera: *Duke Bluebeard's Castle";* György Kroó, "Ballet: *The Wooden Prince";* and György Kroó, "Pantomime: *The Miraculous Mandarin."* Under *Vocal Music,* includes Vera Lampert,"Works for Solo Voice with Piano"; Miklós Szabó, "Choral Works"; and György Kroó, *"Cantata profana."* Under *Orchestral Music,* includes: Günter Weiss-Aigner, "Youthful Orchestral Works"; Malcolm Gillies, "Two Orchestral Suites"; Günter Weiss-Aigner, "The 'Lost' Violin Concerto"; Malcolm Gillies, "Portraits, Pictures and Pieces"; Malcolm Gillies, *"Dance Suite";* János Kárpáti, "The First Two Piano Concertos"; Vera Lampert, *"Second Violin Concerto";* Elliott Antokoletz, *"Concerto for Orchestra";* and Sándor Kovács, "Final Concertos." Contains illustrations, a chronology of Bartók's life and works, select bibliography, basic information on contributors, index of Bartók's works, and general index.

1159. Halász, Péter. "Bartók Seminar and Festival: Szombathely." *Hungarian Music Quarterly* 1/3-4 (1989): 43-44.   914.39105 H893 ISSN 0238-9401

    Report on the amplification of this ongoing summer series originally intended for the study of Bartók's music. States that the most important event of this year turned out to be the musicological conference for Hungarian and foreign participants in preparation for the launching of the *Béla Bartók Complete Critical Edition*. Informs us that "László Somfai, head of the Bartók Béla Archives in Budapest, introduced the great recent developments in the philology of Bartók manuscripts, then musicologist András Wilheim, pianist Imre Rohmann and conductor Miklós Szabó, the editors in charge of the volumes under preparation, reported on the present state of their work. According to the plans, at least six volumes will be ready by 1991 for examination by the international advisory council as regards their editorial principles."

1160. International Bartók Colloquium 1995. Held in Szombathely, Hungary (July 3-5, 1995).

    Part of the International Bartók Seminar and Festival in Szombathely. Program director: László Somfai. Participation by European, American, and Australian scholars. Basic topics and lectures included: *Keynote address*--László Somfai, "Perspectives of Bartók Studies in 1995"; *Source studies* (Chair: László Somfai)--Klára Móricz, "Operating on a Fetus: Sketch Studies and Their Relevance for the Interpretation of Bartók's Music"; László Vikárius, "In Search of the Meaning of Corrections in Bartók's Compositional Process"; Dorrit Révész, "Text, Versions, and Recycling in Bartók's Writings"; Sándor Kovács, "'Wir können sie in drei verschiedene Phase einteilen'--Einige Gedanken über Bartóks Volksliedaufzeichnungen"; *Biography, musical background, reception* (Chair: Tibor Tallián)--Malcolm Gillies, "Redrawing Bartók's Life"; János Breuer, "Bartók im Dritten Reich"; Vera Lampert, "Bartók's Music on Record: An Index of Popularity"; Péter Laki, "Poetic Criticism and Critical Poetry in Bartók's Hungarian Reception"; *Style analysis (I)* (Chair: Malcolm Gillies)--Iván Waldbauer, "Theorists' Views on Bartók, from Edwin von der Nüll to Paul Wilson"; Benjamin Suchoff, "The Genesis of Bartók's Musical Language"; Elliott Antokoletz, "Organic Development and the Interval Cycles in Bartók's *Three Studies* Op. 18"; János Kárpáti, "Perfect and Mistuned Structures in Bartók's Music"; *Style analysis (II)* (Chair: Elliott Antokoletz)--Tibor Tallián, "Das holzgeschnitzte Hauptwerk"; Carl S. Leafstedt, "'Judith' in *Bluebeard's Castle*: The

Significance of a Name"; David Schneider, "Toward Bridging the Gap: The Culmination Point as a Fulcrum Between Analysis and Interpretation"; András Wilheim, *"'...more exactly than a biography...':* Analytical Notes on Bartók's Realistic Music of 1907/1910"; *Style analysis (III)* (Chair: Iván Waldbauer)--Judit Frigyesi, "'Folk-music Themes' in Bartók's Compositions"; Ferenc László, "Rumänische Stilelemente in Bartók's Music"; Maria Anna Harley, "On *Natura naturans:* Arch Forms and Nightingales in Bartók's Music"; Jürgen Hunkemöller, "Der Klage-Topos im Komponieren Bartóks"; *Bartók interpretation* (Chair: János Kárpáti)--Victoria Fischer, "Articulation Notation in the Piano Works of Béla Bartók: Evolution and Interpretation"; János Mácsai, "Neue Ergebnisse in der Forschung von Bartóks Tonaufnahmen"; László Somfai, "Idea, Notation, Interpretation: Written and Oral Transmission."

1161. International Bartók Conference. Held at Radford University, Virginia (April 6-9, 1995).

In conjunction with the fifteenth annual Bartók-Kabalevsky International Competition, György Sándor, guest pianist and judge (see item no. 1140). Conference participation by Hungarian, American, and Australian scholars. Basic topics included: style-analytic problems; sources of Bartók's musical language; recent research into issues and problems in the editions; and ethnomusicological sources of Bartók's arrangements. Lectures included: László Somfai (Budapest Bartók Archive), "Definitive Authorized Version vs. Authentic Variant Forms in Bartók's Music"; Elliott Antokoletz (University of Texas at Austin), "Organic Expansion and Classical Structure in Bartók's *Sonata for Two Pianos and Percussion";* György Sándor (Juilliard School of Music), "Harmonic and Formal Analysis of the *Sonata* and Other 'Ambiguous' Aspects of Bartók's Piano Music"; Péter Bartók and Nelson Dellamaggiore (Bartók Records), "Revision of Béla Bartók's *Viola Concerto* as Part of a Program of Correcting Published Editions of His Works"; Malcolm Gillies (University of Queensland), "Bartók's Tonal Mosaics"; Benjamin Suchoff (Former Head of the New York Bartók Archive; University of California, Los Angeles), "The Genesis of Bartók's Musical Language: Art Music and Folk Music Sources, 1900-1910"; John Novak (Austin, Texas), "The Benefits of 'Relaxation": The Role of the 'Pihenő' Movement in Béla Bartók's *Contrasts ";* Victoria Fischer (Elon College), "Bartók's Piano Notation: Sources, Evolution and Interpretation"; and David Yeomans (Texas Women's University), "Background and Analysis of Béla Bartók's *Colinde Sz. 57, 1915."* Conference also included a performance of Bartók's *Contrasts* by the *Sonsa Trio:* Corine Cook (violin), Donald L. Oehler (clarinet), and Victoria Fischer (piano). Panel discussion on "Bartók's Position and Influence in the

Twentieth Century" included Elliott Antokoletz, Malcolm Gillies, György Sándor, László Somfai, and Benjamin Suchoff.

1162. International Bartók Festival and Congress of the Detroit Symphony Orchestra. Held in Detroit, Michigan (March 10-21, 1981).

The Congress (March 12-14) coincided with the first weekend of Detroit's "International Bartók Festival," in which many national and international artists joined the Detroit Symphony to present major selections from Bartók's dramatic and orchestral works, all six string quartets and other chamber music, and many piano and vocal works. The Congress included lectures by scholars from Hungary, England, and the United States: Ellwood Derr, "Bartók in Detroit;" László Somfai, "Manuscript versus Urtext, The Primary Sources of Béla Bartók"; Vera Lampert, "The Present State of Bartók Research"; Glenn Watkins, "Bartók in the 1920s"; Christopher Rouse, "Bartók and Percussion"; József Ujfalussy, "Bartók and Debussy"; Paul Wilson, "The Atonal Vocabulary of Bartók's *Second Violin sonata";* Dénes R. Bartha, "Refined 'Quatrain'-Type Thematic Patterns in Bartók's Music"; Benjamin Suchoff, "Folk Music Sources in Bartók's Works"; Elliott Antokoletz, "Symmetrical Transformations of the Folk Modes in Bartók's Music: a Study of Selected Pieces and Their Sketches"; Todd Crow, "Bartók's *Fourteen Bagatelles:* Thoughts from a Performer's Perspective"; Richard Parks, "Harmonic Resources in Bartók's 'Fourths' (Mikrokosmos V/131)"; Jonathan W. Bernard, "Space and Symmetry in Three Works of Bartók"; János Kárpáti, "Third Structure and Polytonality in Bartók's *First Sonata for Violin and Piano";* György Kroó, "Symphonic Poem, Ballet, Pantomime-- The Development of Bartók's Dramaturgy as Reflected in the Genesis of His Stage Works"; Tibor Tallián, "Models of Self-Expression in Béla Bartók's Essays. A Study of the Sources, Subjects and Motives"; and David Drew, "Bartók and His Publishers."

1163. International Bartók Seminar and Festival. Held in Szombathely, Hungary (July 7-25, 1986).

Entitled "Bartók--New Music," these sessions included concerts and workshops. The organizers of the Seminar, looking back over two decades--in cooperation with the Budapest Bartók Archívum and the Savaria Symphony Orchestra--in 1985 decided to include other twentieth-century composers in addition to Bartók. In addition to Hungarian performers, musicology and analysis was conducted by Ernő Lendvai, László Somfai, and András Wilheim.

1164. International Bartók Symposium. Held in Budapest, Hungary (September 28-30, 1981).

Symposium held at the "Bartók Béla Emlékház" [Béla Bartók Memorial House], as part of the Bartók Centennial Celebration. After the opening address by József Ujfalussy, the program included the following: Elliott Antokoletz, "Pitch-Set Derivations from the Folk Modes in Bartók's Music"; Peter Petersen, "Bartók und Lutosławski: Vergleich;" András Szentkirályi, "Bartók and the Twentieth Century"; Tibor Tallián, "'Um 1900 nachweisbar:' Skizze zu einem Gruppenbild mit Musikern"; János Kárpáti, "Tonal Divergences of Melody and Harmony: A Characteristic Phenomenon of Bartók's Musical Language"; András Wilheim, "Bartók's Exercises in Composition"; János Breuer, "Die Beziehungen zwischen Bartók und Milhaud"; Sandor Kovács, "Formprobleme des Bartók-Serly Bratschenkonzertes"; László Dobszay, "Absorption of Folk Song in the Bartók Composition"; Mária Domokos, "Ethnomusikologische Klassifikationen von Bartók"; Ilkka Oramo, "Bemerkungen zu einigen Paradigmen der Bartók-Forschung"; Judit Frigyesi, "Between Rubato and Rigid Rhythm: A Particular Type of Rhythmical Asymmetry as Reflected in Bartók's Writings on Folk Music"; Vera Lampert-Deák, "Bartók's Choice of Theme for Folk Song Arrangement"; Ivan Waldbauer, "Intellectual Construct and Tonal Direction in Bartók's 'Divided Arpeggios'"; demonstrations and discussions, introduced by László Somfai, including I. "'Bartók Record Archives:' Bartók Plays Bartók" II. "Quellenmaterial der Bartók Werke und Volksliedsammlungen" III. "Studien von jungen Musikologen"; Bertalan Pethő, "Bartók's Secret Path"; Günter Weiss-Aigner, "Tonale Perspektiven der jungen Bartók"; Frank Michael, "Analytische Anmerkungen zum 2. Klavierkonzert"; Hans Winking, "Klangflächen bei Bartók bis 1911. Zu einigen stilistischen Beziehungen in den Orchesterwerke Bartóks zur Orchestermusik des späten 19. und frühen 20. Jahrhunderts"; András Batta, "Gemeinsame Nietzsche-Symbol bei Bartók und bei R. Strauss"; Theodor Hundt, "Barocke Formelemente im Kompositionsstil Bartóks"; Günter Händel, "Dynamik und Energetik in den Klangbildern von Bartóks Rondo I and Improvisation II"; Lidia Kristiansen, "Cherty edinstva v interpretatsii fol'klora Bartókoy teoretikom i tvortsom" [The unity of interpretation of folklore by Bartók--theorist and creator]; Yves Lenoir, "The Destiny of Bartók's Ethnomusicological Research Immediately Prior to His Stay in the United States"; and a demonstration by Albert Simon of his analytical approach to Bartók's music. This symposium is published in *Studia musicologica* 24/3-4 (1982). See the review of the published symposium lectures by Malcolm Gillies in *"Studia musicologica. 24/3-4: Report of the International Bartók Symposium Budapest 1981.* Ed. by László Somfai. pp. [304]. (Akadémiai Kiadó, Budapest, 1982.)." *Music and Letters* 66/4 (October 1985): 373-375.

1165. *International Musicological Conference in Commemoration of Béla Bartók 1971,* ed. József Ujfalussy and János Breuer. Budapest: Editio Musica; Melville, New York: Belwin Mills, 1972. 230p. ML410.B29 I61 [Editio Musica]   ML410.B26 I5 [Belwin Mills]

Collection of articles in English, German, and French on Bartók's music. György Kroó, in his "Closing Report," summarizes the organization of the conference (lectures are grouped in three categories), the international make-up (its scope and limitations), focus on landmarks in Bartók research in the past decade, problems in the separation of Bartók materials between America and Hungary, the most significant publications of the Hungarian and American Bartók Institutes, and general literature on Bartók and his music. An appendix lists the program of the conference. Includes the following: László Orbán, "Bartók's Message Has Never Been More Topical Than Today"; György Lukács, "Bartók und die ungarische Kultur" [Bartók and Hungarian culture]; Dénes Zoltai, "Bartók in Sicht der Frankfurter Schule" [Bartók in light of the Frankfurt School]; Jaroslav Volek, "Bartók--Determination of a period"; János Kovács, "Heiliger Dankgesang in der lydischen Tonart, und Andante religioso"; Erich Kapst, "Zum Tonalitätsbegriff bei Bartók" [Bartók's conception of tonality]; János Kárpáti, "Le désaccordage dans la technique de composition de Bartók" [The role of scordatura in Bartók's technique of composition]; László Somfai, "A Characteristic Culmination Point in Bartók's Instrumental Forms"; Halsey Stevens, "The Sources of Bartók's Rhapsody for Violoncello and Piano"; Robert Schollum, "Stilkundliche Bemerkungen zu Werken Bartóks und der 2. Wiener Schule" [Stylistic observations concerning works by Bartók and the Second Viennese School]; Hartmut Krones, "Stilkundliche Betrachtungen auf soziologischer Basis inbesondere dargestellt am Beispiel Béla Bartók" [Stylistic reflections based upon sociology, with particular reference to the example of Béla Bartók]; Benjamin Suchoff, "Béla Bartók: Man of Letters"; György Kroó, "On the Origin of *A fabol faragott kiralyfi"*; Bence Szabolcsi, "Bartók and World Literature"; Ivan Martynov, "Quelques pensées sur Bartók" [Several thoughts regarding Bartók]; János Demény, "Ady-Gedichtbände in Bartóks Bibliothek" [The volumes of poetry by Ady in Bartók's Library]; Erik Tawaststjerna, "Sibelius und Bartók: einige Parallelen" [Sibelius and Bartók: several parallels]; Izrael Nest'yev, "Prokofiev and Bartók: Some Parallels"; Ferenc Bónis, "Bartók und der Verbunkos" [Bartók and the *verbunkos*]; József Ujfalussy, "Gemeinsame Stilsicht in Bartóks und Kodálys Kunst" [A common stylistic aspect of Bartók's and Kodály's art]; Antal Molnár, "Die Bedeutung der neuen Osteuropäischen Musik" [The significance of the new music of Eastern Europe]; János Breuer, "Die Zeitgenössische ungarische Musik auf dem Pfade Bartóks" [Contemporary Hungarian music following the path of Bartók]; István Szelényi, "Bartók und Modalität" [Bartók and modality];

Ladislav Burlas, "The Influence of Slovakian Folk Music on Bartók's Musical Idiom"; Stoyan Djoudjeff, "Bartók, promoteur de l'ethnomusicologie balkanique et sud-est européene" [Bartók--promoter of Balkan and Southeast European ethnomusicology]; Oskár Elschek, "Bartóks Beziehung zur Volksmusik und Volksmusikforschung" [Bartók's relationship to folk music and folk music research]. Includes facsimiles and music examples. See also Erich Kapst's report on the conference in: "Internationale Bartók-Konferenz in Budapest" [The International Bartók Conference in Budapest]. *Musikgesellschaft* 21/7 (July 1971): 458-460.

1166. *La revue musicale,* Special Issue no. 224. Paris: Richard-Masse, ed., 1955. 222p.   780.5 R328   ISSN 0035-3736

Special issue devoted largely to Bartók, the man and the work. Includes: "Béla Bartók, L'homme et l'œuvre, 1881-1945:" 7-19, including brief commentaries on different aspects of his multifaceted activities by Claude Delvincourt, Roger Delage, Louis Durey, Géza Fríd, Tibor Harsányi, Jacques Ibert, Joseph Kosma, Darius Milhaud, and Francis Poulenc. Also includes: Gisèle Brelet, "L'esthétique de Béla Bartók," 21-39; "Bartók, pionnier de la musicologie," 41-57; "Écrits de Béla Bartók" (on Hungarian music and two letters), 61-75; Lajos Hernádi, "Béla Bartók le pianiste, le pédagogue, L'homme," 77-90; Suzanne Demarquez, "Souvenirs et réflexions," 91-97; "Souvenirs de collaboration avec Béla Bartók" (including essays by André Gertler, Erich Doflein, and F. Lopes Graça), 99-115.

1167. *Liszt-Bartók: Second International Conference: Budapest 1961. Studia musicologica* 5 (1963). pp. 339-596   781.05 St92 ISSN 0039-3266

Collection of papers given at the musicological conference in 1961, includes 21 essays on Bartók in the second part of the publication. This part deals with Bartók's compositions and his activities in researching and collecting folk song material. Includes essays by Gerald Abraham, György Bodnár, Ferenc Bónis, Ladislav Burlas, Chao Feng, János Demény, Denijs Dille, M. Gorczycka, Pál Járdányi, György Kerényi, Görgy Kroó, Lajos Lesznai, Izrael Nest'yev, S. Petrov, J. Racek, Adnun A. Saygun, Bence Szabolcsi, József Ujfalussy, Zeno Vancea, Jaroslav Volek, and John Weissmann. See the review of the publication of this conference by Ernő Balogh, in *Music Library Association Notes* (Fall 1965): 707-708.

1168. *Magyar zenetörténeti tanulmányok 3. Mosonyi Mihály és Bartók Béla emlékére* [Essays in the history of Hungarian music, In memory of Mihály Mosonyi and Béla Bartók], ed. Ferenc Bónis. Budapest: Zeneműkiadó, 1973. 364p.   ML55 S992 B6

According to Vera Lampert, *RILM Abstracts* No. 1702 (1974), this issue includes a collection of essays, letters, and documents. The abstractor states that *"RILM* numbers in parentheses refer to abstracts of individual articles appearing in this issue of *RILM."* The following includes the authors' names and translations of non-English titles: Kálmán Isoz, "The History of the Rózsavölgyi Publishing House, 1850-1908" and "Béla Bartók and Twentieth-Century Hungarian Music"; Rezső Alberti, "The History of the Rózsavölgyi Publishing House, 1918-1949"; János Demény, "Information Concerning the Cultural History of Bartók's Birthplace"; László Somfai (3834); Zsuzsanna A. Nemes, "Documents Concerning the Relationship between Bartók and Hubay"; Bálint Vázsonyi, "Data on the Relationship between Bartók and Dohnányi"; Ernő Lendvai (2842); János Breuer, "Data on the Origin of Két portré"; György Kroó, "Concerning the Origin of A fából faragott királyfi"; Denijs Dille, "Memories of Zoltán Kodály"; Pál Gergely, "Béla Bartók's Seven Years at the Hungarian Academy of Sciences"; and Benjamin Suchoff, "The Computer and Bartók Research in America." See the reviews by: István Raics in *Muzsika* (Budapest) 16/12 (December 1973): 38-39; and Vera Lampert, in *Magyar zene* (Budapest) 15/1 (March 1974): 96-98.

1169. *Magyar zenetörténeti tanulmányok 4. Kodály Zoltán emlékére* [Essays in the history of Hungarian music. In memory of Zoltán Kodály], ed. Ferenc Bónis. Budapest: Zeneműkiadó, 1977. 457p. ML55 S992 B6

Includes articles on Bartók by János Breuer, János Demény, Ernő Lendvai, and Arisztid Valkó. Also, contains summaries of the articles in English.

1170. *Magyar zenetörténeti tanulmányok: Szabolcsi Bence 70. születésnapjára* [Studies in Hungarian musical history. Dedicated to Bence Szabolcsi on his 70th birthday], ed. Ferenc Bónis. Budapest: Zeneműkiadó Vállalat, 1969. 433p. ML55 S992 B6

Contains the following articles: Denijs Dille, "Bartók és Kodály első találkozása" [The first meeting of Bartók and Kodály]; György Kroó, "Adatok 'A Kékszakállú herceg vára' keletkezéstörténetéhez" [Some data on the genesis of *Duke Bluebeard's Castle*]; László Somfai, "Bartók egynemű kórusainak szövegforrásáról" [On the sources of Bartók's male and female choruses]; Margit Tóth, "Egy népi énekes dallamainak változása Bartók óta" [Variations in a folk singer's melodies since Bartók]; and József Ujfalussy, "Az Allegro barbaro harmoniai alapgondolata és Bartók hangsorai" [The harmonic idea of the *Allegro barbaro* and Bartók's scales].

1171. *Melos* 5-6 (May-June 1949). pp. 129-155.   780.5 M492

Contains the following secondary and primary source items: Erich Doflein, "Béla Bartók," which presents a discussion of Bartók's stylistic development; "Drei Briefe von Béla Bartók" [Three letters of Béla Bartók], including "Bartók in Paris," "Bartók im Völkerbund," and "Bartók am Schönenberg"; Béla Bartók, "Der Einfluss der Volksmusik auf die heutige Kunstmusik" [The influence of folk music on the art music of today]; Ludwig Lesznai, "Béla Bartóks Leben 1881-1945" [Béla Bartók's life 1881-1945]; John S. Weissmann, "Béla Bartók und die Volksmusik" [Béla Bartók and folk music]; and "Béla Bartóks Werk" [Béla Bartók's work], compiled by Erich Doflein, revised by György Ligeti, which includes a catalogue of Bartók's works, arrangements, and scholarly publications.

1172. *Melos en musiktidskrift* (Stockholm) 3 (Spring-Summer 1995). 90p.   ISSN 1103-0968

Contains the following items: Lars Forssell, "Bartók Variations (A Poem)"; Vahid Salehieh, "Editor's Preface"; Malcolm Gillies, "Bartók as Correspondent"; Yehudi Menuhin, "Bartók--The Man Remembered"; Dorothy L. Crawford, "Bartók's Expressionism"; Irina Nikolska, "An Interview with Ivan Martynov"; Carl-Gören Ekerwald, "Béla Bartók in 1919"; György Sándor, "Recollections of Béla Bartók"; Mikhail L. Muginshtein, "Courage and Tragedy of Cognition: Bartók's 'Bluebeard's Castle'"; Mattias Gejrot, "Béla Bartók--a 'Classical' Composer?"; János Kárpáti, "Dramatic Turn Instead of Thematic Process: An Aspect of Bartók's Instrumental Dramaturgy"; Kjell Espmark, "Béla Bartók Against the Third Reich (A Poem)"; André Gertler, "Bartók and Hubay"; László Somfai, "Experimenting with Folkmusic-Based Concert Sets, Béla Bartók's Arrangements Reconsidered"; and Björn Westberg, Göran Södervall, Nils-Göran Olve, "Béla Bartók's Music on Record, Recommended Recordings." Contains cover photo of Bartók in London 1936 (Bartók Archives, Budapest).

1173. *Musica/realtà 2. Bartók e la didattica musicale* [*Musica/realtà 2*. Bartók and didactic music], atti a cura di Franco Masotti. Milano: Edizioni Unicopli, 1981. 156p.   H51.767

Congress program on Bartók at Ravenna, Teatro Alighieri e Musica/Realtà during the Bartók Centennial, from October 30 to November 1, 1981. Articles dealing specifically with Bartók include: Luigi Pestalozza, "Bartók e la musica del '900" [Bartók and the music of '900]; Silvano Sardi, "Valore di studio del 'Mikrokosmos'" [Value of the study of "Mikrokosmos"]; Gino Stefani, "Livelli di competenza musicale in Bartók" [Levels of musical competence in Bartók]; Boris Porena, "Micro-strutture, criteri elementari del 'Mikrokosmos'" [Micro-structure, elementary criteria of

"Mikrokosmos"]; Peter Varnai, "Béla Bartók: contrasto e unità" [Béla Bartók: contrast and unity].

1174. Musicology Congress of the International Music Council of UNESCO. Held in Budapest, Hungary (October 2-5, 1981).

Title of Congress: "The Composer in the Twentieth Century--In Commemoration of the 100th Anniversary of the Birth of Béla Bartók." Organized by the Hungarian National Committee of IMC. Simultaneous translation of the lectures from and into English, French, German, Hungarian, and Russian. All the topics in the six round table lectures and discussions were relevant to Bartók, but those dealing directly with the composer were "Bartók Reconsidered" and "Analysis of Bartók's Style." Also, included evening programs of many Bartók works presented in various concert halls and theaters. See János Breuer's "Musicological Congress of the International Music Council Budapest 2-5 October, 1981." *Studia musicologica* 24 supplement (1982): 5-7, for a complete summary of the Congress.

Musik der Zeit. Eine Schriftenreihe zur zeitgenössischen Musik.

See item No. 132.

1175. *Musikblätter des Anbruch* (Vienna) 3/5 (1921). H22.955

Special issue devoted to studies of Bartók's music.

1176. *Musik-Konzepte* 22 , ed. Heinz-Klaus Metzger and Rainer Riehn. (Munich) (November 1981). 153p. ISBN 3883770884 ML410.B26 B44

Volume devoted to reprinted articles by and about Bartók and his works. Articles include: Béla Bartók, "Revolution und Evolution in der Kunst" [Revolution and evolution in art]; René Leibowitz, "Béla Bartók oder die Möglichkeit des Kompromisses in der zeitgenössischen Musik" [Béla Bartók or the possibility of compromise in contemporary music]; Ulrich Dibelius, "Abweichung--Gegensatz--Zusammenschluss. Beobachtungen an Béla Bartóks Streichquartetten" [Variation--contrast--synthesis. Observations on Béla Bartók's string quartets]; Peter Petersen, "Bartóks Sonata für Violine solo. Ein Appell an die Hüter der Autographen" [Bartók's *Sonata for Solo Violin*. An investigation into the preservation of the autographs]; Siegfried Mauser, "Die musikdramatische Konzeption in 'Herzog Blaubarts Burg'" [The musical-dramatic conception in "Duke Bluebeard's Castle"]; Peter Petersen, "Über die Wirkung Bartóks auf das Schaffen Lutosławskis" [Beyond the influence of Bartók to the creations of Lutosławski]; Theodor W. Adorno, "Über Béla Bartók. Aufsätze und Auszüge aus Kritiken, zusammengestellt von Rainer Riehn" [About Bartók. Essays and abstracts on criticism, compiled by Rainer Riehn]; and a comprehensive bibliography and list of works.

1177. *The New York Times* (Friday, November 3, 1995): section on "The Living Arts," B10.

Commentary, entitled "Bartók on Compact Disk: As Ever, a Fresh and Fearless Composer," by *Times* classical-music critics on some of their favorite recordings of Bartók's works. Alex Ross discusses recordings of the "Orchestral Works," James R. Oestreich the "Solo Concertos," Allan Kozinn the "Chamber Works," Anthony Tommasini the "Piano Works," Kenneth Furie the "Stage Works," and Bernard Holland the "Archival Material." Reviews include brief stylistic comments on the music itself in addition to the performances.

1178. Per Béla Bartók Italia 1981, il musicista, il recercatore, il didatta. Held at the Teatro La Fenice in Venice, Italy (October 14-17, 1981).

Included concerts, international and national conventions, seminars, exhibits, publications, and recordings. Lectures included: Roberto Leydi, "Bartók ricercatore"; Luigi Nono, "Bartók compositore;" Enzo Beacco, "Bartók didatta"; Balint Sárosi, "La musica popolare ungherese"; Aurelio Milloss, "Bartók e 'Il mandarino meraviglioso'"; Benjamin Suchoff, "The Impact of Italian Baroque Music on Bartók's Music"; Ernő Lendvai, "Modality in the Music of Verdi and Bartók"; József Ujfalussy, "Liszt, Debussy, Bartók--Multimodalität und Polymodalität"; Tibor Tallián, "'Un desiderio dello sconosciuto,' Il popolismo del giovane Bartók"; Eberhardt Klemm, "Das Spaetwerk von Bartók"; Luigi Pestalozza, "Bartók: nazione e società"; László Somfai, "Peasant Music Influence Beyond Folklorism--The Case of Béla Bartók"; and Franco Donatoni, "Presenza di Bartók."

1179. *Proceedings of the International Bartók Colloquium: Szombathely, July 3-5, 1995. Studia musicologica* 36/3-4 (1995), ed. László Somfai.   781.05 St92   ISSN 0039-3266

Collection of papers given at the International Bartók Colloquium in Szombathely, Hungary, in 1995, includes 15 essays in Part I and 7 essays in Part II. Part I includes: László Somfai, "Perspectives of Bartók Studies in 1995"; Elliott Antokoletz, "Organic Development and the Interval Cycles in Bartók's *Three Studies*, Op. 18"; János Breuer, "Bartók im Dritten Reich"; Victoria Fischer, "Articulation Notation in the Piano Music of Béla Bartók: Evolution and Interpretation"; Malcolm Gillies, "Redrawing Bartók's Life"; Malcolm Gillies, "Bartók Analysis and Authenticity"; Maria

Anna Harley, "Natura naturans, natura naturata and Bartók's Nature Music Idiom"; Jürgen Hunkemöller, "Der Klage-Topos im Komponieren Bartóks"; János Kárpáti, "Perfect and Mistuned Structures in Bartók's Music"; Sándor Kovács, "'*Wir können sie in drei verschiedene Phasen einteilen'*: Einige Gedanken über Bartóks Volksliedaufzeichnungen"; Vera Lampert, "Bartók's Music on Record: An Index of Popularity"; Ferenc László, "Rumänische Stilelemente in Bartóks Musik. Fakten und Deutungen"; Carl S. Leafstedt, "Judith in *Bluebeard's Castle:* The Significance of a Name"; János Mácsai, "Neue Ergebnisse in der Forschung von Bartóks Tonaufnahmen"; Klára Móricz, "Operating on a Fetus: Sketch Studies and Their Relevance to the Interpretation of the Finale of Bartók's *Concerto for Orchestra.*" Part II includes: Dorrit Révész, "Text, Versions, and Recycling in Bartók's Writings, A Progress Report"; David E. Schneider, "Toward Bridging the Gap: The 'Culmination Point' as a Fulcrum Between Analysis and Interpretation"; László Somfai, "Idea, Notation, Interpretation: Written and Oral Transmission in Bartók's Works for Strings"; Tibor Tallián, "Das holzgeschnitzte Hauptwerk"; László Vikárius, "Corrections *versus* Revision: In Search of the Meaning of Alterations to the 'text' in Bartók's Compositional Sources"; Iván Waldbauer, "Theorists' View on Bartók from Edwin von der Null to Paul Wilson"; András Wilheim, "'. . . more precisely than a biography . . .' Bartók's *Real* Music in 1907-1910."

1180. "Sesja Bartókowska" [The Bartók session]. *Zeszyty naukowe. Państwowa wyższa szkoła muzyczna w Warszawie 2.* Warszawa: Państwowa Wyższa Szkoła Muzyczna, 1967. 178p.

Not examined. According to Kornel Michałowski, *RILM Abstracts* No. 2996 (1968), this is "a collection of lectures and discussions from a conference organized by the State College of Music in Warsaw, December 1966. The Polish and Hungarian authors (Zygmunt Folga, Pál Járdányi, Ernő Lendvai, Leon Markiewicz, Jan Stęszewski, Janusz Urbanski, Maciej Załewski) discuss the connections of Bartók's work with the world of nature, its connection with dodecaphony, the structure of consonances in his works, his influence on Polish music, the audiovisual problems in his work, and his role in ethnomusicology and in the classification of folk tunes."

1181. "Sesja Bartókowska" [The Bartók session], ed. Franciszek Wesełowski. *Państwowa wyższa szkoła muzyczna w Łódzi. Zeszyt naukowy1.* Łódz: Państwowa Wyższa Szkoła Muzyczna, 1969. 246p.

Not examined. According to Kornel Michałowski, *RILM Abstracts* No. 1922 (1969), this is "a collection of essays delivered at a session devoted to the works of Bartók at the State College of

Music in Łódz, May 1966. Seven authors discuss analytical problems relative to the composer's chamber works (especially the string quartets) as well as performance questions concerning the sonata for violin solo and the duos for two violins."

1182. Somfai, László. "Opening Address." *Studia musicologica* 24/3-4 (1982): 261-262. 781.05 St92 ISSN 0039-3266

For the Report of the International Bartók Symposium, Budapest 1981. Mentions three international Bartók conferences (1961, 1971, 1981), some of the renowned participants, places held, size and focus, and problems in Bartók research.

1183. *The Stage Works of Béla Bartók,* ed. Nicholas John. Sponsor: Martini. *Operaguide* 44 (New York: Riverrun; London: Calder, 1991). 112p. ML 410 B26 S78 ISBN 0-7145-4194-X ML410 B26 S78

Contributions include: Paul Banks, "Images of the Self: Duke Bluebeard's Castle"; Simon Broughton, "Bartók and World Music"; Keith Bosley and Peter Sherwood, translators, "Annie Miller [The Ballad of Anna Molnár]"; Julian Grant, "A Foot in Bluebeard's Door"; Mike Ashman, "Around the Bluebeard Myth"; Thematic Guide [to *A kékszakállú herceg vára (Duke Bluebeard's Castle)*]; "'A kékszakállú herceg vára' libretto by Béla Balázs, 'Duke Bluebeard's Castle' translation by John Lloyd Davies"; Ferenc Bónis, "The Wooden Prince: A Tale for Adults"; "'A fából faragott királyfi' scenario by Béla Balázs, 'The Wooden Prince' translation by István Farkas"; Ferenc Bónis, "The Miraculous Mandarin: The Birth and Vicissitudes of a Masterpiece"; "'A csodálatos mandarin' scenario by Menyhért Lengyel, 'The Miraculous Mandarin' translation by István Farkas"; and John Percival, "Bartók's Ballets." Contains selective discography by David Nice, selective bibliography, music examples, photos, tables.

1184. *Studia memoriae Bélae Bartók sacra* [Sacred studies in memory of Béla Bartók], 2nd ed. by Zoltán Kodály, Benjamin Rajeczky, and Lajos Vargyas. Budapest: Aedes Academiae Scientiarum Ungaricae, 1956. 544p. 2/1957, 3/1959. 780.92 B285R

Memorial volume dedicated to works on folk music, some involving Bartók and others dealing with cultures with which Bartók was not associated. Includes articles on Bartók by Sabin Dragoi, Pál Járdányi, József Kresánek, Béla Avasi and others. Contains 26 essays, dealing with three basic categories: 1) the music of the ethnic groups of Hungary and her neighbors; 2) the music of other cultures and continents; and 3) speculations of the nature of scale, tonality and musical structure. See the reviews by: Alfredo Bonaccorsi in *Quaderni della Rassegna musicale* 4 (1968): 179-180;

and Klaus P. Wachsmann in the *International Folk Music Journal* 9 (1957): 78-80.

1185. *Studia musicologica*, ed. József Ujfalussy. Budapest: Akadémiai Kiadó, since 1961.   781.05 St92   ISSN 0039-3266

Quarterly publication of the Hungarian Academy of Sciences. Includes articles in several European languages, most frequently in English, German, French, and occasionally Russian. Articles often cover aspects of Bartók's life, aesthetics, style, and works. Early issues devoted entirely to Bartók were the centenary volume 23 (1981) and volume 24/3-4 (1982). The latter two fascicles include, respectively, the 1981 lectures presented at the International Bartók Symposium held at the Bartók Memorial House in Budapest (September 28-30) and at the Musicology Congress of the International Music Council of UNESCO in Budapest (October 2-4). The most recent fascicles devoted to Bartók, 36/3-4 (1995), include the 1995 lectures presented at the International Bartók Colloquium in Szombathely (July 3-5). See the critical review by Malcolm Gillies of volume 24/3-4 in *Music and Letters* 66/4 (October 1985): 373-375.

1186. *Tempo* (London) 13-14 (1949-1950). 47p., 47p.   780.5 T249 ISSN 0040-2982

Special issues of this quarterly review of contemporary music devoted to Bartók. Includes articles on his life and works, in an attempt "to give a clear impression of the man--through his own words, through the words of people who knew him, through photographs (some of which have never been published before)." Items are as follows: Béla Bartók and Denijs Dille, "The Life of Béla Bartók"; Béla Bartók, "Some Early Letters"; Ralph Hawkes, "Béla Bartók: A Recollection By His Publisher"; Béla Bartók, "On Collecting Folk Songs in Turkey"; Mátyás Seiber, "Béla Bartók's Chamber Music"; Sándor Veress, "Bluebeard's Castle"; Gustav Oláh, "Bartók and the Theatre"; John Weissmann, "Bartók's Piano Music"; Béla Bartók, "The Influence of Peasant Music on Modern Music"; Francis F. Clough and G. J. Cuming, "The Music of Béla Bartók on Records"; Halsey Stevens, "A Bartók Bibliography" and "Béla Bartók: Chronological List of His Works." See the reprint of these combined issues, *Béla Bartók: A Memorial Review*. New York: Boosey & Hawkes, 1950. 95p.

1187. Weissmann, John S. "Bartók Festival in Budapest." *Music Review* 10/1 (February 1949): 36-37.   780.5 M9733   ISSN 0027-4445

Summary of the first world-wide musical event in the new Hungary (October 10-31). Discusses divisions of the festival into performances of works by Bartók, by foreign composers, new

Hungarian compositions, etc. Describes participants, works performed, and place of performance (e.g., three stage works of Bartók at the Opera House), with some reference to audience reception.

1188. ----------. "Report from Budapest." *Tempo* (London) 10 (Winter 1948-1949): 21-22.   780.5 T249   0040-2982

Author was present at the "Bartók Competition of October, 1948," and at the "Festival of Contemporary Music" that followed it. Reviews the works performed.

1189. *Zeneelmélet, stíluselemzés. A Bárdos Lajos 75. születésnapja alkalmából tartott zenetudományi konferencia anyaga* [Music theory, style analysis. Papers presented at the Conference of Musicologists held in celebration of the seventy-fifth birthday of Lajos Bárdos]. Budapest: Zeneműkiadó, 1977.

Includes articles on Bartók by János Breuer, János Kárpáti, Imre Olsvai, László Somfai, and Ilkka Oramo.

1190. *Zenei szemle* (Budapest).   HA2.398

Essays by and on Bartók in many issues since 1/9 (November 1917).

1191. *Zenetudományi tanulmányok* [Musicological studies]. Special Issues, ed. by Bence Szabolcsi and Dénes Bartha. Budapest: Akadémiai Kiadó. No. 2: *Erkel Ferenc és Bartók Béla emlékére* (1954); No. 3: *Liszt Ferenc és Bartók Béla emlékére* (1955); No. 7: *Bartók Béla megjelenése az európai zeneéletben* (1914-1926), *Liszt Ferenc hagyatéka* (1959); No. 10: *Bartók Béla emlékére* (1962).

As stated in the review by John Weissmann in the *International Folk Music Journal* 17/1 (1965): 38-41, the last issue "includes part of János Demény's Bartók Documentation, an important publication, not least for music folklorists." In realizing the "need of accessible documents to accompany and supplement the Bartók correspondence for the future biography, he conceived the plan of collecting and publishing all written contemporary records of Bartók's life and work." The documentation, except for letters, includes programs, newspaper communiques and reviews, criticisms published in printed matter contemporary with the events discussed, as well as statements of friends, colleagues and others who had come in contact with the man and his work. See also the reviews by: Halsey Stevens (of No. 7) in *Music Library Association Notes* (December 1959): 55-56; and (of No. 3) in the same journal (September 1957): 569-570.

4. Computerized Data Bases for Analysis and Research

1192. Jackson, David Lowell. "Horizontal and Vertical Analysis Data Extraction Using a Computer Program." Ph.D. diss. University of Cincinnati, 1981. 423p.

Uses a computer program to analyze the third movement of Bartók's *Fourth String Quartet.* Also, contains illustrations, bibliography, and appendices for general information on the computer.

1193. Osborn, F.E. Ann. "A Computer-Aided Methodology for the Analysis and Classification of British-Canadian Children's Traditional Singing Games." *Computers and the Humanities* 22/3 (1988): 173-182.   QA 76 C5185

Employs Bartók's methodological approach to classification as the basis for defining the musical features of British Canadian children's traditional songs, and to develop a music education program in Canada. Contains music examples, bibliography.

1194. Suchoff, Benjamin. "A GRIPHOS Application of Bartók's Turkish Folk Music Material." *Spectra Publication* 1. Stony Brook: State University of New York, Center for Contemporary Arts and Letters, 1975. 14p.   MT-92.B37 S9

Discusses the development of a scholarly apparatus in the form of permuted indices for Bartók's Turkish folk music material by means of a General Retrieval and Information Processor for Humanities-Oriented Studies, developed by Professor Jack Heller of the State University of New York at Stony Brook. These permutations and the approach to the construction of the data base from which others were derived are the subjects of this essay. Analysis of Bartók's Turkish manuscript was concerned with the melodies and their morphology, the poetic texts and their translations, data regarding performance, and general aspects of the collection. Contains tables, bibliography.

1195. ----------. "Aplicárea calculatoarelor electronice la etnomuzicologica bartókiana" [The use of the electronic computer in the Bartókian ethnomusicological method]. *Muzica* (Romania) 20/11 (November 1970): 10-14.   ISSN 0580-3713

According to Elena Zottoviceanu, *RILM Abstracts* No. 1306 (1971), this article "describes the examination by computer of Bartók's ethnomusicological dating and the problems revealed by the publication of Rumanian folklore collections. A lexical index of musical material is necessary for the classification of variants.

Bartók's system is based on grammatical principles: structural analysis, determining the framework of sections, etc."

*Suchoff, Benjamin. "Bartók, Ethnomusicology, and the Computer."
See item no. 406

1196. ----------. "The Computer and Bartók Research in America." *Journal of Research in Music Education* 19/1 (Spring 1971): 3-16. 780.705 J826   ISSN 0022-4294

According to the author, *RILM Abstracts* No. 1831 (1971), this article is "a summary of research work undertaken thus far in computational musicology and computational ethnomusicology toward automation of the New York Bartók Archives in terms of information retrieval. Discussion of thematic indices and data bank construction of Bartók's Hungarian, Romanian, and Serbo-Croatian folk music material, and his six string quartets, is illustrated by various examples of research instruments and computer printouts, including permuted bibliographic files." Contains illustrations, facsimiles, and music examples. Also published in *Magyar zenetörténeti tanulmányok 3. Mosonyi Mihály és Bartók Béla emlékére,* ed. Ferenc Bónis. Budapest: Editio Musica, 1973.

1197. ----------. "Computer Applications to Bartók's Serbo-Croatian Material." *Tempo* (London) 80 (Spring 1967): 15-19.   780.5 T249 ISSN 0040-2982

A computer-written index of Bartók's *Serbo-Croatian Folksongs.* Also includes analysis for the classification of the melodic variants, their folk characteristics, and the methodological approach. Contains illustrations, facsimiles, and music examples.

1198. ----------. "Computer-Oriented Comparative Musicology." *The Computer and Music* (1971): 193-206.   ML55 C75

According to the author, *RILM Abstracts* No. 1996 (1971), this article is a "presentation of specific details concerning procedures and programs used in the comparison of different musical materials by means of electronic data processing. The procedures are based on Bartókian methods in ethnomusicology. The materials: Bartók's Serbo-Croatian and Romanian folk music collections, Harry B. Lincoln's (State University of New York at Binghamton) collection of frottole incipits, and Earle Hultberg's (State University of New York at Potsdam) collection of incipits from Cabezon works. The programs: lexicographical indexing of incipits, string length distribution, signed digit frequency of occurrence, substring interval extraction, and interval type distribution. Conclusion: similarity in melodic contour among the materials seems to point toward this feature as perhaps a folk-based or folk-styled characteristic of the art melodies." Contains illustrations, facsimiles, and music examples.

1199. ----------. "Computerized Folk Song Research and the Problem of Variants." *Computers and the Humanities* 2/4 (March 1968): 155-158.   QA 76 C5185

Discusses a computerized extension of Bartók's systematic scientific examination of the morphological aspects of folk music material. Statistical methods form the base on which the bulk of Bartók's conclusions are drawn.

1200. ----------. "Some Problems in Computer-Oriented Bartókian Ethnomusicology." *Ethnomusicology* 13/3 (September 1969): 489-497.   781.05 Et38

Discusses the importance of the computer in determining melodic variants so basic to Bartók's folk-music research. Bartók's own methodological approach is the basis for the computerized thematic indices of his Romanian and Serbo-Croatian folksong collections. The resulting indexes are intended to demonstrate the relation of melodic variants through their intervallic design. Contains illustrations, music examples, and bibliography. Also published in Romanian as "Únele probléme privind folósírea masinilor electronice de calcul la materialul etnomuzicologic al lui Béla Bartók." *Revista de etnografie și folclor* 14/5 (1969): 343-352, and in Hungarian as "A bartóki népzenekutatás és az elektronikus számítógépek." *Muzsika* 13/7 (July 1970): 6-8; 8 (August 1970): 4-6.

AUTHOR-TITLE INDEX

This index contains entries for all authors, joint authors, editors, book titles in the original language, and titles of special journals or issues devoted to articles on Bartók. The following are excluded: names of translators; and titles of articles and dissertations as initial entries. Citations are indicated by item number. Entries referred to in the annotations are indicated by item number plus the letter "n." The few occurrences of items appearing with asterisk rather than item number are indicated by the following item number plus the letter "p." Entries referred to in the Introduction are indicated by footnote number, designated by "n." plus the number.

In the listing of entries, initial definite and indefinite articles in all languages are included in the title, but are ignored in the alphabetical filing. However, in listings of articles, essays, and books subsumed under one author, definite and indefinite articles are accounted for in the local alphabetizing. Diacritical markings in all languages are ignored in filing, except in German, where letters with the umlaut are considered to be followed by *e* (*ä* is equivalent to *ae, ö* to *oe,* and *ü* to *ue*).

Abraham, Gerald. "Bartók and England," 253; "Bartók String Quartet No. 6," 517
Adorno, Theodor W. "Béla Bartóks Drittes Streichquartett," 683; "Über Béla Bartók. Aufsätze und Auszüge aus Kritiken, zusammengestellt von Rainer Riehn," 1176n
After the Storm: The American Exile of Béla Bartók (Sturrock), 254
Agárdi, Péter. "Révai József Bartók Béláról, kiadatlan levelek," 684
Agawu, V. Kofi. "Analytical Issues Raised by Bartók's Improvisations for Piano, Op. 20," 518
Alberti, Rezső. "The History of the Rózsavölgyi Publishing House, 1918-1949," 1168n
Albrecht, Jan. "Das Variations- und Imitationsprinzip in der Tektonik von Bartóks Bratschenkonzert," 519
Almárné-Veszprémi, Lili. See Veszprémi, Lili Almárné
Andraschke, Peter. "Folklora in kompozicija," 877
Antokoletz, Elliott. "'At last something truly new': Bagatelles," 520, 1158n; *Bartók in Retrospect,* 1138; "Bartók's *Bluebeard:* The Sources of Its 'Modernism,'" 604n, 685; "Bartók's Humanistic Philosophy as Reflected in His Musical Aesthetics: The Fusion of

Divergent Folk- and Art-Music Sources," 1157n; "Bartók's Improvisations, Op. 20: From 'Folksong Arrangement' to 'Composing with Folk Tunes,'" 1157n; "Béla Bartók in Eastern Europe and the United States," 207; "Concerto for Orchestra," 521, 1158n; "Middle-period String Quartets," 522, 1158n; "Modal Transformation and Musical Symbolism in Bartók's *Cantata Profana,"* 523, 1138n, 1139n; *Musical Symbolism in the Operas of Debussy and Bartók,* 527; "Organic Development and the Interval Cycles in Bartók's Three Studies, Op. 18," 528. "Organic Expansion and Classical Structure in Bartók's *Sonata for Two Pianos and Percussion,"* 529, 1161n; "Pitch-Set Derivations from the Folk Modes in Bartók's Music," 530, 1164n; "Principles of Pitch Organization in Bartók's *Fourth String Quartet,"* 531, 583n, 1143n; "Rhythmic Form in Three of Bartók's String Quartets," 532; "Symmetrical Transformations of the Folk Modes in Bartók's Music: a Study of Selected Pieces and Their Sketches," 1162n; "The Music of Bartók: Some Theoretical Approaches in the U.S.A.," 524; *The Music of Béla Bartók: A Study of Tonality and Progression in Twentieth-Century Music,* n.2, n.28, n.35, 525, 640n, 1080n; "The Musical Language of Bartók's*14 Bagatelles* for Piano," 526; "The State of Bartók Research in the Centennial Year," 476; "Transformations of a Special Non-Diatonic Mode in Twentieth-Century Music: Bartók, Stravinsky, Scriabin and Albrecht," 533

Apám életének krónikája (Bartók), 210

Arauco, Ingrid. "Bartók's Romanian Christmas Carols: Changes from the Folk Sources and Their Significance," 878; "Methods of Translation in Bartók's Twenty Hungarian Folksongs," 879

Arion 13 (Somlyó), 1129

Arthuys, Philippe. "Béla Bartók, expression du phénomène contemporain," 686

Ashman, Mike. "Around the Bluebeard Myth," 981, 1183n

Austin, William. "Bartók's Concerto for Orchestra," 534; *Music in the 20th Century: from Debussy Through Stravinsky,* 1096

Autexier, Philippe A. *Bartók Béla. Musique de la vie. Autobiographie, lettres et autres écrits choisis, traduits et présentés par Autexier Philippe A.,* 178

Avasi, Béla. "Tonsysteme aus Intervallpermutationen," 535

Babbitt, Milton. "The String Quartets of Bartók," 536

Bachmann, Tibor, and Maria Bachmann. *Studies in Bartók's Music,* 537

Bachmann, Tibor, and Peter J. Bachmann. "An Analysis of Béla Bartók's Music Through Fibonaccian Numbers and the Golden Mean," 538

Bahk, Junsang. "Die Auswirkungen der Volksliedforschung auf das kompositorische Schaffen von Béla Bartók," 880

Balanchivadze, E. "Bartók's The Miraculous Mandarin," 539

Balas, Edith. "Brancuşi and Bartók: A Parallel," 881

Balázs, Béla. "A fából faragott királyfi," 540

Ban, Louise G. *Bartók Béla,* 208

Banks, Paul. "Images of the Self: 'Duke Bluebeard's Castle,'" 687, 1183n
Baraczka, István. "Egy ismeretlen Bartók-levél," 159
The Bard Music Festival Rediscoveries: Béla Bartók and His World (Bard College, Annandale-On-Hudson, N.Y.), 1130
Bárdos, Lajos. "Bartók dallamvilágából," 882
Barna, István. "Bartók II. vonósnégyesének módosított metronóm jelzései," 982
Baróthy, Zoltán. "Bartók Béla Mikrokozmosza az általános iskolai zenehallgatásban," 1059
Bartha, Dénes. "Bartók's View on Tonality," 1143n; "La Musique de Bartók," 541; "Quatrain, a Classical Thematic Structure, Demonstrated in Bartók's Piano Music," 1143n; "Refined 'Quatrain'-Type Thematic Patterns in Bartók's Music," 1162n; "The Use of Pre-Existent Folk Music Materials in Selected Bartók Works," 1143n; *Zenetudományi tanulmányok 2, 3, 7, and 10,* 1191
Bartók, Béla.
  articles:
  "A Biskra-vidéki arabok népzenéje," 22; "A clavecinre írt művek előadása," 16; A fából faragott királyfi: II. A zeneszerző a darabjáról," 23; "A gépzene," 98; "A hangszeres zene folkloreja Magyarországon,"14; "A hegedű duókról," 78; "A hunyadi román nép zenedialektusa," 20; "A Kékszakállú herceg vára: I Szerzők a darabjukról," 27; "A magyar nép hangszerei," 15; "A magyar zenéről," 11; "A népzene (paraszt-zene) fejlődési fokai," 33; "A népzene jelentőségéről," 72; "A parasztzene hatása az újabb műzenére," 71; "A zongora-irodalom remekművei. Scarlatti--Couperin--Rameau, etc.," 57; "Academies, Hungarian; Chamber-Music Players, Hungarian; Hungarian Folk Music; Hungarian Musical Instruments; Hungarian Opera, Pantomime and Ballet; Opera Houses, Hungarian; Orchestras, Hungarian; Publishers, Hungarian; Rumanian Folk Music; Slovak Folk Music," 58; "Aki nem tud arabusul . . .," 43; "Analyse du Deuxième Concerto pour Piano et Orchestre de Béla Bartók par son auteur," 109; "Analyse zum V. Streichquartett," 92; "Antwort auf einen rumänischen Angriff," 94; "Arab Folk Music in the Biskra District," 143n; "Arnold Schönbergs Musik in Ungarn," 38, 142n, 1155n; "Aufbau der Musik für Saiteninstrumente," 102; "Autobiography," 126; "Az összehasonlító zenefolklore," 17; "Az úgynevezett bolgár ritmus," 106; "Az új egyetemes népdalgyűjtemény tervezete," 18; "Bach-Bartók: Preface and Notes to Well-Tempered Clavier," 4; "Bartók Béla, oroszországi útjáról," 64; "Bartók Béla. Önéletrajz," 10; "Bartók válasza Hubay Jenőnek," 32; "Bence Szabolcsi," 120; "Béla Bartók Replies to Percy Grainger," 87; *Búzavirág, magyar férfikórus gyűjtemény Bartók Béla előszavával,* 91; *Cantata Profana. A kilenc csodaszarvas [Cantata Profana. The Nine Miraculous Deer],* 128; "Cigányzene? Magyar zene? (Magyar népdalok a német zeneműpiacon)," 69, 76n, 77n, 81n; "Concerto for Orchestra by Béla Bartók," 122; "Contemporary

Drew, David. "Bartók and His Publishers," 1162n
Dustin, William Dale. "Two-Voiced Textures in the Mikrokosmos of Béla Bartók," 564

Edwards, Lorraine. "The Great Animating Stream of Music," 1065
Eisikovits, Max. "Contribuţii la geneza unor elemente de stil ale creaţiei lui Béla Bartók," 713
Ekerwald, Carl-Gören. "Béla Bartók in 1919," 1172n
Eller, Rudolf. "Über Gestalt und Funktion des Themas bei Bartók," 714
Ellsworth, Ray. "The Shadow of Genius: Béla Bartók and Tibor Serly," 280
Elschek, Alica, and Oskár. *Béla Bartók. Slovenské l'udové piesne,* 191
Elschek, Oskár. "Bartók ako etnomuzikolog," 372; "Bartóks Beziehung zur Volksmusik und Volksmusikforschung," 373, 1165n
Eősze, László. "Aspetti comuni dell'arte poetica di Verdi, Bartók, e Kodály," 438; "Bartók és Kodály levelezése," 165; "Thirteen Unpublished Letters by Zoltán Kodály to Béla Bartók," 166
Erdely, Stephen. "Bartók on Southslavic Epic Song," 374, 1138n, 1139n; "Complementary Aspects of Bartók's and Kodály's Folk Song Researches," 1141n, 1132n; "Folk-Music Research in Hungary Until 1950: The Legacy of Zoltán Kodály and Béla Bartók," 375
Erdélyi Magyarság. Népdalok (Bartók), 183
Erinnerungen an Béla Bartók (Takács), 353
Espmark, Kjell. "Béla Bartók Against the Third Reich (A Poem)," 1172n
Evans, Edwin. "Béla Bartók," 565

Fábián, Imre. "Bartók im Wandel der Zeiturteile," 484; "Bartók und die Wiener Schule," 281; "Bartók und die Zeitgenossen," 439; "Debussy und die Meister der ungarischen Musik," 948
Falvy, Zoltán. "Franz Liszt e Béla Bartók (Béla Bartók su Franz Liszt)," 949
Fancsali, János. "Bartók Béla Sepsiszentgyörgyi hangversenye," 282
Fassett, Agatha. *The Naked Face of Genius; Béla Bartók's American Years,* 283
Ferguson, Donald N. "Béla Bartók," 566
Fin, N. "The Cultivation of Hungarian Folksong in the Works of Bartók," 1146n
Fine, Irving G. "Bartók's New Koussevitzky Number," 715
Finger, Hildegard. "Béla Bartók: *Konzert für Orchester,*" 716
Fischer, John Frederic. "Cyclic Procedures in the String Quartet from Beethoven to Bartók," 717
Fischer, Victoria. "Articulating Bartók's Piano Music: Legato, Portato, Staccato," 1157n; "Articulation Notation in the Piano Music of Béla Bartók: Evolution and Interpretation," 1179n; "Articulation Notation in Bartók's Piano Music: Sources and Evolution," 1066, 1138n, 1161n; *Bartók in Retrospect,* 1138; "Bartók's Piano Notation: Sources, Evolution and Interpretation," 1161n; "Béla Bartók's *Fourteen Bagatelles,* op. 6: Determining Performance Authenticity,"

Hawkes, Ralph. "Béla Bartók, A Recollection by His Publisher," 298, 1186n; "Béla Bartók in der Emigration," 132n, 487
Hawthorne, Robin. "The Fugal Technique of Béla Bartók," 584
Heath, Mary Joanne Renner. "A Comparative Analysis of Dukas's *Ariane et Barbe-bleu* and Bartók's *Duke Bluebeard's Castle*," 736
Helm, Everett. *Bartók*, 230; "Bartók on Stage: Fresh Light on a Long Undervalued Dramatic Trilogy," 488; "Bartók's Musik für Saiteninstrumente," 585; *Béla Bartók in Selbstzeugnissen und Bilddokumenten*, 180; "Béla Bartók und die Volksmusik--zur 20. Wiederkehr von Bartók's Todestag," 893; *Der Mensch Bartók*, 444
Henry, Leigh. "Béla Bartók," 737; "Contemporaries--Béla Bartók," 738
Herbage, Julian. "Bartók's Violin Concerto," 739
Hernádi, Lajos. "Bartók Béla a zongoraművész, a pedagógus, az ember," 299 (in French, 1166n)
Heseltine, Philip. "Modern Hungarian Composers," 300
Hirashima, Naeko. "Barutóko no ongaku no tokushitsu nikansuru ichi kosatsu," 894
Hodges, Janice Kay Gray. "The Teaching Aspects of Bartók's *Mikrokosmos*," 1075
Horn, Herbert Alvin. "Idiomatic Writing of the Piano Music of Béla Bartók," 740
Horváth, Béla. "Bartók és a Nyolcak," 301
Howat, Roy. "Bartók, Lendvai and the Principles of Proportional Analysis," 586, 612n; "Debussy, Ravel and Bartók: Towards Some New Concepts of Form," 587; "Debussy, Bartók et les formes de la nature," 741; "Masterworks (II): Sonata for Two Pianos and Percussion," 588, 1158n
Hrcková, Nada. "Nielen chlebom je človek živy. Po stopách Bélu Bartóka," 302
Hsu, Madeleine. *Olivier Messiaen, the Musical Mediator: A Study of the Influence of Liszt, Debussy, and Bartók.*, 971; "Olivier Messiaen, The Musical Mediator, and His Major Influences Liszt, Debussy and Bartók," 972
Huang, Fung-Yin. "Bartók's Contributions to Piano Pedagogy; His Edition of Bach's *Well-Tempered Clavier* and Impressions of Former Students," 1076
Hundt, Theodor. "Barocke Formelemente im Kompositionsstil Béla Bartóks," 952, 1164n; "Bartóks Satztechnik in den Klavierwerken," 742
Hungarian folk songs: Complete Collection I (Bartók), 198
Hunkemöller, Jürgen. "Bartók analysiert seine 'Musik für Saiteninstrumente, Schlagzeug und Celesta,'" 997; "Bartók und Mozart," 953; "Bartóks Urteil über den Jazz," 743; "Béla Bartók. Musik für Saiteninstrumente," 998; "Choral-Kompositionen von Béla Bartók," 744; "Der Klage-Topos im Komponieren Bartóks," 1160n, 1179n; "Kunstwerk, Bauernmusik und Evolution. Bartók's Vision der Moderne," 445

'Principles of Proportional Analysis,'" 586n, 612; *The Workshop of Bartók and Kodály,* 782

Lengyel, Menyhért. "The Miraculous Mandarin," 613

Lenoir, Yves. "Béla Bartók et George Herzog: Chronique d'une collaboration exemplaire (1940-1945)," 321; "Béla Bartók et le folklore: Le cas de la période américaine (1940-1945)," 909; "Bibliographie de Denijs Dille Sur Béla Bartók," 1112; "Contributions á l'étude de la Sonate Solo de Béla Bartók (1944)," 322; "Folklore et transcendance dans l'œuvre américaine de Béla Bartók (1940-1945): Contributions à l'étude de l'activité scientifique et créatrice du compositeur," 395; "Le destin des recherches ethnomusicologues de Béla Bartók à la vielle de son séjour aux Etats-Unis," 323; "Réflexions critiques sur une édition posthume: B. Bartók, *Rumanian Folk Music.* Ed. Benjamin Suchoff," 496; "Réflexions sur l'activité scientifique de Béla Bartók à la lumière de ses recherches en Amérique," 396; "The Destiny of Bartók's Ethnomusicological Research Immediately Prior to His Stay in the United States," 397, 1164n

Lesznai, Lajos. *Béla Bartók. Sein Leben--Seine Werke,* 232; "Béla Bartóks Leben 1881-1945," 1171n; "Realistische Ausdrucksmittel in der Musik Béla Bartóks," 453

Leydi, Roberto. "Bartók ricercatore," 1178n

Liebner, János. "Bartók utolsó amerikai rádióinterjúi," 181, 324n; "Une œuvre oubliée de Bartók," 324n, 1008; "Unpublished Bartók Documents," 324

The Life and Music of Béla Bartók (Stevens), n.5, n.18, n.23, n.26, 243

Ligeti, György. "Analyse des V. Streichquartetts von Béla Bartók," 614

Lindlar, Heinrich. *Lübbes Bartók Lexicon,* 233; *Musik der Zeit. Eine Schriftenreihe zur zeitgenössischen Musik* 3, 132, 1175p; "Viermal Bartók Musik für Saiteninstrumente Notizen zu einem Interpretationsvergleich," 497

Lipman, Samuel. "Bartók at the Piano," 1009

Liszt-Bartók: Second International Conference: Budapest 1961 (Ujfalussy), 1167

Little, Jean. "Architectonic Levels of Rhythmic Organization in Selected Twentieth-Century Music," 783

Locke, Derek. "Numerical Aspects of Bartók's String Quartets," 616

Lord, Albert B. "Bartók and the Milman Parry Collection," 1141n; *Serbo-Croatian Folk Songs,* 173, 195n; *Serbo-Croatian Heroic Songs,* 175

Lowman, Edward A. "Some Striking Propositions in the Music of Béla Bartók," 615

Lübbes Bartók Lexicon (Lindlar), 233

Lukács, György. "Bartók und die ungarische Kultur," 325, 1165n; "Béla Bartók. On the Twenty-fifth Anniversary of His Death," 326

Lükő, Gábor. "Bartók tudományos öröksége," 398

Lyle, Watson."Béla Bartók. A Personal Impression," 454; "Modern Musicians: III. Béla Bartók. An Interview by Watson Lyle," 455

Olivier Messiaen, the Musical Mediator: A Study of the Influence of Liszt, Debussy, and Bartók (Hsu), 971

Olsvai, Imre. *Népdaltípusok,* 189n; "West-Hungarian (Trans-Danubian) Characteristic Features in Bartók's works," 914

Oramo, Ilkka. "Bemerkungen zu einigen Paradigmen der Bartók-Forschung," 1164n; "Die notierte, die wahrgenommene und die gedachte Struktur bei Bartók," 802; "Marcia und Burletta. Zur Tradition der Rhapsodie in zwei Quartettsatzen Bartóks," 801; "Modale Symmetrie bei Bartók," 628; "Tonaalisuudesta Bartókin bagatellissa Op. 6 No. 1," 629

Orbán, László. "Bartók's Message Has Never Been More Topical Than Today," 241, 1165n

Ordnung und Gestalt. Die Musik von 1900 bis 1950 (Wolff), 876

Orvis, Joan. "Technical and Stylistic Features of the Piano Etudes of Stravinsky, Bartók, and Prokofiev," 630

Osborn, F.E. Ann. "A Computer-Aided Methodology for the Analysis and Classification of British-Canadian Children's Traditional Singing Games," 1193

Paisov, J. "Polytonality in Bartók's Music," 1146n

Panufnik, Andrzej. "Homage to Béla Bartók," 334

Pap, Gábor. *"Csak tiszta forrásból": Adalékok Bartók* Cantata profanájának *értelmezéséhez,* 803

Papp, Márta. "Bartók hegedűrapszódiái és a román népi hegedűs játékmód hatása Bartók műveire," 915

Parker, Beverly Lewis. "Parallels Between Bartók's Concerto for Orchestra and Kübler-Ross's Theory About the Dying," 460

Parker, Mary Elizabeth. "Bartók's Mikrokosmos: A Survey of Pedagogical and Compositional Techniques," 1080

Parks, Richard. "Harmonic Resources in Bartók's 'Fourths' (Mikrokosmos V/131)," 1162n

Párosítók (Kerényi), 189n

Parry, Milman. *Serbo-Croatian Heroic Songs,* 190

Per Béla Bartók Italia 1981, il musicista, il recercatore, il didatta (Venice), 1178

Percival, John. "Bartók's Ballets," 504, 1183n

Perle, George. "Bartók and the Twelve-Tone Modal System," 1143n; "Berg's Master Array of the Interval Cycles," 631; "Symmetrical Formations in the String Quartets of Béla Bartók," 524n, 633; "The String Quartets of Béla Bartók," 632

Pernecky, John Martin. "The Historical and Musico-Ethnological Approach to the Instrumental Compositions of Béla Bartók," 916

Pernye, András. "New Records," 505

Persichetti, Vincent. "Current Chronicle," 634

Perspektiven neuer Musik. Materialien und didaktische Information (Zimmerschied), 1090

Pestalozza, Luigi. "Bartók e la musica del '900," 1173n; "Bartók: nazione e società," 1178n

Themenentwürfe zu dem Violinkonzert aus den Jahren 1936/37," 1027, 1156n; "Egy sajátos kulminációs pont Bartók hangszeres formáiban," 831, 1165n; "Experimenting with Folkmusic-Based Concert Sets, Béla Bartók's Arrangements Reconsidered," 1172n; "Idea, Notation, Interpretation: Written and Oral Transmission in Bartók's Works for Strings," 1160n, 1179n; "In his 'Compositional Workshop,'" 1028, 1158n; "Kompositionsprozess und Quellenlage bei Bartók," 1029; *Magyar népzenei hanglemezek Bartók Béla lejegyzéseivel*, 1118; "Manuscript Versus Urtext: The Primary Sources of Bartók's Works," 1030, 1162n; "Nichtvertonte Libretti im Nachlass und andere Bühnenpläne Bartóks," 1152n; "Nineteenth-Century Ideas Developed in Bartók's Piano Notation in the Years 1907-14," 1031; "Opening Address," 1182; "Peasant Music Influence Beyond Folklorism--The Case of Béla Bartók," 1178n; "'Per finire': Some Aspects of the Finale in Bartók's Cyclic Form," 832; "Perspectives of Bartók Studies in 1995," 1160n, 1179n; *Proceedings of the International Bartók Colloquium: Szombathely, July 3-5, 1995*, 1179; "Quellenmaterial der Bartók Werke und Volksliedsammlungen," 1164n; "Strategics of Variation in the Second Movement of Bartók's Violin Concerto 1937-1938," 651; "Studien von jungen Musikologen," 1164n; "The Budapest Bartók Archives," 1093; "The Development of Thematic Materials in Selected Works by Bartók," 1143n; "The Influence of Peasant Music on the Finale of Bartók's Piano Sonata: An Assignment for Musicological Analysis," 924; "The 'Piano Year' of 1926," 833, 1158n; *Tizennyolc Bartók-tanulmány*, 834; "Über Bartóks Rubato-Stil. Vergleichende Studie der zwei Aufnahmen 'Abend am Lande' des Komponisten," 1155n; "Vierzehn Bartók-Schriften aus den Jahren 1920/21. Aufsätze über die zeitgenössische Musik und Konzertberichte aus Budapest," 142; "Why Is a Bartók Thematic Catalog Sorely Needed?," 1119, 1131n
Somfai, László and Vera Lampert. "Béla Bartók," 242
Somlyó, György. *Arion 13,* 1129
Spinosa, Frank. "Beethoven and Bartók: A Comparative Study of Motivic Techniques in the Later Beethoven Quartets and the Six String Quartets of Béla Bartók," 835
The Stage Works of Béla Bartók (John), 1183
Starr, Lawrence. "Melody-Accompaniment Textures in the Music of Bartók, as Seen in his *Mikrokosmos* ," 652; "Mikrokosmos: The Tonal Universe of Béla Bartók," 653
Staud, Géza. "Ismeretlen Bartók-levelek," 344
Stefani, Gino. "Livelli di competenza musicale in Bartók," 1173n; "Tritono e forma-arco nel 5° quartetto di Bartók," 654
Stehman, Jacques. "Souvenirs sur Béla Bartók by André Gertler," 464
Stenzl, Jürg. "Béla Bartók--'Repräsentant der alten Welt'?" 836
Stephan, Rudolf. "Zur Bartók-Rezeption in den zwanziger Jahren," 507
Stern, Gershon. "Semiotic Levels in Performances of Bartók's *Music for Strings, Percussion and Celesta,* " 837

Westphal, Kurt. "Béla Bartók und die moderne ungarische Musik," 939

Whitaker, Frank. "A Visit to Béla Bartók," 474; "The Most Original Mind in Modern Music," 475

Whittall, Arnold. "Bartók's Second String Quartet," 673

Wightman, Alistair. "Szymanowski, Bartók and the Violin," 873

Wilheim, András. "A Bartók Bibliography, 1970-1979," 1128; "Bartók's Exercises in Composition," 1053, 1164n; "Egy Bartók-kottarészletről," 1054; "Két Bartók-vázlat," 1055; "'. . . more exactly than a biography . . .' Bartók's *Real* Music in 1907-1910," 1160n, 1179n; "Skizzen zu 'Mikrokosmos' Nr 135 und Nr. 57," 1056, 1156n; "Zu einem Handschriften-Faksimile aus dem Jahre 1917," 1057, 1156n

Williams, J. Kent. "Post-Tonal Theory in Bartók's *Mikrokosmos:* Pitch Sets, Other Analytical Techniques," 1157n

Willis, Andrew. "Bartók's Three Etudes, Op. 18: Romantic Technique in a Brave, New World," 1157n; "Overview of Bartók's Piano Music: Styles, Genres, Sources," 1157n

Wilson, Paul Frederick. "Approaching Atonality: Studies and Improvisations," 674, 1158n; "Atonality and Structure in Works of Béla Bartók's Middle Period," 640n, 675; "Concepts of Prolongation and Bartók's Op. 20," 676; "Function and Pitch Hierarchy in Movement II of Bartók's Fifth Quartet," 677; "The Atonal Vocabulary of Bartók's Second Violin Sonata," 1162n; *The Music of Béla Bartók,* 678; "Violin Sonatas," 679, 1158n

Winking, Hans. "Klangflächen bei Bartók bis 1911. Zu einigen stilistischen Beziehungen in den Orchesterwerken Béla Bartóks zur Orchestermusik des späten 19. und frühen 20. Jahrhunderts," 874, 1164n

Winrow, Barbara. "Allegretto con indifferenza. A Study of the 'Barrel Organ' Episode in Bartók's Fifth String Quartet," 680

Wittlich, Gary E. "An Examination of Some Set-theoretic Applications in the Analysis of Non-serial Music," 681

Wolff, Hellmuth Christian. "Béla Bartók und die Musik der Gegenwart," 875; *Ordnung und Gestalt. Die Musik von 1900 bis 1950,* 876

Worbs, Hans Christoph. *Welterfolge der modernen Oper,* 1058

The Workshop of Bartók and Kodály (Lendvai), 782

Xenakis, Iannis. "Homage to Béla Bartók," 334

Yeomans, David. "Background and Analysis of Bartók's Romanian Christmas Carols for Piano," 940, 1138n, 1139n; "Background and Analysis of Béla Bartók's *Colinde Sz. 57, 1915,*" 1161n; *Bartók for Piano: A Survey of His Solo Literature,* 1089

Zágon, G.V. "Briefe an Bartók," 1152n

Zeneelmélet, stíluselemzés. A Bárdos Lajos 75. születésnapja alkalmából tartott zenetudományi konferencia anyaga, 1189

Zenei szemle 8, 1/4, 1190

INDEX OF BARTÓK'S COMPOSITIONS, KEYBOARD EDITIONS AND TRANSCRIPTIONS

Arabic numerals that are preceded by Roman numeral "I," both of which are underlined, indicate the main listing of Bartók's compositions and his editions and transcriptions of keyboard works of other composers in Chapter I; this Roman numeral is used to distinguish the independent numbering system of these items from that of the bibliographic items. Where a Bartók composition, edition, or transcription is referred to in the bibliographic items of Chapters II-V, the number of the bibliographic item is used.

Initial articles, diacritical markings of letters, and Roman and Arabic numerals are included in the title, but only the initial articles are included in alphabetizing.

The original language of a composition determines the main entry, which provides the item number; English translations are also listed, but are cross-referred to the main entry for classification data.

INDEX OF PROPER NAMES

All entries are designated by item number without distinction between occurrence in citation or annotation.

SUBJECT INDEX

Aesthetics. *See under* Compositions

Analytical Studies. *See under* Compositions. *See also* Theories, special

Archives. *See under* Institutions

Art Music

    Bartók's discussions of his own and other traditional and contemporary compositions, 2, 4, 8, 12, 13, 16, 23, 27, 29, 35, 36, 56, 57, 66, 67, 78, 92, 95, 102, 104, 109, 110, 112, 114, 119, 122, 123, 124, 127, 128, 130, 133, 139-142, 149

    Bartók's Editions and Transcriptions of Keyboard Works by Other Composers, catalogue of in Chap. I, 2, 7, 944, 950, 953, 1031, 1076

    influences of on Bartók's music. *See under* Influenced by: art music

Atonality. *See* Theories, special

Autobiography. *See under* Primary Source Categories

Bibliography, extensive, 133, 141, 250, 481, 635, 1096-1128 passim, 1145, 1147, 1171, 1176, 1186

Biography, 133, 135, 162, 207-362 passim, 434, 514, 595, 860, 1120, 1147, 1171, 1185, 1186, 1191

Catalogues, Chap. I passim, 1096-1128 passim

Composer

    Bartók as, 135, 224, 385, 766, 963, 964, 1064, 1083

        philosophy of Bartók as, 416-475 passim. *See also under* Personality, Philosophy, Psychology

Compositional Process. *See under* Primary Source Studies

Compositions

    analytic-theoretical studies of, 133, 132, 144, 228, 229, 231, 235, 238, 239, 251, 309, 316, 322, 357, 372, 451, 457, 463, 478, 499, 517-682, 753, 860, 1010, 1056, 1080, 1120, 1135, 1146, 1164, 1170, 1181

    facsimiles and reprints of. *See under* Primary Source Categories

    historical approach to, 518

    lists of, Chap. I, 133, 153, 236, 250, 635, 1147, 1171, 1176, 1186

    primary sources of. *See under* Primary Source Studies

    style sources and comparisons (with other composers' approaches) of, 131, 239, 240, 244, 245, 250, 281, 295, 304, 333, 343, 347, 420, 421, 425, 438, 439, 446, 479, 557, 563, 570, 584, 586, 609, 611, 630, 631, 633, 636, 644, 648, 661, 718, 722, 735, 749, 752, 759,

760, 764, 772, 783, 787, 797, 802, 810, 811, 818, 822-824, 835, 840, 842, 849, 852, 856, 859, 860, 863, 873, 881, 942-969, 976, 1064, 1141, 1132, 1145, 1152, 1162, 1164, 1165

Stylistic and aesthetic studies of, 683-876, 1147, 1165, 1166, 1173, 1174, 1176, 1185

Computerized Data Bases, 1143, 1192-1200, 1168

Conferences, Congresses, and Festivals:
    devoted to folk-music, 80, 84, 898
    devoted to Bartók, 485, 498, 1129-1191 passim

Discography, 246, 250, 1096-1128 passim

Emigration, 135, 132, 153, 208, 217, 230, 242, 250, 283, 298, 305, 322, 328, 332, 339, 346, 350, 353, 951, 1164

Ethnomusicologist

Bartók as, 133, 135, 174, 218, 220, 224, 228, 230, 235, 250, 269, 276, 320, 327, 336, 340, 361, 363-415, 431, 814, 824, 875, 886, 891, 893, 901, 923, 963, 996, 1083, 1097, 1135, 1141, 1132, 1143, 1147, 1149, 1152, 1156, 1164, 1165, 1166, 1167, 1171, 1180, 1186, 1195, 1198-1200

Eulogistic Articles, 213, 315, 351, 467

Fibonacci Series. *See under* Theories, special

Folk Music Sources and Methodology

Bartók's discussions of, 5, 6, 14, 15, 17, 18, 20-22, 24, 25, 28, 31, 33, 34, 36, 39, 40, 51, 55, 58, 62, 63, 65, 68-74, 77, 79, 80, 81, 83-91, 96, 97, 101, 103, 106, 111, 113, 115-118, 129-133, 140-143, 144-156 passim, 814, 911, 1146

influences of on Bartók's music. *See under* Influenced by: folk music

Golden Section and Fibonacci Series. *See under* Theories, special

Historical Position, 241, 311, 325, 326, 333, 501, 796, 836, 849, 859, 870, 875, 934, 1141, 1132, 1143, 1165

History of Musical Development, 208-362 passim, 632, 1082, 1083, 1171

Homage:
    by Bartók, 60, 120, 121, 964
    to Bartók, 212, 332, 334, 436, 1129, 1142

Humanist

Bartók as, 131, 265, 308, 311, 456, 516, 650, 893, 964, 1141, 1132, 1145, 1157

Hungarian Art Music

Bartók's discussions of, 11, 54, 58, 113, 119, 123, 130, 131
    new, 132

Hungary

musical activities in, 30, 35, 37, 38, 41, 42, 46-50, 53, 58, 60, 142, 264, 331, 892

Journals, Newsletters, and Special Issues, 1129-1191 passim

Influenced by:
  art music, 942-969. *See also the following more specific entries*
  Bach, 701, 734, 842, 894, 943, 945, 957
  Baroque, 952
  Beethoven, 692, 695, 734, 822, 894, 943, 951, 958-961 passim,
    969, 1109
  Brahms, 692, 695, 701, 874, 956
  Busoni, 947
  Debussy, 44, 108, 357, 385, 551, 734, 809, 826, 842, 871, 874,
    894, 943, 946, 947, 948, 955, 957, 1109
  Delius, 947
  Dohnányi, 874
  folk music, 133, 318, 520-533 passim, 605, 606, 652, 657, 662,
    665, 692, 694, 696, 701, 710, 713, 742-748 passim, 767, 809,
    822, 826, 831, 842, 856, 859, 870, 871, 877-941, 945, 951, 955,
    963, 1008, 1040, 1080, 1084, 1085, 1109, 1141, 1132, 1146,
    1164, 1165, 1186, 1198
  Germanic tradition, 44
  Gypsy and/or Verbunkos styles, 801, 883, 892, 1165
  illness, 869
  Italian Baroque music, 951, 963, 1141, 1132, 1178
  jazz, 743
  Kodály, 967
  Liszt, 44, 219, 385, 692, 701, 785, 871, 874, 949, 956, 964, 969
  Ravel, 108, 551, 943, 1109
  Reger, 947
  Schoenberg, 826, 951
  Schumann, 871
  R. Strauss, 44, 357, 785, 826, 874, 947, 955, 965
  Stravinsky, 826, 943, 951
  Wagner, 44, 874, 942, 955
Influences on others, 970-980
Institutions
  archives and special libraries, 273, 429, 428, 471, 476, 493, 494,
    514, 659, 923, 946, 1000, 1002, 1003, 1019, 1032, 1033, 1081,
    1092-1095 passim, 1097, 1098, 1102, 1121, 1143, 1160, 1168,
    1196
  societies and organizations, 1092-1095 passim

Libraries. *See under* Institutions

Manuscripts. *See under* Primary Source Studies
Modality and Polymodal Chromaticism. *See under* Theories, special
Modern Music. *See under* New or Modern Music